An Introduction to Criminal Psychology

This book offers a clear, up-to-date, comprehensive, and theoretically informed introduction to criminal psychology, exploring how psychological explanations and approaches can be integrated with other perspectives drawn from evolutionary biology, neurobiology, sociology, and criminology. Drawing on examples from around the world, it considers different types of offences from violence and aggression to white-collar and transnational crime, and links approaches to explaining crime with efforts to prevent crime and to treat and rehabilitate offenders.

This revised and expanded second edition offers a thorough update of the research literature and introduces several new features, including:

- detailed international case studies setting the scene for each chapter, promoting real-world understanding of the topics under consideration;
- a fuller range of crime types covered, with new chapters on property offending and white-collar, corporate, and environmental crime;
- detailed individual chapters exploring prevention and rehabilitation, previously covered in a single chapter in the first edition;
- an array of helpful features including learning objectives, review and reflect checkpoints, annotated lists of further reading, and two new features: 'Research in Focus' and 'Criminal Psychology Through Film'.

This textbook is essential reading for upper undergraduate students enrolled in courses on psychological criminology, criminal psychology, and the psychology of criminal behaviour. Designed with the reader in mind, student-friendly and innovative pedagogical features support the reader throughout.

Russil Durrant is Senior Lecturer at the School of Social and Cultural Studies at Victoria University of Wellington, New Zealand.

An Introduction to Criminal Psychology

Second Edition

Russil Durrant

Routledge
Taylor & Francis Group

LONDON AND NEW YORK

Second edition published 2018
by Routledge
2 Park Square, Milton Park, Abingdon, Oxon, OX14 4RN

and by Routledge
711 Third Avenue, New York, NY 10017

Routledge is an imprint of the Taylor & Francis Group, an informa business

© 2018 Russil Durrant

British Library Cataloguing-in-Publication Data
A catalogue record for this book is available from the British Library

Library of Congress Cataloging-in-Publication Data
A catalog record for this book has been requested

ISBN: 978-1-138-65095-4 (hbk)
ISBN: 978-1-138-65096-1 (pbk)
ISBN: 978-1-315-62504-1 (ebk)

Typeset in Eurostile and Akzidenz Grotesk
by Saxon Graphics Ltd, Derby

CONTENTS

FIGURES

TABLES

BOXES

ACTIVITIES

RESEARCH IN FOCUS

CRIMINAL PSYCHOLOGY THROUGH FILM

PREFACE

The aim of *An Introduction to Criminal Psychology* is – as its title rather plainly suggests – to introduce the topic of criminal psychology. Although mainly intended for undergraduate students the book may be of wider interest to general readers, policy-makers, and academics from other disciplines who are interested in finding out more about the causes of crime and different ways of responding to criminal behaviour. The word 'psychology' in the title should clue readers in to the main focus of the book, but my aim throughout is to explore how psychological explanations and approaches can be integrated with other perspectives drawn from evolutionary biology, neurobiology, sociology, and criminology. Although pitched at an introductory audience with no prior knowledge of the field one of my aims was to ensure that the book is firmly anchored in the research literature. Unfortunately the picture of crime (and criminology) that we often receive from the media does not necessarily provide a very accurate portrait of crime in society or the activities of criminologists and criminal psychologists (much to the disappointment of many an undergraduate criminology student!). As such, the book has a lot of references, and I hope that it can serve as both an introduction to the topic and a useful reference source.

I well remember one year in teaching my undergraduate course, Criminal Psychology, when having reached the sixth lecture a concerned student appeared at my door during my office hour. She explained that, although she was enjoying the paper, the course was – literally – giving her nightmares. On reviewing the content matter this perhaps was not surprising – we had spent close to 12 hours covering aggression, violence, serial murder, mass murder, sexual violence, genocide, and terrorism, and it wasn't until Lecture seven that – for what probably seemed like a bit of light relief – we turned to the topic of drugs and crime. Several reviewers of the first edition also noted the rather extensive coverage of violence compared to other topics and encouraged me to expand the range of topics covered. The second edition, then, includes two brand new chapters – one on property offending and one on white-collar, corporate, and environmental crime. In addition, the topics of prevention and rehabilitation previously covered in a single chapter now get their own chapter, allowing for a more detailed coverage of these topics. Other changes from the first edition include a thorough updating of statistics and the research base, many new figures and tables, and the introduction of two regular features that will pop up in each chapter: Criminal Psychology Through Film, and Research in Focus.

ACKNOWLEDGEMENTS

I would like to take this opportunity to thank the staff at Routledge for their encouragement and support through the process of writing this book. I would also like to thank the staff at the Institute of Criminology and Tony Ward from the School of Psychology at Victoria University of Wellington. A special thanks to Carolina (who also provided the drawings for Figures 1.3, 1.4, and 1.5), Zoe, Leo, Mavis, and Bea.

VISUAL TOUR
(HOW TO USE THIS BOOK)

Listed below are the various pedagogical features that can be found both in the margins and within the main text, with visual examples of the boxes to look out for, and descriptions of what you can expect them to contain.

LEARNING OBJECTIVES

Each chapter begins with a list of the key areas in which you can expect to gain knowledge through reading the chapter and completing the accompanying activities.

Review and reflect

Pause regularly to review what you have read so far and test your understanding of the material by answering key questions about the chapter.

REVIEW AND REFLECT

1   What role do genes play in the origin of criminal and
2   What are neurotransmitters?
3   What are the implications of biological approaches
    for criminal culpability? Do you think that recent r
    neuroscience implies a more lenient criminal justic

Boxed features

Boxed features appear throughout the text containing helpful extra material for students, such as case studies, discussion questions, and detailed explorations of concepts and real-life events mentioned in the text.

**BOX 1.1 SOME COMMON MISCONCEPTIOI
EVOLUTIONARY EXPLANATIONS
BEHAVIOUR**

Evolutionary explanations have a long and controversial
behavioural sciences (Plotkin, 2004), and many socia
value. However, although there are some legitimate conc
to be addressed when applying evolutionary theory to

Activities

Activities to guide students in considering the wider implications of the concepts, examples or themes discussed in the chapter.

ACTIVITY 1.1 THE CAUSES OF CRIME

Rank the following five possible causes of crime in term:
think they are in explaining criminal behaviour. For examp
'family environment' is the most important cause of crim
'1' next to family environment.

_____

Cause
_____

Research in Focus

Presents a detailed summary of a recent piece of empirical research in the area with a discussion of key methods and findings, connecting the material in the textbook back to the empirical research literature.

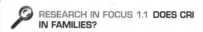

RESEARCH IN FOCUS 1.1 DOES CRI IN FAMILIES?

Title: The familial concentration and transmission of crin

Author: Beaver, K. M.   **Year**: 2013

Source: *Criminal Justice and Behavior*, 40, 139–155

Criminal Psychology Through Film

Provides a brief synopsis of a film relevant to the chapter content and encourages students to consider implications for our study of crime.

CRIMINAL PSYCHOLOGY THROUGH I
Out of the Blue (2006)

Directed by: Robert Sarkies
Starring: Karl Urban (Nick Harvey), Matthew Sunderla
Simon Ferry (Garry Holden)

Chapter summaries

Each chapter ends with a concise summary of important concepts that have been discussed in the chapter.

Further reading

Annotated recommendations of additional readings and primary sources that will expand upon information covered in the chapter in greater depth.

Web resources

Links to online resources that complement and expand upon material covered in the chapter, and invite students to further their understanding of particular topics through additional exploration.

Key concepts

Lists of key concepts can be found at the end of each chapter to assist students in checking their knowledge of the important terms highlighted in each chapter.

Chapter 1

Understanding criminal behaviour

An overview

LEARNING OBJECTIVES

On completion of this chapter you should:

➤ have gained an understanding of what crime is and how it is measured;
➤ understand what criminal psychology is;
➤ recognise the importance of levels of analysis and the different types of explanations that they are associated with;
➤ have gained some understanding of the main types of explanation that will feature throughout this book, including:
  – evolutionary approaches
  – social-structural and cultural approaches
  – developmental approaches
  – psychological approaches
  – biological approaches
  – situational approaches.

Aromoana is a small town in New Zealand with a population of fewer than 300 individuals, located on the remote Otago Peninsula. On 13th and 14th November 1990 it was the location of New Zealand's worst mass murder (vividly depicted in the 2006 film *Out of the Blue* – see Criminal Psychology Through Film 1.1). Over a 34-hour period, local man David Gray ran riot through the town with a rifle shooting anyone that he came across. By the time that Gray was shot dead by the police he had murdered 13 residents and police officers and had wounded a further three individuals. Why did Gray commit this offence? Although this question is deceptively straightforward, providing a complete and coherent answer is not. There is a suggestion that Gray was suffering from paranoid schizophrenia so perhaps aspects of this mental disorder contributed to his offending. However, as we shall see in Chapter 3, the vast majority of individuals with major mental disorders like schizophrenia do not commit violent offences, let alone the kind perpetrated by Gray. Those who knew Gray also reported that he was socially isolated and was obsessed with weapons, war, and survival. Maybe then, something in Gray's mind set, or thinking patterns, contributed to the shooting spree. Prior to the shooting Gray had also had an argument with his neighbour, Gary Holden, over a dog that Gray spent a lot of time walking but Holden had to put down. Perhaps, then, this was an important precipitating or triggering factor. Certainly if Gray survived the mass murder we could ask him what motivated his shooting spree, but any answer that he could provide us would likely be less than complete. Part of the problem in our attempts to explain this mass murder is that we find it very hard to make the imaginative leap from our own minds to that of Grey (assuming that very few, if any, readers of this book have perpetrated a mass murder!). In order to fully understand this and other, more mundane, examples of criminal behaviour we also need to carefully think about the *type* of explanation that we offer. As we shall see in this chapter and throughout this book, a wide range of (often compatible) explanations have been offered to explain why individuals commit crime. In order to understand criminal behaviour, it will be argued, we need to take all of these types of explanation into account.

CRIMINAL PSYCHOLOGY THROUGH FILM 1.1
Out of the Blue (2006)

Directed by: Robert Sarkies
Starring: Karl Urban (Nick Harvey), Matthew Sunderland (David Gray), and Simon Ferry (Garry Holden)

This film vividly depicts the sequence of events as they unfolded on November 13, 1990, in the small coastal settlement of Aramoana on the Otago peninsula. This remote setting was the scene of New Zealand's worst mass murder when local man, David Gray, went on a shooting rampage killing 13 individuals before being shot by police. The film tracks the sequence of events leading up to the mass murder as David Gray, angry over an incident at a bank in town, turns to his cache of weapons and starts shooting members of the community of which he is a part.

Question for discussion

What motivated David Gray to perpetrate this mass shooting? Watch the film and note down the potentially relevant psychological and situational factors that might have played a role.

For further discussion

The residents of Aramoana were strongly opposed to the production of this film and refused permission for it to be filmed in the settlement itself. Some of the police officers were also upset about the way they were depicted in the film. When making films of this nature is there an obligation for filmmakers to adhere to the 'facts', and should those most affected by the actual events have a say in whether the film should go ahead?

The aim of this chapter is to provide a conceptual overview of the various different types of explanation that we will encounter throughout the rest of the book. First, however, we need to take a little time to explain just what we mean by 'crime' and 'criminal behaviour', and how these are defined and measured. We will also discuss the specific contribution of **criminal psychology** to the task of understanding offending. We then consider how the different types of explanation for crime can be organised in a conceptually coherent fashion and introduce some of the main approaches that will feature throughout the rest of this book.

WHAT IS CRIME?

Almost without fail every introductory textbook in criminology begins by addressing this question. The reason for this is pretty straightforward: it is essential that we are clear about the phenomenon that we are studying before we embark on detailed accounts of that phenomenon. What, then, is this thing called crime? The most straightforward approach is to define crime in legal terms. Thus, Munice and Mclaughlin (2001, p. 10) define crime as 'an act or omission punishable by law', and Wikström (2006, p. 63) views crime as 'an act of breaking a moral rule defined in criminal law'. This approach to defining crime has some clear advantages. Most importantly, as long as we have a clear understanding of the criminal law then we will be able to determine with a reasonably high degree of confidence what constitutes criminal behaviour. However, as criminologists have noted, criminal law is far from static, and thus crime is a 'moving target': what constitutes a criminal act depends on when and where it is committed (Newburn, 2013). In short, crime is considered to be a socially constructed class of acts, rather than something that is a 'given' feature of the world. Examples are not hard to come by. The use of various drugs, gambling, homosexuality, prostitution, and spousal rape are all acts that have been punishable by the law (and thus 'criminal') in some times and places but not in others.

This poses an apparent problem for psychological explanations of criminal behaviour. As Wortley (2011, p. 4) notes, 'If someone can be a criminal today but not tomorrow for the same behaviour, then how can anything meaningful be said about their criminal nature'. To address this issue, the criminologist Robert Agnew (2011, p. 187) proposes that crime should be defined as 'acts that cause blameworthy harm, are condemned by the public, and/or are sanctioned by the state'. This definition helps to shift the burden away from acts that are currently proscribed by the law to a wider range of harmful behaviours. A similar way of resolving this problem is to focus more broadly on 'deviant' or 'antisocial' behaviour – that is, behaviour that violates social norms – rather than criminal behaviour per se. Many psychologists, for instance, focus their attention on 'antisocial behaviour', and we will use this term widely throughout this book. Inevitably, of course, there is a significant overlap in what we consider to be 'antisocial' and what we consider to be 'criminal' behaviour although the overlap is not so complete that we can't meaningfully use the term 'criminal *and* antisocial' behaviour.

In many respects the issues in defining crime – important as they are – will not significantly hamper our efforts in this book to provide explanations for criminal behaviour. In part, this is because we are largely concerned with explaining what criminologists term *male in se*, or 'core' offences – those that tend be viewed as more serious, are culturally and historically less relative, and are subject to more severe penalties (Walsh & Ellis, 2007). Murder, rape, serious assault, and robbery are all examples of *male in se* offences. We will also consider a variety of acts that may not always be considered as criminal, including aggressive behaviour, drug use, war, and various types of 'green' crimes. However, these topics are important because either they are related to more serious criminal acts (e.g., violence) or, although not necessarily violations of the law, they may cause significant amounts of harm (e.g., war, 'green' crimes).

Measuring crime and criminal behaviour

The task of measuring crime is important for a wide range of different reasons. Most straightforwardly we are interested in determining just how much crime there is in society and how prevalent different types of crime are. Inevitably we will also be interested in finding out whether crime is increasing or decreasing and whether crime is more prevalent in some places than others. Obtaining clear information about the nature and prevalence of crime in society is also important for the development of theories of crime. A good theory of crime, for instance, will provide a satisfactory account of the most notable patterns in criminal behaviour, such as the over-representation of men and young people in crime statistics. In short, we want to ensure that we have a clear picture of the phenomenon that we want to explain.

Criminologists typically recognise two main approaches to measuring crime: **official crime statistics** and **victim surveys**. Official crime statistics are those that are gathered by law enforcement agencies and are based on offences that are reported to, or otherwise come to the attention of, the relevant law enforcement authorities. All Western countries meticulously collect and publish official crime statistics on a regular basis. In England and Wales these are known as *recorded crime statistics* and are published alongside the results from the *British Crime Survey* (a victim survey – see below). In the United States the official crime statistics are collected by the FBI and are published as the *Uniform Crime Reports*. Recorded crime in New Zealand is presented as *New Zealand Police Statistics*, and in Australia these are held at the *Australian Bureau of Statistics*. These and the official crime statistics from other countries are readily accessible online.

Official crime statistics provide important information about the prevalence of different types of offences in society, and we will draw upon them throughout this book. They do, however, have some well-recognised limitations. Importantly, because they are largely based on criminal offences either that are reported to the police or that the police find out about through other means, they inevitably represent only a *sample* of the total amount of crime in society. The reason for this is straightforward: many offences are simply not reported to the police, and thus they cannot find their way into official crime statistics. Criminologists use the term 'the **dark figure of crime**' to refer to those unreported and undetected offences. To make matters more problematic, some offences are more likely to be reported to, or detected by, the police than are others. Property offences, for instance, such as burglary or motor vehicle theft, are likely to be reported to police as people will typically want to make insurance claims on lost items. Many offences against the person, however, such as sexual and violent offences, may be less likely to be reported as many people may view these as private matters or think that the police will not be able to do anything to help them (Bradley & Walters, 2011; Newburn, 2013). These and other reasons also remind us that we should take care in interpreting trends in official crime statistics over time. The release of the latest crime statistics is typically a newsworthy event, and – if crime rates are seen to be going down – they are often the cause for some mutual backslapping among the incumbent government and law enforcement agencies. However, fluctuations in official crime statistics can occur for a number of reasons that may have little to do with actual rates of crime in society. It is important to keep in mind, therefore, that despite their usefulness, official crime statistics may not necessarily provide the most accurate picture of crime in society (see Table 1.1).

Table 1.1 The limitations of official crime statistics

Limitation		Implications
Unreported crimes are not counted	If crimes are not reported to or detected by police then they will not find their way into the police-recorded statistics	There is a substantial 'dark figure' of crime that includes all those offences that are not reported to police
Not all reported crimes are recorded	Police have substantial discretion in deciding whether or not to record a specific incident	There is a significant 'grey figure' of crime represented by reported but not recorded crime
Reporting rates vary by crime type	Some offences are more likely to be reported than others (e.g., property offences)	Police-recorded crime statistics do not provide a good indication of the relative prevalence of different types of crime
Trends in crime are influenced by a range of factors	Changes in legislation, recording practices, reporting practices, and police numbers and practices all can affect the volume of reported crime	Changes in recorded crime may not accurately portray actual changes in the amount of crime in society over time
Cross-national comparisons are problematic	Different countries have different recording practices, crime types, policing practices, and so forth	With some exceptions it is difficult to compare overall rates of crime between different countries

A second common approach for measuring crime in society is the victim survey. Victim surveys involve obtaining information about the experience of victimisation from a representative sample of the population over a particular time period (usually a year). Researchers are then able to extrapolate from the information provided in victim surveys to estimate how much crime (or, rather, victimisation) there has been in a country as a whole over the relevant time period. Most Western countries also fairly regularly administer victim surveys. In England and Wales this information is captured in the *British Crime Survey*, and in the United States the equivalent survey is referred to as *National Crime Victimization Survey*. The most recent victimisation survey in New Zealand is the New Zealand Crime and Safety Survey (NZCASS) 2015, and Australia conducts an annual *Crime Victimization Survey*. Perhaps unsurprisingly, victim surveys reveal a great deal more crime than are captured in official crime statistics, thus shedding some light on the 'dark figure' of crime. In addition to regular national crime victimisation surveys there are also a plethora of typically more local or more crime-specific victim surveys that attempt to capture the experience of victimisation for certain types of offence or in certain regions. Although victim surveys are enormously useful for understanding crime in society, like official crime statistics they also have their limitations. For example, because they rely on the reporting of victimisation from the public they are subject to the natural limitations of human memory. Moreover, some people may be reluctant to talk about their experiences of victimisation, particularly if they involve sexual offences (see Figure 1.1).

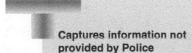

Captures information not provided by Police	Limitations of self-report methodology
• Crime not reported • Information on multiple and repeat victimisation • More accurate measure of long term trends • Information about fear of crime and public attitudes towards crime and criminal justice	• Does not cover certain types of crime (e.g., homicide, 'victimless crimes') • Excludes some type of victims (e.g., children, commercial agencies and individuals who are difficult to contact) • Subject to potential errors or biases in recall and reporting (e.g., fabrication)

Figure 1.1 The advantages and disadvantages of victim surveys.

A third type of study that we will make use of in this book is the self-report study. Whereas victim surveys obtain information about experiences of victimisation, self-report studies involve obtaining information from individuals about their experience as offenders. Self-report studies are often employed as part of longitudinal research designs that track individuals over time and may be particularly useful in mapping changes in offence rates over time for the same individuals (Newburn, 2013). They are also widely used for offences like illicit drug use, which are poorly represented in both official crime statistics and victim surveys. Inevitably, although self-report studies can provide valuable information that may be missed in other types of research, they are limited by the sample employed and the willingness of individuals to disclose information about illegal activities.

Given the strengths and limitations of the three types of approach for measuring crime and criminal behaviour, how should we go about determining the nature and prevalence of crime in society? As with other types of research enquiry, the best approach is to draw on a diverse range of research methods rather than to rely predominantly or exclusively on one source of data. If we can demonstrate similar patterns across different sources of data then we are in a stronger position to claim that the particular phenomenon that we are interested in is a 'robust' one and not simply an artefact of the particular source of data. Throughout this book we will draw on a range of different sources of information about crime, alongside various different research methodologies for understanding criminal behaviour.

WHAT IS CRIMINAL PSYCHOLOGY?

This book is centrally concerned with the application of psychology to our understanding of criminal behaviour. Let us pause for a moment to reflect on what this actually entails. As every introductory psychology textbook will quickly tell us, psychology is 'the science of mental processes and behavior' (e.g., Kosslyn & Rosenberg, 2004, p. 4). Criminology textbooks are rather less concise or uniform in how they define their discipline, but, broadly speaking, criminology is defined as the study of crime, criminal behaviour, and responses to crime (e.g., Newburn, 2013). Criminal psychology, then, critically involves the use of psychology as a science to advance our understanding of the causes of crime. Psychology here refers to the academic discipline of psychology (which includes the study, among other things, of brain processes, development, cognition, personality, social influence, and culture) not just peoples' thinking process and personality (as in the *psychological level of analysis* discussed below). Unfortunately, although there is some agreement regarding the boundaries of 'psychology' and 'criminology', there is no such consensus on what is meant by 'criminal psychology', and there are a number of overlapping terms that are also employed including 'forensic psychology' 'psychological criminology', 'criminological psychology', and 'legal psychology'.

For some (e.g., Blackburn, 1996), the term 'forensic psychology' refers specifically to the application of psychology to the legal system – as reflected in the etymology of the word 'forensic', as 'pertaining to the courts of law'. Other scholars offer a more narrow interpretation of 'forensic psychology' as the 'practice of clinical psychology to the legal system' (Huss, 2009, p. 5). To complicate matters, the term 'forensic psychology' is also used more broadly to embrace the application of psychology to virtually anything related to crime, including our understanding of the causes of crime. Davies, Hollin, and Bull (2008, p. XIII) for instance, suggest that forensic psychology is a 'broach church', with:

> two main aisles: legal psychology covering the application of psychological knowledge and methods to the process of law and criminological psychology dealing with the application of psychological theory and method to the understanding (and reduction) of criminal behaviour.

To confuse matters further, the application of psychology to the investigation of crime and, in particular, the profiling of offenders is sometimes referred to as 'investigative psychology' (Canter & Youngs, 2009), or when coupled with the use of psychology in the training and selection of police the term 'police psychology' can be used (Bartol & Bartol, 2012).

Finally, when psychology is used in prison contexts for the assessment and rehabilitation of offenders it is often called 'correctional psychology' (Bartol & Bartol, 2012).

In the end analysis labels are important because they can help to define what it means to be a criminal or a forensic psychologist, and what people *expect* from this role (Brown, Shell, & Cole, 2015). However, for the purposes of this book it is probably best to think in terms of the specific domains of inquiry and application, rather than get bogged down with what labels should be employed. In other words, we will be focusing on what psychologists have found out about the nature of crime and the criminal justice process and how this knowledge can be most usefully applied. Thus, we will be using the term 'criminal psychology' as the application of psychology as an academic discipline to our understanding of the causes of criminal behaviour (roughly equivalent to Wortley's, 2011, use of the term 'psychological criminology', or Hollin's, 2013, use of the term 'criminological psychology') leaving the term 'forensic psychology' to describe the application of psychology to the legal system.

THE NATURE OF EXPLANATION

Explaining crime

I spent many years teaching university courses in psychology, and when people asked me what I did for a living, the reply 'psychologist' often evoked a defensive reaction, and responses along the lines of 'so you are probably psychoanalysing me right now' were not uncommon. Typically the conversation ended in a somewhat uneasy silence (especially when I responded with a stony-faced 'yes'!). However, since becoming a 'criminologist' I have been astounded at how readily people – often complete strangers – want to tell me their thoughts and feelings on the main causes of crime and how to address the crime 'problem'. Given the attention paid by the media to crime, and the real harms that arise from criminal behaviour, the interest that people have in crime is perhaps not too surprising. Inevitably when people do think about the topic of crime they gravitate towards two fundamental questions: 'why does it occur?' and 'how can it be prevented?' These two questions are, of course, related. One of the reasons that we want to advance our understanding of the causes of crime is because if we know why crime occurs then we will be in a better position to implement approaches to preventing or reducing crime. Specific types of explanation for crime also suggest different ways of responding to crime. If, for instance, you believe that criminals are inherently 'bad' or 'evil' and thus are irredeemable then you are likely to favour responses that involve locking them in prison for as long as possible. On the other hand, if you think that criminal behaviour is related to the way that offenders think about the world then you might support the implementation of rehabilitation programmes designed to change thinking patterns. In short, our theories of crime matter.

Before we start looking at the major theoretical approaches to understanding crime, it is worth pausing for a moment to consider what *you* think are the main causes of crime. Before reading further, complete Activity 1.1.

ACTIVITY 1.1 **THE CAUSES OF CRIME**

Rank the following five possible causes of crime in terms of how important you think they are in explaining criminal behaviour. For example, if you think that the 'family environment' is the most important cause of crime then assign a rank of '1' next to family environment.

Cause	Rank

Family environment
Criminal behaviour is the result of an unstable family environment, abusive parenting and lack of parental supervision.

Biological factors
Criminal behaviour is the result of biological factors such as the genes that people inherit and the way that their brain works.

Psychological factors
Criminal behaviour is the result of psychological factors like impulsiveness, lack of empathy, and low IQ.

Social-structural factors
Criminal behaviour is the result of a lack of educational opportunities, an unfair economic system, poor job opportunities, and other social-structural factors.

Situational factors
Criminal behaviour is the result of opportunities to commit crimes, involvement with antisocial peers, and the use of alcohol and other drugs.

Discussion question

What factors do you think influenced your rankings in this exercise?

The task of identifying the most important causes of crime is, as you will probably have noted, not a straightforward one. First, there is widespread agreement among criminologists, psychologists, criminal justice professionals, and others interested in explaining crime that there is no simple or single explanation for criminal behaviour. In other words, there is nothing that we can definitely point to and say '*that* is why crime occurs'. One important theme of this book, therefore, is that we need to draw on a wide range of different approaches in our endeavours to understand crime. Second, notwithstanding the fact that many offenders demonstrate criminal versatility – that is, they commit a wide range of different offences – our explanations for crime will often need to take into account the particular type of offence under consideration. Thus, our explanations for fraud will, in some respects, differ from our explanations for rape, or serial murder. This is reflected in the fact that although there are many general theories and approaches to explaining crime, there are also a number of crime-specific theories

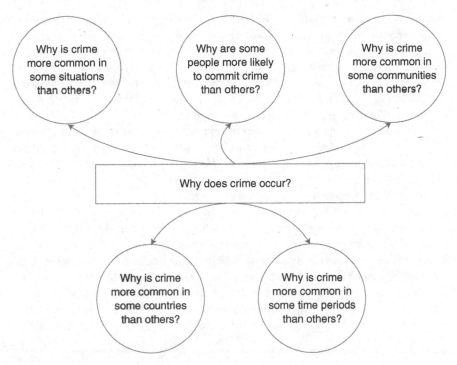

Figure 1.2 Understanding crime: what needs to be explained?

and models that need to be considered. Finally, we need to recognise that the question 'why does crime occur?' hides a number of more fine-grained or specific questions that we want to be able to answer. As illustrated in Figure 1.2, we want to explain why some individuals are more likely to commit crime than others, why crime is more common in some situations than others, and why the frequency of criminal acts vary cross-nationally and historically. We will also want to ask these questions for specific types of offence. For instance, we want to know why men are more likely to commit sexual offences than women and why homicide rates fluctuate dramatically over time. Taken together the questions posed in Figure 1.2 represent some of the most important phenomena that we want our theories of crime to explain.

Levels of analysis and explanations for crime

There is no shortage of explanations for criminal behaviour. Indeed, for the newcomer to the study of criminology there is a somewhat bewildering thicket of 'theories', 'approaches', 'perspectives', and 'models' to navigate their way through. It is essential, therefore, that we find a way to organise this material in coherent fashion. First, it is important that we understand what is meant by a 'theory', 'approach', or 'model'. Very briefly, an approach or perspective is a broad way of looking at or understanding a given topic of study. Thus, we can talk of developmental approaches to understanding crime that focus on how factors across the lifespan of an individual might influence the development of criminal behaviour. A theory can be viewed as a typically more specific set of propositions that specify the key causal processes that give rise to a specific phenomenon. Social control theory, for instance, proposes that crime tends to emerge when individuals are weakly bonded or attached to social institutions. Theories can be employed to generate specific hypotheses (statements that are derived from theories) and predictions (specific statements that are derived from hypotheses). Finally, a model can be considered to be an idealised representation of some feature of the world (just as we have model buildings and model aircraft). In practice, the boundaries between what are viewed as 'theories' and what are considered 'models' are somewhat blurred in the social sciences and vary substantially in terms of their scope and complexity from a very simple single factor, to complex, integrated theories and models.

A relatively simple, but popular, approach for organising the various different perspectives, theories, and models in criminology is to make a distinction between macro-level and micro-level explanations (Muftic, 2009; Rosenfeld, 2011). Macro-level explanations focus on what Rosenfeld (2011, p. 2) terms the 'big picture' – the characteristics of social systems, social institutions, and culture that can account for criminal behaviour. Micro-level explanations, in contrast, focus on features of individuals and their immediate social environments and how these impact on criminal offending. The distinction between macro-level and micro-level explanations is a useful one because it highlights how explanations for crime can be found at different **levels of analysis** (also sometimes referred to as 'levels of explanation' – see McGuire, 2004). A level of analysis can be simply viewed as a particular way of looking at the world that allows researchers to focus on particular phenomena and to frame specific research questions (Durrant & Ward, 2015).

Although the distinction between macro-level and micro-level explanations is useful, it is also somewhat coarse grained and actually leaves out a number of important types of explanation that we will explore in this book. A more relevant framework for understanding different types of explanation draws on the work of the ethologist, Niko Tinbergen (1963). Tinbergen noted that when biologists attempt to explain some characteristic of an organism they can invoke one or more of four complementary types or levels of explanation. First, biologists provide explanations in terms of the evolutionary function of the trait in question. In short, they ask how the characteristic of interest promoted survival and reproductive success and was thus favoured by natural selection. Second, they provide explanations that delineate the evolutionary history of the characteristic in terms of how it has evolved over time from earlier forms. Taken together, these first two types of explanations are often referred to as 'ultimate' explanations, but we will use the term '**distal explanations**' to capture the idea that they reflect processes that have largely occurred thousands or millions of years ago in our ancestral past. The development (or 'ontogeny') of the trait in question represents the third type of explanation, as biologists are interested in explaining how the characteristic emerges during the life-span of the organism. Finally, biologists are interested in unravelling the important **proximate mechanisms** – be they psychological, physiological, or social – that underlie the characteristic of interest.

An example should help to clarify these different types or levels of explanation. Consider incest avoidance in humans. Why do the vast majority of humans avoid having sexual relations with their siblings? Think for a moment why this might be the case.

Siblings often are of a similar age, they have a lot in common, but, with a few media-worthy exceptions, they almost never have sexual relations with one another. The most obvious explanation for this finding is that most people find the thought of sex with their brother or sister extremely unpleasant, if not downright disgusting. Many people will also believe that it is morally wrong. These are clearly proximate explanations because they refer to the psychological processes that help us to understand why sexual relations among siblings rarely occur.

However, the explanatory story is clearly incomplete because we want to be able to explain *why* it is that most people find sexual activity with their siblings so unappealing. An ultimate or distal explanation for this finding focuses on the deleterious effects of in-breeding on reproductive fitness. Having sex with close relations significantly increases your risk of having offspring with harmful characteristics. The evolutionary function of the proximate mechanisms is thus incest avoidance and will have been selected for during our evolutionary history. Finally, we need to consider how it is that individuals become disgusted at the thought of having sex with their siblings, because clearly this is not something present at birth. The most plausible developmental explanation suggests that individuals who grow up in very close proximity to one another (as siblings typically do) develop a natural aversion to sexual relations with one another. On most occasions this is an effective developmental mechanism. However, it also means that other individuals who grow up in close proximity (e.g., age-group cohorts in Israeli kibbutzim) also develop the same aversion while siblings who grow up apart may not (Cartwright, 2000).

In order to flesh out the framework developed by Tinbergen (1963) for human behaviour (including criminal behaviour) we need to add an additional two levels of explanation. The first is implicit in Tinbergen's framework and refers to the immediate situational context of behaviour. This includes both the immediate physical and the immediate social environment. We also need to recognise that, in explaining human behaviour, we need to consider the importance of social-structural and cultural approaches. These two perspectives don't quite fit neatly into our organisational scheme as they can be viewed as both distal *and* proximate explanations for human behaviour as well as being important inputs into developmental processes. Social institutions, for example, clearly have a history: they are the product of changes that occur over decades, centuries, and millennia. The same is the case for what social scientists refer to as **culture** (shared patterns of beliefs, values, norms, and practices) with some cultural practices (e.g., the use of fire) likely to have a history that stretches into millions of years (Wrangham & Carmody, 2010). Social institutions and culture also have immediate proximate influences on human behaviour as behavioural choices are shaped to a significant extent by particular cultural and social structural environments. Returning to our example of incest avoidance, we can see how the tendency to avoid sexual relations with siblings becomes reflected in both cultural norms (which are cross-culturally universal) and legal practices, no doubt reinforcing the aversion that most people have to this behaviour. An illustration of the different levels of analysis discussed here is provided in Figure 1.3. As you can see, the various levels of analysis can be arranged across a dimension that spans more distal to more proximate explanations (with the grey arrow along the bottom illustrating the idea that social structural and cultural explanations span the distal–proximate dimension). The arrows in the diagram reinforce the idea that the various factors identified interact with one another in a complex fashion.

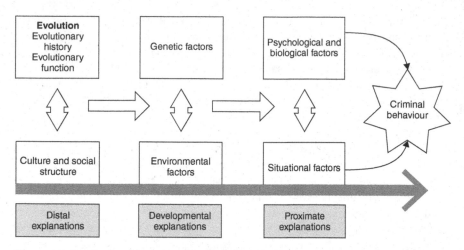

Figure 1.3 Levels of analysis and explanations for crime.

Given the range of theoretical approaches on offer it is natural to ask which is the 'best' approach. However, although there are important criteria for evaluating the worth of a theory, typically speaking, explanations drawn from different levels of analysis are not in direct competition with one another because they provide alternative, but (in principle) *compatible*, explanations for criminal behaviour. In makes no sense, for instance, to say that an approach that focuses on social structure is necessarily a better explanation for crime than one that focuses on developmental process or on neurobiology. Explanations drawn from different levels of analysis are, therefore, all potentially *relevant* for understanding criminal behaviour (to the extent that they are 'correct'). However, some types of explanation may become more *salient* depending on just exactly what we want to explain (Durrant & Ward, 2012, 2015). For example, if we are interested in accounting for cross-national differences in homicide rates, then an explanation that draws on social-structural and cultural approaches is likely to be most salient. This is because the differences in rates of homicide are likely to reflect difference in social structure or culture (rather than, say, personality). If, however, we are interested in explaining why some individuals are more likely to engage in criminal behaviour than others, despite living in the same community, then explanations that focus on individual-level characteristics (e.g., personality) and developmental history become more salient.

Now that we have considered a broad framework for understanding how the different approaches or perspectives to explaining crime can be understood, we turn to a brief overview of the major theoretical approaches themselves, beginning with evolutionary approaches.

REVIEW AND REFLECT

1   What are some of the different types of explanations for crime that you have come across?
2   Organise these different types of explanation into the different levels of analysis described in this chapter.

EVOLUTIONARY APPROACHES

Humans, like all other animals, are the product of evolutionary processes. It follows – fairly straightforwardly some would argue – that we can use the resources of evolutionary theory to help us to understand human behaviour, including criminal behaviour. However, with a few notable exceptions (e.g., Walsh & Ellis, 2007), evolutionary approaches to understanding crime are largely absent from mainstream criminology textbooks and journals. In contrast, there is now a fairly extensive psychological literature on evolutionary approaches to understanding criminal behaviour, and we will draw on this material throughout this book (Daly & Wilson, 1988; Duntley & Shackelford, 2008; Durrant & Ward, 2011, 2015).

Key theoretical constructs

It will be useful first to consider some of the main theoretical constructs that are important for understanding the evolutionary origins of human behaviour.

A good place to start is with the concept of **natural selection**. Although the idea of evolution itself had been around for a long time, there was no clear understanding of *how* evolution worked. Darwin's (1859) notion of natural selection provided an elegant and simple explanation for the process of evolution and can be captured in three general principles: phenotypic variability, differential fitness, and heritability (Durrant & Ellis, 2013). Organisms vary in the physical, psychological, and behavioural (i.e., 'phenotypic') characteristics that they possess. Some of these differences will result in differential fitness – that is, some members of the species will be better able to survive and reproduce due to the specific characteristics that they possess. If these differences are heritable (i.e., reliably passed on from parents to offspring via genes) then the favourable characteristics will become more common in the population than the less favourable characteristics. Inherited characteristics that have been selected for because of their role in advancing survival and reproductive success are known as biological **adaptations** (Buss et al., 1998; Durrant & Ellis, 2013).

Not all adaptations necessarily increase the survival chances of organisms that possess them. Consider the ridiculously elongated tail of the aptly named long-tailed widowbird. Although the bird itself is little bigger than a sparrow, the male sports tail feathers that stretch to some one and half metres, making flying much harder work than it would be with a more modest tail. Another of Darwin's great insights was that such characteristics can evolve through a process that he termed **sexual selection**. Briefly, sexual selection involves the competition that arises over mates and mating, and involves two main processes: mate choice (by one sex for the other), and competition (between members of the same sex). Straightforwardly enough, any characteristic that increases the chance of being 'chosen as a mate' (think the peacock's resplendent tail feathers), or that helps to exclude others from mating through competition (think the large, branching antlers of the red deer used in fighting other males), will be selected for. Furthermore, the sex that experiences greater variance in reproductive success – that is, the sex that can potentially have, on average, more offspring than the other sex – will be subject to stronger sexual selection. Because in mammalian species gestation is internal, and maternal care is largely obligatory (males can not provide milk), males of mammalian species almost inevitably experience greater variance in reproductive rates than females. This is largely why sexual dimorphism (differences in size and strength between males and females) and male–male aggression is widespread (but not universal) among mammalian species (Andersson, 1994). These important insights, as we shall see in Chapter 4 and Chapter 5 of this book, can help us to explain human sex differences in aggressive and violent behaviour (Archer, 2009a)

Another important theoretical construct in applying evolutionary theory to human behaviour is **parental investment theory**. Durrant and Ellis (2013) ask us to 'imagine that a man and a woman each had sexual intercourse with 100 different partners over the course of a year. The man could potentially sire 100 children, whereas the woman could potentially give birth to one or two'. The reason for this discrepancy is rather obvious: the *minimum* male contribution to offspring is a tablespoon of sperm, whereas the minimum female contribution is an egg, nine months of pregnancy, and a potentially dangerous child birth. Throughout much of evolutionary history women were also largely responsible for nursing and caring for infants. In short, because women (and, indeed females of most mammalian species) on average invest significantly more in offspring than men do (they have to carry, give birth to, and feed children) it follows that men, relative to women, can increase their overall reproductive success through access to more mates. This means that there will be greater variance in the reproductive success of men than in that of women – some men will be able to have a large number of offspring, and others may have few or none (Betzig, 2012). These differences in parental investment (Trivers, 1972) have wide-ranging implications for the behaviour of humans and other animals. For the purposes of understanding criminal behaviour the most important implication is that men, relative to women, should be more willing to engage in a variety of risky behaviours in the pursuit of mating opportunities (Campbell, 2013a; Daly & Wilson, 1988). However, human males – somewhat unusually among mammals – often also contribute significantly to the welfare of their offspring, typically in the context of long-term intimate relations with women (Fletcher, Simpson, Campbell, & Overall, 2015; Geary, 2000). Men who invest significantly in long-term relationships may be less prone to engage in risky activities (as they have more to lose) and may be particularly motivated to ensure that the offspring that they are investing in are actually their own. Thus, sex differences in humans may be more muted in many domains than those in other mammalian species (Stewart-Williams & Thomas, 2013). We shall explore some of the potential implications of this idea in Chapter 5 when we discuss evolutionary approaches to understanding intimate partner violence.

Evolutionary psychology

As the biologists Jerry Coyne (2009) and Richard Dawkins (2009) have argued, evolution is, to all extents and purposes, true. Natural and social scientists alike would largely agree that the fact of evolution is largely beyond dispute. However, the application of evolutionary theory to understanding human behaviour is more widely disputed (Durrant & Ward, 2011). Although there are a number of different approaches to applying evolutionary theory to human (and thus criminal) behaviour (Brown, Dickins, Sear, & Laland, 2011; Durrant & Ward, 2015), the most prominent of these is known as **evolutionary psychology**, and thus we will focus on this approach throughout this book. Evolutionary psychology can be simply defined as 'the application of the principles and knowledge of evolutionary biology to psychological theory and research' (Durrant & Ellis, 2013). Evolutionary psychologists also assume that the human mind is composed of a large number of dedicated psychological mechanisms (often referred to as 'modules') that have been selected for because they have increased survival and reproductive success in ancestral environments by solving specific 'adaptive problems'. Thus, evolutionary psychologists employ evolutionary theory (and specific theories derived from evolutionary theory such as parental investment theory) to develop hypotheses about the nature of the human mind and behaviour (Buss, 1995; Confer et al., 2010; Cosmides & Tooby, 2013). One central assumption of evolutionary approaches to understanding crime, therefore, is the idea that criminal behaviour is the outcome of evolved psychological mechanisms. In many – but not necessarily all – cases what we view as criminal behaviours may have been selected for during the course of human evolutionary history.

The ideas of evolutionary psychologists have been subject to intense scrutiny from philosophers, biologists, social scientists, and fellow psychologists alike, and evolutionary approaches to understanding human behaviour have been variously described as genetically deterministic, untestable, unfalsifiable, tautological, and ideologically unsound. Many also doubt the relevance of evolutionary ideas in a world of birth control and medical advancement where 'differential fitness' does not seem to play such an obvious role (see Box 1.1). As discussed in Box 1.1 these criticisms are largely unjustified. However, there does remain some key conceptual and methodological issues that perhaps have yet to be fully resolved by evolutionary psychologists (Durrant & Ward, 2015; Gangestad & Simpson, 2007). The first concerns the identification of adaptations. As we have seen, adaptations are the product of natural selection, and straightforward examples are easy to come by. It is clear, for instance, that the human eye is an adaptation that involves the intricate coordination of mechanisms to produce a clearly beneficial function – sight. It can be rather more difficult, however, to clearly identify *psychological* adaptations, and sometimes evolutionary psychologists are a bit too ready to claim that something is an adaptation without the appropriate evidence being clearly marshalled. We shall revisit this issue when we consider whether rape and war may be considered to be biological adaptations in Chapter 6 and Chapter 7, respectively. Another important issue that has yet to be fully resolved by evolutionary psychologists concerns the way that culture is incorporated into their explanatory accounts. Generally speaking, culture is viewed as one environmental 'input' that may affect how humans' evolved psychological mechanisms process information and subsequently produce behaviour (what is termed 'evoked culture' – see Confer et al., 2010). However, a good deal of human behavioural diversity is the result of what is sometimes referred to as 'transmitted culture': the replication of norms, beliefs, values, practices, and traditions that arise in social groups through a process of social or cultural learning. Transmitted culture is clearly important to understanding human behaviour because our behaviour – including our criminal behaviour – is powerfully shaped by our beliefs, values, attitudes, and traditions. Transmitted culture, although recognised by evolutionary psychologists, has so far played a fairly limited role in their explanatory accounts, although for other evolutionary approaches it is more important (Mesoudi, 2011; Richerson & Boyd, 2005), and Henrich (2016) persuasively argues that the tremendous 'success' of humans as a species is largely due to our capacity for transmitted culture.

BOX 1.1 SOME COMMON MISCONCEPTIONS ABOUT EVOLUTIONARY EXPLANATIONS FOR HUMAN BEHAVIOUR

Evolutionary explanations have a long and controversial history in the social and behavioural sciences (Plotkin, 2004), and many social scientists doubt their value. However, although there are some legitimate conceptual issues that need to be addressed when applying evolutionary theory to human behaviour, there are also a number of criticisms that are less defensible.

Evolutionary explanations are genetically deterministic

One prominent criticism is that evolutionary accounts of human behaviour advance a deterministic view of human nature in which our various behaviours are largely 'fixed' by our genetic heritage. As evolutionary psychologists are quick to point out, this is a 'straw-man' argument, and evolutionary psychologists actively endorse an interactionist perspective that highlights the complex interplay between genetic and environmental factors (Confer et al., 2010).

Evolutionary explanations are ideologically unsound

A second prominent criticism is related to the first: critics have suggested that evolutionary approaches to human behaviour promote a view of the world that implies that human nature is largely fixed by our genetic heritage and therefore supports the social status quo. Recognising that evolutionary approaches emphasise the enormous flexibility of human behaviour helps to defuse this particular criticism. It is also important to understand that adopting an evolutionary perspective on topics like violence or rape does not in any way mean that such acts are either acceptable or justifiable. Evolutionary psychologists note that to make the claim that something is morally justifiable because it is part of our evolutionary heritage is to commit the **naturalistic fallacy** – that is, to incorrectly derive a normative conclusion from a factual premise. In other words, just because some behaviour may be the product of evolution this does not mean that the behaviour is necessarily morally acceptable.

Evolutionary explanations are untestable and unfalsifiable

There are two parts to this criticism. The first suggests that because evolutionary accounts necessarily invoke the operation of selection in the long-distant past we can never subject evolutionary explanations to empirical test. The second part of the criticism suggests that, due to this fact, evolutionary scientists can simply make up any plausible account for the evolutionary origin of behaviour and then change it at will if it fails to find support (thus making evolutionary hypotheses unfalsifiable). A robust rebuttal to these criticism has been provided by Ketelaar and Ellis (2000; see also Confer et al., 2010) who point out that evolutionary scientists go about testing (and refuting) hypotheses in much the same way as any other scientist. As we shall see in this book a number of testable hypotheses regarding criminal behaviour have been derived from evolutionary theory.

Evolutionary explanations are irrelevant in explaining human behaviour

Although many individuals accept the fact of evolution they harbour doubts about the use of evolutionary theory in explaining *human* behaviour. There is no doubt that humans *are* different from other animals in some important respects. Our capacity for higher order cognition, language, and culture has furnished us with an enormous degree of behavioural flexibility. However, it is important to recognise that these capacities are themselves the product of evolution and that our behavioural flexibility is – to some unknown (perhaps unknowable) degree – constrained by our evolved nature. Explanations that draw on consciousness or rationality or culture, therefore, need to be compatible with our understanding of the evolved nature of the human mind.

Evaluation

Although many remain sceptical of the value of evolutionary approaches to understanding criminal behaviour, given that humans are the product of evolutionary history it would seem strange to claim that this fact has *no* relevance for our explanatory theories. Indeed, as we shall see throughout this book, evolutionary approaches can meaningfully contribute to our understanding of many different types of criminal behaviour. The crucial point to recognise is that evolutionary approaches provide 'ultimate' or 'distal' explanations for understanding criminal behaviour and therefore should be typically viewed as complementary rather than competing explanations for crime. Evolutionary explanations are most salient for explaining why humans might be prone to engage in a range of criminal acts including aggression and violence under certain circumstances and why there are such substantial age and gender differences in criminal offending.

REVIEW AND REFLECT

1   Briefly outline the key ideas of parental investment theory.
2   What are the main implications of this theory for our understanding of gender differences in offending?

SOCIAL-STRUCTURAL AND CULTURAL APPROACHES

Mainstream criminological approaches to understanding crime and criminal behaviour have a strong sociological flavour. As such, they draw heavily on social-structural and cultural factors in accounting for crime. The idea of **social structure** refers to the way that society is organised. The term, therefore, can be used to refer to the prevailing political, economic, legal, and other social frameworks and institutions that are in place and how these affect the relations among individuals in ways that influence criminal behaviour. In particular, criminologists are often interested in how specific social-structural arrangements affect particular groups of individuals such as women, ethnic minorities, and those from deprived social backgrounds. Culture is a somewhat nebulous concept but, generally speaking, it is used to refer to shared patterns of beliefs, values, norms, and practices that can define specific social and ethnic groups. Cultural and social-structural explanations are conceptually distinct, but are often combined in mainstream criminological theory. For instance, specific social arrangements may give rise to structural inequalities that lead to the formation of 'sub-cultural' groups defined by specific values, norms, and practices.

As this is a criminal *psychology* textbook it was tempting to leave these theoretical perspectives to one side. However, although they will not get the prominence that they might in mainstream criminology textbooks, they do provide some important explanatory resources that should form part of our explanations for criminal behaviour. In this section we very briefly review some of the main criminological theories of crime, and interested readers are encouraged to pursue the extensive literature on these theories for more detail (see the suggested reading at the end of this chapter).

Key theoretical approaches

Three important theoretical 'traditions' in criminology are represented, respectively, by strain theories, control theories, and sub-cultural and labelling theories.

The central feature that unites strain theories of criminal offending is the idea that 'certain strains or stressors increase the likelihood of crime' (Agnew & Brezina, 2010, p. 96). Strain theorists typically assume that adherence to social norms that prevent criminal behaviour can be largely taken for granted, so the task for criminological theory is to explain under what circumstances individuals will deviate from these norms. Classic strain theorists such as Merton and Cohen argue that humans strive to achieve particular culturally valued goals or objectives such as monetary success and social status. When individuals are deprived of legitimate opportunities to achieve these goals due to poverty, deprivation, or discrimination they experience 'strain' and resort to illegal activities to obtain the goals that they are otherwise denied. More recently, Messner and Rosenfeld (2013) have emphasised how the peculiarities of American culture (which elevates the importance of monetary success) create incentives for crime in individuals who are – for social-structural reasons – 'locked out' of the American dream.

A more recent version of strain theory is provided by Agnew (2006). Agnew's **general strain theory** significantly broadens the scope of strains that might lead to crime to include not only strains that arise from the failure to achieve status and monetary success, but also strains that arise from the loss of positively valued experiences and relationships (e.g., family and friends) and strains that occur from the experience of abuse and victimisation (Agnew & Brezina, 2010). Agnew also points out that strains can be either 'objective' (everyone would experience them as such) or 'subjective' (they are disliked by the specific individual) thus bringing in an important individual difference component into the theory. Why do strains result in criminal behaviour? According to general strain theory, strains lead to the experience of negative emotions such as anger and frustration. This, in turn, can make individuals engage in crime in order to alleviate or assuage these negative emotional states. Although Agnew locates the source of many important strains in prevailing social-structural conditions, general strain theory also has a strong focus on psychological factors and specific developmental contexts.

Control theories form a second important tradition in theoretical criminology. As Paternoster and Bachman (2010, p. 114) note:

> Control theories begin with the assumption that socialization is not fully adequate, and that a person's first inclination is to act on the basis of their own self-interest, which may easily run them afoul of the law since the pursuit of self-interest through crime is very often the quickest and easiest way to need fulfilment.

Conventionally, two main forms of control dominate the theoretical literature: social control and self-control. For social control theorists, like Hirschi (1969, p. 16), crime is more likely to occur when the social bonds that attach individuals to conventional society and which support adherence to social norms are weak or broken. In contrast, individuals who form strong and enduring attachments to others and who adhere to conventional social norms are less likely to commit crime. Sampson's (Sampson, Raudenbush, & Earls, 1997) notion of 'collective efficacy' places the importance of social bonds within a broader community context by noting that communities that demonstrate high levels of social cohesion and the willingness to enforce social norms experience lower levels of crime and antisocial behaviour. Social control theory, therefore, locates the source of control in the relationship between individuals and the community. Self-control theory, in contrast, views control as an internal psychological characteristic that can explain why some individuals are more crime-prone than others (Gottfredson & Hirschi, 1990). We discuss the role of self-control in the section below on psychological approaches.

A third major tradition in criminological theory focuses on how criminal and antisocial behaviour arises through the way that individuals are defined relative to others in 'mainstream society'. Labelling theorists focus on how certain types of behaviour come to be defined as deviant and how this process can influence the subsequent behaviour of the individual who has, as a result, been labelled as a 'criminal' (Munice, 2010). Labelling theorists are interested not only in the 'marking' of specific individuals as deviant or criminal, but also in the wider labelling of particular social and cultural groups. Sub-cultural theorists are also interested in the way that **sub-cultures**, with specific values, norms, and practices can emerge in response to particular social environments that often entail a rejection of mainstream values (Hallsworth & Young, 2010).

Evaluation

There is little question that human behaviour is influenced by both the social-structural and cultural contexts in which we are embedded. Explanations that ignore social-structural and cultural factors will, therefore, be incomplete. However, as McGuire (2004) points out, all social-structural and cultural theories of crime imply the existence of a human agent who possesses certain psychological characteristics that make crime more or less likely. Social-structural and cultural theories of crime are, therefore, most salient for explaining geographical and historical patterns in criminal behaviour and are less important in accounting for individual differences (particularly among individuals who exist within the same culture or social structure but differ in their crime propensity). We will draw on social-structural and cultural theories of crime in various places throughout this textbook in order to explain a range of criminological phenomena.

REVIEW AND REFLECT

1   How might Agnew's general strain theory explain individual differences in offending?
2   What are the implications of the notion of 'collective efficacy' for preventing crime?

DEVELOPMENTAL APPROACHES

Are criminals born or made? That is, does criminal behaviour largely result from the specific genes that people inherit or does it arise from the developmental experiences that individuals are exposed to? I am willing to wager that most people would favour the latter explanation, but as most scholars will recognise, the question is poorly formulated because it is widely recognised that human development is shaped by the complex *interaction* of genetic and environmental factors (Pinker, 2002). Developmental approaches to understanding crime focus on how specific developmental trajectories (which include biological, psychological, social, and cultural factors) can influence criminal behaviour. Developmental approaches to understanding criminal behaviour have become increasingly important, and we devote a whole chapter to these perspectives (Chapter 2). In this section, therefore, we briefly consider some core ideas that will be drawn upon in later chapters.

Social learning theory

The idea that much of human behaviour, including aggression and violence, is largely the product of **social learning** is perhaps the most widely accepted idea in the social sciences. Within psychology this view is linked most clearly to the work of Albert Bandura (1973); in criminology, a version of social learning theory has been developed by Ronald Akers (1977, see Akers & Jensen, 2010). Although there are some differences in these two approaches to social learning, they both are based on a core set of fundamental assumptions. First, human behaviour is largely the product of learning. Second, individuals learn both through their own experiences with the world and also through observing (and imitating) others (what Bandura calls *vicarious learning*). Third, whether a behaviour is learned will depend on (a) the outcome of that behaviour (behaviour with positive outcomes is more likely to be learned) and (b) for vicarious learning, the status of the model or observed individual (models who are similar or high in status will be more likely to be imitated). Although initial formulations of social learning theory focused very much on the learning of behaviour per se, more recent developments emphasise that individuals also learn values, attitudes, beliefs, scripts, and other such cognitions that influence behavioural responses. The idea of social learning is prominent in many theoretical approaches to understanding criminal behaviour, and, as we will see in later chapters, it has been used to further our understanding of a diverse range of crime from domestic violence to terrorism (Akers & Jensen, 2010).

Developmental criminology

As Farrington (2010a, p. 249) explains:

> Developmental and life-course criminology is concerned mainly with three topics: (a) the development of offending and antisocial behaviour from the womb to the tomb; (b) the influence of risk and protective factors at different ages; and (c) the effects of life events on the course of development.

Developmental theories of crime, therefore, are concerned very broadly with how criminal behaviour relates to developmental processes. Thus, research has focused on the relationship between 'normal' developmental processes (e.g., puberty) and antisocial behaviour, as well as how specific developmental experiences (e.g., the experience of child abuse) impact on criminal offending. A good deal of the research focuses on developmental experiences through childhood up to adulthood, but it is also recognised how life experiences during the adult years may impact on criminal behaviour. In Table 1.2 some of the important findings of developmental criminology are outlined (Farrington, 2015). In Chapter 2 we explore these topics in more detail.

Table 1.2 Important findings relating to the development of offending

1   Offending peaks during late adolescence (aged 15–19).
2   Individuals who begin offending at an earlier age commit more offences and have a longer offending career.
3   There is considerable continuity in antisocial and criminal behaviour across the lifespan.
4   A relatively small number of individuals are responsible for the majority of crime.
5   Offenders tend to be criminally versatile and commit a wide variety of different types of offence.
6   Adolescent offenders tend to commit crimes with others, whereas adults tend to offend alone.
7   Important risk factors for offending relate to individual characteristics, and family, school, and community environments.
8   Employment, marriage, and having children are some of the key life events that are related to desistance from offending.
9   As people age they are, on average, less likely to commit crime.

Evaluation

Developmental approaches to understanding criminal behaviour are, by their very nature, interdisciplinary in scope. Because human development is a biosocial phenomenon (i.e., is the result of complex interactions between biological factors and the social environment) developmental approaches to criminology often draw on explanations from several different levels of analysis. Developmental approaches are, perhaps, most salient for explaining individual differences in criminal behaviour. In other words, they attempt to account for differences in criminal propensity as a result of different developmental experiences. Because groups of individuals may also be exposed to the same or similar developmental environments, developmental approaches can also potentially account for variations in offending across time and space. As we shall see in Chapter 11, developmental approaches have also played a prominent role in social crime prevention initiatives.

REVIEW AND REFLECT

1   Are criminals born or made? Review the research carried out by Beaver (2013) in the Research in Focus 1.1 box. Does this research provide an answer to this question? Why? Why not?

RESEARCH IN FOCUS 1.1 **DOES CRIME RUN IN FAMILIES?**

Title: The familial concentration and transmission of crime

Author: Beaver, K. M.   **Year**: 2013

Source: *Criminal Justice and Behavior*, 40, 139–155

Aims: To explore the extent to which crime is concentrated in families

Method: Sample of kinship pairs drawn from the National Longitudinal Study of Adolescent Health; Measures of criminality, parent criminality, family environment.

Key results:
- 5% of criminal families accounted for 53% of all criminal arrests.
- 10% of criminal families accounted for 79% of all criminal arrests.
- Having a criminal father, mother, or sibling significantly increased the odds of a respondent having a criminal arrest.

Conclusion: Crime is concentrated in families and is intergenerationally transmitted

Discussion question

Does this study allow us to say whether genetic or environmental factors were responsible for the familial concentration of crime? What further information might we need?

PSYCHOLOGICAL APPROACHES

What is it about some individuals that make them more likely to commit crimes than others? We have seen in the previous section that developmental approaches have focused on how different developmental trajectories make some individuals more prone to criminal and antisocial behaviour than others. In this section we explore approaches that focus on the individual-level psychological characteristics of people that may make them more or less likely to engage in criminal behaviour. We begin by considering approaches that have examined the personality characteristics of individuals, then turn to an overview of cognitive approaches to understanding criminal behaviour. We close this section with a brief consideration of how psychological or mental disorders might play a role in offending.

Personality

Most people recognise that individuals differ in their characteristic ways of thinking, feeling, and behaving. Some individuals are outgoing and drawn to exciting and risky activities whereas others are shy, withdrawn, and risk averse; some individuals easily get upset when things go wrong, whereas others tend to be more stoic in the face of adversity, and so on. In short, people differ in terms of their personality characteristics or traits. How might these differences relate to differences in the potential for criminal and antisocial behaviour? Two main types of approach have dominated the literature. The first type of approach looks broadly at models of personality based on multiple, essential traits, whereas the second type of approach focuses more narrowly on specific personality traits or characteristics. In both approaches the primary task has been to explore the extent to which certain personality characteristics are related to criminal behaviour.

The essential trait approach

In a famous study carried out in the 1930s, Allport and Odbert (1936, cited in Funder, 2004) counted 17,953 words in a standard dictionary that refer to the personality characteristics or traits of individuals. Clearly we find it easy to come up with terms that describe the personality of others! One important task for personality psychologists has been to attempt to reduce the plethora of trait terms to a few essential traits or characteristics that can capture the major dimensions of personality. One such approach was developed by the psychologist Hans Eysenck and is known as the **PEN model** (McAdams, 2006). Eysenck suggested that there are three major dimensions (or what Eysenck termed 'super-traits') of personality: psychoticism, extraversion-introversion, and neuroticism (note that the first letter of each personality dimension forms the acronym 'PEN'). The last two of these personality super-traits were the first developed by Eysenck with extraversion-introversion capturing individual variation in people's tendency to be sociable, outgoing, dominant, and active, while neuroticism captures individual differences in the tendency to be anxious, moody, irritable, and emotionally unstable. Psychoticism was a late addition to the model and was included, in part, due to Eysenck's interest in antisocial and criminal behaviour. The super-trait of psychoticism captures individual differences in people's tendency to be cold, insensitive, egocentric, and cruel.

An alternative model suggests that human personality can be captured in terms of five fundamental personality dimensions (the so-called '**big five personality traits**') (McAdams, 2006; McCrae & Costa, 1997): openness, conscientiousness, extraversion, agreeableness, and neuroticism (note that the first letter of each of the traits when combined conveniently spell out the word 'OCEAN'). The traits of 'extraversion' and 'neuroticism' in this approach are much the same as Eysenck envisioned them in the PEN model with people high on extraversion tending to be sociable, outgoing, and dominant and people high on neuroticism tending to be moody, emotional, and anxious. The trait of agreeableness refers to individual differences in the tendency to be good natured, trusting, and helpful, and conscientiousness captures individual differences in reliability, task perseverance, and self-discipline. Very roughly, individuals who are low on both agreeableness and conscientiousness would typically be high on psychoticism in the PEN model. The trait of openness has no parallel in Eysenck's model (and is not particularly relevant for understanding criminal behaviour) but refers to individual differences in the tendency to be curious, creative, and untraditional.

Although there remains a fair amount of dispute regarding the fundamental dimensions of human personality (Funder, 2001), the available evidence suggests that the five factor model captures the most important dimensions of personality (although another prominent model suggest that there are *six* fundamental dimensions – see Ashton, Lee, & de Vries, 2014), that personality traits are modestly heritable (see below), are relatively stable over time, and can be used to predict important life outcomes (Costa & McCrae, 1994; Paunonen, 2003). In Chapter 4 we will consider research that has linked Eysenck's super-traits and the big five to criminal behaviour, but you might want to consider in advance which of these personality characteristics in both of the approaches might be most important in explaining offending.

Single-trait approaches

Whereas the essential trait approach attempts to capture the major dimensions of personality, the single-trait approach focuses more narrowly on specific personality characteristics that are viewed as important. A number of these single-traits have been explored in the context of criminal and antisocial behaviour, with a particular focus on impulsivity, empathy, and narcissism.

Consider the following choice. Would you rather I give you $100 now or would you rather wait one year and receive $120. When I pose this question to my class of undergraduate students there is an almost unanimous response: they want the $100 now. Even if I slide the amount to be received in a year's time up to $150 most will still plump for the $100. When I ask my class why they opt for the smaller amount of money in the present their typical response is that they could use the money in the present for necessary (paying the rent) and not so necessary (a night out drinking) reasons. The odd, cynical student also fails to believe that I would actually pay them $150 in a year's time! This question taps into your capacity to delay gratification: that is, to inhibit the motivation to obtain something desirable in the present (the $100) in order to obtain an even greater reward in the future (the $120 or $150). **Delay of gratification** is just one among a somewhat bewildering array of related and partially overlapping psychological constructs including **impulsivity**, **self-control**, self-regulation, **executive functioning**, **risk seeking**, and **sensation seeking** (Cross, Copping, & Campbell, 2011). To confuse matters these various psychological constructs have been measured in an equally bewildering variety of ways with over 100 different self-report questionnaires alone (Duckworth & Kern, 2011). A useful way of organising these different constructs is provided by Cross et al. (2011) who suggest that three main characteristics are captured in the literature: overattraction to reward, undersensitivity to punishment, and difficulties in exerting control over behaviour.

Overattraction to reward relates to differences in approach motivation. Some individuals are simply more motivated to pursue and engage in a variety of risky and exciting activities than are others. Scales that measure risk seeking or sensation seeking tend to capture individual differences in the motivation to pursue risky and rewarding activities. These individual differences are potentially important to understanding criminal behaviour because many risky and exciting activities are either criminal offences (e.g., dangerous driving, drug use, fighting) or associated with criminal behaviour (e.g., binge drinking, gambling). As we shall see, there are both important age (Chapter 2) and gender differences (Chapters 4 and 5) in the motivation to pursue rewards that can, in part, account for individual differences in criminal behaviour. In Chapter 8 we will also see how the biological mechanisms underlying reward can be 'highjacked' by drugs of abuse, which, in part, explains the attractiveness of these substances. Undersensitivity to punishment refers to individual differences in the tendency to be influenced or affected by the negative consequences of behaviour. Individual differences in punishment sensitivity have not played a particularly prominent role in theories of criminal behaviour but are potentially important for understanding why women tend to engage in significantly less crime then men (they tend to be more fearful or concerned about the negative consequences – see Campbell, 2013b; Cross & Campbell, 2011) and why individuals who have 'psychopathic' characteristics may be particularly crime prone (see Chapter 3).

The capacity for self-control or self-regulation features prominently in many theoretical approaches to understanding criminal and antisocial behaviour. Self-control can be defined as 'the capacity to alter or override dominant response tendencies and to regulate behaviour, thoughts, and emotions' (de Ridder et al., 2012, p. 77). The capacity for self-control can be viewed as both a dispositional characteristic that varies among individuals (some people have a better capacity to control their behaviour than others) and a characteristic that varies across situations and that might be influenced by a range of factors including the consumption of alcohol and other drugs (see Chapter 8). The capacity for self-control is related to a wide range of behaviours and outcomes with individuals who are better able to control their behaviour, typically performing better at school and in the workplace (e.g., Daly, Delaney, Egan, & Baumeister, 2015) and having fewer problems with alcohol, gambling, and other problematic behaviours (de Ridder et al., 2012; Tangney, Baumeister, & Boone, 2004). For our purposes, as we shall explore in more detail in Chapters 2 and 4 in particular, the capacity for self-control is an important predictor of antisocial and criminal behaviour. Indeed, one of the better known criminological theories – Gottfredson and Hirschi's (1990) **general theory of crime** – elevates the capacity for self-control as the most important component in understanding criminal behaviour. For Gottfredson and Hirschi (1990) the desire to engage in crime is a given as it reflects a general human tendency to seek immediate gratification. Whether or not individuals do actually engage in criminal behaviour is then dependent on their capacity for self-control given the opportunities afforded by specific situations.

Cognition

Another important psychological approach to explaining criminal behaviour focuses on offender cognition. Cognitive approaches emphasise the importance of attending to the way that offenders think about themselves and the world. Cognitive psychology is a major sub-discipline in psychology that is concerned with a wide array of topics, including memory, language, reasoning, decision making, and intelligence. Most cognitive approaches to understanding criminal behaviour focus, however, on social cognition so we will restrict ourselves to a discussion in this section to the social-cognitive approaches to understanding crime.

Social-cognitive approaches

As Kosslyn and Rosenberg (2004, p. 670) explain, social cognition 'does not focus on the "objective" social world, but instead on how individuals perceive their social worlds, and how they attend to, store, remember, and use information about other people and the social world'. Social cognitive theory, furthermore, assumes that these internal representations of the social world arise largely though learning and can subsequently influence behaviour. Two important constructs in social cognitive theory are **schemas** and **scripts**.

A schema is a collection of learned concepts that relate to a specific domain (Kosslyn & Rosenberg, 2004; Wortley, 2011). We can have schemas for all sorts of domains including objects, people, and roles. Thus if I ask you to think about what an 'office' looks like, you will automatically access your 'office schema' that will contain beliefs about what specific items (chairs, desks, computers) tend to reside in offices. You will also have specific schemas for types of people (offenders, lecturers, politicians, etc.) and particular types of roles (e.g., doctors, police officers). Scripts are viewed by cognitive psychologists as knowledge structures that describe particular sequences of action that are associated with particular events or activities (Goldstein, 2005). Scripts, therefore, are a specific type of schema known as an event schema. Thus we all have scripts for going out to dinner that involve booking tables, waiting to be seated, ordering drinks, ordering food, ordering more drinks, eating the food, ordering more drinks, paying, and so forth. If someone mentions 'going out to dinner' we readily conjure up this script to guide our behaviour. Scripts, in short, can represent and define situations and guide behaviour.

Mental structures like schemas and scripts play an important role in guiding appropriate social behaviour. They can, however, also influence criminal behaviour. In Chapter 4, for example, we explore how exposure to violence during development might contribute to the development of specific scripts for violent behaviour that become readily activated under certain circumstances. In Chapter 6 we also explore how some sex offenders may possess 'distorted scripts' regarding normal sexual relations that contribute to their offending. More generally, we will explore the wider role of offender cognition in the aetiology of criminal behaviour and see how certain ways of thinking about the world and processing social information may contribute to offending behaviour. In Chapter 13 we will also explore the importance of cognitive-behavioural approaches to offender rehabilitation that target patterns of offender thinking in attempts to reduce re-offending.

Psychological disorders

Many people will have the view that there must be something 'wrong' with individuals who engage in serious and persistent criminal behaviour. Indeed the idea that offenders are, in some sense, mentally ill or dysfunctional has a relatively long history in criminology. Vivid media reports of serial and mass murderers (see Chapter 5) certainly lend, on the face of it, credence to this view. Why else, it may be natural to think, would (or could) an individual start shooting others at random at a school or crowded public place, unless they were mentally disturbed? In order to address this question it will be important to establish just what we mean by a 'mental disorder' or 'mental illness' and what the available evidence indicates about the relationship between mental disorder and crime.

In Chapter 3 we will provide a definition of mental disorder and will explore in detail the relationship between mental disorder and crime. As we shall see, although many studies do find a relationship between mental disorder and criminal behaviour the nature of this relationship is in no sense straightforward (Schug & Fradella, 2015). We will also see how certain types of disorders (in particular, certain personality disorders) may be particularly relevant for understanding criminal behaviour.

Evaluation

Psychological approaches to understanding criminal behaviour will feature prominently throughout this book. This not only reflects the fact that this book is about *criminal psychology*, but is also because psychological approaches to explaining criminal behaviour attempt to provide an answer to one of the key questions posed by criminologists and other scholars interested in crime: why are some individuals more likely to engage in criminal offending than others? Psychological approaches attempt to answer this question by locating differences in personality and cognitive characteristics, some of which may relate to specific mental disorders.

REVIEW AND REFLECT

1   What are some of the important personality characteristics that may be related to criminal and antisocial behaviour?
2   What are 'schemas', and how might they be relevant for understanding individual differences in the propensity for offending?
3   Why might individual differences in the capacity for self-regulation impact on so many diverse life domains such as health, employment, and antisocial behaviour?

BIOLOGICAL APPROACHES

The search for the biological correlates of crime has a relatively long, albeit somewhat controversial, history in criminology (Rafter, Posick, & Rocque, 2016). Many of the early leading criminologists – from Cesare Lombroso to William Sheldon – sought to explain criminal behaviour in terms of specific biological characteristics. Lombroso, for instance, argued that criminals were 'throwbacks' to an earlier evolutionary time and could be identified by specific physical characteristics such as protruding jaws and drooping eyes. These early biological approaches to understanding crime, not surprisingly, have been discredited, and biological approaches have been largely neglected for most of the latter half of the twentieth century. However, in recent decades there has been a resurgence of interest in biological explanations for crime (Barnes, Boutwell, & Beaver, 2016; Raine, 2013). In this section we provide a brief overview of the most important biological processes that are relevant for understanding research on criminal behaviour, focusing in turn on genetic factors, neurotransmitters and hormones, and neuropsychological approaches.

Genetic factors

As noted above, Darwin's theory of natural selection is predicated on the idea that for favourable characteristics to be retained in the population they must be reliably passed on from parents to offspring. That is, they must be heritable. Although Darwin failed to accurately identify just how this happened, over a century of research has substantially advanced our understanding of this process with the identification of the gene as the fundamental unit of inheritance. Humans have somewhere in the region of 20,000 to 25,000 genes, which, in combination with each other and the environment, are largely responsible for determining the phenotypical (i.e., manifest or observable) characteristics of each and every person (Beaver, 2009). Most people will recognise that certain physical traits or characteristics tend to 'run in families', with children more likely to resemble their parents than adults in the general population. However, the idea that certain psychological characteristics such as IQ, personality, or, perhaps, an increased propensity for criminal behaviour might be heritable is somewhat more controversial.

One important approach that has been used to explore the heritability of a wide range of psychological characteristics is known as **behavioural genetics** (Plomin, DeFries, McClearn, & McGuffin, 2008). Behavioural genetics involves exploring the extent to which population variations in a given trait (like IQ) can be accounted for by genetic versus environmental factors. **Heritability** is expressed in terms of a coefficient that can range from 0 to 1 and which specifies how much of the variance in the population can be attributable to genetic factors. It is very important to recognise that heritability is a population statistic – it reflects the source of variation in whatever population is sampled – and therefore does not apply to individuals. Thus a heritability coefficient of 0.4 for a given trait allows us to say that 40 per cent of the variation in this trait in this population is due to genetic factors. It does not allow us to infer that genes contribute 40 per cent to the trait in question (Wortley, 2011).

In generating heritability coefficients behavioural geneticists make use of the fact that individuals vary in their degree of genetic relatedness in a fairly consistent fashion. Identical or monozygotic twins share 100 per cent of their genes, siblings share (on average) 50 per cent of their genes as do children with their biological parents, while the genetic relatedness of unrelated individuals is close to zero. Thus, behavioural genetic research involves comparisons on a given trait or characteristics between:

- identical (monozygotic) twins, and non-identical (dizygotic) twins
- identical twins reared together, and identical twins reared apart
- individuals with criminal (biological) parents adopted into non-criminal families, and individuals with non-criminal (biological) parents adopted into criminal families.

The logic of these comparisons is easy to see. For example, if the variation in a given trait is influenced by genetic factors then identical twins should be more similar on that trait than non-identical twins, and there will be little difference between identical twins reared together and reared apart. The extent to which individuals resemble their biological compared to their adopted parents also speaks to the relative amount of variation that is explained by genetic factors. We will look at the relevant research for criminal behaviour in more detail in Chapter 4, but meta-analyses of this research suggest that approximately 40 to 50 per cent of the variance in antisocial and criminal behaviour can be attributed to genetic factors (Moffitt, 2005; Rhee & Waldman, 2002). Thus, although these studies point to a role for genetic factors, they equally highlight the important role of the environment (see Burt & Simons, 2014, for a critique of heritability studies in criminology and the response from Barnes et al., 2014).

Indeed, research in behavioural genetics clearly identifies the crucial role of environmental influences and, perhaps more importantly, highlights the complex *interaction* between genetic and environmental influences. Researchers have highlighted the importance of both gene/environment correlation (rGE) and gene/environment interaction (G × E) in explaining the genetic influences on antisocial behaviour (Rutter, 2007; Walsh, 2009b).

There are three types of rGE: passive rGE, active rGE, and **evocative rGE**. Walsh (2009b, p. 38) provides a good summary of how these effects can shape the development of antisocial behaviour. Passive rGE highlights the fact that parents contribute both genes and environment to their developing offspring. Thus an individual who is born to parents who are both heavily involved in criminal activities is likely both to have personality characteristics that may make him or her more criminal 'prone' as well as to have been raised in a family environment clearly conducive to the development of antisocial attitudes and behaviour. Individuals react to us, in part, due to the way we behave. An individual who consistently behaves in an antisocial manner is likely to evoke negative responses from others, which, in turn, may enhance or magnify these antisocial characteristics. This is an example of evocative rGE as genetically influenced characteristics change the (social) environment in ways that may enhance these characteristics. Finally, humans actively seek out environments that best suit their characteristics including those that have a genetic basis. Someone with strong antisocial tendencies, therefore, is likely to actively pursue friendships and associations with peers who share their characteristics and interests. Through this active rGE process, individuals create environments or niches that are tailored towards their needs and desires.

To date most genetic research on criminal and antisocial behaviour has employed twin and adoption studies to explore the role of genetic factors. However, although this research has proved to be highly informative, it tells us little about just *how* genes actually contribute to the development of particular characteristics. Research in the field of molecular genetics attempts to address this issue. This line of research attempts to locate candidate genes that, in combination with specific environments, play a role in the expression of antisocial and criminal behaviour. Typically the focus is on how genes might influence the development of the brain, with a particular focus on how they can affect the activity of specific neurotransmitters (see below) (Beaver, 2009; Raine, 2013). As we shall explore in more detail in Chapter 3, this line of research emphasises the importance of G × E interactions in the development of antisocial and criminal behaviour: the effect of specific genes on behaviour depends on aspects of the environment (Baker, Tuvblad, & Raine, 2010; Chen et al., 2016). Indeed, it is becoming increasingly clear that environmental factors can influence the way that genes are expressed throughout the lifespan, and a whole field of enquiry, known as **epigenetics**, has arisen to address this fact (see Moore, 2015).

Hormones and neurotransmitters

Other biological research has focused on specific neurophysiological processes, with a good deal of attention paid to the role of **neurotransmitters** and **hormones**. Neurotransmitters are chemical substances that play a critical role in the brain's communication system and hence have an important impact on thinking, emotion, and behaviour. Neurotransmitters are released from the terminal buttons of **neurons** (specialised cells in the brain), cross a small space between the terminal button of one neuron and the receptor of another, known as the **synapse**, and subsequently influence the action of other neurons in the nervous system (see Figure 1.4). Given that the brain has something in the region of 100 billion neurons of various types and over 75 different neurotransmitters the processes involved are enormously complicated (Kolb & Whishaw, 2011).

Fortunately we can avoid most of this detail here, as most research relevant for our understanding of criminal behaviour has focused on two main neurotransmitter systems: the dopaminergic system (relating to the neurotransmitter **dopamine**) and the serotonergic system (relating to the neurotransmitter **serotonin**). The dopaminergic system plays an important role in emotional arousal and pleasure (see Figure 1.5). In Chapter 4 we will explore research that has linked dopamine with impulsivity and

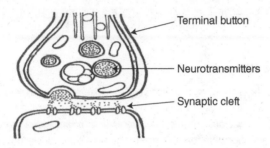

Terminal button

Neurotransmitters

Synaptic cleft

Figure 1.4 The synapse.

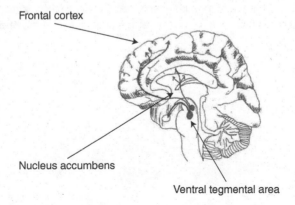

Frontal cortex

Nucleus accumbens

Ventral tegmental area

Figure 1.5 The mesolimbic dopamine pathway.

aggression, and in Chapter 2 we will see that changes in the dopaminergic system may play a role in heightened risk for antisocial behaviour during adolescence. The dopaminergic system is also the target for most drugs of abuse and hence, as we will see in Chapter 8, plays a role in our understanding of drug use and addiction. The serotonergic system plays a role in a number of brain functions, including those relating to sleep, appetite, and impulsive control, and has been implicated in aggressive and violent behaviour.

Whereas neurotransmitters are produced or synthesised in the brain, hormones are chemical substances that are produced in a number of different glands in the human body. They are of relevance for understanding criminal behaviour because hormones act as neuromodulators. In other words, they alter or modulate the effect of neurotransmitters in the central nervous system and hence influence the communication of information in the brain. Important hormones include **testosterone**, oestrogen, and cortisol. Of these, testosterone is the hormone that has been most implicated in criminal behaviour. Testosterone is a sex hormone that is produced in much larger quantities in men than in women and is responsible for influencing the in utero development of male characteristics such as the external genitalia and the masculinisation of the central nervous system. At puberty there is a dramatic tenfold increase in the amount of testosterone produced in the testes. This is responsible for development of male characteristics such as the lowering of the voice, facial and body hair, and muscle mass (Mazur, 2009). In Chapter 3 we will examine the – somewhat complex – relationship between aggression and testosterone in more detail.

Neuropsychology

The brain is a 1.4kg spongy mass that vaguely resembles a prize-winning cauliflower except that the brain is divided into two hemispheres or halves, which are made up of four 'lobes' or parts – occipital, temporal, parietal, and frontal (see Figure 1.6). These four different lobes are responsible for different functions although it is important to recognise that they are richly interconnected with one another, and a number of brain functions are 'distributed' across the brain. The most important mental processes take place in the **cerebral cortex**, which is the convoluted top layer of the brain. The frontal lobe is the part of the brain most relevant for our understanding of criminal and antisocial behaviour, and a particular focus has been on the part of this area known as the **prefrontal cortex**.

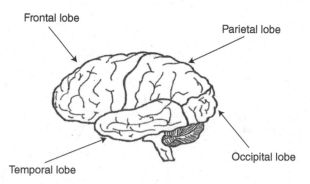

Frontal lobe

Parietal lobe

Occipital lobe

Temporal lobe

Figure 1.6 The lobes of the brain.

The prefrontal cortex is critically implicated in a suite of psychological processes referred to as executive functions. These can be conceptualised as the 'cluster of higher order cognitive processes involving initiation, planning, cognitive flexibility, abstraction, and decision making that together allow the execution of contextually appropriate behaviour' (Ishikawa & Raine, 2003, p. 281). The psychological processes of self-control or self-regulation, which we have discussed earlier, can therefore be viewed as part of the brain's executive functions (Beaver, Wright, & DeLisi, 2007). Although we do not need to delve too deeply into the biological details, it is worth noting here that the prefrontal cortex is typically viewed as comprising several distinct anatomical regions including the orbitofrontal cortex (OFC), the dorsolateral prefrontal cortex (DLPFC), the ventromedial prefrontal cortex (VLPFC), and the medial prefrontal cortex (MPFC) (Yang & Raine, 2009), each of which has relatively specific psychological functions. In Chapter 4 we will examine the frontal-brain hypothesis, which suggests that criminal and antisocial behaviour can be understood in terms of the impaired functioning of the frontal cortex.

Underneath the cortex can be found a number of sub-cortical structures including the hippocampus and an almond-shaped structure known as the **amygdala**. The amygdala is part of the limbic system, which is critically involved in emotion and motivation. The amygdala plays a specific role in the processing and regulation of emotion and is implicated in recognising anger and fear responses in others. As we shall see in Chapter 3, some approaches to understanding psychopathy have focused on amygdala dysfunction as a partial explanation for the development of psychopathic characteristics.

Evaluation

Biological approaches are most salient for understanding individual differences in criminal behaviour. That is, they contribute to addressing the question of why some individuals are more likely to engage in criminal behaviour than are others. There are also potentially clear linkages with the other approaches described in this chapter. Most straightforwardly many biological processes in the brain can be viewed as the instantiation of corresponding psychological mechanisms. Thus the capacity for self-regulation is an important function of the prefrontal cortex (among other structures). Genetic factors can also be firmly located within developmental approaches to understanding antisocial behaviour as researchers have devoted a considerable amount of effort to unravelling the complex G × E interactions that give rise to specific traits and characteristics. Traditionally criminologists have been reluctant to incorporate biological approaches to understanding criminal behaviour. In part, this may be due to a fear that by invoking genetic factors or brain processes we will be inevitably pushed into a determinist view of crime in which nothing can be done to alter or change criminal behaviour (short of science fiction style genetic engineering or neurosurgery). However, if we recognise that contemporary genetic approaches emphasise the complex interaction of genes and environment in development and if we understand that neuropsychological approaches attempt to provide explanations at one specific level of analysis many of these fears should be allayed. Although there are – sometimes formidable – methodological issues in carrying out biological research on crime, as we shall see throughout this book that our understanding of criminal behaviour would not be complete unless we incorporate biological approaches (Chen et al., 2016).

REVIEW AND REFLECT

1   What role do genes play in the origin of criminal and antisocial behaviour?
2   What are neurotransmitters?
3   What are the implications of biological approaches to understanding crime for criminal culpability? Do you think that recent research in genetics or neuroscience implies a more lenient criminal justice response? (You may want to check out recent articles in the *Journal of Law and the Biosciences* for relevant material to address this question.)

SITUATIONAL APPROACHES

The final level of analysis that we will consider in this chapter relates to the situational context of offending. It may seem like stating the obvious but it is important to recognise that crime is always embedded in specific situations. Some human activities, such as breathing, may be influenced by environmental factors, but they essentially occur all the time. Even the most persistent criminals, however, are not always committing offences. It is thus important to explore how criminal behaviour emerges in specific environmental contexts.

The social environment

One important aspect of our environment is the other people that we interact with – that is, our *social* environment. An entire sub-discipline of psychology (social psychology) is largely concerned with how a person's thinking and behaviour are shaped and influenced by their interactions with others. Think for a moment about how your behaviour is different depending on the people that you are interacting with. If, for instance, you are having a formal dinner with your parents and grandparents I wager that your behaviour will be rather different than if you are out celebrating a friend's bachelor or bachelorette party. Why is this case? The reason that your behaviour varies depending on the situation is that the social environment provides information about what kind of behaviour is appropriate or expected. We should not be surprised, therefore, that social environments can also exert an important influence on criminal behaviour. As we shall see in Chapter 2 a significant body of research highlights that importance of peer influence in the criminal behaviour of young people, and there is evidence to suggest that the presence of peers heightens the risk of engaging in antisocial behaviour. In Chapter 7 we will also see how some of the most appalling human acts of collective violence (e.g., genocide, war, torture) are influenced by the social actions of others. In particular, the psychologist Philip Zimbardo (2007) has highlighted how morally reprehensible acts are more readily performed in groups as individuals conform to particular social roles, and responsibility for actions is diffused among members of the group so individual responsibility is diminished. This social process is known as **deindividuation**.

A significant amount of interpersonal crime also emerges in the context of social interactions. Although there is certainly a fair amount of 'predatory' offending in which individuals specifically plan to target a particular victim or location, a large of amount of criminal behaviour is, essentially, unplanned or spontaneous. As we shall see in Chapter 5 many serious violent offences, including homicide, occur in social situations when individuals are frustrated or provoked in some fashion or other. Indeed, it can be difficult in some of these situations to clearly demarcate 'offenders' from 'victims'. It is important to recognise, therefore, that criminal behaviour can emerge out of the relatively normal day-to-day social interactions of family members, friends, and acquaintances.

A number of theoretical approaches draw heavily on the role of social processes but also incorporate individual psychological characteristics. Wikström (2006; Wikström & Treiber, 2016), for instance, has advanced a situational action theory of crime that emphasises the importance of how individual characteristics interact with situational contexts to produce criminal behaviour. As he states: 'To explain crime we need to identify the key individual characteristics and experiences (crime propensities) and the environmental features (crime inducements) that influences whether an individual tends to see crime as an alternative and tends to act upon it' (Wikström, 2006, p. 62). In recent times a distinct 'psychosocial' approach to understanding criminal behaviour has also emerged in which criminal actions are located at the complex interface between 'inner' (mental states and processes) and 'external' (social and cultural relations) worlds (Jefferson, 2010). Within the 'social process tradition' of mainstream criminology there has also been an emphasis on how individuals perceive and respond to their social reality (Walsh & Ellis, 2007). Social learning theory, social bonding theory, and sub-cultural theories (discussed above) all emphasise the importance of social processes in the development of criminal behaviour.

The physical environment and criminal opportunities

Although understandably there has been a large amount of attention devoted to the social environment in theories of criminal behaviour it is important to recognise that criminal acts are also influenced by the wider physical environment that we find ourselves in. Three prominent theoretical perspectives in criminology focus on the important role played by the situation in offending: (a) **rational choice theory**; (b) **crime pattern theory**; and (c) **routine activities theory**. According to the rational choice perspective, criminal behaviour is rational, and offenders, like everyone else, seek to obtain maximum reward for minimum effort. Offenders are thus influenced by the perceived benefits and costs of offending at a given time and place (Cornish & Clarke, 2008, 2014). Property offenders, for instance, will be influenced by such factors as convenience (why drive across town to burgle a house when an opportunity is available three streets over), level of protection (target the house without the security system when the owners are out), and anticipated yield (target houses with expensive and portable items like laptop computers). The central proposition of routine activities theory (Felson, 2008) is that for crime to occur, three things must converge in space and time: (a) a motivated offender; (b) a suitable target; and (c) the absence of an available guardian. The existence of motivated offenders is largely taken as given so inevitably crime will converge on suitable targets (e.g., properties with expensive and portable items) without capable guardians (e.g., no one at home). Felson (2008) also emphasises how people's routine activities provide different opportunities for offending. For example, a family that lives out in the suburbs with two parents that commute to work creates a reliable window for offending during the time that everyone is away from the home during the daytime.

The importance of routine activities is also highlighted in crime pattern theory (Brantingham & Brantingham, 2008), which takes as its basic premise the idea that crime does not occur randomly in time or space but, rather, is patterned: crime is more frequent in some environments than others, and individual offending reflects aspects of an individual's geographical location. Thus, individuals have a typical range of routine activities that operate around different 'nodes' of activity such as school, work, shopping, and recreation. These nodes of activity and the routes that link them represent an individual's 'activity space' or 'awareness space' in which offending tends to occur. Support for crime pattern theory comes from 'journey to crime' research that consistently finds that offenders do not tend to travel long distances to commit crime, but rather offend close to home in areas that they are familiar with (Bernasco, 2010)

Evaluation

Situational approaches to understanding crime are clearly important because they highlight the role that the social and environmental context plays in offending. As such, situational approaches are especially salient for explaining intra-individual differences in offending. In other words they can help to explain the situations that contribute to the offending of an individual at one time rather than another. Although situational perspectives emphasise the role of the situation, offending is always the result of the interactions that occur between persons and the environments in which they are embedded, and thus criminal behaviour can be viewed as the 'emergent' product of people and situations (McGloin, Sullivan, & Kennedy, 2012). As we shall see in Chapter 11, situational approaches to understanding crime have played an important role in some crime prevention initiatives.

REVIEW AND REFLECT

1   How might the routine activities of individuals influence opportunities for criminal behaviour?
2   How can situational theories of offending be utilised to prevent crime?

SUMMARY

Crime can be most straightforwardly defined as 'an act or omission punishable by law' (Munice & McLaughlin, 2001, p. 10), although we need to recognise that what constitutes a punishable offence varies across time and space. Criminologists employ three main approaches for measuring crime: official crime statistics, victim surveys, and self-report studies. Each of these three approaches has their limitations, and, where possible, information about the nature and prevalence of crime should be obtained from a variety of sources.

Criminal psychology can be viewed as the application of psychological science to our understanding of criminal behaviour. In our attempts to provide explanations for crime it is important to recognise that many different types of explanation may be compatible with one another because they focus on different levels of analysis. A useful framework for understanding levels of analysis, adapted from Tinbergen (1963), recognises that we need to consider distal explanations (in terms of evolutionary and cultural history), developmental explanations (in terms of the complex interplay between genes and environment in the developing individual), and proximate explanations (in terms of the important biological, psychological, and situational factors that contribute to criminal behaviour). A summary of the main levels of analysis and key theories and approaches is provided in Table 1.3.

Evolutionary explanations for criminal behaviour have as their starting point the idea that humans are the production of evolution by natural and sexual selection, and hence our behaviour can be understood (in part) in evolutionary terms. Evolutionary psychology is the branch of psychology that focuses on the application of evolutionary theory to understanding human mind and behaviour. Despite an ongoing reluctance

Table 1.3 An overview of the approaches discussed in this chapter

General approach	Level of analysis	Specific theories or approaches	Most salient for explaining
Evolutionary	Distal	Natural selection; sexual selection; parental investment theory	Why humans commit crimes in general; sex and age differences in offending
Social-structural and cultural	Distal; developmental; proximate	Strain theories; control theories; labelling and sub-cultural theories	Geographical and historical patterns in offending
Developmental	Developmental	Social learning theory; developmental theories of offending	Individual differences in offending; patterns in offending across the life span
Psychological	Proximate	General theory of crime; social-cognitive approaches; psychological disorders	Individual difference in offending
Biological	Proximate	The role of genetics, specific brain regions, neurotransmitters, and hormones	Individual difference in offending
Situational	Proximate	Situational action theory; rational choice theory; routine activities theory; crime pattern theory	Intra-individual variations in offending

among most criminologists to consider evolutionary explanations of criminal behaviour they can meaningfully contribute to our understanding of crime. However, evolutionary accounts have their limitations and need to be integrated with explanations from other levels of analysis to advance our understanding of criminal behaviour.

Humans clearly have an evolutionary history that is relevant for our understanding of criminal behaviour. Humans, somewhat uniquely among animals, are also strongly influenced by the cultural and social structural contexts in which they are embedded. Most mainstream criminological theories focus on this level of analysis with three important traditions represented by strain theories, control theories, and labelling and sub-cultural theories, respectively. Strain theorists argue that crime arises when individuals are blocked from achieving legitimate cultural goals and thus resort to criminal offending. Control theorists focus on how weak attachment to mainstream social groups leads to deviant behaviour, and labelling theorists examine the way that mainstream society responds to and labels certain behaviour as deviant.

Developmental approaches to understanding criminal behaviour focus on how particular developmental trajectories might influence criminal behaviour. One important assumption of most developmental approaches is that the learning environment can play an important role in the development of characteristics that may make some individuals more likely to offend than others. Criminal behaviour has also been related to normal aspects of development with the important observation that offending tends to peak in adolescence and young adulthood. Developmental theories of crime thus attempt to account for patterns in offending across the lifespan and how developmental processes may make some individuals more likely to become persistent offenders than others.

One major approach to explaining individual differences in offending focuses on the psychological characteristics of individuals. A good deal of research has explored to what extent specific personality characteristics may make some individuals more likely to offend than others with a prominent role afforded to the capacity for self-control. Social-cognitive approaches to understanding criminal behaviour also focus on the way that offenders tend to perceive their social world and how this might influence the development of criminal behaviour. Some offenders may also suffer from specific mental disorders that may make them more likely to commit crime, although as we shall see in Chapter 3 the relationship between mental disorder and crime is a complex one. Biological approaches to understanding criminal behaviour also tend to focus on individual differences. One line of research has examined how criminal behaviour may be the result of the complex interaction of genetic and environmental characteristics, whereas other research has examined the role of specific neurotransmitters, hormones, and brain regions.

All criminal behaviour occurs within a specific social and environmental context. Thus, situational approaches to understanding criminal behaviour focus on how features of the social and physical environment may facilitate offending. Three prominent theoretical approaches within this tradition are rational choice theory, routine activities theory, and crime pattern theory.

FURTHER READING

Hollin, C. R. (2013). *Psychology and Crime: An Introduction to Criminological Psychology.* London: Routledge.
A useful introduction to criminological psychology.

Newburn, T. (2013). *Criminology* (2nd edition). London: Routledge
Simply the best introductory criminology textbook on the market – seriously monumental in scope.

Piquero, A. R. (ed.), (2016). *The Handbook of Criminological Theory.* Chichester: Wiley Blackwell.
A cutting-edge handbook that provides a good overview of the state of the play in criminological theory.

Raine, A. (2013). *The Anatomy of Violence: The Biological Roots of Crime.* London: Penguin.
A highly readable account of biological approaches to crime written for a general audience by one of the main researchers in the field.

Walsh, A., & Ellis, L. (2007). *Criminology: An Interdisciplinary Approach.* Thousand Oaks, CA: Sage Publications.
In my view, the best U.S.-oriented criminology textbook with a wider scope of coverage than your standard textbook.

Wortley, R. (2011). *Psychological Criminology: An Integrative Approach.* London: Routledge.
An excellent overview of psychological approaches to understanding crime including good coverage of evolutionary, biological, and developmental approaches.

You will find relevant information on the material covered in this chapter in a number of different sources, but four useful journals for criminal and forensic psychology research are: *Legal and Criminological Psychology, Psychology, Crime and Law, Criminal Justice and Behaviour*, and *The Journal of Investigative Psychology and Offender Profiling.*

WEB RESOURCES

A good place to start for general information about criminal and forensic psychology is to explore the homepages (and associated journals) of the various criminal and forensic psychology organisations:

Division of Forensic Psychology (UK): www.bps.org.uk/dfp.
The American Psychology-Law Society (US): www.ap-ls.org.
European Association of Psychology and Law (Europe): http://eapl.eu.
International Association for Correctional and Forensic Psychology: www.aa4cfp.org.

KEY CONCEPTS

- adaptations
- amygdala
- behavioural genetics
- big five personality traits
- cerebral cortex
- crime pattern theory
- criminal psychology
- culture
- dark figure of crime
- deindividuation
- delay of gratification
- distal explanations
- dopamine
- epigenetics
- evocative rGE
- evolutionary psychology
- executive functioning

- general strain theory
- general theory of crime
- heritability
- hormones
- impulsivity
- levels of analysis
- naturalistic fallacy
- natural selection
- neurons
- neurotransmitters
- official crime statistics
- parental investment theory
- PEN model
- prefrontal cortex
- proximate mechanisms
- rational choice theory

- risk seeking
- routine activities theory
- schemas
- scripts
- self-control
- sensation seeking
- serotonin
- sexual selection
- social learning
- social structure
- sub-cultures
- synapse
- testosterone
- victim surveys

Developmental approaches to understanding crime

LEARNING OBJECTIVES

On completion of this chapter you should:

> have a clear idea of the nature and extent of offending across the lifespan;
> be able to provide an explanation for the age–crime curve based on your knowledge of the important biological, psychological, and social changes that occur during adolescence;
> have a good understanding of the key individual, family, and social risk factors associated with offending;
> have developed an understanding of three important developmental theories of offending.

At the tender age of 13, Bailey Junior Kurariki became New Zealand's youngest individual charged with homicide. Kurariki was subsequently convicted for manslaughter for his part in the killing of pizza delivery worker Michael Choy on September 12, 2001, in Papakura, Auckland. Kurariki, then aged 12, acted as a decoy and signalman in the murder, which involved five other teenagers. Labelled by the media as 'the child who shocked a generation' (Boland, 2007), Kurariki came from a difficult family environment and had been repeatedly removed from his family by social services. Due to his behavioural problems, Kurariki had not attended school since the age of ten and was regularly in trouble with the police (Kay, 2002). Bailey Junior Kurariki was eventually released from prison in May, 2008, after serving seven years in prison. However, his troubles with the law continued, and in 2011 he was sentenced to a further 14 months in prison on assault and domestic violence charges.

It seems that each new adult generation laments the state of 'today's' youth. High-profile cases of children who have been convicted of killing, like Bailey Junior Kurariki, inevitably attract a great deal of media coverage. In the United Kingdom, the abduction and murder of two-year-old James Bulger by two 10-year-old boys generated an enormous amount of media attention and provoked various debates concerning the age of criminal responsibility, the state of the nation's youth, and concern over the 'moral decay' of society (Green, 2007, 2008).

These examples raise a number of important questions about the nature of juvenile offending. Just what kind of offences do young people commit, and how much juvenile crime is there? Are adolescents and young adults more likely to offend than older individuals, and, if so, why? How should young people be treated by the criminal justice system, and at what age can we say that an individual is criminally responsible for their crimes? Do young offenders continue on a 'life of crime' as Bailey Kurariki seems to have, or do they desist from offending? Why are some young people more likely to commit crimes than others – what are the important individual, family, and social factors that put some young people at greater risk of offending?

There are four main sections to this chapter. First, we examine the nature of offending across the lifespan with a focus on juvenile offending. One important finding is that crime rates seem to peak during adolescence, and, in the second section, we will examine the important biological, psychological, and social changes that occur during adolescence in an attempt to explain this phenomenon. Some young people are more likely to engage in offending than others, and their offending is of a more serious and persistent nature. In the next section we will examine, in some detail, the most important individual, family, and social risk factors for offending to explain these individual differences. Finally, some of the key developmental theories of offending that have been developed to explain patterns of crime over the lifespan will be reviewed. By the end of this chapter you should have developed a good understanding of the nature of offending across the lifespan and the various approaches that have been developed to explain the patterns that are found.

CRIMINAL OFFENDING ACROSS THE LIFESPAN

Juvenile delinquency and criminal responsibility

It is a fairly straightforward task to provide a clear legal definition of juvenile delinquency. **Juvenile delinquency** is simply any behaviour that violates the criminal law when perpetrated by individuals who have not yet reached the aged of adulthood, as specified in relevant national or state legislation (Bartol & Bartol, 2008). In short, juvenile delinquency refers to criminal acts committed by minors. A social definition of delinquency is, however, broader in scope and encompasses a range of behaviours, such as alcohol and tobacco use, truancy, aggressive acts, petty theft, or other forms of 'misbehaviour' that either are not illegal for adults or are unlikely to come to police attention. Social scientists often prefer to use the term **antisocial behaviour** to refer to this wider range of acts that either violate the rights of others or transgress social norms, but which may not necessarily constitute criminal offences (Bartol & Bartol, 2008; Le Blanc, 2015).

The fact that many of these behaviours are treated differently when perpetrated by young people is reflected in the existence of **status offences** in the United States. Status offences are acts that are legal for adults but, when committed by juveniles, may be subject to various criminal justice responses. The most commons status offences include truancy, running away from home, alcohol use, and incorrigibility (failing to obey parents) (Agnew, 2009). Although status offences are not treated as seriously today as they were several decades ago, their continuing existence reflects a very important point: we treat juvenile delinquents differently from adult criminals. Consider the following real-world example from Norway. A five-year-old girl is playing with her toboggan and is set upon by three male assailants. The girl is held down and is punched, kicked, and stomped upon until she is unconscious. Her attackers leave her to freeze to death in the snow. How do you think the criminal justice system should respond in this example? What kind of sentence should be imposed on the attackers? Your answer will almost certainly depend on the age of the assailants. In this case, the three attackers were all six-year-old boys, and they were not punished in any formal way by the criminal justice system (Green, 2007). Although you may be justly concerned with this case, the fact that the boys were not punished reflects the belief that when young people break the law they should be treated differently from adults.

Table 2.1 Age of criminal responsibility in various countries

Country	Age (years)
Indonesia	8
Bangladesh, Iraq	9
England and Wales, Australia, Switzerland, Northern Ireland	10
Netherlands, New Zealand[a], Canada, India	12
Germany, Italy, Austria, Chile	14
Denmark, Norway, Sweden, Finland, Iceland	15
Portugal, Argentina	16

Note: [a] Except for murder/manslaughter where the age of criminal responsibility is 10.

Source: Child Rights International Network. (2016). Minimum Ages of Criminal Responsibility Around the World. Retrieved from www.crin.org/en/home/ages on May 30, 2016.

When considering the way that the criminal justice system treats young people, most countries make two important distinctions based on age. The first is the **age of criminal responsibility**. This is the age at which someone can reasonably be said to recognise the difference between right and wrong and therefore, in principle, can be held fully responsible for their criminal acts. Below this age, individuals can not be criminally liable for their acts (Urbas, 2000). The age of criminal responsibility varies considerably from country to country, as illustrated in Table 2.1. In the United States there are important state differences in the age of criminal responsibility – from age six in North Carolina to age ten in Colorado, Kansas and a number of other states. Many states do not have *any* specified minimum age (Mays & Winfree, 2006).

Even if a young offender has reached the age of criminal responsibility they are likely to be treated differently from adults as long as they are still considered to be a minor. The second important age, then, relates to the point at which juveniles are treated in the same way as adults by the criminal justice system. This age again varies cross-nationally but is typically set at 17 or 18. Individuals who are under this age are usually dealt with by juvenile or youth courts and typically receive different, and usually less severe, sanctions than would accrue for similar offences if committed by adults (Agnew, 2009; Mays & Winfree, 2006). The existence of separate juvenile justice systems in many countries reflect the important way in which offending is treated differently when committed by individuals who have not yet reached adult status.

The age–crime curve

How much crime do young people commit? The answer to this question depends on the source of data, the country concerned, and the particular historical period under consideration. However, ignoring some of these important differences, we can say with some confidence that young people are responsible for a disproportionate amount of offending in society. In other words, offending rates peak during adolescence.

The peak in crime rates during adolescence is known by criminologists as the **age–crime curve**. First recognised by Quetelet in the nineteenth century (Quetelet, 1833, cited in Loeber, 2012), the age–crime curve describes a characteristic pattern of offending across the life span: offending typically begins between age 8 and 14, peaks in late adolescence (age 15–19), and then declines thereafter (Loeber, 2012; Piquero, Hawkins, & Kazemian, 2012). An example of the age crime curve is provided in Figure 2.1. This graph plots total recorded offences by age in New Zealand in 2015. Rates of overall offending start increasing rapidly from age 15 to 19, peak between ages 20 to 24, and then start to decline precipitously in the 20s and 30s. The data depicted in Figure 2.1 provide a cross-sectional picture of age and crime that is fairly consistent across modern industrialised societies (Agnew, 2003; Piquero et al., 2012). There are, however, some important variations by crime type, gender, ethnicity, and socioeconomic status. For instance, the prevalence of property offending tends to peak earlier than that of violent offending, and white collar offences (see Chapter 10) are more likely to be perpetrated by older individuals.

Despite some variation, the relationship between age and offending is robust (Sweeten, Piquero, & Steinberg, 2013). It is found in both official offending statistics and in studies that use self-report data indicating that the relationship is not due to the different ways that police might treat younger people (Farrington et al., 2013). Moreover, it is not simply the case that young people today are especially criminally inclined. Longitudinal research that tracks the *same* individuals over long periods of time also reveals that the amount of offending is highest during adolescence. An example drawn from the Cambridge Study in Delinquent Development illustrates these points (see Figure 2.2). This graph plots the prevalence of self-report and official offenders obtained for the sample at different ages. Unsurprisingly the percentage of self-report offenders is substantial higher than the percentage of official offenders at each age

Figure 2.1 Total number of recorded offences by age in New Zealand in 2015.
Source: New Zealand Police (2016).

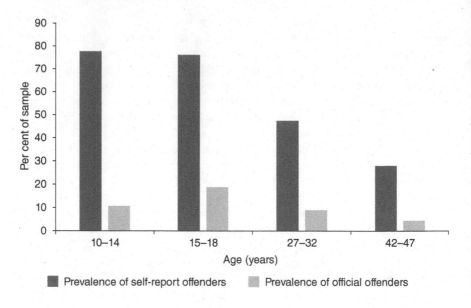

Figure 2.2 The prevalence of self-report and official offenders at different age groups for the Cambridge Study in Delinquent Development.
Source: Farrington et al. (2013; data obtained from Tables 4.1 and 4.3).

group. However, the overall pattern of offending across the lifespan is the same with a clear peak in offending in the ages 10–18 and a subsequent decline thereafter (Farrington et al., 2013). The results from longitudinal studies like the Cambridge study also clearly demonstrate that both the *prevalence* and *frequency* of offending peak during adolescence. In other words, a greater proportion of individuals committed offences during adolescence, and those that offend perpetrate a greater number of crimes during this period.

What factor or factors can satisfactorily explain this peak in offending during adolescence? Before reading the next section it is worthwhile pausing for a moment to consider the reasons that *you* think might explain the age–crime curve (see Activity 2.1).

ACTIVITY 2.1 **EXPLAINING THE AGE–CRIME CURVE**

The peak in offending during adolescence – known as the 'age–crime curve' – is well known to criminologists. Hirschi and Gottfredson (1983) claim that this pattern is a cross-cultural and historical universal and that no variables known to criminology (in 1983) could explain it. Can you do better? What factor or factors do you think can explain this relationship between age and crime?

First, jot down on a spare piece of paper three or four of the key changes that occur during adolescence and which makes this period different from childhood. Then, consider how these changes might be plausibly related to criminal offending. Finally, write down three or four changes that occur during late adolescence/early adulthood (age 20–25). Could any of these changes help to explain the relative decline in offending post adolescence?

Once you have done this, read the section on adolescence to see how many of the changes that you have identified might help us to explain the age–crime curve.

REVIEW AND REFLECT

1   What is the 'age of criminal responsibility'?
2   Describe (and draw) a typical age–crime curve.
3   Hirschi and Gottfredson (1983) claim that the age–crime curve is a universal and invariant feature of human populations. Are there exceptions to this claim?

THE NATURE OF ADOLESCENCE

Adolescence is typically characterised as a period of transition between childhood and adulthood when important biological, psychological, and social changes are occurring. The age boundaries of adolescence are not clear cut, but in Western cultures are usually thought to lie between the ages of around 12 and 13 through to the late teens or earlier twenties (Steinberg, 2014). Dahl (2004, p. 9) defines adolescence as 'that … period between sexual maturation and the attainment of adult roles and responsibilities' to capture the idea that adolescence encompasses both important biological and social changes. The idea that adolescence is necessarily a period of 'storm and stress', as young people try to come to grip with their 'raging hormones', has come under scrutiny in recent years: not all young people experience significant problems during this period, and, although adolescence appears to be a cross-culturally universal development period, its nature and length vary in important ways across cultures and in different historical time periods (Arnett, 1999; Steinberg, 2014). However, there is no doubt that adolescence is a period where there is an increase in parental conflict, risk-taking behaviour, and a range of emotional and behavioural problems (Arnett, 1999; Mata, Josef, & Hertwig, 2016; Steinberg, 2014). As we have seen, criminal offending tends to peak during adolescence. So, too, do risky behaviours like drug use, binge drinking, unprotected sex, car 'surfing', and other such dangerous pursuits that can be readily viewed on YouTube. As Reyna and Farley (2006) concisely summarise: 'The scientific literature confirms the common-sense belief that adolescence is a period of inordinate risk taking' (p. 7). Moreover, these changes can occur very rapidly to often bewildered and beleaguered parents (see Criminal Psychology Through Film 2.1). In order to understand why adolescence is characterised by a heightened risk for many harmful behaviours, including criminal offending, we need to look closely at the inter-related set of biological, psychological, and social changes that are occurring during this period.

CRIMINAL PSYCHOLOGY THROUGH FILM 2.1
Thirteen (2003)

Directed by: Catherine Hardwicke
Starring: Evan Rachel Wood (Tracy), Holly Hunter (Melanie), and Nikki Reed (Evie)

Thirteen-year-old Tracy Freeland lives with her divorced mother, Melanie, and attends a middle school in Los Angeles where she is a good student with a group of caring friends. Tracy's life undergoes a rapid transformation as, determined to 'grow up', she abandons her old group of friends, starts wearing trendy clothes, and hangs out with Evie Zamora who is one of the 'popular' girls at school. This association leads to a range of 'problem' behaviours including shoplifting, drug use, sexual activity, and self-harm. Although the film's narrative is clearly located in the context of a very specific cultural milieu (Los Angeles in the early 2000s) it vividly depicts some of the pronounced changes that occur with puberty and how they might result in antisocial and criminal behaviour.

Questions for discussion

1   Adolescence is a period where individuals are increasingly influenced by peers. In the film *Thirteen* this clearly contributes to Tracy's delinquent behaviour, but does this necessarily have to be the case? What factors are likely to contribute to the negative influence of peers on antisocial behaviour?

2   Why do so many different 'problem' behaviours tend to occur together during adolescence? Tracy and her friend Evie shoplift, use a variety of illicit drugs, engage in under-age sexual activity, and self-harm – do the same underlying mechanisms account for this range of problem behaviours?

The dual systems model of adolescent risk taking

Important biological changes are occurring in the adolescent brain that can help us try and understand the increase in risk-taking and antisocial behaviour during this developmental period. One prominent view of teenage decision making suggests that adolescents fail to *understand* the risks associated with certain behaviours, or, if they do, to underestimate the likelihood that harmful outcomes will happen to them. The idea that teenagers view themselves as bullet-proof supermen (and women) appears to be inaccurate. The available research demonstrates that young people *can* accurately appraise the risk of various behaviours, such as drink driving or unprotected sex. Indeed, if anything, they tend to overestimate these risks (Reyna & Farley, 2006, 2007; Steinberg, 2014). According to the **dual systems model** of adolescent risk taking the peak in criminal and antisocial behaviour and other forms of risk taking that is seen in adolescence can be explained by the differential maturation of two different brain systems: the **socioemotional system** and the **cognitive control system** (Cauffman et al., 2016; Spear, 2013; Steinberg, 2007; Shulman et al., 2016).

The hormonal changes that occur with the onset of puberty lead to key organisational changes in the brain (Peper & Dahl, 2013). More specifically, the socioemotional system, which involves regions of the brain that underlie the experience of reward, becomes hyperactive. What this means is the adolescents demonstrate heightened sensitivity to rewards compared to both children and adults. In short, activities that stimulate the reward system in the brain (see Chapter 1), such as thrill seeking, sexual activity, socialising, and the risky behaviour that characterises much antisocial behaviour, are experienced more intensely during this developmental period. Inevitably this means that adolescents, on average, are more *motivated* to seek out these rewarding activities than individuals at either younger or older ages (Cauffman et al., 2016; Galvan, 2013). Research typically finds that sensation seeking and the mechanisms underlying reward sensitivity peak during mid to late adolescence (ages 14–18), and decline thereafter (Braams et al., 2015; Shulman et al., 2016).

Rewarding, and often risky, activities thus seem to become more attractive to adolescents. However, the cognitive control system that plays a key role in the self-regulation of behaviour is still developing. Research has found that the development of the prefrontal cortex, a region of the brain that is implicated in impulse control, planning, and decision making (see Chapter 1), is not fully developed until the early 20s (Casey & Caudle, 2013; Spear, 2013). More specifically, connections between areas of the prefrontal cortex and other brain regions increase in a linear fashion from childhood into adolescence and are still strengthening into the early 20s (Shulman et al., 2016). This means that although adolescents have better self-regulatory capacities than children they are not as capable of regulating impulses as are adults, particularly in highly emotional or arousing contexts – just the sort of contexts that often lead to risk taking and antisocial behaviour (Cauffman et al., 2016). In sum, according to the dual systems model of adolescent risk taking, adolescence is a period where the rewards of risky behaviour become more attractive, but the capacity to control and regulate behaviour is still developing. This 'imbalance' results in the peak in risk taking and criminal offending characteristic of this developmental period (see Figure 2.3).

Social and cultural changes

The biological changes that have been identified by researchers can help us to understand the increase in risk taking and antisocial behaviour during adolescence, but they are not the full story. Importantly, there are significant *social* changes that are also occurring in the lives of teenagers. Perhaps the most obvious change to parents is that adolescents spend significantly less time with their parents and more time with peers.

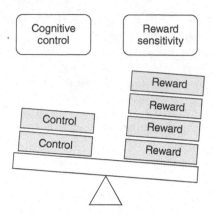

Figure 2.3 The dual systems model of adolescent risk taking. The model suggests that adolescent risk taking is due in part to an imbalance between cognitive control and reward sensitivity.

The young child who wailed at their parent not to go and leave them with the babysitter has been replaced with a young teenager who demands to be dropped off several blocks away from school so as not to be seen with their parents. A greater amount of time spent with peers means that there is significantly less active parental monitoring of teenager behaviour. Less parental monitoring provides greater opportunities for delinquency and antisocial behaviour (Agnew, 2003). We will examine the influence of peers on antisocial behaviour in detail later in this chapter, but it is worth noting that the presence of peers also seems to increase risk taking among adolescents.

A number of studies have found that the presence of peers (even if they are not even physically present) seems to increase the risk taking of adolescents but not adults (Gardner & Steinberg, 2005; Weigard et al., 2014) (see Research in Focus 2.1). Moreover, consistent with the heightened activity of the socioemotional system during adolescence (see above) the presence of peers is related to enhanced activation of the brain systems underlying reward (Nelson, Jarcho, & Guyer, 2016). More generally, adolescents seem especially sensitive to social evaluation – both positive and negative – making this a developmental period where 'fitting in' with one's peers becomes a crucial task (Somerville, 2013). These features of adolescence can help us to understand not only why the presence of peers appears to increase risk taking but also why adolescents are much more likely to commit crimes with others than are adults (Van Mastrigt & Farrington, 2009; Warr, 2002).

Growing levels of independence also increases demands on teenagers. Greater autonomy and the granting of some adult privileges mean that adolescents are more responsible for their behaviour, need to prepare for adult roles by devoting time and effort to their education, and need to navigate their way through social and intimate relationships. These demands, Agnew (2003) argues, occur while adolescents are still developing appropriate coping strategies and can increase levels of 'strain', ultimately leading to delinquent behaviour. Cultural factors can also influence the length of adolescence (and hence extend the risk period for offending) as individuals are both experiencing puberty at an earlier age in Western societies and increasingly delaying the acquisition of major adult roles and responsibilities, like marriage and child raising, until their mid- to late twenties (Arnett, 2000; Moffitt, 1993; Steinberg, 2014).

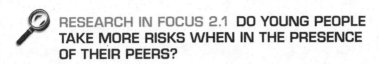

RESEARCH IN FOCUS 2.1 DO YOUNG PEOPLE TAKE MORE RISKS WHEN IN THE PRESENCE OF THEIR PEERS?

Title: Peer influence on risk taking, risk preference, and risky decision making in adolescence and adulthood: An experimental study

Authors: Gardner, M., & Steinberg, L   **Year**: 2005

Source: *Developmental Psychology*, 41, 625–635

Aims: To explore the role of peer influence on risk taking among adolescents

Method: Sample of adolescents (13–16), youths (18–22), and adults (24+) participated in a risk-taking game called 'chicken' either alone or in the presence of peers.

Key results:
- Younger participants engaged in more risky driving than older participants.
- The effects of peers on risk taking was greater for younger participants.

Conclusion: The presence of peers makes adolescents and youths more likely to engage in risky behaviour, whereas peer presence has little impact on adult behaviour.

Discussion question

Why are adolescents but not adults more likely to engage in risky behaviour in the presence of peers?

An evolutionary perspective

From an evolutionary perspective it can be argued that these biological, psychological, and social changes are not simply incidental by-products of development but, instead, have been specifically selected for (Durrant & Ward, 2015). Antisocial and risky behaviour peaks during adolescence and adulthood because this is the time period where young individuals – especially young men – are competing most vigorously for status and resources. In other words there is a focus among young men on 'mating' rather than 'parenting' effort. As men get older, form long-term relationships, and have children then the competitive advantages of risky and antisocial behaviour decline (Kruger & Nesse, 2006; Walsh, 2009a). The finding that risk taking is greater in the presence of peers and that sensitivity to social evaluation is especially pronounced during adolescence reflects the evolutionary function or purpose of risk taking: to obtain social status and signal to others one's reproductive value. Consistent with this evolutionary perspective, heightened risk taking and antisocial behaviour during adolescence are especially pronounced among males, who have more to gain (from an evolutionary point of view) from engaging in risky behaviour than females (Durrant & Ward, 2015; Shulman et al., 2014).

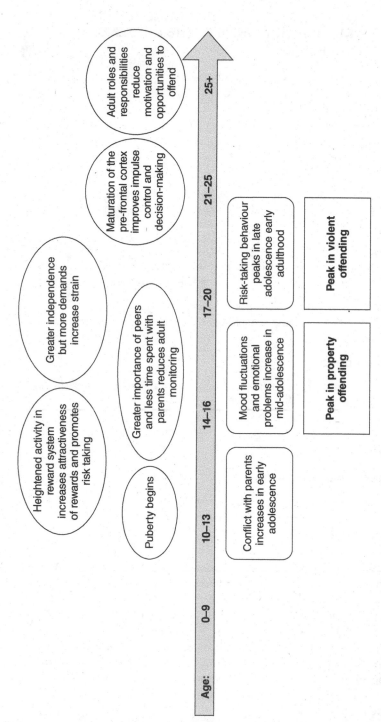

Figure 2.4 Key developmental changes from puberty through to young adulthood.

Summary

The biological, psychological, and social changes that occur during adolescence can help us to understand why this period is characterised by a sharp rise in antisocial behaviour and offending. As individuals reach adulthood, brain regions related to impulse control and decision making become fully developed, risk-taking activities become less appealing, and adult roles and responsibilities limit the opportunities and motivation for offending. Although cultural factors have certainly shaped the nature and, especially, length of adolescence in the modern world, the characteristic features of this developmental period and the biological mechanisms that underpin it have, arguably, been shaped by natural selection and thus represent an aspect of our evolved history. A schematic overview of these key developmental processes is depicted in Figure 2.4 and highlights the interaction of biological, psychological, and social factors in explaining the age–crime curve.

Adolescence is a period where many young individuals engage in antisocial behaviour. It is also a period where the *rate* of offending peaks. However, most young people do not engage in serious offending, and many young people abstain from criminal behaviour entirely. The material presented in this section can help us to explain the spike in offending during adolescence (with important implications for juvenile justice – see Box 2.1), but it can not, by itself, explain why some individuals are more likely to offend (and to become persistent offenders) than others. In the next section we will examine in some detail the various individual, family, and social factors that can help us explain individual differences in offending.

BOX 2.1 ADOLESCENT DEVELOPMENT AND JUVENILE JUSTICE

The research on adolescent brain development, reviewed in this chapter, raises some important implications for how adolescents are treated by the criminal justice system (Steinberg, 2009). One important issue relates to criminal culpability. If young people are more prone to engage in risky behaviours, more susceptible to peer influence, and less able to regulate or control their impulses should they be held to the same standards as adults in determining their moral blameworthiness? The issues raised by this question are no doubt complex. Although criminal responsibility cannot be entirely absolved except in rare cases involving severe mental disorder (see Chapter 3), many criminal justice systems recognise the importance of factors that mitigate or reduce the overall culpability of offending and may result in less severe punishment as a consequence. Given that adolescents as a group have characteristics that may make them more likely to engage in antisocial and criminal behaviour, an argument can be made that they should be treated more leniently by the criminal justice system. As Steinberg (2009, p. 61) argues: 'this does not excuse adolescents from criminal responsibility, but it renders them less blameworthy and less deserving of adult punishment'.

Over the last decade or so, the U.S. Supreme Court has been significantly influenced by research on adolescent neurodevelopment to deliver a number of landmark decisions (see Cohen & Casey, 2014; Steinberg, 2013).

- In 2005 the death penalty was abolished for offenders under the age of 18.
- In 2010 life in prison without parole was deemed unconstitutional for individuals under the age of 18 convicted of non-homicide offences.
- In 2012 life in prions without parole was abolished for individuals under the age of 18 convicted of any crime.

Questions for discussion

1   Do you think that adolescents should be viewed as less culpable for their criminal behaviour and therefore receive more lenient responses from the criminal justice system?
2   What are some other implications of the research on adolescent development for juvenile justice?

REVIEW AND REFLECT

1   How does the dual systems model of adolescent risk taking help to explain the age–crime curve?
2   Not all adolescents engage in risky or antisocial behaviour. Think about a sibling, friend, or acquaintance that appeared to *abstain* from any risky or antisocial behaviour during this developmental period. What factors might have led them to avoid engaging in the same kind of behaviour as their peers?

RISK AND PROTECTIVE FACTORS

Walter and Reuben are two young men, both aged 21, with quite different backgrounds. Reuben grew up in an impoverished family in a disadvantaged neighbourhood. His parents were always fighting, and they eventually separated when he was nine years old. Reuben remembers that his parents often neglected him, but were particularly strict in punishing any misbehaviour, hitting Reuben on many occasions. Reuben was a 'difficult' child who had trouble paying attention in class, had few friends, and did poorly in school. Walter, on the other hand, grew up in a well-off family in a good part of town. Walter recalls that his parents typically set clear boundaries for appropriate behaviour, but that they were always warm and loving. Walter excelled in school and was always a popular member of his class.

Which one of these two young men do you think is most likely to have a history of antisocial behaviour and a criminal conviction for violent crime? You probably chose

Reuben, but take a moment to reflect on this choice. Why did you pick Reuben and not Walter as the likely candidate? In the language of developmental criminology you probably chose Reuben because he possessed more **risk factors** (e.g., family conflict, low socioeconomic status, poor school performance) and fewer **protective factors** (e.g., good neighbourhood) for offending. A risk factor is simply any variable 'that predicts an increased probability of later offending' (Farrington & Welsh, 2007, p. 17), whereas a protective factor is a variable that predicts a *decreased* probability of offending.

In this section we will first explore the idea of risk factors in a little more detail, then we will examine what is known about the major risk factors for antisocial behaviour and criminal offending. The main individual, family, and social risk factors are summarised in Table 2.2.

The nature of risk factors

Before we examine the major risk factors that have been identified by researchers, it is useful to understand the nature of risk factors in a little more detail. One crucial challenge for researchers is to try and distinguish which risk factors are actual *causes* of offending and which are best considered as 'indicators' or 'markers' of offending (Durrant, 2016; Farrington & Welsh, 2007; Rutter, 2003b). Working out which risk factors play a causal role in offending is important because these are the factors that need to be targeted in any prevention initiatives. Farrington and Welsh (2007, p. 19) suggest that three key criteria can help us to determine whether a risk factor plays a causal role in offending:

- The risk factor should be associated with the outcome (e.g., antisocial behaviour or offending).
- The risk factor should precede the outcome.
- The risk factor should predict the outcome after controlling for other variables (i.e., it should have an effect independently of other variables).

Table 2.2 Important risk factors for the development of antisocial and criminal behaviour

Individual	Low intelligence and school failure
	Low self-control/impulsiveness
	Low empathy
	Attention-deficit/hyperactivity disorder (ADHD)
Family	Antisocial parents
	Parental conflict
	Child abuse and neglect
	Harsh or erratic parenting
	Lack of parental monitoring and supervision
Social	Low socioeconomic status
	Association with delinquent peers
	Poor school environment
	Deprived neighbourhood or community

Source: Farrington (2015).

The importance of establishing the causal status of risk factors means that **longitudinal research designs** are often favoured by researchers trying to understand the developmental origins of antisocial behaviour (see Box 2.2 and Table 2.3). Longitudinal research, in principle, can help researchers disentangle some of the many complex relationships that occur among different risk factors. It would be fair to say, however, that researchers currently know a lot about the variables that are *associated* with antisocial behaviour, but a clear understanding of specific causal pathways has yet to be established (Rutter, 2003a, 2003b).

BOX 2.2 LONGITUDINAL AND CROSS-SECTIONAL STUDIES IN DEVELOPMENTAL CRIMINOLOGY

Two main types of study have contributed to our understanding of the nature of juvenile delinquency. The first type is **cross-sectional research**. Cross-sectional research involves taking, as its name suggests, a cross-section of a given population at a given moment in time and measuring or assessing them on a range of relevant characteristics. For example, a researcher might take a sample of 13-year-olds from three different schools and ask them questions about their involvement in antisocial behaviour and the antisocial behaviour of their friends. Although this type of research can often provide us with important information about the nature of juvenile delinquency, it does have a number of drawbacks. Importantly, it can be very difficult to unravel the causal factors that are involved in the development of antisocial behaviour over time. For instance, it is difficult to reliably assess whether it is the association with delinquent peers that results in antisocial behaviour or whether antisocial individuals are simply more drawn to likeminded individuals.

To answer some of the important questions about the development of offending over time we need to conduct longitudinal research. Longitudinal research involves tracking a sample of individuals over time and assessing those individuals on a regular basis. Longitudinal research can start at birth (or even before birth) or at any time during development. As Farrington (2006, p. 123) summarises, longitudinal studies 'provide information about developmental sequences, within-individual change, effects of life events and effects of risk and protective factors at different ages on offending at different ages'. There are now a number of longitudinal research studies in progress (see Table 2.3 for a selection), and they have yielded, to date, a rich source of information that has helped us to understand the development of antisocial and criminal behaviour.

Most research suggests that the predictive power of risk factors tends to be cumulative in nature. That is, the more risk factors an individual possesses the greater the likelihood that they will engage in antisocial and criminal behaviour. For instance, in a study of violence and homicide in young men based on results from the Pittsburgh Youth Study it was found that 'boys with 4 or more risk factors for homicide were 14 times more likely

Table 2.3 A sample of prospective longitudinal studies of offending

Study name	Location	Sample
Cambridge Study in Delinquent Development	London, England	411 boys age 8–9 (including all male students in six London schools of that age) in 1961–1962
National Youth Survey	United States	Representative sample of U.S. adolescents aged 11–17 in 1976
Christchurch Health and Development Study	Christchurch, New Zealand	All 1,365 children born in Christchurch in mid-1977
Pittsburgh Youth Study	Pittsburgh, United States	1,517 boys age 7, 10, or 13 attending Pittsburgh public schools in 1987–1988
Dunedin Multidisciplinary Health and Development Study	Dunedin, New Zealand	1,037 children born in Dunedin in 1972–1973
Glueck Longitudinal Study	Boston, United States	500 male delinquents in correctional schools in 1939–1944 and 500 matched male non-delinquents
Mater University Study of Pregnancy	Brisbane, Australia	7,661 women who gave birth in Brisbane in 1981
New York State Longitudinal Study	New York, United States	976 randomly sampled mothers with a child aged 1–10 in 1975

Source: Farrington and Welsh (2007).

to later commit homicide than violent individuals with fewer than 4 risk factors' (Loeber et al., 2005, p. 1074). Risk factors are, however, not destiny. Individuals burdened with a large number of risk factors may in fact end up as model law-abiding citizens although the *probability* that they will engage in antisocial behaviour is greater than individuals with fewer risk factors.

Individual risk factors

Individual risk factors are those factors that are located in individuals and which help us to understand why some people are more likely to engage in antisocial and criminal behaviour than are others. Key individual risk factors that have been identified by researchers include low intelligence, certain temperamental and personality factors, specific neurodevelopmental disorders, and impaired social and cognitive skills.

Low intelligence
Although the relationship between intelligence and crime has often been downplayed in criminology textbooks, the research clearly supports that idea that low intelligence

is a risk factor for offending. In most studies intelligence is measured by scores on IQ tests, although it needs to be recognised that 'intelligence' is a much broader concept than is typically assessed in such tests (Gardener, 1983). Most longitudinal studies have found a relationship between IQ and crime (Farrington, 2015). For example, in the Cambridge Study in Delinquent Development, verbal and non-verbal IQ measured at age 8–10 predicted later juvenile and adult convictions (Farrington & Welsh, 2007). Some longitudinal studies have found, however, that once other variables are controlled for, IQ is no longer a robust predictor of offending. For instance, in the Christchurch Health and Development Study an association between IQ measured at age 8–10 and criminal offending at ages 18, 21, and 25 was also found. However, this association largely disappeared after other factors, such as early conduct problems and family background, were controlled for (Fergusson, Horwood, & Ridder, 2005).

Most researchers recognise that although IQ is a clear risk factor for offending this relationship is likely to be mediated by other factors. One important candidate is school performance. Individuals with lower IQs typically do not flourish in school environments and are likely to end up with lower levels of educational attainment. Failure at school, in turn, can increase the likelihood that an individual will engage in antisocial and criminal behaviour. Another possibility is that low IQ may simply be part of a broader pattern of cognitive impairment that may predispose some individuals to criminal offending. We also need to consider how above average intelligence may act as a *protective* factor against offending, even among otherwise high-risk individuals (Ttofi et al., 2016). The precise nature of the relationship between IQ and offending has yet to be established. However, it is clear that low IQ, as assessed in childhood, is a clear risk factor for later delinquency, although its effects on criminal offending are likely to be indirect in nature.

Temperament and personality

Personality can be broadly defined as 'those characteristics of the person that account for consistent patterns of feeling, thinking and behaving' (Pervin, Cervone, & John, 2005, p. 6). **Temperament** is a term that is usually applied to describe individual differences in emotional and behavioural responses. Temperament is considered to be strongly influenced by biology and is typically used to describe the behaviour of infants and young children. Clearly individuals differ in their characteristic ways of thinking, feeling, and behaving. Moreover, research suggests that, although personality is not set in concrete, there is a good deal of consistency in people's personality characteristics over time (Pervin et al., 2005). Do differences in personality, particularly those evident in early life, make some individuals more 'crime prone' than others? The answer to this question is, almost certainly, 'yes', and there has been considerable progress in our understanding of those personality characteristics that are most clearly related to antisocial and criminal behaviour.

The personality trait or characteristic that has been most consistently related to antisocial behaviour is low self-control or impulsivity (see Chapter 1). Individuals who are less able to inhibit or control their behaviour are more likely to engage in antisocial and criminal behaviour (e.g., Pratt & Cullen, 2000). Taken together, the characteristics that comprise self-control are what psychologists often refer to as **executive functions**: a collection of cognitive capacities, located in the prefrontal cortex of the brain, that are involved in controlling emotional impulses, planning, weighing up the costs and benefits of actions, and monitoring behaviour (Beaver et al., 2007). It doesn't take too much imagination to see how individuals who are less adept at controlling emotional impulses and who tend not to think about the consequences of their actions are more likely to engage in antisocial behaviour. Research clearly supports the link between low self-control or impulsivity and delinquent behaviour, as measured in a variety of different ways (e.g., Fergusson, Boden, & Horwood, 2015). For example, in the Pittsburgh Youth Study, 400 boys were assessed using a number of different measures of impulsivity, including various cognitive tasks, self-report personality scales, teacher ratings, and videotaped observations. The results of the study indicated that both measures of cognitive impulsivity (cognitive tasks requiring mental control) and behavioural impulsivity (real-world behavioural responses) predicted self-reported delinquency at age 10 and 13, but that the relationship was stronger for measures of behavioural impulsivity (White et al., 1994).

Many aspects of self-control appear to be emerge fairly early in development and are manifest in childhood differences in temperament. Infants who have what has been termed a 'difficult' or 'undercontrolled' temperament – they are more restless, irritable, emotionally labile, and harder to soothe – are at a greater risk for later engaging in antisocial behaviour and delinquent behaviour (Bor, McGee, & Fagan, 2004; Caspi, 2000). For instance, in the Dunedin Longitudinal Study, undercontrolled children at age 3 (as rated by observers), scored lower on self-report personality measures of self-control and harm-avoidance at age 18 and were more likely to engage in criminal behaviour at age 21, as assessed through both self-report and conviction records (Caspi, 2000).

Although most attention has focused on the cluster of personality characteristics relating to self-control, there are also several other personality characteristics that seem to be related to antisocial behaviour and delinquency. For example, a meta-analysis of the relationship between empathy and offending demonstrated that individuals who are less able to understand another person's feelings (what the researchers label 'cognitive empathy') are at a greater risk of offending (Jolliffe & Farrington, 2004). This finding was confirmed in a more recent meta-analysis of 38 studies, which found that the relationship between affective empathy and offending was substantially smaller than the relationship between cognitive empathy and offending (van Langen et al., 2014). However, other research suggests that the capacity to experience others' emotions ('affective empathy') may be a better predictor of at least some kinds of offending (Jolliffe & Farrington, 2007), and the relationship between empathy and *aggression* is relatively weak (Vachon, Lynam, & Johnson, 2014). There is clearly scope for more work in this area, and it may be that the broader concept of 'callous-unemotional' traits, including lack of guilt and empathy, is more important for understanding the development of serious antisocial and delinquent behaviour (Frick, Ray, Thornton, & Kahn, 2014a).

Neurodevelopmental disorders

In the *Diagnostic and Statistical Manual of Mental Disorders–5th edition* (DSM–5; American Psychiatric Association, 2013; see Chapter 3 for an overview), a separate section is devoted to 'Neurodevelopmental disorders'. These are disorders that have a relatively clear neurobiological basis and tend to be diagnosed first in infancy or childhood. Two neurodevelopmental disorders are of particular interest to criminologists: **attention-deficit/hyperactivity disorder (ADHD)** and **autism spectrum disorder (ASD)**.

Children who have enduring problems with inattention, impulsivity, and hyperactivity may be diagnosed with ADHD. The core problems experienced by individuals with ADHD appear to be related to deficits in executive functioning (Barkley, 2006; Brassett-Harknett & Butler, 2007). Children with ADHD are characterised as having persistent and maladaptive problems with inattention (e.g., has trouble concentrating in school and completing tasks and is easily distracted), hyperactivity (e.g., often fidgets in class, talks excessively, and runs about and climbs in situations where it is inappropriate), and impulsivity (e.g., has difficulty in waiting turn and often interrupts or intrudes on others; American Psychiatric Association, 2013, pp. 59–60).

ADHD is estimated to affect somewhere between 3 per cent and 7 per cent of children worldwide, and is much more common among boys (Barkley, 2006). For example, in a recent large-scale Australian study of children and adolescents (aged 4–17) ADHD was the most common disorder of those assessed with an overall 12-month prevalence rate of 7.4 per cent (Lawrence et al., 2015). Although many of the symptoms of ADHD decline with age, a number of children who are diagnosed with ADHD will continue to experience these symptoms throughout their adult life. ADHD is associated with a range of negative life outcomes, including an increased risk for antisocial and criminal behaviour (Brassett-Harknett & Butler, 2007). For instance, in a meta-analysis of 42 studies that measured the prevalence of ADHD in incarcerated populations it was found that this disorder was substantially more common in incarcerated populations (over 30 per cent of individuals in youth prison and 26 per cent in adult prison) than in the general population (Young et al., 2015). This is, perhaps, not unsurprising. As we have seen, low self-control is an important individual-level risk factor for delinquent behaviour, and individuals diagnosed with ADHD tend to have persistent and enduring problems in regulating behaviour. However, it should be noted that many children who are diagnosed with ADHD do *not* engage in serious delinquent behaviour, and there appears to be considerable diversity in the nature, course, and outcomes for these individuals (Barkley, 2016).

Another neurodevelopmental disorder with potential implications for criminal and antisocial behaviour is autism spectrum disorder (ASD). The DSM–5 characterises ASD as a disorder that involves 'persistent impairment in reciprocal social communication and social interaction (Criterion A), and restricted, repetitive patterns of behaviour, interests, or activities (Criterion B), [that are] present from early childhood and limit or impair everyday functioning (Criterion C and D)' (American Psychiatric Association, 2013, p. 53). This diagnostic category subsumes Asperger's disorder – a milder form of autism – which was previously included in the DSM manual. The prevalence of ASD in the general population is reported to be at around 1 per cent (American Psychiatric Association, 2013), although a recent longitudinal study in an Australian sample found prevalence rates of 1.5 to 2.5 per cent (Randall et al., 2015).

There are some plausible theoretical reasons to believe that ASD might be related to offending. In particular, the lack of social insight and ability to 'read' the intentions of others may result in impairments in social interactions that could lead to offending. Individuals with ASD also tend to have deficits in empathy, which, as we have seen, may elevate the risk for offending. High-profile examples of offenders with ASD – such as Adam Lanza, who killed 20 children and six adults at Sandy Hook elementary school in 2012 – reinforce this potential link. However, systematic research linking ASD with offending is thin on the ground, and recent reviews of the literature find little evidence to suggest any more than a weak relationship between this disorder and crime (King & Murphy, 2014). Clearly there is scope for more work on the potential links between ASD and offending.

The origin of individual risk factors

Researchers have made substantial progress in identifying some of the main individual risk factors for antisocial behaviour and criminal offending. The origin of individual risk factors, however, still remains to be explained: *why* are some people more likely to possess the individual characteristics that increase their risk for offending?

Very early developmental experiences are one potential source for some of the individual differences that have been shown to be associated with the development of antisocial behaviour. Important early developmental risk factors include the maternal use of alcohol, tobacco, and other drugs during pregnancy, some types of birth complications, and early exposure to toxic substances (Bor et al., 2004; Fergusson et al., 2015; Green et al., 2008). It is likely that these early developmental factors have an adverse effect on neuropsychological development, although researchers have yet to clearly outline the causal pathways that lead from these risk factors to antisocial behaviour (McGloin, Pratt, & Piquero, 2006).

There is also now abundant evidence that genetic factors play a significant role in the origin of antisocial and criminal behaviour (Baker, Bezdjian, & Raine, 2006; Raine, 2013; Walsh & Bolen, 2012). Much of the evidence for the role of genetic factors in the development of antisocial behaviour comes from twin and adoption studies (see Chapter 1). The results of this research suggest that approximately 40 per cent to 50 per cent of the variance in antisocial and criminal behaviour can be attributed to genetic factors (Moffitt, 2005; Rhee & Waldman, 2007). Moreover, many of the individual correlates of antisocial behaviour that we have examined, such as impulsivity and attention-deficit/ hyperactivity disorder, also appear to have a significant heritable component (Baker et al., 2006). More recent research has focused on identifying candidate genes that might predispose individuals to antisocial behaviour via their effects on the developing brain (see Raine, 2008, 2013).

The finding that antisocial behaviour (and the traits that are associated with antisocial behaviour) has a genetic basis, does not, however, lead us to conclude that such behaviour is somehow genetically *determined*. Indeed, research in behavioural genetics clearly identifies the crucial role of environmental influences and, perhaps more importantly, highlights the complex *interaction* between genetic and environmental factors (Beaver & Connolly, 2013). Gene/environment interactions arise when the effects of genetic factors vary *depending* on the environmental context. For example, adoption studies find that the effects of being raised in an adverse environment (e.g., by antisocial or criminal parents) is significantly greater for individuals who are genetically *disposed* to antisocial behaviour (as indicated by having biological parents who are antisocial) (Baker et al., 2006). Perhaps the most widely known example of a G × E interaction in the development of antisocial behaviour comes from the Dunedin Multidisciplinary Health and Development study. In this study, children who were maltreated were at a significantly greater risk of engaging in antisocial behaviour. However, the presence of a genotype that influenced the expression of monoamine oxidase A (MAOA), an enzyme that functions to metabolise neurotransmitters, moderated this relationship. Specifically, maltreated children with a MAOA gene that conferred low levels of MAOA expression were significantly more likely to develop antisocial behaviour than maltreated individuals with a MAOA gene that conferred high levels of MAOA expression (Caspi et al., 2002). The results of this study have since been replicated (Kim-Cohen et al., 2006), and a recent meta-analysis largely supports the interaction between MAOA and childhood maltreatment on the development of antisocial behaviour (Byrd & Manuck, 2014). It seems increasingly likely that criminal and antisocial behaviour is strongly influenced by a number of such gene/environment interactions, and unravelling these complex interactions is an important task for future research (Beaver et al., 2014; Guo, 2011).

In summary, it is clear that many of the individual characteristics that are associated with the development of antisocial behaviour have a genetic basis. It is equally clear that in order to understand the effects of genetic factors on antisocial behaviour we need to closely examine the way the genes and environment interact. One important feature of the environment in the development of antisocial behaviour in children is that provided by the family.

Family risk factors

Crime runs in families. If you have parents, siblings, and relatives who are engaged in criminal behaviour there is a much greater likelihood that you will also develop a history of offending (Beaver, 2013; Farrington & Welsh, 2007). The concentration of offending in families was clearly demonstrated in the Pittsburgh Youth Study (Farrington et al., 2001). In this longitudinal study of the development of antisocial behaviour in boys, information was obtained from the boys' parents concerning the arrest history of family members. It was found that only 8 per cent of the families accounted for a full 43 per cent of all arrests in the sample. Having a family member (especially a father) who had been arrested also significantly predicted a boy's subsequent delinquency. Why should this be the case? Why is having an antisocial or criminal parent a significant risk factor for offending?

There are a number of possible reasons for the finding that crime tends to be concentrated in families (Farrington & Welsh, 2007; Pardini, Waller, & Hawes, 2015). One possibility is that antisocial family members either directly or indirectly encourage younger family members to engage in crime. There does appear to be some evidence that older siblings may facilitate offending in this way, but there is little evidence that criminal parents actively encourage their children to engage in criminal behaviour. Of course, as social learning theorists would argue, criminal parents may well model antisocial behaviour in ways that increase the likelihood of offending among their children. Another possibility is that antisocial individuals who are engaged in criminal activity are simply bad parents, and it is their ineffective child-rearing methods that account for an increased risk in criminality in their offspring. As we shall see below, there is clear evidence that certain child-rearing methods are important risk factors for offending.

It is also possible that the association between antisocial parents and antisocial children arises because of shared risk factors. For example, poor parents living in deprived neighbourhoods typically rear children who suffer the same effects of socioeconomic deprivation. Parents and children not only share environments, but also share genes. If, as outlined above, genetic factors play a role in the development of antisocial behaviour then it should be no surprise that having antisocial parents is a risk factor for antisocial behaviour in their children. Whatever the reason for the concentration of offending in families, many criminologists argue that the family environment plays an important role in the development of criminal behaviour. In this section we will examine the main family risk factors for offending focusing on disrupted families, parenting practices, and child abuse.

Disrupted families and parental conflict

One common stereotype of the persistent juvenile delinquent is someone who comes from a broken home and is raised by a single parent. Research on the effect of disrupted families consistently supports this general stereotype: children from broken homes *are* at a greater risk of engaging in delinquent behaviour than are those children from intact families (Farrington & Welsh, 2007). The relationship between broken homes and juvenile delinquency is, however, rather more complex than the usual stereotype suggests.

Importantly, children who experience their parents' separation are often exposed to a significant amount of parental conflict. Perhaps it is this exposure to parental conflict or other, indirect, effects of parental separation that can explain the relationship between disrupted families and delinquency. There seems to be clear evidence that exposure to violence between parents is a significant risk factor for later offending (Farrington & Welsh, 2007; Pardini et al., 2015; Stith et al., 2000), and parents who end up separated or divorced may be more likely to experience violence in their relationship.

This suggestion is supported by results from the Cambridge Study: although boys from disrupted families were at a greater risk of engaging in delinquent behaviour they were similar in their delinquent behaviour to boys who came from intact but high-conflict families (Juby & Farrington, 2001). A similar result was found in a cross-sectional study of more than 20,000 Swiss men who were surveyed at 20 years of age and were asked questions about their experience of delinquency and violent behaviour along with information about their family background (Haas et al., 2004). Like the Cambridge study, it was found that men who came from disrupted families were more likely to self-report juvenile delinquency. However, the risk of delinquency was similar for men from disrupted families and those from intact but high-conflict families. In short, it seems that although having a disrupted family environment is a risk factor for offending, the *quality* of the family environment is a much more important variable in explaining the development of delinquent behaviour.

Child abuse and neglect

One feature of the family environment that seems to be strongly related to a number of adverse outcomes, including death, physical injuries, mental health problems, and antisocial behaviour, is the experience of child abuse or neglect (Gilbert et al., 2009; Kerig & Becker, 2015). In a classic study of the effects of child abuse and neglect,

Widom (1989) found that the experience of neglect or physical abuse as a child significantly increased the likelihood of juvenile arrest. This finding has since been replicated in a number of studies with the results supporting what some researchers term the **intergenerational cycle of violence**: experience of violence in the family environment increases the likelihood of subsequent violent and antisocial behaviour (van de Wiejer, Bijleveld, & Blokland, 2014). In a review of the literature on the topic, Maas, Herrenkohl, and Sousa (2008, p. 57) highlighted four key research findings:

1   Physical child maltreatment is the most consistent type of abuse predicting youth violence to date.
2   Compounded types of abuse (e.g., sexual, emotional, physical) and increased severity of abuse appear to increase the likelihood of later youth violence perpetration.
3   Evidence is emerging that childhood maltreatment may be a predictor of intimate partner violence perpetration, particularly for females.
4   Findings indicate that less severe forms of physical punishment and harsh parenting can result in an increased likelihood of later youth violence perpetration.

Research clearly supports a link between the experience of violence in the family environment and later violent behaviour, although it should be noted that not all individuals who are maltreated as children will engage in violence later in life.

There are a number of possible causal mechanisms linking childhood abuse and neglect and latter offending (Farrington & Welsh, 2007). Children exposed to neglect or violence may experience neuropsychological impairments as a result − either through direct damage to the brain or through changes to the physiological stress system. Social learning theorists argue that children are more likely to adopt violent behaviour through a process of modelling and imitation if they are the victims of child abuse or neglect. It has also been argued that abused and neglected children are likely to form weak attachments to their parents, which may reduce self-control and contribute to the development of hostile views of close relationships. Regardless of the precise causal mechanisms, it is clear that the experience of abuse and neglect can have a detrimental impact on child development.

Childrearing methods

Raising a child is hard work. Parents need to be able to discipline their children to ensure that they develop age-appropriate behaviours, but at the same time they need to maintain a warm and loving relationship with their offspring. Research on child-rearing practices consistently finds that poor child-rearing practices are related to antisocial and criminal behaviour (Haapasalo & Pokela, 1999). Parents who employ punitive approaches to discipline (including corporal punishment) and who tend to be cold and rejecting are more likely to have delinquent children. Parents who employ erratic or inconsistent approaches to discipline are also more likely to raise delinquent children. In a meta-analysis of longitudinal studies of risk factors for the development of antisocial behaviour, having a harsh, hostile, and rejecting parent was a strong predictor of subsequent delinquent behaviour (Tanner, Wilson, & Lipsey, 2013). Other important aspects of parenting include **parental supervision** and **parental monitoring**. Parents who are involved in their children's lives and know where they are tend to be less likely to have delinquent children (Farrington & Welsh, 2007). The importance of parenting and the development of positive parent–child relationships also appear to extend well into late adolescence (Hair et al., 2008).

Although the role of parenting practices on the development of delinquent behaviour has been well studied, there remains some debate regarding how parenting actually influences subsequent development. Most researchers have focused on the effect that poor parenting practices have on the development of self-control or attachment relationships. Gottfredson and Hirschi (1990), for example, argue that parents who actively monitor their children's behaviour and who consistently (but not punitively) punish their children for inappropriate behaviour are likely to raise children who develop the capacity to effectively regulate or control their behaviour. Poor adult–child relationships are also likely to foster weak attachment. Children who grow up in a family environment with hostile and rejecting parents may subsequently develop a distorted view of the world and relationships: they come to believe that people are inherently untrustworthy and manipulative. This, in turn, guides their social interactions in ways that promote the likelihood of aggressive, confrontational, and antisocial behaviour. The available research provides some support for both of these views (Cullen et al., 2008; Simons et al., 2007). However, some scholars have argued that a significant portion of the relationship between parenting practices and childhood characteristics (especially self-control) may be the result of shared genetic factors (e.g., Wright & Beaver, 2005).

Social risk factors

The final set of risk factors that we will consider in this chapter relate to the broader social context of adolescent development. We will first examine the relationship between socioeconomic status and juvenile delinquency, and then we will explore the influence of peers, schools, and neighbourhoods on the development of antisocial behaviour.

Socioeconomic status

A mainstay of many major criminological theories is the idea that economic deprivation is an important factor in offending. According to strain theory, for example, the experience of poverty exerts numerous strains on individuals, which, in turn, can result in criminal behaviour. Although research largely supports the idea that low socioeconomic status is a risk factor for juvenile offending, socioeconomic status also tends to be associated with a large number of other known risk factors. It is difficult, therefore, to establish exactly what role economic deprivation plays in the development of criminal behaviour (Farrington & Welsh, 2007).

Findings from the Christchurch Health and Development Study nicely illustrate these points (Fergusson, Swain-Campbell, & Horwood, 2004). Socioeconomic status was assessed in this study using paternal occupation when the participants were under six years old, and offending was measured using self-reports at age 16, 18, and 21 and official convictions at age 18 and 21. The relationship between socioeconomic status and offending was clear: offending rates rise steeply for children from lower socioeconomic backgrounds. However, a large number of other known risk factors such as parental offending, child abuse, and attentional problems were also strongly related to socioeconomic status, and when these factors were controlled for in statistical analyses the relationship between socioeconomic status and offending was not significant.

It seems clear that children who grow up in deprived families are more likely to engage in juvenile delinquency and adult offending. They are also more likely to have attentional and conduct problems, be exposed to poor parenting, experience child abuse, associate with delinquent peers, and have problems at school. Researchers have yet to clearly untangle the casual pathways that lead from economic deprivation to crime, but at the very least, low socioeconomic status represents a significant risk factor for offending.

Peer influences

Associating with delinquent peers is one of the most widely replicated and robust risk factors for juvenile delinquency (Agnew, 2009). Indeed, unlike adults who commit most of their offences alone, juvenile offending frequently occurs in the company of others. Co-offending typically occurs in groups of two to four individuals and is more common for offences like drug use, vandalism, burglary, and auto-theft (Warr, 2002). The *association* between delinquency and having delinquent peers could, however, arise for several different reasons. According to the **facilitation hypothesis**, associating with delinquent peers has a causal effect on delinquent behaviour: the association increases the likelihood of offending. In contrast, the **selection hypothesis** suggests that the relationship between involvement with delinquent peers and delinquent behaviour is largely the result of antisocial individuals *seeking* out like-minded peers to associate with (see Figure 2.5).

Researchers have found some support for both of these propositions, and it seems likely that the relationship between delinquency and association with delinquent peers is reciprocal in nature. That is, adolescents who may be more criminally inclined tend to seek

Facilitation hypothesis

Antisocial peers facilitate or encourage antisocial behaviour

Selection hypothesis

Individuals with antisocial tendencies seek out like-minded others

Figure 2.5 The effect of delinquent peers on antisocial behaviour likely reflects both selection and facilitation effects.

out peers with similar characteristics. Subsequently, the association facilitates offending, often of a minor nature. Involvement in delinquent behaviour may then, in turn, promote association with other delinquent peers who both reinforce delinquent beliefs and attitudes and facilitate subsequent delinquent behaviour (Thornberry et al., 1994). Researchers have typically found that when all of an individual's friends are delinquent and when the delinquent group is highly cohesive, then the effect of having delinquent peers on offending is the greatest (Agnew, 2009). In summary, parents are probably quite justified in being concerned if their children are 'hanging out with the wrong crowd', although children with few antisocial tendencies and who are actively monitored or supervised by their parents are less likely to be members of delinquent peer groups (Ingram et al., 2007; Warr, 2005).

School and neighbourhood factors

Some schools have a bad reputation. Truancy is rife, and antisocial and delinquent behaviour is common. There is no doubt that delinquency is more common in some schools than others (Agnew, 2009). The question remains, of course, as to whether it is the *school* that is responsible for the delinquent behaviour or whether it is simply the fact that delinquent youth tend to end up attending the same schools (you might like to think of several reasons why this might be the case). As Farrington and Welsh (2007) summarise for the results of the Cambridge Study, 'it was … very noticeable that the most troublesome boys tended to go to the high delinquency-rate schools, while the least troublesome boys tended to go the low delinquency-rate schools' (p. 83). Researchers do, however, tend to agree that the actual school environment does exert a modest direct effect on the risk for delinquency (Agnew, 2009). Agnew (2009) lists the following features of schools that tend to be associated with *lower* levels of delinquency (pp. 246–247):

- Small schools with good resources.
- Schools with good discipline (rules are consistently, but not harshly enforced – physical punishment tends to be associated with higher rates of delinquency).
- Schools that provide opportunities for student success and praise student accomplishments.
- Schools with high expectations for students.
- Schools with pleasant working conditions for students.
- Schools with good cooperation between the administration and teachers.
- Schools with strong community involvement.

Schools, then, differ in their rates of delinquency depending on the sorts of characteristics outlined above. There are also clear differences between communities or neighbourhoods in their rates of antisocial and delinquent behaviour (Elliott, Dupéré, & Leventhal, 2015; Foster & Brooks-Gunn, 2013). Again, however, we run in to the same problem of interpretation: do certain neighbourhoods or communities cause or facilitate offending or is it simply the case that the most delinquent individuals and families end up living in the same area? Criminologists have identified a number of characteristics of neighbourhoods that appear to be related to offending. Offending tends to be more common in urban areas characterised by poverty, physical disorder, and residential instability. Sampson et al. (1997) conceptualise that these environments are low in

collective efficacy. In other words, there are low levels of informal social control as individuals are less willing to enforce social norms and sanction antisocial behaviour. Disadvantaged neighbourhoods also typically have a high concentration of residents with the individual and family risk factors that have been identified in this chapter.

Factors relating to desistance from offending

To date in this chapter we have focused exclusively on those factors and processes that can explain age-related patterns in offending and the risk factors that make some individuals more likely to offend than others. However, if you take another peek at Figure 2.1 you will see that there is an important story to tell about the 'downslope' in offending that occurs from the early to mid-20s onwards. What factor or factors can explain *desistance* from offending, and why are some individuals more likely to desist than others? We have already seen that the improved capacity for self-regulation that occurs in the early 20s as a result of the maturation of the neurobiological mechanisms underlying self-control can explain part of the reduced prevalence of offending, but what other factors might be important?

It is fair to say that we know a lot more about the risk factors for offending than we do about the factors that might contribute specifically to desistance. However, criminologists generally recognise that engagement with prosocial activities and institutions such as marriage, work, and parenting are often related to desistance from offending (Kazemian, 2015). Most studies find that marriage is consistently related to reductions in offending, although the relationship depends to some extent on the age at which individuals marry and the quality of their relationship (Theobald & Farrington, 2009, 2011; although see Skardhamar et al., 2015). The relationship between parenting and reductions in offending is not quite so robust: research suggests that, for males, becoming a parent is related to reductions in offending although the prophylactic effect of parenting may be relatively short-lived (Theobald, Farrington, & Piquero, 2014). Finally, there is general agreement that gaining meaningful, stable employment is consistently related to reductions in offending (Kazemian, 2015). Although marriage, parenting, and employment are all related to reductions in offending we do need to be wary of potential 'selection' effects: it is not always clear whether engagement with prosocial institutions is a cause or a consequence of reduced offending (or other developmental changes that explain both). We shall have more to say about the factors underlying desistance in our review of the literature on rehabilitation and reintegration in Chapter 13.

REVIEW AND REFLECT

1   Select three different risk factors for antisocial behaviour from the ones that are discussed in this chapter (see Table 2.2). For each risk factor clearly explain (a) *how* this risk factor might lead to offending; and (b) how an understanding of this risk factor may help us to *prevent* the development of antisocial behaviour.
2   Think about your own school experience. What features of your school do you think might have either facilitated or prevented delinquency?

DEVELOPMENTAL THEORIES OF OFFENDING

Developmental theories of offending, as their name suggests, are concerned with the development of antisocial and criminal behaviour across the lifespan. Developmental theories are typically focused on explaining why individuals start offending, what factors maintain offending, and why individuals desist from offending. Most developmental approaches are based on the findings from longitudinal studies and, as such, incorporate the main risk factors for antisocial and criminal behaviour that we have discussed in the previous section. There are a large number of developmental and life course theories of offending (McGee & Farrington, 2016), but in this section we will limit our attention to three of the more prominent approaches.

Farrington's integrated cognitive antisocial potential (ICAP) theory

Farrington's (2003, 2005) integrated cognitive antisocial potential (ICAP) theory provides a useful integration of developmental risk factors for understanding antisocial behaviour. The central theoretical construct of ICAP is the idea of **antisocial potential** (AP). Farrington proposes that individual differences in the probability of offending can be explained in terms of individual differences in long-term AP: some individuals have high levels of long-term AP and are therefore more likely to engage in antisocial and criminal behaviour than are individuals with low levels of long-term AP. What determines an individual's level of AP? Drawing on known risk factors for offending, Farrington suggests that individuals high in AP will typically have a large number of relevant risk factors for offending such as low income, antisocial parents, adverse family environments, and impulsive personalities. These risk factors influence levels of AP through the social modelling of antisocial behaviour, poor attachment and socialisation, and high levels of strain.

Individuals who are high on long-term AP are more likely to engage in antisocial and criminal behaviour. Clearly, however, they are not *constantly* offending. ICAP explains within-individual variation in antisocial behaviour via the concept of short-term AP. The level of short-term AP is determined by the interaction of long-term AP and key situational factors such as the mental state of the individual (are they bored, angry, frustrated, drunk?), the presence of male peers, and suitable opportunities for offending. According to ICAP, ultimately whether or not an individual engages in antisocial behaviour will depend on the cognitive processes of the individual. When the subjective benefits of antisocial behaviour outweigh the costs and the perceived probabilities of getting caught are low then antisocial behaviour is more likely to occur. Finally, the consequences of offending may lead to an increase in long-term AP through learning, reinforcement, or (if apprehended by the criminal justice system) labelling effects.

In sum, ICAP incorporates the known risk factors for offending into a psychological model of antisocial behaviour that explains persistent individual differences in the probability of offending over time in terms of individual differences in long-term AP, and within individual variations in offending due to differences in short-term AP. To test your understanding of this theory review the case study presented in Activity 2.2, and answer the first two questions.

ACTIVITY 2.2 APPLYING DEVELOPMENTAL THEORIES OF OFFENDING

At the age of 19 Michael was arrested for murder. After consuming alcohol and other drugs, he stabbed and killed an international male tourist during a street robbery. Michael told the police that he needed the money to buy heroin.

Michael's mother remembers him as a restless infant and a difficult child who was irritable and had problems paying attention. Michael's natural father abandoned the family when he was 8 years old. Michael recalls that he was a violent man, who drank heavily, repeatedly assaulted his mother, and sexually abused Michael's older sister, Leanne. Michael's stepfather was even worse and physically abused Michael. Michael was a poor student and regularly skipped school to hang out with his friends. His teachers described him as someone who could never pay attention, bullied the other kids and seemed to act on 'the spur of the moment' with no thought for the consequences.

By the time he ran away from home at the age of 15 he was drinking heavily, experimenting with drugs, and stealing cars. By the age of 18 Michael was addicted to heroin and had two prior arrests for theft. After serving 16 years of his sentence for murder, Michael was released from prison. Initially he had problems adapting to life on the outside: he couldn't get a job, started drinking heavily, and came under police notice for a string of property offences. However, at the age of 39, Michael got a regular job and married the women he had been seeing for the past year. Since that time, Michael has 'settled down', no longer drinks, and has not been in trouble with the police.

Questions

1   According to Farrington's ICAP theory would Michael be high or low on antisocial potential? Why?
2   What factors might have increased Michael's short-term antisocial potential prior to committing murder at age 19?
3   According to Moffitt's taxonomy, is Michael likely to be a life-course persistent or an adolescent-limited offender? Why?
4   Provide an example of what Sampson and Laub (2005) would could a 'turning point'.

Moffitt's dual developmental pathway theory

One of the most well-known developmental theories of offending is Moffitt's dual developmental pathway theory (Moffitt, 1993, 2006). The central idea of this theory is that there are two main groups of offenders: **life-course persistent** (LCP) **offenders** and **adolescent-limited** (AL) **offenders**. LCP offenders, according to Moffitt (2006, p. 277), are 'few, persistent, and pathological'. These individuals, who are overwhelmingly male, demonstrate considerable continuity in their antisocial behaviour over the life course, although the form that their antisocial behaviour takes will change over time. As Moffitt (1993, p. 679) summarises, this includes 'biting and hitting at age 4, shoplifting and truancy at age 10, selling drugs and stealing cars at age 16, robbery and rape at age 22, and fraud and child abuse at age 30'. LCP offenders are, according to the theory, responsible for a disproportionate amount of offending. For example, in the Dunedin study, the group identified as LCP offenders represented only 10 per cent of the males in the sample but were responsible for 53 per cent of self-reported violent offences and 45 per cent of violent convictions by the age of 26 (Moffitt et al., 2002).

What factors contribute to the development of LCP offending? According to Moffitt (1993, 2006), the persistent antisocial behaviour of LCP offenders has its origins in early childhood neuropsychological deficits. These include low IQ, reading difficulties, impulsivity, hyperactivity, and attention problems. Moffitt argues that these pervasive neurodevelopmental problems arise through a combination of genetic factors and adverse family environments (including economic deprivation, poor parenting, parental conflict, and child abuse).

The second major group of offenders in Moffitt's theory are referred to as adolescent-limited (AL) offenders. As this name implies, for these individuals offending is typically confined to adolescence and early adulthood. Unlike their LCP counterparts, AL offenders are typically not saddled with the same kind of early neuropsychological problems and adverse family environments. As a consequence they do not demonstrate serious antisocial behaviour during childhood. However, they do engage in a significant amount of delinquency during the adolescent years. Moffitt argues that the factors that initiate offending among this group relate to the development of biological maturity (i.e., puberty) at ages 10–13 but the failure to attain full adult status until much later (late teens or early twenties). This creates, what Moffitt (1993) refers to as a 'maturity gap', or children who are 'chronological hostages of a time warp between biological age and social age' (p. 687). During this period deviant peers, who were likely to be socially marginalised during childhood, become attractive role models for AL offenders as they appear to have succeeded in obtaining many of the trappings of adult status (e.g., drinking, smoking, sex, and independence). AL offenders seek out and are influenced by these deviant peers and, as a consequence, engage in antisocial behaviour. However, because they are not burdened with the enduring psychological problems that characterise LCP offenders, they generally desist from offending on attaining adult roles and responsibilities like marriage, work, and children.

In summary, Moffitt's developmental theory attempts to explain two important findings from research in criminology: the persistence in offending over time (individuals show remarkable continuity in their antisocial behaviour), and the dramatic peak in offending during the adolescent years. The first phenomenon is explained in terms of the persistent offending of LCP offenders, while the second phenomenon is explained in terms of the offending behaviour of AL offenders. To test your understanding of this theory you should revisit the case study presented in Activity 2.2 and answer Question 3.

Sampson and Laub's life course theory of crime

The final theory that we will consider in this section in Sampson and Laub's life course theory of crime (Sampson & Laub, 2005, 2016). Unlike Moffitt, Sampson and Laub (2005, 2016) reject the idea that there are distinct groups of offenders, such as life-course persistent offenders. Rather, they emphasise the ongoing importance of social bonding throughout the lifespan to understanding antisocial and criminal behaviour. Weak social bonds are the main explanation for offending in Sampson and Laub's theory, although the nature and importance of social bonding change throughout the life course. Thus, children who grow up in families with weak or inconsistent discipline and a lack of parental monitoring form weak attachments to their parents and are at risk for antisocial behaviour. As the child ages, family bonding remains important, but so too is attachment to the school environment. During adulthood social bonding remains important although the primary sources of social bonding relate to work, spouse, and children. In short, the more weakly an individual is socially bonded to others and society the greater likelihood they will engage in antisocial and criminal behaviour.

Central to Sampson and Laub's (2005, 2016) theory of offending is the idea that change is always possible. This is the case even for individuals who may grow up with weak attachments to family and society and who subsequently engage in a significant amount of criminal behaviour. In this context, Sampson and Laub (2005) emphasise the importance of '**turning points**': certain life events such as marriage, work, or military service can allow an individual to 'knife off the past from the present' (p. 17) and contribute to a desistance from offending. In short, the concept of human agency is a critical aspect of Sampson and Laub's life course theory of crime. Humans have the capacity to guide and direct their own lives, and regardless of their background they are not inevitably locked into a life-long pattern of antisocial and criminal behaviour.

To test your understanding of the key ideas in Sampson and Laub's (2005, 2016) theory have a look again at the case study in Activity 2.2 and answer Question 4.

REVIEW AND REFLECT

1   Which of the three developmental theories of offending that we have reviewed in this chapter do you think provides the best explanation for the pattern of offending that we find across the lifespan? Why?

SUMMARY

The term 'juvenile delinquency' refers to behaviour that violates the criminal law when perpetrated by minors. Social definitions of juvenile delinquency tend to be broader in scope and embrace a range of antisocial behaviour committed by young people.

One robust finding in criminology is that offending peaks during adolescence. This phenomenon is known as the 'age–crime curve'. There are a number of factors that can help us explain this peak in offending during adolescence. Important biological changes in the developing adolescent brain result in the increased attractiveness of risky and exciting activities. However, the areas of the brain that are involved in decision making and that regulate impulsive control are not fully developed, making risky behaviour more likely. Antisocial behaviour is also facilitated during adolescence through greater involvement with peers, less adult supervision, and the strain experienced by adolescents as they try and cope with the demands imposed during this developmental period.

Risk factors are variables that predict antisocial behaviour or criminal offending. Important individual risk factors include low IQ, low self-control or impulsiveness, low empathy, and ADHD. Broadly speaking, individuals who are less able to control or regulate their behaviour and who are less concerned about harming others are at greater risk for engaging in antisocial behaviour. It is likely that many important individual risk factors arise through a complex interaction of genetic and environmental variables.

Important family risk factors for the development of antisocial behaviour include having antisocial parents, parental conflict, child abuse, and poor child-rearing methods. Research consistently finds that children who grow up in family environments where they are exposed to violence and neglect tend to be more likely to engage in juvenile delinquency and criminal behaviour. It is likely that these types of environment result in weak attachment to parents, lead to the development of attitudes and beliefs favourable to antisocial behaviour through social learning, and reduce the capacity for self-control. Social risk factors that have been identified by researchers include low socioeconomic status, association with delinquent peers, and adverse school and neighbourhood environments.

A number of different developmental theories have been developed in an attempt to explain patterns in the continuity and desistance in offending across the lifespan. The theories developed by Moffitt and by Farrington both provide good explanations for the onset and continuity in offending and why some people are at greater risk for offending than others. Sampson and Laub focus more on *desistance* from offending (regardless of age and criminal history) in terms of changes in levels of formal and informal social control. It is anticipated that our understanding of the risk factors for antisocial behaviour and the developmental trajectories for offending will be enhanced as we gather more information from prospective longitudinal research studies.

FURTHER READING

Carlsson, C., & Sarnecki, J. (2016). *An Introduction to Life-Course Criminology.* London: Sage Publications.
A useful general overview of life-course criminology.

Steinberg, L. (2014). *Age of Opportunity: Lessons from the New Science of Adolescence.* Boston, MA: Houghton Mifflin Harcourt.
An excellent and highly readable overview of the burgeoning literature on adolescent brain development, with implications for prevention, justice, and public policy.

Farrington, D. P. (2015). The developmental evidence base: Psychosocial research. In D. A. Crighton & G. J. Towl (eds.), *Forensic Psychology* (2nd edition) (pp. 62–181). Hoboken, NJ: John Wiley & Sons.
A convenient and up-to-date review of relevant developmental risk factors by one of the towering figures in the field.

McGee & Farrington, D. P. (2016). Developmental and life-course theories of crime. In A. R. Piquero (ed.), *The Handbook of Criminological Theory* (pp. 336–354). Chichester: Wiley-Blackwell.
This chapter is a good resource for developmental and life course theories of offending.

For a special issue on the teenage brain see *Current Directions in Psychological Science* (2013), 22, 79–161.

Useful journals to check out include: *Journal of Developmental and Life Course Criminology*, *Journal of Adolescence*, and *Developmental Psychology*.

WEB RESOURCES

A wealth of useful information can be obtained from the websites of some of the major longitudinal studies discussed in the chapter. For example, see the websites for the Dunedin Multidisciplinary Health and Development Study (http://dunedinstudy.otago.ac.nz) and the Pittsburgh Youth Study (www.lifehistorystudies.pitt.edu).

 KEY CONCEPTS

- age–crime curve
- age of criminal responsibility
- adolescent-limited offenders
- antisocial behaviour
- antisocial potential
- attention-deficit/ hyperactivity disorder (ADHD)
- autism spectrum disorder (ASD)

- cognitive control system
- collective efficacy
- cross-sectional research
- dual systems model
- executive functions
- facilitation hypothesis
- intergenerational cycle of violence
- juvenile delinquency
- life-course persistent offenders

- longitudinal research designs
- parental monitoring
- parental supervision
- protective factors
- risk factors
- selection hypothesis
- socioemotional system
- status offences
- temperament
- turning points

Mental disorder and crime

LEARNING OBJECTIVES

On completion of this chapter you should:

➤ have developed a clear idea of what mental disorder is and the main types of mental disorder that have been identified;
➤ understand the relationship between mental disorder and crime;
➤ be familiar with the construct of psychopathy and its relationship to offending;
➤ have developed an understanding of some of the main factors that give rise to psychopathy.

John always seemed happy as a child. He had a delightful curiosity about the world around him, laughing excitedly when he discovered something new to play with. He had an active imagination, and invented games where he acted out his fantasies of being the hero in the movies and TV shows he watched. He played with the children in his neighbourhood in the usual ways you would expect for a boy growing up in a middle-class family in a small town. As a teenager, however, John became moody and withdrawn. He went through periods when he spent most of his time in his room, listening to music on his headphones. As his adolescence unfolded, he was often irritable, and would snap at his parents with sarcastic and hostile remarks if they attempted to draw him into conversation or suggested that he become more active with others. He became sullen and sometimes lethargic. His hygiene suffered, as he would neglect to bathe or change into clean clothes.

In his early twenties, his parents began to think that something might be seriously wrong with John. He would alternate between periods when he appeared to shut down mentally and emotionally, and other times when he would become acutely agitated. During these times he would be fearful that others were trying to harm him, even though no one else seemed to think that his suspicions were very realistic. He started to show more unusual behaviours. His speech was sometimes incoherent and bizarre. He talked about sinister people with evil intentions. He insisted on installing a deadbolt lock on his bedroom door. His parents didn't know what to do about John. There were no psychiatric services in their small town, and John refused to travel to the larger town nearby where there was a mental health clinic. They thought perhaps that he was using drugs, but they never found direct evidence of this.

One night John went into his parents' bedroom after they were asleep. He had one of his father's golf clubs, which he used to repeatedly strike his parents around the head, killing them. He then apparently went into a bathroom and threw up. Finally, he went into the back yard, naked, climbed into a tree, and waited. This is where the police found him in the morning. The explanation he subsequently gave for his behaviour was that his parents had become vampires. He believed that not only was he in danger, but that his parents were part of a network of vampires that would eventually kill everyone. He believed that his only option was to kill his parents, essentially in order to save the world.

This case study provides a dramatic and disturbing example of a murder committed by someone with an apparently serious mental illness. To what extent, however, is this case in any way typical? Are individuals with mental disorder at a greater risk of offending than people in the general population? And, if this is the case, what characteristics of what mental disorders might be linked to a greater risk for criminal behaviour? In this chapter, we tackle these important but difficult questions. In order to get a clearer picture of mental disorder we first review this concept and discuss some of the major mental disorders that are recognised. We then review what the research has to tell us about the nature of the relationship between mental disorder and crime. In the final part of the chapter we explore the concept of psychopathy and discuss the role that psychopathic characteristics have to play in criminal behaviour.

THE CONCEPT OF MENTAL DISORDER

There are many different terms that we could use to describe someone like John, whose case opened this chapter. Clinicians (i.e., psychiatrists and clinical psychologists) would say that John is suffering from a **mental disorder**, or **mental illness**. In the context of the legal system, a defence lawyer might argue that John is insane, is mentally deficient, or has diminished capacity. Colloquially, of course, there are many – largely pejorative – terms that could be applied, such as 'mad' or 'crazy'. Those individuals that work in the legal system are typically most concerned about issues of criminal responsibility, or whether an individual can reasonably be said to be responsible for their criminal actions. These sorts of considerations are obviously of great importance for forensic psychologists. In this chapter, however, we will focus on the concept of mental disorder from a clinical perspective, as we are largely concerned with how the characteristics of mental disorders may make some individuals more likely to engage in crime.

What, then, do we exactly mean by the concept of *mental disorder*? This question, perhaps not surprisingly, has generated a substantial amount of heated debate over the years. Some have argued that there is no such thing as 'mental disorder' – it is just a label applied to individuals who deviate from social norms. Others have defined mental disorder in terms of deviance from *statistical* norms, or simply in terms of whatever mental health professionals treat (Wakefield, 1992). For the purposes of this chapter we can largely sidestep these debates and accept the definition of mental disorder that is provided in the DSM–5 (see Box 3.1):

A mental disorder is a syndrome characterized by clinically significant disturbance in an individual's cognition, emotion regulation, or behaviour that reflects a dysfunction in the psychological, biological or developmental processes underlying mental functioning. Mental disorders are usually associated with significant distress or disability in social, occupational, or other important activities. An expectable or culturally approved response to a common stressor or loss, such as the death of a loved one, is not a mental disorder. Socially deviant behaviour (e.g., political, religious, or sexual) and conflicts that are primarily between the individual and society are not mental disorders unless the deviance or conflict results from a dysfunction in the individual, as described above.

(American Psychiatric Association, 2013, p. 20)

There are four key elements to this definition:

1   Psychological dysfunction (there is a breakdown in cognition, emotional, and/or behavioural functioning).
2   Personal distress (this is associated with individual distress or impairment).
3   Atypical or not culturally expected (it is something that typically lies outside what is normally expected within the relevant cultural context).
4   Not merely socially deviant (it is something that is not just the result of social deviance or conflict with society).

As noted above, there remains plenty of debate concerning this definition and other such attempts to define mental disorder (see Paris, 2013, for a thoughtful analysis). In John's case, however, these criteria can be easily applied: there is obviously some kind of dysfunction in John's thought processes (John suffers from **delusions** and **hallucinations**), which have led to impairment (he is unable to live by himself) in ways that are not culturally expected (most people in our culture – despite the success of the *Twilight* books and movies – do not really believe in the existence of vampires), and although his behaviour is clearly socially deviant this appears to be related in important ways to John's dysfunctional thought processes.

BOX 3.1 ASSESSING MENTAL DISORDERS

The two systems most frequently used for classifying mental disorders are the Diagnostic and Statistical Manual (DSM) of the American Psychiatric Association and the International Classification of Diseases (ICD) manual of the World Health Organization. The current DSM is in its fifth edition, and is referred to as the DSM–5 (American Psychiatric Association, 2013), while the ICD is in its tenth edition and is referred to as the ICD-10 (World Health Organization, 2002a). Although there are some differences between the ICD and DSM in their classification of certain mental disorders they are largely similar and for ease of exposition we shall be primarily focusing on the DSM in this book.

The DSM–5 remains a largely categorical classification system that divides mental disorders into different types based on specified sets of criteria with defining features of each disorder. In other words, mental disorders are conceptualised as discrete entities with necessary and sufficient defining characteristics. This approach has a number of important pragmatic advantages: it allows for the standardisation necessary for scientific research and enables clear communication among clinicians. However, many of the mental, emotional, and behavioural attributes of humans are distributed along a continuum, with no clear boundaries between what is normal and what is abnormal. Another way to look at mental disorders is to employ a dimensional system that classifies clinical presentations based on a quantification of different attributes rather than the assignment of people to categories (see the diagram below). In a system like this, someone might be assessed as having a particular *level* of depressive symptoms. In developing the DSM–5 there was some thought given to incorporating a more dimensional approach to diagnosis. However, ultimately, this approach was rejected, although the DSM–5 does include symptom severity scales which provide an element of dimensionality (Wakefield, 2016). Although dimensional approaches are not typically employed in clinical practice, they are relevant for understanding the relationship between mental disorder and crime, particular when we consider the association between personality disorders and offending (Widiger & Trull, 2007).

The criteria for mental disorders specified in the DSM are meant to serve as guidelines, which are applied using clinical judgement to reach a diagnosis. Although clinical judgement is the product of training and experience, there is, inevitability, an element of subjective interpretation in the use of diagnostic criteria. The point here is that the diagnosis of mental disorders sometimes lacks the precision and certainty of other medical diagnoses, like cancer or heart disease. This issue introduces a note of caution in our understanding of the relationship between mental disorder and crime.

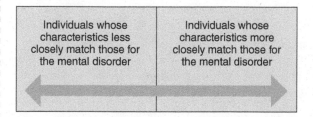

Population of individuals without the mental disorder

Population of individuals with the mental disorder

(a) Categorical approach to classification – an individual either has or does not have the mental disorder.

Individuals whose characteristics less closely match those for the mental disorder

Individuals whose characteristics more closely match those for the mental disorder

(b) Dimensional approach to classification – individuals can have characteristics (symptoms) that are more or less characteristic of the disorder with no clear boundaries between disordered and non-disordered.

MAJOR MENTAL DISORDERS

The case description that began this chapter clearly suggested that something was
seriously wrong with John – that is, John was suffering from a mental disorder.
From a clinical point of view, we can be a little more precise: John was diagnosed as
having schizophrenia. What does this actually mean? Essentially this diagnosis means
that the cluster of symptoms experienced by John allows us to use the DSM–5 or
the International Classification of Diseases–10th Revision (ICD–10) (World Health
Organization, 2002a) to classify him as having schizophrenia because he 'fits in' with the
relevant criteria for this disorder (see Box 3.1 for more on the classification of mental
disorders). There are hundreds of disorders listed in the current DSM. However, for
the purposes of understanding the relationship between mental disorder and criminal
behaviour, a subset of disorders will be focused on in this chapter, and throughout this
book (see Table 3.1).

Schizophrenia spectrum and other psychotic disorders

A number of mental disorders are grouped in the DSM–5 under the broad category
of schizophrenia spectrum and other psychotic disorders. These include schizophrenia,
delusional disorder, brief psychotic disorder, schizophreniform disorder, and
schizoaffective disorder. We shall, however, focus on the first two of these disorders,
as they feature most prominently in research looking at links between mental disorders
and offending.

   Schizophrenia is a serious mental disorder characterised by a broad range of
cognitive and emotional dysfunctions. The DSM–5 specifies that for a diagnosis of
schizophrenia to be made the individual must experience two or more of the following
symptoms for a significant portion of time during a one-month period, with at least one
symptom from the first three listed (American Psychiatric Association, 2013):

1   Delusions (beliefs that would be viewed by most people as misrepresenting reality.
     For example, John's belief that his parents were vampires is an example of a
     delusion).

2   Hallucinations (perceptual experiences without any actual input from the environment. These can occur in any sensory modality, but auditory hallucinations are most common).

3   Disorganised speech (speech that is incoherent or difficult to follow, including frequent and somewhat illogical changes of topic called loose association or derailment).

4   Grossly disorganised or catatonic behaviour (this can include unusual behaviour and postures, agitation, and immobility).

5   Negative symptoms (these include affective or emotional flattening where emotional expressions and reactions are absent or limited; avolition – a lack of motivation; and anhedonia, an apparent inability to experience pleasure).

In addition, the individual must show evidence of social and/or occupational dysfunction (e.g., inability to maintain work or personal relations) during the period since the onset of the disturbance and experience signs of the disturbance for at least six months.

In many respects, schizophrenia remains a poorly understood mental disorder. It is likely to be caused by a complex combination of genetic and neurobiological factors, along with psychosocial stressors (Butcher, Hooley, & Mineka, 2015). Schizophrenia is a chronic disorder that afflicts approximately 0.3–0.7 per cent of the population (American Psychiatric Association, 2013). Through a combination of antipsychotic drugs and psychosocial treatment, the experience of symptoms can be successfully reduced, although treatment rarely involves full recovery (Barlow & Durand, 2005).

Table 3.1 Mental disorders in the DSM–5

Disorder type	Examples	Textbook coverage
Neurodevelopmental disorders	Autism spectrum disorder Attention-deficit/hyperactivity disorder	Chapter 2
Schizophrenia spectrum and other psychotic disorders	Schizophrenia Delusional disorder	This chapter
Bipolar and related disorders	Bipolar I disorder Bipolar II disorder	This chapter
Depressive disorders	Major depressive disorder	This chapter
Disruptive, impulse control, and conduct disorders	Intermittent explosive disorder Conduct disorder	This chapter
Substance-related and addictive disorders	Alcohol use disorder Opioid use disorder	Chapter 8
Personality disorders	Antisocial personality disorder Borderline personality disorder	This chapter
Paraphilic disorders	Paedophilic disorder Sexual sadism disorder	Chapter 6

Note: The disorders presented here are those that are most relevant for understanding the link between mental disorder and crime. For a complete list of disorders see the DSM–5 (American Psychiatric Association, 2013).

Delusional disorder is another mental disorder that features in research on the link between mental disorder and crime. The central characteristic of delusional disorder is the experience of one or more delusions over a period of one month or longer (American Psychiatric Association, 2013). However, individuals with delusional disorder do not display the major cognitive and affective impairments seen in schizophrenia and, aside from the impact of the delusions, may be able to function relatively successfully in society. Seven different types of delusional disorder, based on the prominent theme of the delusion, are recognised in the DSM–5, including the *persecutory type* (delusions that the person, or someone to whom the person is close, is being malevolently treated in some way), the *erotomanic type* (delusions that another person, usually of higher status, is in love with the individual), and the *grandiose type* (delusions of inflated worth, power, knowledge, identity, or special relationship to a deity or famous person). Delusional disorder is a relatively uncommon mental disorder with a lifetime prevalence of around 0.2 per cent (American Psychiatric Association, 2013).

Bipolar and depressive disorders

Depressive disorders are characterised by the presence of 'sad, empty, or irritable mood, accompanied by somatic and cognitive changes that significantly affect the individual's capacity to function' (American Psychiatric Association, 2013). In the DSM–5 individuals who experience severe depression are diagnosed as having a major depressive episode. The core symptoms of this disorder included a significantly depressed mood, diminished interest in normally pleasurable activities, alterations in eating and sleeping patterns, fatigue, feelings of worthlessness, and recurrent thoughts of death (American Psychiatric Association, 2013). Severe depression can be an extremely debilitating disorder and is relatively common, affecting somewhere around 17 per cent of population, with rates significantly higher for women than for men (Butcher et al., 2015).

Whereas severe depression in characterised by an ongoing depressed mood, individuals who experience a 'distinct pattern of abnormally elevated, expansive, or irritable mood and abnormally and persistently increased goal-directed activity or energy, lasting at least 1 week and present most of the day, nearly every day' (American Psychiatric Association, 2013, p. 124) are said to experience a manic episode. In addition to elevated mood, manic episodes are characterised by a decreased need for sleep, distractibility, talkativeness, flight of ideas, and excessive involvement in pleasurable, but detrimental, activities (such as unrestrained buying and sexual indiscretions). Individuals who experience either severe depression or mania but not both are described as having a unipolar mood disorder. Individuals who experience both depressed and manic episodes are diagnosed as suffering from a bipolar disorder (American Psychiatric Association, 2013). The aetiology of mood disorders is complex and is thought to involve the interaction of biological, psychological, and social factors (Barlow & Durand, 2005).

Disruptive, impulse-control, and conduct disorders

Disorders that feature a failure to control impulses and emotions are grouped together in the DSM–5 under the broad label of 'disruptive, impulse-control, and

Table 3.2 Disruptive, impulse-control, and conduct disorders

Disorder	Core features
Oppositional defiant disorder	'A pattern of angry/irritable mood, argumentative/defiant behaviour, or vindictiveness lasting at least 6 months'[a]
Conduct disorder	'A repetitive and persistent pattern of behaviour in which the basic rights of others or major age-appropriate societal norms are violated'[b]
Intermittent explosive disorder	'Recurrent behavioural outbursts representing a failure to control aggressive impulses'[c]
Pyromania	'Deliberate and purposeful fire setting on more than one occasion'[d]
Kleptomania	'Recurrent failure to resist impulses to steal objects that are not needed for personal use or for their monetary value'[e]

Source: American Psychiatric Association (2013): [a] p. 462; [b] p. 469; [c] p. 466; [d] p. 476; [e] p. 478.

conduct disorders'. These disorders are of particular interest for criminal psychologists because they feature characteristics or behaviours that are closely or directly related to delinquent and criminal behaviour. The five most relevant disorders in this diagnostic grouping are listed in Table 3.2.

Along with attention-deficit/hyperactive disorder (discussed in Chapter 2), **oppositional defiant disorder** and **conduct disorder** are among the most common mental health problems for which children and adolescents are referred to mental health services (Frick & Nigg, 2012). Oppositional defiant disorder (ODD) is characterised by a persistent pattern, lasting at least six months, of angry/irritable mood (loss of temper, touchy, angry), argumentative/defiant behaviour (argues with authority, defies rules and requests from authority, annoys others), and/or vindictiveness (American Psychiatric Association, 2013). Of course, we all lose our temper, get annoyed, and argue with authority figures (e.g., parents) on occasion, but according to the DSM–5 what marks ODD from normal behaviour is the persistence and frequency of the symptoms that are inconsistent with normal developmental variation. And, if you are thinking that the pattern of behaviour characteristic of ODD perfectly captures your relationship with a brother or sister when you were a child, the DSM–5 specifically excludes behaviour exhibited during interactions with a sibling. The DSM–5 reports prevalence rates of ODD varying from 1 to 11 per cent, and although the disorder can be diagnosed among adults it is usually employed for children and adolescents.

ODD is often – although not inevitably – seen as a developmental precursor to conduct disorder (CD) which is characterised by a persistent pattern of behaviour involving the violation of others' rights and/or societal norms in one or more domains. Individuals diagnosed with conduct disorder often experience multiple problems with adjustment throughout their life and are at an elevated risk for engaging in antisocial and criminal behaviour (Frick & Nigg, 2012). Indeed, a diagnosis of **antisocial personality disorder** (see below) requires evidence of CD prior to the age of 15, suggesting a strong developmental relationship with later antisocial behaviour. However, it should be noted that CD, although typically first diagnosed from middle childhood to middle adolescence, can also be diagnosed among adults, and not all children who receive a diagnosis of CD will go on to engage in serious antisocial or criminal behaviour. One-year prevalence rates of 2 to 4 per cent are reported in the DSM–5 (American Psychiatric Association, 2013), and a recent survey of parents and carers of over 6,000 children and adolescents (age 4–17) in Australia found that 2.1 per cent of the sample met the diagnostic criteria for CD (Lawrence et al., 2015).

As is the case with many of the mental disorders discussed in this chapter there is much debate over the conceptual validity of the categories discussed in this section, with much of the discussion concerned with distinguishing disordered behaviour from behaviour that can be considered developmentally 'normal' (see Frick & Nigg, 2012; Wakefield, 2016). For instance, many of the behavioural patterns that feature in the diagnostic criteria for ODD – loss of temper, argumentativeness, failure to comply with requests from authority – may be relatively common during some developmental periods (e.g., the 'terrible twos', adolescence) and among some individuals (I can think of a few university professors!) resulting in the potential for over-diagnosis. However, like antisocial personality disorder (discussed below) and the clinical construct of psychopathy (explored in detail later in the chapter) both ODD and CD have strong links to the expression of antisocial and criminal behaviour.

Three other disorders, catalogued alongside ODD and CD and with clear potential links to offending, are **intermittent explosive disorder, pyromania**, and **kleptomania**. A failure to control impulsive aggression is a core feature of intermittent explosive disorder (IED), which is estimated to affect some 3–7 per cent of the population in the United States (American Psychiatric Association, 2013; Coccaro, 2012). Individuals with this disorder display aggressive outbursts – involving either physical or verbal aggression – that are not premeditated and are out of all proportion to potential provocations or other eliciting stimuli. Moreover, aggressive outbursts are typically preceded by physiological symptoms such as a racing heart, hot flashes, and sweating along with a sense of being out of control (Kulper et al., 2015). Given that outbursts of aggression are central to this disorder, it is perhaps not surprising that a diagnosis of IED is related to an elevated risk of violent offending and the destruction of property. Pyromania and kleptomania are also disorders that involve the failure to regulate or control impulses, but in specific domains: firesetting for pyromania and stealing for kleptomania. Both of these disorders involve a heightening tension or arousal prior to perpetrating the act and a sense of gratification or relief after the act is perpetrated. Little is known about the prevalence, aetiology, and course of these two disorders although they are both rare in the general population (American Psychiatric Association, 2013). Although a link between a diagnosis of pyromania and arson may seem inevitable it is important to note that not all firesetting is illegal, and most cases of arson are not perpetrated by individuals with pyromania (Burton, McNiel, & Binder, 2012). A similar distinction should be made between individuals diagnosed with kleptomania and 'garden variety' shoplifting or theft as the underlying motivations to offend are quite distinct. However, clearly there is a link between kleptomania and property offending with an estimated 4 to 25 per cent of individuals arrested for shoplifting likely to meet the diagnostic criteria for kleptomania (American Psychiatric Association, 2013).

Personality disorders

The term *personality* refers to individual differences in the characteristic ways in which people think, feel, and behave. According to the DSM–5, a **personality disorder** 'is an enduring pattern of inner experience and behaviour that deviates markedly from the expectations of the individual's culture' (American Psychiatric Association, 2013, p. 646). Moreover, this enduring pattern 'is inflexible and pervasive across a broad range of personal and social situations ... and leads to clinically significant distress or impairment in social, occupational, or other important areas of functioning' (American Psychiatric Association, 2013, p. 646). The DSM–5 lists a total of ten distinct personality disorders, which are gathered together into three different 'clusters' that reflect underlying similarities (see Figure 3.1).

Of all the mental disorders listed in the DSM, the existence and description of personality disorders have, perhaps, been the most contentious. Most of the debate has centred on whether we can reasonably say that there exists a discrete, categorically defined set of disorders that we can label as personality disorders or whether such disorders are best conceived of as extreme or maladaptive variants of normal personality traits (Samuel & Widiger, 2008; Widiger & Trull, 2007). Although the DSM–5 has retained a largely categorical approach to understanding personality disorders (Gotzsche-Astrup & Moskowitz, 2016), additional material has also been provided on dimensional approaches (see Box 3.1). This issue need not concern us too much in this chapter. However, it is worth mentioning because if there is a relationship between personality disorders and criminal offending, then we might expect to see general relationships between personality traits and antisocial behaviour if such disorders reflect the maladaptive endpoints on a continuum.

What, then, *is* the relationship between personality disorders and offending? The answer to this question is not straightforward. In a systematic review of the relationship between personality disorders, violence, and antisocial behaviour, Yu, Geddes and Fazel

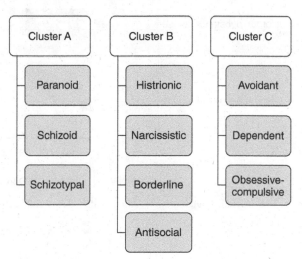

Figure 3.1 The three main clusters of personality disorder.
Source: American Psychiatric Association (2013).

(2012) found that when all personality disorders were considered there was a three-times greater risk of violent outcomes than in the general population. Similarly, in a cross-sectional survey of over eight thousand adults in Great Britain the risk for self-reported violence was significantly greater for individuals with either Cluster A or Cluster B, but not Cluster C, personality disorders (see Figure 3.2) than for the general population (Coid, Gonzalez, et al., 2016). However, although Stone (2007) has suggested that any personality disorder (with the exception of avoidant personality disorder) can be related to offending, the most relevant personality disorder for understanding crime is antisocial personality disorder (ASPD) (Glenn, Johnson, & Raine, 2013).

As illustrated in Table 3.3, most of the characteristic features of ASPD are explicitly related to antisocial behaviour. Individuals with ASPD tend to be deceitful, impulsive, irresponsible, and reckless, acting in ways that show little concern for others. It is not difficult to see how someone with these characteristics may be more likely to engage in criminal behaviour. Indeed, studies consistently and unsurprisingly find a strong relationship between a diagnosis of ASPD, violence, antisocial behaviour, offending, and reconviction (Coid, Gonzalez, et al., 2016; Shepherd, Campbell, & Ogloff, 2016; Yu et

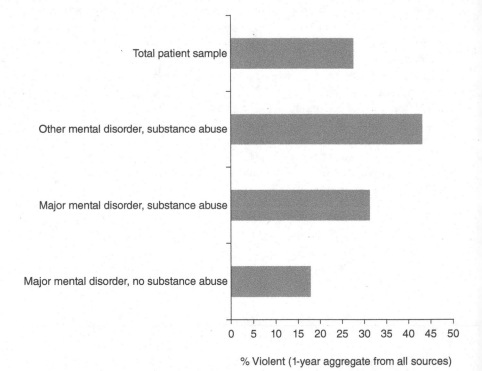

Figure 3.2 Prevalence of violence among mental health patients discharged from psychiatric facilities.

Notes: *Major mental disorder*: diagnosis of schizophrenia, other psychotic disorders; mood disorders; *substance abuse*: diagnosis of substance abuse or dependence; *other mental disorder*: diagnosis of a personality or adjustment disorder.

Source: Based on the data provided by Steadman et al. (1998, Table 4, p. 398).

Table 3.3 Diagnostic criteria for antisocial personality disorder

A. There is a pervasive pattern of disregard for and violation of the rights of others occurring since age 15 years, as indicated by three (or more) of the following:
  1 Failure to conform to social norms with respect to lawful behaviours as indicated by repeatedly performing acts that are grounds for arrest.
  2 Deceitfulness, as indicated by repeated lying, use of aliases, or conning others for personal profit or pleasure.
  3 Impulsivity or failure to plan ahead.
  4 Irritability and aggressiveness, as indicated by repeated physical fights or assaults.
  5 Reckless disregard for safety of self or others.
  6 Consistent irresponsibility, as indicted by repeated failure to sustain consistent work behaviour or honour financial obligations.
  7 Lack of remorse, as indicated by being indifferent to or rationalising having hurt, mistreated, or stolen from another.
B. The individual is at least age 18 years.
C. There is evidence of conduct disorder with onset before age 15 years.
D. The occurrence of antisocial behaviour is not exclusively during the course of schizophrenia or a manic episode.

Source: American Psychiatric Association (2013, p. 659). Reprinted with permission from the Diagnostic and Statistical Manual of Mental Disorders, Fifth Edition, (Copyright ©2013). American Psychiatric Association. All Rights Reserved.

al., 2012). Indeed, in the study conducted by Coid, Gonzalez, et al. (2016), although only four per cent of the sample were diagnosed with ASPD, they were responsible for 22 per cent of all the violent incidents reported. It is, however, important to point out that not all individuals with ASPD will be serious offenders.

One personality disorder that many will be familiar with through depictions in the media, but which does not feature in the DSM, is **psychopathy**. Although psychopathy shares many of the characteristics that are present in ASPD it nonetheless also has important features that distinguish it from this disorder. Because of the importance of psychopathy to understanding criminal behaviour we will examine this personality disorder in much more detail in the second part of this chapter.

REVIEW AND REFLECT

1 What are the key characteristics or symptoms of schizophrenia?
2 What are impulse-control disorders?
3 Consider the diagnostic criteria for antisocial personality disorder. Which of these criteria are closely linked to an elevated risk for offending?

THE ASSOCIATION BETWEEN MENTAL DISORDER AND CRIME

On April 16, 2007 a Virginia Tech student, Seung-Hui Cho, shot to death 32 students and faculty and wounded a further 24 before committing suicide. The Virginia Tech mass murder remains one of the deadliest university mass-shooting in U.S. history (see Chapter 5). In the aftermath of this mass murder, Cho's history of mental illness came to light. He was diagnosed with major depression in the 8th grade and was prescribed antidepressants. He was also briefly committed to a psychiatric hospital in 2005, and many had commented on his 'bizarre' behaviour in the period leading up to the shooting (Flynn & Heitzmann, 2008). To what extent did Cho's mental health problems contribute to his mass murder of 32 individuals, and is his case in anyway typical? That is, are people who suffer from mental illness more likely to commit criminal offences, especially of a violent nature? The image of the insane, deranged killer is certainly a stock feature of films about crime, and the public apparently endorse the idea of a relationship between mental disorder and dangerousness (Jorm, Reavley, & Ross, 2012; Link, Phelan, et al., 1999; Metzl & MacLeish, 2015). However, as is usually the case, the real story is considerably more complex, and it is very important to look closely and critically at what the empirical research tells us about the link between mental illness and criminal offending. There are at least three good reasons why this task is important. First, a clearer understanding of the relationship between mental disorder and crime will contribute to the development of more informed criminal justice policy around such controversial issues as civil commitment, the provision of mental health care, and defences relating to criminal responsibility (Hodgins, 2008; Monahan, 1992). Second, understanding the link between mental disorder and crime can inform us about the importance of treatment in reducing criminal offending (Bean, 2008). And third, accurate information should be able to contribute to a better public understanding of mental disorder that may counter an entrenched stereotypical belief about dangerousness that currently contributes to the stigmatisation of individuals with mental disorders (Jorm et al., 2012; Link, Phelan, et al., 1999).

As a number of scholars have noted, the task of unravelling the relationship between mental illness and crime is a formidable one, beset with methodological problems (Bean, 2008). In order, therefore, to address the relationship between mental disorder and crime it is necessary first of all to be clear about the specific questions that we want to ask. One question is: 'which mental disorders might be related to criminal offending?' Relatively few studies have been carried out that examined a broad range of discrete mental disorders and explored their relationship with criminal offending. Some have examined a particular disorder, such as schizophrenia. A number of studies and reviews of the research literature have looked at the relationship between *major mental disorders* and crime. Unfortunately, exactly what constitutes the major mental disorders in these studies has not always been consistent. Other research has included substance use disorders such as alcohol dependence. The key point here is that we need to pay attention to the type of mental disorder that is being studied and how those mental disorders are defined and measured.

A second question to consider before examining the relationship between mental disorders and crime is: 'which crimes might be related to mental disorder?' Few studies have been done that examine a range of criminal behaviour. Most large-scale studies have focused on violent crime, so this is an area we know more about. A related issue concerns the source of information about crime (see Chapter 1). Not all crimes are reported to police, or result in arrests or convictions that will show up on official records. In other words, there is a significant degree of uncertainty about the actual prevalence of criminal behaviour. This uncertainty includes how much crime goes unrecorded, whether different types of crime have different degrees of under-recording, and whether those with mental disorders are more or less likely to have their criminal behaviour show up in official records (Ballard & Teasdale, 2016).

Bearing these issues in mind, three main kinds of studies have been carried out to examine the relationship between mental disorder and crime. The first type of study looks at the prevalence of criminal behaviour among samples of people with mental disorder. The second sort of research examines the prevalence of mental health problems among criminal offenders. The third type of research explores the prevalence of criminal behaviour and mental disorder in the general population. Each of these three types of research have their limitations, as we shall see below, but collectively they can provide a clearer picture of the association between mental disorder and crime.

Criminal behaviour in the mentally disordered population

There have been a number of studies that have used samples of mentally disordered individuals – usually drawn from psychiatric hospitals – to see whether the prevalence of offending is higher among this group of individuals than in the general population. The most carefully designed and well-known study of this type is the **MacArthur Risk Assessment Study** (Steadman et al., 1998). This research involved 1,136 male and female patients who were discharged from a hospital in the United States with a diagnosis of one or more mental disorders. These individuals were monitored every ten weeks for a year, and information was obtained about their self-reported aggressive and violent behaviour. Importantly, self-reported violence was augmented with reports from critical informants (typically friends and family) and official arrest records to get a clearer picture of the pattern and prevalence of violent behaviour. Critically, this study also included a comparison group of 519 individuals who resided in the same neighbourhoods in which the patients were living. This enabled the researchers to examine whether the prevalence of violence was higher in the patient sample than in the comparison group, while controlling for social context.

There were two main findings in this research. First, the prevalence of violence was significantly higher among patients with a major mental disorder who also abused drugs than in those mentally disordered patients who did not abuse drugs. As can be seen in Figure 3.2, 17.9 per cent of individuals with a major mental disorder engaged in violence over the year compared to 31.1 per cent of individuals with a major mental disorder *and* substance abuse. It would appear that substance abuse heightens the risk for violence among individuals with a major mental disorder. The second main finding was that the prevalence of violence among patients without substance abuse problems was *not* significantly higher than that for the comparison group members who also did not abuse drugs. In other words, mentally disordered individuals *without* substance abuse problems were no more likely to commit violent acts than other individuals drawn from the same community who also did not have drug problems. Finally, it is worth noting that most incidents of violence in both patient and comparison groups were directed at family members and occurred in the home.

Other studies that have drawn on samples of mentally disordered offenders have tended to find a *higher* rate of offending than that in the general population. For instance, in one study involving a sample of 6,644 individuals with serious mental illness (schizophrenia and other psychotic disorders, mood disorders, and other disorders), 23.6 per cent had at least one arrest over a ten-year period, and 8.9 per cent had been arrested for a violent offence. This translates to an overall arrest rate of 775 per 1,000 individuals compared to an estimated community arrest rate of 341 per 1,000 individuals over the same period (Cuellar, Snowden, & Ewing, 2007). This study also found that individuals diagnosed with schizophrenia or other psychotic disorders were significantly more likely to be arrested for violent crimes than individuals with other mental disorders, who were more likely to be arrested for drug offences. Similar results have been found in other studies that have focused on the risk for violence among samples of individuals diagnosed with schizophrenia or other psychotic disorders, and the available evidence seems to indicate that the presence of these disorders is a relatively small, but significant, risk factor for violent offending (Fazel & Grann, 2006; Fazel, Långström, Hjern, Grann, & Lichtenstein, 2009; Swanson et al., 2006; Wallace, Mullen, & Burgess, 2004) (see Research in Focus 3.1). This research also finds that the co-existence of substance abuse and a major mental disorder significantly elevates the risk for violence, and the association between schizophrenia (and other psychotic disorders) and the risk of violence is relatively small for patients who do not also have co-existing substance abuse problems (Fazel et al., 2009).

It should also be noted that this research shows that relatively few violent crimes are committed by mentally disordered individuals. For instance, Fazel and Grann (2006) calculated that approximately 5 per cent of violent offences in Sweden over a 13-year period were committed by individuals with a severe mental illness (schizophrenia and other psychotic disorders). Finally, it is worth pointing out that the relationship between psychotic disorders such as schizophrenia and violence is greater for those who are experiencing their first episode of psychosis and for individuals who are not currently receiving treatment (Silverstein et al., 2015). In sum, although we should exercise some caution in interpreting the available research, it would seem that the risk for offending (particularly violent offending) is higher among the mentally disordered population than it is in the general population.

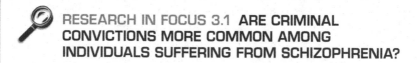

RESEARCH IN FOCUS 3.1 ARE CRIMINAL CONVICTIONS MORE COMMON AMONG INDIVIDUALS SUFFERING FROM SCHIZOPHRENIA?

Title: Criminal offending in schizophrenia over a 25-year period marked by deinstitutionalisation and increasing prevalence of comorbid substance use disorders

Authors: Wallace, C. et al.   **Year:** 2004

Source: *American Journal of Psychiatry*, 161, 716–727

Aims: To investigate criminal offending among a sample of individuals diagnosed with schizophrenia

Method: 2,861 patients admitted for schizophrenia in Victoria (AU) were compared to community comparison sample on criminal convictions.

Key results:
- Patients with schizophrenia accumulated more criminal convictions.
- These patients also experienced more substance abuse problems.

Conclusion: In this sample, schizophrenia was associated with a higher rate of criminal convictions. The relationship is likely to reflect the action of multiple factors, including substance abuse.

Discussion question

Why does the presence of substance abuse problems likely heighten the risk for violence among individuals diagnosed with schizophrenia?

Mental disorders in the criminal population

A second common approach to assessing the relationship between mental disorder and crime is to examine the prevalence of mental disorder among samples of offenders. An example of this kind of study is provided by Silver, Felson, and Vaneseltine (2008). Using results from the Survey of Inmates in State and Federal Correctional Facilities in the United States, Silver et al. (2008) compared the prevalence of violent and sexual offences among inmates with mental health problems (assessed through self-reported experience of mental health treatment or admission to mental health treatment) with that among inmates without such problems. They found that the prevalence of violent and sexual offences was significantly higher among inmates with mental health problems, even after controlling for other relevant variables such as prior offending, victimisation, and alcohol and drug problems. The authors of this study concluded that 'mental health problems are more strongly associated with assaultive violence and sexual offences than with other types of crime' (Silver et al., 2008, p. 424).

Research on the most serious form of violent offending – homicide – is also consistent with the idea of an elevated risk of mental disorder among samples of violent offenders. For example, in a study of 1,594 individuals convicted of homicide in the England and Wales between 1996–1999 it was found that 5 per cent (85 individuals) were diagnosed with schizophrenia, compared to a community prevalence rate for schizophrenia of approximately 0.3–0.9 per cent (Meehan et al., 2006). A similar result was found in a study of 1,087 homicide offenders in Austria: the relative risk of committing a homicide was greater for individuals with schizophrenia or delusional disorder (Schanda et al., 2004).

Although there is some inconsistency in the results found from this type of study, one fairly clear and robust finding is that prevalence of mental disorder is significantly higher in the criminal justice population than in the general population (Sirdifield et al., 2009). Research also suggests that individuals with a mental disorder are also more likely to *re-offend* than those without a mental disorder. Chang et al. (2015) followed up a cohort of over 47,000 offenders released from prisons in Sweden between 2000 and 2009 and found that the presence of a psychiatric disorder (including personality disorders and substance use disorders) significantly increased the risk for violent re-offending even after controlling for relevant demographic (e.g., gender and age) and criminological factors (e.g., offence history).

Mental disorders and crime in the general population

A third type of study attempts to avoid some of the problems of using samples of offenders or mental health patients and focuses on the relationship between mental disorder and crime in the general population. An important early study was carried out using the Epidemiological Catchment Area (ECA) sample of over 10,000 individuals drawn from the community in three cities in the United States (Swanson et al., 1990). A structured diagnostic interview was employed to assess the presence of mental disorder, and violence was measured using a series of self-report questions. The results of this study indicate that whereas 2 per cent of individuals without mental disorder committed violence in the previous year, some 11–13 per cent of individuals with a major mental disorder (major depressive disorder, mania, schizophrenia) reported violence in the same time period. The prevalence of violence was even higher among individuals with a substance use disorder.

More recent epidemiological studies largely replicate these findings: individuals with serious mental illness are more likely to engage in violence than are members of the general community (Alden et al., 2007; Arsenault et al., 2000; Silver & Teasdale, 2005; Swanson, 1994). For example, in a replication of the ECA study described above, Van Dorn, Volavka, and Johnson (2012, p. 488) found a 'statistically significant, yet modest relationship between SMI (schizophrenia, bipolar disorder, and major depressive disorder) and violence' although the relationship was stronger for those also with a substance use disorder.

In sum, research that has drawn on community or population samples tends to support the findings of other types of research: serious mental illness (especially psychotic disorders) is associated with an increased risk for (particularly violent) offending.

Summary and limitations of the research

What can we safely conclude about the relationship between mental disorder and offending based on the research reviewed above? Before we can address this question it is important to consider some of the main limitations of the studies that have been carried out. First, and perhaps most importantly, the majority of research has been conducted using 'special' populations: typically convicted and/or incarcerated offenders and mental health patients. As Bean (2008) notes, studies on convicted offenders have an inbuilt bias: they tell us more about the action of the criminal justice system than they necessarily do about the relationship between mental disorder and crime. Indeed, this is a problem for all studies that use conviction data to establish a link between mental disorder and crime. There is every reason to believe that certain individuals are more likely be arrested and convicted than others, and it is highly likely that people with mental disorders may be at an elevated risk for arrest because they are less able to avoid detection by law enforcement (and may have other characteristics such as low socioeconomic status and residence in deprived neighbourhoods that put them at a greater risk for arrest).

Studies that use psychiatric populations also have their limitations. Individuals who end up undergoing treatment for a mental health problem are not necessarily representative of all of those individuals with mental disorder in the community. These issues are compounded by inconsistent use of psychiatric diagnoses and varied measures of offending. Despite these limitations, the available recent research does provide a reasonably consistent picture of what is known about the association between mental disorder and criminal offending. The main conclusions that can be drawn are as follows:

- There appears to be a general association between major mental disorder and criminal offending.
- The association is strongest between schizophrenia (and other psychotic disorders) and violent offending.
- The co-occurrence of mental disorder and substance abuse problems significantly heightens the risk for violence.
- The overall association between any major mental disorder and any type offending is relatively small in magnitude (especially after controlling for substance abuse and personality disorder).
- Most individuals with major mental disorders (including schizophrenia) do NOT engage in violent or other criminal behaviour.
- Most violent offenders do not have a major mental disorder.

In sum, relatively few crimes are committed by individuals with major mental disorders, and relatively few individuals with major mental disorders commit crime. However, individuals with major mental disorders (especially schizophrenia and other psychotic disorders) do have an elevated risk of (especially violent) offending. Demonstrating an *association* between mental disorder and offending, however, leaves many questions unanswered. Importantly, it is essential to establish just *how* mental disorder might contribute to a heightened risk for criminal offending. In the next section we turn to a discussion of the various factors that can explain this relationship.

REVIEW AND REFLECT

1   Do you think that the public believe that people who have a major mental disorder are dangerous? If so, why do you think that this belief occurs?

2   What are the three main types of research evidence that have been used to explore the association between mental disorder and offending? What are some of the advantages and disadvantages of these three different approaches?

3   Briefly summarise what the research tells us about the relationship between mental disorder and criminal offending.

EXPLAINING THE RELATIONSHIP BETWEEN MENTAL DISORDER AND CRIME

In the preceding section we have reviewed research that, despite some inconsistencies and methodological problems, clearly indicates that there is an association between mental disorder and offending. We have also seen that this association appears to be stronger for some mental disorders (mainly schizophrenia and other psychotic disorders) and some crime (predominantly violent crimes). Another consistent theme is that the co-occurrence of substance abuse problems significantly heightens the risk for offending. Finally, we need to recognise that severe mental illness tends to be associated with a range of other factors like low socioeconomic status, residence in deprived neighbourhoods, and problematic relationships with others (including a significantly heightened risk for being the victim of crime – see Box 3.2) that independently increase the risk for offending (Hiday, 1997; Silverstein et al., 2015). Given these findings, how can we go about *explaining* the relationship between mental illness and crime? In other words, why is it that an association between mental disorder and offending occurs?

BOX 3.2 MENTAL DISORDER AND VICTIMISATION

A large amount of research has been directed at the question of whether individuals with mental disorders are more likely to engage in criminal violence. Surprisingly, relatively few studies have focused on whether people with severe mental disorder are more likely to be *victims* of violent crime. What evidence that we do have indicates that people who have a severe mental illness are at a significantly greater risk of being a victim of violent crime, compared to individuals in the general population (Choe, Teplin, & Abram, 2008). For example, in a UK population based sample of over 8,500 individuals the experience of mental disorder significantly elevated the risk of experiencing both criminal and violent victimisation (Hart et al., 2012). There are a number of potential explanations for these findings. People with severe mental illness may be less able to protect themselves and their routine activities or lifestyle characteristics may render them more vulnerable to victimisation. It is also possible that public perceptions of dangerousness may lead some individuals to engage in 'self-protective violence directed against a person exhibiting symptoms of mental disorder' (Teasdale, 2009, p. 530).

Question for further discussion

Think about the last time that you witnessed someone in your community engaging in a clearly 'odd' or 'bizarre' fashion (and thus perhaps displaying symptoms of a major mental disorder). How did people respond and how might their responses potentially result in an increased risk for victimisation for the individual concerned?

A number of frameworks have been developed to account for the relationship between mental disorder and crime (e.g., Bean, 2008; Hiday, 1997, 2006). Hiday, for instance, suggests that we can understand the association between mental illness and offending in terms of either (a) direct pathways – mental illness, or the symptoms of mental illness, directly lead to or cause offending; or (b) indirect pathways – mental illness tends to lead to other things, such as substance abuse or social deprivation, which in turn cause offending. Implicit in Hiday's framework is also the idea that mental illness and offending are related in part because of (c) common causal factors – there are variables, such as social deprivation, that might cause or result in both a heightened risk for mental illness and a heightened risk for offending. These three models are shown in Figure 3.3, and in the following section we will review evidence in support of each of these alternatives. Before we look at this evidence it is worth noting that all three models are likely to capture something about the relationship between mental illness and crime.

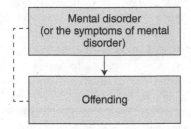

(a) Direct pathway – mental disorder causes or leads to offending

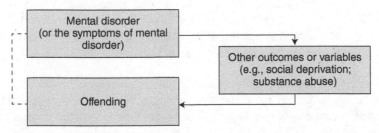

(b) Indirect pathway – mental disorder leads to other outcomes that cause offending

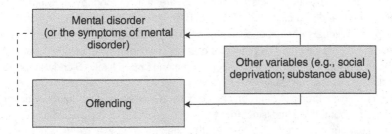

(c) Common cause – a variable or variable cause, or lead to, both mental disorder and offending

Figure 3.3 Three models for explaining the relationship between mental disorder and offending.

Direct pathways

According to the direct pathway model, the association between mental disorder and offending is due to the fact that the symptoms or characteristics of mental illness lead to or result in a heightened risk for offending. What sort of characteristics might put individuals with mental disorder at a risk for offending? For a small number of disorders very specific symptoms may elevate the risk for criminal offending. For instance, many of the disruptive, impulse-control, and conduct disorders discussed earlier in the chapter have symptoms or characteristics that are directly (e.g., kleptomania) or very closely (e.g., pyromania, intermittent explosive disorder) related to offending. However, in this section we will look at the more widely studied relationship between characteristics of major mental disorders (schizophrenia spectrum and other psychotic disorders; bipolar and depressive disorders) and offending with a specific focus on how hallucinations and delusions may increase the risk for violent offending.

Hallucinations are a relatively common feature of psychotic disorders such as schizophrenia, although they also occur in a range of other mental disorders such as mood disorder, personality disorders, and dissociative disorders (McNeil, 1994). There are certainly a number of clinical case studies that have linked certain types of hallucinations to an increased risk of violent offending. Of particular relevance is a type of hallucination known as a **command hallucination**. An individual who experiences a command hallucination believes that they are being directed (e.g., by God or Satan) to carry out certain acts. The content of command hallucinations might include harm to others, but they also may include directions to harm the self or to engage in other, non-violent acts (Barrowcliff & Haddock, 2006; McNeil, 1994).

It may seem intuitively plausible that experiencing a command to harm others will increase the risk for violent offending, but the available evidence in support of this idea remains patchy at best. In a review of 17 studies that examined the link between hallucinations and violence, Bjørkly (2002b, p. 612) concluded that:

- There is no evidence that auditory command hallucinations are dangerous per se.
- There is some, but so far inadequate, evidence that voices ordering acts of violence toward others may increase compliance and thereby be conducive to violent behaviour.

Importantly, not all (or even most) commands are acted upon by individuals who experience command hallucinations (Barrowcliff & Haddock, 2006). It may be that for a sub-group of individuals who experience commands to behave violently to others there is an increased risk of violence. The presence of other psychotic symptoms – in particular, delusions – may make compliance to violent commands more likely (Bjørkly, 2002b).

Delusions are another common symptom of individuals who suffer from psychotic disorders like schizophrenia. A delusion can be conceptualised as a 'pathological belief' in the existence of something that is not true (or is not supported by the available evidence). For instance, in our case study that opened the chapter, John was clearly experiencing a delusion that his parents were vampires. In this case, the delusion appeared to play a role in John's offending. Individuals with severe mental illness may experience a range of different delusional beliefs, some more bizarre or unrealistic than others. Most of these delusional beliefs are likely to have little impact on the risk of offending. Indeed, most of the focus has been on persecutory delusions (the belief that others are out to harm you), and so-called **threat/control override** (TCO) delusions. TCO delusions are characterised by the belief that others are out to harm you (threat), and/or that there are outside forces that are controlling your mind (control).

Several studies have found that the presence of TCO symptoms make individuals more likely to engage in aggressive and violent behaviour (Link, Monahan, et al., 1999; Link & Stueve, 1994). For instance, in a study using both a community and patient sample, Link and Stueve (1994) found that the TCO symptoms significantly predicted violence after controlling for demographic characteristics and other psychotic symptoms. However, not all studies have supported the relationship between TCO symptoms and violence (Applebaum, Robbins, & Monahan, 2000; Witt, van Dorn, & Fazel, 2013), and it is likely that only a subset of individuals with such symptoms are at a greater risk of harming others. Other studies have explored, more generally, the role of persecutory delusions and paranoid ideation on the risk for violence among individuals with major mental disorders. Coid, Ullrich, et al. (2016), in a large population-based study in the UK, found that paranoid ideation was significantly associated with violence in their sample. In a longitudinal study of prisoners in the UK, Keers et al. (2014) found that schizophrenia was significantly related to violence but only in the absence of treatment, with the experience of persecutory delusions being the key symptom explaining the relationship between untreated schizophrenia and violence.

In a comprehensive review of the studies that have looked at the relationship between delusions and violence, Bjørkly (2002a) concluded that both persecutory delusions and TCO symptoms are risk factors for violence, but that the available evidence remains somewhat limited. Indeed, Skeem et al. (2016), using data from the MacArthur Violence Risk Assessment Study, found that the experience of psychosis only preceded 12 per cent of violent incidents in the sample of individuals with major mental disorder. This suggests that, although some of the specific symptoms of schizophrenia and other psychotic disorders may play a role in some violent offending, they cannot fully explain the relationship that is found between major mental disorders and violent offending.

Indirect pathways and common cause explanations

It is likely that the relationship between mental disorder and offending can be explained, in part, due to the fact that mental health problems are associated with a number of other outcomes and variables that independently predict offending. Probably the most important other variable in this context is substance abuse. As we have seen, individuals with substance use problems and a serious mental illness are more likely to offend than individuals with a mental illness alone. In part, this is because substance use problems themselves (as reviewed in Chapter 8) are strongly associated with an increased risk for offending. This finding is important because a relatively high proportion of individuals with a serious mental illness also have a co-occurring substance use problem (Adamson et al., 2006; Mueser et al., 2006). For example, it is estimated that approximately 50 per cent of individuals with schizophrenia also have a substance use disorder – over three times the rate found in the general population (Green et al., 2007).

The relationship between serious mental illness and substance use problems is not straightforward. Individuals with schizophrenia and other mental disorders may use drugs to self-medicate the symptoms of their disorder (Khantzian, 1997), and/or they may be more sensitive to the effects of psychoactive substances, therefore promoting their use. In other words, mental illness may increase the risk for substance use problems, which in turn increases the risk for offending.

The chronic use of some drugs, such as amphetamines and cocaine, can also result in acute mental health problems, including psychotic symptoms such as delusions and hallucinations (McKetin, McLaren, Lubman, et al., 2006). There is also an accumulating body of evidence to support the idea that the use of some drugs might precipitate or exacerbate the symptoms of mental illness in vulnerable individuals (Arseneault et al., 2004). In short, drug use can cause or worsen mental health problems. Finally, we need to recognise that serious mental illness and substance use problems are likely to share common risk factors such as early trauma and abuse, adverse living conditions, stress, and social deprivation (Mueser & Drake, 2007). This means that part of the association between mental disorder and violence arises because substance use problems increase the risk for offending and share the same or similar risk factors as the development of mental disorder.

Individuals with a serious mental illness are also more likely to live in deprived neighbourhoods, have low socioeconomic status, and experience high levels of social stress (Silver, Mulvey, & Monahan, 1999; Silver & Teasdale, 2005). Because the experience of social deprivation and social stress are independently related to a greater risk of criminal offending, part of the relationship between mental disorder and crime might be due to the relatively greater proportion of mentally disordered offenders who are socially disadvantaged. The available research provides some support for this idea. For example, Silver et al. (1999) drew on data from the MacArthur Risk Assessment Study to explore the role of neighbourhood disadvantage in the perpetration of violence by individuals with a serious mental disorder discharged from hospital. The results of the study clearly indicated that: (a) patients discharged from hospital were more likely to reside in a disadvantaged neighbourhood than the general population; and (b) patients discharged from hospital who resided in a disadvantaged neighbourhood were more likely to engage in violence than patients who did not. In another study of 3,438 individuals drawn from the community, Silver and Teasdale (2005) demonstrated that the experience of socially stressful life events and the absence of social support predicted the likelihood of violence among all individuals in the sample. Importantly, the magnitude of the association between mental disorder and violence found in this research was significantly reduced after controlling for levels of social stress and social support. In other words, part of the reason that people with a mental disorder are more likely to engage in violence is because they also experience much higher levels of social stress and have less social support.

The available research can not at this stage untangle the causal relationships among social deprivation, social stress, mental disorder, and violence. It is likely, however, that the experience of a serious mental disorder causes or leads to an increased risk for social deprivation and social stress, which in turn increase the risk for violence. From the perspective of general strain theory (see Chapter 1) it can be argued that the life strains or stressors that are strongly associated with the experience of mental disorder play a key role in the elevated risk for criminal offending and violence among this population (see Link et al., 2016). It is also likely that social deprivation, social stress, and a lack of social support contribute to the development (or exacerbation) of mental health problems. In other words, the relationship between social disadvantage and mental disorder is probably bi-directional in nature.

Any consideration of the relationship between mental disorder and offending must also take into account of the fact that many individuals with a major mental disorder also meet the diagnostic criteria for one or more personality disorders (Witt et al., 2013). For instance, data from the WHO World Mental Health Survey indicate that approximately 16.5 per cent of individuals with a major mental disorder (which included anxiety disorder, mood disorder, externalising disorder, substance use disorder) also meet the diagnostic criteria for one or more personality disorders (Huang et al., 2009). Individuals suffering from schizophrenia are more likely to also experience a personality disorder than are individuals from the general population. Of significance for our discussion here is the significant amount of overlap between major mental disorders and antisocial personality disorder (ASPD) (Huang et al., 2009). This relationship is important because there is a strong association between these personality disorders and criminal offending (Derefinko & Widiger, 2008). A quick review of the diagnostic criteria for ASPD (Table 3.3) clearly indicates why this is the case: individuals with ASPD tend to be impulsive, deceitful, aggressive, and irresponsible, showing little concern with the rights of others. We will examine the relationship between ASPD and the closely related construct of psychopathy and criminal offending in the next section. At this point, all we need to note is that part of the relationship between serious mental illness and offending can be accounted for due to the overlaps between these disorders and personality disorders such as ASPD.

A final indirect pathway between mental disorder and offending may arise due to the way that others respond to individuals with severe mental illness. As Hiday (1997, 2006) notes, the odd or bizarre symptoms that are characteristic of some mental disorders may result in tense situations with others that can escalate into violence. Given research that suggests the public perceive that people with certain mental disorders are dangerous, it is not surprising that such encounters may heighten the risk for violence. The fact that people suffering from a mental disorder are at a significantly greater risk of being a victim of violent crime (see Box 3.3) highlights this point: people with mental health problems may be more likely to find themselves in situations where social encounters result in violent outcomes. This point was clearly illustrated in a study by Ballard and Teasdale (2016) utilising data from the MacArthur Violence Risk Assessment Study. Individuals in the patient sample were over three times more likely to experience victimisation than the community controls, and the experience of victimisation was a significant predictor of violence after controlling for other variables.

Making sense of the direct and indirect pathways between mental disorder and offending is no simple task because the causal relationships among all of the relevant variables are complex and have yet to be fully mapped out. This complexity is nicely illustrated in one recent review of the literature on the relationship between psychosis and violence that highlighted 41 possible causal pathways (Lamsma & Harte, 2015)! Although there may be some direct relationship between some mental disorders and some types of offending (mainly psychotic disorders and violence), a significant part of the relationship between mental disorder and crime is accounted for by co-occurring conditions or factors such as substance abuse, personality disorder, social deprivation, and victimisation. A schematic overview of these relationships is provided in Figure 3.4, although the overlaps indicated in the figure should be viewed as illustrative rather than definitive. Indeed, some studies suggest that the relationship between mental illness and violence can be *fully* accounted for by other variables or factors that are more general risk factors for violence (e.g., Elbogen, Dennis, & Johnson, 2016). The importance of this point can not be underestimated: if we are wanting to gain a clearer picture of the mental disorder and crime relationship and take steps to reduce offending among mentally disordered offenders then we also must address (or at the very least assess) other co-occurring problems such as substance abuse and social deprivation.

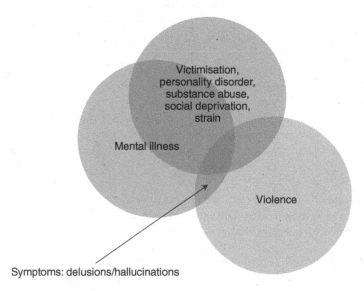

Figure 3.4 A schematic overview of the relationship between mental illness, other factors and conditions, and violence.

REVIEW AND REFLECT

1   Draw diagrams to illustrate (a) a direct pathway between mental disorder and offending; and (b) an indirect pathway between mental disorder and offending. Use these diagrams to explain to someone else why the relationship between mental disorder and offending arises.

2   How might the experience of victimisation heighten the risk for violence among individuals with major mental disorders?

3   What are the main symptoms of schizophrenia and other psychotic disorders that may be directly related to an elevated risk for violence?

PSYCHOPATHY

The idea that some individuals can be viewed as 'pure evil' has an enduring historical appeal. These putative individuals, although few in number, are capable of perpetrating the most heinous acts, apparently without any remorse or guilt. The term 'psychopath' is the modern equivalent, and for most readers this term will readily conjure up examples drawn from the movies (see Criminal Psychology Through Film 3.1), authoritarian dictators (think Stalin or Idi Amin), or even friends, family members, or colleagues (see Oakley, 2007). Researchers have shown no less interest in the construct of psychopathy, and there is an enormous scholarly literature on all aspects of psychopathy. But, what exactly does it mean to describe someone as a 'psychopath'? What are the characteristic features of this disorder, and how do they relate to criminal behaviour? In the remainder of this chapter, we will examine the nature and prevalence of psychopathy and explore its relation to criminal offending. We will also consider current theoretical explanations for the origin of psychopathy and raise the vexed issue of whether psychopaths can be treated.

CRIMINAL PSYCHOLOGY THROUGH FILM 3.1
No Country for Old Men (2007)

Directed by: Joel and Ethan Cohen
Starring: Jarvier Bardem (Anton Chigurh), Tommy Lee Jones (Sheriff Ed Tom Bell), and Josh Brolin (Llewelyn Moss)

Based on Cormac McCarthy's novel of the same name, *No Country for Old Men* depicts a convoluted story involving a botched drug deal, large sums of money, and lots and lots of graphic violence. One of the central characters is Anton Chigurh, brilliantly played by Jarvier Bardem. Hired to recover the drug money stumbled upon by Llwelyn Moss, Chigurh provides a vivid onscreen portrait of someone who would, in all probability, comfortably pass the PCL–R threshold for psychopathy (with points to spare) as he calmly racks up a two-figure body count while displaying barely a flicker of emotion, let alone remorse or guilt. *No Country for Old Men* won four Grammy awards, including best picture and best performance by an actor in a supporting role (Jarvier Bardem).

Questions for discussion

1   What are some of the other films that provide depictions of psychopaths? How are these depictions similar and how do they differ?
2   Watch the film *No Country for Old Men* while you have the items in the PCL–R by your side (see Table 3.4). What characteristics are clearly depicted in the movie, and what further information would you need to determine whether Chigurh really was a psychopath?

The nature and extent of psychopathy

Psychopathy has been conceptualised as a personality disorder characterised by a core set of affective, interpersonal, and behavioural features. As Hare (2001, p. 6) outlines:

> On the interpersonal level, psychopaths are grandiose, arrogant, callous, dominant, superficial, and manipulative. Affectively, they are short-tempered, unable to form strong emotional bonds with others, and lacking empathy, guilt or remorse. These interpersonal and affective features are associated with a socially deviant lifestyle that includes irresponsible and impulsive behaviour, and a tendency to ignore or violate social conventions and mores.

Individuals with these psychopathic characteristics have long been recognised in diverse cultures throughout history (Cooke, 2008; DeLisi, 2016). Current views of psychopathy build on the pioneering work of Hervey Cleckley, who in his book, *The Mask of Sanity* (1964), described a set of 16 personality characteristics that describe the psychopath (see Table 3.4). The most widely employed current approach to assessing psychopathy is the Hare Psychopathy Checklist Revised (PCL–R). The items on the PCL–R are organised into four underlying facets: interpersonal, affective, lifestyle, and antisocial, which capture the core characteristics of psychopathy (see Table 3.4). This 20-item measure is employed by trained observers (typically clinicians) who rate the individual on each item based on information derived from semi-structured interviews with the individual and key informants (e.g., family members, co-workers), along with available file evidence. Each of the 20 items is rated on a 3-point scale (0 = item does not apply; 1 = item applies somewhat; 2 = item definitely applies) so total scores can range from 0–40 with a score of 30 or higher, considered the cut-off point for a diagnosis of psychopathy (Hart & Hare, 1997).

Table 3.4 The characteristics of psychopathy

Cleckley's 16 personality characteristics[a]	The four facets of the PCL–R[b]
1. Superficial charm and good 'intelligence'	Facet 1: Interpersonal • Glibness/superficiality, charm • Grandiose sense of self worth • Pathological lying • Conning/manipulative
2. Absence of delusions and other signs of irrational thinking	
3. Absence of 'nervousness' or psychoneurotic manifestations	
4. Unreliability	
5. Untruthfulness and insincerity	
6. Lack of remorse or shame	Facet 2: Affective • Lack of remorse or guilt • Shallow affect • Callousness/lack of empathy • Failure to accept responsibility for own actions

7. Inadequately motivated antisocial behaviour
8. Poor judgment and failure to learn by experience
9. Pathological egocentricity and incapacity for love
10. General poverty in major affective reactions

Facet 3: Lifestyle
  • Need for stimulation/proneness to boredom
  • Parasitic lifestyle
  • Lack of realistic long-term goals
  • Impulsivity
  • Irresponsibility

11. Specific loss of insight
12. Unresponsiveness in general interpersonal relations
13. Fantastic and uninviting behaviour with drink and sometimes without
14. Suicide rarely carried out

Facet 4: Antisocial
  • Poor behavioural controls
  • Early behavioural problems
  • Juvenile delinquency
  • Revocation of conditional release
  • Criminal versatility

15. Sex life impersonal, trivial, and poorly integrated
16. Failure to follow any life plan

Additional PCL–R items
  • Promiscuous sexual behaviour
  • Many short-term marital relationships

Source: ᵃCleckley (1976, cited in Skeem et al., 2011, Table 1); ᵇHare (2003, cited in Skeem et al., 2011, Table 2).

The core construct of psychopathy (as measured by the PCL–R) has been largely developed in a North American context. However, research suggests that it can be extended to other cultural groups, although the absolute scores on the PCL–R may not be equivalent (Cooke & Michie, 1999; Cooke et al., 2005). It has been suggested, for example, that the cut-off score for a diagnosis of psychopathy should be 25 in the United Kingdom (rather than 30 as is the case in North America). A recent review of the PCL–R by Neumann, Hare, and Pardini (2015) suggested that the proposed four facets of psychopathy reliably emerge in a range of different (although largely Western) cultural contexts around the world. The characteristics of psychopathy – or at least an emerging set of psychopathic traits – have also been recognised in children and adolescents (Salekin & Frick, 2005) and can be measured using the Psychopathy Checklist Youth Version (PCL: YV). It should, however, be noted that there remains a vibrant debate in the academic literature regarding how best to characterise and measure psychopathy with some scholars challenging the widespread acceptance and use of the PCL–R and associated scales (Skeem et al., 2011).

A recent challenge to the four-factor structure of psychopathy championed by Hare and colleagues has been provided by the **triarchic model of psychopathy** (Patrick &

Drislane, 2014). According to this model, three underlying constructs can capture the core features of psychopathy: disinhibition, meanness, and boldness. As described by Patrick and Drislane (2014, p. 628):

> *Disinhibition* entails impulsiveness, weak restraint, hostility and mistrust, and difficulties in regulating emotion. *Meanness* entails deficient empathy, lack of affiliative capacity, contempt toward others, predatory exploitativeness, and empowerment through cruelty or destructiveness ... *boldness* entails proclivities toward confidence and social assertiveness, emotional resiliency, and venturesomeness.

These three constructs are conceptualised as the 'building blocks' from which various ways of capturing psychopathy can be constructed. Thus, different psychopaths may have different configurations of these three underlying features, which can then, perhaps, account for the diverse 'images' of psychopathy that have been presented: from the successful 'corporate' psychopath (low on disinhibition, but high on meanness and boldness) to the chronic offender (high on all three constructs, but especially disinhibition) to the sadistic serial murderer (especially high on meanness) (see Skeem et al., 2011).

Psychopathy is typically viewed as a personality disorder, although it does not (as yet) feature specifically in the DSM. The closest diagnosis listed in the DSM–5 is antisocial personality disorder (ASPD), and if you take another quick look at Table 3.3 you will note a significant overlap in the way that ASPD and psychopathy are assessed. This overlap, however, is only partial, and the two constructs are not identical. For instance, in a study of 136 patients in a secure forensic psychiatric facility in Australia, whereas over 65 per cent of the sample with psychiatric traits received a diagnosis of ASPD (*Diagnostic and Statistical Manual of Mental Disorders–Fourth Edition, Text Revision, DSM–IV–TR*; American Psychiatric Association, 2000), only five per cent of patients with ASPD were high in psychopathic traits. Although the definition of ASPD has come closer to that of psychopathy in the latest version of the DSM it still focuses more on antisocial behaviour at the expense of some of the core affective and interpersonal features of psychopathy, and there appears to be good reasons to distinguish between these two constructs in terms of their underlying causes (Walsh & Wu, 2008).

Relatively few individuals in society can be classified as psychopaths. Most research has been conducted with samples of offenders, so reliable information about the prevalence of psychopathy in the wider population is not currently available. However, it is roughly estimated that less than 1 per cent of males (and even fewer females) in the population would be classified as psychopaths (Blair, Mitchell, & Blair, 2005). In contrast, the prevalence of ASPD in the community is estimated to be approximately 4.5 per cent for men and 0.8 per cent for women (Derefinko & Widiger, 2008). When we turn to research that has examined the prevalence of ASPD and psychopathy among samples of offenders, quite a different picture emerges. According to Hare (1996), approximately 80 per cent of the U.S. prison population meet the diagnostic criteria for ASPD, and somewhere between 15 and 25 per cent can be classified as psychopaths based on their PCL–R scores. Although these figures may be somewhat on the high side, there is no doubt that there is a moderate to strong association between psychopathy and offending, as we shall see in the next section.

Psychopathy and offending

It shouldn't take more than a moment's reflection to see that someone who possesses the characteristics that are measured by the PCL–R is likely to be at an elevated risk of offending. If someone is impulsive, is prone to boredom, and lacks self-control they may be more prone to offend against others, and if they lack remorse and empathy they are not likely to be concerned about the consequences of their actions. Indeed, some of the items in the PCL–R are specifically related to criminal offending (e.g., criminal versatility, juvenile delinquency) so they are going to clearly predict offending. The available research evidence certainly provides support for a moderate to strong relationship between psychopathy and offending (DeLisi, 2016; Hare, 1999; Hare et al., 2000; Neumann & Hare, 2008; Salekin, 2008), and some scholars have argued that the construct of psychopath can be used to fashion a unified theory of crime (DeLisi, 2016). In general, the research suggests that individuals who meet the cut-off point for psychopathy:

- have higher rates of criminal recidivism
- start their criminal careers at an earlier age
- commit more offences
- have higher rates of violent offending
- have higher rates of sexual offending (especially among offenders who victimise adults *and* children)
- may engage in more sadistic violent and sexual offending
- are at an elevated risk for committing sexual homicide.

Because most research has been conducted on offender samples, it is difficult to evaluate how many individuals who meet the criteria for psychopathy do *not* engage in serious offending. Therefore, despite the robust relationship between psychopathy and offending, it is important to keep in mind that psychopathy does not *equate* with criminality (Polaschek, 2015; Skeem & Cooke, 2010; Skeem et al., 2011), and some individuals with psychopathic traits may experience significant occupational and interpersonal success (Lilienfeld, Watts, & Smith, 2015). We should remember, then, that not all psychopaths are criminals (and, of course, not all people who commit crimes are psychopaths). Rather, psychopathy is an underlying personality disorder that has core characteristics that make offending more likely, but not inevitable.

The origins of psychopathy

The core features of psychopathy are widely agreed upon, and a large body of research supports the conclusion that individuals with these characteristics are more likely to commit crime. A key question that remains to be addressed concerns the origins of these characteristics: What causes psychopathic traits, like lack of empathy, callousness, and impulsivity? Theories of psychopathy have been largely dominated over the last couple of decades by biological approaches. In this section, we first explore evolutionary approaches to understanding psychopathy and then discuss two prominent accounts that focus on biological processes.

For many psychologists psychopathy is best conceptualised as a pathology or disorder. However, although psychopaths are often responsible for causing significant amounts of harm to others, it is not entirely clear that psychopathy is particularly harmful to the individual themselves, at least certainly not in the same way that other mental disorders like schizophrenia or depression clearly are. Indeed, some evolutionary psychologists have argued that psychopathy can be viewed as an adaptive strategy that may increase reproductive success in some contexts (Mealey, 1995). Thus, the characteristics of psychopathy – risk taking, need for stimulation, lack of guilt, promiscuous sexuality – may contribute to activities (e.g., a large number of sexual partners) that could plausibly increase reproductive success. However, these characteristics often also entail costs (e.g., poor investment in offspring, formal sanctions, and increased risk of mortality) so it is not entirely clear that psychopathic characteristics would have been specifically selected for. In a comprehensive review of the possible evolutionary origins of psychopathy, Glenn, Kurzban, and Raine (2011) conclude that the currently available evidence does not allow us to clearly distinguish between the possibility that psychopathy is a genuine pathology and the idea that it might represent a suite of traits that have been selected for during our evolutionary history.

Although the putative evolutionary origins of psychopathy are somewhat unclear, there has been substantial progress in unravelling some of the important proximate biological mechanisms that underpin psychopathy. One important early approach to understanding psychopathy was the **low arousal hypothesis** (Lykken, 1957). According to this perspective, psychopaths are characterised by abnormally low levels of physiological arousal. In particular, they show deficits in the capacity to experience fear or anxiety. Although you may think that this might be a good thing (particularly around exam time!), a relative inability to experience fear or anxiety impairs the capacity to learn to avoid averse and damaging situations. It also means that such individuals are hard to socialise, because they do not respond to punishment. Low physiological arousal has also been hypothesised to be related to a proneness to boredom and the need for stimulating experiences in order to bring arousal levels up to optimum levels. Consistent with low arousal theory, research suggests that psychopaths have a low resting heart rate and low electrodermal activity (a physiological measure of arousal to specific tasks) (DeLisi, 2016; Lorber, 2004).

Another important neurobiological model of psychopathy is the **violence inhibition model** (VIM) (Blair et al., 2005). For most individuals, witnessing fear or distress in others is emotionally upsetting, reflecting out capacity for empathy and perspective taking. We are able to place ourselves in another person's position and react to their adverse emotional states. Moreover, distress in others serves to inhibit aggression or harmful acts, because we do not like to see others suffer. According to VIM, it is this capacity that is impaired in individuals with psychopathy: cues of distress and sadness in others are simply not recognised, and hence they tend to be ignored. At a neurobiological level, this deficit is hypothesised to reflect impaired amygdala functioning. Ultimately, the failure to recognise and respond to distress in others inhibits normal moral development and may facilitate the particularly 'cold-blooded' and sadistic nature of violence perpetrated by some psychopaths (Kirsch & Becker, 2007).

The available biological research on brain abnormalities in psychopathy tends to provide some support for the VIM. Studies that have used imaging technology to assess brain function support the contention that psychopaths tend to show impairments in both prefrontal areas and the amygdala, along with connections between sub-cortical and cortical structures (Blair, 2013, 2015). A number of other brain abnormalities have also been identified, and it is likely that psychopathy is characterised by multiple neurobiological deficits. However, some caution should be exercised in the interpretation of these findings. Most imaging studies use small samples, co-occurring problems such as alcohol and drug abuse are not always robustly controlled for, and there is often variation in the way that psychopathy is assessed (Weber et al., 2008).

Neurobiological research highlights the brain regions that may be associated with the underlying cognitive and affective symptoms of psychopathy such as shallow affect, lack of empathy, and impulsiveness. However, this research cannot tell us *why* individuals with psychopathy possess these characteristics. In other words, we need a theory that unravels the origins of psychopathic characteristics. There is an emerging consensus that the development of psychopathy reflects a complex interaction of genetic and social factors. The emergence of psychopathic characteristics, especially so-called callous-unemotional traits (lack of guilt, empathy, and shallow affect), have been demonstrated in young children to be a major risk factor for the development of psychopathy (Frick et al., 2014b). Some evidence supports the idea that there is an important genetic component to the development of these psychopathic characteristics (Blair et al., 2006; Viding et al., 2005). However, it is also likely that the social and family environment play an important role in the development of psychopathy. For instance Farrington (2007), in a review of data from the Cambridge Study of Delinquent Development, found that elevated PCL: SV (a screening version of the PCL–R) scores were related to a host of family (e.g., poor supervision, physical neglect) and social (e.g., low social class, poor housing) risk factors. It may be, as Blair et al. (2006) argue, that the core emotional dysfunction found in psychopathy is under stronger genetic influence, while the more broadly behavioural and antisocial characteristics are influenced more by the social environment. Certainly, there is no currently available evidence to suggest that psychopathic characteristics are in any sense fixed in concrete (see Box 3.3 for a discussion of whether individuals with psychopathic traits can be 'treated').

BOX 3.3 CAN PSYCHOPATHS BE TREATED?

Given the strong relationship between psychopathy and offending, effective strategies to reduce recidivism among psychopaths are clearly needed. However, many researchers have been pessimistic about the possibility of treating or rehabilitating individuals with psychopathy. Cleckley (1964, pp. 477–478), writing in the fourth edition of the *Mask of Sanity*, for example, observed:

I have now ... had the opportunity to observe a considerable number of patients who .... were kept under treatment not only for many months, but for years. The therapeutic failure in all such patients observed leads me to feel that we do not at present have any kind of psychotherapy that can be relied upon to change the psychopath fundamentally.

Others have, more recently, echoed this view, and some research actually seems to suggest that traditional treatment approaches may actually make psychopaths *more* likely to offend than if they were not treated at all (Harris & Rice, 2007). However, not all researchers have given up the possibility of treating psychopaths. Salekin (2002), in a review of 42 treatment studies, suggests that the pessimism regarding the possibility of treating psychopaths is unfounded, although a lack of methodological consistency in the available research limits any firm conclusions. Certainly, the affective and interpersonal characteristics of psychopathy can make treatment difficult: psychopaths rarely see anything wrong in their behaviour so they are not particularly motivated to change. Probably the safest conclusion at this stage is that, although there is no solid evidence in support of the idea that psychopaths can be treated, there is also no convincing evidence to suggest that they *can't* be treated. As Polaschek (2014, p. 300) aptly summarises in a recent discussion on the treatment of psychopathy:

> Psychopaths have sometimes been excluded from criminal-justice interventions because of beliefs about psychopathy's immutability and their untreatability. A small and recent research literature suggests that populist ideas about psychopaths and their treatability largely lack substance – findings that should open the way for a revitalization of research on psychopathy, treatment and change. This revitalization is sorely needed.

REVIEW AND REFLECT

1   What is psychopathy, and how is both similar to, but different from, antisocial personality disorder?
2   What are the three components of the triarchic model of psychopathy?
3   Are their 'successful' psychopaths? What characteristic of psychopathy might contribute to success in the corporate world?

SUMMARY

Major mental disorders of relevance for understanding the relationship between mental disorder and crime include schizophrenia and other psychotic disorders, substance use disorders, mood disorders, and some personality disorders.

The idea that people suffering from a major mental disorder are inherently dangerous appears to be well entrenched among the public, perhaps heightened by the dramatic cases that are often presented in the media. The true picture is, however, considerably more complex. Although research consistently (but not universally) finds that there is an association between mental disorder and criminal offending, the overall size of this relationship is small and tends to be strongest for some disorders (especially psychotic disorders) and some types of offending (especially violent offending). It is very important to keep in mind that most people who suffer from a mental disorder (including schizophrenia and other psychotic disorders) are no more likely to behave violently or to commit a crime than individuals who do not have a mental disorder.

The research on mental disorder and offending suggests that there are both direct and indirect pathways that can explain the relationship. Certain symptoms of mental disorder – especially persecutory delusions, and threat/control override symptoms – may make some individuals with mental disorder more likely to engage in violence. Individuals who suffer from a mental disorder are also more likely to have co-occurring substance use problems, meet the diagnostic criteria for a personality disorder, and experience greater amounts of social deprivation and social stress. Because these co-occurring characteristics are all related to an elevated risk for offending, a substantial part of the relationship between mental disorder and violent crime can be accounted for by these characteristics and not the experience of the major mental disorder per se.

The mental disorder that shows the strongest and most robust relationship with criminal offending is psychopathy. Psychopathy is a personality disorder characterised by a core set of interpersonal (grandiose, arrogant, and callous), affective (lacking guilt and anxiety), and behavioural (irresponsible and impulsive) characteristics. Psychopathy, as measured by the Hare Psychopathy Checklist Revised (PCL–R), is a strong predictor of criminal behaviour, especially violent offending. Current aetiological theories of psychopathy have focused on deficits in key neurobiological structures such as the amygdala and the prefrontal cortex that probably arise as a result of a complex set of interactions between genetic and social factors.

FURTHER READING

Schug, R. A., & Fradella, H. F. (2015). *Mental Illness and Crime*. Thousand Oaks, CA: Sage Publications.
This book provides a comprehensive, up-to-date and accessible overview of the literature on mental illness and crime. The authors provide useful tables that summarise the available research for each major mental disorder.

Paris, J. (2013). *The Intelligent Clinician's Guide to the DSM–5*. Oxford: Oxford University Press.
For those interested in thinking more closely about the nature of mental disorder itself and how it is presented in the DSM–5 this book is a great place to start.

DeLisi, M. (2016). *Psychopathy as Unified Theory of Crime*. New York, NY: Palgrave MacMillan.
A comprehensive review of psychopathy and its relationship to criminal offending.

Silverstein, S. M., Del Pozzo, J., Roché, M., et al. (2015). Schizophrenia and violence: Realities and recommendations. *Crime Psychology Review*, 1, 21–42.
A good detailed account of the relationship between schizophrenia and violence, with implications of this research for practitioners, policy makers, and the criminal justice system.

Skeem, J. L., Polaschek, D. L. L., Patrick, C. J., & Lilienfeld, S. O. (2011). Psychopathic personality: Bridging the gap between scientific evidence and public policy. *Psychological Science in the Public Interest*, 12, 95–162.
An excellent overview of recent work on psychopathy with implications for public policy. Strongly recommended as a starting point for those interested in learning more about psychopathy.

There are plenty of journals in which you will find work on mental disorder and crime. Some of the main ones include: *American Journal of Psychiatry, Criminal Justice and Behaviour, Clinical Psychology Review, Clinical Psychological Science*, and *Schizophrenia Bulletin.*

WEB RESOURCES

This is the homepage for the MacArthur Research Network, which contains links to the MacArthur Risk Assessment Study described in this chapter: www.macarthur.virginia.edu/home.html.

This website provides a comprehensive list of articles on psychopathy including links to a number of full-text versions: www.hare.org.

 KEY CONCEPTS

- antisocial personality disorder
- command hallucination
- conduct disorder
- delusions
- delusional disorder
- hallucinations
- intermittent explosive disorder
- kleptomania
- low arousal hypothesis
- MacArthur Risk Assessment Study
- mental disorder
- mental illness
- oppositional defiant disorder
- pyromania
- personality disorder
- psychopathy
- schizophrenia
- threat/control override delusions
- triarchic model of psychopathy
- violence inhibition model

Aggression and violence

LEARNING OBJECTIVES

On completion of this chapter you should have developed a good understanding of:

➤ the important conceptual distinctions between aggression, violence, and violent crime, and between different types of aggression;
➤ the major theoretical approaches to explaining aggression and violence, including:
  – evolutionary approaches
  – social-structural and cultural approaches, including sub-cultures of violence, the culture of honour hypothesis, and strain theory
  – psychological approaches, including the cognitive neoassociation model, script theory, and the social information processing model
  – biological approaches, including the role of genes, hormones, neurotransmitters, and specific regions of the brain
  – key situational and environmental factors that are related to aggression and violence;
➤ integrated theories of aggression and violence, specifically the general aggression model.

It is not hard to come up with examples of aggression and violence. Consider the following: A man pulls out a knife and demands money from a shopkeeper; a shopkeeper, frightened for his life, pulls out a baseball bat and hits a robber over the head with it; a heated dispute between two young men in a bar results in one man killing the other with a handgun; a women, upset at her unfaithful husband, cuts him in the face with a knife; a young parent neglects the physical and psychological needs of his infant daughter; a high school student spreads a malicious rumour about a class mate; a participant in a social psychology experiment selects an especially fiery hot sauce to administer to a fellow participant; a serial killer targets young men whom he rapes and kills; a grandfather sexually abuses his 8-year old granddaughter; a solider aims his machine gun at the advancing enemy line, killing dozens of soldiers.

These cases illustrate the important point that aggressive and violent acts represent a varied, or heterogeneous, group of behaviours that vary by context, motive, and the amount of harm inflicted on others. In our attempts to understand and to *explain* violent crime, therefore, it will be important to consider a wide range of theoretical perspectives and how they apply to different forms of violent offending. Over the next four chapters we will explore the topic of aggression and violence in all its myriad forms. In Chapter 5 we will look at specific types of violent crime, Chapter 6 tackles the literature on sexual violence, and Chapter 7 explores the topic of collective violence. In this chapter, however, we engage with the more general theoretical approaches to understanding aggression and violence. We begin by addressing some of the important conceptual issues relating to the definition and classification of aggression, violence, and violent crime. The main part of this chapter is taken up with the challenging task of explaining aggression and violence, and we will consider a wide range of theoretical approaches (see Chapter 1 for an overview). These include evolutionary theory, social-structural and cultural factors, psychological process, biological mechanisms, and the situational context of violent offending. We conclude the chapter by looking at how many of these different theoretical approaches might be integrated to provide explanations for aggression and violence, looking specifically at the general aggression model.

CONCEPTUAL ISSUES

Consider the list of behaviours presented at the start of this chapter. These are all acts that result in, or have the potential to result in, harm to others. But do they all count as instances of aggression, or even violence? As we shall see, there is no straightforward answer to these questions because the concepts of 'aggression' and 'violence' have been defined in different ways. Moreover, as these examples illustrate, the class of acts that we might consider as aggressive or violent encompasses a diverse range of human behaviour. This is an important point because it suggests that there is unlikely to be any single or simple *explanation* for violent behaviour. However, let's begin by considering some of the main attempts to define and classify aggression and violence.

A fairly standard working definition of **aggression** is offered by Baron (1977, p. 7): 'Aggression is any form of behaviour directed toward the goal of harming or injuring another living being who is motivated to avoid such treatment.' There are several key features to this definition that psychologists typically agree upon (Anderson & Bushman, 2002). First, intention is crucial. If I accidentally harm you by mowing the lawn as you walk by, causing stones to fly up and hit you in the face, my act is not one of aggression. Accidental injuries clearly do not count. A second key aspect of this definition is that harm includes both physical and psychological harm. The intentional use of insults and verbal abuse, therefore, count as instances of aggression. Finally, for the act to count as aggression the individuals must be motivated to avoid that harm. A drill-wielding dentist, despite deliberately causing pain, is not behaving aggressively because the intent is not to cause harm, and the patient, in an obvious sense, accepts the pain as something they need to endure. It is important also to note what this definition *excludes*. Our everyday use of the term 'aggression' may be employed to describe someone who is angry, or having hostile thoughts, or who is overly competitive but we should reserve the term aggression for certain types of behaviour, not patterns of thinking or emotional states (Warburton & Anderson, 2015).

Violence can be conceptualised as 'aggression that has extreme harm as its goal' (Anderson & Bushman, 2002, p. 29), or as 'destructive physical aggression intentionally directed at harming other persons or things' (Bartol & Bartol, 2008, p. 146). These definitions highlight that all instances of violence are also instances of aggression but that violence involves behaviours that are more harmful in nature, typically involving more extreme physical aggression. Some have argued for a more expanded concept of violence that also captures instances of structural violence (e.g., the deprivation that might arise from specific economic policies) (Lee, 2015). However, although there is substantial merit in broadening the scope of the term violence, for ease of exposition we will employ the definition employed in this chapter as it best captures the phenomena that we will mainly be concerned with. Finally, criminal violence can be viewed as violence that is prohibited by the law. Although much violence is, therefore, criminal violence there are clearly instances of violent acts that are legitimised by the state (e.g., punishment, and the use of reasonable force by the police) that do not count as instances of criminal violence (see Figure 4.1). Before reading further, check your understanding of these definitions by completing Activity 4.1.

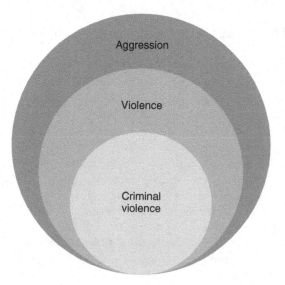

Figure 4.1 The relationship between criminal violence, violence, and aggression.

ACTIVITY 4.1 CONCEPT CHECK

Consider the following examples. According to the definitions supplied in the text indicate whether they are examples of aggression, violence, and/or criminal violence.

	Aggression	Violence	Criminal violence
A man assaults his wife with a cricket bat, breaking her collarbone.			
A heroin trafficker, caught by a customs officer in Singapore, is caned and sentenced to death.			
A builder accidentally drops a hammer from a construction site wounding a bystander.			
A school bully verbally abuses a classmate.			

Now that we have considered some key definitions of aggression and violence we are in a position to further explore specific types of aggressive and violent acts. Four important typologies of aggression and violence will be considered (see Table 4.1):

1 Physical, verbal, and relational aggression.
2 Direct aggression, indirect aggression.
3 Hostile and instrumental aggression.
4 Aggression motivated by instrumental reasons, dominance, revenge, sadism, and ideology.

The distinction between physical and verbal aggression is pretty straightforward. Physical aggression simply involves aggressive acts that result in some amount of physical harm to victims. A punch is a clear example of physical aggression. Insults, derogatory comments, threats, and other such acts are, by contrast, examples of verbal aggression (sometimes also referred to as 'psychological aggression'). In these instances there is intent to harm another individual who is motivated to avoid that harm, but the mode of harming is verbal rather than physical in nature. **Relational aggression** encompasses acts that intend to harm the victims' social status or self-esteem, such as spreading malicious rumours about someone else's sexual behaviour (Archer & Coyne, 2005). Aggression can also manifest either directly or indirectly. **Direct aggression** involves acts (either physical or verbal) that are carried out by a perpetrator and are clearly directed at a victim who is typically present. **Indirect aggression**, in contrast, involves attempts to cause psychological harm to someone else through social manipulation in ways that are typically covert and often occur in the physical absence of the victim (Archer & Coyne, 2005). Indirect aggression typically involves acts of relational aggression: a teenager who deliberately excludes a peer from a social group, a man who rubbishes the ideas of a work colleague behind his back, and a woman who spreads a malicious rumour about one of her acquaintances might all be said to be engaging in indirect aggression.

Another long-standing distinction has been made between **hostile aggression** (also known as affective, expressive, angry, impulsive, or reactive aggression), and **instrumental aggression** (also known as predatory, cold-blooded, pre-meditated, or proactive aggression). The distinction is typically based on three key factors (Bushman & Anderson, 2001): (a) the goal of the behaviour; (b) the level of emotional arousal involved; and (c) the amount of planning or premeditation involved. Hostile aggression is characterised by strong emotional arousal (usually anger or fear), occurs in response to a perceived threat, is typically impulsive or spontaneous, and is primarily directed at harming the victim. A prototypical case of hostile aggression would involve a bar-room brawl, where one man responds to a perceived insult by punching another man in the face. Instrumental aggression involves the use of aggression to obtain a pre-meditated goal or objective and is carried out in the absence of high levels of emotional arousal. Robbery is typically considered an example of instrumental violence: it is usually (but not always) planned, and the ultimate goal is to obtain goods and money, not to harm others, although such harm might result as a 'by-product' of the primary objective.

Table 4.1 Typologies of aggression and violence

Typology	Description	Example
Direct	Aggression perpetrated at a victim who is present	Joshua hits Kyle over the head with a bottle
Indirect	Aggression perpetrated at a victim who is not immediately present	Kyle spreads a rumour behind Joshua's back about his sexual inadequacies
Physical	Aggressive acts that involve some level of physical harm to victims	Joshua hits Kyle over the head with a bottle creating a wound that requires five stitches
Verbal	Aggressive acts that do not result in direct physical harm to victims	Prior to being hit over the head by Joshua, Kyle yells at him and threatens to take a sledge hammer to his new car
Relational	Aggressive acts designed to threaten the social status or esteem of victims	Kyle spreads a rumour about Joshua's sexual inadequacies to Ruby, a woman that Joshua likes
Hostile	Aggression that is typically impulsive, occurs in the response to an immediate threat, and involves high levels of emotional arousal with the aim of hurting or getting back at the victim	Insulted by Kyle's threat, Joshua becomes enraged and attacks Kyle with a bottle aiming to hurt him as much as possible
Instrumental	Aggression that is typically planned, does not involve high levels of emotional arousal, with harm to the victim a 'by-product' of the primary goal	In order to pay for his expensive legal bills, Joshua holds up a service station, threatening the attendant with a hunting knife

This typology has been widely employed by psychologists. However, it has also been subject to criticism. For instance, Bushman and Anderson (2001) note that both forms of violence often co-occur in a given instance: a robber might experience significant arousal and gain pleasure from harming victims even though this is not the main goal of the attack; and although much so-called expressive violence may seem to have no ultimate goal from the outside, from the perpetrator's perspective the goal of saving face or restoring justice is the legitimate end goal with violence simply the means to achieve it. The distinction between hostile and instrumental aggression, however, is still of some value in that it can be employed to differentiate different types of aggressive response and different types of violent offender (Meloy, 2006). However, it may be better to conceptualise aggression on a continuum – from more impulsive, emotional, and reactive to more controlled, planned, and instrumental – rather than thinking in terms of a strict dichotomy between hostile and instrumental aggression (see Figure 4.2). It also needs to be recognised that both forms of aggression may be present in any given situation (Bushman & Anderson, 2001; Meloy, 2006).

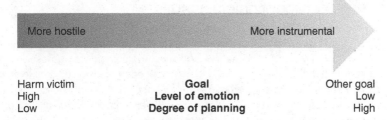

Harm victim	**Goal**	Other goal
High	**Level of emotion**	Low
Low	**Degree of planning**	High

Figure 4.2 Hostile and instrumental aggression can be viewed on a continuum.

Finally, we can – very roughly – categorise aggression and violence in terms of the core causes or underlying motivations while recognising that any given instance of violence or aggression may have multiple underlying causes. According to Pinker (2011), in a scheme adopted from the social psychologist Roy Baumeister, there are five root causes or motivations for violence. First, violence might arise for purely instrumental or predatory reasons – aggression, violence, or the threat of violence can simply be an effective way of getting what you want. This is true of both humans and other animals. The lion that pulls down the gazelle after a frantic pursuit has no personal grudge against the gazelle, she just wants her dinner. Similarly, humans also engage in instrumental violence to get what they want: whether it is a two-year-old pushing a younger child out of the way to get a favourite toy or a robber threatening a shop owner with a gun to get at the cash register. Second, a lot of violence is also perpetrated not to obtain some obviously tangible benefit, but in order to dominate or exercise power over others. A lot of male–male aggression, as we shall see in more detail in Chapter 5, is fundamentally about dominance or status. Third, humans and other animals also employ violence to exact retaliation or revenge on others for actual or perceived wrongs. This is, of course, the violence that is routinely perpetrated by the criminal justice system, but revenge is a well-embedded feature of social life – what have you imagined doing to a driver that cuts you off without signalling and makes you engage in an emergency break? The fourth category is violence for the pure pleasure of it. This is somewhat of a disturbing and perhaps puzzling motive, but it is clear that for some people in some situations there is pleasure to be obtained in harming others (Baumeister, 1997). Finally, a good deal of inter-group violence, in particular, is perpetrated in the service of an underlying ideology or belief system. Examples are not hard to come by for anyone who reads the news, and we shall tackle this underlying motive in more detail in Chapter 7.

Now that we have considered some of the important conceptual issues in defining aggression and violence (see also Box 4.1 for an overview of key methodological issues), we turn to look at the different theoretical approaches that have been developed to explain aggression and violence.

BOX 4.1 METHODOLOGICAL ISSUES

Imagine that you are a criminal psychologist interested in exploring the relationship between playing violent video games and the development of aggressive and violent behaviour in adolescents. What kind of methods would you employ to study this topic? There are – as you can imagine – a number of different approaches you could use. One approach would be to design an experiment. Participants could be randomly assigned to two groups: the first group could play a violent video game like Grand Theft Auto, and the second group could play a non-violent video game like Spyro. Both groups of participants could then be put in a context where aggressive behaviour is likely to occur, and the amount of aggression displayed by the two groups would be measured. If the violent video game group displayed more aggressive behaviour than the non-violent video game group then you might have some support for the idea that playing violent video games increases aggression.

Experimental laboratory approaches have a number of virtues. Most importantly you can carefully control and measure all relevant variables. Experimental research also allows you to make claims about causal relationships between the variables that you have measured. However, laboratory aggression paradigms also have a number of drawbacks. The most critical issue concerns the measurement of aggression – just how do you get participants to display aggression and violence in a laboratory context? You could get your participants to hurl insults at each other until a fist fight ensues and then measure the number of punches and the damage that they cause, but this design is unlikely to make it past a university's ethics committee! Researchers therefore have developed a number of different ways of operationalising aggression in the laboratory, such as the administration of electric shocks, or blasts of white noise against others (who typically are confederates of the experimenter, or don't actually exist at all; see Ritter & Eslea, 2005).

Critics of laboratory aggression research argue that such approaches are flawed because adequate measures of aggression have not been employed. Hence, the results of such studies cannot be extrapolated to our understanding of aggression and violence in the 'real world' (Ferguson & Rueda, 2009; Tedeschi & Quigley, 1996). Other researchers have vigorously defended the use of experimental research paradigms (e.g., Bushman & Anderson, 1998). Probably the safest approach at this stage is to accept that laboratory approaches to studying aggression have some value in informing us about aggression and violence in the real world, but that they inevitably have their limitations, and therefore they should be used as only *one* source of information in the development and testing of theories about aggression and violence.

Other approaches to studying aggression and violence include the use of official crime statistics, victim surveys, longitudinal studies, archival and documentary research, and in-depth qualitative studies involving interviews with offenders and victims. All methodological approaches have both virtues and limitations, and, where possible, the best approach is to adopt a strategy of 'triangulation' where the result from studies using different methodologies are employed, rather than relying on a single source of information (Lee & Stanko, 2003; Warburton & Anderson, 2015).

REVIEW AND REFLECT

1   Does it matter how we define terms like 'aggression' and 'violence'? Why?
    Why not?
2   What are some of the problems in distinguishing between 'hostile' and
    'instrumental' aggression?
3   The next time you watch the news or browse the news online consider the
    potential underlying root causes or motives of any stories relating to violence.

EVOLUTIONARY APPROACHES

Aggression and violence are not uncommon features of social life in modern Western societies. Moreover, although the *rates* of violence may differ, the available evidence indicates that violence is a cross-culturally and historically universal feature of human society (McCall & Shields, 2008; Nivette, 2011b). In short, it can be argued that the *capacity* for aggression and violence is part of the behavioural repertoire of our species, just as it is for many other animals including our closest genetic relative, the common chimpanzee. An evolutionary perspective suggests that the psychological and physiological mechanisms that underlie aggression are biological adaptations: they have been selected for because they increased the survival and reproductive success of individuals in ancestral environments (see Chapter 1). In other words, the capacity for aggression and violence is an evolved characteristic of our species (Archer, 2009b; Buss & Shackelford, 1997; Daly & Wilson, 1988; Liddle, Shackelford, & Weekes-Shackelford, 2012).

How might have aggression and violence promoted survival and reproductive success? Unlike earlier evolutionary conceptions of aggression as a simple 'drive' or instinct, Buss and Shackelford (1997) argue that human aggression is a context-sensitive strategy that is employed in a variety of specific situations in order to solve particular 'adaptive problems'. These might include such things as the co-option of resources from others, defence against attack from others, the negotiation of status and power hierarchies, and the deterrence of long-term mates from sexual infidelity (Buss & Shackelford, 1997, pp. 608–611). Central to an evolutionary approach to aggression, then, is the premise that, in the evolutionary currency of reproductive fitness, the benefits of aggression (in specific circumstances) outweigh the costs, and hence mechanisms underlying aggression have been selected for.

Evolutionary approaches can help us to understand why humans have an enduring capacity for aggression and violence under particular circumstances. In other words, evolutionary theory can provide the 'ultimate' explanation for aggression (see Chapter 1 for a distinction between ultimate and proximate explanations). An evolutionary perspective can also potentially help to advance our understanding of the particular patterns of aggression and violence that are found. The most robust finding in the literature on aggression and violence relates to gender differences: men are, in general, more aggressive and violent than are women (one exception is relational aggression, which shows little in the way of a gender differences – Archer & Coyne, 2005). Meta-analyses of sex differences in aggression consistently support the idea that men are more aggressive than women (Archer, 2004), and the data on violent offending and homicide also clearly indicate that men are more likely to be perpetrators of violent crime than are women. Importantly, men are also more likely to be the *victims* of violent crime, especially homicide (see Chapter 5 for details). Of course, there are no surprises here: everyone 'knows' that men are more violent than women – but, why is this?

A number of scholars have argued that sex differences in aggression and violence – particularly the preponderance of male–male violence – can be accounted for by the process of sexual selection (Archer, 2004, 2009a; Daly & Wilson, 1990; Puts, 2010). From this perspective, the preponderance of male–male violence can be viewed as the outcome of competition between rival males for status and resources. This doesn't mean that men always fight 'over women'; rather, males compete with each other for dominance, status, and physical resources, which correlate reliably with mating opportunities and overall reproductive success, or at least would have done in ancestral environments. The seemingly 'trivial' nature of the disputes that occur between men (e.g., perceived slights and insults) that can result in serious violence and homicide can be viewed, from this perspective, as conflicts over something of ultimate value: reproductive success. Male violence may also be adaptive in other contexts, and we will explore evolutionary approaches to understanding intimate partner violence in Chapter 5, sexual violence in Chapter 6, and collective violence in Chapter 7.

Campbell (2006, 2007, 2013a) argues that the proximate mechanisms underlying sex differences in aggression and violence relate to the fact that women experience greater fear of the outcomes of violence and exhibit relatively greater control over feelings of anger and frustration. From an evolutionary perspective this makes sense: because they experience less variance in reproductive success, women have less to gain and more to lose (in evolutionary terms) from engaging in risky behaviour, including violence, than do men. Moreover, women are more pivotal in ensuring the survival of offspring than are men, and hence we would expect them, on average, to be more risk-averse. As Cross and Campbell (2011, p. 391) put it: 'Women's lives are precious commodities. When an ancestral mother risked her life, she risked the lives of her descendants in each of whom she has invested more than any father.'

It is important to recognise that taking an evolutionary perspective on aggression and violence does mean that violence is somehow obligatory or inevitable. Certainly, evolutionary accounts suggest that everybody has the *capacity* for violence, but whether this is expressed depends on specific circumstances (which are potentially amenable to change). It is also important to understand that adopting an evolutionary perspective on violence does not in any way mean that violence (in general) is either acceptable or justifiable (see Chapter 1). Finally, although evolutionary accounts can further our understanding of why aggression occurs in specific contexts, in order to provide a complete account of aggressive and violent behaviour we need to consider the proximate psychological and physiological mechanisms than underlie aggressive behaviour and the particular situational, developmental, and social contexts in which violence occurs.

REVIEW AND REFLECT

1   What are some of situations where the use of aggression might have been effective in promoting survival and reproductive success in humans in ancestral environments?

2   We know that males exhibit higher rates of aggression and violence than do females, and evolutionary psychologists have argued that this reflects, in part, stronger selection pressures on males for intra-sexual competition. What are some other differences between males and females that could be explained using the same evolutionary logic?

SOCIAL-STRUCTURAL AND CULTURAL APPROACHES

Violence is an inescapable fact of human social existence, and occurs in all human societies. However, as we will explore in Chapter 5, rates of violence vary substantially across different time periods, among different nations, and between different regions and communities within nation states. What factor or factors can explain these large historical and regional differences in rates of violent offending? Broadly speaking, two types of explanation have been offered by social scientists to account for this variation. The first type of explanation focuses on how differences in specific attitudes, values, beliefs, practices, and norms (in short, differences in 'culture') influence the prevalence of violent crime. The second type of explanation looks to specific social-structural features such as poverty, inequality, and demographic characteristics to account for variations in violent crime. In this section we examine these two types of explanation in more detail and look at some of the prominent theoretical explanations that have been developed, in part, to account for variations in violent offending. It should be noted, however, that cultural and social-structural explanations are not mutually exclusive, and a number of theoretical perspectives combine these accounts in order to explain the patterns in violent offending that are found.

Cultural approaches

A social-cognitive approach, as we shall discuss later in the chapter, identifies the important role that violent-related attitudes, beliefs, norms, and scripts (acquired via social learning) can play in understanding individual differences in aggression and violent behaviour. An individual that has positive attitudes towards violence believes that violence is appropriate in a wide range of contexts, and someone who has a large number of readily accessible violent-related scripts will be more likely to commit a violent offence than someone who does not share these attitudes, beliefs, and scripts. It follows, fairly straightforwardly, that *group* differences in violent-related attitudes, norms, beliefs, and scripts can plausibly explain the neighbourhood, regional, and national differences in violent crime rates that are found. Consistent with this idea, in a study involving 19 nations and four regional areas in the United States, it was found that differences in the reported acceptability of killing under certain circumstances predicted national and regional differences in homicide rates (McAlister, 2006). Two main theoretical ideas have dominated cultural approaches to understanding violent crime: The **sub-cultures of violence** theory and the **culture of honour thesis**.

Sub-cultures of violence theory

According to the sub-cultures of violence theory, formulated by Wolfgang and Ferracuti (1967, cited in Brookman, 2010), high rates of violence arise among certain groups of society (typically lower class males) who share a certain set of values, beliefs, and norms that are conducive to violence. In particular, it is argued that among certain sub-cultures violence is seen as an acceptable, even obligatory, means of maintaining respect and resolving conflicts. In short, violence is a legitimate way of achieving and maintaining status among peers. This idea has been most thoroughly developed by Elijah Anderson (1994, 1999) in his work on 'street culture' in the United States, or what he terms 'the code of the streets'. As Anderson (1994, p. 82) explains:

> the street culture has evolved what may be called a code of the streets, which amounts to a set of informal rules for governing interpersonal public behaviour, including violence. The rules prescribe both a proper comportment and a proper way to respond if challenged. They regulate the use of violence and so allow those who are inclined to aggression to precipitate violent encounters in an approved way.

To illustrate, imagine that you are walking down the street, minding your own business, when someone approaches you from the opposite direction. You look up to find that they are looking directly at you, maintaining eye contact for what feels to you like an uncomfortably long period of time. What do you do? If you are like most middle-class individuals, you will probably look away and walk past the person concerned without a further thought. However, for individuals inculcated in the code of the street, maintaining eye contact for too long will be perceived as both a threat and a challenge: one that requires a – potentially violent – response in order to retain respect.

This sub-culture of violence is viewed by Anderson as a 'cultural adaptation' to an environment in which there is a profound lack of reliable third-party enforcement (i.e., police), and in which there is little opportunity for social and economic success through conventional means. This results in individuals having to 'take care of themselves' in social encounters through the use of violence (and the threat of violence) and to seek status through their success in projecting a tough and violent persona to their peers. Research in the United States has provided some support for these key features of the sub-culture of violence theory. In one study involving over 700 African Americans, for instance, it was found that individuals who live in neighbourhoods where 'street culture' is more pronounced and who endorsed the 'street code' (e.g., agreed with statements like 'when someone disrespects you, it is important that you use violence against him or her to get even') were more likely to engage in violence even after controlling for other related variables such as neighbourhood disadvantage, family socioeconomic status, parenting factors, and prior violent offending (Stewart & Simons, 2010). More recent research has explored how Anderson's 'code of the streets' can be valuably extended to other cultural contexts including deprived communities in Scotland (Holligan, 2015) and street children in the Ukraine (Naterer, 2015), suggesting that the theory has some cross-cultural value in accounting for aggression and violence perpetrated by males in economically and socially deprived contexts.

The culture of honour thesis

Whereas the 'code of honour' thesis was developed to account for community differences in violent crime, a similar theoretical approach – the 'culture of honour thesis' – has been offered as an explanation for *regional* differences in violent crime rates in the United States. Specifically, it is argued that the higher rates of homicide in the American South are the result of a particular set of cultural factors that guide behaviour among Southern men (or more accurately Southern *White* men) (Nisbett, 1993). Nisbett maintains that Southern men adhere to a 'culture of honour': they believe that violence is an appropriate, and indeed expected, way to respond to insults, disputes, and arguments. Threats to personal and family honour, for these individuals, are viewed as fundamental threats to status and reputation and must be dealt with accordingly. The origin of this culture of honour, according to Nisbett (1993), resides in the settlement of the Southern region of the United States by largely Scots and Irish immigrants who have come from primarily herding (as opposed to farming) communities in the British Isles. Because herders have their wealth sunk into livestock, which are highly mobile and therefore easily rustled, and because they tend to inhabit sparsely populated regions without effective rule of law, it was incumbent on individuals to 'cultivate a posture of extreme vigilance toward any act that might be perceived as threatening in any way, and respond with sufficient force to frighten the offender and the community into recognizing that they are not to be trifled with' (Nisbett, 1993, p. 442). Due to the ongoing socialisation of children into this 'culture of honour' this suite of violent-related attitudes, beliefs, and norms has been retained in Southern states in the United States, and putatively can account for regional differences in homicide rates.

Support for the culture of honour thesis comes from a variety of different sources, as outlined below:

- Regional differences in homicide rates support the contention that argument- or dispute-related homicides (but not those that occur in the context of robbery) are higher in the Southern states and in places with a greater concentration of Southern white men (Lee et al., 2007; Lee & Shihadeh, 2009; Ousey & Lee, 2010).
- In experimental contexts, Southern men are more likely to respond to insults with (a) heightened physiological arousal in readiness for violence; and (b) more aggressive and dominant behaviour (Cohen et al., 1996).
- At the county level, communities with a greater prevalence of Scottish-Irish immigrants in the nineteenth century have higher rates of argument-related homicides (Baller, Zevenbergen, & Messner, 2009).

Honour cultures are not restricted to the American South, and, in a similar fashion to 'the code of the streets' discussed above, honour cultures may emerge reliably in contexts where conditions are harsh and where social institutions – such as the rule of law – are weak (Nowak et al., 2016). However, despite the widespread evidence that a 'culture of honour' does exist in the American South and that it may have an influence on rates of lethal violence, it is important not to neglect the potential role that economic and social factors might have on regional differences in homicide rates (Daly, 2016; Daly & Wilson, 2010).

Social-structural approaches

Social-structural approaches to understanding crime in general and violent crime in particular are prominent in criminology although they tend to play a more limited role in psychological theorising. In this section we first examine some of the main social-structural correlates of violent crime before turning to several prominent theoretical approaches for understanding the relationship between these correlates and violent crime.

In a classic study that investigated the structural correlates of homicide rates across 50 states, 904 cities, and 259 metropolitan areas in the United States, Land, McCall and Cohen (1990) found three factors that reliably predicted differences in homicide rates: resource deprivation, population structure, and percentage of divorced males. Areas that were more deprived and less affluent experienced higher homicide rates. More populous (and more densely populated) areas and those that had a higher percentage of divorced males also had higher rates of homicide. Since this landmark pieces of research there have been a large number of studies that have explored the relationship between social-structural characteristics and homicide rates. Consistent with the findings of Land et al. (1990), resource deprivation has emerged as one of the most important predictors of homicide rates: those neighbourhoods, cities, regions, and states that are less affluent and more deprived tend to have a greater incidence of homicide than more affluent and less deprived regions. There is, however, some debate about whether absolute deprivation, or what some scholars call 'concentrated poverty', is more important than relative deprivation (e.g., income inequality) in predicting homicide rates (Daly, 2016; Daly, Wilson, & Vasdev, 2001; Kubrin, 2003). In a partial replication and extension of the study by Land et al. (1990), McCall, Land, and Parker (2010) also confirmed the importance of population structure and percentage of divorced males in predicting differences in homicide rates.

Although much of the research that has examined structural correlates of violent offending has been conducted in the United States, there are now also a number of cross-national studies that include a range of different countries. In general, the results of this research are consistent with the findings from the United States, with measures of relative deprivation such as income inequality the most robust predictor of homicide rates (Jacobs & Richardson, 2008; McCall & Nieuwbeerta, 2007). For instance, McCall and Nieuwbeerta (2007) examined the structural correlates of homicide in a study of 117 cities in 16 European countries and found that deprivation and population structure (population size and density) were the best predictors of homicide rates. A review of 65 cross-national studies confirmed that relative deprivation is the most robust predictor of homicide rates (Pridemore & Trent, 2010), and a meta-analysis by Nivette (2011a) found a number of significant predictors of cross-national homicide rates including poverty, income inequality, divorce rate, population growth, and infant mortality.

Another line of research has looked at the importance of social cohesion on rates of violent offending and has usually focused on neighbourhoods or communities as the main ecological unit of study (as opposed to cites, states, or countries in the research reviewed above). A fairly consistent finding in this research is that low levels of social cohesion are related to higher rates of violent crime. Communities that are socially disorganised and have low levels of collective efficacy (i.e., a willingness among community members to supervise children, enact informal social control, and maintain public order) are characterised by relatively high rates of violent crime (Mazerolle, Wickes, & McBroom, 2010; Sampson, 2012; Sampson et al., 1997). For example, in a study of 82 neighbourhoods in Brisbane, Australia it was found that a measure of collective efficacy explained 30 per cent of the variation in rates of self-reported violent victimisation (Mazerolle et al., 2010).

Social disorganisation and strain theory

Two prominent theoretical approaches in criminology have been employed to account for the relationship between social-structural characteristics and violent crime rates. The social disorganisation perspective highlights how intense urbanisation, poverty, and socially disorganised neighbourhoods contribute to crime through the weakening of social bonds and informal mechanisms of social control. Support for this perspective comes from the research that suggests that more densely populated areas with low levels of collective efficacy and a large percentage of disrupted families have higher rates of violent crime. In these communities there tend to be low levels of parental supervision of children and limited exercise of informal mechanisms of social control. The central tenet of strain theory is that stressors and strains (arising from inequality, poverty, discrimination, and marginalisation) reduce an individual's capacity to cope and to achieve cultural goals through legitimate means. Violence, from this perspective, can be viewed as a way for individuals to obtain status and resources that are otherwise denied to them (Agnew, 2007). Consistent with strain theory is the fairly robust finding that measure of economic deprivation, including absolute poverty and income inequality, consistently predict rates of violent crime.

REVIEW AND REFLECT

1   What is the culture of honour thesis and how can it explain regional differences in homicide rates in the United States?
2   What is collective efficacy and how might it account for neighbourhood differences in violent crime?
3   What are some of the major cross-national predictors of homicide rates?

PSYCHOLOGICAL APPROACHES

It is just one of those days. First, mistakenly setting your alarm clock for 7.00 pm instead of 7.00 am you sleep in and miss the first hour of an important two-hour exam. You go to see your lecturer to explain, but she is less than sympathetic and refuses to take your lateness into consideration in marking the exam. You then have lunch with your partner who informs you that your relationship is over. Finally, waiting in the over-heated and un-air-conditioned university café someone boisterously pushes past you causing your plate of spaghetti to splatter over your new white t-shirt. The offender turns around, and instead of apologising, simply laughs. What is going through your head at this point? Are you likely to respond to this provocation with an angry comment or perhaps even an act of violence? Almost certainly this will depend on who you are and the specific thoughts and emotions that you are experiencing.

Psychological approaches to understanding aggression and violence focus largely on the cognitive and emotional processes within individuals and how individuals respond to their immediate social environment. One line of work has tried to identify the individual difference factors that can explain why some individuals are more likely to use aggression and violence than others. Other theoretical approaches have focused on the psychological processes that go on inside the individual in specific circumstances that might give rise to aggressive behaviour, and how cognitive and emotional processes relating to aggression develop over time.

Personality and aggression

As we will discuss in the section on situational approaches, aggression and violence are more likely to occur in certain contexts rather than others. However, these contexts do not inevitably result in aggression: confronted with the scenario presented at the start of this section, some individuals, but not others, are more likely to respond in an aggressive or violent fashion. This suggests that there are important individual differences in aggressive and violent behaviour.

Evidence for the role of personality characteristics on aggressive behaviour comes from findings that indicate that there is a fair amount of stability in aggressive behaviour over time. Longitudinal studies have consistently found that individuals who are more aggressive as children are also more aggressive and more likely to engage in violent crime as adolescents and as adults (Farrington, 1991; Huesmann et al., 1984; Moffitt et al., 2002). For instance, in the Cambridge Longitudinal Study (see Chapter 2), it was found that teacher ratings of aggression at age 12–14 predicted subsequent convictions for violent crime (Farrington, 1991). There are a number of possible factors that can account for this continuity in aggression and violence over time, but one possibility is that certain individuals have relatively enduring personality characteristics that make them more likely to engage in aggressive behaviour.

Although a relationship has been found between certain core personality characteristics and aggression, typically speaking the overall effects of personality traits on aggressive and violent behaviour tend to be relatively weak. Research that has used Eysenck's three factor 'PEN' model of personality (see Chapter 1) has found mixed support for relationships between the three core personality characteristics (psychoticism, extraversion, and neuroticism) and aggression (Cale, 2006; Miller & Lynam, 2001), with the strongest association typically found for psychoticism. Other research that has been based on the big five personality traits has found that of these five factors, only neuroticism, agreeableness, and conscientiousness have been shown to be related to aggression and violence. Although specific findings depend on the kind of research conducted, generally it is found that both conscientiousness and agreeableness are negatively related to aggression. In other words, individuals who are less conscientious and who are less agreeable are more likely to engage in aggressive behaviour. On the hand, the personality dimension of neuroticism seems to be positively related to aggression and violence (Bartlett & Andersen, 2012; Bettencourt, Talley, Benjamin, & Valentine, 2006; Miller & Lynam, 2001).

In addition to attempts to link the major dimensions of personality with aggression, a number of researchers have identified single-factor individual difference characteristics that they believe are especially important in understanding aggressive behaviour. These include self-control, narcissism, and empathy.

The idea that individuals who have a limited capacity to control or regulate their behaviour are more prone to engaging in violent and antisocial behaviour is the core postulate of Gottfredson and Hirschi's (1990) general theory of crime and features prominently in psychological approaches to understanding aggression and violence (Baumeister & Boden, 1998; Baumeister & Vohs, 2016; Denson, de Wall, & Finkel, 2012). Baumeister has argued that although many individuals might experience the kind of situational factors – provocation, frustration, rejection – that increase the likelihood of aggressive responding, most of the time people manage to control or restrain their aggressive impulses. Aggression, from this perspective, can often be viewed as a failure in self-regulation. People who are low in **self-control** are more likely to have engaged in violence and other criminal acts, and respond to provocation with aggression. Factors that tend to reduce or limit the capacity for self-regulation such as the use of alcohol, sleep deprivation, low blood glucose, and prior efforts at self-control also tend to be associated with aggression and violence in both laboratory and real-world contexts (Denson et al., 2012; Gailliot & Baumeister, 2007). According to the 'strength model of self-regulation' the capacity to regulate or control behaviour is reliant on a limited resource that, when taxed, weakens self-regulatory capacities (Baumeister & Vohs, 2016). Thus, aggression and violence may be more likely in circumstances where individuals' capacity for self-regulation are depleted.

A self-control approach to understanding aggression can, therefore, help to explain both inter- and intra-individual differences in aggression and violence. In other words, individuals who are less able to restrain their aggressive impulses are more likely to respond to specific situations with aggression or violence (inter-individual differences), and individuals whose self-regulatory resources are depleted may also be more likely to aggress (intra-individual differences). Of course, the capacity for self-control is not the only important factor in understanding aggression, but it is the factor that is often most proximal to the aggressive act. We also need to recognise that the capacity for self-control is more relevant for understating impulsive or hostile aggression than for instrumental aggression.

One long-held idea in psychology is that individuals who suffer from low self-esteem are more likely to engage in aggressive and violent behaviour, and many therapeutic efforts have been directed at raising the self-esteem of offenders. This idea was vigorously challenged by the social psychologist Roy Baumeister and his colleagues in the 1990s (Baumeister, Bushman, & Campbell, 2000; Bushman & Baumeister, 1998). They argued that it is *high* rather than low self-esteem that makes an individual more prone to violence. Specifically, they suggest that individuals with high but unstable self-esteem (i.e., individuals who tend to have a somewhat insecure and inflated view of themselves) are more likely to engage in aggression when this view of themselves is threatened by others. 'Violent men', suggest Baumeister et al. (2000, p. 26), 'seem to have a strong sense of personal superiority, and their violence often seems to stem from a sense of wounded pride'. The relationship between self-esteem and violence, however, is by no means straightforward. Some studies support the idea that low self-esteem is a risk factor for aggression and violence, whereas others find that high self-esteem is a more important factor (Ostrowsky, 2010; Walker & Bright, 2009). In part these different findings are likely to reflect the use of different methodologies and different ways of measuring self-esteem. However, one fairly consistent finding is the relationship between **narcissism** and aggression (Lambe et al., 2016).

Narcissism is a personality type characterised by a grandiose feelings of self-worth, a sense of entitlement, low empathy, and an exaggerated need for the admiration and love of others. Thus, narcissists can be viewed as individuals who have a particular type of high self-esteem characterised by feelings of superiority and a need for that superiority to be recognised. When insulted, rejected, or otherwise slighted by others, narcissists may be especially prone to aggression and violence (Ostrowsky, 2010). In a recent, systematic review of the relationship between narcissism and aggression, Lambe et al. (2016) found that narcissism was a significant predictor of violence in clinical, forensic, and student populations. Moreover, there was support for the idea that individuals high on narcissism are particularly likely to aggress following a threat to their ego, and the combination of narcissism and low self-control may be especially strongly related to violence (Larson et al., 2015).

Another personality characteristic that has been associated with violent offending is **empathy** (see Criminal Psychology Through Film 4.1). Empathy has been defined in a range of different ways (Maibom, 2014), but one fairly common conceptualisation presents empathy as the capacity to 'understand and share in another's emotional state or context' (Cohen & Strayer, 1996, p. 988). Research suggests that individuals who are low in empathy are at a higher risk of violent offending (Jolliffe & Farrington, 2004). However, a more recent meta-analysis of the literature on empathy and aggression found that although there is a relationship, it is a surprisingly weak one (Vachon et al., 2014). In other words, a reduced capacity for empathy may play a role in accounting for individual differences in aggression and violence, but it is a less important role than many have previously thought. This conclusion, on the face of it, may seem somewhat surprising: individuals who are less able to recognise and share the cognitive and affective state of others should be less concerned about their suffering, and hence they will be less likely to restrain aggressive responses. However, what may be more important than the *capacity* for empathy per se is the degree to which individuals actually *care* about the harm and suffering of others, which will depend on a host of other factors including the situational context and their relationship with those individuals (Ward & Durrant, 2014).

CRIMINAL PSYCHOLOGY THROUGH FILM 4.1
The Revenant (2015)

Directed by: Alejandro G Iñárritu
Starring: Leonardo DiCaprio (Hugh Glass), Tom Hardy (John Fitzgerald), and Will Poulter (Jim Bridger)

Violence is hardly an unusual feature of films. In fact, it can be hard to locate movies that do *not* contain violence. However, the filming techniques employed in *The Revenant*, heightened by a stunning soundtrack by Ryuichi Sakamoto, take the vicarious experience of violence to a whole new level. The visceral response to the opening scenes in which a company of early nineteenth-century trappers are attacked by an Arikara war party in the remote American wilderness reminds us that the human capacity for empathy can play an important role in moderating the use of aggression and violence. Judging by the number of audience members with hands over their eyes in the movie theatre that I saw this film the intensity of the violence and the (simulated, yet realistic) suffering displayed by the characters was simply too much to deal with.

Question for discussion

While watching this movie reflect on your emotional responses to the scenes involving violence. Why do you think that you respond in this way?

It seems clear that personality – an individual's relatively enduring tendency to think, feel, and behave in particular ways – can influence their likelihood of engaging in aggression and violence. However, whether or not aggression occurs will also clearly depend on the presence of specific social and situational factors. A good deal of the focus of personality approaches to aggression and violence has also been on the role of specific traits or personality characteristics. However, we can think of personality more broadly to encompass such things as beliefs, values, goals, norms, and particular life histories (McAdams, 2006). If personality is viewed in this more inclusive fashion then it is clear that cognitive processes and their development become important components of a psychological approach to understanding aggression and violence.

Social-cognitive theories

The core premise of social-cognitive theories is that aggression is related to social cognition. In other words, the way that individuals think about and process social information can affect the likelihood of engaging in aggressive behaviour.

Cognitive neoassociation theory

One influential cognitive model of aggression has been proposed by Berkowitz (1990, 1993). The central idea of the **cognitive neoassociation theory** is that negative affect (frustrations, provocations, hot temperature, bad mood) is the primary source of anger and aggression. Negative emotional states, maintains Berkowitz (1990, p. 496), are linked to 'anger-related feelings, ideas, and memories, and also with aggressive inclinations'. When an individual experiences an aversive event (such as frustration) this triggers these anger-related thoughts and feelings and makes aggressive behaviour more likely. Whether an individual actually behaves in an aggressive fashion will depend on a range of additional factors including their appraisal of the situation and the outcome of possible responses. The cognitive neoassociation theory can account for the importance of aversive events in triggering aggression, and it also provides an explanation for the so-called weapons effect – because aggressive concepts are linked in memory the mere sight of a gun is likely to make other aggression-related thoughts, feelings, and action plans more accessible.

Script theory

Another important social-cognitive approach to aggression is script theory (Huesmann, 1988, 1998) (see Chapter 1). According to Huesmann, aggressive behaviour is largely the result of the learning of aggressive scripts. Huesmann (1988) suggests that children who grow up in environments where they are exposed to a lot of aggressive behaviour and who readily employ aggression themselves develop 'a network of cognitive scripts for social behaviour emphasizing aggressive responding' (p. 13). In other words, aggressive scripts become 'chronically accessible' and are activated in a wide range of situations at the expense of non-aggressive scripts. This results in an increased likelihood that aggression will be employed in any given situation.

Social information processing model

A third important social-cognitive model of aggression is the **social information processing model** (Crick & Dodge, 1994). Central to this model is the idea that aggressive behaviour occurs in social situations due to the way that individuals cognitively process information. Specifically, it is proposed that there are five key steps in the processing of social stimuli (although the steps do not have to proceed in a strict linear fashion). These steps and their potential relationship to aggressive behaviour are depicted in Figure 4.3. Essentially, individuals encode and interpret social cues and develop and evaluate alternative response options based on their memory store of knowledge, rules, schemas, and scripts. The model was developed as a general model of children's social adjustment, but it has been widely employed in the context of understanding aggressive behaviour, particularly in children and adolescents.

Whether a given social situation will give rise to an aggressive response will depend on each stage of social processing. For example, some individuals may preferentially attend to (Step 1) and interpret (Step 2) cues in ways that make aggression more likely. Some children, argue Dodge (2006), develop a **hostile attribution bias** that leads them to interpret ambiguous social cues as hostile. For instance, a child with a hostile

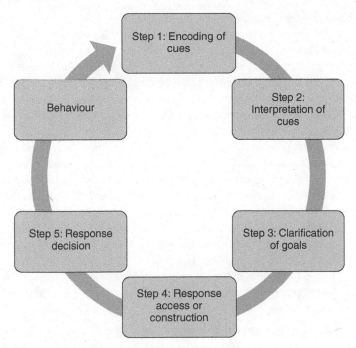

Figure 4.3 The social information processing model of aggression.
Source: Dodge (2006).

attribution bias may interpret an offhand, largely ambiguous social comment such as 'I like your new haircut' as a sarcastic slight on his appearance and hence a threat to his self-image, whereas another child may interpret the comment as a compliment. Hostile attribution biases are associated with reactive or hostile aggression, rather than with proactive or instrumental aggression, and hence increase the risk of aggressive responses to perceived provocations (rather than aggressive behaviour in general). A growing body of research now supports the important role of hostile attributions in the development of reactive aggression in children (De Castro et al., 2002; Dodge et al., 2015). Ultimately, whether specific social situations give rise to aggression will depend on access to (Step 4), and evaluation of (Step 5), different behavioural response options. Individuals who have readily accessible scripts for aggressive behaviour, who believe that aggression in morally acceptable in the specific social situation, and who believe that they have the capacity to behave aggressively in order to obtain favourable outcomes will be most likely to behave in an aggressive fashion (Fotaine & Dodge, 2006). Key features of the social information processing model overlap with Huesmann's script theory outlined above, and both draw from Berkowitz's cognitive neoassociation model. Central to all three models is the idea that aggression can be understood in terms of the outcome of specific cognitive processes. Moreover, individual difference in aggression can be understood, in part, in terms of the development or learning of specific aggression-related attitudes, values, beliefs, and scripts.

A social learning perspective

The idea that much of human behaviour, including aggression and violence, is largely the product of social learning is widely accepted in the social sciences. Applying social learning theory to the development of aggression is relatively straightforward. Consider a young boy who grows up in a violent and abusive family environment embedded in a lower socioeconomic community characterised by high rates of violence and other antisocial behaviour. This individual will, inevitably, be exposed to a large number of violent models: his parents, siblings, and peers. He is, therefore, likely to develop positive attitudes towards violence, accept that violence is normative, and have many highly accessible aggression-related scripts. He may also learn through his own experience that the use of violence is the only way to obtain the rewards he needs in this particular environmental context. Support for the core ideas of social learning theory comes from a number of studies that indicate that growing up in a violent family is a significant risk factor for aggressive behaviour and violence (e.g., Ehrensaft et al., 2003; Widom, 1989). Somewhat more controversially there is also a body of research that indicates that exposure to media violence is an important risk factor for aggression and violence (see Box 4.2 for a detailed discussion; also see Research in Focus 4.1). In sum, different developmental histories give rise to differences in aggression-related cognitive processes that in turn can increase or decrease the likelihood that an individual will behave in an aggressive fashion in a given situation.

BOX 4.2 EXPOSURE TO MEDIA VIOLENCE AND THE DEVELOPMENT OF AGGRESSIVE AND VIOLENT BEHAVIOUR

If you are like most individuals living in Western society, you will have been exposed to a significant amount of violent media over the course of your life. You will have almost certainly watched thousands of films and television shows that prominently feature violence, you will have been exposed to violent music videos, and you will have spent many hours playing video games with violent content. Is this exposure an important risk factor for the development of aggressive and violent behaviour? This deceptively simple question has generated a significant body of research and has divided academic opinion. Whereas some scholars have adamantly argued that the evidence overwhelmingly supports the conclusion that exposure to violent media is an important risk factor for aggression and violence (Anderson et al., 2010; Anderson et al., 2015; Huesmann, 2007; Prot et al., 2016), other scholars deny that there is any clear evidence that suggests a link between exposure to media violence and, especially, violent offending (Ferguson et al., 2013; Ferguson, 2015; Savage, 2004; Savage & Yancey, 2008). Consider the following two quotes from respected academics published in respected, peer-reviewed academic journals at about the same time:

> Research on violent television and films, video games, and music reveals unequivocal evidence that media violence increases the likelihood of aggressive and violent behavior in both immediate and long-term contexts.
>
> (Anderson et al., 2003, p. 81)

... It is concluded here that, despite persistent published reviews that state the contrary, the body of published, empirical evidence on this topic does not establish that viewing violent media portrayals causes crime.

(Savage, 2004, p. 99)

Who is right? Although ultimately, we will 'want to see the numbers', a good place to start in considering this question is theory: are there good theoretical reasons for believing that exposure to violent media will increase the risk of aggression and violence. I think that the answer to this question is a clear 'yes'. Social cognitive theories of aggression indicate that, in the short term, exposure to media violence should prime aggression-related cognitions, increase emotional arousal, and provide an opportunity to mimic or copy aggressive behaviour. In the long term, repeated exposure to violent media should result, through observational learning, in the development of aggression-related attitudes, beliefs, values, norms, and scripts (Bushman & Huesmann, 2006). Of course we need to recognise that media is just *one* source of social learning and therefore may not be the most important factor in the development of aggression-related concepts. Certainly, however, the relationship between exposure to media violence and aggression is consistent with the core ideas of social-cognitive theories of aggression and violence.

Summarising the large, sometimes inconsistent, body of empirical literature on media violence effects is no simple task. Very broadly speaking the available evidence from experimental, cross-sectional, and longitudinal research indicates that exposure to media violence is positively related to both short-term and long-term increases in aggressive behaviour (Anderson et al., 2015; Anderson et al., 2010; see Research in Focus 4.1). However, the evidence for a relationship between exposure to media violence and violent *offending* is much less robust (Browne & Hamilton-Giachritsis, 2005; Savage, 2004). Moreover, as Ferguson (2015) has argued with specific reference to violent video games there are a number of reasons why we should be somewhat cautious about making strong claims concerning the relationship between violent media and aggression, including methodological problems with experimental studies and the fact that rates of violent offending have been declining over the past 20 years as violent video game play has been on the rise. In short, exposure to media violence is probably one factor that contributes to aggressive and violent behaviour, but it is unlikely to the most important factor in the aetiology of violent offending.

Further reading

To get a flavour of the violent media debate have a look at two recent special issues on the topic that include target articles and commentaries (and responses to commentaries!). Read one of these target articles and responses and note down what you think are the key areas of dispute among the authors and how those disputes might be resolved through further research.

Target Article 1

Anderson, C. A., Bushman, B. J., Donnerstein, E., et al. (2015). SPSSI research summary on media violence. *Analyses of Social Issues and Public Policy*, 15, 4–19.

Plus five commentaries and a response published in *Analyses of Social Issues and Public Policy* (2016), 16(1), 407–423.

Target Article 2

Ferguson, C. J. (2015). Do angry birds make for angry children? A meta-analysis of video game influences on children's and adolescents' aggression, mental health, prosocial behaviour, and academic performance. *Perspectives on Psychological Science*, 10, 646–666.

Plus five commentaries and a response published in the same issue of *Perspectives on Psychological Science*.

 ## RESEARCH IN FOCUS 4.1 DOES THE REPEATED PLAYING OF VIOLENT VIDEO GAMES INCREASE AGGRESSION?

Title: The more you play, the more aggressive you become: A long-term experimental study of cumulative violent video game effects on hostile expectations and aggression behaviour

Author: Hasan, Y., Bégue, L., Scharkow, M., & Bushman, B. J.   **Year**: 2013

Source: *Journal of Experimental Social Psychology*, 49, 224–227

Aims: To explore the effects of cumulative video game play on aggression

Method: Participants played either a violent or a non-violent video game for 20 minutes a day over three consecutive days and were assessed for hostile expectations and aggression after each period of game play. Hostile expectations were assessed by an evaluation of responses to the completion of story stems, and aggressive behaviour was operationalised as the intensity and duration of noise selected by participants against an opponent in a competitive reaction time task.

Key results:
- Both hostile expectations and aggression significantly increased over the three days of the experiment for participants playing the violent video games but not for those participants playing the non-violent video games.
- The increase in aggression over the three days was partly mediated by (due to) the increase in hostile expectations.

Conclusion: The cumulative playing of violent video games increases aggressive responses, perhaps in part due to an increase in hostile expectations.

Discussion question

Does this study allow us to say whether the playing of violent video games increases the risk for aggression? What further information might we need?

REVIEW AND REFLECT

1   How can we use the idea of self-control or self-regulation to explain both individual and intra-individual differences in aggression?
2   What are the key steps in Crick and Dodge's social information processing model, and how do they relate to the likelihood of aggressive behaviour in children?
3   Based on research that has explored the impact of exposure to violent media and the development of aggressive and violent behaviour, do you think that there should be greater controls on access to this media?

BIOLOGICAL APPROACHES

On September 13, 1848 railroad worker Phineas Gage was the victim of an unfortunate accident: A dynamite explosion propelled a metre-long iron bar through his left cheek and up through his frontal lobes, landing some 25 metres away. Not surprisingly Phineas was somewhat dazed after this accident, but after recovering from the immediate effects it was evident that his general verbal and cognitive abilities were largely unimpaired. However, his personality had undergone some significant changes. Prior to the incident he was described by the attending physician John Harlow (1868, cited in MacMillan, 2008) as a man of 'temperate habits' with an 'iron will' and a 'well-balanced mind', whereas afterwards he became 'impatient of restraint or advice that conflicted with his desires' and 'fitful, irreverent, grossly profane'. In short, although the available documentary evidence is somewhat scant, after his accident Phineas appeared to be impaired in his capacity to control and regulate his behaviour. This well-known case provides a vivid example of how biological factors (in this case, brain damage) may relate to aggression and violence. In this section we briefly review some of the main biological approaches for understanding human aggression and violent offending, focusing first on the neuropsychology of violence and then turning to the role of hormones and neurotransmitters (see de Almeida, Cabral, & Narvaes, 2015, for a review).

The neuropsychology of aggression and violence

The crucial brain region that appears to have been damaged in the case of Phineas Gage is a structure known as the prefrontal cortex (see Chapter 1). The prefrontal cortex, as we have seen, is critically implicated in a suite of referred psychological processes, including the capacity to regulate or control behaviour (Beaver et al., 2007). Not surprisingly, given the relationship between self-control and violent and antisocial behaviour reviewed above, the idea that damage to, or impaired functioning of, prefrontal areas is associated with an increased risk for aggression and violence is now well supported in a number of clinical cases and research studies (Raine, 2013). For instance, Raine, Buchsbaum, and LaCasse (1997) used positron emission tomography to measure brain activity in a sample of 41 convicted murderers (who had all pleaded not guilty by reason of insanity) and a matched control group. Among other differences, it was found that the murderers had significantly lower glucose metabolism in prefrontal areas than did controls, suggesting an impaired ability to control and regulate behaviour. Reviews of the literature suggest that individuals with a history of aggression and violent behaviour have reduced functioning in a number of specific regions of the prefrontal cortex (Bannon, Salis, & O'Leary, 2015; Bufkin & Luttrell, 2005; Yang & Raine, 2009), leading Bufkin and Luttrell (2005, p. 181) to conclude: 'The consistency with which prefrontal disruption occurs across studies, each of which investigated participants with different types of violent behaviours, suggest that prefrontal dysfunction may underlie a predisposition to violence.' Impaired prefrontal functioning, furthermore, appears to be most relevant for understanding impulsive or hostile aggression rather than instrumental aggression.

Although the prefrontal cortex has been the focus of most of the research on the relationship between neuropsychological functions and violence, it is worth noting that researchers have also implicated a number of other brain regions. These include parts of the limbic system, in particular the almond-shaped structure known as the amygdala. The amygdala is involved in the processing and regulation of emotion and appears to play a crucial role in recognising anger and fear responses in others. Individuals who are unable to efficiently process this emotional information may fail to interpret relevant social cues appropriately, which could result in an increased propensity for violence (e.g., the recognition of fear in others may serve to inhibit the use of violence) (de Almeida et al., 2015; Marsh & Blair, 2008).

Although there is a significant body of evidence linking neuropsychological impairments to aggression and violence it is important to recognise that neuropsychological deficits are neither necessary nor sufficient for violence to occur (Séguin, Sylvers, & Lilienfeld, 2007). In other words, some individuals with specific neuropsychological impairments may not be more prone to aggression and violence, and many individuals who engage in aggression and violence do not have any obvious neuropsychological problems.

Hormones and neurotransmitters

Other biological research has focused on specific neurophysiological processes, with a good deal of attention paid to the role of specific neurotransmitters and hormones.

Neurotransmitters

The neurotransmitter serotonin has an important inhibitory function in the brain and is critically involved in the control and regulation of affect and behaviour. In other words, serotonin is implicated in the capacity for self-regulation or self-control. Given that an impaired ability to exercise self-control, as we have seen, is related to aggression and violence, it is perhaps not surprising that research typically finds that low levels of serotonin are related to aggression and antisocial behaviour in humans (Moore, Scarpa, & Raine, 2002). Individuals who have impaired serotonergic systems, therefore, may be less able to resist aggressive impulses and may be more prone to reactive or impulsive forms of aggression and violence (Glick, 2015). A recent meta-analysis of the relationship between serotonin and aggression found a small inverse relationship across the studies: in other words, lower levels of serotonin were related to an increased risk for aggression, anger, and hostility (Duke et al., 2013). However, a relationship between serotonin and aggression has not been found in all studies, and the functioning of the serotonergic system is extraordinarily complex (Olivier & van Oorschot, 2005). It is also important to recognise that the serotonergic system does not operate in isolation, and there are likely to be complex interactions with other neurotransmitters such as dopamine (Seo, Patrick, & Kennealy, 2008) and hormones, such as testosterone and cortisol (Montoya et al., 2012). Clearly more research is needed in order to establish what role serotonin might play in aggression and violence and how this is related to other aspects of brain functioning.

Hormones

Of all the potential biological factors that are thought to be related to human aggression and violence perhaps none is as well known as the male sex hormone testosterone (see Chapter 1). Indeed, the media happily report on 'testosterone fuelled violence' in contexts involving hyper-masculinity. If testosterone is related to violent offending it might be a convenient explanation for both gender differences in violent behaviour and for the high prevalence in violent crime that occurs among adolescent males (Ellis, 2005). As we shall see, however, the relationship between testosterone and violence is by no means straightforward.

Most researchers now agree that there is no simple one-to-one relationship between testosterone and violent behaviour. Studies that have attempted to find a relationship between levels of circulating testosterone and violence have produced somewhat inconsistent results. Meta-analyses of the research do typically find a relationship between levels of testosterone and aggressive and violent behaviour, but the magnitude of the relationship is relatively small and fluctuates from study to study (Archer, Birring, & Wu, 1998). One interpretation of these results suggest that testosterone may be directly related to dominance, status, and competition and is thus only *indirectly* related to aggression and violence (Carré & Olmstead, 2015; Mazur, 2009). Specifically, it is hypothesised that testosterone plays a prominent role in dominance contests between men. According to the 'challenge hypothesis', levels of testosterone surge in readiness to engage in conflicts over dominance and status (Archer, 2006b). After the conflict, it is proposed that the testosterone level of victors remains high, whereas that of the losers reduces. Because, as we have seen, violence is a common feature of status disputes among young men in particular, we should expect to find some relationship between aggression and testosterone level. However, because levels of testosterone fluctuate depending on specific social contexts, many studies may not find a clear relationship between circulating levels of testosterone and violence.

In an attempt to explain the somewhat inconsistent results that have been found in studies linking testosterone to aggression and violence a number of scholars have advocated for a dual-hormone hypothesis that implicates both testosterone and the stress hormone, **cortisol** (Mehta & Prasad, 2015). Specifically, as illustrated in Figure 4.4, it is argued that the relationship between testosterone and various status-seeking behaviours depends on levels of cortisol. When there is an imbalance between testosterone and cortisol, such that levels of testosterone are high, and levels of cortisol are low, then there is an increased risk for a range of status-seeking and dominance-related behaviours, including aggression, risk taking, and violence. Evidence for the dual-hormone hypothesis has emerged in a range of different studies, and it has become clear that the relationship between testosterone and aggression is complex and is influenced by a number of different factors, including levels of cortisol (Carré & Olmstead, 2015).

Genetic factors

As we have discussed in Chapter 1 there is accumulating evidence that genetic factors play a role in antisocial and criminal behaviour. Behavioural genetic research has emphasised that something in the region of 40–50 per cent of the variance in antisocial behaviour can be attributed to genetic factors. More recent research, however, has attempted to locate candidate genes that predispose certain individuals to aggressive and violent behaviour via their effects on developing brain systems (Raine, 2013). As discussed in Chapter 2, variation in the MAOA gene appears to be related to an increased risk for violence, especially when individuals had experienced serious maltreatment as children (Dorfman, Meyer-Lindenberg, & Buckholtz, 2014). However, candidate gene studies in general have produced rather inconsistent results, and in a recent systematic

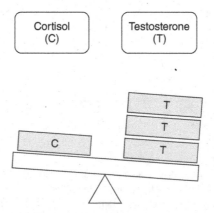

Figure 4.4 The dual-hormone hypothesis. The hypothesis suggests that a risk for aggression occurs when levels of testosterone are high, and levels of cortisol are low.

review of the literature, Vassos, Collier, and Fazel (2014) concluded that there was little or no evidence for a strong association between any candidate genes and aggressive and violent behaviour. Research on this topic in many ways is still in its infancy, and – like most biological risk factors – it is probable that the relationship between candidate genes and behavioural outcomes reflects complex interactions that have yet to be fully mapped out in any detail.

REVIEW AND REFLECT

1   Why is damage to the prefrontal cortex associated with a heightened risk for aggression and violence?
2   What is the dual-hormone hypothesis, and how can it explain the relationship between testosterone and aggression?
3   If we can uncover clear biological 'markers' for aggression and violence how might this influence our efforts at crime prevention?

SITUATIONAL APPROACHES

Every act of violence occurs in a specific situational context. Moreover, most – but certainly not all – acts of aggression and violence can be viewed as responses to specific situations or experiences. It is important, then, to understand the social and environmental contexts that can both trigger aggression and make aggression more likely to occur.

Social and environmental antecedents of aggression

Some instances of violence, as we have seen, are predominantly instrumental in character: individuals deliberately engage in violence in order to obtain specific, often tangible, rewards. Armed robbery is a case in point. A great deal of aggression and violence, however, is not planned – it occurs in *response* to specific situations. In particular, situations that involve frustration, provocation, and rejection have been shown to be important antecedents to acts of aggression and violence.

Frustration
One prominent and influential psychological theory of aggression is the **frustration-aggression hypothesis** (Dollard et al., 1939). According to Dollard et al. (1939) when individuals are blocked or thwarted from obtaining specific, desirable goals they experience frustration. In turn, frustration increases the likelihood that an individual will become angry and behave in an aggressive fashion. In his reformulation of the frustration–aggression hypothesis, Berkowitz (1988, 1993) emphasises that the amount of frustration experienced depends on: (a) the importance of the goal that is thwarted; and (b) how completely the individual is prevented from obtaining that goal. Thus, if getting a good

grade on your criminal psychology essay is extremely important to you, and you are prevented from handing in your essay on time (thus incurring a hefty late penalty) because your dog swallowed your memory stick with the only copy of the essay, you are likely to experience a significant amount of frustration. Berkowitz (1988) notes that this experience of frustration, because it is aversive, results in negative affect that, in turn, increases the probability of an aggressive response (perhaps even directed against the offending canine). Although research supports a relationship between frustration and aggression (Berkowitz, 1993), it is important to point out that aggression is not an *inevitable* response to experiencing frustration, and other actions are also possible. This point should be clear from our discussion of individual differences in the propensity for aggression.

Provocation

Another important situational antecedent of aggression is provocation (Baron, 1977; Berkowitz, 1993). Imagine that you are in a long queue at the bank waiting patiently when somebody cuts in front of you, turns around, and insults you by casting derogatory remarks about you appearance and parentage for no apparent reason. How are you likely to feel? Most individuals in this situation are likely to experience a significant amount of anger (although fear may also be a common response). They may also be likely to respond in an aggressive fashion towards the perpetrator – either verbally or physically. A good deal of both experimental and real-world research indicates that insults, slights, and other forms of provocation are common instigators of aggression and violence (Baron, 1977; Berkowitz, 1993). Indeed, analyses indicate that many acts of serious violence, including homicide, result from a series of provocations between two individuals (Luckenbill, 1977; Polk, 1999). Luckenbill (1977), for example, argues that violence – particularly male/male violence – can be viewed as 'situated transactions' that take the form of a sequence of escalating exchanges between the victim and the perpetrator. The following example provides a typical illustration of this idea (Luckenbill, 1977, p. 183):

> The offender and friend were passing by a local tavern and noticed the victim, a co-worker at a food-processing plant, sitting at the bar. The offender entered the tavern and asked the victim to repay a loan. The victim was angered by the request and refused to pay. The offender then pushed the victim from his stool. Before the victim could react the bartender asked them to take their fight outside. The victim followed the offender out the door and, from behind, hit the offender with a brick he grabbed from a trash can immediately outside the door. The offender turned and warned the victim that he would beat the victim if he wouldn't pay up and continued his aggressions. The victim then struck the offender in the mouth, knocking out a tooth.

This example also illustrates the importance of 'saving face' and demonstrates how seemingly trivial exchanges may result in serious violence through a reciprocal pattern of provocations and responses between the victim and the offender.

Rejection

Another important – although somewhat neglected – social antecedent of aggression is rejection (Leary, Twenge, & Quinlivan, 2006). A teenager ostracised by his peers at school, a worker made redundant by her boss, and a husband spurned by his wife in favour of another man are all examples of social rejection that may result in the increased likelihood of aggression and violence. In a comprehensive review of the literature on rejection and aggression, Leary et al. (2006) conclude that both experimental studies and research on real-world violence support a link between the experiences of rejection and aggression. For instance, in one study of 15 school shootings in the United States it was found that in 13 cases the perpetrators had experienced interpersonal rejection prior to their offending (Leary et al., 2003). The evidence clearly supports the idea that rejection can be an important social antecedent of aggression and violence. *Why* rejection appears to an important antecedent of aggression is, however, a matter of dispute, and it is important to recognise that aggression is not the only response (or, even the most common response) to experiences of rejection. One important recent finding is that there are individual differences in *rejection sensitivity* such that some individuals may be more sensitive to the experience of rejection and more likely to aggress as a consequence (Bondü & Richter, 2016).

Environmental factors that increase the likelihood of aggression

It is clear that certain situations tend to provoke aggression. The experience of frustration, provocation, and rejection are three important antecedents of aggression. Certain environmental contexts also make aggression more likely, even though they might not be direct instigators of aggression. One of the most widely studied examples concerns the presence of weapons. In a classic study carried out by Berkowitz and LePage (1967) male participants who had experienced electric shocks (supposedly from another participant) were given the opportunity to shock this individual in turn. Participants delivered significantly more shocks when in the presence of weapons (a rifle and a revolver lying on the table in front of them) than when no object was present (or in the presence of neutral stimuli – i.e., a pair of badminton racquets). Berkowitz and Le Page (1967) suggested that this **weapons effect** was probably the result of the largely unconscious stimulation of aggressive thoughts. Given the widespread existence of guns in social life (especially in an American context) the finding that the mere presence of weapons elicits greater aggression is an extremely relevant one. Not all studies have consistently found a weapons effect; however, reviews of the literature generally conclude that aggressive responding *does* increase when aggression-related cues are present (Benjamin & Bushman, 2016), especially when participants have been negatively aroused prior to their exposure to the cues (Carlson, Marcus-Newhall, & Miller, 1990). It is likely that the main mechanism whereby the presence of weapons increases aggressive behaviour is through an increase in the accessibility of aggression-related thoughts.

Another environmental characteristic putatively linked to aggression and that has attracted a considerable amount of research attention is temperature. In particular, it is hypothesised that extremely hot environmental conditions increase the likelihood of aggression and violence. As Anderson (2001) notes, the idea of a link between heat and violence has a long history and is illustrated in terms such 'hot under the collar', 'hot headed', and 'my blood is boiling'. The evidence for the relationship between heat and aggression is somewhat mixed. However, both experimental studies that have manipulated temperature in the laboratory and field studies that have examined the impact of temperature on violent crime rates generally support the idea that temperature is significantly positively related to aggression and violence. For instance, research has found that violent offending is more common in (a) the hotter months of the year; (b) in hotter years than in cooler years; and (c) in warmer geographical regions in the United States (see Anderson, 2001; Anderson & Anderson, 1998). Not all scholars have unequivocally supported a straightforward relationship between heat and violence, and it is clearly important to rule out alternative explanations for the relationship, such as the idea that individuals are simply more likely to be engaged in activities that increase the likelihood of violence during warmer weather. However, enough evidence has accumulated to indicate that heat is one factor that increases the risk of violence, with potentially serious ramifications in the context of global warming (see Van Lange, Rinderu, & Bushman, 2016) (Chapter 10). Anderson (2001) favours a fairly straightforward explanation for this finding by suggesting that high temperatures make people more 'cranky', which in turn increases the likelihood that social interactions will result in hostility that potentially escalates into violence.

REVIEW AND REFLECT

1   Think back to the last time that you felt angry or had aggressive thoughts. What specific situation were you in, and why do you think that this situation led to your aggressive cognitions?
2   How might you design a study to test the potential relationship between heat and aggression? What factors would you need to control to ensure that your study provided an adequate test of the 'heat hypothesis'?

GENERAL THEORIES OF AGGRESSION

In addition to the various different approaches to explaining aggression and violence that we have explored in this chapter there have also been several attempts to develop general theories of aggression and violence. We shall consider one of the more prominent general approaches: the general aggression model.

The general aggression model

One of the better known examples of a general theory of aggression is provided by Anderson and Bushman (2002) in their **general aggression model** (GAM), which is described as a 'dynamic, social-cognitive, developmental model that includes situational, individual (personological), and biological variables and provides an integrative

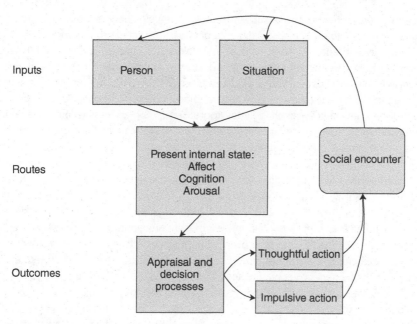

Figure 4.5 The general aggression model.
Source: Anderson and Bushman (2002, p. 34). Reproduced with permission of Annual Review of Psychology, Volume 53 © Annual Reviews, www.annualreviews.org.

framework for domain specific theories of aggression (Anderson & Carnagey, 2007, p. 173). As outlined in Figure 4.5, the GAM focuses on accounting for specific episodes of aggression and involves three main foci: inputs (persons and situations), routes (internal states), and outcomes (appraisal and decision-making processes).

According to Anderson and Bushman (2002, p. 35) 'person factors include all those characteristics a person brings to the situation, such as personality traits, attitudes, and genetic predispositions'. Thus, person factors encompass the range of personality characteristics such as self-control, narcissism, and empathy that we know are related to aggressive and antisocial behaviour, along with specific attitudes, beliefs, values, scripts, and goals that arise through developmental processes such as social learning and which may facilitate aggressive behaviour. Person factors therefore summarise all that we know about the psychological, developmental, and biological factors that are related to aggression and violence. Individuals with certain person factors may be more likely to behave aggressively, but whether they do or not depends on specific situational contexts. Thus, important situational factors in the GAM include many that we have discussed earlier in the chapter, including provocation, frustration, and the presence of aggressive cues, along with specific incentives for aggression and the use of alcohol and other drugs.

These input variables (person and situation factors) do not directly cause aggressive behaviour but, rather, influence behaviour through the internal states that they cause. Internal states include current affective, cognitive, and arousal processes. Consider an individual with low self-control, low levels of empathy, and attitudes favourable to violence (person inputs) who is subject to provocation by a peer (situational input). This individual is likely to experience hostile thoughts, activate scripts for violence (cognition), feel hostility and anger (affect), and be physiologically aroused and ready for action (arousal). Ultimately, whether or not these internal states result in thoughtful versus impulsive action will depend on appraisal and decision-making processes (outcomes). Immediate appraisal is relatively automatic and occurs outside of conscious awareness. Immediate appraisal may result in either aggressive or non-aggressive outcomes but is largely dependent on present internal states. Reappraisal may occur if there is enough time or cognitive resources and if the outcome is viewed as important and unsatisfying. Reappraisal may involve the generation of alternative explanations for the situation or result in the activation of different scripts, schemas, or memories. This will lead to more thoughtful action, which may or not be aggressive, but is likely to result from a more considered view of the situational context. Thus our aggressive-prone individual when provoked may simply respond to their present emotional state and lash out at the source of provocation. If reappraisal occurs they may come to view the initial provocation as less threatening or generate more viable alternative response options (perhaps by remembering the negative consequences that occurred the last time they hit someone).

The GAM provides a useful integration of psychological, biological, and situational approaches to aggression as well as outlining the processes that may result in aggressive behaviour. Recent applications of the model have outlined how it can potentially provide explanations for intimate partner violence, inter-group conflict, and even the impact of global environmental change on violence (de Wall, Anderson, & Bushman, 2011). Although a significant amount of research on aggression is consistent with the GAM, relatively little research has explicitly tested the key causal processes of the model. There may also be some scope to broaden the model to more explicitly incorporate the role of both evolutionary and cultural factors.

REVIEW AND REFLECT

1 Briefly outline the main features of the general aggression model.
2 How might the general aggression model be employed to inform interventions aimed at reducing aggressive and violent behaviour?

SUMMARY

Aggression can be viewed as purposeful behaviour that involves physical or psychological harm to others; violence is aggression that has extreme (typically physical harm) as its goal; and criminal violence is violence that is prohibited by the law. A large number of different theoretical approaches have been employed to explain aggression and violence.

From an evolutionary perspective, the capacity for aggression and violence is viewed as a universal, evolved characteristic of our species. The psychological and physiological mechanisms that underlie aggression have evolved because they promoted survival and reproductive success in particular situations. Evolutionary psychologists have focused, in particular, on how violence between males is the product of a history of sexual selection involving competition for status and resources. It should be emphasised that an evolutionary approach to violence neither implies that it is inevitable nor implies that it is morally justifiable.

Although the capacity for violence may be an evolved characteristic of our species, the nature of aggression and violence is also strongly influenced by cultural and social-structural factors. According to the sub-cultures of violence theory, certain communities have higher rates of violence because individuals (especially men) in these communities have developed a 'code of the streets', which fosters the use of violence as a legitimate way to maintain status and to respond to disputes. A similar idea is at the core of the **culture of honour thesis**, which maintains that regional differences in violent offending in the United States can be explained, in part, as a result of the persistence of a 'culture of honour' in the Southern states that dictates the use of violence in response to insults, threats, and arguments. Violence is also strongly associated with specific social-structural characteristics of communities, regions, and nation-states. In particular, areas that are economically deprived tend to have higher rates of violent crime, plausibly because these environments generate greater levels of 'strain' and provide fewer opportunities for the achievement of cultural goals through legitimate means.

Cultural and social-structural approaches can, therefore, help us to explain some of the macro-level patterns in aggression and violence across different geographical regions and historical time periods. In order to account for individual differences in offending, however, we need to consider some of the proximate psychological and biological factors identified by researchers.

A good deal of evidence indicates that some individuals are more prone to the use of aggression and violence than are others in any given situational context. Specifically, individuals who are low in conscientiousness and agreeableness and high in neuroticism are more likely to engage in aggressive and antisocial behaviour. Low self-control, narcissism, and low empathy are further personality traits that have been linked to the use of aggression and violence. Broadly speaking, individuals who are less able to regulate their behaviour, who view themselves as superior to other people, and who are less concerned about the suffering of others are more likely to employ aggression and violence in specific situational contexts.

Social-cognitive approaches to understanding aggression and violence focus on how specific aggression-related beliefs, attitudes, norms, and scripts influence the way individuals respond to certain situational contexts. Individuals who have readily accessible aggression-related scripts and who have positive attitudes towards the use of violence are more likely to respond in an aggressive or violent fashion. According to the social information processing model of aggression, the way that individuals interpret and process information is also an important factor in understanding individual differences in the propensity for violence. The development of aggression-related cognitions can be understood from a social learning perspective in terms of how individuals acquire specific beliefs, attitudes, norms, and scripts from their familial and social environments. Those individuals who are exposed to violence in the family and community (and, perhaps, in the media) are more likely to develop cognitions that are conducive to the use of aggression and violence.

Another approach to understanding individual differences in the propensity for violence focuses on identifying the key biological correlates of aggressive behaviour. One line of research has identified the importance of the prefrontal cortex. Damage to, or impaired functioning of, this part of the brain has been associated with a diminished capacity for self-regulation and a greater propensity for violent behaviour. Other lines of research have focused on the role of neurotransmitters like serotonin, and hormones such as testosterone. Our current knowledge of the role that these hormones and neurotransmitters play in aggressive behaviour is still limited, but available evidence indicates that low levels of serotonin are related to aggression and that testosterone may play an important role in the expression of dominance and hence is implicated in violence between men.

Violence is also more likely to occur in some situational contexts than others. Researchers have identified that situations involving frustration, provocation, and/or rejection are particularly likely to be related to aggression and violence. According to the frustration–aggression hypothesis, for instance, aggression arises when individuals are blocked from attaining goals. Moreover, certain environmental conditions – in particular the presence of weapons and high temperatures – make aggressive and violent behaviour more likely.

If we want to develop a complete understanding of aggression and violence we must be willing to embrace a range of different theoretical perspectives that are drawn from different levels of analysis. The general aggression model provides one of the more comprehensive integrated models of aggression that has been developed to date and focuses on how person and situational factors interact to generate cognitive and affective states that can lead to aggressive and violent behaviour.

FURTHER READING

Raine, A. (2013). *The Anatomy of Violence: The Biological Roots of Crime.* New York, NY: Pantheon Books.
Adrian Raine provides a comprehensive, yet accessible overview of biological approaches to violence.

Pinker, S. (2011). *The Better Angels of our Nature: Why Violence Has Declined.* London: Penguin.
A highly readable and engaging historical perspective on violent crime and the factors that are associated with its decline. Essential reading.

Daly, M. (2016). *Killing the Competition: Economic Inequality and Homicide.* New Brunswick, NJ: Transaction Publishers.
A recent book-length treatment of the idea that inequality is a major driving factor in explaining violent crime rates. Daly also provides a good overview of evolutionary approaches to understanding violence.

Warburton, W. A., & Anderson, C. A. (2015). Aggression, social psychology of. In *International Encyclopaedia of the Social and Behavioural Sciences* (2nd edition, Vol. 1, pp. 373–380). Oxford: Elsevier.
A really useful overview of social psychological approaches to aggression.

De Wall, C. N., Anderson, C. A., & Bushman, B. J. (2011). The General Aggression Model: Theoretical extension to violence. *Psychology of Violence*, 3, 245–258.
A review of the general aggression model and its theoretical extension to explaining different types of violent crime.

There are a number of journals devoted to research and reviews on aggression and violence, including: *Aggressive Behaviour*, *Aggression and Violent Behaviour*, and *Psychology of Violence*.

WEB RESOURCES

The World Health Report on Violence is a useful global overview of violence in human society and can be downloaded from: www.who.int/violence_injury_prevention/violence/world_report/en.

Some useful information can also be obtained from the website of the International Society for research and aggression at: www.israsociety.com.

The centre for the study of violence also contains some useful information with a focus on media effects research: www.psychology.iastate.edu/faculty/caa/csv/index.htm.

 KEY CONCEPTS

- aggression
- cognitive neoassociation theory
- cortisol
- culture of honour thesis
- direct aggression
- empathy
- frustration–aggression hypothesis

- general aggression model
- hostile aggression
- hostile attribution bias
- indirect aggression
- instrumental aggression
- narcissism
- relational aggression
- self-control

- social information processing model
- sub-cultures of violence
- violence
- weapons effect

Violent offending

LEARNING OBJECTIVES

On completion of this chapter you should:

➤ have developed a good understanding of the nature and extent of violent offending;
➤ understand the main contexts in which community violence occurs and be able to identify the key features and causes of male/male violence, and robbery;
➤ recognise the main types of family violence, the risk factors associated with different types of family violence, and the main theoretical approaches to understanding why family violence occurs;
➤ be familiar with the nature and extent of school violence;
➤ understand the main types of multiple homicide and the main theoretical approaches to understanding mass and serial murder.

Chris and Crue Kahui were born on 20 March, 2006 and died less than three months later on 18 June 2006 in Auckland Starship Hospital. The twins' mother returned home after being away overnight and, concerned about some bruises on their faces, took them to their local GP who ordered that they be taken immediately to hospital. Rather than follow this advice the parents went to McDonald's first and then home for several hours before taking the twins to hospital, where they were eventually taken off life support. The death of any young child is a sad occurrence, but what made this case especially tragic was that they did not die of 'natural causes'. The Clinical Director of Starship Hospital noted that both twins had suffered extensive brain injuries and that they had multiple skull fractures. In addition, Chris had a fractured femur and multiple fractured ribs. These injuries, it was noted, were consistent with 'being slammed against something' (Imogen, 2011). In short, the Kahui twins were clear victims of serious child abuse. However, to date there have been no convictions in this case. The boys' 21-year-old father was initially charged with their murder but was eventually acquitted, although a coroner's report in 2012 indicated that the injuries occurred when he was in sole custody of the twins and thus that he was the likely culprit.

This case attracted an enormous amount of media attention and was followed by a number of equally tragic cases of fatal child abuse in New Zealand, including three-year-old Nia Glassie who, over a period of three weeks before she ultimately died, was beaten, kicked, and put in a clothes dryer by family members (Vance, 2011). These cases and others like them raise some important questions about the nature of violent crime in society. How common is violent crime, and in what contexts does it occur? Why would family members willingly abuse and neglect their own children? And what factors are associated with different types of violent crime?

In this chapter we build on the general theoretical approaches to understanding aggression and violence presented in the previous chapter to consider the nature, extent, and causes of violent crime in society. We begin with a general overview of the nature and extent of violent offending, highlighting the different contexts in which violence occurs. We then explore the most prevalent different types of violence, looking in turn at community violence, family violence, school violence, and the special case of multiple homicide. For each of these types of violence we will examine the key conceptual issues involved, and review theoretical approaches to understanding why they occur.

THE NATURE AND EXTENT OF VIOLENT OFFENDING

The nature of violent offending

As we have already noted, violence occurs in a number of different contexts (see Criminal Psychology Through Film 5.1). At the broadest level, the World Health Organization (2002b) classifies violence into three categories: self-directed violence, interpersonal violence, and collective violence (see Figure 5.1). Self-directed violence involves self-harm and suicide. Although this is clearly an important topic, it is not one that we will consider in this chapter. Collective violence refers to violent acts that are perpetrated by groups of individuals (or individuals representing groups) against other groups of individuals. The violence that occurs in the context of war, acts of genocide, and terrorism are typically viewed as instances of collective violence. We explore these topics in Chapter 7. Finally, interpersonal violence is violence that occurs between individuals and is the focus of this chapter. Interpersonal violence can be further categorised into three main categories: robbery, violence against the person, and sexual offences (Newburn, 2013). Theories of sexual offending are covered in Chapter 6 so we will not consider this type of violent crime in the present chapter. Crimes that involve violence against the person can be further sub-divided based on the context in which they occur. These contexts include the school and workplace, the family (parent, child, and elder violence), and the community (stranger and acquaintance violence). The theories of aggression and violence that we reviewed in the previous chapter are relevant for all of these contexts; however, violent offending in different contexts has also attracted a number of specific theories that we will consider in more detail in this chapter.

Violent crime, then, can be differentiated by the primary target of the violence and the context in which it occurs. Violent crimes can also be categorised in terms of specific legal boundaries. These focus on the different nature and gravity of the offence. The exact number of different types of violent offence varies widely among different national and state jurisdictions. However, the most widely recognised category is **homicide**, which can be defined as 'the killing of a human being, whether the killing is lawful or unlawful' (Brookman, 2010, p. 217). Homicide can be sub-divided into two main categories: (a) **criminal homicide** (the killing of another human that is prohibited by the law); and (b) **non-criminal homicide** (killing that is not prohibited by the law – e.g., capital punishment). Criminal homicide can be further sub-divided into acts of **murder** that involves the intentional killing of another person, and **manslaughter** where the killing of another person was not specifically intended. Manslaughter itself can be further divided into two categories: voluntary manslaughter (referred to as non-negligent manslaughter in the United States) and involuntary manslaughter (negligent

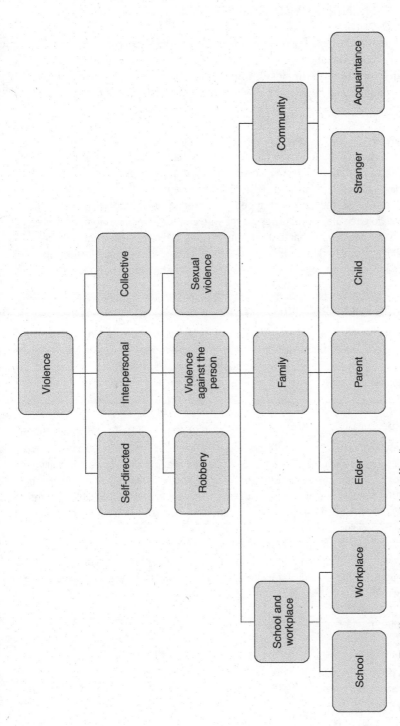

Figure 5.1 The different contexts in which violent offending occurs.
Source: World Health Organization (2002b).

CRIMINAL PSYCHOLOGY THROUGH FILM 5.1
Once Were Warriors (1994)

Directed by: Lee Tamahori
Starring: Rena Owen (Beth Heke), Temuera Morrison (Jake 'the muss' Heke), Julian Arahanga (Nig Heke), and Mamaengaroa Kerr-Bell (Grace Heke)

Once Were Warriors is one of the most iconic of all New Zealand films. Centred on the Heke family, the film teases out issues relating to interpersonal relationships and ethnic identity amidst violence, poverty, and alcohol abuse. Based on the novel by Alan Duff (1990) of the same name, *Once Were Warriors* features many of the different types of violence illustrated in Figure 5.1: domestic violence (Jake brutally beats his wife Beth), community violence (Jake also brutally beats up a bar patron, among others), sexual violence (Grace's 'uncle Bully' rapes her), self-directed violence (Grace, in response to the rape, commits suicide), and collective violence (Nig is initiated into a gang).

Question for discussion

Some of the violence perpetrated in the movie is depicted as normative, or at least accepted (e.g., Jake the Muss's pummelling of an annoying patron in the local pub), while other types of violence are not. Why might serious violence be deemed as appropriate in some contexts (and among some social groups) but not others?

manslaughter in the United States) (see Figure 5.2). The boundaries between murder and voluntary manslaughter are not particularly clear cut (and can be very hard to determine in practice) but essentially voluntary manslaughter involves the killing of another person without 'malice aforethought' – in other words, without a specific planned intent to kill. Involuntary manslaughter involves cases where someone is killed as a result of recklessness or negligence. For instance, someone who drinks a significant quantity of alcohol and crosses the centre line causing an accident that results in the death of the other driver may be convicted of involuntary manslaughter.

Other types of violent crime (excluding sexual offences) that are typically included in crime statistics in the United States, the United Kingdom, Australia, Canada, and New Zealand, include:

- attempted murder
- robbery
- assaults
- kidnapping/abduction
- intimidation and threats
- hate crimes.

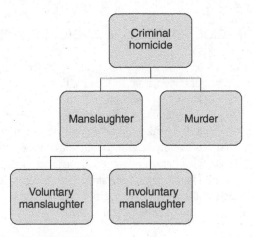

Figure 5.2 Legal categories of homicide.

It is worth noting, however, that different countries (and different states within countries) vary both in their list of violent offences and in the particular legal definitions that circumscribe these violent acts. This suggests that both cross-state and cross-national comparisons should be undertaken with some caution when based on official crime statistics.

The extent of violent crime

There is a considerable amount of violent crime in society. In England and Wales for instance, official crime statistics indicate that there were just over a million violence against the person offences recorded by the police in the year ending June, 2016 (Flatley, 2016a). Victim surveys, by illuminating the 'dark figure' of crime, tend to provide still higher counts of violent crime with an estimated 1,292,000 violent incidents in England and Wales in the year ending June, 2016 (Flatley, 2016a). In the latest version of the New Zealand Crime and Safety Survey there were an estimated 512,000 assaults, 17,000 robberies, and 401,000 offences involving the threat of force with less than 30 per cent of these incidents reported to police (Ministry of Justice, 2015).

As noted in Chapter 1, we must be cautious in drawing comparisons among countries based on either recorded crime statistics or victim surveys. A more reliable way of obtaining an overall picture of cross-national and historical patterns in violent crime is by examining homicide statistics. Homicide statistics are typically viewed as more reliable than other crime statistics because they are less subject to reporting and recording biases and omissions (although international comparisons still need to be taken carefully due to differences in legal definitions – Brookman, 2010). Rates of homicide vary both among countries and over time within the same country (see Box 5.1). Internationally, homicide rates vary substantially, with the highest rates occurring in Africa and the Americas and lower rates occurring in Europe and Asia (see Figure 5.3). Countries with very high rates (measured per 100,000 individuals in the population) include Honduras (90.4), Jamaica (39.3), and South Africa (31), and countries with low rates include Japan (0.3), Austria (0.9), and Singapore (0.2) (United Nations Office on Drugs and Crime, 2013).

BOX 5.1 HOMICIDE RATES: A 500-YEAR PERSPECTIVE

Is the world becoming an increasingly more violent place to live? Despite the impression that is often obtained from the media, the answer to this question – in Western countries at least – is a resounding 'no'. Rates of violent crime have actually been falling in many countries from the early- to mid-1990s onwards (Farrell et al., 2010), and if we take a much longer term perspective then it is clearly apparent that our society is considerably less violent than it was 500 years ago (Eisner, 2003). Although estimating historical rates of homicide is a tricky endeavour, the overall picture is fairly clear: current homicide rates in Europe, as illustrated in the graph below, are around 30 times lower than they were in the fifteenth century (Eisner, 2003).

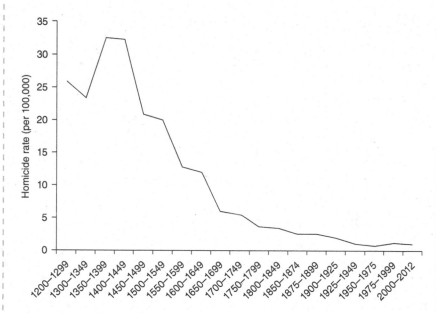

Mean homicide rates in European regions between 1200 and 2012 (excluding Corsica and Sardinia).
Source: Eisner (2014, Table 4)

Discussion question

What factor or factors do you think can explain the declining rates in homicide over the last 500 years? (See Eisner 2013 and Pinker 2011 for an extended discussion.)

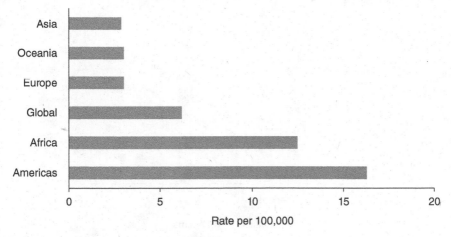

Figure 5.3 Homicide rates by region (2012 or latest).
Source: United Nations Office on Drugs and Crime (2013).

Despite differences in the rate of homicide in different countries, the overall *pattern* of homicide is relatively similar. Men are much more likely to be perpetrators of homicide than are women. Statistics repeatedly confirm that over 90 per cent of all homicides are perpetrated by men (Brookman, 2010; United Nations Office on Drugs and Crime, 2013) (see Figure 5.4). Men are also more likely to be the *victims* of homicide. For instance, 75 per cent of the victims of homicide globally are male, although the proportion of male victims varies by country and by region (United Nations Office on Drugs and Crime, 2013) (see Figure 5.4). In other words, the vast majority of homicides involve men killing other men. Indeed, only 3 per cent of all homicides in England and Wales between 1998 and 2008 involved women killing other women (Brookman, 2010). Both homicide victims and perpetrators are also more likely to be *young* males, with rates typically highest for men in their twenties (see Figure 5.5). The relationship between the victim and the offender differs substantially depending on the gender of both the perpetrator and the victim. Men are much more likely to kill and be killed by friends, acquaintances, and strangers. Women, on the other hand, are much more likely to be killed by intimate partners and family members, and when women do commit homicide their victims are also more likely to be intimates and family members (Brookman, 2010). The primary mode of homicide differs somewhat by country. In Australia and the United Kingdom most homicides are the result of stabbings or beatings, whereas in the United States the murder weapon is overwhelmingly likely to be a firearm. Finally, official crime statistics often record a primary 'motive' or 'context' in which homicide occurs. Obtaining accurate information on offender's motive can be difficult, but where a motive is recorded it is most likely to be labelled as resulting from an 'argument'.

In sum, violent crime is a relatively common occurrence in Western societies, although lethal violence is relatively rare, and rates of violent crime appear to be declining in many countries (and are considerably lower than they were 500 years ago). Violent crime is also clearly patterned in important ways. It we consider the most serious form of violent crime, homicide, we see that men – especially young men – are overwhelmingly likely to be both the perpetrators and the victims of homicide.

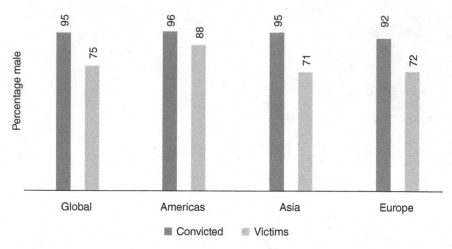

Figure 5.4 Percentage of male victims and perpetrators (convicted) of homicide (2011 or latest year).
Source: United Nations Office on Drugs and Crime (2013).

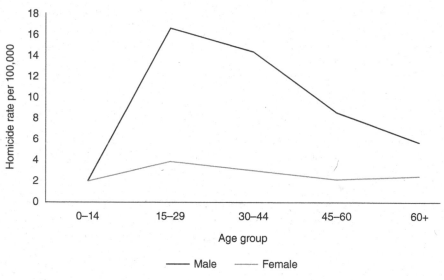

Figure 5.5 Global homicide rates by sex and age group.
Source: United Nations Office on Drugs and Crime (2013).

REVIEW AND REFLECT

1   What is the difference between 'murder' and 'manslaughter'? Why can it be hard in practice to distinguish between these two types of criminal homicide?
2   Why do you think that homicide rates are significantly higher in the Americas than in other geographical regions?

COMMUNITY VIOLENCE

A significant proportion of violence in society occurs among strangers and acquaintances in community contexts. As the homicide statistics reviewed above clearly indicate, community violence (as opposed to family violence – see below) is largely a male affair. In this section we consider some of the main theoretical approaches to understanding male/male violence and then turn to a brief overview of the nature of robbery.

Male/male violence

One of the most robust findings in criminology is that men kill other men much more frequently than women kill other women and that this gender difference is most pronounced when we consider homicides that occur among strangers or acquaintances (rather than intimate partners or family members). For example, in an influential cross-cultural review of 35 studies of same-sex homicide, Daly and Wilson (1988) found that the proportion of such homicides involving male perpetrators and male victims was over 90 per cent in all but one of the samples. It is worth pausing for a moment to reflect on these figures. The fact that men are the more violent (and, indeed, more criminal) sex will hardly be news to any readers, but it is also important to recognise that homicide victims are also overwhelmingly likely to be male, particularly when we exclude homicides that occur among intimate partners and family members. Under what circumstances do men engage in violent conflict with other men, and why is it men, rather than women, who are both the perpetrators and the victims?

One important finding is that male/male homicide often appears to occur in the contexts of arguments, disputes, and apparently 'trivial altercations'. Consider the following two examples:

> In a dice game, the victim and the offender had a $2 bet, which the victim refused to pay. After both left the game, the offender fired three shots from his car, fatally wounding the victim as he walked along the street.
>
> (Wolgang, 1958, cited in Polk, 1999, p. 8)

> EJF stabbed to death DJC at a notorious Edmonton hotel. They had been drinking. They argued over a glass of beer. They pushed one another prior to the fatal attack. Bouncers separated the two but as EJF was being pulled away from DJC he reached round a corner with his knife and stabbed DJC in the heart. He could not see DJC but knew where he was. It was a fatal stab in the dark.
>
> (Silverman & Kennedy, 1993, cited in Polk, 1999, p. 7)

As Jones (2008) notes, confrontational homicides involving men have a number of typical features. First, they appear to arise over what seem like minor or trivial matters. Second, they often occur within public spaces in front of bystanders. Third, the victims and perpetrators have often been drinking. Finally, weapons such as firearms and knives are often involved. It is also worth noting that these kind of homicide are more likely to involve young men from socially and economically disadvantaged backgrounds

(Daly, 2016; Daly & Wilson, 1997). Many of these homicides follow a similar pattern: a reciprocal series of escalating 'provocations' get 'out of hand', resulting in the death of one of the protagonists (Luckenbill, 1977; Polk, 1999) (see Chapter 4).

One possible explanation for why these types of homicide typically involve male victims and perpetrators is to suggest that men – especially young men – are simply more prone to engage in risk-taking and impulsive behaviour than are women. The evidence in support of this view is overwhelming (Byrnes, Miller, & Schafer, 1999; Cross et al., 2011). As reviewed by Cross et al. (2011), men participate in extreme sports, abuse alcohol and drugs, engage in a diverse range of criminal activities, drive more recklessly, have more accidents, and die from external causes at higher rates than do women. Two main differences between men and women appear to drive these findings. First, men are more *motivated* to seek out rewarding and risky activities, and, second, women seem to be more anxious or concerned about the *consequences* of risky activity and inhibit their behaviour accordingly (Campbell, 2006; Cross et al., 2011). At a proximate level, therefore, men are more attracted to, and less averse to, risk. However, we still need to explain just why these gender differences exist and why it is conflicts between *men* who are acquaintances or strangers that are more likely to result in homicidal outcomes.

One prominent theoretical perspective in criminology highlights the importance of '**masculinity**' in understanding same-sex violence. Broadly speaking, some scholars have argued that prevailing social-structural contexts reinforce the notion of male hegemony or dominance and create environments in which men are socialised to accept violence as a legitimate, indeed appropriate, way of responding in certain situations (Messerschmidt, 1993; Schrock & Schwalbe, 2009). The use of violence is one way that men can assert their 'manhood', and thus masculinity can be viewed as dynamic risk factor for violent offending (Whitehead, 2005). This perspective can be useful in helping us to understand why male/male violence appears to arise over relatively trivial disputes and why it often occurs in a public forum. Polk (1995, 1999) has argued that confrontational violence between men takes the form of '**honour contests**' where the precise material details of the conflict are less important than the need to maintain reputation or status by not backing down or yielding, particularly in front of an audience often involving other men.

The view that masculinity plays a crucial role in confrontational homicides between men is essentially based on the idea that men conform to certain social roles that are embedded in particular cultural contexts. In crude terms, men are doing what they have been socialised to do. As Polk (1999) notes, however, clearly not all men respond in the same way to apparent challenges to their honour, and they can successfully maintain their status or reputation without resorting to violence. This suggests that particularly social environments, or 'sub-cultures', such as those highlighted in Anderson's (1999) work on 'the code of streets' (reviewed in Chapter 4) may promote particular ways of responding to conflict as men need to assert their dominance through violence in order to signal to others that they are not the sort of individual that can be 'pushed around'. The fact that male/male violence is more prominent among men who come from deprived backgrounds lends support to this view as these individuals may have more to gain from resolving disputes with violence, particularly when there is a relative absence of third-party enforcement (i.e., the police).

Evolutionary psychologists have also argued that lethal violence that occurs between men can be understood in terms of the need to maintain or achieve status, although the origins of that motivation are located in the evolutionary history of our species rather than (or in addition to) specific cultural environments (Daly, 2016; Daly & Wilson, 1988, 1997). Drawing on sexual selection and parental investment theory (see Chapter 1), evolutionary psychologists argue that men who were able to succeed in competitive conflicts with other men would have been at a reproductive advantage, and hence we should expect men to be more prone to engage in risky, competitive activities, particularly against their male rivals (Archer, 2009a, 2009b). Of course this doesn't mean that all men should be indiscriminately violent. Young unmarried males with limited resources, for instance, will have more to gain (and less to lose) from competitive conflict with other men, and hence we should expect violent interactions to be most common among this group (Daly, 2016; Daly & Wilson, 1997). We might also expect that competitive violent conflicts are more prevalent in cultural environments where there is a lack of third-party policing, and hence men must be ready to resolve conflicts and disputes themselves.

The evolutionary picture sketched here is somewhat complicated by the fact that status in humans can be achieved through multiple routes, not all of which involve physical dominance (Cheng & Tracy, 2014). However, studies that have explored morphological differences between men and women provide clear evidence for the importance of physical contests between men in human evolution. Males are slightly taller than females on average, but they are significantly stronger than women and have greater lean muscle mass (Lassek & Gaulin, 2009; Puts, 2016). As Puts (2010, p. 161) summarises: 'Men are larger, stronger, faster, and more physically aggressive than women, and the degree of sexual dimorphism in these traits rivals that of species with intense male contests.' This strongly suggests that aggression between males reflects sexual selection processes that have favoured risky competitive interactions among males more so than among females (Puts, 2016).

Violence between strangers and acquaintances is largely a male affair: men are overwhelmingly both the perpetrators and the victims of both lethal and non-lethal same-sex violence. At the proximate level this is likely to reflect the fact that men tend to be more willing to engage in a variety of risky behaviours, whereas women tend to be more risk averse. These differences are likely to reflect, at an evolutionary level of analysis, greater selection pressures on men for competitive conflict with other men. To what extent competitive conflict involves the use of violence will, however, depend on variety of contextual factors including specific social-structural arrangements and prevailing cultural norms (Kruger, Fisher, & Wright, 2014).

Robbery

Robbery is an offence that involves the threat or use of force to appropriate cash or goods from others. As such, robbery encompasses a range of different crimes including 'mugging', 'carjacking', 'bag-snatching', and 'armed robbery' (Bennett & Brookman, 2010). Robbery is, therefore, clearly a violent offence although one that typically has a seemingly fairly straightforward instrumental objective: to obtain money or other valuable goods.

The nature and prevalence of robbery varies in important ways cross-nationally, although again we should be careful in making comparisons due to differences in the way that robberies are reported and recorded. According to the Uniform Crime Reports 2015 (U.S. Department of Justice, 2016) in 2015 there were 327,374 robberies (or

101.9 per 100,000 individuals) in the United States resulting in an estimated US$390 million in losses. Firearms were used in approximately 40.8 per cent of robberies, and just under 40 per cent occurred on the street or highway. In England and Wales there were 50,236 robberies in 2014/2015 (Flatley, 2015), and previous research has indicated that around 50 per cent of robberies in England and Wales occur on the street. Around a third involve a weapon of some type, although only 3–4 per cent of robberies involve a firearm of any kind (Bennett & Brookman, 2010). Internationally, robbery rates are highest in Latin America where, on average, 7 per cent of the population are victims of robbery offences per year (van Dijk, 2008). Robbery offenders may target a range of different items with the most common being cash. Mobile phones are another common item that is stolen (Bennett & Brookman, 2010). As with almost all types of offending, robbery offenders tend to be male. For instance, in the United States 85.6 per cent of robbery offenders arrested in 2015 were men (Uniform Crime Reports, 2015: U.S. Department of Justice, 2016). Interestingly, robbery victims are also more likely to be males, with research in the UK indicating that approximately 71 per cent of robberies involve male perpetrators and male victims (Bennett & Brookman, 2010).

Why do individuals commit robbery? The answer to this question may seem straightforward: offenders use force in order to obtain desired items without having to pay for them. This response, however, only provides a partial explanation for why individuals commit robbery offences. Certainly research on street robbery finds that individuals are motivated by the simply desire to obtain money and other goods (Jacobs & Wright, 1999; Wright, Brookman, & Bennett, 2006). However, this research suggests that other reasons are also important. For example, in a study that involved in-depth interviews with 86 active robbers in St Louis, Missouri, it was found that although the desire for money was a key motivating factor, the money was mainly used to support a hedonistic, fast-paced lifestyle involving conspicuous consumption and drug use rather than as a way of obtaining a liveable income (Jacobs & Wright, 1999). Similarly, a study of 27 convicted robbers in England and Wales found that an important motivation for robbery was the purchase of high-status items like expensive cars. Some offenders also noted that it was the 'buzz' or excitement of the robbery that attracted them (Wright et al., 2006). As noted by one participant: 'Oh, yeah! Its like, "that bugger didn't want to give the keys up for nothing!", "Had to beat him to death", and all that. We get a buzz off it. I love it. Love the cars and the buzz' (Wright et al., 2006, p. 9).

These findings were supported by a recent Australian study of 14 individuals convicted of armed robbery (Taylor, 2016a). Although financial gains certainly featured in the motivations underlying robbery for this group of offenders, the thrill or 'rush' of offending was also an important component. Some street robberies may also have a 'moralistic' component to them, as perpetrators deliberately target individuals who they perceive to have wronged them in the past, or in order to obtain relative increases in status (Jacobs & Wright, 2008). In sum, although we should not ignore the purely pecuniary benefits of street robbery as an important motivating factor it appears that other factors – the support of a hedonistic lifestyle, status, excitement, and street 'justice' – are also important.

Summary

In this section we have reviewed violent offences that typically occur in the community between individuals who are largely either strangers or acquaintances. Both lethal and non-lethal forms of violence can occur in a range of contexts in the community, but a large proportion of such offences involve conflicts or disputes between young men and the forced appropriation of resources. Robbery may often have a clear instrumental objective, and confrontational violence may on the surface seem to be largely 'expressive' in character; however, both types of offending largely involve male victims and perpetrators and thus, in part, may reflect a broader pattern of male dominance and competition for status and resources that can be understood as the outcome of both specific evolutionary and cultural processes.

REVIEW AND REFLECT

1   From an evolutionary perspective why is male/male violence much more common than female/female violence?
2   What are some of the main reasons that individuals commit robbery offences?

FAMILY VIOLENCE

The importance of families in most people's lives cannot be underestimated. Humans have a strong need 'to belong' (Baumeister & Leary, 1995), and close, loving relationships with partners, parents, siblings, children, grand-parents, and other relatives are an integral part of human existence. However, perhaps paradoxically, the family is also an environment in which a significant amount of – sometimes lethal – conflict occurs (see Table 5.1). For example, in Australia, around 40 per cent of all homicides occur among family members, with intimate partners most likely to be the victims of family homicide (Cussen & Bryant, 2015) (see Figure 5.6). It is generally recognised that family violence should include all harmful acts perpetrated by a family member against another family member including physical attacks, sexual violence and abuse, psychological/emotional abuse, controlling behaviours, and neglect (Gelles, 2007; Tolan, Gorman-Smith, & Henry, 2006). If we accept this broad definition, then it is perhaps unsurprising that family violence is one of the most prevalent form of violence in most Western countries. Family violence can also be distinguished from other forms of violence in that victims and perpetrators typically have an ongoing relationship that usually exists both prior to and after violent episodes. Unlike other forms of violence there are also substantive and ongoing debates concerning what constitutes criminal violence within the family context, with many forms of violence accepted or condoned within the family that would be criminalised in other contexts (Tolan et al., 2006). In this section we will review the relevant literature on the main forms of family violence, looking in turn at intimate partner violence, violence against children, and elder abuse.

Table 5.1 Terms used to describe homicides involving different offender–victim relationships

Neonaticide	The killing of an infant in the first 24 hours of life
Filicide	The killing of a child by a parent (father or mother)
Siblicide	The killing of a sibling
Parricide	The killing of one's parents (father or mother)
Matricide	The killing of one's mother

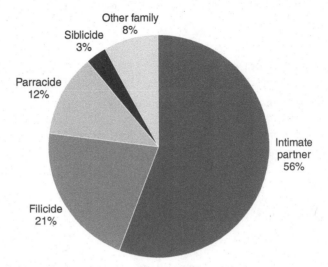

Figure 5.6 The proportion of different types of family victims of homicide in Australia between 2002 and 2003 and 2011 and 2012.
Note: *N* = 1158.

Intimate partner violence

The nature and extent of intimate partner violence
Intimate partner violence (IPV) can be said to refer to 'any behaviour within an intimate relationship that causes physical, psychological or sexual harm to those in the relationship' (World Health Organization, 2002a, p. 89) and includes acts of physical aggression, psychological abuse, sexual violence, and various different controlling behaviours. Other terms that have been commonly employed in the literature to cover similar ground include 'domestic violence', 'spousal abuse', 'domestic abuse', and 'dating violence'. The term 'intimate partner violence', however, is suitably inclusive and encompasses a range of different types of intimate relationships (dating, cohabiting, married, same-sex) and covers violence perpetrated by both male and female partners.

Two important issues have dominated attempts to provide a clear picture of the prevalence of IPV in society. The first concerns the overall frequency of IPV: just how common is violence between intimate partners? The second concerns gender differences: are men or women most likely to be the perpetrators? Clear answers to these two questions are difficult to come by because different studies employ different methodologies, and, importantly, the scope of acts covered vary significantly with some studies focusing on more serious acts of physical violence while other studies cover a wider range of behaviours including relatively minor acts of physical aggression, psychological abuse, and controlling behaviours. A good place, to start, however, is by considering the statistics on intimate partner homicide. In Table 5.2 information is provided on the number of intimate partner homicides in the United States and Australia. It is clear from these data that significantly more females are victims of intimate partner homicide than are males – approximately three quarters of victims in both Australia and the United States are female. Globally, around 15 per cent of all homicides are perpetrated by an intimate relationship partner although a much greater proportion of female homicide victims are killed by their intimate partners, compared to male homicide victims (who, as we have seen above, are most likely to be killed by other men) (Stöckl et al., 2013).

Homicide statistics provide an invaluable window on the nature of IPV in society, but a more thorough picture can be obtained by considering the results of victim surveys. It should be cautioned, however, that cross-national comparisons are problematic because of differences in methodology. Here are the figures for several victim surveys in England and Wales, New Zealand, and the United States:

• 5.8 per cent of women and 3.1 per cent of men report being the victim of partner abuse in England and Wales in 2009 (Flatley et al., 2010).
• 7 per cent of women and 6 per cent of men report being victims of a confrontational offence by a partner in New Zealand in 2006 (Mayhew & Reilly, 2007).
• 4.1 per cent of women and 0.9 per cent of men reported being victims of intimate partner violence in the United States in 2009 (Truman & Rand, 2010).

There are several things to note about these figures. First, IPV is a relatively common phenomenon. Indeed, in the UK approximately 33 per cent of women and 22 per cent of men have experienced intimate partner violence in their lifetime (Hoare & Jansson, 2008, cited in Robinson, 2010), and in a World Health Organization (2005) multi-site study of violence against women, the proportion of women who had experienced

Table 5.2 Intimate partner homicide victims by gender in Australia and the United States

	Total number (%) of male and female victims	
	United States[a] (2015)	Australia[b] (2002/03 to 2011/12)
Female victims	1,005 (79%)	488 (75%)
Male victims	265 (21%)	166 (25%)
Total victims	1,270 (100%)	654 (100%)

Source: [a]U.S. Department of Justice (2016). [b]Cussen and Bryant (2015).

physical or sexual violence by an intimate partner in their lifetime ranged from 15 per cent (Japan) to 71 per cent (provincial Ethiopia). The second key finding both from victim surveys and from recorded crime statistics is that women are more likely to be victims of intimate partner violence than are men.

However, the issue of gender differences in the perpetration of IPV is rather more complex than this picture suggests and has been the source of much heated debate. Some scholars, for instance, have argued that male violence tends to be viewed more seriously than female violence and thus is more likely to be both prosecuted by the criminal justice system and reported on in victim surveys that focus on criminal acts (Felson & Feld, 2009). A large number of, largely population-based, studies have employed an assessment measure known as the **Conflict Tactics Scale** that asks a number of questions concerning the resolution of conflict in intimate relationships including the use of various forms of physical aggression. Studies that have employed this measure consistently find that, in Western nations, men and women are roughly equally likely to perpetrate violence against their intimate partner (Archer, 2002; Straus, 2008, 2011), leading the developer of the Conflict Tactics Scale to conclude:

> when it comes to partner violence, women physically assault male partners at about the same rate, and with about the same intensity as men assault female partners. Although women are injured more often, about a third of the injuries are sustained by men ...
>
> (Straus, 2008, pp. 203–204)

One way of resolving the apparent discrepancy regarding gender differences in IPV is to recognise that a significant proportion of violence among intimate partners can be considered '**common couple violence**' and often occurs in the context of ongoing disputes and arguments and is largely symmetrical in nature: men and women are roughly equally likely to be both perpetrators and victims (M. P. Johnson, 2006, 2008). However, a relatively smaller proportion of IPV involves what M. P. Johnson (2006) terms '**intimate terrorism**' and is characterised by an enduring pattern of control and abuse. Intimate terrorists, M. P. Johnson (2006) argues, are significantly more likely to be males, and the violence that results may be particularly serious (although see Straus & Gozjolko, 2016, for research on female perpetrated 'intimate terrorism' violence). This picture is complicated somewhat by research that suggests that a more heterogeneous range of intimate partner violence types are needed to capture the range of contexts in which violence occurs in close relationships (Ali, Dhingra, & McGarry, 2016). Regardless of how this dispute regarding gender symmetry is resolved (see Straus, 2011), four important things stand out from the literature on IPV. First, a significant proportion of violent crime in society occurs among intimate partners. Second, men and women are both perpetrators and victims of IPV. Third, women suffer more severe consequences from IPV and are more likely to be killed by an intimate partner. Fourth, although women are significantly less likely to be violent than men in general, when they are violent it is often directed against an intimate partner. Less is known about violence in same-sex intimate relationships, although an emerging body of research has begun to address this issues (see Box 5.2).

BOX 5.2 VIOLENCE IN SAME-SEX INTIMATE RELATIONSHIPS

Criminology, like much of the social sciences, has largely focused on the experiences of heterosexual individuals or implicitly assumed that participants in studies have preferences for opposite-sex relationship partners. As a consequence we know surprisingly little about the experiences of lesbian, gay, and bisexual individuals from a criminological perspective. An emerging body of research has, however, addressed the issue of same-sex domestic violence although variability in the kinds of methods employed does limit the conclusions that we can currently draw from this research. Broadly speaking, the full range of acts that constitute intimate partner violence in heterosexual relationships are also present among same-sex relationship partners. Estimates of prevalence vary wildly but seem very roughly in line with prevalence figures for heterosexual relationships. In addition to the risk factors identified for opposite-sex relationship partners, specific or unique aspects have also been highlighted for same-sex couples, including the additional stresses that can accompany experiences of discrimination or abuse that arise from being a marginalised sexual minority (for relevant research and discussion, see Badenes-Ribera et al., 2016; Finneran & Stephenson, 2012; Mason et al., 2014; Stiles-Shields & Carroll, 2015).

Risk factors

IPV may, as we have seen, be a relatively frequent occurrence but this should not obscure the fact that there are important individual differences in the likelihood of being both a perpetrator and a victim of intimate partner violence. In this section we therefore look at some of the main risk factors for IPV. Because the vast majority of research has examined risk factors for male violence against female partners we shall focus exclusively on this context here.

In Table 5.3 some of the most important perpetrator, victim, relationship, and societal risk factors for male intimate partner violence are illustrated (see Aldridge & Browne, 2003; Stith et al., 2004; Stöckl et al., 2013; World Health Organization, 2002b, for reviews). Perhaps unsurprisingly, men who perpetrate intimate partner violence, including intimate partner homicide (IPH), are more likely to have general antisocial personality characteristics, have a history of violence, abuse alcohol and other drugs, and be unemployed. One very important specific risk factor for IPV and IPH relates to possessiveness and sexual jealousy. Men who are extremely jealous and engage in controlling behaviours such as limiting the autonomy of their partners, constantly checking up on them, and controlling financial resources are more likely to perpetrate violence against their partner. This finding was clearly illustrated in a study of over 8,000 Canadian women in 1993 who reported on a range of controlling behaviours exhibited by their partners as well as their experience of intimate partner violence (Wilson, Johnson, & Daly, 1995). The study found that women who had experienced more controlling behaviours (e.g., had male partners that were jealous and limited contacts with friends and family) were also significantly more likely to be victims of intimate partner violence.

Table 5.3 Risk factors for intimate partner violence

Perpetrator risk factors	*Antisocial personality characteristics*
	History of violence Alcohol and drug abuse Possessiveness and sexual jealousy Stalking Unemployment
Victim risk factors	Age
Relationship risk factors	Separation or threat of separation Cohabitation Age discrepancy between partners Presence of step children
Societal risk factors	Gender empowerment and cultural attitudes towards women

Sources: Derived from reviews by Aldridge and Browne (2003); Stith et al. (2004); Stöckl et al. (2014); World Health Organization (2002b).

A number of studies have also found that women who are younger in age are at a heightened risk for intimate partner violence, and the relative risk of violence increases with greater age discrepancy between female and male partners (Shackelford, Buss, & Peters, 2000; Wilson, Johnson, & Daly, 1995). Intimate partner violence is also more prevalent when stepchildren are present and when the couple are in a cohabiting as opposed to in a married relationship (Shackelford & Mouzos, 2005). Another important relationship risk factor is separation or threat of separation. That is, when a woman threatens to end her relationship or actually leaves her partner she is at a heightened risk for intimate partner violence, including intimate partner homicide (Johnson & Hotton, 2003). Moreover, men who stalk their former partners are at an especially high risk for perpetrating intimate partner violence. Finally, important societal risk factors for violence against women in intimate relationships include cross-cultural differences in gender empowerment and attitudes towards women. For example, in a comprehensive review of intimate partner violence in 52 nations, Archer (2006a) found that in countries in which there were greater gender inequalities and where there were more sexist attitudes and greater approval for wife beating there were relatively more female than male victims of intimate partner violence.

Theoretical approaches

Now that we have explored the nature and extent of intimate partner violence and looked at some of the main risk factors, we turn to a discussion of three of the more prominent theoretical perspectives that have been employed to understand violence that occurs between intimate partners: (a) evolutionary approaches; (b) social-structural and feminist perspectives; and (c) social learning approaches.

From an evolutionary perspective, intimate personal relationships deliver important benefits to both males and females. For both partners, an enduring close relationship increases the chances of their children surviving and, ultimately, reproducing themselves. However, evolutionary psychologists also highlight how intimate relationships are contexts in which conflict emerges: 'contrary to ideals of romantic harmony, sexual conflict is predicted to be common and pervasive, and to occur in identifiable regions or "battlegrounds" in intimate relationships' (Buss & Duntley, 2011, p. 418; Buss & Duntley, 2015). Partner-directed violence, therefore, can be viewed as one strategy that can potentially solve persistent 'adaptive problems' that emerge in the course of intimate relationships. In particular, evolutionary psychologists have argued that one of the most important adaptive problems faced by males is **paternity certainty**: although females can always be completely certain that their offspring are their own, males can never be sure (Archer, 2013). Thus it is argued that a strong tendency for males to be concerned with the sexual fidelity of their partners, to monitor their whereabouts, and to use coercive tactics to control their partner's behaviour – what Wilson and Daly (1996) call '**male sexual proprietariness**' – has been selected for during the course of human evolution.

An evolutionary perspective can help us to understand some of the important research findings on IPV. Separation or the threat of separation and real or perceived infidelity are important risk factors for IPV because these contexts are likely to signal to men the loss of a 'valued reproductive resource' or 'the risk of directing paternal investments to another man's child' (Wilson & Daly, 1996, p. 2). Evolutionary psychologists also argue that younger partners are at a greater risk of IPV because they are relatively more valuable in reproductive terms (i.e., they are statistically more likely to be able to produce viable offspring).

Most evolutionary theorists have focused almost exclusively on IPV perpetrated by males, but how might an evolutionary approach address the finding that, in Western nations at least, there is a significant degree of gender symmetry in the perpetration of violence between intimate partners? Why would women use violence in intimate personal relationships? It is important to recognise that in evolutionary (and indeed non-evolutionary) terms, intimate relationships have important benefits for women that are threatened if they have a partner who is abusive and violent, who does not contribute significantly to the relationship, and who diverts time and resources to other women. In short, violence and the threat of violence may also be a strategy employed by women to protect themselves and their offspring and to ensure paternal investment (see Cross & Campbell, 2011, for a more detailed discussion).

Although an evolutionary approach may be able to shed some light on the phenomenon of IPV it is important to recognise that violence in intimate relationships is not somehow 'genetically hard-wired' and should be viewed as just one strategy among others that is more or less likely depending on specific social and environmental contexts (Buss & Duntley, 2011, 2015). Furthermore, some men (and some women) are, as noted above, more likely to perpetrate IPV, suggesting that it is essential to consider individual risk factors. In sum, evolutionary approaches should be viewed as complementing other important theoretical perspectives.

Another prominent theoretical approach to understanding IPV asserts that male perpetrated violence against partners is the result of social-structural arrangements that reinforce the idea that women should be subjugated to the needs of men and that wives should be viewed as their husbands 'property'. Thus feminists have noted that patriarchal social arrangements create an environmental context in which male violence against intimate partners is not only condoned but, until quite recently in most Western countries, was also exempt from legal sanctions in most cases (Dobash & Dobash, 1979). Feminist approaches have been invaluable in generating changes in the way society responds to intimate partner violence and are supported by studies that find a relationship between measures of female dis-empowerment and patriarchal ideology and the prevalence of male-directed partner violence (see Archer, 2006a; Sugarman & Frankel, 1996).

Critics, however, have noted that feminist and social-structural perspectives fail to provide adequate explanations for female perpetrated intimate partner violence or violence that occurs in same-sex relationships. Moreover, in Western societies at least, Felson (2002) argues that there are strong norms against the use of violence against women, suggesting a limited role for patriarchal values in these contexts. However, as Johnson (2011) argues, although a significant proportion of violence in intimate relationships may be 'common couple violence' there is still a small but highly significant group of men who engage in 'intimate terrorism' and who may be especially likely to endorse traditional gender roles.

Both feminist and evolutionary approaches emphasise the tendency for men to use violence to coerce and control their intimate relationship partners, although they differ as to the origin of these tendencies. Clearly not all men (or all women for that matter) use violence in their intimate relationships, suggesting that individual difference factors must play an important role. A social learning perspective on intimate partner violence emphasises how individuals who grow up in families in which they witness or experience violence are more likely to become perpetrators of violence themselves. Variously known as the 'cycle of violence theory', the 'intergenerational transmission of violence', or simply the 'social learning theory of violence' this perspective draws on general principles of learning to highlight how exposure to violence may increase the propensity to aggress against intimate partners (Sellers, Cochran, & Branch, 2005). As noted in Chapter 4, individuals raised in violent households may come to hold attitudes and beliefs favourable to violence and develop chronically accessible violent-related scripts that emphasise the use of aggression to resolve conflicts. Support for a broad social learning perspective comes from studies that find a relationship between violent exposure and the perpetration of intimate partner violence.

The three perspectives considered here contribute some important insights in to the origin of violence in close relationships. The tendency for some men to engage in a pattern of abuse and controlling behaviours may well reflect an extreme form of male 'sexual proprietariness' that is reinforced and heightened in certain social-structural contexts and may be more prevalent for those individuals who themselves have grown up in abusive family environments. The recognition that a significant proportion of violence in intimate relationships is perpetrated by women, although still an object of debate, emphasises the need to consider a range of different theoretical perspectives and the need to explore how the dynamics of specific relationships may promote violence. Flynn and Graham (2010), for instance, suggest that it is important to recognise the role of background characteristics (e.g., upbringing, beliefs, personality), current life circumstances (e.g., stress, alcohol and drug abuse, marital unhappiness), and immediate precipitating factors (e.g., provocation, intoxication, communication issues) in understanding violence that occurs among partners. Understanding these factors may contribute to recognising the way that men and women experience different strains or stresses in their relationship and how these might result in intimate partner violence (e.g., Eriksson & Mazerolle, 2013).

Violence against children

The nature and extent of violence against children

We opened this chapter with a particularly vivid and disturbing example of violence, resulting in the death of two young children. Three terms have been commonly, although somewhat inconsistently, used to describe the killing of children. **Neonaticide** is the killing of an infant in the first 24 hours after birth, **infanticide** refers to the killing of young children, and **filicide** is the more general term used to describe the killing of a child by a parent or caregiver (Porter & Gavin, 2010). The term **familicide** is employed to describe the killing of an intimate relationship partner and children (see Box 5.3). Fortunately the killing of children by parents and other caregivers is relatively rare, although a significant proportion of filicides may go unreported, particularly when they involve infants in their first 24 hours of life. In a recent review of the literature, Porter and Gavin (2010) report that incident rates for filicides in Western nations range from between 2.1 per 100,000 to 6.9 per 100,000 (p. 100, Table 1). Although some children are killed 'deliberately' by their parents, many child homicide victims die as the result of physical assaults, neglect, and deprivation.

BOX 5.3 FAMILICIDE

The killing of multiple family members is referred to as a 'familicide' (Liem & Reichelmann, 2014; Wilson, Daly, & Daniele, 1995). Familicides are particularly tragic events, but fortunately they are also not common. In a large archival study of homicide in Canada, and England and Wales, Wilson, Daly, et al. (1995) found that out of 19,562 homicide victims, 279 were the victims of familicide. Given their relative rarity, little is known about the causal factors that lead to an individual killing their partner and children. However, perpetrators are overwhelmingly likely to be males, and close to half of perpetrators also kill themselves along with their partner and children. Wilson, Daly, et al. (1995) propose that there are two main types of familicide perpetrators. The first type refers to those who are primarily motivated to kill their intimate partner due to a perceived grievance and kill their children as a way of getting back at the partner. The second type of familicide perpetrator is someone who may be more likely to be suffering from depression and who kills his partner and family as a way of 'saving them' from some perceived impending disaster. Wilson, Daly, et al. (1995) argue that both types may reflect an extreme manifestation of 'male proprietariness' as in both cases 'the killer apparently feels entitled to decide his victims' fates' (p. 289). In a study of 238 cases of familicide in the United States, Liem and Reichelmann (2014) found that 17 per cent were largely motivated by 'spousal revenge', while 45 per cent fitted the category of 'despondent husbands' consistent with the second type of familicide offender proposed by Wilson, Daly, et al. (1995). In addition, they identified two other types of perpetrator: 'parracide' offenders (13 per cent of the sample) who mostly killed parents and siblings; and 'diffuse conflicts' (24 per cent of the sample), which involved the killing of various different family members including in-laws, cousins, and so forth.

Although the violent death of children is particularly disturbing, it is essential to recognise that violence against children encompasses a range of harmful acts (Gelles, 2007). These include:

- physical abuse – acts resulting in physical harm, including death
- sexual abuse – acts involving the use of children for sexual gratification
- emotional abuse – acts that involve verbal or emotional abuse
- physical neglect – the failure to provide adequate care for children
- educational neglect – the failure to meet the educational needs of children
- emotional neglect – the failure to meeting the emotional needs of children.

Establishing just how frequent these acts are is no easy task as family violence against children often goes unreported. The reasons for this are relatively straightforward: parents and other caregivers may be strongly motivated not to report such violence, and children may be unable or afraid to do so. More generally, there may simply be a lack of clear recognition that the acts are criminal in nature and therefore should be reported to the police. One recent attempt to synthesise findings from international studies estimated prevalence rates from self-report studies, finding:

- a rate of 226 per 1,000 for physical abuse
- a rate of 127 per 1,000 for sexual abuse
- a rate of 363 per 1,000 for emotional abuse
- a rate of 163 per 1,000 for physical neglect
- a rate of 184 per 1,000 for emotional neglect (Stoltenborgh et al., 2015).

These authors concluded that 'child maltreatment in all its forms is a global phenomenon of considerable extent, touching the lives of millions of children' (Stoltenborgh et al., 2015, p. 48).

Risk factors

The characteristics of individuals who perpetrate filicides vary depending on the age of the victim. Neonaticides are largely perpetrated by mothers who are more likely to be young, unmarried, socially disadvantaged, and unemployed. Although some women who kill their newborn offspring may be suffering from severe mental illness, this appears to be the exception rather than the rule (Porter & Gavin, 2010). Neonaticides by fathers are rare, but the killing of older children by their fathers is more common and is more likely to occur in the context of ongoing child abuse and neglect, and male perpetrators often have a history of antisocial behaviour (Stanton & Simpson, 2002). Stepfathers are also statistically more likely to kill children in their care than biological fathers, and having one or more stepparents is an important risk factor for child abuse and filicide (Daly & Wilson, 1996; Harris, Hilton, Rice, & Eke, 2007).

A large number of child, family, and social risk factors have also been identified for (non-fatal) child abuse and neglect (Barnett, Miller-Perrin, & Perrin, 2004; Gelles, 2007; Stith et al., 2009). Boys, younger children, and children with disabilities tend to be at a greater risk for child abuse and neglect, although girls are at a higher risk for sexual abuse. Perpetrators are more likely to be younger, be unemployed, have emotional and behavioural problems such as depression, abuse alcohol and other drugs, and be under a significant amount of stress. Child abuse and neglect are also more common where there are frequent arguments and disputes between caregivers. This was clearly illustrated in a longitudinal study in New Zealand in which the risk of child abuse was dramatically higher in families in which parents engaged in physical violence against each other (Moffitt & Caspi, 1998). Important social risk factors for the experience of child abuse and neglect include poverty, social isolation, and neighbourhood disadvantage. Although it is important to recognise that violence against children can occur in all types of families and social environments, child abuse and neglect are more common in socially disadvantaged families in which there are high rates of intimate partner violence.

Theoretical perspectives

A number of theoretical approaches have been developed in an attempt to further our understanding of why violence against children in families occurs. Evolutionary psychologists have noted that conflict between parents and offspring can be expected to the extent that the optimal or ideal amount of investment in offspring from the parent's perspectives does not necessarily agree with the optimal amount of investment from the perspectives of the children themselves (Schlomer, Del Guidice, & Ellis, 2011). In short, offspring may 'want' more investment from parents than parents are 'willing' to give. Although an evolutionary perspective has broad implications for conflicts in families, most of the attention has been focused on step-families. Specifically, Daly and Wilson (1996, 2008) have argued that the elevated risk of abuse and death experienced by step-children arises from a lack of parental (mainly paternal) solicitude as non-genetic parents are less motivated to devote resources to offspring who are not genetically related to them (although note that this is not a 'conscious' strategy). This idea has generated a fair amount of controversy among scholars, with the suggestion that step-fathers may simply be more likely to have characteristics (e.g., antisocial traits) that heighten the risk for violence against children (Temrin et al., 2011). Of course many step-fathers are also kind and loving towards their step-children, and clearly most step-parents do not abuse, let alone kill, their non-genetic offspring.

An evolutionary perspective highlights some of the more 'distal' factors that may contribute to violence against children; however, most approaches focus on how family dynamics and social contexts may promote family violence in general and violence against children in particular. Bronfenbrenner's (1977, 1986) ecological framework provides a good example of this approach. Bronfenbrenner argues that human development can be conceived of as a chronological process involving the reciprocal dynamic interactions between the developing child and a series of nested environments. Children spend a significant amount of time with their family, and clearly this family environment plays a central role in child development. Children also spend time in other environments such as school, health care, with peers, and with extended families. The interaction between a child and any of these specific environments is referred to as a microsystem, with the interrelations among these important contexts conceptualised as the child's mesosystem (i.e., a system of microsystems). Moreover, child development is not only affected by the different environments that they interact with, but also by the different environments in which their parents spend their time (e.g., work and recreational contexts), and by other structures and institutions such as the mass media, community, and government. These various influences are referred to as the exosystem, which in turn is embedded in the wider cultural and social-structural context, known as the macrosystem. In terms of understanding child abuse and neglect, Bronfenbrenner's model highlights the importance of attending to a broad range of factors that extend beyond the family to embrace community, cultural, and social-structural contexts. Although the complexity of the ecological perspective provides a challenge to researchers, studies have found that child abuse, neglect, and homicide are related to various community and social-structural characteristics such as economic deprivation and neighbourhood disadvantage (Diem & Pizarro, 2010; Zuravin, 1989).

Elder abuse

The topic of family violence has spawned a vast scholarly literature devoted to understanding the frequency, causes, and consequences of violence between intimate partners and violence directed against children. A relatively neglected, but increasingly important, area concerns elder abuse, defined by the World Health Organization as 'a single or repeated act, or lack of appropriate actions, occurring within any relationship where there is an expectation of trust which causes harm or distress to an older person' (World Health Organization, 2002b, pp. 126–127). The neglect and abuse of the elderly is an under-reported criminal offence, and relatively little is known about its nature and extent. One study involving over 2,000 older people in the UK found that 4 per cent had experienced elder abuse in their own homes and that it was typically perpetrated by close family members (Mowlam et al., 2007, cited in Williams, 2010). In the United States, one study found that over 58 per cent of elders had experienced some form of neglect, and over 15 per cent had experienced physical abuse (National Center on Elder Abuse, 1999, cited in Bartol & Bartol, 2008), and it is clear that the abuse of the elderly is not an uncommon occurrence. Elderly people most at risk include those that are socially isolated and functionally impaired, and perpetrators of elder abuse are more likely to be caregivers suffering from stress, have a history of violence, and have substance abuse problems (Tolan et al., 2006).

Summary

Although families are often loving and safe environments, they are also contexts in which a significant amount of violence occurs. Violence most commonly occurs between intimate partners, against children, and against the elderly. From an evolutionary perspective, much of this violence reflects the conflicts of interest that arise among family members. The proximal causes of violence typically relate to a more familiar cluster of risk factors that reflect the experience of poverty and social disadvantage.

REVIEW AND REFLECT

1   What are some of the main risk factors for male perpetrated intimate partner violence?
2   What are the main points of similarity and difference between evolutionary and feminist approaches to explaining intimate partner violence?
3   What do the terms 'neonaticide', 'infanticide', and 'filicide' refer to?

SCHOOL VIOLENCE

The attack on Columbine High School on April 20, 1999 by two of its students – Dylan Klebold and Eric Harris – resulted in the death of 15 individuals (including the two perpetrators) and the wounding of 24 others. This school shooting, and others like it in the United States in the 1990s, generated an enormous amount of media attention and helped to attract attention not only to the – fortunately rare – phenomenon of school shootings but to the nature of school violence more generally. In some respects it is perhaps not all that surprising that violence is a feature of the school environment. After all, children in Western countries spend a significant amount of their time at school. In this section we review the available evidence on this topic.

In the wake of the Columbine shooting, fear of violence in schools – perhaps not surprisingly – soared in the United States. School shootings, as discussed below, are relatively rare. However, less severe forms of violence in schools, including threats, abuse, property damage, and bullying, are much more prevalent. Victimisation studies in the United States suggest that for 12–18-year-olds the risk of victimisation is higher in the environments in and around schools despite individuals spending less time in these contexts (Gottfredson & Gottfredson, 2007). International studies also highlight the prevalence of bullying in the school environment (Due et al., 2005; Due, Holstein, & Soc, 2008). Bullying is characterised by 'targeted intimidation or humiliation ... typically [where] a physically stronger or socially more prominent person (ab)uses her/his power to threaten, demean, or belittle another' (Juvonen & Graham, 2014, p. 161), and is a relatively common feature of school environments (Zych, Ortega-Ruiz, & Del Ray, 2015). For example, in an international survey of over 123,000 students in 28 countries, Due et al. (2005) found that the prevalence of students who had been bullied once during the last school term ranged from 6.3 per cent among girls in Sweden to 41.4 per cent for boys in Latvia. Another analysis of two international bullying victimisation studies involving an expanded sample of 66 countries and territories found that on average around a third of all students had been bullied at least once in the last one to two months (Due et al., 2008). Given that the experience of being bullied heightens the risk for a range of negative physical and psychological outcomes (see Research in Focus 5.1), including suicide, these figures are of particular note.

RESEARCH IN FOCUS 5.1 **WHAT ARE THE PSYCHOLOGICAL AND PHYSICAL CONSEQUENCES OF BEING BULLIED?**

Title: Bullying and symptoms among school-aged children: International comparative cross sectional study in 28 countries

Author: Due et al.   **Year**: 2005

Source: *European Journal of Public Health*, 15, 128–132

Aims: To investigate the psychological and physical effects of being bullied

Method: International cross-sectional survey of 123,227 students age 11, 13, and 15 years from representative sample of schools in 28 countries in Europe and North America.

Key result:
* Exposure to bullying increased the risk for a range of physical and psychological symptoms (see diagram below).

Conclusion: 'There was a consistent, strong and graded association between bullying and each of 12 physical and psychological symptoms among adolescents in all 28 countries.'

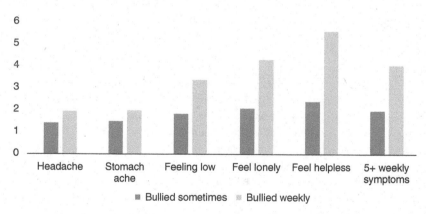

Odds of experiencing symptoms for individuals bullied sometimes or weekly (1 = Not bullied).

Risk factors for the perpetration of school violence have focused variously on characteristics of individuals, families, schools, and communities. In a review of the risk factors for school bullying, Ttofi and Farrington (2010) found that a number of individual factors heightened the risky for bullying, including poor academic performance, impulsivity, attention problems, and low empathy. Given that these factors are related to general antisocial and delinquent behaviour (see Chapter 2) it is perhaps not surprising that individuals who are impulsive, lack empathy, and do poorly at school should be at a higher risk of victimising their peers. Perpetrators of bullying are also more likely to come from families characterised by poor and/or abusive parenting (Ttofi & Farrington, 2010). The characteristics of school and community environments may also heighten the risk for school violence. Research in the United States suggests that schools that have clear rules and enforce them fairly and non-punitively have lower levels of both student and teacher victimisation. Perhaps not surprisingly, schools embedded in communities with high levels of poverty and social disorganisation tend to have higher rates of school violence (Gottfredson & Gottfredson, 2007).

REVIEW AND REFLECT

1   How common was bullying at the school that you went to, and how was it addressed (if at all) by the teachers and school administrators?

MULTIPLE HOMICIDE

The vast majority of homicides involve a single victim and a single offender. When an offender (or, sometimes, several offenders) is responsible for the death of multiple victims, the term multiple murder or **multiple homicide** is employed. It is generally recognised that there are three main types of multiple homicide: **serial murder**, **spree murder**, and **mass murder** (Fox & Levin, 2005). Serial murder refers to the killing of three or more individuals with a 'cooling off' period in between the murders. Spree murder involves the killing of several people over the period of several hours or days, perhaps in different locations, but viewed as part of the same killing episode. When several people are killed in a single episode at the same location, it referred to as mass murder. Although some scholars have argued that the boundaries between these three types of multiple homicide are somewhat blurred (Fox & Levin, 2005), generally speaking it is possible to make a relatively clear distinction between serial murderers on the one hand and those individuals that perpetrate spree or mass murder on the other hand (Hickey, 2002) (see Figure 5.7). In this section we review the relevant literature on multiple homicide, looking at the nature and extent of multiple murder and the different theoretical explanations that have been developed to explain the different types of this relatively rare, but extremely damaging, criminal act.

Serial homicide

Tedy Bundy, John Wayne Gacy, and Alexander Pichushkin are all examples of serial murderers. Ted Bundy, who killed over 22 women in the United States in the 1970s, targeted young women whom he would abduct, kill, and then have sex with their corpses. John Wayne Gacy was responsible for the death of over 30 boys and young men

Mass murder	Serial murder
• Usually arrested or killed at the crime scene • Often commits suicide after the crime • Kills several individuals in a short period of time • Firearms are usually employed • Killers are often motivated by revenge	• Eludes arrest and detection • Kills several period over a period of time with a 'cooling off' period in between murders • Killing is usually not perpetrated with firearms • Murders often have a sexual component • Victims are more likely to be female

Figure 5.7 Some of the key differences between mass and serial murderers.

between 1972 and 1978 whom he would also rape, beat, and torture. Known as the 'chessboard killer' for his aim to kill one person for every square on a chessboard (64 in total), Alexander Pichushkin killed over 48 individuals in Russia between 1992 and 2006, targeting primarily elderly homeless men, but also women and children (Egger, 2002; Hickey, 2002). Serial murderers generate a morbid fascination among the public as illustrated in the numerous books and films dedicated to the topic. Undoubtedly part of this interest resides in an attempt to understand and to explain these often bizarre crimes.

The nature and extent of serial homicide
The precise extent of serial homicide in Western societies is unknown. However, it is estimated that serial murderers account for approximately somewhere between 2 and 7 per cent of all murder victims per year in the United States (Miller, 2014a; Walsh & Ellis, 2007). In a study of serial murders in Australia between 1989 and 2006 it was found that there were 52 victims of serial murder and 13 different offenders, accounting for 1 per cent of all homicide victims during this period (Mouzos & West, 2007). No country appears to be immune to the phenomenon of serial murder (see Table 5.4) although serial murderers only account for a small fraction of all homicide deaths globally.

The typical offender in the United States is a Caucasian man (although see Box 5.4), in his twenties to forties, although some research seems to indicate that African Americans appear to be over-represented among serial murderers (Walsh & Ellis, 2007). Victims are typically stranger and more likely to be female, although offenders often have specific targets, with prostitutes and the homeless common victims (Miller, 2014a). Killing is normally premeditated and clearly planned, with offenders aiming to avoid detection. Killing is sometimes accompanied by a range of diverse, ritualistic behaviour such as the collection of trophies, posing of the body, the mutilation of body parts, and cannibalistic behaviour (Miller, 2014a; Schlesinger et al., 2010). Several attempts have been made to develop typologies of serial murder, but Miller (2014a) suggests that there are four basic subtypes of serial killers: sexual sadists, delusional killers, custodial killers, and utilitarian killers (see Figure 5.8).

Table 5.4 Serial killers: some notorious examples from the twentieth century

Serial killer	Country	Years	Number of victims
Andrei Chikatilo	Soviet Union	1978–1990	50+
Ted Bundy	United States	1973–1978	22+
Ivan Milat	Australia	1989–1994	7
Harold Shipman	England	1975–1998	218+
Anatoly Onoprienko	Ukraine	1989–1996	52
Robert Pickton	Canada	1997–2001	6–52

Sources: Howard (2010); Walsh and Ellis (2007).

BOX 5.4 FEMALE SERIAL KILLERS

Like all other violent offences, males are overwhelmingly likely to be the perpetrators of serial murder. However, although rare, women have also been known to kill three or more individuals and thus 'qualify' as a serial murderer. Perhaps the best-known example is Aileen Wuornos, subject of the film *Monster*, who killed seven men over a two-year period. Relatively little is known about female serial killers, although it seems as though they are more likely to target children and family members, employ poison as a means to kill their victims, and are rarely sexually motivated (see Farrell, Keppel & Titterington, 2011, 2013). In a recent study of 64 female serial killers in the United States active between 1821 and 2008, it was found that half of the sample employed poison as a means to kill their victims, and 40 per cent were suffering from some form of mental illness (Harrison et al., 2015).

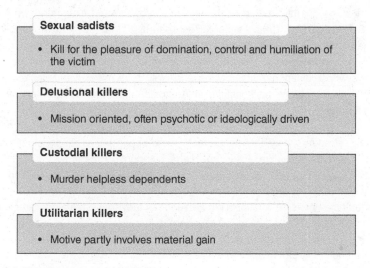

Sexual sadists

- Kill for the pleasure of domination, control and humiliation of the victim

Delusional killers

- Mission oriented, often psychotic or ideologically driven

Custodial killers

- Murder helpless dependents

Utilitarian killers

- Motive partly involves material gain

Figure 5.8 The major types of serial killer.
Source: Miller (2014b).

Theories of serial killing

The rare and unusual nature of serial murder has impeded attempts to develop coherent theoretical approaches to understanding this crime. In part, this is because of the difficulty of identifying characteristics that differentiate serial murderers from other violent offenders (apart from the nature of their crimes) (DeLisi & Scherer, 2006). However, various biological, developmental, cognitive, social-structural, and situational characteristics have been suggested to play a role in serial murder (Allely et al., 2014; Miller, 2014b).

It may be that serial murderers are more likely to have neurobiological deficits such as impaired functioning of the prefrontal cortex, although research in this area is limited (Miller, 2014b). Most researchers highlight the important role of developmental factors, and serial murderers often report experiences of childhood abuse, neglect, and deprivation (Chan & Heide, 2009; Egger, 2002; Hickey, 2002). Of course, this is true of a very large number of individuals who do not go on to become serial murderers.

Although many individuals will find it hard to believe that serial murderers could be anything but 'insane', only relatively few such killers suffer from mental disorders such as schizophrenia. However, the presence of psychopathic traits such as callousness, lack of guilt, low empathy, and sensation seeking are more common, and personality disorders such as antisocial personality disorder, psychopathy and narcissistic personality disorder are prevalent among serial murderers. For perpetrators of sexual homicide, various sexual paraphilias are common (Chan & Heide, 2009) (see Chapter 6). Paraphilias that may feature among serial sexual murderers include **necrophilia** – a strong urge to have sexual relations with corpses (Stein, Schlesinger, & Pinizzotto, 2010) – and **erotophonophilia** – sexual gratification derived from killing (Arrigo & Purcell, 2001). Although the precise set of factors that give rise to these and other sexual paraphilias that may be present in serial murderers is unclear, most researchers highlight the important role of developmental factors such as abuse (especially sexual abuse), neglect, and deprivation. These experiences, in turn, may give rise to the development of deviant sexual fantasies, particularly ones that involve themes of power and control, which are subsequently reinforced through masturbation and elaborated on over time (Arrigo & Purcell, 2001; Chan, Heide, & Beauregard, 2011).

Finally, it is also likely that situational and social-structural factors may play a role in serial homicide (Miller, 2014b). For instance, many serial murderers target individuals whose disappearance may be less likely to be noted. Ivan Milat, for instance, targeted foreign tourists backpacking in Australia, and other serial murderers often target prostitutes, runaways, and the homeless for the same reason. Modern social environments that allow for the interaction of large numbers of individuals who are, effectively, 'strangers' may, therefore, create more opportunities for serial murderers to target certain types of victims (DeFronzo, Ditta, Hannon, & Prochnow, 2007). DeFronzo et al. (2007) also suggest that social environments that are more likely to endorse the use of violence (so-called 'sub-cultures of violence' – see Chapter 4) may elevate the risk for multiple homicide. In support of these ideas they found that, in a sample of 151 male serial killers in the United States, variables that were related to a higher number of suitable victims (e.g., degree of urbanisation in the state in which the killings mainly occurred) and socialisation in a more violent sub-culture (i.e., growing up in a Southern region of the United States) predicted the rate of serial homicide offenders.

One attempt at a comprehensive integrated model of serial killing is provided by Hickey's (2002) **trauma control model**. Hickey argues that in order to understand the phenomenon of serial murder it is important to consider a range of different factors and processes. Thus, he argues that serial murderers are likely to have a number of predispositional factors that may be biological (e.g., genetic), psychological (e.g., mental disorder), and sociological (e.g., family dysfunction) in nature. However, although these factors may increase the chance that an individual will become a serial murderer it is the experience of one or more trauma events that play a key causal role. These trauma events may include 'unstable home life, death of parents, divorce, corporal punishments, sexual abuse, and other negative events that occur during the formative years' (Hickey, 2002, p. 108). These trauma events may, in combination with predispositional factors, lead to feelings of failure, rejection, worthlessness, and low self-esteem in the developing child. As a result a process of dissociation may occur whereby the traumatised individual constructs 'masks, facades, or a veneer of self-confidence and self-control' (Hickey, 2002, p. 109), or the trauma event may be suppressed entirely so that it is blocked from conscious awareness.

A crucial aspect of the model concerns the development of 'low self-esteem fantasies' where feelings of rejection, worthlessness, and low self-esteem lead to the development of an active fantasy life centred on feelings of power and control over others. These fantasies may become increasingly violent over time and often have an explicitly sexual component. Essentially, the fantasies represent a mechanism whereby the individuals can retain some sense of control over their life and vent feelings of anger and revenge. Various facilitators such as alcohol, drugs, pornography, and occult literature may feed into these fantasies and influence their development. Ultimately, the serial murderer ends up acting out their fantasies, and a homicide results. It is during the homicide that trauma events may resurface, contributing to the further development of violent fantasies, and homicidal behaviour in a cyclical fashion.

Hickey's model provides a reasonably comprehensive attempt to explain the phenomenon of serial murder and certainly seems to fit some cases quite well. To what extent individuals do actually 'split off' traumatic events from conscious awareness remains a contentious issue in psychology, and inevitably the empirical evaluation of the model is hampered by the rare and unusual nature of this type of criminal offending. Indeed, serial murder can be considered what Taleb (2007) calls a 'black swan' event: a rare and unusual occurrence that may be explainable in retrospect, but is almost impossible to predict (Griffin & Stitt, 2010).

Mass homicide

On July 22, 2011 at a summer camp on the island of Utoya, not far from Norway's capital Oslo, 32-year-old Anders Behring Breivik shot dead 77 attendees of a youth meeting of the Norwegian Labour Party. The mass killing is the worst in Norway's history, and Breivik, a right-wing extremist, appeared to be motivated by an ideological hatred of Muslims and left-wing liberals. Fortunately, horrific events like the one in Norway in 2011 are relatively rare. However, mass homicides do periodically occur and, like serial murder, are not restricted to any particular country or geographical region. Fox and Levin (2005) identified 636 incidents of mass murder (episodes involving the killing of four or more victims) in the United States between 1976 and 2002, resulting in the death of 2,869 individuals or on average just over 100 victims a year. In a more recent study, Huff-Corzine et al. (2014) examined incidents of mass murder involving four or more victims (excluding the perpetrators) in the United States between 2001 and 2010 and identified a total of 444 offenders and 1,410 victims. Although mass murder may appear to be particularly common in the United States, it is certainly not unknown in other countries. For instance, in China between 2000 and 2011 it was estimated that there were 696 victims of mass murder – although unlike in the United States the most common weapon was not a gun, but a knife (Hilal et al., 2014).

Although mass murders are united by the killing of multiple individuals in a single killing episode, they vary significantly in terms of motive and context. No widely agreed typology of mass murder has been developed, but a number of different types have been identified in the literature (e.g., Holmes & Holmes, 1992). These include:

- *family slayer or annihilator* – an individual (almost always a man) who kills his wife and children
- *pseudo-commando* – an individual obsessed with weaponry who often kills in order to exact revenge for some perceived injustice
- *psychotic killers* – individuals who may be suffering from psychotic disorders such as schizophrenia
- *disgruntled employees* – individuals who have often been dismissed from their place of employment and are motivated to exact revenge on their employers and others
- *the disciple* – individuals who commit mass murder at the behest of a charismatic leader, perhaps as part of a cult
- *school shootings* – mass killings that occur on school or university campuses by current or former students
- *ideological mass murderers* – individuals who are motivated to kill for ideological reasons
- *gang killings* – killings that occur in the context of gang disputes.

Approaches to understanding mass homicide

Our theoretical understanding of what motivates individuals to engage in mass homicide remains limited for some of the same reasons that plague our understanding of serial murder (e.g., the problem of explaining rare events). However, several studies have identified a number of important factors associated with mass homicide (Meloy et al., 2004; Palermo, 1997). Perpetrators tend to be male and vary in age. They may also suffer from a mental disorder, with psychotic disorders more common among adult perpetrators and depression more prevalent in adolescent perpetrators of school shootings. However, in many cases no clear psychiatric history can be identified. Perpetrators often have a morbid fascination with guns, weapons in general, and war (Knoll, 2010). In general, the idea of revenge or 'payback' is a common motif among mass murders as the act is often precipitated by experiences of rejection, failure, or ostracism (Fox & DeLateur, 2014). Thus mass murder may be seen as a last desperate attempt to exert control or obtain status in the face of rejection (Harrison & Bowers, 2010).

School shootings

School-related homicides represent the most extreme form of violence in schools. In the United States between 1999 and 2006, 116 students were killed in school-related events (Wike & Fraser, 2009). School homicides include those that involve single perpetrator and single victims and those that involve the killing of a number of students in a single event, such as the mass murder at Columbine High School. In a review of school shootings in the United States, Wike and Fraser (2009) note the following risk factors:

- access to, and fascination with, weapons
- depression, anger and suicidal ideation
- the experience of rejection by peers and others
- the experience of victimisation.

Taken together, the portrait of a 'typical' school shooter is a young male with access to and an interest in weapons who may be suffering from depression and suicidal thoughts and has been rejected, ostracised, or victimised by his peers. However, this 'profile' probably matches a large number of male adolescents in Western countries, and developing good theoretical accounts of school shootings is made problematic by their rarity. In one attempt to develop a model of mass school shootings, Thompson and Kyle (2005) highlight how ineffective guardianship inhibits moral development and weakens pro-social orientation in youth. If these adolescents are subsequently marginalised by peers they may be blocked from obtaining a positive sense of self, and, as a consequence, they pursue alternative means to obtain a sense of personal significance. School environments dominated by cliques and the marginalisation of children perceived to be 'losers' may facilitate this process. Although this model appears to fit some school shootings (for example, Harris and Kelbold, the perpetrators of the Columbine mass homicide, were reported to have said 'Isn't it going to be fun to get the respect we are going to deserve' – cited in Thompson & Kyle, 2005, p. 426), inevitably theoretical accounts of school shootings are hampered by a lack of good quality data and will tend to identify characteristics that are relatively common in school populations (see also Levin & Madfis, 2009).

REVIEW AND REFLECT

1   What are the main differences between serial and mass murder?
2   Research an example of a mass murder. What factors do you think were most important in explaining why this mass murder occurred?
3   Do you think that we will ever be able to develop a satisfactory explanation for serial murder?

SUMMARY

Violence occurs in a range of different contexts and involves different combinations of victims and perpetrators, including strangers, acquaintances, and family members. Violent crimes can also be differentiated based on the nature and gravity of the offending, with an important distinction between made between murder (the intentional killing of another person) and manslaughter (the killing of another person that was not intended). Official crime statistics and victims surveys clearly indicate that there is a substantial amount of violent crime in society, although instances of lethal violence are comparatively rare with rates mostly in the region of one to two homicides per 100,000 individuals each year. Men − especially young men − are overwhelmingly likely to be both the perpetrators and victims of homicide, and men are most likely to kill and be killed by acquaintances and strangers.

The prevalence of male/male violence can be understood in terms of the greater propensity for men (compared to women) to engage in risky, impulsive behaviour. A large number of violent crimes between men take the form of 'honour contests' and often arise over relatively trivial incidents or disputes. From a sociological perspective this reflects the socialisation of men in environments that promote dominance, violence, and other characteristics associated with 'masculinity'. Evolutionary psychologists have argued that the preponderance of male/male violence reflects sexual selection on men for competitive conflicts relating to status or dominance. Another prevalent form of community violence is robbery, which also often involves male perpetrators and male victims. Robbery offences are committed for a variety of reasons, including financial gain, excitement, and status.

A significant proportion of violence in society also occurs among family members. Three main forms of family violence are intimate partner violence, violence against children, and elder abuse. Intimate partner violence involves a range of harmful physical and psychological acts directed against relationship partners. Rates of intimate partner violence in general are roughly equally likely to perpetrated by females as by males (in Western societies at least). However, the available research indicates that women are more likely to be victims of more serious intimate partner homicide, including homicide, especially when they have partners who engage in jealous controlling behaviours. From an evolutionary perspective, male perpetrated intimate partner violence is hypothesised to be one 'solution' to the adaptive problem of paternity uncertainty. Particular social-structural contexts that emphasise the dominance of men over women and growing up in an abusive family environment are important risk factors that further heighten the risk of male perpetrated intimate partner violence.

Violence against children encompasses a range of acts that include physical abuse, sexual abuse, emotional abuse, and neglect. The killing of children − referred to as filicide − is fortunately a relatively rare occurrence, although rates in Western countries range between 2.1 to 6.9 deaths per 100,000 every year. Women are more likely to kill younger children (especially in the first 24 hours of their life) and are more likely to be younger, unmarried, and socially disadvantaged. Men are more likely to kill older children and tend to have a history of antisocial behaviour. A large proportion of filicides occur in the context of ongoing abuse and neglect. Although less widely studied than intimate partner violence or child abuse and neglect, elder abuse is another form of family violence that involves ongoing abuse and neglect of older people, typically by caregivers and family members.

Multiple homicide involves the killing of more than one individual by a perpetrator or perpetrators and covers instances of serial, spree, and mass murder. Serial homicide involves the killing of three or more individuals with a 'cooling off' period in between murders. Fortunately serial murder is rare, accounting for a small fraction of the total number of homicides. Our theoretical understanding of serial murder remains limited, although Hickey (2002) has provided a useful model that emphasises the role of early childhood trauma and the development of increasingly violent fantasies. Mass murder involves the killing of three or more individuals as part of the same killing episode. Like serial murder, mass murder is also rare but can have a huge impact on communities. There are a number of different 'types' of mass murderer but our theoretical understanding of this act remains limited.

FURTHER READING

Daly, M. (2016). *Killing the Competition: Economic Inequality and Homicide*. New Brunswick, NJ: Transaction Publishers.
A superb, highly readable overview of the role of economic inequality in promoting homicide. The book also includes an excellent overview of evolutionary approaches to violence.

United Nations Office on Drugs and Crime (2013). *Global Study on Homicide*. World Health Organization. Retrieved from www.unodc.org/gsh/ on February 1, 2017.
Everything you wanted to know about global homicide patterns can be found here.

Fox, J. A., & DeLateur, M. J. (2014). Mass shootings in America: Moving beyond Newtown. *Homicide Studies*, 18, 125–145.
A thoughtful overview of key issues in understanding and responding to mass murder.

Juvonen, J., & Graham, S. (2014). Bullying in schools: The power of bullies and the plight of victims. *Annual Review of Psychology*, 65, 159–185.
Good review of the literature on bullying in schools.

Miller, L. (2014a). Serial killers I: Subtypes, patterns, and motives. *Aggression and Violent Behavior*, 19, 1–11.

Miller, L. (2014b). Serial killers II: Development, dynamics, and forensics. *Aggression and Violent Behavior*, 19, 12–22.
The research literature on serial murder is patchy at best, but these two articles by Miller are useful places to start.

There are many journals that include material on violent offending. Some of the more prominent include: *Homicide Studies*, *Violence against Women*, *Child Abuse Review*, and *Aggression and Violent Behavior*.

KEY CONCEPTS

- common couple violence
- Conflict Tactics Scale
- criminal homicide
- erotophonophilia
- familicide
- filicide
- homicide
- honour contests

- infanticide
- intimate partner violence (IPV)
- intimate terrorism
- male sexual proprietariness
- manslaughter
- masculinity
- mass murder

- multiple homicide
- murder
- necrophilia
- neonaticide
- non-criminal homicide
- paternity certainty
- serial murder
- spree murder
- trauma control model

Sexual offending

LEARNING OBJECTIVES

On completion of this chapter you should have developed a good understanding of:

➢ the nature and extent of sexual offending;
➢ the important characteristics of both adult and child sex offenders;
➢ the major theoretical approaches to understanding sexual offending, including:
  – evolutionary approaches
  – social-structural and cultural approaches
  – social-cognitive approaches;
➢ some of the main integrated models of sexual offending, including:
  – Marshall and Barbaree's integrated theory
  – Finkelhor's precondition model
  – Hall and Hirschmann's quadripartite model
  – Malamuth's confluence model
  – Ward and Beech's integrated theory of sexual offending.

Joseph Thompson is one of New Zealand's worst serial rapists. During a 13-year period from 1983 to 1995, Thompson was responsible for the rape of over 40 women, including girls as young as ten years old. His typical modus operandi was to stalk his victims, and when he believed the time was right he would break into their homes and, taking a knife from the kitchen, would then rape his victims. He was also an opportunist offender, and many of his rapes took place outside as the situation arose. Justice Fisher, commenting on the trial that sentenced Thompson to 30 years in prison, noted 'It is difficult to think of any person who has brought more pain and misery to so many people in New Zealand's history'. After being arrested by the police and confessing to his crimes (including some that the police had not linked to Thompson), Thompson was given an opportunity by the police to account for his behaviour. In the video of this interview, the quietly spoken Thompson provided a detailed account of his own history of child sexual abuse and neglect. He also noted that his sexual offending was driven by a strong 'need' for sex, at one point describing it akin to a hungry man in search of a 'feed'.

Thompson's case highlights a number of important issues that we will engage with in this chapter. First, it demonstrates the enormously harmful and damaging impact that sexual offending can have on victims, their families, and the community. Second, although all forms of sexual offending cause harm, they can be arrayed along a spectrum from the relatively less harmful (e.g., indecent exposure) to the extremely serious, such as rape and sexual homicide. Indeed, sexual offences cover a range of acts that vary in terms of their seriousness, the victim targeted (children vs. adults; males vs. females), and the relationship between the offender and the victims (e.g., strangers, acquaintances, intimate partners, family members). This suggests that our explanations for sexual offending will need to be broad enough to account for this diversity. Third, Thompson's case highlights the fact that many (although not all) sexual offenders have been the victim of sexual abuse and other negative developmental experiences. However, it is worth noting that, although we will review a wide range of theoretical explanations for sexual offending, no explanation can reasonably serve as an excuse or exoneration for the offence. Understanding the causal factors that underlie sexual offending will, though, provide us with the necessary information to develop more effective approaches to prevention and rehabilitation.

In this chapter we first focus on some important conceptual and legal issues relating to sexual offences. We then turn to an overview of the prevalence of sexual offending, noting the difficulties in obtaining reliable information about the extent of sexual offending society. We then outline some of the important characteristics of sexual offenders, before turning to an in-depth exploration of some of the theoretical perspectives that have been employed to explain sexual offending. A wide range of different theoretical approaches are covered in this chapter including evolutionary perspectives, social-structural and cultural approaches, and social-cognitive approaches. There are also a number of integrated perspectives that have been specifically developed to explain sexual offending and we review these in the final section of the chapter.

THE NATURE AND EXTENT OF SEXUAL OFFENDING

Of all the types of criminal behaviour that we consider in this book, sexual offences are probably the most difficult to clearly conceptualise. They are also, for a variety of reasons that we discuss below, difficult to measure. In this section we explore the important conceptual and legal issues that relate to sexual offending and then outline what the different approaches to measuring sex offending can tell us about the overall prevalence of these types of offence.

Conceptual and legal issues

One of the most influential definitions of sexual violence was provided by Liz Kelly (1988, p. 41) who defined it as:

> Any physical, visual, verbal or sexual act that is experienced by the woman or girl at the time or later as a threat, invasion or assault that has the effect of hurting her or degrading her and/or takes away her ability to control intimate contact.

This conceptualisation of sexual violence clearly identifies that there is a continuum of sexual offending that ranges from pressure to have sex through to rape. This insight is an important one as there are a wide range of different behaviours that can be understood as instances of sexual violence. The definition also clearly focuses on females as victims and (implicitly) males as perpetrators. As we shall see, although the vast majority of instances of sexual violence conform to this pattern, males can also be victims, and females can be perpetrators, so gender-neutral definitions of sexual violence may be preferable.

The different legal categories of sexually violent offences also reflect a considerable diversity of behavioural acts. This is clearly illustrated in the sample of sexual offences listed in the Sexual Offences Act (2003) for England and Wales (Table 6.1). As you can see by the examples provided in Table 6.1, sexual offences can be distinguished by their type, the victim of the act, and the relationship between victim and offender. **Rape** in the Sexual Offences Act (2003) refers to the non-consensual penetration of the vagina, mouth, or anus of another person by a penis and thus is an offence that can only be perpetrated by men, although the victim may be male or female. **Sexual assault** is a more inclusive legal category that involves non-consensual sexual touching of another person. Other offences that do not involve direct physical contact with victims include voyeurism, exposure, and possession and dissemination of indecent photographs of children (see Box 6.1). The nature of the terms used to describe these acts and the legal boundaries of the acts do, however, vary from country to country so it is important to clearly identify the relevant legal statutes.

Table 6.1 Examples of offences in the Sexual Offences Act (2003) (England and Wales)

Offence type	Examples
Rape	Rape
Assault	Sexual assault Assault by penetration
Causing sexual activity without consent	Causing a person to engage in sexual activity without consent
Rape and other offences against children under 13	Rape of a child under 13 Sexual assault of a child under 13
Child sex offences	Sexual activity with a child Causing a child to watch a sex act
Abuse of a position of trust	Abuse of a position of trust: causing a child to watch a sex act
Familial child sex offences	Sexual activity with a child family member
Offences against persons with a mental disorder impeding choice	Sexual activity with a person with a mental disorder impeding choice
Abuse of children through prostitution and pornography	Causing or inciting child prostitution or pornography
Exploitation of prostitution	Controlling prostitution for gain
Trafficking	Trafficking in the UK for sexual exploitation
Preparatory offences	Administering a substance with intent
Sex with an adult relative	Sex with an adult relative: penetration
Other offences	Exposure Voyeurism Sexual penetration of corpse

Source: Sexual Offences Act (2003).

BOX 6.1 SEXUAL OFFENDING AND THE INTERNET

The widespread availability and use of the internet have created a raft of criminal opportunities that can be hard to classify and difficult to police. Of particular relevance for this chapter is the use of the internet in the context of sexual offences against children. Beech et al. (2008) outline three main ways in which the internet can be employed:

1   The dissemination of sexually abusive images of children.
2   Communication with other individuals who have sexual interest in children.
3   The development and maintenance of online paedophilic networks.

It is almost impossible to quantify the number of sexually abusive images of children that might be available on the internet, but they are likely to number in the hundreds of thousands, if not millions. The content of these images varies considerably, from naked images of children to representations involving indecent sexual acts (Beech et al., 2008). It is important to recognise that possession and dissemination of such images support the sexual exploitation of children, and many countries have implemented legislation to criminalise these acts. The internet may also be used by individuals with sexual interests in children to communicate with like-minded others, in so-called 'paedophile networks'. The inherent anonymity of the internet can make the identification and prosecution of individuals who participate in such networks a difficult task.

To what extent are offenders who only view and download childhood pornography different from offenders who only, or also, commit contact offences against children? In a comprehensive meta-analysis of 30 independent samples, Babchishin, Hanson, and VanZuylen (2015) found that child-pornography-only offenders compared to contact offenders had less access to children, scored lower on indicators of antisociality, and were more likely to possess psychological barriers to contact offending such as victim empathy. The results of this meta-analysis suggest that offenders that restrict their criminal activity to childhood pornography may have a number of situational and psychological barriers to committing contact offences, perhaps suggesting a possible avenue for interventions with this group of offenders.

Most jurisdictions also make clear distinctions based on the nature of the victim, with an age of consent providing a basis for establishing that an individual is capable of freely giving their consent to sexual acts. Sexual acts with individuals below the age of consent (which varies significantly from jurisdiction to jurisdiction) are deemed by definition to be coercive. In the United Sates, sexual intercourse with a female under the age of consent is referred to as **statutory rape** (Bartol & Bartol, 2012). Many jurisdictions further classify offences based on the age of the victim with offences against children under the age of 13 categorised differently from those perpetrated against older children. Offences are also classified based on the relationship between the victim and the offender with many jurisdictions recognising offences that involve an abuse of a position of trust or that are perpetrated against family members.

There is perhaps no other category of offence that has shown as much cross-cultural and historical variation as have sexual offences (D'Cruze, 2012; McGregor, 2012). This is most vividly and disturbingly illustrated in laws against rape. Cross-culturally, rape laws are highly variable. Some countries permit marital rape, and others exonerate the perpetrator from charges of rape if they subsequently marry the victim. Female victims of rape in some countries can even be subject to *punishment* for the acts perpetrated against them (McGregor, 2012). The history of laws against rape in the Anglo-American legal system provides some similar examples. Indeed, it was not until the 1980s and 1990s in most Western countries that husbands could be legally accountable for raping their wives (McGregor, 2012).

Prevalence of sexual offending

In Chapter 1 we noted that criminologists refer to the amount of crime that is not captured in official crime statistics as 'the dark figure of crime'. The size of this dark figure is offence specific with some offences better represented by official crime statistics than others. For a variety of reasons, sexual offences tend to be less likely to be recorded in official crime statistics than many other offences. Some individuals may feel ashamed or embarrassed and therefore will not report being the victim of a sexual offence, and some victims (especially children) may not fully comprehend the illegal nature of the acts perpetrated against them. Many sexual offences occur within a familial context so some individuals may perceive that the offending is a 'private matter' and will not want to involve the authorities (Hollin, Hatcher, & Palmer, 2010). Some victims may also feel that the police will not take them seriously (a perception unfortunately that has some basis in reality) or will believe (again, with some reason) that the whole experience of reporting, testifying, and so forth is likely to be an especially harrowing one (Jordan, 2012). Ultimately, what this means is that we need to be cautious in interpreting official crime statistics for sexual offences and that it important also to employ victim surveys and other sorts of studies in order to obtain a clear picture of the prevalence of sexual offending in society.

In England and Wales in the year ending March 2015, there were a total of 88,106 sexual offences recorded by the police. Of these offences, 41 per cent involved rape (Flatley, 2016c). Women comprised 90 per cent of rape victims in police recorded statistics with the vast majority of those (70 per cent) being under the age of 30 (Flatley, 2016b). The British Crime Survey also includes a self-completion model on experience of sexual assault that can provide a clearer idea of the prevalence of sexual violence. Responses on the questions in this module indicate that approximately 2 per cent of individuals aged 16–59 are sexually assaulted each year (Flatley, 2016a). In the United States in 2015 there were 90,185 forcible rapes reported to law enforcement agencies, making a rate of 38.6 per 100,000 individuals in the population (Uniform Crime Reports: U.S. Department of Justice, 2016). Results from the National Crime Victimization Survey in the United States revealed an estimated 431,840 rapes and sexual assaults in 2015 with women making up to close to 90 per cent of the victims. Various studies indicate that the *lifetime* prevalence of sexual victimisation is relatively high with the National Violence Against Women Survey revealing that 15 per cent of adult women in the United States report being the victim of rape at some time in their lives (cited in Bartol & Bartol, 2012, p. 307).

Rates of sexual violence vary substantially cross-nationally as revealed by the World Health Organization's Multi-Country Study on Women's Health and Domestic Violence Against Women (World Health Organization, 2005). The results of this study revealed that:

- The prevalence of reported sexual abuse from a partner ranged from 6 per cent in Japan and Serbia and Montenegro, to 59 per cent in Ethiopia.
- Between 4 per cent (Serbia and Montenegro) and 21 per cent (Namibia city) of women reported being sexually abused before the age of 15.
- Over 14 per cent of women in the United Republic of Tanzania, Ethiopia, Peru, and Bangladesh reported that their first experience of sexual intercourse was forced.
- Between 10 per cent and 12 per cent of women in Peru, Samoa, and the United Republic of Tanzania reported experiencing sexual violence by a non-partner since the age of 15.

Providing a clear summary of the overall prevalence of sexual violence in society is a difficult task, but a few general points can be made. First, although sexual offences are relatively rare compared to other types of offence (such as violent and property offences) they involve a significant number of victims each year, and the lifetime prevalence figures for the experience of sexual victimisation are disturbingly high. Second, women are overwhelmingly likely to be the victims of sexual offences. Third, victims are most likely to know their perpetrator. Fourth, the experience of sexual victimisation for women varies significantly cross-culturally.

CHARACTERISTICS OF SEXUAL OFFENDERS

As we have noted in the previous section, sexual violence encompasses a range of different acts perpetrated against individuals of different ages. Sexual offenders are a similarly diverse group although they are commonly divided into two main types of perpetrator: those that offend against adults (especially adult women) and those that offend against children. Offenders who tend to offend against adults are typically referred to as **adult sex offenders** or **rapists** (reflecting the fact that most of the crimes are directed against women). Offenders who tend to offend against children are variously referred to in the literature as **child sex offenders**, **child molesters**, and **paedophiles**. As discussed in more detail below, the term 'paedophile' is a diagnostic label rather than a type of offender, and in this chapter we will largely use the terms 'adult sex offender' and 'child sex offender' to refer to individuals that offend against adults and children (under the age of legal consent), respectively. It is, however, important to recognise that some individuals may offend against both adults and children. For example, in one study of 1,345 adult male sexual offenders who had been discharged from England

and Wales between 1992 and 1996, 8 per cent had offended against *both* adults and children (Cann, Friendship, & Gozna, 2007)

Adult sex offenders

The most obvious characteristic of adult sex offenders is that the vast majority are male (although see Box 6.2). Because rape is usually legally defined in ways that preclude female offenders, all rapists are male. The vast majority of all sexual assaults and other forms of sexual offending that involve adult victims are also perpetrated by men. Adult sex offenders typically share many of the same characteristics of offenders in general. They are more likely, for example, to come from a low socioeconomic background, be unemployed, and be less educated (Gannon et al., 2008; World Health Organization, 2002b). They are also likely to engage in a wide variety of different types of offences and have convictions for both sexual and non-sexual offences (Gannon et al., 2008). Adult sex offenders are also more likely to be characterised by adverse developmental experiences that often involve a history of sexual abuse, physical abuse and neglect, and exposure to violence (Levenson & Socia, 2015; Simons, Wurtele, & Durham, 2008). For example, in a sample of 137 incarcerated rapists at the Colorado Department of Corrections, it was found that, as children, 43 per cent had experienced sexual abuse, 68 per cent had experienced physical abuse, and 78 per cent had been exposed to domestic violence (Simons et al., 2008). In a recent meta-analysis of 17 studies that measured experience of child sexual abuse, it was found that adult sex offenders were significantly more likely to experience sexual abuse than non-sex offenders, although there was no difference for experience of physical abuse (Jespersen, Lalumière, & Seto, 2009). Adult sex offenders, then, are overwhelmingly likely to be male and share many of the characteristics of offenders in general, although they are perhaps more likely to have experienced sexual abuse as children.

BOX 6.2 FEMALE SEX OFFENDERS

Most sex offenders are male. Hence, most theories of sexual offending are theories that have been designed to explain male sexual offending. It is important to recognise, however, that women do also perpetrate sexual offences. Getting a clear picture of the prevalence of female perpetrated sexual offending is problematic for a range of different reasons. However, it is likely that somewhere in the region of five per cent of sexual offenders are female (Cortoni & Gannon, 2016). Relatively little is known about the characteristics of female sex offenders but, like their male counterparts, they are likely to be a relatively heterogeneous group of offenders. In an attempt to draw together what is known about female sex offenders a review of studies was undertaken by Colson et al. (2013). They found that approximately half of the offenders had themselves experienced sexual abuse and were likely to come from violent or unstable families, and around 50 per cent suffered from a mental disorder.

Clearly more work is needed on the nature of female sexual offending in order to better inform assessment, treatment, and prevention efforts.

Questions for discussion

1   Why are males overwhelmingly more likely to commit sexual offences than females?
2   Can explanations for male sexual offending be applied to females? Why? Why not?

Child sex offenders

Child sex offenders, like those that offend against adults, are most likely to be men (see Criminal Psychology Through Film 6.1). Individuals who offend against children can be distinguished from adult sex offenders in a number of important respects, although there is also a clear overlap in terms of the risk factors for both types of offender (Whitaker et al., 2008). Generally speaking, compared to adult sex offenders, child sex offenders tend to be older and better educated with a less extensive and versatile criminal history (Gannon et al., 2008). Furthermore, although both adult and child sex offenders are more likely to have a history of childhood sexual abuse than other types of offender, child sex offenders are more likely to have experienced sexual abuse than adult sex offenders (Jesperson et al., 2009; Simons et al., 2008). For instance, in the study carried out by Simons et al. (2008) close to three quarters of the sample of child sex offenders had experienced some form of sexual abuse (see Research in Focus 6.1).

Child sex offenders are often further categorised based on characteristics of the victim such as age, gender, and relationship to the offender (Bickley & Beech, 2001). Familial offenders sexually offend against family members such as children, whereas extra-familial offenders target non-family members. Some offenders may specifically target boys whereas others target girls. However, although there is some utility in categorising offenders in this way, there is also a significant amount of cross-over in offender–victim relationships. Perhaps the most common categorisation is based on the age of the victim, with a distinction made between 'paedophiles' (those with a sexual interest in pre-pubescent children) and 'hebephiles' (those with a sexual interest in pubescent children). We will look at paedophilia and pedophilic disorder in our discussion of sexual paraphilias in the next section; however, it is worth noting that there is often significant age diversity in the victims of child sex offenders whether they be considered paedophiles or hebephiles (Stephens et al., 2016). Making accurate assessment of the age preferences of sex offenders can also be problematic (Marshall, 2006) (see Box 6.3).

CRIMINAL PSYCHOLOGY THROUGH FILM 6.1
The Woodsman (2004)

Directed by: Nicole Cassell
Starring: Kevin Bacon (Walter), Kyra Sedgwick (Vicki), and Mos Def (Lucas)

Thoughtful depictions of child sex offenders in the popular media are few and far between. *The Woodsman*, however, tackles a difficult topic in an insightful – even compassionate – fashion. Walter, a convicted child molester, is released in to the community (to an apartment rather unrealistically located opposite from an elementary school). He finds work and starts a relationship with a co-worker, Vicki. However, Walter's live begins to unravel as his history is revealed to his work colleagues, he loses his job, and he is faced with temptations to re-offend.

Question for discussion

1   What are some of the barriers for child sex offenders to reintegrating back in society?
2   Do community members have a right to know if someone convicted of child sexual offending moves to their neighbourhood?

RESEARCH IN FOCUS 6.1 HOW DO THE DEVELOPMENTAL EXPERIENCES OF CHILD AND ADULT SEX OFFENDERS VARY?

Title: Developmental experiences of child sexual abusers and rapists

Author: Simons, D. A., Wurtele, S. K., & Durham, R. L.   **Year**: 2008

Source: *Child Abuse and Neglect*, 32, 549–560

Aims: To identify the distinct developmental experiences associated with child sexual abuse and rape

Method: Information about developmental experiences obtained from a sample of 269 sexual offenders (137 rapists and 132 child sexual abusers) from the Colorado Department of Corrections.

Key results:
*   Child sexual abusers reported more frequent experiences of child sexual abuse whereas rapists reported more frequent experiences of physical abuse, domestic violence, and emotional abuse.

Conclusion: Child sexual abusers' developmental histories were characterised by heightened sexuality, whereas rapists' childhood histories were more indicative of violence.

Discussion question

How might the different developmental experiences of child and adult sex offenders contribute to an explanation of these two types of offenders?

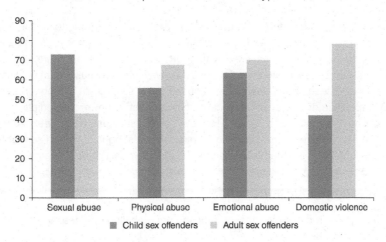

Results of the study by Simons et al. (2008) showing the percentage of individuals experiencing different forms of adverse child experiences among child and adult sex offenders.

In sum, it is possible to identify certain characteristics of sex offenders and to distinguish between different types of sex offender. However, it is important to recognise that sexual offenders are a heterogeneous group. In other words, there is a considerable amount of variability in the characteristics that sex offenders possess, and, although we can make distinctions based on victim characteristics, there is a substantial overlap or crossover in types of sex offender (Cann et al., 2007). These facts point to the importance of developing theories of sexual offending that can accommodate the variability in types of offender.

Sexual paraphilias

There seems to be no widespread agreement as to what counts as 'normal' sexual interests, and there is substantial cross-cultural and historical variability in what constitutes 'appropriate' sexual behaviour. However, the DSM–5 recognises a range of specific sexual interests and behaviours that are referred to as **paraphilias** and are defined as 'an intense and persistent sexual interest other than sexual interest in

BOX 6.3 PHALLOMETRIC ASSESSMENT AND THE MEASUREMENT OF DEVIANT AROUSAL

The assessment of deviant sexual preferences (e.g., for pre-pubescent children or for rape) can be done through a variety of means, including self-report. However, one common approach is **phallometric testing**. Phallometric testing involves the use of an apparatus known as the penile plethysmograph, which measures penile erection responses to visual or auditory stimuli of different types (Marshall & Fernandez, 2000). Paedophilic sexual interests, for example, can in principle be determined by measuring arousal to an auditory tape that describes sexual activity with young children. Men who demonstrate greater arousal to the tape, as measured by their erectile responses, are more likely to have deviant sexual preference for sexual activity with pre-pubescent children. Phallometric testing has been used to successfully distinguish among different types of offender and appears to have some predictive power in predicting re-offending (Blanchard et al., 2006). However, as Marshall and Fernandez (2000) note, the psychometric properties of phallometric testing is less than desirable, and the approach is potentially open to faking on the part of participants.

Discussion question

How might individuals fake their response during phallometric testing, and how might this problem be overcome?

genital stimulation or preparatory fondling with phenotypically normal, physical mature, consenting human partners' (American Psychiatric Association, 2013, p. 685). **Paraphilic disorders** are paraphilias that result in either distress or suffering to the individual or to others as a result of the specific sexual interests or behaviours. For our purposes, we are interested in paraphilic disorders that either are criminal offences or are closely related to sexual offending. Table 6.2 provides a list of relevant paraphilic disorders that includes voyeuristic disorder, exhibitionistic disorder, and frotteuristic disorder (Beech, Miner, & Thornton, 2016; Krueger & Kaplan, 2016). Relatively little is known about the prevalence, course, or aetiology of most paraphilic disorders listed in the DSM–5; however, a substantial amount of research has been directed at one particular paraphilic disorder: **pedophilic disorder** (Stinson & Becker, 2016).

An individual can receive the diagnosis of pedophilic disorder if they have 'experienced, for at least 6 months, recurrent and intense sexually arousing fantasies, sexual urges, or behaviours involving sexual activity with a prepubescent child or children (generally age 13 or younger)' (American Psychiatric Association, 2013, p. 697). In addition, the individual needs to have acted upon these urges or they have caused substantial distress. Finally, the person must be at least 16 years of age and five years older than the child or children who is the subject of the sexual fantasies, urges, or behaviours. The prevalence of pedophilic disorder is unknown although perhaps 3–5 per cent

Table 6.2 Examples of paraphilic disorders in the DSM–5

Disorder	Description	Potential relationship to criminal behaviour
Paedophilic disorder	Sexual fantasies, urges, and/or behaviour directed at children 13 years and under	Yes, if acted upon
Voyeuristic disorder	Behaviours that involve observing non-consenting others naked or engaged in sexual activities	Yes
Exhibitionistic disorder	Recurrent fantasies, sexual urges, or behaviours relating to the exposure of one's genitals to others without consent	Yes, if acted upon
Frotteuristic disorder	Recurrent fantasies, sexual urges, or behaviours involving touching and rubbing up against a non-consenting person	Yes, if acted upon
Sexual masochism disorder	Sexual arousal to being humiliated, beaten, bound, or made to suffer	Not usually, but can depend on specific circumstances
Sexual sadism disorder	Sexual arousal from the physical and/or psychological suffering of others	Yes, if acted upon with non-consenting others
Fetishistic disorder	Sexual interest in or arousal to non-living objects (e.g., shoes, feet, underwear)	Not usually, but can depend on specific circumstances
Otherwise specified paraphilic disorder	Any other specific (typically rare) paraphilia e.g., necrophilia (sexual activity with corpses), coprophilia (sexual arousal to being defecated upon or defecating on others)	Depends on specific paraphilia and associated circumstances
Unspecified paraphilic disorder	Likely presence of a paraphilic disorder but insufficient information available to make diagnosis	Depends on specific circumstances

Source: Beech et al. (2016, Table 1); American Psychiatric Association (2013).

of men report some sexual interest in pre-pubescent children (Stinson & Becker, 2016). The age of the children for which the category of pedophilic disorder applies remains an area of some contention as puberty is a process rather than an event and varies both among and between populations. However, the disorder attempts to capture a group of (largely) men with clear sexual interests in, and often preferences for, children who have not yet gone through puberty. It is important to note, however, that not all child sex offenders meet the criteria for pedophilic disorder as their offending may not be driven by specific sexual preferences for pre-pubescent children. Moreover, not all individuals with pedophilic disorder are offenders as some individuals may not act upon their sexual interests or urges in ways that violate the criminal law.

REVIEW AND REFLECT

1   What are some of the reasons why it is so difficult to get accurate information about the prevalence of sexual offending in society?
2   What does research indicate are some of the main differences between adult and child sex offenders?
3   What is pedophilic disorder?

THEORETICAL APPROACHES TO UNDERSTANDING SEXUAL OFFENDING

We turn now to an examination of some of the main theoretical perspectives that have been developed to understanding sexual offending. In this section we explore three main prominent theoretical perspectives: evolutionary approaches, social-structural and cultural approaches, and social-cognitive approaches.

Evolutionary approaches

There have been a number of attempts to apply evolutionary theory to understand the origins of sexual offending (Goetz, Shackelford, & Camilleri, 2008; McKibbin et al., 2008; Thornhill & Palmer, 2000). Almost all of these approaches focus on adult sex offending (specifically rape), and thus we will focus on this type of sexual offending here. Evolutionary approaches to understanding rape have generated a considerable amount of controversy, with critics suggesting that an evolutionary perspective might be used to legitimise rape. However, as discussed in the opening chapter, we need to remember that there is an important difference between generating an evolutionary *explanation* for rape (or for other forms of criminal behaviour) and providing a *justification* for that behaviour. To conflate explanation with justification is to commit the naturalistic fallacy. It is important, therefore, to consider evolutionary approaches (like all other perspectives) on their scientific merit. What, then, do evolutionary theorists suggest about the origin of rape, and what evidence is there to support their conclusions?

In their book, *A Natural History of Rape*, Thornhill and Palmer (2000) argue that two plausible evolutionary hypotheses can be made regarding rape. The first suggests that rape is an evolutionary adaptation that has been specifically selected for during our evolutionary history because of the reproductive benefits that would accrue to men who rape. The second hypothesis suggests that rape is a by-product of other evolved adaptations and therefore has not been specifically selected for, but can be understood in the light of other evolutionary adaptations.

Let us first consider the possibility that rape may be an evolved adaptation. Thornhill and Palmer (2000) argue more specifically that rape may be a conditional strategy that is only employed in specific circumstances. In other words, they suggest that all men may have evolved psychological adaptations for rape but they are only activated in particular contexts. More specifically, they argue that men who lack the status or opportunity to obtain sexual partners through non-coercive means may resort to coercion (see McKibbin et al., 2008, for a more detailed discussion of different contexts). There is clearly an evolutionary logic to this argument as men who sexually coerce women into having sex may increase their chances of having offspring. The demographic characteristics of rapists and rape victims also provide some prima facie support for the adaptation hypothesis. As we have seen, adult sex offenders are more likely to have less education, come from lower socioeconomic backgrounds, and possess general antisocial characteristics, suggesting that they may have relatively lower status. Rape victims are overwhelmingly likely to be young women and therefore are statistically more likely to conceive.

However, there are also some major problems with the idea that rape may be an evolved adaptation. First, the chances of conception given one act of intercourse are low. Although estimates vary, and some authors claim that conception is more common after rape (Gottschall & Gottschall, 2003), most studies find that less than 5 per cent of unprotected sexual acts result in conception (with even fewer, of course, resulting in viable offspring) (Wilcox et al., 2001). In other words, the evolutionary 'benefits' of rape (in terms of increasing reproductive success) are relatively small. Importantly, for a characteristic to be favoured by natural selection the benefits must outweigh the costs (given alternative options). In the case of rape, the costs for rapists potentially include retaliation from the victim, victim's husband, and victim's kin. It is not at all clear, therefore, that the benefits of rape would have outweighed the costs, especially given alternative non-coercive strategies for obtaining a mate (Smith, Borgerhoff Mulder, & Hill, 2001). Moreover, as Thompson (2009) points out, most men who rape actually have considerable sexual experience and therefore seem able to obtain mates through other means. Indeed, as we noted above, a significant proportion of rapes occur within the context of intimate relationships. In sum, although we are not in a position to entirely reject the idea that rape may have been specially selected for, the available evidence does not currently provide strong support for the suggestion (Ward & Siegert, 2002a).

The idea that rape is, in some sense, a by-product of other evolved adaptations is perhaps more plausible. The fact that rape (and, indeed, other forms of sexual offending) is overwhelmingly perpetrated by men suggests that certain male characteristics make men more likely to commit this type of crime. A general tendency for men (relative to women) to be willing to engage in relatively impersonal sexual relations and to dominate and control the sexual behaviour of women (especially their intimate partners) may make men more likely to engage in rape given certain circumstances (see discussion of Malamuth's confluence model below). However, the likelihood of men engaging in coercive sexual behaviour will depend on their individual level characteristics, developmental experience, and the particular cultural environments in which they are embedded (Ward, Polaschek, & Beech, 2006). In other words, although certain psychological characteristics of men may have been selected for during our evolutionary history that make rape more likely, and which can help us to understand the pattern of rape that is found, we also need to carefully integrate evolutionary explanations with those at other levels of analysis to provide a comprehensive account of adult sexual offending.

REVIEW AND REFLECT

1   What are some of the arguments for and against the idea that rape has been selected for in humans?
2   Do some research to find out how common rape and sexual coercion are in other species (especially other primates). What, if anything, can this information tell us about rape in humans?

Social-structural and cultural approaches

Another prominent approach to explaining sexual offending focuses specifically on how features of our social and cultural environment may make rape and other forms of sexual offending more likely. Social-structural and cultural approaches to understanding sexual offending have also largely focused on rape (although see Cossins, 2000) and have been dominated by various feminist theories that view rape as primarily motivated by male power and dominance, not sexual desire. It is important to recognise that there are a variety of different feminist perspectives, but broadly speaking they argue that rape can only be understood within the broader context of a patriarchal social structure and the power relations between men and women. More specifically, it is argued that prevailing social structures support male authority and dominance and that rape is one tool among others to keep women 'in their place'. As Brownmiller (1975, p. 5) asserts: 'Rape is nothing more or less than a conscious process of intimidation by which all men keep all women in a state of fear'.

Feminist theories have had a significant impact on the way we view rape, and they have been instrumental in helping to change laws about the legality of sexual violence, especially in the context of marriage relationships. Feminist theories have also highlighted the broader role of cultural norms, beliefs, and laws that are supportive of sexual violence in the aetiology of sexual offending. It is fairly easy to see, for example, that cultures that regard marriage as entailing the obligation on women to be always sexual available, or that support the ideology of male superiority and male honour have increased levels of sexual violence. Feminist scholars have also highlighted the role that pornography might play in shaping attitudes towards women and therefore making rape more likely (see Box 6.4) and how adult sexual offending may be shaped by specific sub-cultural environments. For example, among some sub-cultural groups (e.g., certain gangs) rape can be viewed in normative terms as a 'rite of passage' for male gang members who also endorse highly negative attitudes towards women that support their sexual offending. A good example of this comes from Philip Bourgouis's (1995) ethnographic study of Puerto Rican crack cocaine dealers in El Bario Harlem in which he describes in disturbing detail the seemingly routine nature of gang rape and how men who are socialised into these sub-cultural groups develop particular 'rape myths' such as the idea that women somehow enjoy being raped.

BOX 6.4 PORNOGRAPHY AND SEXUAL OFFENDING

Does the consumption of pornography play a causal role in the aetiology of sexual offending? In other words, are men who use pornography on a regular basis more likely to sexually aggress against women? Before reading on, take a moment to reflect on this question and jot down several reasons why you think that there might be a causal relationship between pornography use and sexual violence and several reasons why you think there might not be a causal relationship.

In order to address the relationship between pornography and sexual offending we first of all must clarify just what we mean by pornography. According to Hald, Malamuth, and Yuen (2010, p. 15), pornography 'refers to sexually explicit materials intended to create sexual arousal in the consumer', with an important distinction drawn between non-violent pornography as 'sexually explicit material without any overt coercive control' and violent pornography in which 'nonconsensual, coercive, and/or violent sexual relations are explicitly portrayed'. There is no doubt that, in Western countries, pornography is readily available and easily accessible to consumers whether through traditional print media, videos, or via the internet. A study of 200 Australian 16- and 17-year-olds, for instance, found that 73 per cent of the males in the sample had been exposed to X-rated videos (classified as 'R-18'), 84 per cent had experienced 'inadvertent' online exposure and 38 per cent had deliberately sought out pornography on the internet (cited in Bryant, 2009).

For many feminist scholars the harms associated with exposure to pornography are clear: pornography reinforces entrenched patriarchal values that highlight the social subordination of women to men. Pornography, by depicting women as constantly sexually receptive and, in more violent genres, receptive to non-consensual sexual relations also reinforces certain 'rape myths' that might contribute to sexual offending. Itzin (2002, p. 25) provides a particularly vivid account of the harms of pornography:

> The harm, however, is that in pornography (soft and hard) women are reduced to their genitals and amuses, and now their anuses as genitals, fully exposed to the camera and graphically displayed in public, legs spread, inviting sexual access and penetration, presented as sexually voracious and sexually insatiable, passive and servicing men sexually ... Inevitably, men's use of pornography leads to men seeing and treating women like pornography.

Although there are plausible theoretical linkages between pornography use and sexual aggression, demonstrating a clear causal relationship is not a straightforward task (Seto, Maric, & Barbaree, 2001). Meta-analyses generally support the idea that there is an association between pornography consumption and attitudes supportive of sexual violence against women (e.g., rape myths) in both experimental (Allen et al., 1995) and non-experimental studies (Hald et al., 2010), although the size of the relationship tends to be quite small, being stronger for the consumption of violent pornography. There is also some evidence that men who consume more pornography are also more likely to sexually aggress against women (Vega & Malamuth, 2007). It seems evident, however, that pornography increases the risk of sexual aggression predominantly among those men who are already predisposed to sexually aggress against women (Kingston et al., 2009; Vega & Malamuth, 2007), or among individuals low in agreeableness (Hald & Malamuth, 2015). In sum, although some scholars vigorously challenge the idea that pornography plays any kind of causal role in the aetiology of sexual offending (Ferguson & Hartley, 2009), there is enough evidence to suggest that the use of pornography is one risk factor for sexual offending (Hald et al., 2014). The most plausible explanation for this finding is that pornography consumption contributes to pre-existing implicit theories regarding women, rape, and sexual relations that themselves contribute to sexual aggression.

Feminist theories, although important, cannot provide a complete explanation for rape, because the focus on social-structural and cultural factors doesn't allow us to understand individual differences in the risk of sexual offending among men. Certainly, a strong case can be made that some cultures (and sub-cultures) may be more 'rape-prone' and that social-structural arrangement can make rape more likely by fostering specific beliefs and attitudes towards women and through legal structures that historically have legitimated rape and continue to make the prosecution of this crime difficult. Although evolutionary theorists and feminist scholars are typically highly critical of each other's work, there are some interesting points of convergence between the two different approaches. Importantly, both approaches generally view adult sex offending in the context of a general male desire to control and dominate women. For feminist scholars this control is largely to do with simple power relations and emerges out of historically embedded social structures, whereas for evolutionary psychologists the motivation to dominate is ultimately about obtaining sexual access to females and has an evolutionary history. Both approaches, however, focus mainly on some of the distal causes of rape, and it is important to also examine the more proximate developmental and psychological factors that can help us to understanding sexual offending.

REVIEW AND REFLECT

1   What are some aspects of society that you think might facilitate or support sexual violence against women?
2   How have attitudes towards sexual violence changed over the last 20 to 30 years?

Social-cognitive approaches

Another prominent approach to understanding the aetiology of sexual offending focuses on social cognition. Social-cognitive approaches explore the way that individuals think about and process social information, and they have been developed to understand sexual offending against both adults and children. The general theoretical approach to understanding offending against these two different groups of victims is the same: the attitudes, beliefs, and values that an offender holds, and how these attitudes and beliefs are organised in memory and subsequently influence the processing of social information, are argued to play a key causal role in offending (Gannon et al., 2008). However, the specific content of social cognitions will differ. Thus, a social-cognitive approach to rape focuses on the specific attitudes, beliefs, and values that individuals hold relating to women, sexual relations, and rape, whereas a social-cognitive approach to child sexual offending will focus on attitudes and beliefs regarding children and sexual relations. In sum, a social-cognitive perspective emphasises that the attitudes and beliefs that men hold (and how these subsequently influence social information processing) play an important causal role in sexual offending (Drieschner & Lange, 1999; Gannon, Ward, & Collie, 2007).

As discussed in the previous section, feminist scholars argue that certain social-structural arrangements lead to the development of various 'rape myths' such as the idea that women who dress in a certain way are simply 'asking to be raped'. Similarly, it is argued that some men hold specific attitudes and beliefs regarding children and sexual relations, such as the idea that children 'initiate sexual relations' or that 'sexual relations with children isn't harmful'. These attitudes and beliefs are typically referred to in the academic literature as **'offence-supportive beliefs'** or **'cognitive distortions'**. Various scales have been developed in an attempt to measure these attitudes and beliefs that support sexual offending, including the *Rape Myth Acceptance Scale*, *Adversarial Sex Role Stereotyping Scale*, *Acceptance of Interpersonal Violence Scale* (Burt, 1980), *Rape Scale*, and the *Molest Scale* (Bumby, 1996) (see Table 6.3). Ward and colleagues (Polaschek & Ward, 2002; Ward & Keenan, 1999) have argued that it is fruitful to conceptualise the interconnected patterns of beliefs and attitudes that sex offenders might hold as **'implicit theories'**. Implicit theories, much like scientific theories, are knowledge structures that help an individual to understand and predict aspects of their social environment. Importantly, it is argued that implicit theories are 'relatively coherent and contain a number of beliefs and concepts that are interconnected' and 'guide the interpretation of evidence so that observation is theory-laden rather than theory neutral' (Polascheck & Ward, 2002, p. 391). Thus, a man who believes that when a woman says 'no' she is really just playing 'hard to get' and that women are 'always interested in sex' may dismiss a women's rejection of his sexual advances. Similarly, a man who believes that 'children can sometimes act seductively' and that 'children can enjoy sexual relations with adults' will interpret the fact that the child did not tell anyone about the sexual offending as evidence that no harm was done. A number of implicit theories have been postulated for both adult Polaschek and Ward (2002) and child sex offenders (Ward & Keenan, 1999), and we will examine these in turn.

Table 6.3 Scales measuring offence-supportive beliefs

Scale	Sample items	Type of sexual offender
Rape Myth Acceptance Scale[a]	'When women go around braless or wearing short skirts and tight tops, they are just asking for trouble' 'A woman who goes to the home or apartment of a man on their first date implies that she is willing to have sex'	Adult
Adversarial Sexual Beliefs Scale[a]	'A woman will only respect a man who will lay down the law to her' 'Most women are sly and manipulating when they are out to attract a man'	Adult
Acceptance of Interpersonal Violence Scale[a]	'Being roughed up is sexually stimulating to many women' 'Sometimes the only way a man can get a cold woman turned on is to use force'	Adult
RAPE Scale[b]	'Women who get raped probably deserved it' 'Part of a wife's duty is to satisfy her husband sexually whenever he wants it, whether or not she is in the mood'	Adult
MOLEST Scale[b]	'I believe that sex with children can make the child feel closer to adults' 'Sometimes children don't tell that they were involved in sexual activity because they are curious about sex or enjoy it'	Child

Source: [a]Burt (1980); [b]Bumby (1996).

Drawing on various scales that have been developed to measure rape-supportive beliefs, Polaschek and Ward (2002) suggest that five implicit theories play an important role in sexual offending against women (Table 6.4). The first implicit theory is the idea that '*women are unknowable*'. Men who hold this theory believe that women are fundamentally different from men and that these differences cannot be understood. This implicit theory is likely to foster impersonal relationships with women that avoid intimacy. Men may also believe that women are inherently sly, manipulating, and deceptive and thus that when women say 'no' they really mean 'yes'. The idea of '*women as sex objects*' is the second implicit theory identified by Polaschek and Ward (2002). Men who hold this implicit theory are likely to believe that women are essentially sexual beings who are constantly sexually receptive. Thus a man who holds this implicit theory may believe that 'a woman can enjoy sex even when it is forced upon her' and that rape is not really harmful as long as the victim is not physically injured. A third implicit theory is that '*male sex drive is uncontrollable*'. A man who holds this particular implicit theory may feel that he is not in control of his sexual behaviour and that when a woman dresses in a certain way she is, somehow, instigating rape because a man cannot be expected to control his sexual energy in the face of such 'provocation'. In interviews with the New Zealand police, the

Table 6.4 Implicit theories held by adult and child sex offenders

Adult sex offenders[a]	Child sex offenders[b]
Women are unknowable	Nature of harm
Women as sex objects	Children as sex objects
Male sex drive as uncontrollable	Uncontrollability
Entitlement	Entitlement
Dangerous world	Dangerous world

Source: [a]Polascheck and Ward (2002); [b]Ward and Keenan (1999).

serial rapist Joe Thompson, described in the opening vignette of this chapter, clearly illustrated this particular implicit theory as he described his urge to sexually offend by comparison to a hungry man seeking out food to eat. The fourth implicit theory is that of 'entitlement'. A man who holds this theory will believe that 'men should have their needs, including their sexual needs, met on demand' (Polaschek & Ward, 2002, p. 398). Finally, men might also hold a more general implicit theory that it is a 'dangerous world' and that people are simply out to get what they can regardless of others. Holding this implicit theory tends to promote a callous and indifferent attitude towards others.

The implicit theory framework provided by Polaschek and Ward (2002) provides a useful way of organising and conceptualising some of the important social-cognitive processes that might be found among sexual offenders. What evidence is there that men who sexually offend against adults actually hold these particular implicit theories? Two studies have provided some useful preliminary information. The first study was carried out by Polaschek and Gannon (2004) on a sample of 37 convicted rapists in New Zealand and was based on the coding of interview transcripts for the presence of the five implicit theories. It was found that the most common implicit theory in the sample was 'entitlement', identified in 68 per cent of the interview transcripts, followed by 'women as sex objects' and 'woman are unknowable' (see Figure 6.1). The second study explored the presence of each of the five implicit theories in a sample of 28 men convicted of sexual homicide in the United Kingdom using a similar methodology (Beech, Fisher, & Ward, 2005). As shown in Figure 6.1, among this sample of men, 'dangerous world' and 'male sex drive as uncontrollable' implicit theories were the most common, perhaps reflecting the more violent nature of the offence.

Of course, it must be noted that these studies did not include samples of non-offenders (or non-sexual offenders) so it is unclear how common these implicit theories are in either the criminal or the general population. Indeed, attempts to show that men who sexually offend against adult women are more likely to hold offence-supportive cognitions (like rape myths) than men in general have generated somewhat patchy results (Drieschner & Lange, 1999). This is likely to reflect, in part, the use of questionnaires: sexual offenders may simply not answer items in an honest way. Indeed, experimental studies that have attempted to shed light on cognitive processing suggest that rapists and rape-prone men (as assessed through acceptance of rape myths) have a tendency to ignore or misinterpret women's social behaviour, with a particular problem in correctly identifying cues to rejection (see Gannon, 2009, for a review).

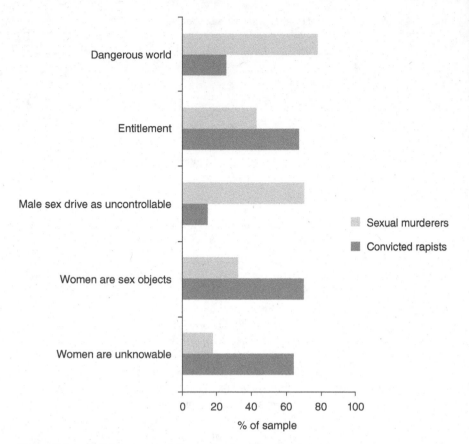

Figure 6.1 Implicit theories of adult sex offenders from two samples.
Source: Sexual murderers (Beech et al., 2005); convicted rapists (Polaschek & Gannon, 2004).

The ideas that sexual offenders hold implicit theories that play a causal role in their offending has also been applied to child sex offenders. Ward and Keenan (1999) suggest that five implicit theories may be important (Table 6.4). The first of these implicit theories is *children as sex objects*. Men who hold this implicit theory believe that people in general, including children, are sexual beings who are motivated to desire sexual relations with others. Thus a child sexual offender might claim that the child victim 'imitated sex' or that the child was 'flirting with him by walking around with few or no clothes on'. The second implicit theory is that of *entitlement*. Men who hold this implicit theory believe that some individuals are more valuable than others and that they should be allowed to have their needs met, including their desire for sex if they so wish. Thus a child sex offender might believe that a 'man is justified in having sex with his children if his wife doesn't like sex'. A third implicit theory is *uncontrollability*. According to this implicit theory, the world is essentially uncontrollable, and things just 'happen' to people largely outside of their own control. Thus a child sex offender may believe that they are not in control of their sexual offending because they were drunk or under stress or because they were sexually abused as a child. Essentially they come to believe that external factors beyond their control are responsible for their offending. The idea that there are various types of harm and that sexual activity is unlikely to harm other people is captured in the fourth implicit theory – *nature of harm*. Men who hold this implicit theory may believe that their sexual offending didn't really harm the child and may rationalise that because the child didn't tell anyone it can't have really hurt them. Finally, men may also hold the implicit theory termed *dangerous world*, which, as described above for adult sex offenders, captures a general view that the world is a dangerous place, and people are out to get whatever they can for themselves.

Evidence that child sex offenders hold these implicit theories and that they may play a role in their offending comes from a variety of sources. Studies that have involved interviews with child sex offenders, which are subsequently coded for the presence of the five implicit theories, find that a significant proportion of child sex offenders hold beliefs and attitudes consistent with these implicit theories (Keown, Gannon, & Ward, 2010; Marziano, Ward, Beech, & Pattison, 2006) (see Box 6.5). Questionnaire-based research that has compared child sex offenders with controls on scales such as Bumby's (1996) MOLEST scale have also found significant differences, with controls less likely to endorse items. However, it is worth noting that even child sex offenders tend to disagree with statements on this scale, it is just that control participants disagree more strongly (Gannon, 2009). As with questionnaire research on adult sex offenders it is hard to control for impression management biases as child sex offenders may not answer items entirely honestly. New methods to try and tap the thinking processes of child sex offenders have focused on cognitive tasks that may show for the evidence of implicit theories. For example, Keown, Gannon, and Ward (2008) explored whether child sex offenders respond more rapidly to a word completion task involving words that are consistent with the implicit theories that may hold compared to community comparisons. These studies have, however, produced mixed results to date, and there remain important questions about how best to measure the attitudes and beliefs that child sex offenders might hold (Keown et al., 2010).

Summary

A social-cognitive approach to understanding sexual offending is not only intuitively compelling (as we expect people's attitudes, beliefs, and values to have some causal impact on their behaviour), but is also reasonably well supported in the available research. Moreover, a social-cognitive approach clearly identifies important targets for treatment as attempts can be made to challenge and modify offence-supportive thinking in ways that might help to reduce re-offending among sex offenders (Helmus et al., 2013). Further research is needed in validating the implicit theories identified by Polaschek and Ward (2002) and Ward and Keenan (1999) in different offender samples (and with suitable controls), and there is scope to explore in more detail just how such implicit theories arise during development. There also remain some important questions as to what extent offenders' implicit theories operate as important causal processes in offending as opposed to capturing post-offence rationalisations or justifications for offending. Ultimately, as with the other approaches described in this section, a social-cognitive approach is unlikely to provide us with the complete picture, and there is a need to integrate social-cognitive approaches with other perspectives.

BOX 6.5 CHILD SEX OFFENDING IN THE CLERGY: EVIDENCE FOR COGNITIVE DISTORTIONS

As several high-profile cases have illustrated, child sexual offending may be relatively common in the Roman Catholic Church. Given the nature of the offending and the secrecy that is often shrouded over such offences within the Catholic Church, it is, however, hard to come by accurate prevalence figures. Certainly, research on the topic is relatively limited. However, a study by Saradjian and Nobus (2003) involved the interviewing of 14 convicted child sex offenders in the United Kingdom, of which 11 were Catholic priests, one was a Protestant vicar, and two were Christian missionaries. Qualitative analysis of the interviews revealed a number of cognitive distortions, consistent with the framework developed by Ward and Keenan (1999). Listed below are examples taken from the interviews in terms of the implicit theory that they illustrate.

* *Nature of harm*
  'It was love and physical expression of affection rather than sexual abuse.'
  'How could it be that bad if he [God] allows it!?'
* *Children as sex objects*
  'Teenage boys are full of sex, and they want it.'
* *Entitlement*
  'As a priest, everything is alright.'
  'I'm feeling down; I need cheering up.'
* *Uncontrollable*
  'God has called me to be a priest. I believe this fully. When he called me, he knew what I was like, what my needs were, and how I could have them met.'

Questions for discussion

1   What features of the Roman Catholic Church in particular might facilitate sexual offending against children?
2   How have specific religious beliefs informed the implicit theories held by this sample of child sex offenders?

REVIEW AND REFLECT

1   What are 'implicit theories', and how might they help us to understand the causes of sexual offending?
2   How might implicit theories be targeted in treatment contexts so as to reduce the likelihood of re-offending?

INTEGRATED MODELS OF SEXUAL OFFENDING

A number of theorists have attempted to develop integrated models or theories of sexual offending that draw on aspects of the three approaches described above, along with other key elements. Some of these models have been developed specifically to explain sexual offending against adults, and some for sexual offending against children, and some are more general models of sexual offending. In this section we review these various different models, noting their domain of application (children, adults, or both).

Finkelhor's precondition model

One of the most influential integrated models of sexual offending against children was developed by Finkelhor (1984) and is typically referred to as Finkelhor's four preconditions model. As this name suggests, Finkelhor argued that four preconditions must be met before child sexual offending can occur. As illustrated in Figure 6.2 the first precondition refers to the motivation to sexually offend against children. Before sexual offending can occur, men must, in some sense 'want to' sexually offend against children. Finkelhor suggested that three main motivations can be found among child sex offenders. First, men may seek to have sex with children to satisfy their emotional needs, which are perceived to be best met with children (emotional congruence). Second, men might find sex with children sexually arousing. Third, men might seek to have sex with children because they are unable to meet their sexual needs in other ways (blockage). These motivations may occur separately and, according to Finkelhor, can be used to identify different types of child sex offenders based on their primary motivation.

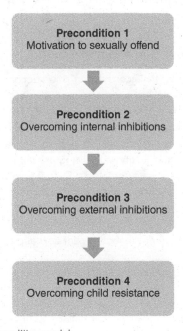

Figure 6.2 Finkelhor's precondition model.

The second precondition that needs to be met is overcoming internal inhibitions. That is, the offender must be able to negate or suppress their disinclination to offend despite the fact that they may be motivated to do so. A number of factors can, potentially, overcome such inhibitions, including alcohol and drug use, stress, access to pornography, and low self-control. Once internal inhibitions are overcome, then the next step involves negotiating external factors or obstacles that might prevent offending. Some child sex offenders engage in extensive planning to overcome such obstacles and may invest substantial time into 'grooming' children to facilitate offending. Other factors that might assist the offender in overcoming external obstacles include low parental monitoring and family dysfunction (which may make potential victims both more vulnerable and more available). Finally, the offender must overcome any resistance provided by the child. This might be achieved in a variety of ways including the giving of gifts, the use of pornography, threats, and the use of force.

In sum, Finkelhor's (1984) model highlights the important motivations that might drive some individuals to offend against children (Precondition 1) along with the important processes involved in overcoming internal inhibitions (Precondition 2), external inhibitions (Precondition 3), and the resistance of the child (Precondition 4). In a clear critical evaluation of Finkelhor's model, Ward, Mann, and Gannon (2007) note that it has a number of virtues including the identification of the main problems experienced by child sex offenders (e.g., sexual arousal to, and emotional identification with, children) and the processes (and associated risk factors) that might result in offending. However, the origins of the motivation to offend are not fully developed in the model. Moreover, it is not clear from research on child sex offenders that most of them have any trouble in overcoming internal inhibitions given the motivation to offend, and thus the model 'fails to do justice to the heterogeneity of offenders' psychological and behavioural features' (Ward et al., 2006, p. 29).

Hall and Hirschmann's quadripartite model

The second model that we shall consider in this section in Hall and Hirschman's quadripartite model. This model has been employed, with some modifications, to explain sexual offending against both children (Hall & Hirschman, 1992), and adults (Hall & Hirschman, 1991). Essentially, Hall and Hirschman (1991, 1992) argue that there are four primary 'motivational precursors' that drive sexual offending: physiological sexual arousal, cognitions that justify sexual aggression, negative affective states or affective dyscontrol, and personality problems. First, it is suggested that physiological sexual arousal can be an important motivating factor in sexual offending. For child sex offenders this sexual arousal might reflect deviant sexual preferences for children whereas as for adult sex offenders the physiological arousal might be perceived as especially compelling but may not reflect deviant sexual preferences for rape. In most cases, Hall and Hirschman argue, physiological sexual arousal is not sufficient to result in sexual violence against either adults or children.

Importantly, cognitions that justify sexual aggression may play an important role in promoting offending. Essentially these are what we have referred to above as 'cognitive distortions' or 'offence-supportive beliefs': patterns of thinking that result in appraisals that make offending more likely. A third motivational precursor is negative affective states or affective dyscontrol. For men who sexually offend against children it is suggested that these negative emotional states are likely to reflect depression, whereas anger and hostility may be more prominent among men who sexually offend against adults. Physiological sexual arousal, cognitive distortions, and affective dyscontrol are argued to be primarily variables that reflect the specific state of the offender and thus are dependent on specific situational contexts. In many cases these three variables also interact with the fourth motivational precursor – personality problems – to promote offending. Personality problems – for example, antisocial personality disorder – are argued to be more enduring characteristics of sexual offenders that are likely to reflect adverse developmental environments.

In sum, the quadripartite model highlights the importance of four motivational precursors in the aetiology for sexual offending against both children and adults. Hall and Hirschman (1991, 1992) also argue that, although each of these four components may be present, often one of the motivational precursors is more 'potent' and therefore is the key motivational factor. Furthermore, this key motivational factor can serve to define specific subtypes of offending, thus capturing the heterogeneous nature of sexual offenders. For example, one child sexual offender may be largely motivated by physiological sexual arousal to children – he has preference for sexual activity with children and strong sexual urges to realise this preference. He may also have cognitive distortions, negative emotional states, and general personality problems that facilitate offending but his primary motivating factor relates to his physiological sexual arousal. In contrast, another offender may be largely motivated to offend to alleviate negative emotional states such as depression, and physiological sexual arousal may play a relatively limited role in his offending.

As Ward et al. (2007) note, the quadripartite model does an excellent job in identifying four important aetiological components of sexual offending. It also provides scope to account for the diversity found among sexual offenders in a way that can potentially guide treatment programmes (e.g., by identifying the core problem that needs to be addressed during treatment). The mechanisms underlying the four key factors, however, are never fully elaborated upon (e.g., just why do some men have sexual preference for children?), and there is scope to explore in more detail how the four factors interact with one another.

Marshall and Barbaree's integrated theory

Most of the theoretical approaches that we will consider in this chapter focus on either sexual offending against children or sexual offending against adults. Marshall and Barbaree's (1990; Marshall & Marshall, 2000) integrated theory of sexual offending is different in this respect as it is a truly *general* theory of sexual offending that can be applied to both child sex offenders and adult rapists. In brief, Marshall and Barbaree propose that early developmental experiences create vulnerabilities that heighten the risk for being sexually abused. Being sexually abused, in turn, can lead to early sexualisation and the use of masturbation as a coping strategy. Conditioning processes may then entrench deviant sexual fantasies (e.g., rape, sex with children) that result in a predisposition to sexually offend. Disinhibiting factors such as alcohol abuse, and situational triggers like negative affective states, may then result in sexual offending.

Let's look at some of the important processes identified in this theory in more detail. Central to the aetiology of sexual offending in Marshall and Barbaree's (1990) theory is the development of vulnerabilities that arise from adverse early experiences. Children who grow up in dysfunctional family environments, characterised by abuse and neglect, are more likely to develop insecure parent–child attachments resulting in low self-esteem, feelings of worthlessness, and potentially mistrusting and hostile views of relationships in general. These developmental experiences may lead to heightened sexualisation as masturbation is used as a tool to deal with negative emotional states. In short, deprived of effective coping strategies, adolescent males turn to masturbation, which reliably generates (short-lived) feelings of pleasure and thus can divert attention, albeit briefly, away from negative emotional states and experiences. The frequency of masturbation, coupled with feelings of low self-esteem and, for some individuals, early sexual experiences with adults, results in the development of deviant sexual fantasies that may particularly revolve around feelings of power and control. During puberty sexual and aggressive impulses may also become 'fused' in the vulnerable adolescent resulting in the development of violent sexual fantasies. These fantasies become entrenched due to repeated masturbation and are thus 'positively reinforced' through a conditioning process as the deviant sexual fantasies reliably result in feelings of pleasure (masturbation to orgasm).

As a result of these developmental experiences an individual may be predisposed to sexually offend. Whether or not they do actually commit a sexual offence depends on the presence of disinhibiting and situational factors. Important disinhibiting factors include the use of alcohol and other drugs, and the presence of offence-supportive cognitions. Alcohol (as discussed in Chapter 8) reliably impairs the capacity to regulate behaviour, and thus deviant sexual preferences may be more likely to find expression. Offence-supportive cognitions, as we have seen in the section on social and cognitive approaches above, comprise various attitudes, beliefs, and values that are conducive to sexual offending (e.g., rape myths). Important situational triggers that can play a role in sexual offending include negative emotional states and the availability of suitable victims. As Marshall and Marshall (2000, p. 258) note, 'negative mood states appear to trigger deviant fantasies in sexual offenders, which in turn lead them to seize or seek to create an opportunity to offend'. In short, when inhibitions to offend are removed and when opportunities become available men who are predisposed to sexually offend may be especially likely to commit a sexual offence.

As Ward et al. (2007) note, Marshall and Barbaree's (1990) theory of sexual offending is an important achievement as it manages to integrate a range of factors into a coherent theoretical account of the development of sexual offending. Importantly, the theory identifies the key developmental factors that heighten the risk for sexual offending and is clearly in line with an extensive body of research, reviewed above, that suggests that experiences of physical and sexual abuse are important risk factors for sexual offending. What is perhaps less clear in the theory is why some men end up sexually offending against adults while others offend against children – in other words, the theory does not effectively specify the different aetiological pathways that may give rise to sexual offending (Ward et al., 2007). However, despite these issues, Marshall and Barbaree's integrated theory has contributed significantly to our understanding of sexual offending and has been the basis for various therapeutic programmes designed to rehabilitate offenders.

Malamuth's confluence model

Why do some men sexually aggress against adult women? Malamuth and colleagues (Malamuth, 2003; Malamuth et al., 1995) argue that two important theoretical constructs, which they refer to as **hostile masculinity** and **impersonal sex**, are central to answering this question. Hostile masculinity refers to a personality profile characterised by 'a) an insecure, defensive, hypersensitive, and hostile-distrustful orientation, particularly toward women, and b) gratification from controlling or dominating women' (Malamuth et al., 1995, pp. 353–354). Thus men who conform to this hostile masculinity profile tend to be distrustful and hostile towards women and are strongly motivated to exert power and control over them through various means, including sexual aggression. For these men 'sexual aggression may be a mechanism for reaffirming one's own sense of masculine superiority by demonstrating the ability to control women' (Malamuth et al., 1995, p. 354). The construct impersonal sex refers to a strong preference for non-committal, impersonal sex. Men with this orientation tend to avoid long-term intimate relationships in favour of numerous impersonal sexual relations with low levels of intimacy. Support for the importance of these two constructs in the aetiology of sexual offending has been found in a number of studies carried out by Malamuth and colleagues. In short, both cross-sectional and longitudinal studies (primarily carried out on U.S. college students) have found that hostile masculinity and impersonal sex both predict the likelihood of (self-reported) sexual aggression against women. Moreover, the *confluence* of hostile masculinity and impersonal sex provides the best predictor of sexual aggression.

Malamuth's confluence model not only highlights the important proximate factors – hostile masculinity and impersonal sex – that may contribute to sexual offending, but also identifies the important evolutionary, developmental, and cultural processes that, in combination, give rise to these two constructs. From evolutionary theory, Malamuth notes that paternity uncertainty has plausibly selected for male characteristics that involve the control and domination of women's sexual behaviour. He also highlights that, due to fundamental differences in parental investment, men, relative to women, are likely to possess psychological mechanisms that favour relatively impersonal sex. Thus, men are likely to possess evolved psychological characteristics that underlie the two key constructs of hostile masculinity and impersonal sex. Malamuth (1996) also emphasises that, although these psychological mechanisms may be universal in men, the extent to which they are expressed depends critically on particular developmental pathways and cultural contexts. More specifically, men who grow up in abusive and neglectful family environments are more likely to develop hostile and adversarial attitudes towards social relationships in general, and women in particular. Exposure to cultural environments that reinforce the dominance and control of women, including the consumption of violent pornography, leads to the further development of hostile attitudes towards women and preferences for impersonal sex. In sum, Malamuth and colleagues have developed a model of sexual aggression against women that manages to integrate both proximate (hostile masculinity, preference for impersonal sex) and distal (evolutionary theory, developmental experiences) causal factors, within a coherent theoretical framework.

Ward and Siegert's pathway model

One of the important findings concerning sex offenders in general, and child sex offenders in particular, is that they are a heterogeneous group. In other words, there are differences among child sex offenders in terms of the type of offending, the motivations to offend, and the key causal factors underlying offending behaviour. It follows that theoretical accounts of sexual offending should take this diversity into consideration. Ward and Siegert's (2002b) pathways model of sexual offending attempts to account for the heterogeneous nature of child sex offenders by proposing a number of distinct aetiological pathways, each of which is dominated by a predominant causal factor (see Figure 6.3).

Based on a substantial body of research, Ward and Siegert (2002b) propose that four important sets of 'clinical phenomena' characterise child sex offenders. These are: (a) intimacy and social skills deficits; (b) deviant sexual preferences and arousal; (c) difficulties in controlling and regulating emotional states; and (d) cognitive distortions or offence-supportive beliefs. These four sets of clinical problems are conceptualised to be *vulnerability factors* that are argued to arise from a complex interaction of biological, developmental, and cultural processes that include adverse developmental environments and social contexts. Ultimately whether sexual offending occurs will depend on the interaction of these vulnerabilities with specific situational or triggering factors. Importantly, although each of these four sets of vulnerability factors are hypothesised to be present in all episodes of sexual offending, it is suggested that one (or sometimes more) of these factors is the primary aetiological factor that drives sexual offending for a given offender, and thus there are multiple aetiological pathways each characterised by a primary dysfunction.

Ward and Siegert (2002b) propose that there are four aetiological pathways each characterised by a primary deficit, with a fifth pathway that involves multiply dysfunctional mechanisms. Thus, for Pathway 3 the primary deficit involves problems with intimacy and social relations. For men characterised by this pathway, their offending against children is primarily driven by a need to develop an intimate personal relationship rather than

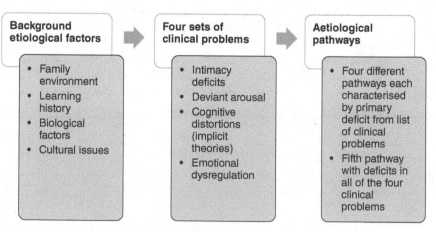

Figure 6.3 The pathways model of child sexual offending.
Source: Ward and Siegert (2002b).

arising from deviant sexual preferences (i.e., they may prefer to have sexual relations with adults, but find adult relationships unavailable or difficult to develop). For these men, offending will typically start during adulthood and may be triggered by rejection. In contrast, Pathway 1 involves multiple dysfunctional mechanisms. These child sex offenders hold severely distorted sexual scripts (sex with children as 'normal') that are likely to reflect a history of child sexual abuse. They also have problems in developing social relationships and controlling emotional states and are likely to have various offence-supportive beliefs relating to children. These men may actively choose children as their preferred sexual partners (i.e., are relatively 'pure' paedophiles), and their sexual offending will typically begin at an early age.

By proposing multiple aetiological pathways, the pathways model provides a conceptually coherent account of child sex offending that can account for the heterogeneous nature of child sex offenders. The recognition that the sexual offending of different sex offenders may be predominantly 'driven' by different causal factors also provides guidance for clinicians as they can target specific deficits or problems during treatment. To date, however, there has been little research carried out to verify the presence of the different aetiological pathways, and there is scope for further theory development, particular in terms of elaborating how the different set of clinical problems may interact to make some men vulnerable to sexual offending (Ward et al., 2007).

Ward and Beech's integrated theory of sexual offending

The final model of sexual offending that we will consider in this chapter is Ward and Beech's (2006; Ward, Fisher, & Beech, 2016) integrated theory of sexual offending (ITSO). This theory is perhaps the broadest in scope of the various theories and models discussed in this chapter. It has been developed to explain sexual offending in general (i.e., against both adults and children) and attempts – as its name implies – to integrate biological factors (e.g., evolution, genetics, neurobiology) with ecological and situational factors (e.g., personal circumstances, and the social, physical, and cultural environment) within a developmental framework to account for the psychological systems that give rise to core clinical problems that lead to sexual offending.

Drawing from Pennington's (2002) neuroscientific account of human behaviour, Ward and Beech (2006) propose that three interacting functional neurobiological systems are responsible for the clinical symptoms that are associated with sexual offending (social skills/intimacy deficits, distorted cognitions, deviant sexual arousal, emotional deregulation). The *motivation/emotional system's* primary function is to adjust the organism's motivational state to changing environmental contexts in the pursuit of specific goals. This system interacts with the *action selection and control system*, which plans and implements behaviour in accordance with goals, and the *perception and memory system*, which processes incoming information and integrates this with existing information in memory. These three neuropsychological systems are, in turn, hypothesised to be influenced by developmental processes that involve the complex interplay of biological (brain development) and environmental (what Ward & Beech, 2006, refer to as the 'ecological niche') factors. Moreover, ecological niche factors not only influence the development of the three neuropsychological systems outlined above, but also interact with these systems to affect behaviour.

This is clearly a complex theory, but a few examples will help to clarify the key processes involved. Consider a child who is brought up in a sexually abusive and neglectful family environment. These developmental experiences may impact on normal process of brain development (themselves influenced by genetic and evolutionary factors that may, for instance, be different for males and females and provide weak predispositions towards impersonal sex or sexual proprietariness) to generate disturbances in the three interlocking neuropsychological systems. For instance, the individual may struggle to form normal relationships with others and to manage emotional states arising from disturbances in the motional/emotional system (emotional states may be poorly recognised and goals inappropriately identified). They are also likely to experience deficits in the action selection and control system that lead to problems in regulating or controlling behaviour. Finally, their perception and memory system may well contain offence-supportive beliefs and deviant sexual scripts that support sexual offending (e.g., the belief that sex with children is normal, or that women 'enjoy' being raped). Because this individual may be motivated to pursue certain goals (e.g., sexual intimacy) through inappropriate means (sexual offending), possess cognitions that support offending, and have a limited capacity to regulate their behaviour when given certain environmental contexts (e.g., the availability of suitable victims) they will have an increased likelihood of sexual offending. Ultimately, the offence behaviour of an individual will feedback into their 'ecological niche' by, for instance, furthering their social isolation or, perhaps, through identification with like-minded individuals.

The ITSO is a relatively new explanatory account of sexual offending and therefore has not been subject to rigorous empirical testing. However, the theory is certainly consistent with research on sexual offenders. By attempting to integrate a diverse range of biological, psychological, developmental, and social/cultural factors the theory, however, provides a useful starting point for further research and theoretical elaboration.

Evaluating theories of sexual offending

No one could accuse social scientists for their failure to develop theory. Indeed, as this chapter has clearly illustrated, for any given phenomenon – like sexual offending – there is typically a legion of different theories, models, and approaches to draw from. Navigating our way through this theoretical thicket is, at times, somewhat daunting. However, it is possible to step back from the three broad theoretical 'approaches' (evolutionary, social-structural/cultural, and social-cognitive) and the six models and theories that we have examined in this chapter (see Table 6.5 for an overview) and identify important points of connection and to outline what is required for any good theory of sexual offending.

First of all, theories of sexual offending need to clearly clarify the important proximate psychological and emotional characteristics that play an important causal role in sexual offending. The available research suggests that they include intimacy/social skills deficits, deviant sexual arousal and interests, emotional regulation problems, and offence-supportive cognitions. Theories also need to identify the important situational factors that might facilitate or trigger sexual offending. These facts include negative emotional states, alcohol and drug problems, opportunities, and available victims.

A complete theory of sexual offending will also need to outline how and why the psychological processes that put individuals at risk of sexual offending arise. This

Table 6.5 Theoretical approaches to understanding sexual offending: a summary

Approach/theory/model	Primary focus (adult or child victims)	Key concepts
Evolutionary	Adults	Parental investment theory, sexual proprietariness, paternity certainty
Social-structural/cultural	Mainly adults	Patriarchy, rape myths, sub-cultures
Social-cognitive	Adults and children	Offence-supportive beliefs, cognitive distortions, implicit theories
Finkelhor's precondition model	Children	Emotional congruence, blockage, internal inhibitions, external inhibitions
Marshall and Barbaree's integrated theory	Adults and children	Developmental vulnerabilities, insecure attachment, fusion of sex and aggression, disinhibiting factors
Hall and Hirschmann's quadripartite model	Adults and children (different models)	Physiological sexual arousal, cognitions that justify sexual aggression, negative affective states or affective dyscontrol, and personality problems
Malamuth's confluence model	Adults	Hostile masculinity, impersonal sex
Ward and Siegert's pathway model	Children	Clinical phenomena, aetiological pathways, primary deficit
Ward and Beech's integrated theory of sexual offending	Adults and children	Motivation/emotional system, action selection and control system, perception and memory system

requires a focus on important developmental processes and how they are shaped by specific developmental pathways and by specific social and cultural inputs. The available evidence clearly supports a prominent role for the experience of adverse developmental environments on later sexual offending. In particular, children who have been physically and, perhaps especially, sexually abused are more likely to develop insecure attachments, hostile views of the world, and specific attitudes and beliefs that may facilitate offending. A broader cultural environment that promotes certain views of women and sexual relations is likely to feed into developmental processes and the emergence of specific attitudes and beliefs that may put individuals at greater risk of offending. Finally, a complete theory of sexual offending will need to recognise that humans are the product of evolution and that certain evolved characteristics of men may make certain forms of sexual offending more likely under certain circumstances. These points should lead to the development of integrated theoretical accounts of sexual offending that can successfully address multiple levels of analysis.

REVIEW AND REFLECT

1   What are the two key theoretical constructs in Malamuth's confluence model of rape?
2   What are some of the main advantages of Ward and Siegert's (2002b) pathway model?
3   Compare and contrast two of the specific models discussed in this section. How are the models similar, and how do they differ? Which model do you think provides the best explanation for sexual offending and why?

SUMMARY

Sexual offences encompass a relatively wide range of criminal acts from comparatively minor behaviours such as indecent exposure through to the serious interpersonal crime of rape. There are significant cross-national differences in the way that different sexual offences are defined although distinctions are typically made based on the gravity of the offence, the nature of the victim, and the relationship between victim and offender. Estimating the prevalence of sexual offending is difficult because a significant proportion of sexual crimes are not reported or recorded and therefore fail to make their way into official crime statistics. However, a range of studies clearly indicate that a significant proportion of all women are victims of sexual offences at some time in their life and that these are most likely to be perpetrated by individuals known to the victim.

Sex offenders are most commonly differentiated based on the age of the typical victim: adult sex offenders are those individuals who largely sexually offend against adults, and child sex offenders are those individuals who typically offend against children. Child sex offenders are also often further characterised based on the age of their victims and their relationship to them. Men with specific and recurrent sexual interests in pre-pubescent children are termed paedophiles. Although there is a considerable overlap in the characteristics of both types of offender, adult sex offenders tend to resemble the offender population more generally. Both adult and child sex offenders are likely to have experienced adverse developmental experiences as children, especially childhood sexual abuse.

A number of broad approaches have been utilised to advance our understanding of sexual offending. These include evolutionary approaches, social-structural and cultural approaches, and social cognitive approaches. Some evolutionary psychologists have argued that rape may be a biological adaptation that has been specifically selected for. However, the available evidence for this claim is somewhat mixed, and it may be more plausible to view rape as the 'by-product' of other evolved mechanisms, such as a tendency for men to control the sexuality of women. Feminist scholars also emphasise the tendency for men to exert dominance and control over women although they see the origin of this tendency as arising from specific social-structural arrangements. A social-cognitive approach to understanding sexual offending focuses on how the way that individuals think about and process social information can influence their behaviour. More specifically, it is argued that both adult and child sex offenders may hold specific offence-supportive beliefs or implicit theories that contribute to their offending behaviour. Thus adult sex offenders may come to accept certain rape myths such as the idea that 'when women say no they really mean yes', and child sex offenders may believe that their actions do not really harm their victims. Although there is some support for the existence of such offence-supportive beliefs or implicit theories and their role in the aetiology of sexual offending, more research is needed.

A number of specific theories of sexual offending have also been developed that, in various degrees, integrate explanations from different levels of analysis although most focus on relatively proximate psychological processes. Finkelhor's precondition model of child sexual offending outlines four key 'pre-conditions' that must be met for sexual offending to occur, Hall and Hirschman argue that there are four primary 'motivational precursors' that drive sexual offending, and Marshall and Barbaree focus on the development processes that can give rise to sexual offending. Each of these theoretical perspectives highlights the role that individual psychological factors can play in the aetiology of sexual offending and thus attempts to explain why some individuals are more likely to become sexual offenders than others. A recent attempt to integrate some of the key features of these three models into a more comprehensive model of child sex offending is provided by Ward and Siegert in their pathways model. A key feature of this model, and one that can help to account for the heterogeneous nature of sexual offending, is the existence of multiple offence pathways each characterised by a primary deficit. Finally, Ward and Beech's integrated model of sexual offending represents an ambitious effort to integrate biological, psychological, developmental, and social factors into a comprehensive theory.

FURTHER READING

Brown, J. M., & Walklate, S. L. (Eds.). (2012). *Handbook on Sexual Violence*. London: Routledge.
A good overview of a range of issues related to sexual offending.

Ward, T., Polaschek, D. L. L., & Beech, A. R. (2006). *Theories of Sexual Offending*. Hoboken, NJ: John Wiley & Sons.
A comprehensive critical overview of theories of sexual offending.

Hald, G. M., Seaman, C., & Linz, D. (2014). Sexuality and pornography. In D. L. Tolman & L. M. Diamond (eds.), *APA Handbook of Sexuality and Psychology* (Vol. 2, pp. 3–35). Washington, DC: American Psychological Association.
An excellent review of the literature on pornography, including its relationship to offending.

Beech, A. R., Miner, M. H., & Thornton, D. (2016). Paraphilias in the DSM–5. *Annual Review of Clinical Psychology*, 12, 383–406.
A comprehensive and critical analysis of paraphilias in the DSM–5.

Lussier, P., & Cale, J. (2016). Understanding the origins and development of rape and sexual aggression against women: Four generations of research and theorizing. *Aggression and Violent Behavior*, 21, 66–81.
Nice summary of recent theoretical work on rape and sexual aggression.

Relevant journals include: *Sexual Abuse: A Journal of Research and Treatment, Trauma, Violence & Abuse*, and *Journal of Sexual Aggression*.

KEY CONCEPTS

- adult sex offenders
- child molesters
- child sex offenders
- cognitive distortions
- hostile masculinity
- impersonal sex
- implicit theories
- offence-supportive beliefs
- paedophiles
- pedophilic disorder
- paraphilias
- paraphilic disorder
- rape
- rapists
- sexual assault
- statutory rape

Collective violence

LEARNING OBJECTIVES

On completion of this chapter you should:

➤ have developed a clear understanding of the nature and extent of different forms of collective violence, including war, terrorism, genocide, and gang violence;
➤ be familiar with prominent evolutionary approaches to collective violence;
➤ be able to recognise the important social-structural and cultural factors that play a role in understanding collective violence;
➤ have an understanding of the key psychological and situational processes that contribute to episodes of collective violence.

Rwanda is a small, densely populated Central African nation that, during April, May, and June of 1994 become the focal point for one of the most brutal genocides in human history (see Criminal Psychology Through Film 7.1). The Rwandan indigenous population is largely made up of two ethnic groups: the minority Tutsis, traditionally cattle owners and given political favour by Belgian colonists prior to independence in 1959, and the majority Hutus, traditionally agriculturists and labourers. After gaining independence a Hutu-dominated political order was established in Rwanda, leading to discrimination and episodes of mass killing directed against Tutsis. As a consequence many Tutsis fled to Uganda where they formed the Rwanda Patriotic Front, a military organisation that launched periodic attacks into Rwanda (Dutton, Boyanowsky, & Bond, 2005; Jones, 2011).

Despite this history of ethnic conflict, Hutus and Tutsis lived in the same communities, attended the same churches, and married one another. What social harmony existed between Tutsis and Hutus, however, was shattered after the plane carrying President Habyarimana was shot down near the Rwandan capital, Kigali. This incident was the catalyst that unleashed an unprecedented paroxysm of killing: in a period of no more than 12 weeks, over 800,000 Tutsis and moderate Hutus were mutilated, raped, and murdered. Although many of the killings were perpetrated by Hutu army and militia forces, thousands of 'normal' Hutu men, women, and children participated in the killing, often using machetes to hack their victims to death. In terms of the sheer rate of killing, the Rwandan genocide was unprecedented as something in the order of 9,000 men, women, and children were killed every day over the three-month period, a rate significantly higher than that which occurred during the Nazi Holocaust (Jones, 2011). Disturbingly, despite the sobering lessons of the Holocaust, and other genocidal episodes in human recent history, the United Nations failed to provide any meaningful intervention, leading to the UN Secretary General Kofi Annan admitting in 2004 that 'the international community failed Rwanda, and that must leave us always with a sense of bitter regret and abiding sorrow' (cited in Jones, 2011, p. 347).

CRIMINAL PSYCHOLOGY THROUGH FILM 7.1
Hotel Rwanda (2004)

Directed by: Terry George
Starring: Don Cheadle (Paul Rusesabagina), Sophie Okonedo (Tatiana Rusesabagina), and Joaquin Phoenix (Jack Daglish)

Hotel Rwanda focuses on the plight of hotelier Paul Rusesabagina, his family, and over a thousand refugees seeking shelter at the Hôtel des Mille Collines while the Rwandan genocide unfolds in all its horror around them. The film not only depicts the sheer terror of the events that occurred in 1994 but also highlights the manifest failure of the international community to do anything to avert or arrest the genocide. The makers of *Hotel Rwanda* later partnered with the UN foundation to create the International Fund for Rwanda to help survivors of the genocide (see www.globalproblems-globalsolutions-files.org/unf_website/PDF/unf_overview_2005.pdf).

Questions for discussion

1 Why did the international community fail to prevent or stop the genocide in Rwanda, and how might have things been different?
2 Director Terry George has said that 'the goal of the film is not only to engage audiences in this story of genocide but also to inspire them to help redress the terrible devastation'. What role do films and other media potentially have to play in facilitating help for those affected by the Rwandan genocide and other similar acts of collective violence?

The Rwandan genocide is, of course, not an isolated example. The historical record clearly illustrates that the human capacity for genocide, war, terrorism, and other forms of collective violence is an important source of suffering, misery, and death in human history. This raises a disturbing, but important question: how is possible that, under some circumstances, so many apparently 'ordinary' individuals are capable of such extreme acts of harm? In this chapter we attempt to provide some preliminary answers to this question. It must be noted, however, that compared to the voluminous literature devoted to understanding interpersonal violence, there is a relative paucity of psychological and criminological research on the origins of collective violence (Winterdyk, 2009). We begin the chapter with a definition of collective violence and briefly outline the four main types of collective violence that we will be focusing on in this chapter: war, genocide, terrorism, and gang violence. We then turn to consider whether the human capacity for collective violence may reflect something about the evolutionary history of our species. Although an evolutionary approach is important for understanding collective violence it is crucial to recognise that every war, genocide, or terrorist act occurs within a broader social, political, and cultural context. As such it is essential that we examine the important role of situational influences and the wider social-structural and cultural context. The main part of this chapter is taken up with a consideration of the prominent psychological and situational approaches to understanding collective violence. Drawing on classic and contemporary research in social psychology we examine the role of authority figures and the psychology of inter-group relations in the genesis of collective violence. We then consider how Bandura's (1999) model of moral disengagement can shed light on the psychological processes that enable war, genocide, and terrorism to occur. We close the chapter with a consideration of the key situational processes that can facilitate acts of collective violence and can help us to understand why, in certain contexts, many individuals are willing to engage in harmful acts directed against others.

THE NATURE AND EXTENT OF COLLECTIVE VIOLENCE

What is collective violence?

In the previous three chapters we have focused exclusively on acts of interpersonal violence. In other words we were looking at acts of violence perpetrated largely by individuals directed largely against other individuals for 'personal' reasons (whether instrumental or expressive in nature). Collective violence also often involves acts of violence perpetrated by individuals directed against other individuals. However, the crucial – albeit somewhat imperfect – distinction is that the individuals concerned are, or are perceived to be, members of particular *groups*. Thus the World Health Organization (2002b, p. 215) defines collective violence as:

> The instrumental use of violence by people who identify themselves as members of a group – whether this group is transitory or has a more permanent identity – against another group or set of individuals in order to achieve political, economic, or social objectives.

Crucially, acts of collective violence are typically characterised by what Kelly (2000) calls *social substitutability*: they are not directed against specific individuals *as* individuals, but rather because those individuals are members of particular groups. Thus, for perpetrators of collective violence it is not important who is targeted as long as they are a member of a particular group (although in some contexts there will be boundaries that circumscribe 'legitimate targets', which may, for instance, exclude women, children, and civilians). Inevitably, as with most definitions, there will be some grey areas. For instance, certain 'hate crimes' may be perpetrated against others of a particular race or sexual orientation because they belong to those 'groups', although the individuals perpetrating the violence may not be acting in an obviously collective fashion on behalf of a particular group. Prototypical examples of collective violence are more straightforward and include the four that we will focus on in the chapter: war, genocide, terrorism, and gang violence. These forms of collective violence are, however, not the only types that we could consider, and rioting, revolutionary violence, and state-sponsored violent oppression may all be considered examples.

War

For the nineteenth-century political theorist and Prussian army officer, Karl von Clausewitz (1780–1831), war is 'an act of violence intended to compel our opponents to fulfill our will' and thus was simply 'the continuation of politics by other means'. This definition pithily captures the essence of armed conflict between large, organised groups of protagonists (states, nations, empires) for largely political and economic reasons. Prototypical examples are not hard to find. The two World Wars of the twentieth century clearly involved large-scale organised armed conflict between allied groups of protagonists. However, not all wars are so easily characterised. The Korean War, for instance, resulted in the death of over two million individuals, yet the United States never formally declared war, and the United Nations officially labelled it a 'police action' (Barash & Webel, 2009). Moreover, since the Second World War most instances of armed conflict have not occurred between or among nation states but rather have occurred *within* states (Pettersson & Wallensteen, 2015; Pinker, 2011). Once we take into consideration the rich anthropological literature on armed conflict – including pitched battles, raiding, and ambushes – between small groups of hunter-gatherer bands (Gat, 1999, 2015; LeBlanc, 2003) then it might appear that a clear definition of war is hard to find. Although definitional issues are important, particularly when we consider whether certain acts of war should be considered to be 'crimes' (e.g., Kramer & Michalowski, 2007), they need not detain us too much here. Although we need to pay attention to the particular social, cultural, and political contexts, the psychological processes underpinning armed conflict between groups of protagonists are likely to share important similarities across the various examples of war considered here.

Organised armed conflict between opposing groups of protagonists – that is, war – is a prominent feature in human recorded history. Archaeological and paleoanthropological research also indicates that war occurred prior to the development of writing and the keeping of historical records (Keeley, 1996; Lee, 2016). The remains of fortifications, rock paintings that depict battle scenes, and mass burials all suggest that collective violence has been a feature of human societies for at least the last 10,000 to 12,000 years, although many would argue that it has occurred throughout human evolutionary history (Gat, 2006, 2015). Quantifying the harm wrought by war in human history is a challenging task, and obtaining accurate figures for the total number of war-related deaths is probably impossible. Matthew White (2012), in his sobering book *Atrocities: The 100 Deadliest Episodes in Human History*, provides 'body counts' for some of the worst acts of collective violence in recorded history including the Second World War (66 million), The Taipang Rebellion (20 million), and the First World War (15 million). Regardless of the precise figures we can confidently assert that war is a relatively frequent feature of human societies (see Table 7.1 for a list of major armed conflicts in the twentieth century) and that it is responsible for an enormous amount of pain, suffering, and death. Moreover, war not only involves harm to combatants, but often also includes the wounding, rape, and killing of civilians (Dutton et al., 2005). It is tempting to conclude that large-scale military conflict of the kind witnessed in the first half of the twentieth century may be a thing of the past. Certainly, there appears to have been a decline in major inter-state armed conflicts since the end of the Second World War, although the number of intra-state or civil wars has increased during the same time period (Pinker, 2011; Themnér & Wallensteen, 2011). Overall, though, there does appear to have been a decline in the number of deaths arising from armed conflict over the last 50 or 60 years (Lacina, Gleditsch, & Russett, 2006), although these numbers do show considerable fluctuation with a significant upswing in battle-related deaths in 2013–2014 (Pettersson & Wallensteen, 2015). However, although the nature of war has changed considerably over the last 100 years (not least due to the development of nuclear weapons), and research suggests an overall declining willingness of individuals to fight for their country (Inglehart, Puranen, & Welzel, 2015), it is probable that war, in some form or other, will remain a feature of our future just as it has been of our past.

Table 7.1 Major armed conflicts of the twentieth century

1899–1902	Boer War
1904–1905	Russo-Japanese War
1914–1918	The First World War
1917–1921	The Russian Revolution
1931–1945	The Sino–Japanese Wars
1936–1939	The Spanish Civil War
1939–1945	The Second World War
1947–1949	The Chinese Civil War
1949–1953	The Korean War
1954–	Ongoing Civil Wars in Africa
1967	The 'Six Day' War
1954–1991	The Cold War
1954–1975	The Vietnam War
1979–1996	The Soviet War in Afghanistan
1982	The Falklands War
1980–1988	The Iran–Iraq War
1991	The Gulf War
1990–1999	Civil Wars in Yugoslavia

Source: Collins Atlas of Military History (2006).

Genocide

Most people reading this book will be familiar with the concept of **genocide**. However, unlike the notion of 'war', genocide was a phenomenon that remained unnamed until Raphael Lemkin (1900–1959) coined the term in the 1940s, and tirelessly lobbied to have it recognised as a crime by the United Nations (Jones, 2011). The essence of genocide involves the intent by a particular social group (or nation state) to destroy or to eliminate another social group, often, but not always, through mass murder. Genocide thus describes a particular behavioural phenomenon, but it is also a clearly articulated legal concept, as outlined in the 1948 Convention on the Prevention and Punishment of the Crime of Genocide (see Table 7.2). There are several important things to note about the United Nations Convention on Genocide. First, the target group can be based on a variety of different characteristics such a nationality, ethnicity, race, or religion. This highlights the fact that genocide involves the targeting of a relatively clearly delineated social group regardless of how membership to those groups is determined. Second, although genocide typically involves the mass killing of target group members, its scope is much broader than this and includes a variety of strategies – the prevention of reproduction, the forced transfer of children, the imposition of certain, harmful 'conditions of life' – designed to destroy the existence of the group. Indeed, Goldhagen (2009) has argued that what unites these, and other acts, is a desire to *eliminate* another social group. This may be achieved through a variety of means, including the mass deportation of people from a particular area, a phenomenon that has been referred to as 'ethnic cleansing' (Altchison, 2010).

Table 7.2 The United Nations Convention on Genocide

Article I
The Contracting Parties confirm that genocide, whether committed in time of peace or in time of war, is a crime under international law which they undertake to prevent and punish.

Article II
In the present Convention, genocide means any of the following acts committed with intent to destroy, in whole or in part, a national, ethnical, racial or religious group, as such:
(a) Killing members of the group;
(b) Causing serious bodily or mental harm to members of the group;
(c) Deliberately inflicting on the group conditions of life calculated to bring about its physical
     destruction in whole or in part;
(d) Imposing measures to prevent births within the group;
(e) Forcibly transferring children of the group to another group.

Article III
The following acts shall be punishable:
(a) Genocide;
(b) Conspiracy to commit genocide;
(c) Direct and public incitement to commit genocide;
(d) Attempt to commit genocide;
(e) Complicity in genocide. .

Source: International Humanitarian Law (2012).

Like war, genocide is not a phenomenon that is restricted to the modern world, and episodes of genocide have occurred periodically throughout history (van Wees, 2010). Again, like war, genocide has been the cause of a barely calculable amount of suffering, pain, and death. Rummel (cited in Adler et al., 2004) estimates that there have been something in the order of 192 million deaths from genocide in the twentieth century alone and some 325 million deaths throughout recorded history. Prominent genocides in the twentieth century include, but are not restricted to:

*   the mass deportation, forced conversion, rape, and massacre of Armenians and other minority Christian groups in the Ottoman Empire from 1915–1923
*   the Jewish Holocaust under the Nazi regime in which up to 6 million Jews were murdered during a five-year period between 1941 and 1945
*   the systematic incarceration and extermination of millions of 'class enemies' and other groups under Stalin in the Soviet Union and Mao in China
*   the forced expulsion and mass killing of Cambodians under the Khmer Rouge in which over a fifth of the Cambodian population died between 1975 and 1979
*   the Rwandan genocide in 1994 in which over 800,000 men, women, and children were slaughtered.

The recent genocide in the Darfur region of Sudan (Hagan, Rymond-Richmond, & Parker, 2005) suggests that, like war, genocide is a phenomenon that unfortunately shows no sign of disappearing in the twenty-first century and is undoubtedly the product of a complex set of individual- and group-level processes (Owens, Su, & Snow, 2013).

Terrorism

The events of September 11, 2001 involving the attack on the twin towers in New York in which close to 3,000 individuals were killed brought the topic of terrorism to the forefront of political agendas in the United States and other Western nations. In the United States Code of Federal Regulations (cited in Federal Bureau of Investigation, 2006) **terrorism** is defined as:

> the unlawful use of force and violence against persons or property to intimidate or coerce a government, the civilian population, or any segment thereof, in furtherance of political or social objectives.

The FBI further sub-divides terrorism into two categories: domestic terrorism (relating to individuals operating within the United States) and international terrorism (terrorism that occurs outside of the United States or crosses national borders). As Schmid (2011) notes, however, 'terrorism' is a 'contested concept', and over 250 different definitions have been provided. In an attempt to capture the core academic consensus on what terrorism is, Schmid (2011, p. 86) offers the following 'revised academic definition of terrorism':

> Terrorism refers on the one hand to a doctrine about the presumed effectiveness of a special form of tactic of fear-generating, coercive political violence and, on the other hand, to a conspiratorial practice of calculated, demonstrative, direct

violent action without legal or moral restraints, targeting mainly civilians and non-combatants, performed for its propagandistic and psychological effects on various audiences and parties.

This definition captures the idea that terrorism is a particular type of physical violence that is centrally concerned with the generation of fear among targeted parties. Terrorist acts may be perpetrated by a wide range of different actors for a diverse array of purposes although often these will be political in nature. Terrorism, then, is a particular type of collective violence that is typically employed in situations that involve asymmetrical power relations between protagonists such that ordinary military action would be impossible or impractical. Marsden and Schmid (2011, p. 173) note a number of different attempts to provide typologies of terrorism including those defined by:

- type of actor (e.g., state terrorism, state-sponsored terrorism, revolutionary terrorism)
- type of method involved (e.g., suicide terrorism, cyberterrorism)
- motive (e.g., religious terrorism, political terrorism)
- geographic range (e.g., domestic terrorism, international terrorism).

As this discussion should make clear, the scope of terrorist acts is broad in nature, and there are a wide variety of terrorist groups in action with different methods, motives, and targets. A number of attempts have been made to keep track of terrorist acts (Bowie & Schmid, 2011) with one prominent effort captured in the Global Terrorism Database (LaFree & Dugan, 2007). This database contains information about over 150,000 terrorist incidents that have occurred between 1970 and 2015, and reflects the growing interest among criminologists in explaining acts of terrorism (Freilich & LaFree, 2015).

Gang violence

The topic of gangs – especially youth gangs – has long been of interest to criminologists. Whether it is 'the mods' and 'the rockers' in the UK in the 1960s, 'the crips' and 'the bloods' in Los Angeles, or 'the mongrel mob' in New Zealand, criminal activities by gangs and inter-gang conflict have been a feature of criminological research and theory. There is considerable disagreement among scholars, however, about what actually constitutes a 'gang', and numerous different definitions have been suggested (Melde, 2015). One influential definition was provided by Klein (1971, p. 13, cited in Melde, 2015) who suggested that a gang is:

any denotable adolescent group of youngsters who (a) are generally perceived as a distinct aggregation by others in their neighbourhood, (b) recognize themselves as a denotable group (almost invariably with a group name) and (c) have been involved in a sufficient number of delinquent incidents to call forth a consistent negative response from neighbourhood residents and/or enforcement agencies.

As you can see from this – clearly youth-focused – definition, what constitutes a gang is a group of individuals who see themselves, and are seen as, a definable group who also engage in some form of antisocial behaviour. Definitional issues preclude any clear picture of the prevalence of gangs or of gang membership. However, according to the 2012 National Youth Gang Survey, there were over 30,000 gangs and 850,000 gang members in the United States in 2012 (Listenbee, 2014).

Gang membership, almost by definition, is a potential risk factor for antisocial behaviour, including violent offending (O'Brien et al., 2013). For the purposes of this chapter our main concern is with inter-gang conflict. This form of violence can clearly meet the definition of collective violence that we have presented: individuals engage in violence against others on behalf of, or together with, a particular social group against others because of their membership in a particular social group. Clearly inter-gang conflict is an important problem in some locations. Gang membership can sometimes be defined, and often reinforced, by reference to other gangs and conflicts over territory, the 'right' to engage in certain types of criminal activities, and retaliation for prior 'offences' often feature in gang conflict (Maher, 2010). In this respect, gangs operate in similar ways to other definable groups that engage in collective violence, and it is likely that there are similar psychological and social mechanisms that underlie such violence.

Summary

Collective violence involves the organised targeting of specific groups of individuals by other groups. As such, although collective violence shares many of the characteristics of interpersonal aggression and violence, the targets of collective violence are often strangers, and death is often the primary objective. The protagonists and targets of collective violence may be specific ethnic, political, or religious groups, organisations, and states. Although the indiscriminate killing of civilians including women and children is a feature of many instances of collective violence, most acts are perpetrated by men (McDonald, Navarrete, & van Vugt, 2012). Given the enormous harm that arises from acts of collective violence, developing explanations for this form of violence is clearly an important task.

REVIEW AND REFLECT

1   How is collective violence different from the sort of violence that we explored in Chapters 4, 5, and 6?
2   What are the key features of genocide?
3   Go to the Global Terrorism Database website (see the link at the end of this chapter), and have a look at some of the maps showing terrorist actions. Where is terrorism most common in the world, and why do you think this is the case?

EVOLUTIONARY APPROACHES

The seeming ubiquity of war, genocide, and other forms of collective violence in human history has led many scholars to the conclusion that our capacity for inter-group violence is firmly rooted in the evolutionary history of our species (Gat, 2006; Van der Dennen, 1995; Wrangham & Peterson, 1996). In short, many have argued that our capacity for collective violence is an evolutionary adaptation: it has been selected for during our evolutionary history because those individuals (or groups) who participated in collective violence were reproductively more successful than individuals (or groups) who did not. Collective violence is, however, a costly activity, which involves a significant risk of mortality for protagonists. It follows, therefore, that in order for it to have evolved, the benefits (in evolutionary terms) must have outweighed the costs. What might be some of the reproductive advantages that could accrue through the use of organised group violence? Most evolutionary hypotheses assume that the benefits of collective violence would have included better access to food and other resources through the expansion of territory, safety through the elimination of threats from other groups, and increased reproductive opportunities for men through the abduction of women, rape, and more in-group reproductive partners (because successful male warriors may obtain more mates) (Gat, 2006, 2009, 2015; Glowacki & Wrangham, 2013; Van der Dennen, 1995; Wrangham, 1999).

Four main sources of evidence are drawn upon to support the idea that collective violence may have been selected for in our evolutionary history (Durrant, 2011):

- the historical and pre-historical record of war, genocide, and other forms of collective violence
- patterns of fighting and inter-group conflict among hunter-gather groups and small-scale societies
- inter-group violence in other species, especially chimpanzees
- proximate psychological mechanisms and processes that appear to be 'designed' for collective violence.

As we have noted in the previous section, war and genocide are apparently ubiquitous features of the historical record (Gat, 2006). The idea that war is somehow intrinsically tied to the development of agriculture and the rise of complex, stratified societies is challenged by the findings that collective violence also appears to be prominent in the archaeological record. For instance, the Oftnet site in Bavaria, dated to around 7,720 years ago, contains a mass grave of some 38 humans who were apparently bludgeoned to death, indicating that they were killed in an episode of collective violence (LeBlanc, 2003). It is important to note, however, that although conclusive evidence for warfare emerges in many places, dating back to the last 10,000 years or so, the extent of this evidence varies from place to place, and we have little conclusive evidence for the existence of collective violence prior to about 12,000 years ago (Ferguson, 1996).

The anthropologist Margaret Mead (1940) suggested that war should be viewed as a cultural 'invention' and that it is typically absent from simple hunter-gatherer societies. As attractive as this scenario appears, it is, unfortunately, contradicted by the available evidence. For instance, Ember and Ember (1996) examined the evidence for warfare in a comprehensive sample of 186 largely pre-industrial societies. They found that war was a relatively constant feature of 38.6 per cent of the sample, occurring at any time during the year. In 27.6 per cent of the sample war was, however, largely 'absent or rare' (i.e., occurring less that once every ten years), although many of these societies had been 'pacified' by external powers, and war may therefore have been suppressed. Thus, although war may be rare or absent for long periods of time among some hunter-gatherer societies (Fry, 2007), it remains a relatively common phenomenon (Gat, 2015).

Collective violence in hunter-gatherer societies takes two main forms: 'pitched battles' and 'raids' (Gat, 2006; Keeley, 1996). Pitched battles involve large numbers of men coming together to face off against one another, as the following description of war among highland agriculturists in New Guinea illustrates (Gat, 2006, p. 124):

> The familiar, formal prearranged battles between communities involved arrow shooting or spear throwing from afar, with the combatants taking cover behind large shields. Called 'small fights' or 'nothing fights' by the Maring, one of those highland peoples, these battles were noisy and could last days and even weeks, but they were much like 'tourneys' (tournaments) and 'deaths or serious injuries in them were rare'. Sometimes 'nothing fights' could escalate to 'true fights' involving close-quarter weapons such as spears and axes.

A somewhat more lethal form of violence is the raid or the ambush where a small group of men from one tribe or clan will enter the territory of another clan (typically under the cover of darkness) and deliberately kill individuals that they find (see Chagnon, 1988). The specific motives for warfare in small-scale societies typically include revenge, the procurement of resources, the abduction of women, and defence (Gat, 2006; Glowacki & Wrangham, 2013; Le Blanc, 2003). For evolutionary psychologists the widespread existence of collective violence among hunter-gatherer groups suggests that such forms of violence may have been prevalent throughout most of our evolutionary history in which our ancestors lived in small, hunter-gatherer groups. However, we should be somewhat cautious in extrapolating from living hunter-gatherer groups as they may not be representative of the kinds of hunter-gatherer groups that were prominent throughout our evolution (Ember & Ember, 1996).

A third source of evidence used to support the idea that collective violence in humans has an evolutionary basis comes from research on lethal inter-group aggression among chimpanzees. In his observations on *Man's Place in Nature* Mark Twain noted that 'man is the only animal that deals in the atrocity of atrocities, war' (Twain, 1966, p. 179). This view was clearly refuted when the remarkable observations of inter-group violence among chimpanzees came to light in the 1970s. Although aggression, violence, and killing are common in a wide range of species, primatologists documented for the first time the coordinated use of violence perpetrated by one group of chimpanzees against members of other chimpanzee groups (Wrangham, 1999; Mitani, 2009). Specifically, groups of male chimpanzees have been observed to engage in apparently deliberate border patrols of their territory and to make deep incursions in to the territory of other chimpanzee groups, deliberately killing males of the other group that they encounter. According to Wrangham's (1999, p. 11) **imbalance of power hypothesis**, 'the function of unprovoked intercommunity aggression (i.e., deep incursions and coalitionary attacks) is intercommunity dominance'. Establishing dominance over other chimpanzee groups may, Wrangham argues, deliver specific evolutionarily benefits such as better access to food resources, safety, and access to females (see also Pandit et al., 2016). The relevance of this research for understanding the evolution of collective violence in humans is clear to many researchers. Because chimpanzees are humans' closest living relatives (sharing a common ancestor approximately 5–6 million years ago), it is possible that the capacity to engage in coalitional aggression or collective violence is a characteristic that was present in our common ancestor and has been retained in both the chimpanzee and human lineages (Wrangham, 1999). We should, however, be somewhat cautious in accepting this hypothesis as we simply do not know enough about the social and group structure of all of the hominid species ancestral to humans, and so we cannot know with any degree of certainty whether they also engaged in collective violence.

A final important source of evidence used to support the idea that collective violence has evolved in humans is the presence of proximate psychological processes that clearly facilitate inter-group conflict. We will discuss these proximate psychological mechanism in more detail below, but of particular importance is the strong human tendency to preferentially favour in-group members (what Choi & Bowles, 2007, term **parochial altruism**) and to be somewhat distrustful and hostile towards out-group members (what is known as **xenophobia**). To what extent these process have evolved to *specifically* facilitate inter-group conflict is, however, a matter of some debate. Plausibly, the tendency to favour in-group members and be distrustful of out-group members would have had other evolutionary benefits such as ensuring individuals cooperate with others with whom they share a common fate (i.e., in-group members) and to avoid those who might impose various costs such as violence or the spread of disease (Faulkner et al., 2004). It is also very likely that *cultural* evolutionary processes have played an important role in the historical development and maintenance of large-scale warfare. Human groups who were better able to coordinate themselves successfully in military encounters against other groups would have led to the spread of these groups and the cultural traits (e.g., norms for self-sacrifice, in-group cohesion, cooperation with strangers) that would have facilitated such success (Zefferman & Mathew, 2015). Indeed, some scholars have argued that collective violence has played a crucial role in the emergence of large-scale groups over the last 10,000 years or so (Morris, 2014; Turchin, 2016).

For many social scientists that idea that war and other forms of collective violence may have an evolutionary basis is an abhorrent one. Indeed, in the *Seville Statement on Violence*, drafted in 1986 by a group of 20 leading scientists, the potential biological basis for war is explicitly rejected: 'It is scientifically incorrect to say that we have inherited a tendency to make war from our animal ancestors ... violence is neither in our evolutionary legacy or in our genes ... warfare is a product of culture' (cited in Adams, 1989, p. 120). However, the apparent cross-cultural and historical ubiquity of war and other forms of collective violence would suggest that warfare is not entirely a 'cultural invention' and that it has some evolutionary basis. It is unclear at this stage whether our capacity for collective violence has been specifically selected for (i.e., is an evolutionary adaptation) or is better viewed as a by-product of other evolved characteristics of our species that emerges under particular social and situational contexts (Durrant, 2011).

SOCIAL-STRUCTURAL AND CULTURAL APPROACHES

Attempts to explain war, genocide, terrorism, and other forms of collective violence have often focused very broadly on social-structural and cultural factors. Indeed, political scientists have invested a considerable amount of effort into understanding the societal-level factors that contribute to war and inter-group conflict. Space doesn't allow us to dig too deeply in to this literature but we touch on a few key approaches.

Social-structural approaches

Because acts of collective violence such as war, genocide, and terrorism involve conflict between groups of individuals it seems reasonable to assume that such conflicts can be instigated and shaped by a range of political, economic, societal, and demographic factors (World Health Organization, 2002b). Potentially important political factors include a lack of democratic processes and unequal power relations in society. Certainly democracies are not immune to engaging in armed conflict as the U.S.-led coalition's invasion of Iraq has illustrated. However, democratic processes tend to (albeit imperfectly) reduce conflict in society through the use of legal processes and regular multi-party elections. When it comes to violence directed against the internal population of a country then it is clear that most of the worst examples (the Stalinist purges, the genocide in Cambodia, the Cultural Revolution in Mao's China) occur in non-democratic regimes that allow autocratic leaders to wield power largely unchecked. There is also some fairly sound empirical evidence to support the idea that – since the twentieth century at least – democracies are less likely to engage in inter-state armed conflict, especially against other democracies (Pinker, 2011; Russett & Oneal, 2001). More generally, instances of collective violence are often associated with political instability and may be more frequent in emerging states that lack the relevant democratic checks and balances. For instance, Fahey and LaFree (2015) found that a country-level measure of social disorganisation significantly predicted terrorist attacks in a sample of 101 countries between 1981 and 2010. This study suggests that in countries where there is a breakdown in both formal and informal processes of social control, terrorist actions become more likely.

A large literature has also focused on the role that various economic factors might play in the instigation and maintenance of armed conflicts and other types of collective violence. For instance, it has been argued that economic globalisation may result in economic inequality that can lead to inter-group conflict due to competition over scarce natural resources that may be unequally distributed (World Health Organization, 2002b). This argument appears to make a greater deal of sense: when certain populations are economically deprived relative to others and when crucial natural resources are scarce or unequally distributed then it seems logical that groups may engage in armed conflict to rectify these inequalities. The available evidence in support of these economic factors is, however, somewhat mixed, and it is not clear that resource scarcity is a major driver of inter-group conflict. Indeed, conflict may be more common when resources are locally abundant and highly profitable (e.g., diamonds, oil), especially in politically unstable states (Mildner, Lauster, & Wodni, 2011; Theisen, 2008). Of course, it needs to be recognised that *perceptions* of economic inequality may be more important in driving inter-group conflict, particularly among groups with a history of violence. It is also important to note that globalisation may also result in perceived threats to religion, traditional family roles, and social structures that may promote acts of collective violence.

A good recent example of an approach to understanding collective violence that links social-structural with psychological factors is provided by Agnew's (2010) general strain theory of terrorism (see Chapter 1 for a discussion of general strain theory). Agnew (2010, p. 131) argues that terrorism arises from 'collective strains': those experienced by members of specific social, religious, or ethnic groups. Strains that are more likely to lead to terrorist acts include those that are high in magnitude, unjust, and caused by more powerful others. Social groups that have experienced deprivation, violence, and discrimination from more powerful social groups may thus be more likely to have members that are willing to engage in terrorist acts. This is because serious and long-standing strains tend to lead to negative emotional states such as anger, humiliation, and hopelessness, which in turn can motivate individuals to pursue membership in terrorist groups as a way of coping. One important implication of this general strain theory of terrorism is that it may be possible to reduce the prevalence of terrorism by enacting policies that ameliorate some of the strain experienced by terrorist groups.

Cultural approaches

In our efforts to explain instances of collective violence it is impossible to ignore the role of specific values and belief systems. Indeed, some of the most harmful acts of collective violence in history have been strongly influenced by specific belief systems or ideologies. An **ideology** can be defined as 'an interrelated set of moral and political attitudes that possesses cognitive, affective and motivational components. That is, ideology helps to explain why people do what they do; it organises their values and beliefs and leads to political behaviour' (Tedin, 1987, cited in Jost, 2006, p. 653). For example, the appalling death toll resulting from the Holocaust was, in part, a consequence of a specific set of ideological beliefs related to the notion of 'racial superiority', the 'pollution' of the Aryan race by inferior genetic stock, and the need to create 'lebensraum' (or living room) for the German people. This example also highlights the important role of leaders in promoting and disseminating particular belief systems (see Padilla, Hogan, & Kaiser, 2007).

From the outside, many instances of collective violence appear highly irrational: individuals willingly risk their lives in the service of particular values, beliefs, or causes that to others might seem irrelevant or even absurd. The anthropologist Scott Atran and colleagues have argued that individuals sometimes behave as 'devoted actors': their actions cannot be predicted from any reasonable assessment of costs and benefits but, instead, reflect their commitment to sacred causes or values (Atran & Ginges, 2012; Atran, Sheikh, & Gómez, 2014) (see Research in Focus 7.1). Sacred values are values that brook no compromise and thus are not subject to negotiation. They operate instead as obligatory moral rules that outweigh any consideration of costs and benefits. Sacred values are often bound up with specific religious belief systems, but secular societies also have forms of sacred values as well (e.g., freedom, democracy) that, under certain circumstances, might be worth fighting – and dying – for.

RESEARCH IN FOCUS 7.1 WHAT FACTORS PROMOTE THE WILLINGNESS TO FIGHT?

Title: For cause and comrade: Devoted actors and willingness to fight

Authors: Atran, S., Sheikh, H., & Gómez, A.   **Year**: 2014

Source: *Cliodynamics: The Journal of Quantitative History and Cultural Evolution*, 5, 41–57

Aims: To explore to what extent 'sacred values' and 'identity fusion' can predict the willingness to make costly sacrifices on behalf of a social group.

Method: 260 individuals were interviewed in two Moroccan neighbourhoods, which have previously been associated with recruitment to jihadi groups in Syria. Participants completed measures that assessed their degree of identity fusion with their 'family-like' friends, the extent to which they viewed Sharia as a sacred value, and their willingness to make costly sacrifices for Sharia (along with additional measures).

Key result:
* Individuals who viewed Sharia as a sacred value and who were completely fused with their social group were more willing to make costly sacrifices for Sharia.

Conclusion and implications: Sacred values and identify fusion interact to predict the willingness to engage in costly sacrifices on behalf of one's social group. 'Devotion to a sacred cause, in conjunction with unconditional commitment to comrades, may be what allows low-power groups to endure and often prevail against materially stronger foes' (Atran et al., 2014, abstract, p. 41).

REVIEW AND REFLECT

1   How does Agnew's general strain theory of terrorism help us to understand the origin of terrorist acts?
2   What are 'sacred values', and how might they contribute to specific cases of collective violence?

PSYCHOLOGICAL APPROACHES

The idea that humans may, in some sense, be 'naturally' inclined to engage in collective violence under certain circumstances is disturbingly illustrated in Christopher Browning's (1992) influential study of Reserve Battalion 101. From 1942, this unit of 500 or so ordinary middle-aged men from Hamburg, many with families of their own, were responsible for the shooting of over 38,000 defenceless Jews and the deportation of thousands more despite the fact that superior officers were willing to excuse those men who were 'not up to the task'. Browning's research and the widespread participation of individuals in episodes of genocide and other forms of collective violence provide strong evidence to suggest that the perpetrators in these events are not suffering from any form of psychopathology or mental illness but rather are, to all extent and purposes, normal (see Box 7.1). However, despite the apparent ease in which the members of reserve Battalion 101 went about their collective killing of innocent civilians there is also a substantial body of research that suggests that humans are typically reluctant to kill their fellow human beings, even in times of inter-group conflict. Dave Grossman (1995), for instance, notes that a significant proportion of soldiers either fail to fire their weapons or deliberately aim to miss their opponents during episodes of armed conflict. The human capacity for compassion and empathy means that we typically avoid harming others where possible, and strong normative proscriptions against killing need to be overcome in order to perpetrate the harms seen in war, genocide, terrorism, and other instances of collective violence (Littman & Paluck, 2015).

BOX 7.1 ARE SUICIDE TERRORISTS 'CRAZY'?

It seems obvious to some people that terrorists in general, and suicide terrorists in particular, must be suffering from some sort of psychopathology. How else could they bring themselves to indiscriminately maim and kill not only 'innocent' civilians, but also themselves? The available evidence, however, suggests otherwise. Although research using actual samples of terrorists is limited for obvious reasons, what research there is provides no support for the idea that suicide terrorists are more likely to suffer from psychopathology. Indeed, it seems that, in most respects, perpetrators of suicide terrorism are pretty much like other individuals in the populations from which they are drawn (Atran, 2003).

How is it, then, that humans can overcome this reluctance to harm others under certain circumstances? In this section we consider some of the prominent psychological approaches to understanding collective violence that have attempted to address this question.

In-groups and out-groups

One of the classic and most widely cited studies in social psychology was conducted in the summer of 1954 and is known as the 'robber's cave' experiment (Sherif et al., 1961). The participants were 11-year-old boys who attended a summer camp in 1954. At the start of the camp the boys were randomly assigned to one of two groups. A sense of group identity quickly developed in each of the two groups. In the second phase of the experiment the two groups competed against each other for prizes. Conflict soon started to develop between the two groups, including name calling and property damage. In the final stage of the experiment the two groups were brought together to work on superordinate goals that required members of the two groups to cooperate. Conflict subsequently declined. This study illustrates some important characteristics of group psychology. First, and perhaps most importantly, humans can readily and rapidly identify with 'in-groups' even when such groups are arbitrarily defined. Second, competition between groups can facilitate inter-group conflict. And, third, when members of different groups are required to coordinate their behaviour to serve common goals, conflict typically declines. What are the implications of this study, and others like it, for understanding real-world instances of collective violence?

The first important point to recognise is that the human capacity to engage in coordinated collective action and to differentiate in-groups from out-groups is a necessary precondition for collective violence as we have defined it in this chapter (Durrant, 2011). For instance, during periods of armed conflict it is necessary to be able to distinguish those that one is fighting with and for ('us' or the 'in-group') from those that one is fighting against ('them' or the 'out-group'). Just how humans accomplish this cognitive task is a matter of some debate, but it is likely that our sense of group or collective identity is based on perceptions of coordinated activity, common fate, collective history and shared norms, values, and attitudes (David & Bar-Tal, 2009). In other words, we identify with individuals with whom we interact with in a cooperative fashion and who are similar to us in important respects.

Not only do humans have the ability to distinguish in-groups from out-groups but there is also a wealth of social psychological research that suggests that we have a strong tendency to favour in-group members and to view them in a positive light at the same time as we tend to view out-group members more negatively (Hogg & Abrams, 2003). This phenomenon has been referred to as parochial altruism, or **ethnocentrism**: the tendency to favour and preferentially interact with members of one's in-group (Choi & Bowles, 2007). **Social identity theory** emphasises how an individual's self-concept is connected to their identification with a particular social group or groups (Hogg & Abrams, 2003). Think for a moment about the social groups that you identify with. If you are like most people your own identity is partly bound up with these social groups. In other words, you care about your social group and will have a tendency to favour your social group over others.

A considerable body of research suggests that the nature and extent of an individual's identification with a social group can influence both intra- and inter-group behaviour. For example, in a series of studies it was found that the degree of 'identity fusion' that individuals had with their group was positively related to pro-social behaviours towards group members, and endorsement of self-sacrificial behaviour, including a greater willingness to die for their country (Swann et al., 2014; Swann, Gómez, Dovidio, et al., 2010; Swann, Gómez, Huici, et al., 2010). In other words, the greater individuals identified with their own national group the more likely they were to engage in behaviours that benefited in-group members even at the expense of members of other groups. In another study, Ginges, Hansen, and Norenzayan (2009) explored a range of factors that might predict support for suicide terrorist attacks in samples of Palestinian Muslims, including religious attendance and prayer to God. They found that the best predictor of support for suicide attacks was religious attendance, suggesting that commitment to a particular social group (what they term 'coalitional commitment') is more important than religious belief per se. It seems clear that the tendency for humans to identify with particular social groups and to favour these groups over others plays an important role in many instances of collective violence, including terrorism (Schwartz, Dunkel, & Waterman, 2009) (see Research in Focus 7.1).

Of course, relationships between members of different groups are not always negative, and most of the time interactions between groups are cooperative, or at least not overtly hostile. Under what circumstances, then, does our tendency towards 'parochial altruism' turn into inter-group conflict? According to **realistic group conflict theory**, when groups compete for scarce resources then conflict is more likely to arise. More generally, when group members perceive that they are *threatened* by out-groups conflict is more likely to occur, even if the nature of the threat is symbolic rather than realistic (Riek, Mania, & Gaertner, 2006). The existence of threats may also promote the categorisation of unfamiliar individuals as out-group members (Miller, Maner, & Becker, 2010).

Conflict between groups may also be more prevalent among groups that have a past history of conflict as previous instances of violence may serve as the basis for ongoing hostilities in a mutually reinforcing fashion – in other words, violence begets violence and may reinforce perceptions of group identity (Littman & Paluck, 2015). Osama bin Laden, for instance, deliberately invoked memory of the Crusades to garner support for actions against Western targets. Invoking memories of historical victimisation for a particular group may also serve to lessen collective guilt for current transgressions. For example, in a series of studies carried out by Wohl and Branscombe (2008) it was found that reminding individuals of past victimisations from out-groups (e.g., the holocaust for Jewish participants, September 11 attacks for American participants) resulted in a reduction in guilt for current harmful actions perpetrated by the in-group (e.g., against Palestinians for Jewish participants and against Iraq for American participants).

An intriguing line of recent research has also explored the potential biological underpinnings of ethnocentrism. De Dreu and colleagues (De Dreu et al., 2010; De Dreu et al., 2011) suggest that the neuropeptide **oxytocin** may play an important role in ethnocentrism and inter-group behaviour. Oxytocin operates as both a hormone and a neurotransmitter, and previous research suggests that it plays a role in trust and affiliative behaviour, particularly among family members. De Dreu et al. (2010) also found, however, that an intranasal dose of oxytocin to male participants (control group members received a placebo) promoted greater in-group trust and, when threatened, more out-group distrust, suggesting that oxytocin may play a critical role in the regulation of inter-group behaviour. Consistent with these findings, a recent study found that levels of oxytocin were elevated in chimpanzees prior to and during periods of inter-group conflict, suggesting a role for the oxytocinergic system in promoting in-group cohesion during bouts of inter-group conflict in our closest living relative (Samuni et al., 2017).

Other research has explored emotional responses during periods of inter-group conflict and their potential neurobiological underpinnings (Cikara & van Bavel, 2014). Consider your emotional response to the success and failure of your favourite sports team: when they win you are likely to experience pleasure, and when they lose you are likely to experience negative emotions. Given the way that individuals identify with the sports teams that they support, this is hardly surprising. However, consider your emotional responses to the successes and failures of a *rival* sports team. If you are like many sports fans you experience pleasure in their failure (or what the Germans term *Schadenfreude*), even when they are not participating against your own team. You are also likely to feel displeasure when the rival team are successful (the Germans have another great word for this experience: *Glückschmerz*). These experiences highlight what psychologists refer to as inter-group empathy bias: the tendency to feel less empathy for out-group members than for in-group members and to even feel counter-empathy (or pleasure) in the suffering of out-group members (Chang, Krosch, & Cikara, 2016; Cikara, 2015; Cikara et al., 2014). These experiences have been shown to have a related neurobiological basis. For example, in one study baseball fans in the United States viewed baseball plays while undergoing functional magnetic resonance imaging (fMRI) scans that measured activity in different regions of their brain. Among other results, it was found that areas of the brain associated with reward were more active both when the favoured team succeeded and when the rival team failed. Moreover, activation levels in response to the rival team's failure were associated with self-reported willingness to engage in various types of aggressive behaviour against the rival team (Cikara, Botvinick, & Fiske, 2011).

The importance of understanding the psychological (and physiological) processes that underlie inter-group interactions cannot be overstated. Collective violence depends on the human capacity to be able to categorise individuals into social groups and is strongly driven by the tendency for humans to favour in-group members and experience hostility against out-group members. Identifying the contexts in which negative inter-group attitudes and behaviours develop will be crucial in our attempts to reduce the harm that arises from inter-group conflict.

Mechanisms of moral disengagement

Most people, most of the time, are reluctant to engage in behaviour that physically harms others. As Bandura (1999, 2002) notes, our sense of self-worth is tied up, in part, with our belief that we are moral agents who behave in ways that are in accordance with our moral standards. As we have seen, certain situational contexts and a strong human tendency to favour in-groups over out-groups can combine to promote collective violence that involves the infliction of harm against others. Bandura argues that various

Reprehensible conduct	Detrimental effects	Victim
• Moral justification • Advantageous comparison • Euphemistic labelling • Displacement of responsibility • Diffusion of responsibility	• Minimising, ignoring or misconstruing the consequences	• Dehumanisation • Attribution of blame

Figure 7.1 Mechanisms of moral disengagement.
Source: Bandura (1999).

social-cognitive mechanisms are activated that allow individuals to maintain their sense of moral self-worth even in the face of extremely harmful behaviour. As outlined in Figure 7.1 these mechanisms focus variously on the reprehensible conduct itself, on the detrimental effects of the conduct, or on the victim.

One of the striking features of many, perhaps most, instances of collective violence is that perpetrators typically view their conduct as *morally justified*. As Baumeister and Vohs (2003, p. 93) note, 'it may be startling to realize that many of the perpetrators of the most horrific acts of violence in the twentieth century were actually motivated by positive ideals'. The enormous death tolls wrought by the Stalinist purges in the Soviet Union and Cultural Revolution in Mao's China were putatively carried out in order to obtain a communist society free of hate, suffering, and inequality. Many terrorists also see their activities as a legitimate, even obligatory, response to perceived injustices and oppression. Even when the harm of the acts are recognised by protagonists they are often downplayed as less harmful than alternative acts in the process of *advantageous comparison*. A good example comes from the American-led coalition's invasion of Iraq, which was variously justified as protecting the free world from the weapons of massive destruction that Iraq supposedly possessed and removing an evil dictator from power. Language can also be employed to make reprehensible conduct seem less harmful through a process of *euphemistic labelling*. Thus, the death of innocent citizens becomes 'collateral damage' and bombing sorties as 'servicing the target' (Bandura, 1999). As we have discussed above, harmful acts are easier to perpetrate when individuals do not feel morally responsible for them. Moral responsibility for reprehensible conduct and the detrimental effects of reprehensible conduct can be disengaged when responsibility for the conduct is either *displaced* (e.g., an individual was acting under a legitimate authority) or *diffused* (e.g., an individual was acting as part of a group).

The detrimental effects of collective violence can also be minimised, ignored, or misconstrued thus making such harmful acts easier to perpetrate. As Bandura (1999, p. 199) notes, 'it is easier to harm others when their suffering is not visible and when injurious actions are physically and temporally remote from their effects'. All the aircrew of the *Enola Gay* (the Boeing B-29 superfortress bomber that dropped the atomic bomb on Hiroshima on August 6, 1945) could see as they flew away was a large mushroom-shaped cloud billowing on the horizon. On the ground, where 70 per cent of the city was obliterated, causing over 80,000 casualties, the images would have been rather different. In short, the modern mechanisms of war allow for the killing of thousands of individuals at a distance thus reducing any 'natural' disinclination to inflict harm that might otherwise be engaged.

A third set of mechanisms work to disengage moral responsibility by focusing on how the victims are perceived. In many contexts of collective violence the victims may be blamed by the perpetrators who might believe that the violence was provoked, incited, or otherwise deserved. In many instances of collective violence there is also a strong tendency to *dehumanise* victims. **Dehumanisation** can take several forms, but centrally involves denying victims full human status. This may involve viewing them as less than human, like animals, or machine-like (Haslam, 2006; Smith, 2011). The use of propaganda during wartime provides a disturbing insight into this process as enemies are routinely depicted as bestial or animal like, or portrayed as vermin or lice that need to be eradicated. Dehumanisation is a powerful mechanism of moral disengagement because individuals are likely to feel less morally responsible for harmful acts if they are perpetrated against groups of individuals who are not viewed as 'fully human' (Haslam & Stratemeyer, 2016). In combination, the mechanisms of moral disengagement provide a variety of strategies that individuals employ to prevent or alleviate the moral self-censure that might otherwise accompany harmful acts, and some research suggests that they may play an important role in attitudes towards war (Aquino et al., 2007; Jackson & Gaertner, 2010).

Clearly there are a number of important psychological processes that can facilitate conflict between groups. However, for much of the time people live happily – often side by side – with individuals from diverse social, ethnic, and religious groups. Unlike chimpanzees where harmonious relations between groups are highly unusual, humans, most of the time, get along with their neighbours. This suggests that there are particular situational contexts and social processes that can foster or facilitate inter-group conflict. In the next section we consider some of these contexts and processes in more detail.

REVIEW AND REFLECT

1   What do we mean by the term 'ethnocentrism'?
2   How might 'identity fusion' contribute to instances of collective violence?
3   Track down some examples of propaganda posters that were employed in World War II. Can you find examples of 'dehumanisation' and how might this have facilitated acts of collective violence during the war?

SITUATIONAL APPROACHES

As we have seen in Chapter 4 and Chapter 5 it is possible to provide explanations for serious acts of criminal violence, like homicide. However, interpersonal homicide is a rare phenomenon: most people will happily live out their lives without killing anybody. Inevitably, this means that the key task is to explain why some individuals are more likely to perpetrate serious violent crimes than are others. The central explanatory task for theories of collective violence is somewhat different. We want to be able to explain why, under certain specific circumstances, very large parts of the population (the male population at least) are willing to injure, maim, and kill their fellow human beings. In short, although we also will look at the psychological processes underlying collective violence, it is essential to understand the specific situational factors that tend to facilitate war, genocide, terrorism, and other such instances of collective violence.

Social influence

Imagine that you are a participant in one of the most famous experiments in psychology. You arrive at the laboratory located at a prestigious university to be greeted by the researchers dressed in white coats. You are assigned the role of 'teacher', and a fellow participant is assigned the role of 'learner'. You discover that your task is to participate in a study on learning in which you are required to teach pairs of words to the learner. If the learner fails to provide the correct answer you will be required to give them increasingly severe electric shocks using a shock generator that contains an array of switches that run from 15 through to 450 volts. The learner is taken to an adjacent room, and the experiment begins. It soon becomes clear that the task for the learner is not all that straightforward, and you are required to administer increasingly severe electric shocks. The learner appears uncomfortable with the procedure, and you hear his yelps of pain as you give him higher and higher shocks. At one point he screams for the experiment to stop, mentioning a recently diagnosed heart problem. How would you proceed? At what point would you stop administering electric shocks or would you go all the way up to 450 volts even as the 'learner' becomes suspiciously quiet?

This experiment and others like it were carried out by Stanley Milgram in the 1960s and early 1970s and are collectively known as 'the **obedience experiments**' (Milgram, 1963; Blass, 2004). Although the 'learner' was actually a confederate of the experimenter who didn't have a heart problem, and the shock machine generated no shocks, the participants were not aware of these facts. The remarkable and often-cited finding from Milgram's first series of studies was that a full 65 per cent of participants were willing to proceed with the experiment up to what would be an intensely painful maximum of 450 volts. This experiment vividly illustrates the 'power of the situation' in influencing human behaviour, with several key processes at work (Miller, 2004). Importantly, the study demonstrated that individuals are willing to inflict harm on others if directed to by a legitimate authority figure. Once the 'learner' started screaming many participants became distressed and expressed their desire to stop the experiment. However, repeated requests that 'the experiment requires that you continue' from the experimenter were typically enough for participants to continue. For Milgram, this illustrated the tendency for individuals to obey authority figures, in part because their own responsibility for the harmful acts could be 'displaced' to the experimenter.

In variations on the basic experimental design Milgram also illustrated that individuals were more likely to proceed to the maximum shock when the 'learners' were physically distant and inaudible and when they had previously witnessed other 'teachers' (actually confederates) deliver the maximum shock. Levels of obedience, by contrast, declined when the 'teachers' were in closer physical proximity to the learners, when they had previously seen other 'teachers' (again confederates) refuse to participate, and when the instructions were delivered by a 'peer' not a white-coated experimenter. It seems that levels of obedience are therefore influenced by the legitimacy of the authority figure, the proximity to the individuals experiencing the painful shocks, and perceived social norms (whether others had complied or not).

The influence of this series of experiments in social psychology has been enormous (Benjamin & Simpson, 2009; Miller, 2016) (see Box 7.2), but what are the implications for our understanding of collective violence? For Milgram (1965, p. 75) who, in part, developed the experimental paradigm in an attempt to understand the Holocaust, the conclusion was disturbingly clear:

> If in this study an anonymous experimenter could successfully command adults to subdue a fifty-year-old man, and force on him painful electric shocks against his protests, one can only wonder what government, with its vastly greater authority and prestige, can command of its subjects.

Although it is important not to overplay the comparisons between a series of laboratory studies and real-world instances of collective violence, such as the Holocaust, some important connections can be discerned (Berkowitz, 1999; Miller, 2004; Zimbardo, 2003). Most acts of collective violence are the end result of a chain of commands issued by authority figures. Although, as Goldhagen (1996) has argued for the Holocaust, it is typically not simply a case of individuals 'obeying orders' because of the fear of the consequences, the very fact that harmful acts are authorised by authority figures allows individuals to displace their moral responsibility for those acts on others. A related point concerns the power of social norms. In the obedience experiments participants are behaving as they believe they are 'expected' to behave, a point highlighted by greater rates of compliance in conditions where participants witness another 'teacher' administer 'electric shocks' up to the highest level. The tendency to act in accordance with perceived norms is disturbingly illustrated in many instances of collective violence such as genocide and terrorism (Roth, 2011). For example, in one study of 35 incarcerated Middle Eastern terrorists, participants indicated that involvement in terrorist groups was *expected* (Post, Sprinzak, & Denny, 2003). As one individual noted: 'Anyone who didn't enlist during that period (intifada) would have been ostracized' (Post et al., 2003, p. 178).

The Milgram obedience studies also illustrate the tendency for individuals to act in accordance to specific social roles. This point was vividly illustrated in another classic study in social psychology, carried out in 1971: the Stanford prison experiment (Zimbardo, 2003, 2007). In this experiment, college students in the United States, screened and cleared for any mental health problems, were randomly assigned to play the role of either guard or prisoner in a simulated prison environment. Guards were issued with military style uniforms and mirror sunglasses, while the prisoners were clothed in shapeless smocks branded with their prison ID numbers. Within a short space of time, the participants appeared to act in accordance with their prescribed roles, as Zimbardo (2003, p. 40) explains:

Pacifistic young men were behaving sadistically in their role as guards, inflicting humiliation and pain and suffering on other young men who had the inferior status of prisoners. Some "guards" even reported enjoying doing so. Many of the intelligent, healthy college students who were occupying the role of prisoner showed signs of "emotional breakdown" (i.e. stress disorders) so extreme that five of them had to be removed from the experiment within the first week.

As a result, Zimbardo called the experiment off after six days.

This experiment illustrates how individuals can engage in harmful behaviour that is in accordance with the roles that they perceive are defined by the social situation. It also highlights how harmful action may be more likely when individuals act in groups in contexts where individual accountability is diminished, a process heightened by the wearing of similar 'uniforms'. Social psychologists call this phenomenon **deindividuation**, and it is prominent in many instances of collective violence. During armed conflicts, for instance, similarly dressed individuals act in a coordinated way in accordance with their role as 'soldiers'. Just like the Stanford prison experiments, although with more deleterious consequences, in times of war guards may act in particularly brutal ways against prisoners as illustrated in the tortures inflicted on Iraqi prisoners of war at Abu Ghraib. In sum, a body of now classic work in social psychology has illustrated the power of the situation in shaping human behaviour as individuals tend to conform to social roles, perceived norms, and the orders of legitimate authorities in ways that facilitate acts of collective violence.

BOX 7.2 REPLICATING MILGRAM

In teaching the Milgram obedience studies to classes of undergraduate psychology and criminology students I typically ask whether individuals believed that *they* would continue with the experiment up to the 450 volts or whether the experiment would produce similar results if conducted today. Most students tend to believe that they would resist the pressure to continue shocking up to the full amount and that if the study was run today the results would be rather different. For years I would have to –somewhat wistfully – announce that 'for ethical reasons, of course, the study cannot be replicated today'. However, in 2006, psychologists Jerry Burger (2009) did just that – replicated the Milgram obedience experiments. They argued that, because 79 per cent of Milgram's subjects continued to the full 450 volts once they heard the learner's protests at 150 volts, it would be possible to reconduct the experiment but terminate rapidly at the 150-volt mark. This would both prevent the prolonged stress experienced by Milgram's participants as they worked their way up to 450 volts but would also give a good indication of how many participants would continue if they were not stopped by the experimenter. The results? Of the 29 men and 41 women who participated in Burger's replication, 70 per cent continued the experiment past the 150-volt cut-off point and were stopped by the experimenter. As Burger (2009, pp. 9, 10) concluded:

> My partial replication of Milgram's procedure suggests that average Americans react to this laboratory situation today much the way they did 45 years ago … in line with those who point to the power of situation variables to overcome feelings of reluctance.

Questions for discussion

1   Why do you think it can be so difficult to resist the power of situational forces even in contexts that involve the infliction of harm on others?
2   Do you think that knowing about the Milgram studies would influence your behaviour in similar real-world situations?

Social processes

Although, as we have seen, situational contexts can exert a powerful influence over human behaviour, the process of 'turning' normal individuals into perpetrators of collective violence often involves a process of socialisation that takes place over time. This is clearly illustrated in work on involvement in terrorist organisations (Horgan, 2008; Kruglanski et al., 2014; Moghaddam, 2005; Silke, 2008). One model of involvement in terrorism suggests that there are three key phases in the 'radicalisation' process (Doosje et al., 2016) (see Figure 7.2).

The first phase, 'sensitivity', highlights how individual feelings of uncertainty and a quest for significance embedded within a broader economic and political context that might involve cultural threat can motivate individuals to identify with particular terrorist groups. This process is more likely when individuals have friends and family members who are sympathetic with, or otherwise involved in, terrorist groups. The second phase, 'group membership', involves a sense of belonging or fusion with the radical group.

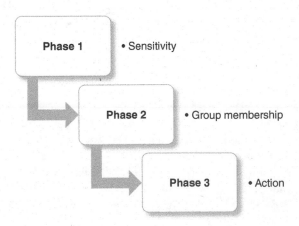

Figure 7.2 The radicalisation process in terrorism.
Source: Doosje et al. (2016).

This process is often facilitated via initiation rituals, the breaking of former group ties, and immersion in group norms and values. In Phase 3 of the radicalisation process individuals engage in violent acts against other groups. Individuals are psychologically prepared to engage in violence as identification with the group entails the acceptance of violent actions as legitimate responses to out-group members.

This model provides a useful framework for understanding how individuals become involved in terrorism, and, like other scholars, the authors note that the involvement with terrorist organisations is often a gradual process (Silke, 2008). More generally, the model emphasises that individuals often have to be socialised into accepting acts of collective violence, and often the process is an incremental one. Soldiers, for instance, typically undergo extensive training in relatively cloistered environments that, among other things, helps to reduce inhibitions against killing (Grossman, 1995). Many instances of genocide also proceed through a comparatively gradual series of stages. The wholesale killing of Jewish people and others during the Holocaust, for instance, was preceded by an extensive propaganda campaign, discriminatory laws, acts of non-lethal violence, and forced deportation. We also see this process at work in the Milgram obedience studies as the incremental nature of the harm inflicted (the escalating voltage of the electric shocks) facilitated the process as each additional level of shock applied was only slightly higher than the one before (complete Activity 7.1 to test your understanding of the key psychological and situational processes involved in collective violence).

REVIEW AND REFLECT

1   Describe the key research findings of Milgram's obedience studies? What are the implications of this research for understanding instances of collective violence?
2   How might individuals be 'socialised' into engaging in terrorist acts?

ACTIVITY 7.1 UNDERSTANDING THE RWANDAN GENOCIDE: KEY PSYCHOLOGICAL AND SITUATIONAL PROCESSES

Read through the following extracts from Hatzfeld's (2005) research with some of the perpetrators of the Rwandan genocide in 1994. For each extract identify the key psychological and situational processes that we have explored in this chapter and that might have contributed to the killing.

Excerpt 1

After the plane crash [in which the Rwandan president was killed] we no longer worried about who had followed the teachings of the presidential party or the teachings of a rival party ... Suddenly Hutus of every kind were patriotic brothers without any partisan discord ... We gathered in teams on the soccer field and went out hunting as kindred spirits.

(Hatzfeld, 2005, p. 13)

Excerpt 2

We no longer saw a human being when we turned up a Tutsi in the swamps. I mean a person like us, sharing similar thoughts and feelings. The hunt was savage, the hunters were savage, the prey was savage ...

(Hatzfeld, 2005, p. 42)

Excerpt 3

We became more and more cruel, more and more calm, more and more bloody. But we did not see that we were becoming more and more killers. The more we cut, the more cutting became child's play to us ... We stopped thinking about obligations and advantages − we thought only about continuing what we had started.

(Hatzfeld, 2005, p. 45)

Excerpt 4

In the evening, we told about Tutsis who have been obstinate, those who had got themselves caught, those who had got away. Some of us had contests ... We had sessions with girls who were raped in the bush. Nobody dared protest that. Even those who were edgy about it, because they had received blessings in church for example, told themselves it would change nothing since the girl was marked for death.

(Hatzfeld, 2005, p. 89)

SUMMARY

Collective violence entails the organised use of violence by individuals who identify themselves as members of a particular social group against individuals of another social group. Prototypical examples include war, genocide, and terrorism. War can be conceptualised as organised armed conflict between opposing groups and has been a prominent feature of human societies across cultures and throughout history. Genocide has also been a prominent feature of human history and involves the attempt by one social group to eliminate another social group. Terrorism is a particular type of collective violence, typically perpetrated by weaker social groups against stronger social groups, with the purpose of generating fear among targeted parties to further particular political objectives. In combination, war, genocide, terrorism, and other forms of collective violence, such as gang violence, are responsible for an enormous among of suffering and death in human history.

The ubiquity of war, genocide, and other forms of collective violence in human history has prompted some researchers to argue that our capacity for inter-group violence has an evolutionary basis. In other words, it has been suggested that our capacity for collective violence has been selected for during the course of our evolutionary history because of the specific benefits that might accrue to groups willing to engage in these forms of violence. The existence of coordinated coalitional aggression among our closest living evolutionary relative, the chimpanzee, provides some support for the idea that collective violence may have featured throughout our evolutionary history. However, the available evidence does not allow us to clearly determine whether collective violence has been specifically selected for or if it is a by-product of other evolved characteristics.

Although the main focus of this chapter is on the psychological and situational processes that can help us understand instances of collective violence, it is important to recognise that acts of war, genocide, and terrorism occur in specific social and political contexts and often reflect a history of antagonisms between different groups. It is thus important to explore the social-structural conditions – such as economic deprivation, inequality, and social threat – and cultural belief systems (e.g., anti-Semitism) that can contribute to acts of collective violence.

Psychological approaches to understanding collective violence have focused on the cognitive processes that underpin acts of collective violence. Of crucial importance is the apparently enduring human tendency to partition the social world into in-groups and out-groups. Moreover, there is a strong tendency to favour in-group members and display hostility or distrust to members of the out-group. Although inter-group relations are not necessarily – or even typically – hostile, conflict may be more likely when group members more strongly identify with the in-group and when they perceive that they are threatened by the out-group. An emerging line of research suggests that aspects of our inter-group psychology may be underpinned by specific neurophysiological processes with an important role identified for the neuropeptide, oxytocin. Typically speaking, humans tend to view themselves as moral agents and therefore behave in ways that accord with their moral standards. Bandura highlights how various 'mechanisms of moral disengagement' can allow individuals to maintain this view of themselves while perpetrating harmful acts against others.

Situational approaches to understanding collective violence emphasise the 'power of the situation' in shaping human behaviour and hence can provide an explanation for why instances of collective violence are typically perpetrated by otherwise 'normal' individuals. Several classic studies in social psychology, including the Milgram obedience studies and the Stanford prison study, illustrate how individuals may come to engage in harmful behaviour against others when they act according to the perceived roles and norms demanded by the situation. Involvement in acts of collective violence is also shaped by powerful social processes that serve to socialise individuals into perpetrating violent acts.

FURTHER READING

There is now an enormous literature devoted to war, genocide, and terrorism. Good single-volume overviews of genocide are provided by Jones (2011) and Bloxham and Moses (2010). For those interested in exploring the vast literature on terrorism, the book by Martha Crenshaw (2011) is a good place to start. A general social scientific overview of war is provided by Owens et al. (2013). For evolutionary approaches to collective violence see Lopez (2016) and Gat (2015). There is a huge psychological literature on inter-group relations and inter-group conflict but Littman and Paluck (2015) offer a good review of the relevant psychological and social processes. For an overview of inter-group empathy bias see Cikara (2015), and for a review of work on the role of identity fusion start with Swann and Buhrmester (2015).

Crenshaw, M. (2011). *Explaining Terrorism: Causes, Processes, and Consequences*. London: Routledge.
A useful introduction to terrorism.

Jones, A. (2011). *Genocide: A Comprehensive Introduction* (2nd Edition). London: Routledge.
A good source for information about genocide.

See the special issue of *Science* (May 18, 2012, Vol. 336) for an accessible collection of articles on inter-group conflict and collective violence.

Cikara, M. (2015). Intergroup schadenfreude: motivating participation in collective violence. *Current Opinion in Behavioral Sciences*, 3, 12–17.
A short accessible overview of the work on inter-group empathy bias.

Gat, A. (2015). Proving communal warfare among hunter-gatherers: The quasi-Rousseauan error. *Evolutionary Anthropology*, 24, 111–126.
A useful starting point for considering evolutionary approaches to collective violence.

Littman, R., & Paluck, E. L. (2015). The cycle of violence: Understanding individual participation in collective violence. *Advances in Political Psychology*, 36, 79–99.
A good review of the relevant psychological and social processes involved in inter-group conflict and collective violence.

Research on all facets of collective violence and inter-group conflict can be found across a diverse range of psychological, criminological, and other social scientific journals. Two journals dedicated to such research are: *Journal of Peace Research* and *Terrorism and Political Violence*.

WEB RESOURCES

Global Terrorism Database: www.start.umd.edu/gtd.
For a list of the worst atrocities in human history, see http://necrometrics.com/pre1700a.htm.
On the Stanford prison experiment, see www.prisonexp.org.

KEY CONCEPTS

- dehumanisation
- deindividuation
- ethnocentrism
- genocide
- ideology
- imbalance of power hypothesis

- obedience experiments
- oxytocin
- parochial altruism
- realistic group conflict theory
- social identity theory

- terrorism
- xenophobia

Drugs and crime

LEARNING OBJECTIVES

On completion of this chapter you should:

➤ have developed an understanding of how drugs are classified, patterns of drug use, and the distinction between drug use and misuse;
➤ understand the different theoretical approaches to explaining drug use and misuse;
➤ be familiar with relevant literature that demonstrates an association between drug use and crime;
➤ be able to describe three important models for explaining the association between drugs and crime.

On January 21, 2003 at 8.30 a.m. Antonie Dixon downed a cocktail of orange juice, cocaine, and methamphetamine at a house in Pipiroa on the Hauraki Plains, New Zealand. Dixon's violent crime spree began later that day when he attacked his girlfriend Renee Gunbie with a hammer, breaking her arm. Then, wielding a samurai sword, he sliced off Gunbie's right hand before attempting to scalp her, later telling psychiatrist Karl Jansen that 'God told him to' ('God ordered Dixon', 2005). Dixon also attempted to decapitate former girlfriend, Simone Butler, mutilating both her hands with the sword as she raised her arms to protect herself. He then stole a car and drove to the car park of a shopping centre where he shot to death James Te Aute with a home-made sub-machine gun. He later picked up a hostage, but finally surrendered to police in the early hours of the next day (Cleave, 2005). Although Dixon pleaded not guilty by reason of insanity to these assaults and murder, he was subsequently found guilty and sentenced to life imprisonment with a 20-year non-parole period (Leigh, 2007). Dixson died in prison in 2009.

The role that methamphetamine (known in New Zealand as 'P' or 'Pure') played in this crime spree is clearly illustrated in the subsequent news media's coverage of the assaults and murder. Headlines in the *New Zealand Herald* proclaimed 'Drug "pure" linked to sword attacks and gunshot death' (Wall & Horwood, 2003, para 1) and 'A powder keg ignited by P' (Cleave, 2005, para 1). The New Zealand police also clearly fingered methamphetamine in the genesis of Dixon's offending: 'Police who dealt with Dixon are confident they know exactly what turned him from a troubled petty criminal who aspired to notoriety into a homicidal madman: the drug P, a pure form of methamphetamine' (Cleave, 2005, para 14). Dixon, however, had a long history of involvement in crime, with over 150 convictions for various offences including theft and assault. What role, then, did methamphetamine play in the events of January 21, 2003? Would Dixon have committed these crimes even without consuming methamphetamine, or were the attacks directly attributable to his consumption of this drug?

The sale, manufacture, and use of many drugs, such as cocaine, cannabis, and methamphetamine, are crimes in themselves. Drug use, as the case of Antonie Dixon illustrates, has also been *associated* with other kinds of offences such as theft, assault, and murder. The relationship between drug use and crime, however, is not straightforward: clearly not everyone who consumes methamphetamine becomes a sword wielding 'homicidal madman', yet the use of such drugs may heighten the risk for aggression and violence for some individuals. To fully understand the role that drugs play in offending we need to carefully examine a number of important contributing factors such as the type of drug, the type of crime, the user, and the social context of use.

Drugs are a virtually ubiquitous feature of human cultures, and their use has been recorded throughout history. From the ingestion of hallucinogenic fungi among the Aztec of Central America to the kava ceremonies of the South Pacific to the more familiar contemporary Western consumption of alcohol, tobacco, cannabis, and cocaine, humans have been attracted to substances that have the alluring capacity to alter consciousness (Durrant & Thakker, 2003). Drug misuse, however, is a major social problem in many countries. Globally, there are over 200,000 drug-related deaths every year, and an estimated 29 million individuals suffer from a drug use disorder (United Nations Office on Drugs and Crime, 2016b). Drug use has also been strongly linked to crime, and tackling drug use and drug-related offending is an important objective for government policy.

In this chapter we will explore the nature and extent of drug use in society and look at some of the theories that have been used to explain why people use and become addicted to psychoactive substances. We will then examine the research that suggests that there is a relationship between drugs and crime, before exploring in detail different theoretical models that have been used to explain this relationship.

WHAT ARE DRUGS?

Most people have an intuitive idea of what is meant by the term 'drugs'. In medicinal contexts, the term may make people think of pharmaceutical products like aspirin, Prozac, or even Viagra. In the context of crime, the term 'drugs' is likely to conjure up rather different images of recreationally used substances such as cannabis, cocaine, and heroin. Durrant and Thakker (2003, p. 14) define drugs as 'any substance, whether natural or artificial in origin, which, when taken into the body in sufficient quantities, exerts a non-negligible effect on a person's perceptions, cognition, emotion, and/or behaviour'. Although this definition is somewhat longwinded it captures the idea that the kinds of drugs that psychologists (and, indeed, criminologists) are primarily interested in are *psychoactive* drugs, especially those that are used in recreational or non-medicinal contexts.

Drug classification and the effects of drugs

The number of substances, of natural or artificial origin, that have the capacity to alter perception, cognition, and behaviour is truly staggering. The ethnobotanist Richard Schultes (1990), for example, documents around a hundred hallucinogenic plants that are native to North and South America alone. Many additional substances have also been developed in the laboratory over the last 150 years, including crystal methamphetamine, LSD, and ecstasy (3,4-methylenedioxy-methamphetamine, MDMA), and this process continues at a seemingly increasing rate (see Box 8.1). There are a number of different ways that these substances can be classified (Abadinksy, 2014; Maisto, Galizio, & Connors, 2004, pp. 4–5; Julien, 1998). One straightforward way is to make a distinction between legal and illegal drugs. This distinction is obviously important from a criminological perspective as the sale and use of some drugs can be punished by the criminal justice system. The legal status of drugs is discussed in more detail below. Different drugs also have characteristically different physiological and psychological effects on users due to the way that they act on the central nervous system. In Table 8.1 the main pharmacological classes of drugs are illustrated with examples, typical mode of use, and characteristic short-term effects.

Table 8.1 The pharmacological classification of psychoactive drugs

Class of drugs	Examples	Methods of ingestion	Typical short-term effects[a]
Opiates	Opium, morphine, heroin	Ingested, smoked, sniffed, injected	Euphoria, pain relief, sedation, relaxation, depressed respiration, nausea, constipation, pupil constriction.
Stimulants	Cocaine, crack cocaine, amphetamine, methamphetamine, caffeine (ecstasy)	Ingested, snorted, smoked, injected, (ingested)	Elation, excitement, increased energy, alertness, reduced fatigue, insomnia, increased heart rate and blood pressure, increased sweating, paranoia, repetitive behaviours (euphoria, emotional warmth, increased heart rate and blood pressure, increased body temperature).
Depressants	Alcohol, barbiturates, GHB	Ingested	Euphoria, relaxation, disinhibition, impaired perception and thinking, sedation.
Hallucinogens	LSD, Mescaline, psilocybin	Ingested	Perceptual distortions, enhanced sensory awareness, labile emotions, disturbed cognition, anxiety and panic, pupil dilation.
Cannabis	Marijuana, hashish	Oral, smoked	Euphoria, relaxation, altered perceptions, altered time perception, impaired short-term memory, blood-shot eyes, increased heart rate.

Sources: [a]Julien (1998); Maisto et al. (2004); Mosher and Atkins (2007).

BOX 8.1 NEW PSYCHOACTIVE SUBSTANCES

Nature has been bountiful with its range of plants (and other organisms – e.g., fungi, toads) that, when ingested, generate psychoactive effects. The vast majority of these substances are illegal in most countries, and their possession, sale, and use attract criminal penalties. In large part to avoid these sanctions, the ingenuity of human chemists have generated even more drugs that have the capacity to alter consciousness – these are typically referred to as **new psychoactive substances** (NPS). The growth of NPS has been quite extraordinary: in 2005 around 16 NPS were reported; this figure has since skyrocketed to over 550 (Reuter & Pardo, 2016b). Governments have been unsure how to deal with these NPS, although in recent years the default strategy appears to be a simple prohibition on all psychoactive substances that are not otherwise exempt (e.g., alcohol, nicotine, and drugs used for medical purposes). This approach has been criticised by many as excessive and unhelpful in reducing drug-related harm (see Barratt, Seear, & Lancaster, 2017; Reuter & Pardo, 2016a, 2016b; Soussan & Kjellgren, 2016).

Question for discussion

Why have governments been so quick to prohibit NPS without a detailed analysis of their potential harms and benefits?

Drugs are commonly classified in terms of their typical psychopharmacological effects on users. However, there is no simple one-to-one relationship between the ingestion of a drug and the subjective experience of that drug's effects. Rather, the nature of the drug experience is shaped not only by the drug itself and how it is administered, but also by characteristics of the user and the context of use (Maisto et al., 2004).

The legal status of drugs

A distinction is drawn in most countries between legal and illegal substances. Drugs that are legal in most countries, such as alcohol and tobacco, are also subject to certain restrictions on sale and purchase (such as age), but within these restrictions their sale and use are not subject to criminal sanctions. Illegal drugs are often further classified into separate 'classes', which are related to different levels of penalty that an individual is subject to if they are convicted for sale, manufacture, or possession of that substance. The basis for these classification schemes varies in different countries. In the United States, drugs are assigned to classes based on their potential for abuse, likelihood of dependence, and accepted medical use. In the United Kingdom, drug classification is based on actual misuse, potential for misuse, and the harmfulness of the drug. And in New Zealand, drugs are allocated to different schedules based on the risk that they pose to individuals or society.

The harmfulness of drugs is the primary rationale for the division between legal and illegal drugs and the classification of illegal drugs into separate classes. However, it has been noted that the legal status of drugs does not map cleanly onto the harmfulness of different drugs when evaluated in an objective fashion (Room, 2006). Ranking drugs in terms of their harmfulness is not a simple task. Significantly, the concept of harm is not a unitary one (MacCoun & Reuter, 2001). Different drugs are harmful in different kinds of ways. Some drugs, such as heroin and alcohol, put users at a much greater risk of dying from a drug overdose than do other substances such as cannabis, LSD, and magic mushrooms (Gable, 2004). If risk of addiction was our criterion for harmfulness, however, then heroin, cocaine, and tobacco might rank as our most harmful drugs (Nutt et al., 2007).

One attempt to quantify the harmfulness of different drugs is provided by Nutt et al. (2007). Using a combination of 'physical harm', 'risk of dependence', and 'social harms', the authors constructed a scale to measure the harmfulness of a range of psychoactive substances, both licit and illicit. The outcome of this analysis for selected drugs is illustrated in Figure 8.1. There are two key implications that can be drawn from this study. First, as the authors note, the study did 'not provide justification for the sharp A, B, or C divisions of current classifications in the UK Misuse of Drugs Act' (Nutt et al., 2007, p. 1051). Second, the currently legal substances, alcohol and tobacco, were rated as more harmful than many illicit drugs including cannabis, LSD, and ecstasy, questioning the legal demarcation between these different substances.

This study and other similar attempts to evaluate the harmfulness of drugs (e.g., Gable, 2004) and the rationale of current classification schemes raise important questions about the way drugs are regulated in society. While it should be recognised that the harmfulness of drugs can be influenced by their legal status (e.g., legal drugs are more widely used, and illegal drugs may be used less often but in more dangerous ways), it is clear that the sharp division between licit and illicit substances and the finer gradations between illegal drugs are not firmly grounded in any objective measure of the harmfulness or dangerousness of these substances (Room, 2006).

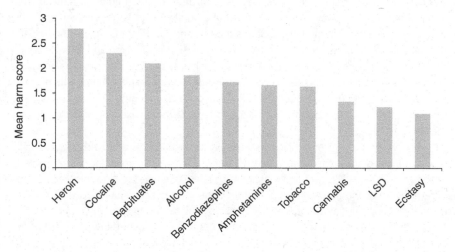

Figure 8.1 Mean harm scores for ten drugs.
Source: Adapted from Nutt et al. (2007).

In part motivated by challenges to prevailing views about the harms of different psychoactive substances, along with the often negative impacts of drug prohibition, a number of jurisdictions in recent times have experimented with the legalisation of specific drugs, notably cannabis. Voters in Colorado and Washington supported a legal market in cannabis in 2012, and a number of other states have since followed this lead. Globally, there appears to be a growing view that the existing model of drug prohibition needs to be changed (e.g., Global Commission on Drug Policy, 2016). However many have voiced concerns about the public health implications of drug legalisation (Hall, 2016; Room, 2013), and finding a balance between harms of prohibition and the potential harms of legalisation remains a gnarly issue for policy makers world-wide.

REVIEW AND REFLECT

1   Imagine that you could reclassify all psychoactive substances from scratch. Which drugs would you make illegal and why?

WHO USES DRUGS?

If we accept that the term 'drugs' includes licit substances such as alcohol, tobacco, and caffeine, then it is clear that almost everyone in Western cultures has tried a drug at least once in their life, and many individuals use drugs on a daily basis. In this section, however, we will largely focus on the use of illicit drugs, although some comparisons will be made with the use of alcohol where relevant.

Many Western countries regularly collect data on the use and misuse of illicit substances, along with other drug-related information such as attitudes towards drugs, the cost of illicit substances, and so on. A good deal of information is derived from national population surveys of adults and young adults, using large samples and self-report questionnaires. In the United States the National Survey of Drug Use and Health provides annual information on drug use among those 12 and over, and the Monitoring the Future Study provides yearly data focused primarily on drug use among secondary school students and young adults. In England and Wales annual information about illicit drug use among those aged 16–59 is provided by the British Crime Survey, and other countries such as Canada, Australia, and New Zealand have similar (although less regular) surveys.

The prevalence of lifetime illicit drug use – those individuals who have taken specific drugs at least once in their life – for England and Wales, Australia, and New Zealand is shown in Table 8.2. Direct cross-national comparisons need to take into account the different year of the survey and the different age ranges sampled; however, a number of general conclusions can be drawn. Cannabis is by far the most commonly used illicit drug with from 30 per cent (England and Wales) to 45 per cent (New Zealand) of the population having used cannabis at least once in their life. No other illicit drug has been used by more than 15 per cent of the population. To put these *lifetime* illicit drug

Table 8.2 Prevalence of lifetime illicit drug use

Drug	Australia[a] (%)	England and Wales[b] (%)	New Zealand[c] (%)
Cannabis	34.8	29.2	46.4
Cocaine	8.1	9.8	3.6
Amphetamine/ methamphetamine	7.0	10.3	7.2
Ecstasy	10.9	9.2	6.2
Heroin/opiates	1.2	0.9	n/a

Sources: [a]Age 14 years and over (Australian Institute of Health and Welfare, 2014); [b]age 16–59 years (Lader, 2015); [c]age 16–64 years (Ministry of Health, 2010).

prevalence figures in perspective, it is worth noting that 80.7 per cent of Australians aged 14 and over (Australian Institute of Health and Welfare, 2014) and 81.2 per cent of New Zealanders aged 12–65 (Ministry of Health, 2007) report using alcohol in the *last year*, and in most Western countries more people have consumed alcohol in the past year than have tried illicit drugs in their lifetime.

In comparison, a relatively small proportion of the population reports using illicit drugs in the last year or last month. For example, in England and Wales 3.7 per cent of individuals aged 16–59 years report using cannabis in the last month, and less than 1 per cent report using cocaine (Lader, 2015). The use of illicit drugs is, however, more common among some portions of the population than others. In general, men are more likely to consume illicit drugs than women, and adolescents and young people are more likely to be recent drug users. The robust relationship between age, sex, and recent illicit drug use is shown for England and Wales in Figure 8.2. This graph clearly illustrates that the use of drugs in the past year is much more common among 16–24-year-olds, with the prevalence of recent drug use declining sharply with age. It also demonstrates that males are more likely to use illicit drugs than females, although the reasons why this is the case remain a matter of some debate (e.g., Becker, McClellan, & Reed, 2016; Fattore & Melis, 2016).

Although the validity of self-report surveys of illicit drug use is generally recognised by researchers, they are likely to under-report the use of illegal substances for several important reasons. First, many respondents may not feel comfortable in responding to questions about an activity that, after all, is illegal. They may, therefore, deny or minimise their drug-taking experiences. This may be especially likely for self-reported use of 'harder' drugs such as heroin and cocaine, which carry stiffer penalties in most countries. Second, population-based surveys may fail to sample a number of high-risk groups such as prisoners, the homeless, and those heavy drug users with 'chaotic' lifestyles (Mosher & Atkins, 2007; Newcombe, 2007).

In sum, despite the limitations of population-level self-report surveys, they provide a fairly consistent picture of illicit drug use in largely English-speaking Western countries. Somewhere between a third and a half of all individuals try an illicit drug at least once in

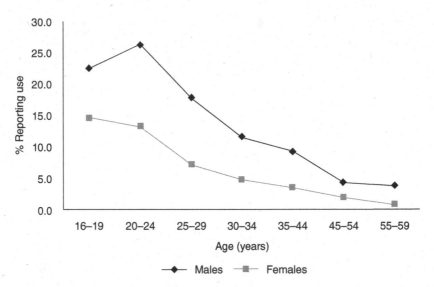

Figure 8.2 The prevalence of last year use of illicit drugs in England and Wales by age and sex. *Source:* Lader (2015).

their life, with cannabis by far the most frequently tried substance. Less than a tenth of the population report using an illicit drug in the last month, and the weekly use of alcohol is more common in the general population than the lifetime rates of trying any illicit drug. Drug use is, however, more common among some portions of society, especially adolescents and young adults.

REVIEW AND REFLECT

1   Review the lifetime prevalence data for selected illicit drugs depicted in Table 8.2. Why do you think that cannabis is by far the most widely used illicit drug in these countries?

2   Review the prevalence of last year drug use by age and sex in Figure 8.2. This pattern appears to be similar to gender and age differences in offending more generally – do you think there are similar explanations for drug use as well?

DRUG USE AND MISUSE

As the prevalence figures outlined in the previous section indicate, most individuals *use* psychoactive substances (including alcohol) at some time in their life. At what point can we consider that this drug use becomes drug *misuse*? The answer to this question is not straightforward. Many consider *any* use of illicit drugs as necessarily constituting drug misuse, but this perspective rests on the legal status of drugs rather than the actual harms they cause to individuals or society. Figure 8.3 provides a broader view of drug use and misuse that recognises that individuals can use drugs, including illicit drugs, without necessarily experiencing any significant problems. Of course, many individuals *do* have problems with drug use: drugs are used more frequently and with more negative social, health, and legal consequences than users often anticipate. In the DSM–5 a **substance use disorder** is described as a 'cluster of cognitive, behavioral, and physiological symptoms indicating that the individual continues using the substance despite significant substance-related problems' (American Psychiatric Association, 2013, p. 483).

In order to be diagnosed with a substance use disorder for any particular substance an individual must experience two or more of the 11 symptoms depicted in Table 8.3 in the last 12 months. As illustrated in Table 8.3 there are four main clusters of issues that can arise with problematic drug use: impaired control over the use of the drug, social impairment, use despite risks, and pharmacological indicators including tolerance and withdrawal. The DSM–5 criteria allows for a substance use disorder to be diagnosed along a continuum from less to more severe and recognises that multiple problems that often arise with problematic drug use.

Using the DSM–5 criteria for substance use disorders, in the United States it was estimated that 21.5 million individuals aged 12 years and over (9 per cent of the population) met the criteria for a substance use disorder in 2014. Of these individuals, approximately 17 million had an alcohol use disorder, 7.1 million had an illicit drug use disorder, and 2.6 million had an alcohol *and* illicit drug use disorder (Center for Behavioral Health Statistics and Quality, 2015).

In addition to substance use disorders outlined above, which relate to repeated patterns of drug use, other problems can arise from occasional use or the acute effects of drugs. For example, an individual who may not have a substance use disorder may end up in an emergency room department due to paranoia brought on by the ingestion of methamphetamine or due to health problems as the result of the excessive consumption of alcohol. Figure 8.3 captures the idea that other drug-related problems can arise in addition to those relating to drug dependence and drug abuse.

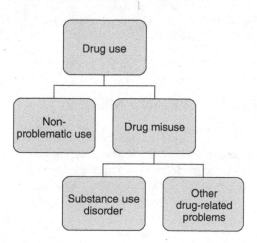

Figure 8.3 Drug use and misuse.

Table 8.3 DSM–5 criteria for substance use disorder

Impaired control	Social impairment	Risky use	Pharmacological indicators
Taken more/longer than intended	Important activities given up because of use	Recurrent use resulting in physically hazardous behaviour	Tolerance
Desire/unsuccessful efforts to quit use	Recurrent use resulting in failure to fulfil important role obligations	Use despite knowledge of problems associated with use	Withdrawal
Craving for substance	Continued use despite recurrent social problems associated with use		
Great deal of time taken by activities involved in use			

Sources: American Psychiatric Association (2013); MacCoun (2013).

Drug use can be thought of as occurring on a continuum: from relatively moderate, non-harmful patterns of use though to the increasingly harmful patterns of use characterised by a severe substance use disorder. Even though a single episode of drug use may lead to drug-related problems, most of the harms associated with drug use in society – including, as we shall, see, much of drug-related crime (Bennett & Holloway, 2005) – is the result of the regular, heavy consumption of drugs among individuals who meet the criteria for a substance use disorder.

REVIEW AND REFLECT

1   What are the diagnostic criteria for a substance use disorder according to the DSM–5?

THEORIES OF DRUG USE AND MISUSE

Why do people use and misuse drugs? Before we examine some of the major approaches that have been developed in order to answer this question, think about your own experience of drug use. What factors led you to try a drug for the first time (and remember, alcohol, tobacco, and caffeine are all drugs)? Or, conversely, why did you decide *not* to try a drug? What factor or factors led you to continue drug use, or to desist from the use of drugs once you had started using? A moment's reflection will probably lead you to the conclusion that the answer to the question posed at the start of this section is not likely to be particularly straightforward. The reason why people take drugs depends both on the type of drug used and the stage of drug use considered. The reason why a 14-year-old has a puff on a cigarette for the first time with her friends at a party is likely to be very different from the reasons why a dependent heroin user seeks another shot. In thinking about the different approaches to explaining drug use we need to keep in mind that a theory that accounts for trying drugs or using drugs recreationally may not explain why someone who is dependent on drugs continues to use despite the profoundly negative consequences of their drug use (West, 2001). Different theories of drug use, like any behavioural phenomenon, are also drawn from different levels of analysis. In this section we will look at biological, psychological, and social-structural and cultural approaches to understanding why people use and misuse psychoactive substances.

Biological approaches

Consider the following scenario. A rat is put in a Skinner box, and every time it pushes down a small metal bar it receives a dose of cocaine. The rat appears to like what it gets and continues to push down the bar, neglecting opportunities for feeding and mating. Under some conditions the rat will continue to self-administer cocaine to the point of exhaustion or even death (Koob & Le Moal, 2006). A wide range of different drugs are reliably self-administered by a number of different animal species, suggesting that drugs act on basic brain mechanisms in ways that promote use.

According to the positive-reinforcement model of drug use (Meyer & Quenzer, 2005), drugs are taken because they generate positive emotional states. In short, people take drugs because they make them feel good. Researchers have found that, although different drugs act on different neurotransmitter systems in the brain, most drugs of abuse appear to increase levels, either directly or indirectly, of the neurotransmitter dopamine in an area of the brain known as the mesolimbic dopamine pathway (Picciotto, 1998). However, the evidence for dopamine activation is strongest for stimulant drugs like cocaine and amphetamine, and it is likely that other neurotransmitter systems also play a critical role (Nutt et al., 2015). Nesse and Berridge (1997) have argued that the mesolimbic dopamine pathway might reflect a natural reward pathway that has evolved to signal the presence of adaptively relevant stimuli to organisms, like food, sex, and water. Drugs of abuse, it is suggested, effectively 'hijack' this system, producing a profound sense of pleasure that promotes repeated use (Durrant et al., 2009).

There is no doubt that the ability of drugs to produce positive emotional states can encourage their repeated consumption. However, individuals who use drugs over a long period of time tend to report experiencing *less* pleasure from drug use even though their *craving* for the drug increases. Part of the reason why they continue to use drugs is to avoid the negative consequences of aversive withdrawal symptoms that occur if drug use is discontinued. This does not appear to be the whole story, however. According to the **incentive-sensitisation model** (Robinson & Berridge, 2001, 2003) it is important to make a distinction between drug *liking* and drug *wanting*. Robinson and Berridge (2003) suggest that the pleasure of drug use (liking) declines over time, and the craving for drugs (wanting) increases, as a result of changes in the nervous system that arise from repeated drug use. Specifically, they suggest that the mesolimbic dopamine pathway, discussed above, is critically involved in the process of **incentive salience**: it is associated with making certain stimuli salient and in motivating the organism to seek out those stimuli. According to this view, **addiction** to drugs is characterised by a pathological wanting brought about by drug-induced changes to these critical brain pathways. Moreover, it is suggested that these changes persist even after prolonged periods of drug abstinence, accounting for the high rates of relapse to drug use among dependent users (Lüscher, 2016).

Other physiological changes brought on by excessive drug use can contribute to the process of drug dependence. Researchers have argued that chronic drug use can reduce dopamine activity in the mesolimbic dopamine pathway and raises reward thresholds (Koob, 2006). This means that individuals dependent on drugs experience less pleasure out of normal activities in life, and the use of drugs become a more important way of producing positive, and alleviating negative, emotional states. The chronic use of drugs may also lead to neural changes in other parts of the brain, including the prefrontal cortex (Dackis & O'Brien, 2005; Fattore & Melis, 2016). As the prefrontal cortex is implicated in decision making, impulsive control and risk assessment, impairment to this region may further reduce the ability of individuals to control their drug use.

A biological perspective views drug dependence as a chronic relapsing brain disease (e.g., Leshner, 1997). Drug use is repeated due to the action of drugs on natural reward systems in the brain. Over time, chronic drug use produces changes in the brain that increase the salience of drug use and impair decision-making processes. Individuals dependent on drugs become locked into a cycle of addiction that results in long periods of compulsive drug taking and high rates of relapse. A biological approach, however, has less to say about why individuals choose to try drugs in the first place, and it is important to recognise the role that psychological, social, and cultural factors play in both the initiation and maintenance of drug-taking behaviours.

Psychological approaches

Some individuals are more likely to use and misuse drugs than are others. A good deal of research has focused on elaborating the psychological and social risk factors that increase the likelihood that an individual will use drugs and/or have drug-related problems. These risk factors can be conveniently categorised into three broad areas: (a) individual factors; (b) family factors; and (c) school, peer, and community factors.

One important personality factor that has been associated with drug use is sensation seeking. **Sensation seeking** has been defined as 'the need for varied, novel, and complex sensations and experiences and the willingness to take physical and social risk for the sake of such experiences' (Zuckerman, 1979, p.10). Individuals who score high on sensation-seeking scales are more likely to try illicit drugs and use drugs in risky ways. Sensation seeking is one of a number of traits, including impulsivity and low self-control that fall under the broad category of behavioural undercontrol (Hesselbrock & Hesselbrock, 2006). Individuals who tend to seek out risky and exciting activities, become bored easily, and who are less able to control impulsive behaviours are more likely to seek out drugs and engage in risky drug use.

The tendency to experience negative affect is also a risk factor for the development of substance use problems. Individuals who suffer from depression, for instance, may attempt to 'self-medicate' by using drugs to alleviate their low mood (Hesselbrock & Hesselbrock, 2006). Although the nature of the causal relationship between problem drug use and depression has not been firmly established, there is well replicated and robust *relationship* between substance use problems and a number of psychiatric disorders including schizophrenia, bipolar disorder, anxiety disorders, and depression. Epidemiological studies, for instance, suggest that the lifetime prevalence of substance use disorders is approximately 50 per cent for those suffering from bipolar disorder or schizophrenia and 25–30 per cent for those with depression or an anxiety disorder, compared to 10–15 per cent among individuals who do not suffer from any mental illness (Mueser et al., 2006).

A number of family factors have also been associated with adolescent substance use. These include parental substance use, low parental monitoring, and family conflict (Hesselbrock & Hesselbrock, 2006). For example, a cross-national study of over 40,000 adolescents in the United States and Australia found that poor family management, family conflict, and a family history of substance use all predicted the regular use of cigarettes and alcohol and the use of cannabis in the last 30 days among adolescents (Beyers et al., 2004). Research supports the idea that substance use problems tend to run in families. In part, this is likely to reflect a genetic contribution to the development of drug problems, although most researchers note the *interaction* of genetic and environmental factors in the aetiology of substance use problems (Hasin, Hatzenbuehler, & Waaxman, 2006). Individuals with a genetic propensity to develop drug problems, for instance, may be more likely to grow up in family environments in which their parents also engage in problematic drug use.

Perhaps one of the most widely recognised risk factors for adolescent drug use is peer influence. Most studies find that adolescents who have friends who use illicit drugs, or who approve of drugs are more likely to use themselves (Jenkins & Zunguze, 1998). For example, in a study of psychosocial risk factors for substance use in adolescents in six European countries, it was found that having friends that use cannabis or other drugs more than doubled the odds for using cannabis or other drugs for both boys and girls (Kokkevi et al., 2007). However, research rarely teases apart the different causal pathways that lead to the finding that peer drug use is an important risk factor. Do individuals who have friends who use drugs become drug users themselves, or do people select friends who share their drug-taking predilections? It is likely that adolescents, to some extent, seek out like-minded peers, and this accounts for some of the relationship between adolescent drug use and drug-using peers.

The psychological and social risk factors reviewed in this section suggest that drug misuse arises out of an interaction between individual-level factors and the developmental environment. Some individuals may be more likely to experiment with drugs or become problem drug users as a result of personality factors that may, in part, have a genetic origin. Specifically, some individuals may be more likely to seek out the rewarding characteristics of drug use (e.g., high sensation seekers) and find that ability of drugs to alleviate negative emotional states more attractive (e.g., those suffering from mental health problems). These points highlight the importance of integrating psychological and neurobiological approaches to substance use and substance use disorders (Baskin-Sommers & Hearon, 2015). The social environment also plays a critical role in the use and misuse of psychoactive drugs. Social learning theory suggests that individuals may be more likely to use drugs if others in their social environment – especially parents, siblings, and peers – model their use, or possess pro drug attitudes and beliefs (see Box 8.2 for the potential role of the media in modelling drug use). Drug use can also be influenced by the broader cultural context in which individuals are embedded.

BOX 8.2 DRUGS AND THE MEDIA: DO REPRESENTATIONS OF DRUGS IN FILMS AND MUSIC ENCOURAGE USE?

Drug use has been widely depicted in music and film since the early part of the twentieth century. Numerous songs, including Fats Waller's 'The Viper's Drag', Neil Young's 'Needle and the Damage Done', and Cypress Hill's 'Hits from the Bong', depict the use of illicit psychoactive substances. The representation of illegal drug use in films has been somewhat more limited until the latter half of the twentieth century, although the 1955 classic *The Man with the Golden Arm* provided a frank depiction of heroin addiction. Later, a spate of films such as *Trainspotting*, *Leaving Las Vegas*, *Blow*, *Drug Store Cowboy*, *Requiem for a Dream*, *Traffic*, and *Candy* have focused explicitly on drugs and drug-related issues (see Criminal Psychology Through Film 8.1).

According to social learning theory, exposure to representations of drug use in the media may promote drug use, especially if drugs are used by high-status models and lead to positive outcomes. What evidence do we have that media representations of drug use may encourage use?

Researchers have found that smoking is often depicted positively in films, with little or no attention given to the negative effects of tobacco use (Charlesworth & Glantz, 2005). Exposure to smoking in movies may also increase the initiation of tobacco use among adolescents (Dalton et al., 2003). Similar findings have been reported for the representation of alcohol in films: alcohol is typically portrayed positively, and exposure to alcohol use in films predicts the early onset of alcohol use among adolescents (Sargent et al., 2006). Very little research, however, has explored the potential impact of representations of illicit drug use in films. Some researchers have noted that drugs are often depicted inaccurately in the film media (e.g., Boyd, 2002); however, there is little evidence to support the idea that drugs are portrayed in an overly positive fashion. Indeed, Shapiro (2005) notes that films about drug use tend to follow a similar cautionary narrative: drugs are depicted at first as being fun, but they typically lead to ruin.

Media effects should never be ignored. Although the influence of the media on behaviours such as drug use is likely to be very small overall, it is important to recognise how different individuals respond to the same media depiction in different ways. Think about this the next time you watch a film involving drug use or listen to drug-related song lyrics. Ask your friends (and parents!) whether they think that drugs are portrayed in a positive fashion and whether they are more (or less) likely to use drugs as a result.

CRIMINAL PSYCHOLOGY THROUGH FILM 8.1
Requiem for a Dream (2000)

Directed by: Darren Aronofsky
Starring: Ellen Burstyn (Sara), Jennifer Connelly (Marion), Jared Leto (Harry), and Marlon Wayans (Tyrone)

Requiem for a dream provides a vivid and disturbing portrait of drug use – both legal and illegal – set in the United States. This narrative is clear. Drugs are used first for seemingly harmless reasons: diet pills to help Sara fit in to her red dress, and pleasure and good times for Marion, Harry, and Tyrone. However, things turn quickly turn sour, and drug use has a negative outcome for each of the four central characters: Sara's use of prescribed amphetamines results in psychosis and hospitalisation, Marion ends up prostituting herself for heroin, Harry has his arm amputated as a result of injecting heroin, and Tyrone is arrested for drug dealing. Visually engaging, the film introduces a number of interesting cinematographic techniques (humorously lampooned in the *Simpson*'s episode 'I'm spelling as fast as I can') that effectively heightens the viewers' emotional responses to the narrative.

Questions for discussion

1   Is the narrative portrayed in this film realistic?
2   Do film makers have a responsibility to portray the negative side of drug use?

Social-structural and cultural approaches

The use of opiates was common among American soldiers in the Vietnam War. Although less than 1 per cent had been addicted to opiates prior to going to Vietnam, over 50 per cent tried opiates while in Vietnam, and approximately 20 per cent subsequently became addicted. However, on returning to the United States very few servicemen continued their heroin use, with rates of addiction dropping to pre-Vietnam levels (Robins, Helzer, & Davis, 1975; Robins & Slobodyan, 2003). If we accept the idea that addiction is a powerful, physiologically driven process then these findings seem hard to understand. However, it is important to recognise that the social and cultural context can strongly influence patterns of drug use. In particular, as Durrant and Thakker (2003, p. 167) note: 'often complex and frequently contradictory sets of norms and values govern *what* are acceptable drugs to take, *who* are allowed to take them, *where* and *when* drugs should be consumed, and what *behaviours* that arise from their consumption might be allowed.' Opiates use in Vietnam was comparatively acceptable and normative, whereas opiate use in the United States did not fit in with acceptable norms and roles and so was typically not continued.

The role of culture is perhaps most clearly recognised in patterns of alcohol use in different societies. Many cultural groups – such as Muslims and Mormons – proscribe the consumption of alcohol outright, whereas others have norms that prescribe moderate drinking and condemn drunkenness (e.g., Jewish culture) (Heath, 2000). Much to the concern of public health advocates, many English-speaking Western cultures such as in Australia, New Zealand, and Great Britain have norms that find heavy binge drinking largely acceptable. Indeed, for young men in New Zealand the consumption of alcohol in many contexts is essentially obligatory, and those men who refuse to drink may be subject to abuse and discrimination (see Paton-Simpson, 2001).

Sociological approaches to explaining drug use and misuse also draw heavily on a range of social-structural theories such as anomie, strain theory, and social disorganisation (Bahr & Hoffmann, 2015; Shaw, 2002). The finding that drug-related problems tend to disproportionately fall on the poorer and more marginalised sectors of society suggests that the experience of poverty, unemployment, discrimination, and marginalisation may contribute to the development of drug-related problems. The relationship between drug use and neighbourhood disadvantage has been identified in research (e.g., Boardman et al., 2001), and involvement in deviant activities such as drug dealing may provide opportunities for marginalised youth that are not available through alternative means (Bourgois, 1995).

As was highlighted at the start of this section, there is no simple or single explanation for why individuals use and misuse drugs. Some kinds of explanations may be better placed to explain why drugs are tried, whereas others can further our understanding of how substance use disorders develop. Many scholars now recognise that in order to fully understand the enduring appeal of psychoactive substances we need to take a multi-disciplinary approach that encompasses biological, psychological, social, and cultural factors (Abadinsky, 2014; Durrant & Thakker, 2003).

REVIEW AND REFLECT

1   How does the incentive salience model account for the fact that repeated drug use occurs even though dependent drug users may experience less pleasure from drug use over time?

2   Think about the notion of 'peer pressure' in relation to the initiation of drug use. To what extent do you think that young people are overtly *pressured* to try drugs in order to 'fit in' with peer groups? How else might peers contribute to drug use among adolescents?

THE ASSOCIATION BETWEEN DRUGS AND CRIME

The idea that drugs and crime are related to each other is firmly entrenched. The association of drug use with criminal offending has been supported in a large number of different studies, and government crime reduction strategies pay particular attention to tackling 'drug-related' crime (Bennett & Edwards, 2015; Brownstein, 2015; McSweeney, Hough, & Turnbull, 2007). Although it is widely recognised that the use of alcohol and other drugs is *associated* with criminal offending, the nature of this relationship is complex. We look in detail at *how* drugs and crime might be related in the next section, but first it is important to consider the research that supports a strong association between drugs and offending. Research on three different populations will be considered (e.g., see McSweeney et al., 2007):

1   Drug use by offenders.
2   Offending among problem drug users.
3   Offending and drug use in the general population.

Some of the best evidence that is available to support an association between drug use and offending comes from **arrestee drug abuse monitoring programmes**. These programmes run in a number of countries, including the United States, the United Kingdom, Australia, South Africa, and New Zealand, and involve detailed interviews with samples of arrestees (suspected offenders that have been arrested by the police) about their drug use and offending. Arrestees are also asked to provide a urine sample to test for the presence of different drugs. Urinalysis allows for a more objective measure of drug use than does self-report. However, it is important to note that although many illicit drugs can be detected in urine samples for up to 1 to 2 days after use, heavy cannabis use can be detected for up to 20 days: a fact that should be taken into consideration when comparing positive tests for different substances (Wilkins et al., 2004).

It is clear from these studies that the percentage of arrestees testing positive for different illicit drugs in Australia, the United States, New Zealand, and England and Wales is substantially higher than the prevalence of self-report drug use in the general population. An illustration of these general findings is provided for the New Zealand drug use monitoring programme in Figure 8.4. As you can see by comparing the results from this figure with those presented in Table 8.2 the reported use of drugs in the last 12 months by arrestees is significantly greater than the reported *life*time prevalence in the general population. Similar results are found from the Australian drug use monitoring programme: In 2013–2014, 73 per cent of the sample tested positive for any drug (excluding alcohol), with 46 per cent testing positive for cannabis, 34 per cent testing positive for methamphetamine, and 20 per cent testing positive for opiates (Coghlan et al., 2015). Even if we take into account the fact that arrestees are likely to be young men (who have a higher general use of illicit drugs), drug use is significantly more common among offenders than in the general population.

Substance use *problems* are also highly prevalent among samples of arrestees. In the United States, for instance, 39.1 per cent and 28.6 per cent of male arrestees were deemed 'at risk' for drug and alcohol dependence, respectively (Zhang, 2003). Similar figures were found among Australian arrestees. Using DSM–IV (American Psychiatric Association, 2000) criteria for drug dependence, 46 per cent of the total sample was assessed as being dependent on drugs and 31 per cent dependent on alcohol (Mouzos et al., 2007). These figures are particularly important, because research has shown that problem drug use is likely to be especially strongly associated with criminal offending (e.g., Bean, 2014; Bennett & Holloway, 2005).

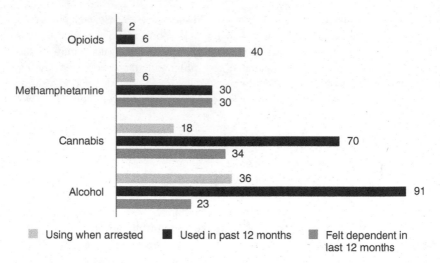

Figure 8.4 Main drugs used by detainees in New Zealand, 2013.
Source: Wilkins, Jawalke, Barnes, et al. (2013).

It is clear from the results of arrestee drug abuse monitoring programmes that drug use and drug use problems are common among individuals who have been arrested. Drug use and misuse are also highly prevalent in samples of prison inmates. In the United Kingdom, Ramsey (2003) found that 73 per cent of a sample of male prisoners had used an illicit drug in the year prior to imprisonment, and over 50 per cent reported taking illegal drugs daily or nearly every day. In Australia, 60 per cent of prisoners sampled in 2004 reported a history of injecting drug use (Australian Institute of Health and Welfare, 2007), and the Drug Use Careers of Offenders (DUCO) female study found that among a sample of 470 women incarcerated in Australian prisons, 62 per cent were regular drug users at the time of their arrest, and 55 per cent were dependent on drugs (H. Johnson, 2006). Similar results were found in a recent New Zealand study of substance use and other mental disorders among prisoners. An extraordinary 87 per cent of prisoners had a lifetime diagnosis of a substance use disorder, and 47 per cent had a past year diagnosis – rates of over seven times higher than in the general population (Indig, Gear, & Wilhelm, 2016)

The use and misuse of drugs are common among offenders. Offending is also prevalent in samples of problem drug users. In the United Kingdom, for instance, 61 per cent of a sample of 1,075 drug misusers in treatment reported having committed crimes (other than drug possession) in the three months prior to their treatment (McSweeney et al., 2007). The association between drugs and crime is also illustrated in this study by the fact that the number of individuals engaged in criminal offending sharply declined after 1 year of being admitted into treatment – presumably, in part, because they were less likely to be using drugs (e.g., Gossop et al., 2003). In another study of 560 problem drug users admitted to treatment in Scotland it was found that 18 per cent had committed an assault in the previous three months (Neale, Bloor, & Weir, 2005). This research also found that 25 per cent of the sample had been a *victim* of assault in the last six months, suggesting that problem drug users may be at greater risk of offending *and* victimisation.

Research that has examined the association between drug use and offending in the general population largely supports the conclusions drawn from studies on samples of offenders and samples of problem drug users. In a cross-sectional telephone survey of 1,000 adults in Ontario, Canada, for example, Wells, Graham, and West (2000) found that heavy alcohol use was associated with experiences of threats and physical aggression. A longitudinal study of a cohort of 1265 individuals in Christchurch, New Zealand also found that alcohol abuse was associated with both violent and property offending: the number of self-reported violent and property offences increased with the number of symptoms of alcohol abuse in the sample (Boden, Fergusson, & Horwood, 2013; Fergusson & Horwood, 2000) (see Research in Focus 8.1). Results of the Youth Lifestyle Survey in the United Kingdom provide further evidence for an association between drug use and offending. Among a sample of 4,848 young people in England and Wales aged between 12 and 30 years, drug use emerged as one of the most important risk factors for offending. Among 12–17-year-olds, for example, past year drug users were five times more likely to be 'serious or persistent' offenders than their non-drug-using peers (Flood-Page et al., 2000).

RESEARCH IN FOCUS 8.1 WHAT IS THE RELATIONSHIP BETWEEN ALCOHOL MISUSE AND OFFENDING?

Title: Alcohol misuse and criminal offending: Findings from a 30-year longitudinal study

Authors: Boden, J. M., Fergusson, D. M., & Horwood, L. J.   **Year**: 2013

Source: *Drug and Alcohol Dependence*, 128, 30–36

Aims: To explore the relationship between the misuse of alcohol and criminal offending in a longitudinal population sample

Method: Information about alcohol abuse and dependence and various offending outcomes at different ages were drawn from members of the Christchurch Health and Development Study, a longitudinal study of a birth cohort of 1,265 children.

Key results:
- There was a strong relationship between the number of symptoms of alcohol abuse and dependence and a range of criminal outcomes.
- After controlling for a range of other relevant factors this relationship was only significant for two categories of offending: (a) assault; and (b) property damage, vandalism, and arson.

Conclusion: 'The results suggest a causal association between alcohol misuse and "impulsive" crimes such as assault and property damage/vandalism/arson, with estimates suggesting that AAD [alcohol abuse and dependence] accounted for approximately 9.6–9.9% of these types of reported offending in the cohort' (from the abstract, p. 30).

It is clear from the research reviewed in this section that drugs and crime go together. Drug use is more prevalent in the offending than in the non-offending population. Offending is also more prevalent among problem drug users, and offending and drug use are associated in studies of the general population. In the next section the nature of the relationship between drugs and crime is explored in more detail.

REVIEW AND REFLECT

1   What are the main sources of evidence used to establish an association between drug use and offending?
2   What are some of the potential limitations of these sources of information?

UNDERSTANDING THE RELATIONSHIP BETWEEN DRUGS AND CRIME

As anyone who has taken an introductory course in statistics will know, the fact that two variables are associated or 'correlated' with each other does not tell us anything specifically about the nature of the *causal* relationship between those two variables. Leaving aside the fact that the use, sale, and possession of some drugs are offences in themselves (drugs *are* crime), most scholars recognise three or four different causal models that could potentially explain the relationship between drugs and (other sorts of) offending (Bean, 2014; Bennett & Holloway, 2005; McSweeney et al., 2007). These different models are depicted in Figure 8.5. The 'drugs causes crime' model suggests that the use of drugs causes or leads individuals to commit crime; for example, a dependent heroin user may engage in acquisitive offending in order to support their habit. The 'crime causes drugs' model indicates that the relationship goes the other way around: involvement in crime and criminal networks leads individuals to use drugs. Whenever we find a robust relationship between two variables, like drugs and crime, we also need to consider the possibility that the two variables are not causally related at all and that other factors (such as personality, social background, or situation) might account for the association. This is the 'common cause model'.

Before we look at these models in more detail and discuss some of the relevant research, it is worth reflecting for a moment on what *you* think is the relationship between drugs and crime. Consider the three models displayed in Figure 8.5. Rank these three models in terms of how important you think they are in accounting for the association between drugs and crime discussed in the previous section. How did you come up with these rankings? Would they differ if you considered different drugs or different kinds of offending?

In doing this exercise you will probably recognise that there is nothing straightforward about the relationship between drugs and crime. The first point to note is that the different causal models are not mutually exclusive. There is no one model that accounts for all of the association between drugs and crime. Rather, each model helps to potentially

Model 1: Drugs cause crime

The use of drugs leads to or causes crime.

Model 2: Crime causes drug use

Involvement in crime leads to or causes drug use.

Model 3: Common cause

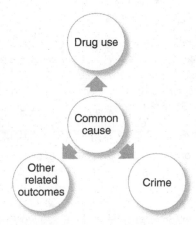

Drug use and crime are related because a common factor causes or leads to both drug use and crime among other related outcomes.

Figure 8.5 Explaining the relationship between drugs and crime.

explain part of that relationship. Second, the nature of the relationship will depend on the combination of drug, offence, offender, and stage of drug use. The drugs cause crime relationship, for instance, may be more relevant for explaining alcohol-related violence among problem drinkers, whereas the crime causes drug use model might help us to understand how young offenders become involved in the use of drugs such as heroin and cocaine. The third crucial point is that, although we can talk of 'drugs causing crime' or 'crime causing drug use', we need to recognise that the term 'cause' does not mean that there is any kind of *necessary* relationship between drugs and crime. Not all, or even most, drug users engage in criminal offending, and not all offenders use or misuse drugs (Bean, 2014). Like most explanations in the social and behavioural sciences the idea of 'cause' in the drugs–crime nexus should be interpreted in a probabilistic rather than deterministic fashion: the use of some drugs may increase the probability of offending for some individuals in some contexts. Keeping these points in mind, let us examine the first model presented in Figure 8.5: drugs cause crime.

Drugs cause crime

The most influential model used to understand the impact of drugs on crime is Goldstein's (1985) tripartite model. Although Goldstein originally developed his model to understand the links between drug use and violence, his model can be employed to understand the relationship between drugs and crime more generally. .Goldstein suggested that drugs and violence can be related in three different ways.

1   **Psychopharmacological model** – The action of some drugs on some individuals can result in changes in cognition, mood, and behaviour that may lead to offending.
2   **Economic compulsive model** – Drug users engage in economically motivated crime in order to obtain money to purchase drugs.
3   **Systemic model** – offending is seen as an intrinsic component of involvement in the sale and distribution of illegal drugs.

Psychopharmacological model

Research on drug use, aggression, and violent behaviour generally finds that alcohol is the substance that is most frequently associated with violent crime (Rossow & Bye, 2013; Tomlinson, Brown, & Hoaken, 2016). Large-scale victim surveys in the United Kingdom, Australia, and the United States strongly support the role of alcohol in violent offending (Dingwall, 2006). Alcohol has also featured prominently in other studies of violent offending. For instance, Shaw et al. (2006) in a study of the role of alcohol and other drugs among 1,594 homicide perpetrators in England and Wales found that alcohol played a 'minor' role in 39 per cent and a 'major' role in 6 per cent of homicides. The comparable figures for other drugs were 15 per cent and 1 per cent, respectively. The attribution of responsibility in this study was based on an assessment of the effects of alcohol and other drugs on the user's state of mind prior to committing the crime, and so provides some information about the psychopharmacological effect of drug use on offending.

Of course, studies like the ones cited above cannot tell us anything definitive about the *causal* role of alcohol in offending. Because alcohol is a legal substance, however, there have been a large number of experimental studies that have examined the influence of alcohol and which *can* provide useful information about alcohol's causal role in the instigation of aggression (see Exum, 2006, for a review). A typical experimental study runs something like this. Participants are brought in to the lab, and half are randomly assigned to receive a small quantity of alcohol, and the other half receives a placebo (an inert beverage that putatively contains alcohol). Then, participants engage in an activity that allows researchers to assess levels of aggression. One of the most prominent approaches is the 'competitive reaction-time paradigm'. In this design, participants engage in a competitive reaction time task that allows participants to give electric shocks or blasts of white noise to opponents (who do not typically exist). Aggression is typically operationalised as the level of shock or noise that participants are willing to administer. Although the results of this research tend to vary depending on methodological, individual, and contextual factors, Exum (2006) in a review of previous reviews and meta-analyses of the literature concluded that the 'findings reviewed here indicated that alcohol had a causal influence on violent behaviour' (p. 141).

The effect of alcohol on aggression and violent behaviour is typically explained in terms of one or more of the following mechanisms (Hoaken & Stewart, 2003; Boles & Miotto, 2003):

1 Disinhibition of fear.
2 Impaired executive functioning.
3 Alcohol expectancies.

As most people will be aware, alcohol has the – often appealing – capacity to reduce or alleviate feelings of stress and anxiety. This disinhibition of normal fear mechanisms may promote aggression if individuals fail to appropriately assess levels of threat in the environment and are less concerned about the potential consequences of confrontation. Alcohol also has an equally widely recognised capacity to impair decision-making processes. The consumption of alcohol tends to alter the capacity to accurately assess the risks and benefits of different courses of actions, to control impulses, and to consider the future consequences of behaviour (Giancola, 2000, 2013). According to the **alcohol myopia model** this occurs because alcohol has the effect of narrowing attentional resources so that individuals focus on the 'most salient, easy-to-process, immediate, and thus attention grabbing cues in the environment' (Giancola et al., 2010, p. 266), which in certain drinking contexts will largely involve hostile cues. People's *beliefs* about the effects of alcohol on behaviour may also play a role in alcohol-related aggression and violence. If, for instance, a person believes that alcohol makes them more aggressive then, according to alcohol expectancy theory, they are more likely to behave in an aggressive fashion.

As anyone who has consumed alcohol will be aware, the relationship between alcohol, aggression, and violence is by no means inevitable. Most drinking occasions do not lead to aggression and violence. It is clear, then, that the relationship between alcohol consumption and aggression is moderated by other factors. Important individual-level factors that have been identified in research include dispositional aggressivity, hostility, irritability, impulsivity, and low empathy (Giancola, 2002, 2013). Relevant contextual factors include provocation and drinking environment (Leonard, Quigley, & Collins, 2003). Many of these factors come together to account for alcohol-related violence: impulsive, aggressive individuals may tend to drink together in bar-room environments in which there is a reputation for violence and in which provocation may be more likely to occur.

Psychostimulants such as cocaine, amphetamines, and methamphetamines have often been associated with violent crime, especially in the media (e.g., Jenkins, 1999). Acute doses of psychostimulant drugs result in an increase in alertness, activity, excitability, and irritability. Chronic heavy use of drugs like methamphetamine may result in drug-induced psychosis characterised by impulsivity and paranoia. These psychological states are certainly consistent with the idea that the use of psychostimulants might be causally related to aggression and violence, although unlike alcohol, the evidence for a strong causal link is not well established (Hoaken & Stewart, 2003; McKetin, McLaren, Riddell, et al., 2006).

In a study of amphetamine users seeking treatment, Wright and Klee (2001) found that 47 per cent of their sample reported having committed a violent crime, and over half of these indicated that their violence was associated with their use of amphetamine. These results were largely mirrored in a more recent study of 205 methamphetamine users in Los Angeles County (Sommers & Baskin, 2006) in which it was found that 45 per cent of the total sample had committed a violent crime, and 27 per cent reported having committed violence while under the influence of methamphetamine. It is clear from these studies that violence is not necessarily an inevitable outcome of methamphetamine use, as most users have not engaged in violence. However, Sommers and Baskin (2006) conclude that 'methamphetamine use may heighten the risk for violence' (p. 93). As was the case with alcohol, the role of situational and individual-level factors probably moderates the relationship between psychostimulants and violent behaviour. In Sommers and Baskin's study, for example, 64 per cent of those individuals who report committing a violent crime also indicated that they had committed violent crimes prior to the methamphetamine-related violence. Situational factors also clearly play a role, although the consumption of methamphetamine may exaggerate or escalate otherwise minor provocations.

Although there is some evidence to support a psychopharmacological link between psychostimulants and crime, there is not much support for the idea that the ingestion of other major drugs of abuse like cannabis, ecstasy, or heroin leads individuals to commit crime. Despite the allusion to cannabis-crazed axe-wielding maniacs in the anti-marijuana film of the 1950s, *Reefer Madness*, most scholars conclude that cannabis tends to inhibit or reduce the expression of aggression. Although some studies do find a positive relationship between cannabis use and aggression these results are likely to be due to the presence of other factors (see the common cause model, Tomlinson et al., 2016) A similar conclusion is drawn about the effects of opiates, such as heroin. Withdrawal from opiates may increase irritability and aggression although there is little research evidence to support any kind of strong link between this psychological state and violent offending (Boles & Miotto, 2003; Hoaken & Stewart, 2003). Although most research has focused on the influence of drugs on offenders' psychological states, it is important to recognise how drugs can also be used on victims to facilitate crime. Box 8.3 explores this topic in more detail.

Economic compulsive model

According to the economic compulsive model, some drugs users may engage in offending in order to obtain money to support their drug use. Illicit drugs, especially substances like heroin, cocaine, and methamphetamine, are extremely expensive. Golub and Johnson (2004) in a study of Manhattan arrestees (interviewed in 2000–2002) found that users of both heroin and crack cocaine had spent just under $1,500 on drugs in the past 30 days. The NEW-ADAM programme includes questions concerning illegal income over the last 12 months. Approximately half of all arrestees interviewed reported obtaining some illegal income in the last year. For non-drug-using arrestees the mean amount of illegal income was £5,763. For users of drugs other than heroin, crack, and cocaine the mean amount of illegal income was £8,290, and among those arrestees who had used heroin, cocaine, *and* crack in the last 12 months, the mean income was £24,338. Heavy users of these drugs, therefore, need to either have a substantial legal income or else resort to crime in order to fund their drug use. Research supports the idea that at least some drug users engage in economically motivated offending in order to purchase drugs.

BOX 8.3 DRUGS AND SEXUAL ASSAULT: THE DANGERS OF DRINK SPIKING

The role of alcohol and drugs in sexual offending has long been recognised. It has been estimated, for instance, that approximately half of all cases of sexual assault in the United States involve the use of alcohol by the perpetrator, victim, or both (Abbey et al., 2001; see also Lorenz & Ullman, 2016). A more recent concern has arisen from the use of drugs – especially the powerful sedatives, GHB and Rohypnol – to facilitate sexual offending by rendering a victim incapacitated or unconscious. Because these drugs are usually slipped into the unwitting victim's drink, this phenomenon has become known as 'drink spiking'. In a recent study conducted in Australia it was estimated that between 3,000 and 4,000 incidents of drink spiking occurred over a one-year period and that a third of these incidents involved sexual assault (Taylor, Prichard, & Charlton, 2004). Drink spiking is an important issue in many countries, and efforts at preventing drink spiking have focused on raising awareness through public health campaigns.

Of arrestees in the NEW-ADAM programme who reported a connection between their drug use and crime, over 80 per cent claimed that they committed crimes in order to obtain money to purchase drugs (Bennett & Holloway, 2006), and 87 per cent of those that used heroin and committed an acquisitive crime in the last 12 months perceived that these were related (Holloway & Bennett, 2004). Of course, we should be wary of assuming any kind of straightforward relationship between illegal drug use and economically motivated criminal offending. Many drug users started offending prior to their involvement in drugs (Bennett & Holloway, 2005), and by no means all heavy users of drugs like heroin and cocaine will resort to illegal activities to fund their drug use.

Systemic model

According to the systemic model, crime is simply an intrinsic component of involvement in illegal drug markets. Drug-related violence, for instance, may occur due to disputes over territorial rights for drug dealing, unpaid debts, and punishment of low-level drug dealers for selling adulterated products by those higher up in the illegal drug hierarchy (Brownstein, Crimmins, & Spunt, 2000).

Why are illegal drug markets often characterised by high levels of violence? Perhaps the most important reason is the absence of third-party enforcement. If you are sold a faulty piece of merchandise at a hardware store you can either return it and get your money back, or, ultimately, resort to the law to recover your losses. If you are sold a bag of crack cocaine and find out that it is largely soap shavings, however, then you have no such options for legal recourse. Other factors also contribute to high levels of violence crime in illegal drug markets including the value of drugs, an environment of low trust, the indirect consequence of drug use, and the participation of individuals who may be more prone to aggression and violence in the first place (MacCoun, Kilmer, & Reuter, 2003; Reuter, 2016).

Table 8.4 The relationship between different drug types and different models of crime

	Psychopharmacological model	Economic Compulsive Model	Systemic Model
Alcohol	✓✓✓	✓	✓
Cannabis	✓	✓✓	✓✓
Heroin	✓	✓✓✓	✓✓
Cocaine	✓✓	✓✓✓	✓✓
Crack cocaine	✓✓	✓✓✓	✓✓✓
Methamphetamine	✓✓	✓✓	✓✓
LSD	✓	✓	✓✓

✓✓✓ = Strong evidence of a link between drug and crime

✓✓ = Moderate evidence of a link between drug and crime

✓ = Limited or no evidence of a link between drug and crime

Levels of systemic violence do, however, vary substantially over time and across different drug markets. The crack cocaine market in the United States in the 1980s, for instance, was particularly violent. Goldstein et al. (1997), for instance, calculated that 39 per cent of all homicides and 75 per cent of drug-related homicides in New York City in 1988 were due to the illegal market in drugs, primarily crack cocaine. The dramatic amount of systemic violence associated with the crack cocaine market might have been partly due to its novelty as prospective dealers jostled for market share and market order (Brownstein et al., 2000). Other drug markets might be characterised by fairly low levels of systemic violent crime. For instance, Wilkins and Casswell (2003) argue that the illegal market in cannabis in New Zealand is unable to be controlled by organised crime in any kind of systematic way. This means that there are a relatively large number of local growers and dealers who make small amounts of profit, and disputes over market share are less likely to occur.

Which of the three 'drug causes crime' models discussed in this section is most important for explaining the drugs–crime connection? The answer to this question is that it depends on the drug, the specific context of use, and available research evidence. In Table 8.4 a schematic overview of the support for each of the three models for different drug types is illustrated. The strength of the relationship shown should be considered indicative only as the details not only vary across different contexts (e.g., in Prohibition era United States alcohol would be strongly associated with systemic crime), but are likely to change as more research is carried out and our understanding of the drugs–crime relationship is improved.

Crime causes drug use

The second model that we will consider is the idea that involvement in crime causes, or leads to, drug use. On the surface this might seem a strange proposition: how can crime *cause* drug use? There are a number of possible links here. First, a number of researchers have noted how drugs might be used in order to facilitate criminal offending. Drugs might, for example, provide the necessary 'Dutch courage' that enables offenders to commit crimes, or drugs might be used in order to provide a handy excuse or rationale for offending. Second, drugs may be used as way of celebrating the successful commission of a crime, with offenders 'rewarding' themselves with drugs from the money produced by offending. Third, crime might lead to drug use because offenders get caught up in criminal networks in which drug use and drug dealing may be both more prevalent and more acceptable (Bean, 2014; Bennett & Holloway, 2005).

There is some evidence to support the broad idea that involvement in crime may lead to drug use. Studies, for example, suggest that involvement in criminal behaviour typically precedes the use of 'hard' drugs such as heroin, cocaine, and crack (White, 2015). This suggests that involvement in offending may facilitate or lead to the use of these drugs. Pudney (2002) for instances, in a review of results from the Youth Lifestyles Survey of 3,901 young people in the UK concluded that 'There is a reasonably clear tendency towards a chain of events beginning with crime and truancy, and only later developing into drug use' (p. 10). However, the use of substances like cannabis or solvents tends to come before involvement in criminal offending, indicating that initiation into drug use and crime may reflect more general age-related patterns of involvement in problem behaviours (Bennett & Holloway, 2005). Qualitative studies also provide some support for the idea that drugs are used to either facilitate or celebrate offending. Hammersley et al. (1989) in a study of opiate users found, for instance, that their participants described rewarding themselves with crack cocaine for the successful commission of a crime:

> I mean it's like every time I make a good bit of money, I just buy a lot ... 'cause I've made myself a bit of money ... so it's not to get the coke, it just what you do to celebrate doing a good job.
>
> (p. 1041)

Involvement in criminal offending may, therefore, lead to drug use through a number of different channels.

Common causes and evaluating the different perspectives

The third main model for explaining the association between drug use and crime is the idea that drugs and crime do not directly cause each other but rather they are associated because a common factor or factors is related to both. Relatively little attention has been specifically paid to the common cause model among scholars, but a good deal of evidence (some that has been reviewed earlier in this chapter) suggests that drug use and crime share, in part, a common aetiology. Simply put, the risk factors for problem drug use overlap considerably with the risk factors for delinquency and criminal offending. Behavioural undercontrol, abusive and inconsistent parenting, low school achievement, and involvement with delinquent peers are factors that are related to both drug misuse and involvement in crime. Part of the association between drug use and crime, then, is likely to be spurious: drugs and crime go together because the sort of individuals who are most likely to misuse drugs are also those who may be more likely to commit crime. Very few studies have attempted to account for the common factors associated with both drug use and offending in order to estimate the unique effects of drugs on crime.

In a longitudinal study of a birth cohort in New Zealand, however, Fergusson & Horwood (2000) examined the relationship between alcohol abuse and crime after controlling for a large number of possible confounding factors such as socioeconomic background, family functioning, and conduct problems. Although much of the relationship between alcohol abuse and crime could be accounted for by these factors, even after they were controlled for, an association between alcohol abuse and crime still remained. This suggests that, although common factors might explain much of the relationship between alcohol and crime, the use of alcohol itself also contributes directly to offending.

There is clearly more research to be done in understanding the relationship between drugs and crime. However, a few general conclusions can be drawn. First, the use of some drugs, for some individuals, does tend to contribute to offending. Alcohol is the drug that appears to have the strongest psychopharmacological link to offending, although there is some evidence the use of psychostimulants, such as methamphetamine, may heighten the risk of offending for some individuals. The heavy use of some drugs, such as heroin, crack, and cocaine also appear to contribute to offending as some users engage in crime in order to obtain money to purchase drugs. The illicit nature of the drug economy also contributes to crime, although this depends to a considerable degree on the nature of the specific drug market. Involvement in crime can also lead to drug use, although the evidence base for this relationship is less robust. Certainly involvement in criminal sub-cultures is likely to make illegal drugs both more acceptable and more available. Some offenders also use drugs to facilitate their offending or to celebrate the successful commission of an offence. The strong association between drugs and crime is also driven, in part, through a range of common factors that predict both drug use and criminal offending. The overall picture that is beginning to emerge is that crime and drug misuse have common origins, but that once offending or drug use is established they tend to mutually reinforce each other: problem drug use contributes to offending, and offending facilitates the use of drugs.

REVIEW AND REFLECT

1   Outline with examples Goldstein's tripartite framework
2   What drug shows the strongest relationship between psychopharmacological use and violence?
3   What are the important features of illicit drug markets that heighten the risk for violence?

SUMMARY

Drugs can be classified based on their typical pharmacological effects on users. The main types of drugs include opiates, stimulants, depressants, hallucinogens, and cannabis. It is also important to recognise that the effects of drugs depend not only on the drug itself, but also on aspects of the user and the context of use. Drugs can also be classified in terms of their legal status. A basic division can be drawn between legal and illegal substances, and illicit drugs are further classified in terms of risks to users and society. Recent research suggests that the simple demarcation of illegal drugs into different 'classes' and the division between legal and illegal drugs are not firmly based on any objective evaluation of the harms of different psychoactive substances.

Cannabis is by far the most commonly tried illicit drug in Western countries, with other substances, such as cocaine, heroin, and ecstasy tried by less than 15 per cent of the population in any English-speaking Western country. Far fewer individuals use drugs on a regular basis, but adolescents and young adults are more likely to self-report illicit drug use in the last month than are older individuals.

Drug use can be considered as occurring on a continuum. Many people use drugs with no or relatively few problems. Problematic drug use can occur due to the adverse consequences that arise from the acute effects of drugs and from patterns of repeated drug use. Substance use disorder is recognised in the DSM–5.

A number of different theories have been developed to explain why people use and misuse drugs. Biological approaches focus on the way that drugs act on critical neurotransmitter systems in the brain. From a biological perspective, drug dependence can be characterised as a chronic relapsing brain disease. A psychological perspective emphasises the influence of a range of individual, family, and social risk factors for drug use. Socio-cultural approaches highlight the important role that social context can have on drug use and drug use problems. Most researchers recognise that, in order to fully understand why individuals use and misuse drugs, a multidisciplinary perspective needs to be taken.

Research clearly supports the idea that drug use is associated with criminal offending. Studies that have looked at the offending population find that drug use and misuse are common. Research that has examined crime among problem drug users and crime and problem drug use in the general population also generally support the idea that drugs and crime 'go together'. It is important to recognise, however, that these studies, by themselves, cannot tell us anything about the causal relationship between drugs and crime.

Three main models have been proposed to explain the relationship between drugs and crime: (a) drugs lead to crime; (b) crime leads to drugs; and (c) a common cause accounts for the relationship. The 'drugs causes crime' model can be further categorised in terms of three models: (a) the psychopharmacological model; (b) the economic compulsive model; and (c) the systemic model.

Research supports the idea that the use of alcohol is, to some extent, pharmacologically related to violent offending. However, the relationship between alcohol and violent crime is moderated by a number of individual and contextual factors. There is some support for the idea that the use of psychostimulants may also make an individual more likely to engage in violent crime, but there is little evidence for a psychopharmacological link between other drugs such as cannabis, ecstasy, and heroin and violent crime.

Because illicit drugs are extremely expensive, some drug users may engage in acquisitive offending in order to support their drug use. Studies of offenders provide some support for the idea that heavy users of drugs like heroin, crack, and cocaine commit crimes, in part, to obtain money to purchase drugs.

Illegal drug markets are often characterised by high levels of violence. The absence of third-party enforcement, the cost of the drugs involved, and an environment of low trust all contribute to the violence that is intrinsic to many illegal drug markets. It is important to note, however, that levels of violence vary considerably across different drug markets and at different times.

The association between drugs and crime can also be understand in terms of the way involvement in crime may lead to the use of drugs. Association with criminal networks and the use of drugs to carry out and celebrate crime are some of the mechanisms that can explain this link. Many of the risk factors for criminal offending are also risk factors for drug use and misuse, suggesting that at least part of the relationship between drugs and crime is due to presence of common causes. It is also worth recognising the way that drugs and crime might be reciprocally related, as involvement in crime may lead to drug use, which, in turn, can contribute to offending.

FURTHER READING

Abadinksy, H. (2014). *Drug Use and Abuse: A Comprehensive Introduction* (8th edition). Belmont, CA: Wadsworth.
Now in its eighth edition, this book provides what its title promises – a comprehensive introduction to drug use and abuse.

Bean, P. (2014). *Drugs and Crime* (4th edition). London: Routledge.
Thoughtful and detailed analysis of the relationship between drugs and crime from a critical perspective.

McMurran, M. (ed.). (2013). *Alcohol-Related Violence: Prevention and Treatment.* Chichester: Wiley. Excellent collection of chapters on the nature and scope of the relationship between alcohol and violence with good coverage of approaches for prevention and treatment.

Tomlinson, M. F., Brown, M., & Hoaken, P. N. S. (2016). Recreational drug use and aggressive behaviour: A comprehensive review since 2003. *Aggression and Violent Behavior*, 27, 9–29. Cutting-edge review of the literature on drug use and aggressive behaviour.

WEB RESOURCES

The Beckley Foundation Drug Policy Programme provides useful information about drug policy (www.internationaldrugpolicy.net) and The Foresight Brain, Science and Addiction and Drugs site includes a number of useful reviews concerning the psychological, biological, and sociological origins of substance use and misuse (www.foresight.gov.uk/Previous_Projects/Brain_Science_Addiction_and_Drugs/index.html).

General information about drugs can be obtained from a number of useful websites, including:

The Australian Drug Foundation: www.adf.org.au.
The New Zealand Drug Foundation: www.nzdf.org.nz.
DrugScope: www.drugscope.org.uk.
National Institute of Drug Abuse: www.nida.nih.gov/NIDAHome.html.

✳ KEY CONCEPTS

- addiction
- alcohol myopia model
- arrestee drug abuse monitoring programmes
- economic compulsive model
- incentive salience

- incentive-sensitisation model
- new psychoactive substances
- psychopharmacological model
- sensation seeking
- substance use disorder
- systemic model

Property offending

LEARNING OBJECTIVES

On completion of this chapter you should:

➤ have a good general understanding of the nature and prevalence of the main types of property offending including burglary, shoplifting, vehicle-related theft, arson, vandalism, and graffiti;
➤ recognise some of the main theoretical explanations for burglary and shoplifting;
➤ understand the main approaches for understanding arson include the multi-trajectory theory of adult firesetting

We have, to this point in the textbook, focused largely on various forms of violent offending. Although violent crimes cause an enormous amount of harm in society, official police statistics remind us that they are not the most common type of offence (although victim surveys can tell us a somewhat different story). Indeed, various forms of economic or acquisitive offending make up the majority of offences recorded by police. For this reason, such offences are often referred to by criminologists as 'volume crime' (Newburn, 2013). Property crime, fairly straightforwardly, entails the illegal acquisition or destruction of property that is not owned by the individual. In this chapter we will consider research on a range of different types of property offending.

We begin with an overview of the nature and extent of property offending in society and general theoretical approaches to understanding this form of crime. We then turn to a more detail discussion of specific types of property crime focusing, in turn, on burglary, shoplifting, vehicle-related theft, and arson. Although purely psychological approaches have had less impact in this area than for forms of violent crime, many of the explanations we have encountered so far also feature in explanations for property crime. Given the ubiquitous nature of property crime, clearly attempts to advance our understanding of this form of offending is important.

THE NATURE AND EXTENT OF PROPERTY OFFENDING

What is property crime?

Humans are a devious species, and there are various ways that another person's property can be acquired through illegal means. We have already discussed robbery, or the use of force to obtain property from others, in the chapter on violent offending so we will not revisit that topic here. Other forms of offending that involve the illegal acquisition of another's property and resources such as fraud, embezzlement, and other instances of so-called white-collar crime are discussed in detail in the following chapter. Here, we confine ourselves to a relatively small range of 'garden variety' property crimes that, together, constitute a significant volume of all offences recorded by the police and hence are the focus of significant activity in the criminal justice system.

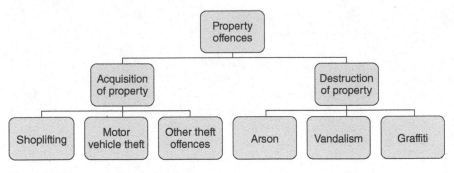

Figure 9.1 The range of property offences.

Different countries categorise property offences in different ways. In the United States, for example, the taking of property from someone else without their consent is referred to as *larceny*, with a distinction made between grand and petit larceny based on the value of the property taken (Brown, Esbensen, & Geis, 2015). In Figure 9.1 the main forms of property offending that feature in the criminological literature are outlined, although these categories do not necessarily map cleanly on to specific *legal* distinctions in different countries. Very broadly, we can make a distinction between offending that involves the acquisition of property and offending that involves the destruction or harming of property. **Burglary** entails illegal entry into a property with the purpose of acquiring others' resources or property. **Shoplifting** entails the acquisition of goods or property from a commercial enterprise without the use of force (when it becomes robbery). **Motor vehicle theft** involves the theft of cars, motorcycles, snowmobiles, and other forms of motorised transport and/or the theft of property from those vehicles. Other forms of illegal property acquisition include pocket picking, purse snatching, theft of bicycles, and so on. Some types of property offending involve the destruction of property rather than its acquisition, including **arson**, **vandalism**, and **graffiti**.

The prevalence of property offending

We have already noted that property offences are often referred to as 'volume crime' because they are relatively common compared to other sorts of offending. As you will be aware by now, establishing a clear picture of the frequency of any form of crime is a difficult task, and cross-national comparisons are especially difficult for property offences due to different definitions, variability in policing, and so forth (see Chapter 1). However, in this section we provide a brief overview of the prevalence of property offences in the United States, England and Wales, Australia, and New Zealand.

The sheer extent of property crime in society is possibly best appreciated by considering the most recent data released from the FBI Uniform Crime Reports 2015 (U.S. Department of Justice, 2016) for the United States. In total in 2015 there were just under 8 million recorded property crimes in the United States, or 2,487 per 100,000 inhabitants, resulting in estimated losses of 14.3 billion dollars. These included:

- 1,579,527 burglaries resulting in $3.6 billion in losses
- 5,706,346 larceny thefts resulting in $5.3 billion in losses

- 707,758 motor vehicle thefts resulting in losses of $4.9 billion
- 41,376 arsons.

In England and Wales, we find for the year ending June 2016 that there were 3,702,000 theft offences in total and 1,255,000 instances of criminal damage (Flatley, 2016a). In Australia, for 2013 there were 203,438 burglary offences, 52,979 motor vehicle thefts, and 482,900 other theft offences (Australian Institute of Criminology, 2016). In New Zealand in 2014 the police recorded:

- 53,265 instances of unlawful entry with intent/burglary, break, and enter
- 49,121 instances of motor vehicle theft and related offences
- 64,188 other theft offences.

In combination, these property offences represented just under 50 per cent of all offences recorded by the police in 2014 (New Zealand Crime Statistics, 2015).

Suitably numbed by this barrage of statistics, the picture established should be pretty clear: there is a huge volume of property offences occurring every year. Interestingly, the volume of property offending is actually much *lower* than it used to be. Indeed, the prevalence of property offending in Western countries has been declining dramatically over the last ten to 20 years – a phenomenon that has generated much interest among criminologists (see Box 9.1). Given how common property offences are you might expect a commensurate amount of criminological research and theory directed at this type of crime. However, this is not the case: although there is a reasonable body of research and theory to draw upon, property offending has not received nearly as much attention from criminologists and criminal psychologists as have other types of crime. We will consider research on the specific types of property crime illustrated in Figure 9.1 in more detail later in the chapter, but it will be useful to start with a brief general overview of theoretical approaches to property offending.

BOX 9.1 THE GREAT PROPERTY CRIME DECLINE

As illustrated in the graph below for Australia, there has been a significant decline in the volume of property offences over the last decade or more. This phenomenon is not restricted to Australia, and declines in crime more generally and in property offending more specifically have been noted for the United States, Canada, New Zealand, and much of Western Europe (Brown, 2015). These trends challenge the public perception, often reinforced in the media, that the crime 'problem' is getting worse. Documenting these trends, however, has proven easier than explaining them. There has been no shortage of theoretical efforts to account for the decline in property crime but to date no widely accepted consensus has been reached. Possibly the most promising explanation for the decline in property offending has been provided by Farrell and colleagues who argue that essentially the drop in property offending is the result of significant improvements in security, especially for motor vehicles (see Farrell, Tilley, & Tseloni, 2014; Farrell et al., 2010).

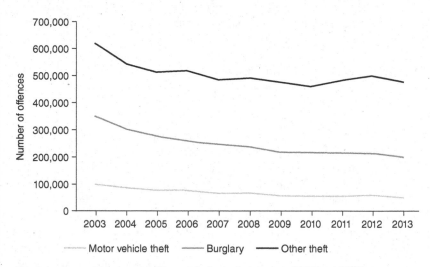

Number of recorded property offences in Australia between 2003 and 2013.

Question for discussion

Review the work by Farrell and colleagues on 'the security hypothesis' for the crime drop. Are you convinced by their arguments? Why? Why not? Can the security hypothesis satisfactorily explain the drop in both property and other forms of offending?

REVIEW AND REFLECT

1   What are some of the main types of property crime?
2   Why do you think that property offences are the most common type of offence in recorded police statistics?
3   Before reading further, how would *you* explain why property offending occurs?

Theoretical approaches: overview

When Willie Sutton (1901–1980), an infamous bank robber in the United States, was asked by a reporter why he robbed banks, he purportedly replied: 'because that is where the money is'. Although Sutton subsequently denied that he responded in this fashion the saying has since morphed into 'Sutton's law', a heuristic used by medical students to remind them to focus on the most likely diagnosis. Clearly explanations for property offending have to recognise the simple fact that individuals engage in such offending in order to obtain valued goods and resources without having to pay for them. Of course, although there is, as we have noted, a huge volume of such offences, most people, most of the time, are not willing to break the law in order to obtain property without paying for it. It is also fair to say that many individuals who engage in property offending also commit other types of crime so it might be reasonable to conclude that we need to consider both specific explanations for property offending and explanations that more generally account for criminal and antisocial behaviour. For the most part, criminologists have been happy to take the latter option, and general criminological theories have been used to explain property crime and to guide relevant research. In this section we will briefly note some of the main general types of explanations drawing from various levels of analysis before looking at more specific explanations for specific offences later in the chapter.

Evolutionary psychologists have had very little to say about the causes of property offending. Some scholars have noted that the notion of 'property' itself is not restricted to the human species, and many other animals can be said to have territory that they monopolise for the resources that it contains. As such, theft itself is an 'offence' that occurs widely in the biological world (Kanazawa, 2008; Stake, 2004) reflecting the simple logic that one viable route to acquiring reproductively relevant resources is through stealing them. As Kanazawa (2008, p. 160) notes 'That theft is a cultural universal and observed among other species strongly suggests a biological and evolutionary origin'. Whether or not humans have specific psychological adaptations for theft, as Kanazawa suggests, is unclear. Certainly, the appropriation of another's resources, in some contexts, might promote reproductive fitness. However, throughout most of our evolutionary history humans lived in small communities where everyone was known to everyone else, making the *costs* of theft, including the reputation for dishonesty, significant. Certainly, it might be expected that given the right contexts, many – although, perhaps not most – individuals might be tempted to advance their wealth in ways that involve the least effort.

There is a somewhat larger criminological literature on the role of social-structural and cultural factors in property offending. Messner and Rosenfeld (2013), for instance, in their book *The American Dream* argue that the relentless creed of capitalism that emphasises the status value of resources encourages a society that is willing to obtain those resources through whatever means possible. In other words, they argue that society is set up in a way that encourages the linking of status to wealth. As not everyone can acquire such wealth through legitimate channels then property offending is the natural response. It is certainly clear that the proliferation of objects that is such a visible feature of contemporary Western societies inevitably makes theft and other forms of property crime more likely. Furthermore, relatively few property offenders, as we shall discuss in more detail below, offend out of absolute necessity (i.e., they offend in order to have enough to eat – although there are certainly some offenders that fit in to this group), suggesting that it is the status of the stolen property (or its conversion in to cash) that drives offending. Although social-structural and cultural approaches (like evolutionary approaches) are useful in highlighting the more distal explanations for offending we still need to account for why some individuals are more likely to engage in property offending than others and why some contexts appear to facilitate offending.

Efforts to explain property offending have drawn heavily on three theoretical approaches that focus on the role of the situation in shaping behaviour: rational choice theory, routine activities theory, and crime pattern theory. We have briefly explored the key features of these theoretical approaches in Chapter 1 so you may want to quickly look over this material before reading this chapter. Very briefly, rational choice theory assumes that individuals, within the limits of their own abilities and the situational context, make rational decisions about whether to offend. The decision-making processes of property offenders should, therefore, reflect something like a rational choice to offend give the capabilities of the offender and the criminal opportunities afforded by the particular situation. Although routine activities theory specifies three elements for a crime to occur – a motivated offender, a suitable target, and the absence of a capable guardian – it is really the last two of these that are the focus of relevant research: how do changes in suitable targets and the presence of capable guardians influence the patterns of property offending that are found. Finally, crime pattern theory highlights that understanding offending requires us to consider the typical spatial patterns of offenders – their awareness space of criminal opportunities. As we shall see, each of these theories have been pressed in to service to help us understand property offending. Of course, not all individuals who are afforded an opportunity for property offending will take up the opportunity, even if the chances of getting caught are minimal. This suggests that we also need to consider more specific individual psychological characteristics such as moral views regarding the appropriateness of stealing to provide complete explanations for property offending. Two criminological theories that address this gap that we have yet to consider in any detail in this book are **neutralisation theory** and **situational action theory**.

One classic, although perhaps not as widely known, criminological theory that still gets a lot of mileage in understanding offending is neutralisation theory, developed by Sykes and Matza (1957). The core idea is reasonably straightforward: in part, the criminal activities of offenders are undertaken because these individuals are able to employ various psychological strategies – what Sykes and Matza refer to as moral neutralisations – to make their offending less morally culpable in their own eyes. The key idea is nicely summarised by the authors (Sykes & Matza, 1957, p. 666):

> It is our argument that much delinquency is based on what is essentially an unrecognised extension of defences to crime in the forms of justifications for deviance that are seen as valid by the delinquent but not by the legal system or society at large.

In Table 9.1 the five neutralisations identified by Sykes and Matza (1957) are outlined. As we shall see, a number of scholars have utilised this theory (with additional neutralisations) to understand various forms of property offending.

Table 9.1 Sykes and Matza's techniques of neutralisation

Technique	Description
Denial of responsibility	Personal responsibility for the offending is discounted, disclaimed, or denied
Denial of injury	The offender denies that their actions actually caused any harm to others
Denial of the victim	The victim of the offence is redefined as a legitimate target
Condemnation of the condemners	The offender argues that their actions are less blameworthy than those that are responding to their deviance
Appeal to higher loyalties	The violation of the law is justified by virtue of more important moral obligations

Source: Sykes and Matza (1957).

Another, more recent, theoretical approach that emphasises the role of individual moral views is situational action theory. The essence of situational action theory is that crime is ultimately a product of the interaction between individual or person factors and features of the situation (Wikström, 2006). The most important individual factor posited by the theory relates to an individual's moral rules and habits: that is, a person's sense of right and wrong and their typical way of behaving in particular circumstances. Individuals who tend to have moral rules and habits that are commensurate with those that are stated in the law will be less likely to offend even in contexts that make offending easy to get away with – for them crime is simply not a viable action alternative (Wikström & Treiber, 2016a). Of course, sometimes an individual's desires or needs will conflict with their moral beliefs. A second key individual factor involved, then, is the capacity for self-control or self-regulation: when self-control is low offending may be more likely even if it conflicts with the moral rules that an individual holds. Crime propensity then is a combination of an individual's morality and their capacity to exercise self-control. Crime, however, is a product of individual × situation interactions. Crime is more likely when the setting is conducive to offending because either the context is more congruent with an individual's morality (e.g., when peers endorse the criminal act) or external controls (i.e., the likelihood of getting caught) are weak. We will discuss this theory in the specific context of shoplifting outlined below but it should be clear how it is relevant for understanding property offending in general.

REVIEW AND REFLECT

1   Why are rational choice theories so prominent in explanations for property offending?
2   What are the key features of neutralisation theory, and how might this theory be relevant for explaining property offending?

BURGLARY

The nature of burglary and burglars

The definition of burglary varies somewhat among different jurisdictions but the key elements are largely the same. In the FBI Uniform Crime Reports (U.S. Department of Justice, 2016) burglary is defined as 'the unlawful entry of a structure to commit a felony or theft'. This is similar to the definition in the International Crime Victim Survey as 'an incident where someone enters property without permission in order to steal something' (cited in Malby, 2001, p. 4). In English law, burglary used to be defined as 'breaking and entering' with the requirement that an individual actually had to physically break in to a property for a burglary to occur. Following the 1968 Theft Act, burglary was defined as 'illegal entry to premises followed by theft or with the intent to commit an offence' (cited in Malby, 2001, p. 4). Thus an individual can be charged with burglary if they illegally trespass on another's property even if nothing of value is taken.

A common distinction is made between the burglary of private residences – domestic burglaries, and those that are directed as commercial properties – non-domestic burglaries. Distinctions are also sometimes made based on the typical mode of burglary. Where an individual uses force or threat of force (or carries a fire-arm or other weapon) the offence is typically referred to as an *aggravated burglary* and usually attracts harsher sentences. *Distraction burglary* involves an offender tricking their way into a home or other premise usually by affecting a legitimate purpose – for example, pretending to be someone from a gas or electrical company or asking directions to a nearby street. Where a vehicle is used to smash into a shop or other premise this is often referred to as 'ram raiding'. Regardless of the type of burglary, the offence is largely focused on illegally obtaining material resources from some dwelling or structure where the individual has no legal right to be (thus distinguishing the offence from shoplifting, discussed below) (Malby, 2001).

What kind of individuals commit burglaries? The answer is perhaps hardly surprising given everything we know about criminal behaviour in general: burglary offenders are likely to be young, be male, and come from socially disadvantaged backgrounds (Malby, 2001). They are also more likely to have had prior criminal convictions, and the abuse of alcohol and other drugs is a risk factor for burglary offending. Although individuals may commit one-off burglaries, generally speaking burglary is part of a criminal career that involves a range of antisocial and criminal behaviour including the use of violence, drugs, and other offences (DeLisi et al., 2016). These general findings, widely recognised in the literature, were clearly illustrated in a recent study by DeLisi et al. (2016). Drawing on data from the National Survey on Drug Use and Health between 2002–2013 the research explored the characteristics of individuals who self-reported burglary in the last 12 months. Individuals were significantly more likely to be young (age 18–20), male, be on government assistance, and have not graduated from college.

Explanations for burglary

Perhaps unsurprisingly a lot of research on burglary has been guided by the assumptions of rational choice theory. It is assumed that individuals who commit burglary are motivated to obtain material resources and to avoid the risk of detection or prosecution. Research largely bears out these assumptions. The primary motivation for committing a burglary offence is the profit that can be obtained from the objects that are stolen. However, the material gains are not necessarily pursued out of strict 'necessity' but, instead, are often used to support a particular lifestyle, which in many cases involves the use of alcohol and other drugs (Malby, 2001). These points were borne out in a study by Taylor (2014) of 30 domestic burglars in the United Kingdom, who concluded that 'obtaining money, and quickly, was the primary motivation for all of the burglars in this study, except one' (p. 491). For most offenders in this study the profits were used primarily to support a desired lifestyle. As one of the participants noted: 'I did it for the money, the lifestyle. To buy alcohol, to go to parties, clubbing. Nothing else' (Taylor, 2014, p. 491).

Rational choice theory, in combination with routine activities theory and crime pattern theory, can also help us understand how burglars go about their offending and the kinds of places that they target. Bernasco and Nieuwbeerta (2005), combining aspects of these three theories, suggest that residential burglars should preferentially target neighbourhoods and residential dwellings in those neighbourhoods that are: (a) more affluent, and hence are more likely to have desirable goods to steal; (b) accessible and thus require less effort to travel to and from; and (c) poorly guarded, and hence the likelihood of detection are low.

The idea that burglars are more likely to target affluent neighbourhoods has somewhat mixed support with some studies finding a relationship between affluence and offending, while other studies suggest that *less* affluent neighbourhoods are more likely to be burgled (Bernasco & Nieuwbeerta, 2005; Townsley et al., 2015). In one international analysis it was found that less developed (and hence poorer) countries were more likely to experience residential burglary, suggesting that other factors need to be considered in addition to the likelihood of obtaining valued items (Chon, 2017). The second suggestion – that residential burglary will be related to the accessibility of suitable targets – is, however, strongly supported in the literature. A consistent finding is that burglars will target households that are close to where they live, although what constitutes 'close proximity' varies somewhat depending on the particular geographical location (Bernasco & Nieuwbeerta, 2005; Townsley et al., 2015). Moreover, consistent with crime pattern theory offenders will also preferentially target households and neighbourhoods that they have targeted previously. Indeed, when a house has been burgled once it is at a significantly greater risk of being targeted again in the near future (Bernasco, Johnson, & Ruiter, 2015; Lantz & Ruback, 2015). Finally, the proposition that more poorly guarded dwellings are preferentially targeted is also well supported. Offenders will, if possible, burgle houses where no one is home and/or the risk of detection is low (Chon, 2017; Townsley et al., 2015). Interestingly, this idea can help to explain the somewhat paradoxical negative relationship that is found between unemployment rate and property offending – as unemployment rates increase, the prevalence of property offending declines, presumably because it is more likely that there will be a capable guardian to deter offending (Chon, 2017; D'Alessio, Eitle, & Stolzenberg, 2012).

The way that burglars carry out their offending can also be understood in terms of the rational need to obtain the valued objects in a timely and efficient fashion. Indeed, research suggests that offenders follow a cognitive script, which guides their behaviour in ways that maximise rewards given the time available to them (Maguire, Wright, & Bennett, 2010). Although there is some variability in these scripts a fairly consistent approach is to target the master bedroom first as this is where most of the valuables are located, and then to search other rooms where valuable goods are most likely to reside (often avoiding children's bedrooms). As one respondent in the study by Taylor (2014, p. 497) noted: '[straight to] the master bedroom. I would be looking for gold, money, just go for the jewellery box and look in the drawers. After that I would hit the front room – you've got your electrical stuff in there – laptops, plasmas, digital cameras, handbags. Everything'. In general offenders aim to complete their burglary as quickly as possible so as to evade detection although there is a fair amount of individual variation in the strategy that is employed.

Although situational theories perhaps provide the most insight into the pattern of burglary offending that is found, the role of morality has also been explored by some scholars. For example, Taylor (2014) in her qualitative analysis of 30 convicted domestic burglars in the United Kingdom found that burglars appeared to use what she refers to as 'codes of practice' in guiding their offending. These codes of practice featured many of the 'neutralisations' elucidated by Sykes and Matza (1957). For example, a number of offenders employed 'denial of injury' and 'denial of victims' to shape their offending behaviour: their actions were justified as taking from those that could well afford it. As one offender noted: 'I god nicked up in [an affluent area of town] because I used to think they were rich and I was poor and to me that justified it. It dint' feel as bad, they have millions anyway' (Taylor, p. 492). More generally, a number of offenders suggested that their actions were guided by their own specific moral compass noting that they wouldn't target old people's houses or take stuff from children's bedrooms.

Despite being a very common offence, there is much less research on burglary (and other property crime) than on violent offences. Most theoretical work has highlighted the role of situational theories such as rational choice and routine activity theory, although clearly there is scope to explore the role of morality and other individual-level characteristics in shaping offending behaviour. As we shall explore in Chapter 11, our understanding of the dynamics of burglary does, however, suggest specific approaches for crime prevention.

REVIEW AND REFLECT

1   What is burglary?
2   Briefly outline what is known about how burglars go about their offending.
3   How useful do you think that neutralisation theory is for understanding burglary offending?

SHOPLIFTING

The nature and extent of shoplifting

Shoplifting – sometimes colloquially known as the 'five-finger discount' – refers to the crime of theft, where customers (or those posing as customers) steal from retail outlets to which they have legitimate access (Tilley, 2010, p. 48). As such, shoplifting can be distinguished from burglary (which involves trespassing on another's property) and robbery (which involves the threat or use of force). There is no doubt that shoplifting is a common offence, even if it is hard to establish accurate figures for the exact amount of shoplifting that occurs. One review of the literature noted that up to 60 per cent of shoppers admit to shoplifting at least once in their lives, and 30–40 per cent of adolescents are repeat shoplifters (Krasnovsky & Lane, 1998). In New Zealand, between 2009 and 2012, 18,341 individuals were convicted of shoplifting, and New Zealand stores are losing on average between 1 and 2 million dollars a day to this crime.

Like most offences shoplifting is more likely to be perpetrated by males than by females, although some studies report roughly comparable rates of offending between men and women. Younger individuals are also more likely to engage in shoplifting although it can be hard to establish exact prevalence figures (Tilley, 2010). The type of product stolen various considerably over time and place depending on a range of factors including the presence of anti-theft mechanisms and other approaches to improving security. Clarke (1999) suggests that more desirable or CRAVED (concealable, removable, available, valuable, enjoyable, disposable) goods are most likely to be taken (see Figure 9.2), although clearly what counts as a CRAVED item varies over time – for example the higher cost of cigarettes in recent years has made this a more valuable (and therefore disposable) item. Moreover, recent changes in the process of shopping, such as the introduction of self-checkouts, can transform what counts as a removable or available item (see Box 9.2)

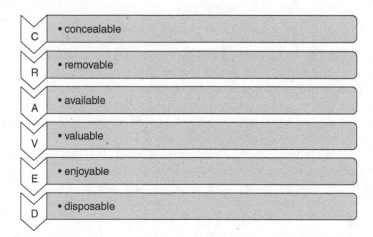

Figure 9.2 Craved items are more likely to be shoplifted.
Source: Clarke (1999).300

BOX 9.2 SELF-CHECKOUTS AND OFFENDING: IS THE TEMPTATION TOO GREAT?

Carrots are cheap. Pretty much anytime of the year in most places you can reliably purchase a kilogram of carrots for very little. Other produce – especially such things as berry fruit, cherries, avocados, and asparagus – can, in contrast, be very expensive. As you scan your kilo of raspberries through the automatic self-checkout swiper at the supermarket a very real temptation might arise: why not pass the berry fruit off as carrots and get them for a lot less. That isn't really stealing is it? As Taylor (2016b) argues, the rise in supermarket self-checkouts has afforded new opportunities for shoplifting that serves as a challenge to existing theories and approaches to this offence. Although research on this topic is limited, studies suggest that 20–30 per cent of shoppers admit to stealing at self-service checkouts at supermarkets (Taylor, 2016b). Strategies employed by these shoplifters include obscuring the bar code while pretending to scan an item, putting items on top of each other so only the bottom one is scanned, and selecting cheaper items from the menu for the more expensive actual item they have chosen – turning raspberries into carrots. Interestingly, many offenders see their actions as 'cheating' rather than theft, suggesting that this offence may, for some individuals, become morally normalised.

Questions for discussion

1   Have you have stolen something through a supermarket self-checkout? If yes, why did you decide to do this, and how did you go about 'beating' the machine?
2   If you were the owner of a supermarket with self-checkouts, what would you do to reduce theft by customers?

So how do potential shoplifters go about their business? The next time you are in a retail store imagine that you plan to take something from the store (but, don't actually take it!). What kind of items might you steal, and how would you go about taking them from the store without getting caught? Research suggests that thieves attempt to evade detection by trying to manage their impression so as to act as normal or 'non-thief' like as possible. In an interesting study by Lasky, Jacques, and Fisher (2015), 39 active shoplifters were interviewed with a focus on establishing how they carried out their offending. Broadly speaking, three key stages were identified: (a) entering and searching for a target; (b) taking the possession and concealing it; and (c) exiting the store with the stolen item. During each stage, participants indicated that they tried to appear as much as possible like normal shoppers. For example, one participant noted how he tried to take a normal route through the store: 'I don't go down the first aisle 'cause when you go in down that first aisle real quick I feel like it looks sketchy. So I go a couple aisles over, kind a shopping round a bit, just looking around like [I] don't really have any kind of particular intention. I'm just kind of walking around looking at stuff like I was just browsing, shopping' (Lasky et al., 2015, p. 300). In order to conceal items participants often noted how they would try and divert attention by bringing out and looking at their phones or by adjusting their facial reactions. Many, but not all, participants indicated that they would also often buy some products as well as the ones they have stolen in order to appear normal.

Explanations for shoplifting

Shoplifting is an offence with a long history: ever since desirable objects have been brought to the same location to sell there has been an ever-present temptation for some individuals to take these objects without paying. As such, it is hardly surprising that, as with burglary, rational choice explanations have predominated for explaining why individuals offend. Indeed, in many respects shoplifting is perceived to be a less risky enterprise than burglary with the chances of getting caught on any particular occasion relatively low (Tilley, 2010). Given the high rates of offending among adolescents there has also been a focus on relevant processes such as peer pressure, and shoplifting is often viewed more broadly as one component in a suite of deviant or antisocial behaviour that includes vandalism, substance abuse, and graffiti (Krasnovsky & Lanc, 1998). However, even though for many the benefits of shoplifting may outweigh the costs, most people, most of the time, don't take advantage of such opportunities. Clearly the costs of detection are greater for some than for others (e.g., those with a greater stake in their reputation), but people's sense of morality can also play an important role in explaining individual difference in shoplifting.

The role of moral neutralisation was clearly illustrated in a qualitative study of 137 apprehended shoplifters by Cromwell and Thurman (2003) (see Research in Focus 9.1). They found widespread use of the five techniques of neutralisation outlined by Sykes and Matza (1957). For example, the use of 'denial of injury' and 'denial of the victim' were common. For example, one participant noted 'they write it off their taxes. Probably make a profit off it. So, nobody gets hurt. I get what I need and they come out O.K. too' (Cromwell & Thurman, 2003, p. 543), clearly denying that any real harm or injury was inflicted. Another participant who indicated that 'stores deserve it. It don't matter if I boost $10,000 from one, they've made 10,000 times that much ripping off people' was obviously denying that there was any real victim in their offending (or, at least, they had it coming to them). In addition to these five techniques of neutralisation the researchers also found evidence for two additional neutralisations identified by Coleman (1998, cited in Cromwell & Thurman, 2003): *the defence of necessity* ('I had no other choice') and *everybody does it*, along with two new techniques identified in their research: *justification by comparison* ('if I wasn't shoplifting I would be doing something more serious'), and *postponement* ('I just don't think about it'). As with research on burglary, it is clear that shoplifting offenders neutralise or rationalise moral qualms they might have about their offending.

The importance of moral values and rules was also found in a study of shoplifting in a sample of 2,911 Austrian school students by Hirtenlehner and Hardie (2016). Using situational action theory to guide their research, the role of morality (beliefs about the wrongfulness of shoplifting), self-control, the moral context (perceptions about peers'

RESEARCH IN FOCUS 9.1 THE NEUTRALISATIONS USED BY SHOPLIFTERS

Title: The devil made me do it: use of neutralisations by shoplifters

Author: Cromwell, P., & Thurman, Q.   **Year**: 2003

Source: *Deviant Behavior*, 24, 535–550

Aims: To explore the moral neutralisations employed by shoplifters

Method: In-depth qualitative interviews with 137 apprehended shoplifters.

Key results:
- Neutralisation techniques were readily employed by participants, with only 5 of the 137 individuals failing to express a justification or neutralisation.
- Nine different categories of neutralisation were identified, including two new methods proposed by the authors.

Conclusion: 'We found widespread use of neutralizations among the shoplifters in our study. We identified two new neutralizations … even those who did not appear to be committed to the conventional moral order, used neutralizations to justify or excuse their behaviour' (Cromwell & Thurman, 2003, p. 547).

moral acceptance of shoplifting – criminogenic peers), and beliefs about the risks of getting caught (deterrence) were explored. In multivariate analyses weak morality, criminogenic peers, and weak deterrence were all significant predictors of shoplifting frequency. Of particular note, beliefs about the moral wrongfulness of shoplifting interacted with beliefs about the risk of getting caught (deterrence) such that those individuals with strong moral beliefs were not tempted to shoplift even if they thought the chances of getting caught were slim. In sum, the researchers concluded that moral elements (both personal morality and the moral context) 'were more important factors in explaining young people's shoplifting involvement than internal and external control' (Hirtenlehner & Hardie, 2016, p. 327), reinforcing the importance of attending to moral beliefs in understanding individual differences in the propensity to engage in property offending.

REVIEW AND REFLECT

1   What is shoplifting?
2   How might research on shoplifting help to prevent or reduce this crime?

VEHICLE-RELATED THEFT

The FBI Uniform Crime Reports defines motor vehicle theft as theft or attempted theft of a motor vehicle, which includes any self-propelled vehicle that runs on land surfaces and not on rails. A similar definition is provided the Theft Act (1968) in the United Kingdom but this act covers all 'conveyances' whether they run on land, air, or water (Brown, 2010). Both jurisdictions exclude the theft of bicycles. More broadly, vehicle crime encompasses both the theft of vehicles and the theft of items *from* vehicles (Brown, 2010). Vehicles may be stolen and then sold or stripped for parts, although a significant proportion of vehicle theft involves the 'temporary' theft of the vehicle for so-called 'joy-riding'. In many respects motor vehicles meet many of the criteria of a CRAVED item: they are (relatively) concealable through alteration, certainly removable and available with the appropriate skills, worth a significant amount of money and hence valuable, capable of generating enjoyment, and relatively easily sold on so – with the right connections – eminently disposable.

Unsurprisingly then, there is a substantial amount of vehicle-related theft in Western countries, although much less than there used to be. If you watch films set in the 1970s, 1980s, or 1990s, stealing cars looks pretty easy: you slip a thin piece of metal down the side of the windshield to force the lock open, then do some magic with the wires, and lo and behold the car is yours. Car theft in the 21st century, however, is much harder work. The introduction of better door locking systems, steering wheel locks, electronic mobilisations, and other security measures has made stealing a car without the key a challenging endeavour for even the most skilled auto thief. These changes are clearly borne out in the precipitous decline in automobile theft even given the increasing number of cars on the road. In Canada, for example, rates of auto theft reached their peak in the late 1990s and have declined ever since – indeed, the volume of such offences has dropped more than 67 per cent between 2003 and 2013 (Hodgkinson, Andresen, & Farrell, 2016). Farrell, Tilley, and Tseloni (2014) have argued that not only have better security measures resulted in the drop in vehicle-related offences but that this drop, in turn, has contributed to a decline in all forms of offending as vehicle theft is seen as a 'gateway' crime that is an important early component of a criminal career. Increasingly, vehicle-related thefts are the result of offenders finding and stealing the keys for cars rather than breaking in to the cars themselves, and car keys have become an increasing focus of burglary offences (Brown, 2010).

As with most other types of property offending, rational choice theories have predominated in explanations for vehicle-related theft, and we have already noted that vehicles are CRAVED items. However, individuals who steal cars to go 'joy-riding' are largely motivated by the excitement or rush of the offence, are engaged in a variety of antisocial and criminal behaviour, and are strongly influenced by their peers (Brown, 2010). These points were illustrated in a qualitative study of 43 Canadian youth with records for auto theft by Anderson and Linden (2014). Some key findings of this study included:

- 88 per cent reported convictions for other offences.
- Only one respondent reported that *none* of his friends stole cars; 37 per cent reported that most of their friends stole cars.
- 65 per cent indicated that they felt pressure from peers to steal cars.

- The most common motivations for offending reported were joy-riding (93 per cent), for transportation (87 per cent), and for the thrill of it (84 per cent).

Clearly the theft of motor vehicles, like other forms of property offending, can be perpetrated for purely instrumental purposes (to obtain a valuable good that can be converted to cash); however, it is often driven by other psychological processes including the search for an 'adrenaline rush' and to fit in to specific peer groups.

ARSON, VANDALISM, AND GRAFFITI

The nature and extent of arson, vandalism, and graffiti

Humans have been controlling and purposely lighting fires for perhaps a million years or longer. The importance of fire in the evolution of our species is highlighted in work by Richard Wrangham and colleagues (e.g., Wrangham & Carmody, 2010) who argue that the invention of fire wrought changes in how we consumed food, with wide-ranging consequences for the evolution of our physical and psychological characteristics (see also Gowlett, 2016). Whether or not we have specific adaptations for fire making or use is unclear, but certainly humans seem to 'drawn' to the lighting and maintaining of fires (see Criminal Psychology Through Film 9.1). Unfortunately for some, this fascination can bring them into contact with the law as their fire lighting leads to the damage of property and loss of lives and hence becomes the criminal offence of arson. Arson, then, involves the intentional lighting of fire with the purpose of damaging property or other objects of value (e.g., forested areas) (BushFIRE Arson Bulletin, 2004). The cost of intentional firesetting in society is substantial especially when we recognise that arson can lead not only to the damage of property and forested areas, but also to the loss of life. Dry regions, prone to bushfires, like California and much of Australia, have a particular interest in furthering understanding of the causes of arson and how best to prevent it. In Australia alone there are an estimated average of 54,000 bushfires a year of which around 30 per cent are suspected of being deliberately lit (BushFIRE Arson Bulletin, 2004).

Both vandalism and graffiti, like arson, involve the illegal damage to, as opposed to acquisition of, property. Vandalism is the broader label and includes a diverse range of acts from littering to the intentional destruction of valuable items and thus includes much of what is considered graffiti (Nordmarker et al., 2016). The term graffiti is much contested in the literature, and it is important to recognise that this label encompasses a potentially diverse range of acts that have a long history in society (Rowe & Hutton, 2012). Very broadly, graffiti, as it is discussed in the criminological literature, refers to 'the marking of other people's property without their consent' (Morgan & Louis, 2009). This definition obscures many of the variations in the practice and products of graffiti from the seemingly ubiquitous urban 'tagging' through to mural art, and political protest (see, for example, the work of Banksy: http://banksy.co.uk/out.asp). This variation was nicely captured in a study by Rowe and Hutton (2012) involving an online survey of 773 New Zealanders (with additional focus groups for smaller numbers) who responded to questions about attitudes towards graffiti. As illustrated in Figure 9.3 a clear majority of

CRIMINAL PSYCHOLOGY THROUGH FILM 9.1
Little Hope was Arson (2013)

Directed by: Theo Love

This documentary vividly captures the fear and drama wrought by a series of arsons directed at churches in East Texas in 2010. The subsequent investigation turns up the two (self-confessed) culprits, but wider issues are raised concerning the nature of community and what happens to those that are marginalised or struggling with their own issues and problems.

Questions for discussion

1   What factors appeared to play a role in the perpetration of these offences?
2   How might Gannon's M-TTAF help to make sense of these incidents?

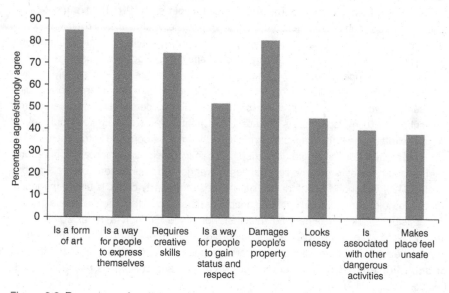

Figure 9.3 Percentage of participants that either agree or strongly agree with eight statements regarding graffiti.
Source: Rowe and Hutton (2012, Table 2).

respondents agreed that graffiti is 'a form of art' and 'a way to express themselves' while simultaneously recognising that it 'damages people's property'. However it is defined, graffiti and other forms of vandalism costs governments a considerable amount of money each year, and some forms are associated with perceptions of disorder and fear of crime among members of the community (Morgan & Louis, 2009).

If we leave aside graffiti that is better viewed as 'urban art' then the profile of the individuals who engage in vandalism and graffiti offences is fairly similar to the general profile of property offenders: they are more likely to be male, young adolescents, relatively less able to regulate behaviour, and involved in a range of antisocial and criminal activities (e.g., Nordmarker et al., 2016; Plenty & Sundell, 2015). Given the ease in which these offences can be perpetrated and the relative youth of offenders many have viewed graffiti as a 'gateway' crime that leads to more serious types of offending. This idea was tested in a longitudinal study by Plenty and Sundell (2015) with a sample of Swedish adolescents. The results suggest that although involvement in graffiti predicted later antisocial behaviour including various forms of property and violent crime, these relationships were largely attenuated after controlling for relevant individual, family, and peer factors. In sum, although committing graffiti at an early age may increase involvement in later antisocial and criminal behaviours this is largely due to shared risk factors relating to features of the individual, family, and peer environment.

Theoretical approaches to explaining arson

The characteristics and associated psychological features of firesetters are generally well recognised in the literature (Barrowcliffe & Gannon, 2016; Ducat & Ogloff, 2011; Gannon & Pina, 2010; Lambie, Ioane, & Randell, 2016; Lambie et al., 2013). Like most other types of property crime, firesetters are more likely to male, young, unemployed, and come from disadvantaged neighbourhoods. Individuals who engage in illegal firesetting are also likely to be involved in a range of other antisocial and criminal activities, mainly related to theft and other property offences. Like many offenders they are also more likely to have experienced adverse family environments, have poor regulation and interpersonal skills, and suffer from various mental health problems including personality, impulse-control, and substance use disorders. As discussed in Chapter 3, a relatively small sub-set of illegal firesetters meet the diagnostic criteria for the impulse control disorder, pyromania.

The motives for firesetting are varied and can included experimentation, boredom, peer pressure, vandalism, crime concealment, revenge, and fraud among others (Lambie et al., 2013). Although firesetting, like other types of property crime, is under-theorised relative to violent crimes, there is a reasonable psychological literature that has explored the aetiological factors underlying this behaviour (see Gannon & Pina, 2010, for a review). Here we consider in detail one important effort to integrate existing theoretical approaches to firesetting into one overarching model – the **multi-trajectory theory of adult firesetting** (M-TTAF) developed by Gannon and colleagues (Gannon, 2016; Gannon et al., 2012).

As summarised by Gannon (2016, p. 28) the M-TTAF conceptualises firesetting 'as being the product of the complex interactions and interrelations between developmental context, psychological vulnerabilities, proximal factors and triggers, moderators, and critical risk factors.' Space precludes anything like a thorough overview of these elements but some of the key processes can be relatively clearly outlined. Various features of the developmental context including the parenting environment, temperament of the individual, opportunities for social learning (especially social, aggressive, and fire-related scripts), and cultural attitudes towards fire can result in a range of psychological vulnerabilities. These include inappropriate interest in fire and fire-related scrips (see

Butler & Gannon, 2015; Gannon & Barrowcliffe, 2012), offence-supportive attitudes (both general and specifically fire-related), emotional regulation issues, and communication problems. These psychological vulnerabilities can be triggered or exacerbated by various triggers such as adverse life experiences and be moderated by other factors such as mental health issues, to be manifested as a corresponding set of critical risk factors that may lead directly to firesetting behaviour.

Specific subtypes of firesetters can also be identified according to M-TAFF by the particular cluster of critical risk factors that individuals hold. As illustrated in Figure 9.4 five 'trajectories' or subtypes of firesetting are proposed, each characterised by a cluster of critical risk factors: antisocial, grievance, fire interest, emotionally expressive/need for recognition, and multifaceted. Individuals in the *antisocial trajectory* are likely to have more general offence support attitudes and beliefs, have self-regulation problems, and commit acts of firesetting out of boredom or to conceal other crimes. The *grievance trajectory* involves individuals with general self-regulation issues who may also have communication problems and inappropriate fire scripts. They are likely to be primarily motivated by revenge or retribution. The third trajectory is *fire interest*. Individuals on this trajectory have inappropriate fire interests or scripts, and set fires as a result of their interest and fascination in fires when bored or stressed, or for thrill seeking. Individuals categorised in the emotionally expressive/need for recognition trajectory are characterised by general communication problems and likely self-regulation issues. Their firesetting is often a cry for help and may be part of an attempt to self-harm or commit suicide. Finally, the multi-faceted trajectory encompasses a range of critical risk factors, and the motivations for firesetting are various.

In sum, the M-TAFF offers a promising theoretical development in our efforts to understand the aetiology of firesetting. By integrating existing theories and by considering multiple levels of analysis the model, in principle, can help us not only to understand why fire-setting occurs but also to recognise clinically significant sub-types of offenders in ways that might lead to effective efforts in prevention and rehabilitation. As the authors themselves note, however, more empirical research is need to confirm many of the key elements of the model.

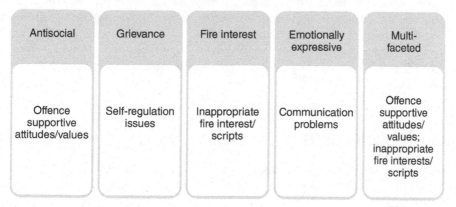

Figure 9.4 Key trajectories and risk factors in the multi-trajectory theory of adult firesetting.
Source: Gannon et al. (2012).

REVIEW AND REFLECT

1   How are arson, vandalism, and graffiti similar?
2   Outline the key elements of M-TAFF.

SUMMARY

In this chapter we have explored a range of different types of property crime and provided a review of attempts to explain this type of offending. Very broadly speaking, property offences can be categorised in terms of whether they involve (a) the illegal acquisition of, or (b) destruction of property. Property crimes are extremely common in society and make up a large proportion of official crime statistics. Attempts to explain property crime have focused unsurprisingly on rational choice and other situational theories, although other levels of analysis are also clearly relevant, and we briefly discussed two useful theoretical approaches: neutralisation theory, and situational action theory.

Burglary involves the unlawful entry of another person's property with the intent to commit a crime. Burglary offenders are much like offenders in general and share many of the same risk factors – they are typically young and male, and come from disadvantaged backgrounds. A rational choice perspective can help us understand the nature and pattern of burglary offending as offenders attempt to obtain rewards while limiting the risks for detection. Burglary offenders may also engage in various moral neutralisations to justify their offending. Shoplifting also involves the illegal acquisition of objects but can be distinguished from burglary because offenders have a legal right to be on the premises that they are stealing from. Again, rational choice theories have dominated explanations for shoplifting, but both neutralisation theory and situational action theory have also proven useful.

In the final section of this chapter we examined offences that involve the destruction (rather than theft) of others' property: vandalism, graffiti, and arson. Offenders of these crimes tend to be young and male, and are more likely to come from disadvantaged backgrounds and have many of the same risk factors for offenders in general. The Multi-Trajectory Theory of Adult Firesetting provides a promising framework for understanding illegal firesetting from a psychological perspective and outlines the key developmental contexts, psychological vulnerabilities, and proximal factors and triggers associated with this offence.

FURTHER READING

Mawby, R. I. (2001). *Burglary.* Cullompton: Willan Publishing.
Although a bit dated, this is an excellent introduction to the topic of burglary.

Tilley, N. (2010). Shoplifting. In F. Brookman, M. Maguire, H. Pierpoint, & T. Bennett (eds.), *Handbook on Crime* (pp. 48–67). Cullompton: Willan Publishing.
A good, single-chapter overview of research on shoplifting.

Gannon, T., Dickens, G., & Doley, R. M. (eds.). (2016). *The Psychology of Arson: A Practical Guide to Understanding and Managing Deliberate Firesetters* (pp. 23–34). New York, NY: Routledge. A comprehensive edited volume covering all aspects of the psychology of arson by the leading researchers in the field.

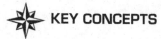 **KEY CONCEPTS**

- arson
- burglary
- graffiti
- motor vehicle theft

- multi-trajectory theory of adult firesetting
- neutralisation theory
- shoplifting

- situational action theory
- vandalism

Chapter 10

White-collar, organised, and environmental crimes

LEARNING OBJECTIVES

On completion of this chapter you should:

- ➤ have an understanding of the nature and extent of white-collar and corporate crime;
- ➤ understand the main theoretical explanations that have been developed to account for white-collar and corporate crime;
- ➤ have an understanding of the nature and extent of organised and transnational crime;
- ➤ have a clear understanding of what 'green criminology' is, and the major issues that engage green criminologists;
- ➤ recognise the potential impact of global environment change on crime patterns and trends.

It is a sad feature of the modern world that the practice of slavery still occurs – even in Western liberal societies such as Australia. In 2010 the married couple Trevor McIvor (aged 63) and Kanakporn Tanuchit (aged 42) were convicted on five offences of possessing and using slaves. The victims were purchased from Thailand and were under the impression that they would be engaged in sex work in Australia, but all were deceived as to the precise nature of the arrangements (Simmons, O'Brien, David, & Beacroft, 2013). On arrival in Australia they were told that they had incurred debts of between $35,000 and $40,000 and that they were required to engage in sex work in a Sydney brothel in order to pay off these debts. The passports of the five victims were confiscated, and they were essentially kept captive in a locked room at the brothel or at the private residence of the offenders (Schloenhardt & Laura-Rose, 2013). Both McIvor and Tanuchit were sentenced to 12 years in prison (Simmons et al., 2013). Sadly, this disturbing case is the just the tip of the iceberg in terms of the scale and scope of human trafficking globally, and both organised and transnational crime cause significant harm to individuals around the world.

In this chapter we tackle the related topics of white-collar and corporate offending, organised and transnational crime, and green criminology. What these topics share is a general focus on offending that involves the exploitations of others (including, in the case of green criminology, the environment) for, typically, financial gain. In some respects the offenders of these types of crime differ from the offenders that we have encountered throughout the book, and the nature and scale of their offending are also often different from the largely interpersonal crimes that we have so far focused on. However, although explanations for these offences differ in some respect from the ones we have encountered to date, there are also many similarities in the psychological processes and situational contexts that tend to foster or facilitate these types of crime. We first tackle the topic of white-collar and corporate crime, before turning to the related issue of organised and transnational crime. We close the chapter with a consideration of a relatively new area, green criminology, and consider the potential impact of global environmental change on offending.

WHITE-COLLAR OFFENDING AND CORPORATE CRIME

The nature and extent of white-collar and corporate crime

Definitional issues

In 2009, financier Bernie Madoff was convicted on a slew of charges including various forms of fraud, submitting false statements, and money laundering and was sentenced to 150 years in prison. Perpetrator of one of the largest 'Ponzi scheme' in history, Madoff managed to convince investors to hand over their money promising guaranteed high returns. Using the money injected by new investors Madoff paid off old investors while siphoning off the extra cash. Inevitably the scheme collapsed leaving an eye-watering shortfall of $65 billion and a lot of angry investors (Yang, 2014). The offence committed by Madoff neatly fits Edwin Sutherland's (1983, cited in Benson & Simpson, 2014, p. 7) classic definition of **white-collar crime** – 'a crime committed by a person of respectability and high social status in the course of his occupation'. Sutherland was motivated to bring attention to a class of offences that, while causing significant amount of harm and the illegal appropriation of large sums of money, went largely under the radar of both law enforcement agencies and criminologists alike.

Although Sutherland's work remains influential in the field, there has been a substantial amount of debate regarding how best to define the kinds of offences that Sutherland was interested in highlighting. It is not clear, for example, whether there should be an exclusive focus on 'high status' offenders, and inevitably there has been disagreement regarding just what constitutes 'high status'. It is also not clear whether there should be an exclusive focus on crimes committed in the course of a person's occupation or whether the net should be cast wider to assume a more diverse range of similar offences (Simpson, 2013). There are also potentially useful distinctions to be drawn between crimes committed by individuals *within* organisations and those committed *by* organisations, which might distinguish 'white-collar crime' from '**corporate crime**' (Newburn, 2013). A much broader definition that attempts to sidestep some of these issues has been provided by Edelhertz, (1970, cited in Benson & Simpson 2014, p. 12) who suggests that white-collar crime is 'an illegal act or series of illegal acts committed by non-physical means and by concealment or guile to obtain money or property, to avoid the payment or loss of money or property, or to obtain business or personal advantage'. Perhaps the clearest approach to gaining an understanding of just what white-collar and corporate crime involve is to consider some more concrete examples (see Criminal Psychology Through Film 10.1).

The scope of white-collar and corporate crimes

You receive an email from a distressed stranger asking for help. The email offers a detailed story about how they have inherited a vast sum of money (say, $5 million), but their government requires that they pay $1,000 in tax in order for the money to be released. Unfortunately they are unable to raise the cash, and time is running out – if you can just front the $1,000 they will happily split the five million dollars with you. It seems almost too good to be true, but hey $2.5 million could come in handy so you forward the cash. It *is* too good to be true – you have been scammed. This is but one example

CRIMINAL PSYCHOLOGY THROUGH FILM 10.1
The Wolf of Wall Street (2013)

Directed by: Martin Scorsese
Starring: Leonardo DiCaprio (Belfort), Jonah Hill (Donnie Azoff), and Kyle Chandler (Patrick Denham)

Based on the stockbroker Jordan Belfort's memoir of the same name, this film provides a fast-paced, comic account of rampant corruption, fraud, and all round greed set in the 1980s and 1990s. After creating the firm Stratton Oakmont, Belfort and his business partner Azoff manage to attract the attention of up and coming young stockbrokers with extraordinary financial success. However, many of their activities are illegal and the FBI attempt to nail Belfort for fraud and other white-collar offences.

Question for discussion

1   How are the actions of Belfort and his colleagues justified? Can you find evidence of moral neutralisations in this film?
2   Was the final outcome for Belfort just? Why? Why not?

of the diverse range of criminal activities that fall under the broad rubric of 'white-collar and corporate crime'. As outlined in Table 10.1 there is a myriad of overlapping activities, schemes, and behaviours that involve some of kind deception or misrepresentation in order to illegally obtain economic advantage. In short, the scope of white-collar and corporate crime simply reflects the limits of the human imagination in unfairly obtaining money, property, or services from others.

Edelhertz (1970, cited in Benson & Simpson, 2014), whose definition of white-collar crime we outlined above, suggests that such offences can be organised in to four basic types (see Figure 10.1). *Personal crimes* involve individuals acting on their own behalf, rather than in the context of a business for personal gain. Income tax evasion provides a common example. *Abuses of trust* entail offences that occur in the context of an individual's occupation such as the embezzlement of money from the business or the taking (or offering) or commercial bribes (see Griffiths, 2016, on bribery in the corporate world). Crimes that occur in the context of advancing business objectives can be viewed as *business crimes* – price fixing, violations of health and safety standards, and deceptive advertising strategies are just some examples. Finally, *con games* involve a diverse range of scams, swindles, and cons that may often serve as a primary source of income for some offenders. Clearly, if we except the broad definition of white-collar crime offered by Edelhertz then we are dealing with a diverse range of activities suggesting that our explanatory accounts of white-collar offending need to also be suitably diverse.

Table 10.1 Some examples of white-collar crime

Income tax evasion[a]	A failure to pay money due to the government as income tax
Fraud	A diverse range of activities perpetrated by individuals, groups, or organisations that involves the appropriation of resources from others by way of concealment, deception, or misrepresentation
Theft from the workplace[b]	The appropriation of money or resources by employees
Fakes, forgery and counterfeiting[c]	Objects that are deliberately made that purport to be what they are not in order to obtain financial gain or facilitate criminal activity, e.g., counterfeit banknotes, fake merchandise, forged documents
Scams[d]	A specific type of consumer-oriented fraud that involve 'orchestrated deception in the service of profit making' (Mackenzie, 2010b, p. 137), e.g., fake lottery schemes
Identity theft[e]	A 'range of offences which involve the criminal acquisition and misuse of an individual's personal data to gain an advantage' (Semmens, 2010, p. 172), e.g., 'phishing' – the use of fake websites to obtain confidential information about individuals such as credit card details
Corporate financial crimes[f]	A diverse range of activities perpetrated by corporations for financial gain, e.g., price fixing, false accounting, insider trading
Deceptive business practices and consumer offences[g]	Activities perpetrated by businesses that violate laws relating to the delivery of consumer services, e.g., the sale of out-of-date food, misrepresenting car repairs

Sources: [a]Minkes and Minkes (2010); [b]Source: Gill and Goldstraw-White (2010); [c]Mackenzie (2010a); [d]Mackenzie (2010b); [e]Semmens (2010); [f]Minkes (2010); [g]Croal (2010).

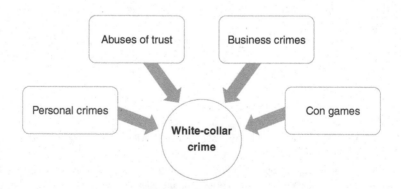

Figure 10.1 Four basic types of white-collar crime.
Source: Edelhertz (1970), cited in Benson and Simpson (2014, p. 12).

The extent and impact of white-collar and corporate crime

Now that we have some sort of idea of what constitutes white-collar and corporate crime it will be useful to briefly consider how prevalent this form of offending is in society. Unfortunately, traditional approaches to gathering information on the extent of white-collar crime are limited in providing us with a clear picture of the extent of these types of crime in society (Newburn, 2013). Newly introduced questions in the British Crime Survey suggest that there is something in the region of 3.6 million fraud offences in England and Wales each year, which contrasts with the 627,825 fraud offences recorded by the police. Data from Financial Fraud UK indicate that there were 1.9 million cases of fraud relating to cards, cheques, and banking (Flatley, 2016a). These figures indicate that (a) fraud offences are extremely common, and (b) most incidents of fraud are not recorded by police. In New Zealand in 2015 there were just over 10,000 convictions for 'fraud, deception, and related offences' which makes an interesting contrast to the just over 16,000 convicted for property and related offences, and just over 9,000 illicit drug offences (New Zealand Statistics, 2017).

Although it is hard to establish the full extent of white-collar and corporate crime in society the impact can be quite substantial. In purely monetary terms the National Fraud Authority (2011, cited in Newburn, 2013) estimated the total losses due to fraud to be in the region of £38 billion a year. However, it must be recognised that many white-collar and corporate crimes also pose a risk to the health and safety of individuals in society through breaches in health and safety regulations. Additionally, corporations are a major source of harm to the environment – a topic we take up later in the chapter.

REVIEW AND REFLECT

1   What are the different ways in which we can define white-collar crime?
2   According to Edelhertz (1970, cited in Benson & Simpson, 2014) what are the four main types of white-collar crime? Give examples of each.
3   Research a well-known example of white-collar or corporate offending (e.g., the executives behind the collapse of energy company Enron). What do you think the impact of this offence on others was?

Explaining white-collar and corporate offending

The deception of others in order to obtain personal gain is not just a feature of the corporate boardroom, capitalism, or, indeed, human society in general. In fact fraud and deception are rife throughout the biological world (Stevens, 2016). Consider the 'underhand' way in which cuckoos propagate their genes. Waiting patiently a female cuckoo will stake out the nest of her mark – say a small wren. When the cuckoo sees the wren fly off in search of food, she will swoop down silently, quickly lay her egg in the nest, shove the egg of the wren over the edge and fly away. What a scam! For little effort the cuckoo not only manages to eliminate a rival's offspring but somehow cons her into incubating her egg and raising her offspring (Davies, 2016). From an evolutionary point of view any strategy that can advance reproductive success (that is, on balance provides more benefits than costs) will be selected for even if it involves various kinds of deception. Perhaps then we should not be surprised that humans, given the appropriate circumstances, will be willing to take advantage of others to promote their own interests. This may be especially the case for white-collar offenders whose actions are located within the highly competitive structure of capitalist societies where those corporations that can generate more profit succeed at the expense of less successful ones (Simpson, 2013). It will be useful to begin our discussion with the ideas of Sutherland before moving on to more recent efforts to account for this type of offending.

Edwin Sutherland's **differential association theory** focuses on how offending results from the learning of norms, values, and specific techniques that are favourable to specific types of offending. In the context of white-collar offending the moral norms that are held and supported by businesses and organisations can be an important component in promoting, or at least facilitating, white-collar crime. In many cases the illegal acts might be viewed as simply a routine or standard way of 'conducting business', and new employees become socialised into accepting this point of view and thus perpetuate both the practices and the norms that support them (Benson & Simpson, 2014; Newburn, 2013). Sutherland's own research lends support to these ideas as has, to some extent, the research of subsequent scholars. For instance, Benson (1985, cited in Benson & Simpson, 2014, p. 74) provides the example of an individual who was convicted for bid rigging, whose response highlighted the normative aspects of his actions: 'It was a way of doing business before we ever got into the business. So, it was like why do you brush your teeth in the morning or something ... It was part of the everyday ... it was a method of survival.'

The comments of this businessman hint at a mode of rationalising or justifying the illegal acts consistent with Sykes and Matza's (1957) neutralisation theory discussed in Chapter 9. Indeed, the techniques of neutralisation identified by Sykes and Matza appear to be prominent in accounts of white-collar offending (Copes et al., 2013; Stadler & Benson, 2012). One example comes from the research of Stadler and Benson (2012) who compared the neutralisation techniques of a sample of white-collar and non-white-collar offenders incarcerated in a Federal prison in the United States. The use of *denial of responsibility* and *denial of victim* were especially prominent among the white-collar offenders although the use of these techniques did not differ significantly from the non-white-collar sample suggesting that such offenders may not differ that much in terms of the techniques of neutralisations employed.

Certainly, white-collar offenders, like other types of offenders, will seek to rationalise or neutralise their criminal actions. Inevitably, explanations for white-collar offending, like property offending in general, will also need to consider the important role that opportunity plays in accounting for individual involvement in these types of crime, along with the very real economic advantages that can accrue to successful offenders. As such, a number of scholars have drawn on situational theories (rational choice, routine activities theory) to account for white-collar offending (Benson & Simpson, 2014; Simpson, 2013). Although there are similarities between white-collar offending and other forms of property offending, Benson and Simpson (2014) highlight how the actions of white-collar offenders have all the appearance of legitimacy as: (a) they have legal access to the location in which the crime occurs; (b) they are separated from the victim (whom they might not even know); and (c) the actions of the offender may appear to an outside observer as perfectly legitimate. Unlike the burglary offender who is clearly transgressing against the law by targeting the property of somebody else, a white-collar offender can affect a patina of legitimacy while engaging in his or her illegal actions. However, even though it may be the case that white-collar offenders are socialised in to their offending, employ neutralisations that make their offending appear more morally palatable, and are afforded relevant opportunities to offend it still remains the case that not all – or even most – individuals faced with the same situations will give in to the temptation to offend. This suggests that we must also consider individual difference factors relating to the personality of offenders.

Psychopathy and personality characteristics

It will be useful, first, to consider how the characteristics of white-collar offenders may differ from other types of offender. Generally speaking, white-collar offenders tend to differ from the 'typical' offender by being older, more educated, employed, less likely to have a criminal history, and less likely to abuse alcohol and other drugs (Ragatz & Fremouw, 2010; Ragatz, Fremouw, & Baker, 2012) (see Research in Focus 10.1). Interestingly, at least some research suggests that white-collar offenders may also be characterised by having greater capacity for self-regulation or self-control (Raine et al., 2012). However, despite these differences, some research also suggests that many white-collar offenders are also likely to have the broadly antisocial personality characteristics that other types of offender have (Ragatz & Fremouw, 2010).

Indeed, there has been considerable interest in the existence of so-called 'corporate psychopaths' (see Chapter 3 for coverage on psychopathy) whose personality characteristics are argued to be advantageous in promoting their success while also contributing to their white-collar offending (Boddy et al., 2015; Perri, 2013). Arguably, individuals who are ruthless, willing to exploit others, deceptive, and lacking remorse may be able to advance their interests in many types of business organisations at the expense of others while taking opportunities to exploit the environment illegally for their own financial gain. However, Smith and Lilienfeld (2013) have urged caution in the widespread acceptance of the importance of the corporate psychopath pointing out that the research base remains limited and to some extent flawed. In short, although some highly successful business leaders who perpetrate white-collar crime may, indeed, have psychopathic characteristics, little is known about the prevalence of such traits among either business leaders or white-collar offenders.

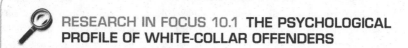

RESEARCH IN FOCUS 10.1 THE PSYCHOLOGICAL PROFILE OF WHITE-COLLAR OFFENDERS

Title: The psychological profile of white-collar offenders: Demographics, criminal thinking, psychopathic traits, and psychopathology

Author: Ragatz, L. L., Fremouw, W., & Baker, E.   **Year:** 2012

Source: *Criminal Justice and Behavior,* 39, 978–997

Aims: To explore how white-collar offenders differ from non-white-collar offenders on psychopathic characteristics, criminal thinking, and criminal lifestyle

Method: Assessment of white-collar-only offenders ($N = 39$), white-collar-versatile offenders ($N = 86$), and non-white-collar offenders ($N = 86$) incarcerated in a Federal prison in the United States.

Key results: Compared to non-white-collar offenders, white-collar offenders have significantly:

- lower levels of criminal thinking
- fewer behaviours consistent with a criminal lifestyle
- fewer drug, but more alcohol, problems.

But there were not significant differences in overall scores on the Psychopathic Personality Inventory.

Question for discussion

How might these personality and lifestyle differences (and similarities) account for the different kinds of offences perpetrated by white-collar and non-white-collar offenders?

REVIEW AND REFLECT

1   What are some of the similarities and some of the differences in the psychological characteristics of white-collar offenders compared to those individuals who commit 'street' crimes?
2   Given our theoretical understanding of why white-collar and corporate crime occurs how might we develop effective strategies for prevention?

ORGANISED AND TRANSNATIONAL CRIME

The nature and extent of organised and transnational crime

The range of activities that fall under the rubric of 'organised and transnational crime' are large and varied. In this section, we consider some of the issues involved in defining organised and transnational crime, note some of the important organised crime groups, and outline some of the main forms of offending.

Definitional issues

There is no widespread agreement regarding what constitutes **'organised crime'**, and the concept remains a contested one (Paoli & Vander Beken, 2014). In the United States the term has traditionally been used to refer to – often large-scale – criminal organisations, like the Mafia (see below) that are engaging in criminal activities for profit. More recent definitional frameworks tend to be quite fluid, recognising the diverse nature of the activities and individuals who are involved. In Table 10.2 criteria employed by Europol to define organised crime are outlined. As you can see, central to the notion is the idea of two or more individuals working together in an ongoing relationship to engage in criminal activities that have the pursuit of profit (or power) as its central goal. Outside of these core criteria there is considerable variation in terms of the structure, size, scope, and organisation of such groups and the kinds of criminal activities that they engage in.

The term **'transnational crime'** appears, on the surface, to have a more straightforward reading: 'transnational crimes have to do with crimes that are commissioned in more than one country, crossing national borders' (Bruinsma, 2015, p. 1). Typically we will think of such crimes as involving the illegal transfer of goods

Table 10.2 EU criteria for what constitutes an organised criminal group (six of the following criteria including the mandatory items)

Mandatory (all)	Non-mandatory (at least two)
Collaboration of more than two people	Each with their own appointed tasks
For a prolonged or indefinite period of time	Using some form of discipline and control
Suspected of the commission of serious criminal offences	Operating on an international level
Motivated for the pursuit of profit and/or power	Using violence or other means suitable for intimidation
	Using commercial or business-like structures
	Engaged in money laundering
	Exerting influence on politics, the media, public administration, judicial authorities, or the economy

Source: Paoli and Vander Beken (2014, p. 22).

(including people) across borders but many forms of cybercrime also readily cross international boundaries and thus can also be considered forms of transnational crime. It should be clear that transnational and organised crime are not the same thing. However, often a criminal enterprise – for example, the illegal trafficking of drugs, wildlife, or humans – is both organised and transnational in character. As such, it makes sense to treat the two together, while noting that they are logically separate (a crime can be organised but not transnational and vice versa).

Organised crime groups and types of organised crime

One approach to the topic of organised crime is through a consideration of **organised crime groups**. In Table 10.3 some of the more widely recognised organised crime groups are briefly outlined. Each of these groups conform to the definition outlined in Table 10.2 but naturally vary in terms of their size, organisation, and the kinds of criminal activities that they are involved in. It is also important to note that organised crime groups evolve over time in response to changing markets and other criminal opportunities, internal dynamics, and the operation of law enforcement activities. For example, whereas the scope and influence of the mafia have declined in Italy, organised crime groups from Nigeria are on the rise and are involved in a diverse range of criminal activities from cybercrime to human trafficking (Williams, 2014).

Another way of thinking about organised crime is to abstract away from specific organisations and to consider the kinds of activities that organised crime groups are involved in. Historically, many organised crime groups – notably the Italian mafia – have made a living through 'protection' and extortion. In short, organised crime groups agree (either explicitly or tacitly) not to resort to violence as long as they receive (e.g., from local businesses) certain sums of money. Related services might be the supply of high-priced goods to businesses, ensuring a near monopoly on certain kinds of business and so forth. Organised crime has also a long history of being involved in various forms of illegal activities relating to drugs, gambling, and prostitution, and the scope of organised crime in these domains – especially illegal drugs – is extensive. 'Money laundering' is another feature of organised criminal activities whereby various financial manoeuvres are made to obscure the (typically illegal) origin of funds and thus protect related profits. In addition to drugs, various other objects including humans, organs, wildlife, antiquities, and arms are illegally trafficked around the word largely run by organised crime networks. Finally, we need to recognise the growing scope and reach of organised cybercrime from email scams through to threats to national security systems (Paoli, 2014). A detailed examination of all these forms of organised criminal activities is not possible in the chapter, but it worth having a look in a bit more detail at the nature, scope, and explanation for **human trafficking**.

Human trafficking

Human trafficking remains an issue of global concern. Between 2012 and 2014 63,251 victims of forced migration were detected in 106 separate countries with over 500 different trafficking flows identified (United Nations Office on Drugs and Crime, 2016a). Individuals are trafficked for a variety of reasons but the most common include

Table 10.3 Some organised crime groups

The Italian mafia	Originating in Sicily in the nineteenth century, the Italian mafia is perhaps the most widely known example of an organised crime group. There are three sets of organisations in Italy referred to as mafia with the most prominent being the *Costa Nostra* located in the western part of Sicily. The mafia are involved in both legal and illegal markets specialising in extortion and the explicit and implicit use of threats to back up transactions in their favour.[a]
The Italian-American mafia	The mafia in the United States trace their origins to the wave of immigration of Italians to cities on the North Eastern seaboard in the nineteenth century. Heavily involved in illegal activities during the Prohibition era, Italian-American mafia groups are considered to be a declining influence among organised crime groups in the United States.[b]
Organised crime in Colombia	The problem of organised crime is deeply entrenched in Colombia. Although best known as the main producer of illegal cocaine to the international market, it is also an important source of counterfeit money, human trafficking and, more recently, cybercrime. Emerging in the 1970s, powerful drug 'cartels' formed that specialised in the cultivation of coca, and its manufacture to coca paste and cocaine and subsequent export to global markets, especially the United States. Notable drug cartels include those located in Medellin and Cali, both sizeable organisations with widespread political influence.[c]
The Japanese Yakuza	The Japanese Yakuza have their origins in seventeenth-century gambling organisations. In 2010 the police estimated that around 80,000 individuals were involved in Yakuza gangs, which are organised by fictive kin relations – e.g., father–son (oyabun-kobun), brother–brother (Kyōdai) – and are marked by a number of specific cultural features including tattoos, the use of finger amputation (yubitsume) for punishment or demonstration of commitment, and participation in a diverse range of ceremonies. Yakuza groups obtain income from a diverse range of both legal and illegal activities including gambling, the distribution of illegal drugs, and protection.[d]
Triads	Triads originated in China as secret societies devoted to fighting the Qing dynasty (1644–1911), but subsequently morphed into criminal organisations involved in a range of illegal activities and most prominent in Hong Kong.[e]

Sources: [a]Paoli (2014); [b]Albanese (2014); [c]Thoumi (2014); [d]Hill (2014); [e]Chin (2014).

trafficking for forced labour and sexual exploitation. Other exploitative purposes include trafficking for organ removal, forced marriage, forced begging, and for child soldiers. As illustrated in Figures 10.2 and 10.3 the majority of victims are female, and the purposes for trafficking vary by the sex of the victim with females most likely to be trafficked for sexual exploitation while males are more likely to be trafficked for forced labour.

Like most types of offending, the majority of individuals convicted of trafficking are males. However, in 2014, 37 per cent of those convicted were females, indicating a relatively high level of female involvement in this offence (United Nations Office on Drugs and Crime, 2016a). This may be, in part, due to the fact that victims and offenders

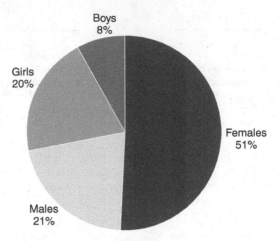

Figure 10.2 Global victims of trafficking in 2014.
Source: United Nations Office on Drugs and Crime (2016a).

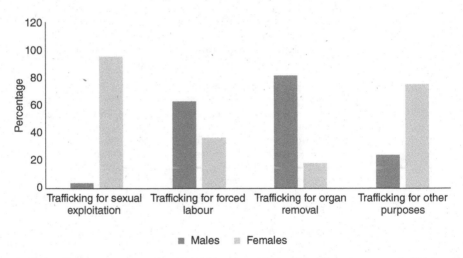

Figure 10.3 The percentage of males and females trafficked for different purposes in 2014.
Source: United Nations Office on Drugs and Crime (2016a).

often are of the same sex and come from similar backgrounds, especially those that might be most visible to law enforcement agencies. The greater relative proportion of female offenders, therefore, may reflect in part the greater overall number of female victims and the role of women in recruiting these individuals (e.g., Simmons et al., 2013).

Various social-structural and cultural factors contribute to the global trafficking of humans (Moloney, 2014). At the broadest level, the flow of goods, services, and peoples that is a feature of globalisation in the twenty-first century facilitates the legal and illegal movement of people and other products to areas where demand arises. In source countries, various social structural and cultural factors such as poverty, attitudes towards women, and conflict can promote opportunities for trafficking that are taken up by criminal organisations (Moloney, 2014). There is limited research on the characteristics of traffickers, but some studies suggest that they may employ various forms of neutralisation similar to other types of offender, and that they may also have elevated scores on measures of psychopathy (Beeson, 2014). Victims of trafficking are likely to experience a range of mental health problems, including depression and post-traumatic stress disorder (Beeson, 2014).

REVIEW AND REFLECT

1   What is organised crime?
2   What are some of the examples of organised and transnational crime?
3   What factors contribute to the global trafficking in humans?

ENVIRONMENTAL CRIME AND GREEN CRIMINOLOGY

The nature and extent of environmental harm and the scope of green criminology

Many scholars have argued that we are now living in the **anthropocene**. The nature, range, and scope of human activities and their impact on the global environment is such that we can view the period in which we now live as dominated by one large mammalian species: *Homo sapiens* (Ruddiman, 2013; Sachs, 2015; Seddon et al., 2016; Williams et al., 2015). If this may seem a little dramatic, consider the following:

*   Humans appropriate something in the order of 25–40 per cent of net primary production (i.e., the products of photosynthesis) for their own purposes.
*   Human activities have led to the global homogenisation of flora and fauna, and biodiversity loss – many consider that we are going through a period of human-caused massive extinction that rivals prior (non-human-caused) episodes.
*   Humans' activities have led to widespread changes to the composition of ecosystems, the pollution of lakes, streams, rivers, and oceans, and changes in the composition of the atmosphere (ozone depletion and increase in the concentration of atmospheric CO_2 and methane).

There is widespread agreement among scientists that these changes are ushering in a future of global climate change, which is likely to result in a raft of adverse consequences for ourselves and other species. Humans are pushing hard against the safe 'operating limits' for our planet, and many would argue that unless appropriate changes are made in the near future then the consequences for human civilisation are likely to be dire (Ehrlich & Ehrlich, 2013; Sachs, 2015).

Given that environmental harm is ultimately the product of human activities, the social sciences – in principle – have a key role to play to help in mitigating this harm and averting the global collapse of human societies. There is no shortage of work in this area (see van der Linden, 2015; Van Vugt, Griskevicius, & Schultz, 2014; Waring, 2016), but here we focus on the potential role that criminology has to play in reducing environmental harm and in understanding (and reducing) the impact of global environment change on human society. **Green criminology** is the term used to describe this sub-field of criminology.

What is green criminology?

White and Heckenberg (2014, p. 8) offer a useful definition of green criminology as 'the study by criminologists of environmental harms ... environmental laws ... and environmental regulation'. Harms to the environment, according to White and Heckenberg (2014), should be conceptualised in the broadest possible manner. Thus, it is suggested that we include: (a) legal conceptions of harm; (b) ecological conceptions of harm; and (c) justice conceptions of harm (see Figure 10.4). Legal conceptions of harm have their basis in local and international laws, rules, and conventions that outline what actions are deemed illegal and punishable by the state. Illegal logging, international trade in endangered wildlife, and the transportation and dumping of hazardous waste are all actions that result in environmental harm and may be subject to criminal sanctions in relevant jurisdictions. Ecological conceptions of harm are informed by a more holistic and less anthropocentric view of environmental harm and are concerned with issues of ecological sustainability. A range of actions and activities, therefore, may contribute to global warming, the pollution of waterways, and the endangerment of species, which, although not technically illegal, result in substantive harm to ecosystems. Finally, justice conceptions of harm extend the notion of human rights (and thus our obligations to ensure that these are met) to non-human animals, ecosystems, and the biosphere. Rather than viewing harm to the environment in terms of how they affect us, a justice conception of harm allows for the intrinsic value of other species and their complex inter-relationships. A more inclusive framework for understanding harm, it is argued, allows us to go beyond anthropocentric views of harms to incorporate a more diverse range of activities that should be of interest to criminologists.

Legal conceptions of harm	Ecological conceptions of harm	Justice conceptions of harm
• Illegal taking of flora and fauna • Pollution offences • Transportation of banned substances	• Problem of climate change • Problem of waste and pollution • Problem of biodiversity	• Environmental rights and environmental justice • Ecological citizenship and ecological justice • Animal rights and species justice

Figure 10.4 Three conceptions of environmental harm.
Source: White and Heckenberg (2014).

A moment's reflection should be enough to recognise both the game-changing nature of green criminology and the potential scope of its subject matter. Through a much more inclusive consideration of harms, green criminology opens up a host of subjects that have received little or no attention from mainstream criminologists (or criminal psychologists for that matter). Here is just a brief sampling of the kinds of topics that have engaged green criminologists to date (from White & Heckenberg, 2014, pp. 14–15):

- deforestation and the accompanying harm to animals, plants, and human communities
- the illegal trafficking in wildlife
- illegal activities relating to fishing
- animal abuse and neglect
- the illegal dumping of toxic waste and harmful effects of pollution
- biodiversity loss and 'ecocide' (see Box 10.1)
- the impact of global environmental change on crime.

Space precludes anything like a thorough analysis of all of these issues, let alone a review of the relevant theoretical approaches employed by green criminologists. Instead, we look in more detail at a topic that has engaged a number of social scientists: the potential impact of global environmental change on crime.

BOX 10.1 ECOCIDE

If homicide is the crime of intentionally and illegally killing another human, and genocide is the crime of intending to destroy or eliminate another social group, what, then, might be the crime of ecocide? According to a proposal for an international law of Ecocide submitted by Higgins (cited in Higgins, Short, & South, 2013, p. 257) to the United Nations Law Commission 'ecocide is the extensive damage to, destruction of or loss of ecosystem(s) of a given territory, whether by human agency or by other causes, to such an extent that peaceful enjoyment by the inhabitants of that territory has been severely diminished.' The call for an international law on ecocide it is argued will help to address urgent issues of responsibility for green crimes that threaten the viability of ecosystems and the human (and other animal) populations that depend upon them.

Environmental change and crime

Even the most conservative estimates suggest that the world in 2050 (or, indeed, 2100) is going to be a very different place from the one that we know today and that human-induced climate change is going to be one major driver of these differences. Due to human activity – in particular the burning of fossil fuels – concentrations of greenhouse gasses (mainly carbon dioxide, but also methane and nitrogen dioxide) are at levels not seen for at least 800,000 years. One of the most important consequences of these changes is a subsequent warming of the earth, and an increase in extreme weather events (Intergovernmental Panel on Climate Change, 2015). The impacts of these changes are being felt in a diverse range of ecosystems around the world and are likely to only worsen as the twenty-first century progresses (although the extent of this depends on how governments collectively respond to this crises), and include:

- an increased risk for extinction for a very large number of species
- threats to food security
- water scarcity
- increase in health problems, particularly in developing countries
- threat to ecosystems, urban environments and human safety
- aggregate economic losses
- the displacement of large numbers of individuals (Intergovernmental Panel on Climate Change, 2015).

A moment's reflection should be enough to recognise that many of these proposed changes have important implications for human behaviour in general, and criminal behaviour more specifically. White and Heckenberg (2014, p. 107) provide a useful analysis of these impacts. They highlight how environmental change is likely to lead to social conflict in a diverse range of contexts, including:

- conflicts over environmental resources (such as water, food, fisheries)
- conflicts linked directly to global warming (e.g., as a result of forced migration of people in low-lying areas to warming-induced rises in sea level)
- conflicts over differential exploitation of resources (bio-piracy, conflicts over energy supplies)
- conflicts over transference of harms (e.g., cross-border pollution).

Although there has been surprisingly little interest among criminologists in bringing the resources of criminology to bear on this issue, Agnew (2012a, p. 26) provides a notable exception. He outlines how climate change is likely to 'foster a range of crimes at the individual, corporate, and state levels' through familiar criminological mechanisms such as increasing strain, reducing social control, and increasing opportunities for crime. Climate change, Agnew (2012b) argues, is also likely to undermine human efforts to mitigate its effects by making meaningful action more difficult as individuals labour under greater strain. This, somewhat bleak, picture has been recently augmented with several efforts to quantify the impact of climate change on crime and conflict. In a review of 55 studies that have explored the impact of changes in temperature and rainfall on conflict, Burke, Hsiang, and Miguel (2015) conclude that each 1-standard-deviation increase in temperature is associated with a 2.4 per cent increase in interpersonal conflict and an 11.3 per cent increase in inter-group conflict. Ranson (2014), in a sophisticated analysis of the role of temperature on criminal behaviour, predicts substantial increases in crime in the United States between 2010 and 2099 including an additional 22,000 murders, 1.2 million aggravated assaults, and 1.3 million burglaries.

One recent effort to provide a psychological model that allows us to understand the impact of climate has been provided by Van Lange, Rinderu, and Bushman (2016).

Their proposed model – climate, aggression, and self-control in humans (CLASH) – hypothesises that higher average temperatures and smaller seasonal variation in temperatures result in faster life history strategies, a greater focus on the present, and lower levels of self-control. In turn, these increase rates of aggression and violence (see Figure 10.5). Let's unpack these proposed processes in more detail. The further you get from the equator the cooler and more seasonal is the temperature. These climatic variables, according to the model, promote more future planning, higher levels of self-control, and slower life history strategies (i.e., less risk-taking, greater investment in parenting, less intra-sexual conflict) as individuals are motivated to engage in long-term planning about the future. In regions closer to the equator the climate is substantially hotter, and there is less seasonal variation. These conditions result in higher levels of stress (due in part to increased exposure to pathogens), lower levels of self-control, and a greater focus on the present because directing your attention to the present makes sense in harsh environments when the future is more uncertain. In turn, faster life histories, lower levels of social control, and a focus on the present are linked to higher levels of aggression and violence as the motivation and capacity to inhibit aggression are diminished. The model is consistent with a wide body of research linking climatic variables with aggression and violence and has clear implications for the potential impact of human-induced climate change on violent offending: higher temperatures are likely to result in an increase in a range of violent offending.

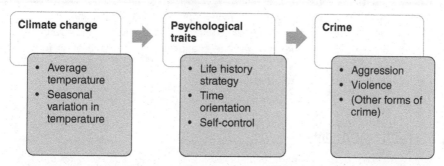

Figure 10.5 Key process in the model of climate, aggression, and self-control in humans (CLASH).
Source: Adapted from Van Lange et al. (2016, Figure 1).

REVIEW AND REFLECT

1   What is green criminology, and what are some of the topics that green criminologists study?
2   What is the likely impact of climate change on crime and conflict?
3   How might criminology as a discipline contribute to reducing or mitigating future climate change and many of its negative impacts on humans and society?

SUMMARY

In this chapter we have reviewed a range of different offences that, in many respects, diverge from those that we have so far considered in this book. In particular, unlike 'street' crime the topics canvassed in this chapter tend to involve a different range of harms and a different 'type' of offender.

We first considered the topic of white-collar and corporate crime noting how these labels – as they are often construed in contemporary research – embrace a wide range of different types of crime from corporate fraud through to email scams. Establishing just how much white-collar crime there is in society is a difficult task but there is no doubt that its impact is substantial. Explanations for white-collar offending focus on the opportunities afforded by specific situational contexts, and the neutralisations that offenders often engage in. A relatively small literature has also considered the psychological characteristics of these types of offenders with the possibility that – at least some – have clear psychopathic traits.

We then explored the closely related topics of organised and transnational crime, briefly noting the kinds of activities that are included and the nature of organised crime groups. A more in-depth examination of human trafficking revealed the scope and impact of this crime internationally and the relative lack of detailed research on the topic.

In the final section of the chapter we considered how the impact of humans on the environment is a topic for the emerging sub-field of green criminology. Green criminologists have turned their attention to a range of activities and practices that – some legal and some illegal – result in harm to non-human animals, and the environment. Mounting concern over the effects of climate change on violence and other forms of crime suggest that this attention is well warranted and is likely to only become more important over the next ten to twenty years.

FURTHER READING

Benson, M. L., & Simpson, S. S. (2014). *Understanding White-Collar Crime: An Opportunity Perspective* (2nd edition). London: Routledge.
A comprehensive and clearly written introduction to the topic of white-collar crime.

Simpson, S. S. (2013). White-collar crime: A review of recent developments and promising directions for future research. *Annual Review of Sociology, 39,* 309–331.
If you are looking for a good article-length introduction to white-collar crime this is an excellent place to start.

Paoli, L. (ed.). (2014). *The Oxford Handbook of Organized Crime.* Oxford: Oxford University Press.
A comprehensive 700-page survey covering most aspects of organised crime. The journals *Trends in Organized Crime* and *Journal of Human Trafficking* are also useful sources on this topic.

White, R., & Heckenberg, D. (2014). *Green Criminology: An Introduction to the Study of Environmental Harm.* New York, NY: Routledge.
An accessible, but thorough introduction to the topic of green criminology, with equal weight afforded to theory, types of transgression, and approaches to intervention and prevention. First author, Rob White, is widely recognised as one of the leaders in this emerging field.

Agnew, R. (2012a). Dire forecast: A theoretical model of the impact of climate change on crime. *Theoretical Criminology*, 16, 21–42.

This is an important contribution on the topic by a leading criminologist. The final sentence of the abstract best sums up the take-home message: 'Even though neglected by criminologists, there is every reason to believe that climate change will become one of the major forces driving crime as the century progresses' (Agnew, 2012a, p. 21).

WEB RESOURCES

The website of the United Nations Office on Drugs and Crime is probably the best place to start. Here you will find information on drug trafficking, human trafficking, money laundering, organised, crime, piracy, and more: www.unodc.org.

The Intergovernmental Panel on Climate Change contains of wealth of relevant information on environmental harm and climate change: www.ipcc.ch.

 KEY CONCEPTS

- anthropocene
- corporate crime
- differential association theory
- green criminology
- human trafficking
- organised crime
- organised crime groups
- transnational crime
- white-collar crime

Crime prevention

LEARNING OBJECTIVES

On completion of this chapter you should:

➤ have developed an understanding of what crime prevention is and be able to distinguish the different ways of categorising crime prevention efforts;
➤ recognise the various different approaches to developmental crime prevention and have developed an understanding of how effective these approaches are;
➤ recognise the various different approaches to community crime prevention and have developed an understanding of how effective these approaches are;
➤ recognise the various different approaches to situational crime prevention and have developed an understanding of how effective these approaches are.

November 26, 2012 was a special day for the residents of New York City: No one was intentionally killed for the entire day – a first, in living memory. In early February 2015 things got even better: there were no murders for 11 days. For a resident of New York in the 1980s and 1990s these would appear incredible statistics. In 1990, for example, there were 2,272 victims of homicide – an average of over six per day. In fact, between 1985 and 2009 crime rates dropped across the board in New York. Homicide was down by 71 per cent, robbery by 80 per cent, and auto theft by 88 per cent (Zimring, 2012). Although crime rates were declining in the 1990s throughout the United States (and, indeed, in much of the Western world), the decline in New York was especially dramatic, much larger than in other American cities. What factor or factors accounted for these reductions in offending? The answer to this question remains a matter of some contention for criminologists. Some have argued that an aggressive form of 'zero-tolerance' policing based on the 'broken windows' hypothesis of situational crime prevention (see later in this chapter) was the key factor. Others dispute this claim, and, indeed, the reasons behind the substantial drop in crime across Western countries from the 1990s have yet to be agreed upon by scholars. What this particular example can tell us, as Zimring (2012) persuasively argues, is that it is possible to achieve dramatic reductions in crime in a relatively short period of time and without recourse to imprisoning more offenders. In short, crime can be prevented.

At the start of each chapter in this book we have considered various case studies of real-world criminal behaviour. These have spanned a variety of different types of offending from drug-trafficking to mass murder. Having reached this point you should have developed a good understanding of the main theoretical approaches to explaining these and other types of crime. In the next chapter we will review research that suggests that, although punishment is a necessary feature of human society, by itself it is not a particularly effective strategy for reducing crime or the harms associated with criminal offending. If we are unlikely to make important gains in reducing crime through punishment, what else can we do? In this chapter we explore a range of different approaches to managing crime and criminal behaviour.

We begin the chapter with a general discussion of approaches to crime prevention. We will examine an important distinction between social, community, and situational approaches to crime prevention and how we can go about effectively evaluating to what extent these different approaches work in reducing offending. We then look at each of these approaches in turn, focusing on the relevant theoretical background, specific approaches, and their relative efficacy in reducing crime. On completion of this chapter you should have developed a good understanding of the different approaches to reducing crime and how effective they are in realising this goal.

WHAT IS CRIME PREVENTION?

When it comes to crime, most people would endorse the adage that 'prevention is better than cure'. If we can, somehow, change the physical and social environment in ways that prevent crime from occurring then we are in a position to avoid the many harms that arise from criminal offending (including the harms associated with the punishment of offenders).

There is no widespread agreement within criminology concerning the precise nature and scope of the term 'crime prevention' (Sutton, Cherney, & White, 2014). One of the most inclusive definitions is provided by Brantingham & Faust (1976, p. 284) who view crime prevention as 'any activity, by an individual or a group, public or private, that precludes the incidence of one or more criminal acts'. This definition, therefore, includes any activity on the part of the criminal justice system (such as punishment or policing) that might result in a reduction in criminal behaviour. Other scholars prefer an approach to defining crime prevention that excludes the activities of the criminal justice system and focuses, instead, on other kinds of activities and initiatives (Sutton et al., 2014). To confuse matters somewhat, other terms such as 'crime reduction ', 'public safety', and 'community safety' are also widely employed in similar contexts (Tilley, 2009). In this chapter we will employed the term 'crime prevention' to refer to all activities and initiatives (excluding the actions of the criminal justice system) that attempt to prevent (or, at least, reduce) criminal and antisocial behaviour.

Crime prevention typologies

Two main typologies are widely employed in the crime prevention literature (see Figure 11.1). The first makes a distinction – adapted from public health initiatives – between primary, secondary, and tertiary crime prevention approaches (Brantingham & Faust, 1976; Lab, 2016). **Primary crime prevention** refers to approaches that are largely directed at the general population and includes such diverse strategies as improved street lighting and universal drug-education programmes in schools. **Secondary crime prevention** involves the development of programmes and initiatives that are targeted as specific 'at risk' groups or locations such as delinquent teenagers or high-crime neighbourhoods. Attempts to reduce crime that focus on offenders (e.g., rehabilitation programmes) are viewed as instances of **tertiary crime prevention**.

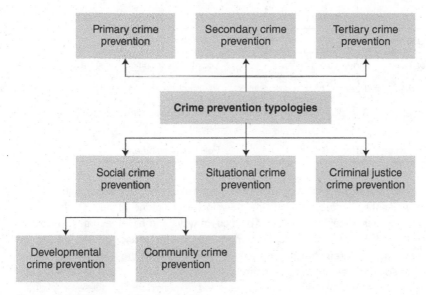

Figure 11.1 Crime prevention typologies.

Another widely employed typology of crime prevention approaches makes the distinction between four different types of approach to crime prevention: developmental prevention, community prevention (which together can be viewed as different types of **social crime prevention**), situational (or environmental) crime prevention, and criminal justice prevention (Welsh & Farrington, 2012). Social crime prevention approaches, broadly speaking, target the more distal causes of crime such as individual characteristics, family environments, and communities. The main aim of **developmental crime prevention** is to prevent the development of criminal behaviour by reducing individual and family risk factors for offending. **Community crime prevention** also focuses on preventing the development of criminal behaviour, but the main target is directed at peers, schools, communities, and institutions. In contrast, **situational crime prevention** initiatives focus on the more proximal causes of crime and attempt to change features of the environment in ways that reduce opportunities for crime. Table 11.1 provides a more detailed overview of these different approaches with some specific examples. In this chapter we will focus, in turn, on developmental, community, and situational approaches to crime prevention. Criminal justice crime prevention will be addressed in Chapter 12, while efforts to reduce crime through the rehabilitation and reintegration of offenders will be considered in Chapter 13.

An evidence-based approach to crime prevention

In the documentary *Scared Straight: Ten Years Later* we are introduced to a number of erstwhile young offenders who participate in a scared straight programme. This programme involves taking individuals in to the heart of a maximum security prison where they gain insight into the life they might end up living if their – typically fairly minor – juvenile transgressions escalate to serious offending. The documentary makes for compelling viewing: the initially cocky young individuals are cowed into silence as they

Table 11.1 Approaches to crime prevention

Approach	Focus	Examples
Developmental	Individuals, families	Social skills training, parent training
Community	Peers, schools, communities	Peer mentoring, community partnerships
Situational	The situation or environment	Crime prevention through environmental design
Criminal justice	Offenders	Policing, punishment

are exposed to what life might actually be like in a maximum security prison. And, it seems to work! At least according to the documentary, follow-ups of the young offenders reveal that they have largely abandoned their delinquent ways and have become law-abiding citizens. Indeed, the interviews reveal that many attribute the change in their ways to the experience in the scared straight programme. On the basis of the documentary should we initiate scared straight programmes more widely? The short answer is no. Although we shouldn't necessarily discount the reported experiences of these individuals, the information provided in the documentary does not allow us to conclude that the programme actually works and therefore should be more widely implemented. In order to make an informed decision we need to ensure that the programme is properly evaluated.

There are three main types of evaluation that we could (and, ideally, should) employ to evaluate the effectiveness of scared straight or any other crime prevention programme: impact (or outcome) evaluations, processes evaluations, and cost–benefit evaluations (or analysis) (Lab, 2016). A **process evaluation** examines the *way* that the implementation was carried out looking at such things as the context, the programme members, and the nature of the implementation. The importance of a process evaluation is that it allows us to determine whether the programme was actually implemented as it was designed to and whether there were other – unexpected – factors that might have threatened its efficacy. A **cost–benefit evaluation** undertakes to find out whether the monetary costs entailed in implementing the programme are outweighed by the monetary savings that it brings. Although calculating the costs involved in designing and implementation programmes is (relatively) straightforward, as you can imagine working out how much money is saved through reductions in offending is rather more complex! However, substantial strides have been made in quantifying the financial impact of crime (on victims, offenders, the criminal justice system), which allows reasonably valid measures of the costs of specific crimes (Dominguez & Raphael, 2015). There is now good evidence that many crime prevention programmes are cost effective: they result in overall monetary savings to society (Welsh & Farringon, 2015). It is clearly important to establish that a programme is cost-effective and that it is implemented appropriately but the bottom line is whether or not it works. An **impact evaluation**, therefore, is crucial to establish whether or not the programme did actually result in a reduction in offending.

There are various ways that programmes can be evaluated, but – where it is possible – evaluations should follow a true experimental design (Lab, 2016). As noted by Bachman and Schutt (2014, p. 161), a 'true' experimental design has three key elements (as illustrated in Figure 11.2):

- at least two comparison groups, one that receives the experimental treatment (the experimental group) and the other receiving no treatment or another form of treatment (the control group)
- random assignment to the two (or more) comparison groups
- assessment of change in the dependent variable for both groups after the experimental condition has been received.

It may not always be possible to meet all of these criteria in practice, especially the element of randomisation. However, it is crucial that there is an appropriate comparison group and that change in the key dependent variable is measured in an appropriate fashion. Why the documentary evidence on scared straight is not reliable of course, is that there was no comparison group to compare (perhaps the young offenders simply 'aged out' of crime), and there was no valid measure of quantitative change in the key outcome variable (in this case, offending). In summary, it is important that we take an evidence-based approach to crime prevention. That is, we need to use appropriate methods to ensure that the prevention programme actually does what it intends to do: prevent crime (see Box 11.1)

BOX 11.1 WHEN CRIME PREVENTION GOES WRONG

Clearly we need to establish whether a programme actually reduces crime or other forms of harm. Although it may not be quite so obvious, we need to also ensure that the programme does no harm. As, the influential criminologist Joan McCord (2003, p. 17) noted: 'Unless social programmes are evaluated for potential harms as well as benefit, safety as well as efficacy, the choice of which social programmes to use will remain a dangerous guess.' Measuring the potentially harmful impacts of crime prevention programmes is, thus, an important task (Braga, 2016). Why might a programme that has – one presumes – been carefully designed, result in harmful outcomes such as an *increase* rather than a decrease in offending? There are a number of possibilities depending on the type of programme, but one relevant process is peer contagion: when groups of at-risk individuals (especially adolescents) complete a programme together some of those individuals may be likely to learn deviant norms and behaviours from others. In a systematic effort to explore the potentially harmful effects of crime prevention programmes Welsh and Rocque (2014) undertook a comprehensive analysis of 15 systematic reviews of different crime prevention programmes to establish the frequency of harmful effects. Overall they found that 3.4 percent of the evaluations were in the undesirable direction (they resulted in more offending or antisocial behaviour). Interestingly, 28.6 percent of evaluations of scared straight programmes resulted in undesirable outcomes (with the rest having no effect at all).

Questions for discussion

1 Why is it important to measure the potentially harmful impacts of crime prevention programmes?
2 Peer contagion is one explanation for harmful outcomes. What might be some others?

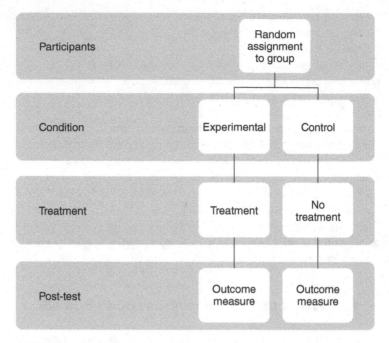

Figure 11.2 The basic logic of experimental design.

REVIEW AND REFLECT

1   What is crime prevention?
2   What are some of the important differences between social and situational crime prevention?
3   Why is it essential to take an evidence-based approach to crime prevention?

DEVELOPMENTAL CRIME PREVENTION

Theoretical background

In Chapter 2 we identified a number of the main risk and protective factors that are associated with criminal and antisocial behaviour. Before reading further, briefly review the risk and protective factors that are associated with individuals and families (Table 2.2). How do you think we might be able to intervene in the lives of individuals and families so as to reduce the prevalence of these risk factors and, thus (hopefully) prevent the development of criminal and antisocial behaviour? As you can imagine, the task posed by developmental crime prevention is a formidable one. However, as Farrington (2010b, p. 95) notes:

The basic idea of developmental or risk-focused prevention is very simple: Identify the key risk factors for offending and implement prevention techniques designed to counteract them.

Developmental crime prevention initiatives, therefore, draw heavily on developmental research and developmental theories of crime. If offending is strongly shaped by the characteristics of individuals and their families in which they are embedded then effective interventions should focus on 'targeting' the relevant criminogenic characteristics so as to reduce their downstream effects on antisocial and criminal behaviour.

Strategies for reducing crime

A large number of social crime prevention initiatives have been developed, and many of these have been subject to reasonably rigorous evaluations that allow us to determine whether or not they are effective in reducing criminal behaviour. Although many programmes target multiple risk factors, and many initiatives are interested in a diverse range of positive outcomes (such as health, employment, education) we will focus here on the effects of such initiatives on reducing crime and antisocial behaviour by looking at programmes that have largely focused on characteristics of individuals and families.

As we have seen in Chapter 2, individual risk factors for antisocial and criminal behaviour include temperamental and personality characteristics (such as low self-control, impulsivity, and low empathy), low IQ, and poor educational outcomes. Preschool enrichment programmes focus primarily on the risk factors of low IQ and poor performance in school, although they may often include other elements, such as parent training. The most well-known preschool programme is the Perry Preschool Project in the United States. Initiated in the 1960s, this programme involved the random allocation of disadvantaged African American preschool children to either an experimental or a control group. The experimental group received weekly home visits and attended a preschool programme on a daily basis. The two groups of students have now been followed up for a period of 40 years, with dramatic results: at both age 27 and age 40 the individuals in the experimental group earned significantly higher incomes and were less likely to have been arrested than individuals in the control group (Schweinhart et al., 2005, cited in Sutton et al., 2008). Other preschool enrichment programmes have shown similarly positive outcomes with the combined results of four studies of preschool enrichment programmes (including the Perry Preschool Project) yielding a 12 per cent reduction in offending in the experimental group compared to the control group (Welsh & Farrington, 2007).

Other programmes focus on the key individual risk factors of low self-control, impulsivity, and low empathy. Child social skills training programmes involve a number of structured sessions that teach children to develop self-control, manage anger, promote victim empathy, and foster social skills. In a meta-analysis of randomised controlled studies of the effectiveness of child social skills training programmes, Lösel and Beelman (2005, p. 102) concluded that 'these studies demonstrate a positive overall effect that is small but robust', although they also noted the need for further research using larger samples with longer follow-up periods.

Some of the most important risk factors for the development of antisocial and criminal behaviour reside in the family. As we have discussed in Chapter 2, children who grow up in family environments characterised by poor parenting practices, harsh discipline, and low parental supervision are at a significantly greater risk for later involvement in crime. It follows that if such family environments can be modified and if parents can be taught effective strategies for raising children, then we should see a reduction in criminal and antisocial behaviour. Various home visitation, parent education, and parent training programmes have been developed to address these issues, and their effectiveness has been evaluated.

In one of the best known home visitation programmes, 400 pregnant women in the late 1970s in the United States were randomly allocated to either the experimental or the control group. The experimental group received on average nine home visits while the mother was pregnant and, on average, a further 23 home visits from birth to the age of two. Home visits involved the provision of information about proper pre-natal and ante-natal care including health care (e.g., information about smoking and drinking), parenting practices, and personal development (e.g., education and employment information). The results of this study were generally positive, with a 15-year follow-up finding that children in the experimental group had fewer arrests and fewer convictions (Olds et al., 1998; see also Olds, Sadler, & Kitzman, 2007). A similar programme is the Early Start home visiting programme implemented in Christchurch, New Zealand (Fergusson et al., 2015). This programme targeted families that faced multiple social and economic problems and involved home visits from family support workers who had qualifications in nursing and social work. These individuals provided support and information on issues relating to child care, health, and education. The outcome of randomised controlled trial indicated positive effects on a number of domains including health, education, and problem behaviour.

Parent education and parent training programmes have also been shown to be successful in reducing criminal and antisocial behaviour (Farrington & Welsh, 2003). Parent education programmes involve teaching parents effective strategies and approaches to raising children. Such strategies include the use of praise and encouragement, setting limits and rules and enforcing them consistently, and dealing with problem behaviour without resorting to physical punishment (e.g., using 'time out' strategies) (Farrington, 2010b). Prominent and widely implemented parent training programmes include the Triple P Positive Parenting programme and the Incredible Years Parenting program. The Triple P program, initially developed at the University of Queensland but now implemented in 25 countries, is an intervention that aims to improve parenting knowledge, skills, and practices in a way that scaffolds problem-solving abilities and enables parents to raise well-adjusted children. The programme is delivered flexibly so that there are five 'levels' of intervention depending on the specific need of the family (McWilliams et al., 2016). A recent review of the evidence supports the effectiveness of this approach (Sanders et al., 2014). The Incredible Years Parenting program is designed for the parents of children who are aged between 2 and 12 and who display significant conduct problems. This programme features a two-pronged approach: parents are provided with information about parenting skills and practices, while children learn appropriate techniques for recognising and managing negative emotional states and related behaviours. A teacher-focused element can also be included to assist in classroom management (Lab, 2016).

What works?

It should be clear by now that many developmental crime prevention programmes are effective in reducing antisocial and criminal behaviour. Although these programmes are often expensive to implement, there is also clear evidence for the cost effectiveness of such programmes: in addition to reducing crime, in the long run they also save money (Welsh & Farrington, 2015). At times, it can be difficult to navigate through the now rich empirical literature on developmental crime prevention, and, inevitably, there is substantial diversity in programme type, delivery, and effectiveness. It is useful, therefore, to look to several recent reviews of the general literature to establish more of a bird's eye view of the field.

Schindler and Black (2015) provide a useful review of early prevention programmes that target child factors (e.g., Head Start REDI and the Chicago School Readiness Project), parent factors (e.g., Nurse-Family Partnership, Family Check-Up), and child *and* family factors (e.g., Perry Preschool, Incredible Years Teaching and Parent Training Program). On the basis of their review they conclude:

> Overall, evaluation science suggests that prevention programs during infancy and childhood can be effective. Those programs that intensively target children's social skills and self-regulation and those that target adult caregivers' skills in behaviour management are particularly promising.
>
> (p. 441)

A similar conclusion was reached in a meta-analysis of early family and parent training programmes by Piquero et al. (2016). Finally, in a systematic review of systematic reviews(!) of developmental and social crime prevention programmes, Farrington, Ttofi, and Lösel (2016) found that the five systematic reviews of individual focused interventions and the eight reviews of family programmes all yielded positive effect sizes – in other words, they were effective at reducing antisocial and criminal outcomes.

Discussion

For many, developmental crime prevention approaches are an attractive strategy for reducing crime. We know that children with certain characteristics who grow up in certain types of family environments are more likely to engage in criminal and antisocial behaviour so the most obvious approach to reducing crime is to make the necessary changes in those individuals and environments. Developmental crime prevention approaches can be particularly appealing because they often result in a range of well-documented benefits such as better educational and work outcomes, alongside a reduction in crime and antisocial behaviour. Given that developmental crime prevention initiatives have been shown to 'work' why are they not more widely implemented? Part of the reason why governments have not devoted more funding to developmental crime prevention initiatives is that they are expensive to implement and tend not to yield immediate reductions in crime. Research has, as we have noted, clearly indicated that many developmental crime prevention programmes are cost-effective in that the savings obtained from reductions in crime outweigh the costs of implementing the programme. Some scholars have also raised concern about the potential stigmatising effects of developmental crime prevention programmes. If such programmes are targeted at specific populations with the stated aim of 'reducing delinquency and crime', then targeted groups may accept the label of 'crime-prone', and the programme will be ineffective. Accordingly, many developmental crime prevention programmes are framed in terms of improving the health and opportunities of certain groups rather than in terms of reducing crime (Sutton et al., 2008).

REVIEW AND REFLECT

1   What is the theoretical logic underlying developmental crime prevention?
2   What are some examples of developmental crime prevention programmes and what specific developmental risk factors for offending do they target?
3   Does developmental crime prevention work?

COMMUNITY CRIME PREVENTION

Theoretical background

Community crime prevention efforts focus on changing aspects of the social environment and related institutions that influence criminal and antisocial behaviour. There is some, inevitable, overlap with both developmental crime prevention and situational crime prevention efforts. In many respects community crime prevention draws upon a similar theoretical background to that of developmental crime prevention. However, whereas developmental crime prevention focuses on addressing risk factors for offending that reside in individuals and families, community crime prevention targets those risk factors that are associated with neighbourhoods, communities, and schools (Welsh & Farrington, 2012).There is also some overlap with situational crime prevention efforts and related theories that are discussed below particularly in terms of programmes that target neighbourhoods and communities. Broadly speaking, community crime prevention efforts attempt to improve social bonding and social cohesion while reducing the negative influence of peers.

Approaches for reducing crime

A range of crime prevention initiatives focus on risk factors associated with schools, peers, and the community. A wide variety of different types of school-based programmes have been developed that variously target school bonding and truancy, teacher classroom management, and bullying (Farrington, 2010b; Kim, Gilman, & Hawkins, 2015). Some of these programs are also designed to include wider community elements in order to provide a more comprehensive set of influences that are likely to shape prosocial behaviour. Two prominent examples include PROmoting School-community-university Partnership to Enhance Resilience (PROSPER), and Communities that Care

(CTC). Other programmes cast their net even wider by incorporating all aspects of a child's ecological system including the family, school, peers, and neighbourhood (Komro et al., 2011). Although these various programmes have somewhat different targets, at the broadest level they are designed to create nurturing environments that foster social bonding and social cohesion.

The evidence base for community-based programmes is not as extensive as that for child and parenting programmes, however many initiatives can be viewed as 'promising' (Kim et al., 2015). There is, however, mixed evidence for the effectiveness of general school-based programmes on antisocial and criminal behaviour (Farrington et al., 2016). Anti-bullying programmes have some demonstrated success (Fox, Farrington, & Ttofi, 2012), although with, perhaps, scope for improvement (see Ellis et al., 2016). Research suggests that drug-education programmes can also be effective, although many widely implemented programmes (e.g., DARE) show little evidence of effectiveness (Ennett et al., 1994). Given that association with delinquent peers is an important risk factor for adolescent offending, programmes that enable young people to resist 'peer pressure' or which involve the use of pro-social peer leaders should be effective in reducing antisocial behaviour. The results to date, however, have been somewhat mixed (Farrington, 2010b) with some scholars claiming that such programmes can be counter-productive (McCord, 2003). Finally, neighbourhood watch programmes that encourage community members to be more involved in crime prevention show some evidence of success, despite the methodological limitations of much of the research (Gill, 2016).

Discussion

Community crime prevention efforts are somewhat of a mixed bag. What they have in common is that they address features of the social environment that resides outside of the family and thus incorporate neighbourhood, school, and peer influences. The importance of the social context on people's lives, including criminal behaviour, is without doubt, and thus community crime prevention efforts should be part of the arsenal of strategies at the disposal of policy makers. The evidence base for their value, although accumulating, is perhaps less robust than that for developmental crime prevention efforts. Perhaps this is due in part to the fact that such initiatives will often target individuals who are older and thus less amenable to change. Changing features of the social environment is, inevitably, a more diffuse way of influencing norms, values, and behaviour than directly intervening in the lives of individuals and families. Programmes that incorporate multiple levels (individuals, families, communities) show substantial promise.

SITUATIONAL CRIME PREVENTION

Consider the following scenario. You are in a clothing store lovingly gazing at a new jacket that you covet, but simply cannot afford. The only staff member in the store leaves the counter and goes out to the back of the store where she cannot see you. Do you take this opportunity to steal the jacket? For many people the answer to this question will be a resounding 'no' regardless of the circumstances. However, before considering stealing the jacket others will want to know whether it is electronically tagged, whether there is closed circuit television (CCTV) in store, whether there are other customers about, and what the exit routes out of the store are like. In short, the decision depends not only on the motivation of the potential offender, but also on the opportunities that the situation affords. Situational crime prevention, then, simply 'seeks to alter the situational determinants of crime so as to make crime less likely to happen' (Clarke, 2008 p. 178).

Theoretical background

Situational approaches to crime prevention draw on four main theoretical perspectives:

- **rational choice theory** (Clarke, 1980)
- **routine activity theory** (Cohen & Felson, 1979; Felson, 2008)
- **crime pattern theory** (Brantingham & Brantingham, 2008)
- **broken windows paradigm** (Wilson & Kelling, 1982; Wagers, Sousa, & Kelling, 2008) (see Box 11.2).

An overview of the first three of these theoretical perspectives was provided in Chapter 1, and a discussion of the broken windows paradigm is provided in Box 11.2. You are encouraged to review these theoretical perspectives before reading further. Clarke (2008) usefully outlines some of the fundamental assumptions of the theoretical approaches that are relevant for situational crime prevention. First, it is assumed that crime results from the interaction of a motivated offender with a specific situation. Situational theories of crime assume that there will always be some individuals willing to commit criminal acts and therefore devote their attention to the specific features of the physical and social environment that make criminal behaviour more likely. Second, crime is always a choice. This may seem a bold claim given that much crime is either impulsive or driven by need. However, as Clarke (2008) points out, even most spur of the moment offences inevitably involve choices about costs and benefits even if they are very rapidly (and perhaps at times unconsciously) evaluated. Third, opportunities play a powerful role in criminal offending. Opportunity is, therefore, an important *cause* of crime and should, therefore, feature prominently in our crime prevention efforts. One final point could be made here about situational theories of crime, and this concerns the spatio-temporal pattern of offending. A good deal of research suggests that offending is not evenly distribution across time and space: it occurs more often at some times and in some locations than at other times and locations (Farrell, 2015). Crime pattern theory and routine activities theory both assume that offending is related to the 'normal' patterns of behaviour that individuals in a community engage in and thus tends to be concentrated in certain locations and during certain time periods.

BOX 11.2 BROKEN WINDOWS HYPOTHESIS

In the late 1960s the social psychologist, Philip Zimbardo, conducted an intriguing set of experiments (cited in Wilson & Kelling, 1982). When a car with its licence plates removed was left abandoned in a poor and rundown area of the Bronx, New York it was rapidly and efficiently stripped and vandalised. A similar car left abandoned in a more affluent suburb in Palo Alto, California however, was left untouched. Until, that is, Zimbardo smashed the car with a sledgehammer, after which the car was rapidly vandalised. The conclusion to be drawn from this experiment is that when there are cues that indicate that deviance is acceptable or normative then restraints on further deviant or antisocial behaviour are removed. As Wilson and Kelling (1982, p. 31) note: 'vandalism can occur anywhere once communal barriers – the sense of mutual regard and the obligations of civility – are lowered by actions that seem to signal that "no one cares".' The central idea of the broken windows hypothesis, then, is that signs of public disorder (including graffiti, run-down environments, minor infractions of rules) lead to the breakdown of informal community controls as fear of crime leads residents to withdraw from public environments. This, in turn, invites further disorder and creates opportunities for more serious criminal behaviour such as drug dealing and robbery (Kelling, 2015; Wagers, Sousa, & Kelling, 2008).

The implications of the broken windows hypothesis for crime prevention are fairly straightforward, if somewhat controversial among criminologists. Wilson and Kelling (1982) argued that in order to prevent a more serious breakdown in public order it is necessary to vigorously police minor infractions and disorderly behaviour such as prostitution, panhandling, and drug use. This idea gave rise to so-called 'broken windows policing' which was vigorously pursued in New York in the 1990s. Although crime did indeed decrease in New York following the implementation of broken windows policing, criminologists still debate to what extent this was due to policing efforts (Wagers et al., 2008). Broken windows theory remains an important guide to the role of disorder in offending and the value that policing that disorder might have on preventing crime. More recent versions tend to emphasise the importance of police working in partnerships with community members rather than a strict 'zero-tolerance' approach (Welsh, Braga, & Bruinsma, 2015).

Questions for discussion

1   Consider some different neighbourhoods where you live. Do you think that the core ideas of the broken windows hypothesis are supported?
2   What are some potential negative consequences of 'broken windows policing'?
3   Read some of the articles in the special issue on the broken windows hypothesis in the *Journal of Research in Crime and Delinquency*, 2015 (volume 52, issue 4). How have the core ideas of broken windows been adapted to improve policing efforts at reducing crime while avoiding some of the negative consequences of 'zero tolerance' policing?

Strategies for reducing crime

Taken together these assumptions suggest that one important strategy for reducing crime is to reduce the opportunities for criminal behaviour. This can be achieved through a diverse range of strategies, as outlined in Table 11.2 (Clarke, 2008). One important strategy is to simply increase the effort of offending. All other things being equal, if offending is more difficult to accomplish then, according to rational choice theory, the benefits of offending are less likely to outweigh the costs. One way of increasing the effort of offending (and thus making benefits harder to obtain) is through **target hardening**: the implementation of locks, bars, screens, and so forth that make desirable items harder to steal. The complex set of screening arrangements in place now at all airports and many other locations provides another example of making offending harder to achieve.

A second strategy that works on the 'benefits' side of the cost–benefit scales is to reduce the rewards of offending. Again this can be achieved through a variety of means. For example, by excluding discs from CDs and DVDs on display, eliminating cash operating systems (e.g., on public transport), and by having removable car stereo systems, the potential rewards of offending are substantially reduced. Offending can also be made more risky and therefore less attractive to would-be offenders. The widespread implementation of CCTV (particularly in the UK) provides a good example of this approach, as does the growing use of alarms systems and private security companies. The risk of offending can also be increased through relatively simple means such as better street lighting and the enhancement of natural surveillance opportunities.

As we discussed in Chapter 4, situational and environmental factors such as provocation, frustration, and heat can all increase the risk for aggression and violence. Situational approaches to crime prevention, therefore, also note the importance of reducing provocations and removing excuses. Provocations can be reduced by such strategies as separate seating for rival sports fans, reducing crowding in bars and other drinking environments, and reducing peer pressure through social marketing that enforces messages against drink-driving and drug use. Excuses for offending can also be removed by clearly providing signs and instructions regarding what is prohibited, and by controlling the sale and use of alcohol and other drugs.

Table 11.2 Situational crime prevention strategies

Key crime prevention strategies	Examples
Increase the effort of offending	Locks, bars, screens, entry control, gating roads
Reduce the rewards of offending	Remove targets, eliminate cash systems, property identification
Increase the risk of offending	CCTV, improved street lighting, increase natural surveillance
Reduce provocation	Separate rival sporting fans, reduce crowding, reduce peer pressure
Remove excuses	Post instructions, alert conscience, control drugs and alcohol

Source: Clarke (2008).

One approach, widely implemented by city councils in Western societies, is known as **crime prevention through environmental design** (CPTED). The central underlying idea of CPTED is that offences can be significantly reduced (if not eliminated) by designing environments and products (see Box 11.3) that discourage or prevent offending. One central idea of CPTED strategies is the notion of **defensible space**, first articulated by the Architect Oscar Newman (Cozens & Love, 2015). According to Newman the concept of defensible space comprises four core elements:

- *territoriality* – environments that create a sense of ownership
- *surveillance* – environments that allow opportunities for monitoring by residents and others
- *image and milieu* – environments that promote a sense of order, space, and maintenance
- *geographical juxtaposition* – the creation of environments that create a sense of security to adjacent spaces (and vice versa).

In principle, by attending to these core principles urban environments can be designed in ways that promote prosocial and discourage antisocial behaviour. For instance, the building of clear signs, fences, and other markers can help to instil a sense of territory and create an environmental milieu that signals to others that the environment is cared for and well maintained; buildings, vegetation, and other features can also be designed so as to increase the natural surveillance of spaces and create a sense of guardianship. So-called 'second generation' CPTED strategies build on these ideas by incorporating

BOX 11.3 DESIGNING PRODUCTS AGAINST CRIME

Many products clearly signal their desirability to would-be criminals: a state of the art mp3 player, a late-model mountain bike, and a handbag zipped open to reveal a cash-filled wallet are all examples of what Clarke (1999) terms CRAVED products (see Chapter 9). One approach to crime prevention focuses on designing such products in ways that decrease the likelihood of offending (Ekblom, 2008).

As Ekblom (2008, p. 205) explains: 'Reducing the probability of crime by product design may work either by making the products objectively harder, riskier, or less rewarding for the offender to exploit, or making them *perceived* as such by the offender.' Examples include fold-away bicycles, theft-resistant bags, and café chairs that enable patrons to secure their bags.

Activity

Log on to the home page of the design against crime research centre (www.designagainstcrime.com) and check out some of the products that have been developed. To what extent do you think they would reduce crime? How would you go about designing a study to evaluate the effectiveness of these products?

elements of social cohesion and community culture in to the mix. Consistent with the notion of collective efficacy, communities in which members are connected, engaged, and cohesive are likely to have lower rates of offending as individuals are more willing to look out for others and informally police deviant and antisocial behaviour (Cozens & Love, 2015).

What works in situational crime prevention?

Having now briefly reviewed situational approaches to preventing crime we need to consider which of the broad range of specific practices that have been adopted are actually effective in reducing offending. Systematic evaluations of situational crime prevention initiatives suggest that a number of strategies can be effective (Bowers & Johnson, 2016; Clarke, 2008; Eck, 2002). There is reasonably good evidence that initiatives that increase the effort of offending (e.g., better security systems) and reduce the rewards of offending (e.g., the elimination of cash operated systems) have had a positive impact on reducing the rates of property (and, perhaps, non-property) offending in Western societies, especially over the last 20 to 30 years (see Farrell et al., 2014). However, systematic reviews of the relevant research have largely focused on a range of strategies that increase the risks of offending.

There is now fairly good evidence that a variety of strategies that enhance public surveillance can reduce offending (Welsh, Farrington, & Taheri, 2015). For instance, the implementation of closed circuit television (CCTV) systems in public spaces has been evaluated in a number of studies with overall positive results: across 44 studies a 16 per cent reduction in crime due to the effects of CCTV was reported. CCTV appears to be particularly effective in reducing property crime such as the theft of cars from public car parks, although studies have also demonstrated positive effects in reducing interpersonal crimes and antisocial behaviour more generally (e.g., McLean, Worden, & Kim, 2013) (see Research in Focus 11.1). Other forms of enhancing public surveillance such as improved street lighting, security guards, and the implementation of defensible space strategies have also yielded positive effects on reducing crime and disorder (Welsh, Farrington, & Taheri, 2015). Certain policing strategies can also contribute to reductions in offending by concentrating police attention to high crime areas. So-called 'hot-spot policing' involves the strategic employment of police to geographical areas that have been identified as particularly crime prone, and there is good evidence that this is an effective strategy for reducing crime, with little evidence of displacement effects (Braga, 2006; Weisburd & Eck, 2004). Another police strategy that focuses attention on particular neighbourhoods is referred to as 'stop, question, and frisk', and, although it may be effective in reducing crime, it has also generated some controversy (see Box 11.4). Many situational crime prevention initiatives, however, are assumed to work, but have not been systematically evaluated, and further research is required to evaluate many situational crime prevention programmes (Bowers & Johnson, 2016).

RESEARCH IN FOCUS 11.1 DO CCTV CAMERAS DETER CRIME AND DISORDER?

Title: Here's looking at you: An evaluation of public CCTV cameras and their effects on crime and disorder

Authors: McLean, S. J., Worden, R. E., & Kim, M.   **Year**: 2013

Source: *Criminal Justice Review*, 38, 303–334

Aims: To explore the impact of CCTV cameras on crime and disorder

Method: Counts of crime and disorder were measured between October 2003 and January 2007 in Schenectady, New York both within the 150-foot 'viewshed' of 11 surveillance cameras and between 150 and 350 feet of the cameras.

Key results:

- Total crime consistently declined within 150 feet of the cameras after they were installed.
- The impact was different for different forms of crime and was greatest for personal rather than property crime.
- The cameras were particularly effective at reducing the total amount of disorder within their 150-foot viewshed.
- Cameras that were more visible were more successful at reducing crime and disorder.

Conclusion: 'Our study suggests that cameras have had effects on crime, even more consistent effects on disorder, and that the visibility of the cameras is associated with its impact on crime and disorder' (p. 303).

BOX 11.4 DO STOP, QUESTION, AND FRISK PRACTICES DETER CRIME?

The police practice of stop, question, and frisk has a long and controversial history in the United States where it has been most widely deployed – most notably in New York City. The practice essentially involves granting police the power of stopping any person who they deem are in the act of committing a crime, or about to commit a crime, and to question and search them. Many have raised concerns that the tactic unduly targets certain segments of the population: ethnic minorities, the young, and those living in disadvantaged neighbourhoods. As such, it has been criticised, in particular, as a method of racial profiling. Leaving this important issue to one side, we can also legitimately ask whether the practice actually works to reduce crime and, if so, why? One of the important underlying assumptions guiding the practice is the finding that crime is heavily concentrated in certain parts of a city. If police are more visible in these locations and have the power to stop, question, and frisk then this should potentially lead erstwhile offenders to avoid criminal activities. Some evidence suggests that stop, question, and frisk practices do, indeed, result in significant (albeit not large) reductions in offending (Weisburd et al., 2016). However, some have challenged these findings as comparisons to alternative policing practices were not made, and others have voiced doubts over whether the practice is unconstitutional in the way that it has been carried out (Nagin, 2016). The ongoing debate regarding stop, question, and frisk practices reminds us that improvements in crime reduction also need to be balanced against the potential harms of specific polices and practices.

Further reading

An excellent special issue of the journal *Criminology and Public Policy*, 2016 (Volume 14, Issue 1) is devoted to this issue and is well worth exploring.

Discussion

As Clarke (2008) notes, many criminologists have shown relatively little interest in situational approaches to crime prevention because they do not appear to get at the 'root' causes of crime such as poverty, inequality, and discrimination. It is certainly true that situational approaches to crime prevention will not eliminate crime from society, in part because they fail to make any meaningful lasting changes in individuals or wider social-structural environments. Situational approaches to crime prevention are also more relevant for certain types of offences – in particular property and public disorder offending and offences that occur in public environments. However, despite these limitations, situational crime prevention strategies are relatively easy to implement, are practical, and show evidence of effectiveness. They should, therefore, form an important part of overall attempts to reduce crime in society.

REVIEW AND REFLECT

1   What are some of the main theoretical perspectives that inform situational crime prevention initiatives?
2   What types of crime do you think are less amenable to situational crime prevention efforts?
3   The next time you visit your local CBD have a good look around the urban landscape: what sort of situational crime prevention initiatives are visible (e.g., CCTV), and how might the environment be improved so as to promote 'defensible space'?

SUMMARY

Crime prevention involves a diverse range of different strategies that aim to reduce criminal and antisocial behaviour. Crime prevention initiatives are usually distinguished on the basis of their primary target: developmental crime prevention approaches target characteristics of individuals and families; community crime prevention focuses on schools, neighbourhoods, and communities; and situational crime prevention efforts focus on changing aspects of the situational context in which offending occurs. Both developmental and community-based crime prevention draw strongly from the developmental literature that has identified the key risk factors for crime. As such, these efforts aim to target risk factors in ways that are likely to lead to a reduction in antisocial and criminal behaviour. Important social crime prevention initiatives include those that provide preschool enrichment, and education and training programmes for parents. Many such programmes have demonstrated clear benefits in terms of reducing criminal behaviour and should form a core component of any systematic effort to reduce the costs of crime in society.

Situational crime prevention draws from a range of theoretical perspectives that emphasise how criminal behaviour is powerfully shaped by a variety of situational and environmental factors. As such, the guiding insight of situational crime prevention approaches is to alter the situational context in ways that make offending less likely. These include increasing the effort, reducing the reward, and increasing the risks of offending. Available evidence suggests that a number of situational crime prevention approaches can, indeed, be effective in reducing crime.

It probably doesn't take a genius to recognise that developmental, community, and situational crime prevention efforts have a complementary role to play in reducing offending and are likely to reinforce each other. By addressing, in turn, developmental, community, and situational risk factors for offending, in principle we can reduce both the number of motivated offenders and the opportunities for offending. Future efforts at crime prevention may also be informed by the growing influence of biosocial criminology (see Box 11.5).

BOX 11.5 BIOSOCIAL CRIME PREVENTION

A biosocial approach to crime prevention may, at first glance, seem an odd proposition. Short of genetic engineering, how can we *change* biological processes so as to reduce the risk for antisocial behaviour? However, it is important to remember the *social* component of the biosocial approach: biological and environmental factors interact – often in complex ways – to produce outcomes, and understanding the nature of these interactions can help us to intervene in more productive ways. Indeed, a number of scholars have highlighted how a biosocial approach can contribute to advances in crime prevention (Gajos, Fagan, & Beaver, 2016; Vaughn, 2016).

One important line of research, with profound implications for crime prevention, concerns the interaction of genes and environments on developmental outcomes. If certain genes make individuals more or less sensitive to particular environmental contexts – including intervention strategies – then there is the potential scope for tailoring the nature and intensity of interventions to different individuals, potentially improving the efficacy of outcomes such as the reduction of crime and other forms of antisocial behaviour. Although more research is needed to better tease out particular gene × environment interactions it is clear that future crime prevention efforts will, to some degree, have to consider how interventions achieve their desired outcome and to what extent this is moderated by genetic differences. As Gajos et al. (2016, p. 694) conclude in their review of this topic:

> As prevention and intervention efforts should be guided by what is known about the causes of crime, then it stands to reason that prevention science research should begin to take seriously the ways in which genetic and environmental factors can be folded into prevention and treatment programs.

Other scholars have raised some concerns with this approach, however, and caution against the specific targeting of prevention efforts based on participants' genotypes (Cleveland et al., 2016).

Other approaches to biosocial crime prevention have focused on reducing exposure to toxins in the environment, such as lead, and in preventing or mitigating the negative effects of early adversity on neurobiological development (e.g., Fisher et al., 2016).

Questions for discussion

1   What are some potential advantages and disadvantages of a biosocial approach to crime prevention?
2   What do you think the future holds for crime prevention? Is anything like the policing approach in the film *Minority Report* ever likely to be realised? (See Criminal Psychology Through Film 11.1.)

CRIMINAL PSYCHOLOGY THROUGH FILM 11.1
Minority Report (2002)

Directed by: Steven Spielberg
Starring: Tom Cruise (John Anderton), Colin Farrell (Danny Witwer), and Samantha Morton (Agatha)

Imagine a future where murders could be prevented before they occurred. This is the world depicted in *Minority Report*, where three special 'pre-cogs' have the ability to reach into the future and determine when murders are going to occur – allowing the police force to stop them in advance and apprehend the (would-be) murderers. Although the plot is somewhat convoluted, the film teases out some of the – perhaps real – issues that might face attempts to prevent crime in the future.

Question for discussion

Although precognition is itself unlikely, it may be possible to determine through various biological measures (brain scans, DNA analyses) which individuals in a population are 'highly likely' to perpetrate serious violent crimes (see Raine, 2013). Would we then have a right (or even an obligation) to arrest or detain these individuals? What are the critical ethical and philosophical issues that are raised by this potential scenario?

FURTHER READING

Lab, S. P. (2016). *Crime Prevention: Approaches, Practices, and Evaluations* (9th edition). New York, NY: Routledge.
Now in its ninth edition this is a comprehensive, wide-ranging introduction to the topic of crime prevention.

Farrington, D. P., & Welsh, B. C. (2007). *Saving Children from a Life of Crime: Early Risk Factors and Effective Interventions*. Oxford: Oxford University Press.
An accessible overview of developmental approaches to understanding and preventing crime.

Weisburd, D., Farrington, D. P., & Gill, C. (eds.) (2016). *What Works in Crime Prevention and Rehabilitation* (pp. 111–135). New York, NY: Springer.
A comprehensive review of systematic reviews of various crime prevention measures, including policing, criminal justice interventions, and offender rehabilitation. Not exactly bedtime reading but a valuable resource for students and policymakers alike.

Cozens, P., & Love, T. (2015). A review and current status of crime prevention through environmental design (CPTED). *Journal of Planning Literature*, 30, 393–412.
A useful single article overview of CPTED covering origins, theoretical background, and effectiveness.

Articles on crime prevention are to be found in most criminology and criminal psychology journals. Good places for browsing include the journals *Criminology and Public Policy*, *Crime Science*, and *Crime Prevention and Community Safety*.

WEB RESOURCES

Provides systematic reviews of crime prevention initiatives: www.campbellcollaboration.org/CCJG/index.asp.
Useful information about the triple p parenting programme: www.triplep.net/glo-en/home.
Useful information about the incredible years parenting programme: http://incredibleyears.com.
The hope page for the 'design against crime' research centre: www.designagainstcrime.com.

 KEY CONCEPTS

- broken windows paradigm
- community crime prevention
- cost–benefit evaluation
- crime pattern theory
- crime prevention through environmental design
- defensible space
- developmental crime prevention
- impact evaluation
- primary crime prevention
- process evaluation
- rational choice theory
- routine activity theory
- secondary crime prevention
- situational crime prevention
- social crime prevention
- target hardening
- tertiary crime prevention

Criminal justice responses to crime

LEARNING OBJECTIVES

On completion of this chapter you should:

➤ have developed an understanding of the nature and scope of criminal justice responses to crime and trends in the use of punishment over time;

➤ recognise the various harms associated with punishment as they relate to offenders, their families, and the community;

➤ understand the main rationales for punishment and the reasons that people punish;

➤ be familiar with the relevant literature on the deterrent effects of punishment and be able to address the question 'does punishment work'?

On December 2, 2005 Vietnamese-born Australian national Van Tuong Nguyen, aged 25, was hanged in Changi Prison, Singapore. Van Nguyen was arrested in Changi airport in 2002 after being found in possession of 396 grams of heroin – more than 25 times the amount that mandates a death sentence in Singapore. Apparently Van Nguyen had agreed to smuggle the heroin in order to pay off the debts of his twin brother Khoa (Timeline: The life of Van Nguyen, 2005). The execution went ahead despite vigorous pleas for clemency from the Australian government, human rights activists, the Australian people, and even the Pope. Australia's attorney general, Philip Ruddock, termed the hanging 'barbaric' (Mother only allowed to hold hands, 2005), and then Prime Minister John Howard warned that the execution would harm the relationship between the people of Singapore and Australia. Singapore's Prime Minister Lee Hsien Loong, however, defended the execution and Singapore's tough stance on drug smuggling as necessary to deter smugglers from using the island as a transit zone for illegal drugs.

> We ... think that drug trafficking is a crime that deserves the death penalty. The evil inflicted on thousands of people with drug trafficking demands that we must tackle the source by punishing the traffickers rather than trying to pick up the pieces afterwards.
>
> (Drug trafficking deserves death penalty, 2005)

This case highlights a number of key issues (Indermaur, 2006). It asks us to consider what form of punishment we deem acceptable. Although the **death penalty** has been outlawed in many countries (see Criminal Psychology Through Film 12.1), during 2015 at least 1,634 individuals were executed throughout the world (excluding the unknown number of executions in China), the highest number executed since 1989 (Amnesty International, 2016). A number of states, including Singapore, also employ corporal punishment (e.g., caning) as a form of punishment. The reaction of human rights groups to Van Nguyen's execution was based, in part, on the belief that the death penalty is an abhorrent form of punishment that has no place at all in the modern world. For others, the Van Nguyen case provoked a sense of outrage because of a perceived discrepancy between the crime and the punishment, not necessarily because of any antipathy towards the use of the death penalty per se. Then Australian Prime Minister John Howard, for example, supported the death penalty for the Bali bomber Amrozi who was involved in the killing of 202 people (including 88 Australians) in the nightclub bombing attack in 2002, while expressing outrage over Van Nguyen's execution. Indeed, opinion polls in Australia reveal that just under half of the population support the death penalty for murder (Roberts & Indermaur, 2007). More broadly, the execution of Van Nguyen prompts us to consider the rationale for punishment in the first place. Just what are the reasons that lead us to believe that certain acts are, in some sense, deserving of punishment? Finally, the case leads us to consider the more pragmatic question of whether punishment can be said to 'work'. One of the stated rationales for the death penalty for drug trafficking in Singapore is to deter would-be offenders. Has this punishment actually realised this goal by reducing drug trafficking in the area, and does punishment, in general, deter individuals from committing crime?

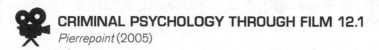

CRIMINAL PSYCHOLOGY THROUGH FILM 12.1
Pierrepoint (2005)

Directed by: Adrian Shergold
Starring: Timothy Spall (Albert Pierrepoint)

Based on the true-life British executioner, Albert Pierrepoint, brilliantly played by Timothy Spall, this film explores the complex set of emotions and cognitive contradictions inherent in the practice of capital punishment. While his role as executioner of war criminals made him a revered figure, by the time he had completed his last execution public opinion towards the death penalty was shifting, and Pierrepoint's own moral orientation towards his work becomes demonstrably more complex.

Question for discussion

1   The death penalty for murder was finally abolished in the United Kingdom in 1965. What factors do you think contributed to the abolition of the death penalty in the UK and many other Western countries in the twentieth century?

2   How might an executioner manage or 'justify' their role in the death of other humans? Are these justifications similar to the justifications that offenders often make for their offending?

Punishment is an integral component of the way that the criminal justice system responds to crime. Punishment can take many different forms – from a monetary fine to a lengthy stretch of imprisonment. The type and amount of punishment meted out also varies considerably among different countries and at different time periods in the same country. In this chapter we will explore the nature and extent of criminal justice responses to crime and examine the so-called 'punitive' turn that punishment has taken in many Western countries over the last decade or so. Punishment, by definition, involves the infliction of harm on others. The social and psychological effects of punishment on offenders and their families is an important topic for forensic psychologists and will also be reviewed in this chapter. We will then examine the key rationales for punishment, from both a philosophical and psychological perspective. Punishment may serve many functions in society, but one of the widely stated rationales for punishment is that it works to deter offenders. We will critically examine this idea by considering whether punishment does, in fact, work to prevent or reduce crime.

THE NATURE AND SCOPE OF CRIMINAL JUSTICE RESPONSES TO CRIME

The pillory was a popular form of punishment in England until it was finally abolished in 1837 (Hitchcock & Shoemaker, 2006). The convicted offender would stand, typically on a raised platform, with head and hands pinned between two solid planks of wood. Members of the public would then pelt the offender with a wide assortment of objects – from rotten eggs to dead cats. The pillory was designed to humiliate or shame offenders and was one of a large number of punishments employed in the pre-modern and early modern periods. The menu of options during this time included fines, corporal punishment (e.g., whipping), execution, transportation, and, increasingly from the early nineteenth century, imprisonment (Hitchcock & Shoemaker, 2006; Roth, 2014).

What all these different acts have in common is that they are 'penalties authorized by the state, and inflicted by state officials, in response to crime' (Hudson, 1996, p. 1). Punishment, then, involves the infliction of pain or unpleasantness that is authorised by an appropriate authoritative source (typically the state) and is directed at an individual who has committed an offence as codified by the laws of the state (Easton & Piper, 2005; Hudson, 1996).

The scope of punishment

Although the pillory is no longer employed as a method of punishment in the modern world, there still remains a wide variety of different options that are used by the criminal justice system in response to crime. In Table 12.1 a selection of these responses is depicted, although some, like corporal punishment and the death penalty, are only employed in a limited number of countries. In most countries non-custodial sanctions are the most widely used method of punishing offenders (Dammer & Fairchild, 2006). For instance, in New Zealand in the year ended June 2016 only 1 in 8 convicted adults received a prison sentence, with the most common sentence being a fine or reparation

Table 12.1 Criminal justice responses to crime

Sentence	Description
Imprisonment	The incarceration of offenders in purpose-built secure facilities.
Commitment to a psychiatric institution	Offenders with serious mental health problems may be involuntarily committed to psychiatric institutions by the criminal justice system.
Warnings	Official remonstrations made by the criminal justice system. They are especially widely used in the context of juvenile justice.
Fines	Monetary penalties imposed on offenders. Fines can take the form of fixed penalties or be calibrated to the offender's ability to pay (so-called 'day fines').
Probation	Probation involves supervision of the offender in the community. Probation takes a wide variety of forms and may include a range of restrictions or conditions, including many of the non-custodial sentences outlined in this table.
Confiscation and forfeiture	The confiscation and subsequent loss of property that has been derived from or used for criminal activity.
Community service	Community service involves the offender performing a set number of hours of unpaid work in the community.
Restitution	The payment of money (or work in kind) to the victim or representative by the offender.
House arrest	Offenders serve a sentence of incarceration in their own home. House arrest can involve various degrees of restriction on the offender.
Electronic monitoring	Offenders are electronically tagged, and their movements can be monitored. Typically used in conjunction with house arrest, probation, and other restrictions to ensure and monitor compliance.
Rehabilitation/treatment	Offenders may be required to participate in treatment or rehabilitative programmes as directed by the criminal justice system.
Corporal punishment	The use of physical punishment such as caning, branding, flogging, and maiming. Globally, corporal punishment is limited to only a few countries.
The death penalty	Execution of offenders.
Restorative justice	Involvement of the victim, offender, and relevant others in the sentencing process. Actual sentences vary widely, but the overall aim is to make the offender accountable for his/her crimes and bring about restoration of the victim and the community.

Source: Dammer and Fairchild (2006).

(33 per cent) (Ministry of Justice, 2016). For lesser offences, warnings and fines are often used, although there are important cross-national differences, with fines much more widely employed in the United Kingdom, Europe, Australia, and New Zealand than in the United States. Fines may take the form of a fixed amount of money or be calculated based on a percentage of the offender's income (Dammer & Fairchild, 2006).

The use of probation has a long history and essentially involves giving the offender an opportunity to remain in the community as long as they abide by certain court ordered restrictions. A condition of probation may involve the offender keeping to a strict curfew, doing unpaid community work, or having to attend a treatment or rehabilitation programme. Probation is a common criminal justice response to crime in many countries. In England and Wales, probation has been subsumed under the Community Order, which applies to all offenders aged 18 and over. The Community Order allows sentencers to pick one or more 'requirements' from a menu of options including unpaid work, curfew, and alcohol and drug treatment (Newburn, 2013). Broadly speaking, the range of non-custodial sanctions that are available to the criminal justice system provide a more cost-effective alternative to prison for less serious offenders while allowing the offender to remain in the community and (ideally) to address the causes of offending (see Worrall & Hoy, 2005).

For more serious offences imprisonment remains the punishment of choice in Western countries. According to the most recent World Prison Population List (11th edition) it was estimated that there are more than 10.35 million individuals currently held in penal institutions throughout the world (Walmsley, 2016). Rates of imprisonment do, however, vary dramatically among countries. The United States has the highest rate of imprisonment in the world (after the Seychelles) with 799 out of every 100,000 individuals incarcerated. As illustrated in Figure 12.1, this figure is significantly higher than any other English-speaking Western country. Prisons and prisoners are typically classified on the basis of a prisoner's perceived level of dangerousness and likelihood of escaping. The most dangerous and escape-prone prisoners are held in maximum security facilities, while those deemed less dangerous are incarcerated in less secure environments (Adler et al., 2007; Newbold, 2007, 2016). A recent development in the United States in the construction of so-called '**supermax prisons**', designed to house inmates who exhibit extremely violent or disruptive behaviour (Pizarro & Narag, 2008). The psychological impact of prisons, including the new supermax prisons, is an important topic for forensic psychologists and is discussed in detail below.

The United States incarcerates a relatively greater proportion of its population than any other country. It is also unique among Western countries in being the only nation to retain the use of the death penalty. The use of the death penalty remains a contentious topic of discussion. Hood (2001) summarises the main objections to the death penalty as follows:

- It violates the fundamental human right to life.
- It does not act as an effective deterrent compared to alternative sanctions such as life imprisonment.
- It cannot be effectively administered without an unacceptable level of arbitrariness and discrimination.
- It conveys an inappropriate and inconsistent message that killing is justified.

Despite these objections, public support for the death penalty remains high in many countries.

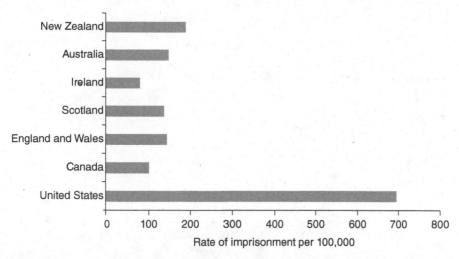

Figure 12.1 Imprisonment rates (per 100,000 population) for selected English-speaking countries. *Source*: Adapted from Walmsley (2016, Figure 1).

Penal trends

The nature and extent of punishment vary not only among different nations, but also within countries over time. One important trend in criminal justice responses to crime that has been identified in most English-speaking Western countries in the late twentieth and early twenty-first century is a shift towards greater **punitiveness** (Pratt et al., 2005). One of the most obvious indicators of this trend can be found in rates of incarceration. This is perhaps most evident in the United States where, as from 1973 'the population behind bars underwent exponential growth, on a scale without precedent in the history of democratic societies' (Wacquant, 2005, p. 5). The number of individuals held in prisons and jails in the United States has increased dramatically over the last decade and a half: from 503,586 in 1980 to just over 2.2 million in 2013 (Bureau of Justice Statistics, 2007; Walmsley, 2016). Similar trends have been evident in other English-speaking Western countries such as Australia, New Zealand, and England and Wales. For example, as illustrated in Figure 12.2 the overall number of individuals incarcerated in New Zealand has over doubled since 1990 despite a modest 35 per cent increase in population (Newbold, 2016). Some predominantly English-speaking countries, such as Canada, appear to have missed this punitive turn, however (Meyer & O'Malley, 2005), and in other European countries, such as Finland, rates of incarceration have actually declined since the mid-1980s (Cavadino & Dignan, 2006). Indeed a number of scholars have highlighted the *contrasts* in punishment regimes in Western English-speaking countries compared to the relatively more humane system identified in Scandinavian countries (Pratt & Eriksson, 2014; although see Barker, 2013).

Rates of incarceration provide some evidence for this punitive turn in criminal justice responses to crime in a number of countries in the late twentieth century. Other indicators include the enactment of harsh penal laws such as **'three strike laws'** in the United States (where, as originally developed, offenders would be given life sentences for a third felony regardless of its severity) and now New Zealand, sexual predator statutes

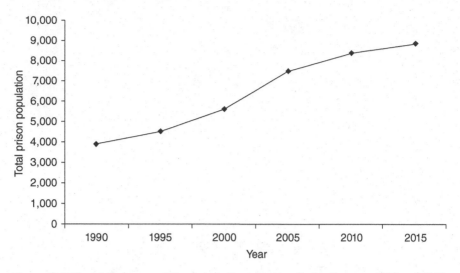

Figure 12.2 The total prison population (selected years) in New Zealand between 1990 and 2015. *Source*: Newbold (2016) and Walmsley (2016).

that allow for indefinite civil detention of certain sex offenders, and mandatory minimum sentences. Alongside these developments we have also seen the return of shaming punishments that involve the public humiliation of offenders (Pratt, 2000, 2006), chain gangs, and the introduction of harsher penal regimes like 'supermax prisons'. Designed to house violent inmates (or those deemed at risk of violence), supermax facilities operate at high levels of security and impose long periods of solitary confinement on inmates (Pizarro & Narag, 2008). Although many scholars agree on the broad contours of this punitive trend, it is important to note that penal developments, as mentioned above, have not been consistently punitive across nations, or within different state jurisdictions within countries like the United States and Australia (Weatherburn, 2016).

The reasons for this punitive turn in many criminal justice systems and the associated rapid rise in prison numbers are undoubtedly complex and are likely to involve a mix of social, political, and economic factors (Cavadino & Dignan, 2006; Pratt, 2006). However, whatever the ultimate *causes* of the increasing punitiveness of the criminal justice system, there have been some clear *effects* in terms of the social and psychological impacts of punishment on offenders.

REVIEW AND REFLECT

1   What are the different ways in which the criminal justice system responds to crime?
2   Why do you think the United States has a much higher rate of imprisonment than other English-speaking nations?
3   What might account for changes in the New Zealand prison population in the twenty-first century?

THE HARMS OF PUNISHMENT

One of the most powerful depictions of prison conditions in the second half of the twentieth century was provided by Jack Henry Abbott in his collection of letters on prison life, *In the Belly of the Beast* (Abbott, 1981). Abbott describes, in vivid detail, his experiences as a prisoner in the United States in the 1960s and 1970s. This included starvation, violence, forced medication, solitary confinement, and profound sensory deprivation. At one point Abbott describes an extended period spent in solitary confinement in a so-called 'blackout cell':

> I was in *total* darkness. Not a crack of light entered that cell *anywhere* ... I counted twenty-three days by the meals ... I heard someone screaming far away and it was me. I fell against the wall, and as if it were a catapult, was hurled across the cell to the opposite wall, Back and forth I reeled, from the door to the walls, screaming. Insane.
> (Abbott, 1981, pp. 26–27)

Although the conditions in most modern Western prisons are not as dire as those described by Abbott, a considerable body of research has documented the harmful social and psychological impacts of prisons on inmates (Liebling & Maruna, 2005).

The effects of imprisonment on offenders

In his classic work on prison life, Gresham Sykes (1958, cited in Welch, 2004) listed some of the most important pains of imprisonment. These include:

- deprivation of liberty
- deprivation of goods and services
- deprivation of heterosexual relationships
- deprivation of autonomy
- deprivation of security.

Although the public sometimes claim that prison is a 'soft option' (Roberts & Hough, 2005), even the most humanely run prisons deprive inmates of a number of important social and psychological experiences, as Sykes has outlined. Importantly, prisons separate inmates from family members and the community and impose tightly regimented routines that can result in a loss of autonomy among prisoners (Irwin & Owen, 2005). The prison environment is also often an extremely violent one, contributing to a sense of fear and insecurity. In one study of 7,221 male and 564 female prisoners in the United States, it was found that over a six-month period 20 per cent of the sample had experienced some form of physical violence, a rate 18 to 27 times higher than that found in non-incarcerated populations (Wolff, Blitz, Shi, Siegel, et al., 2007). Another study of prison violence in four correctional institutions in the United Kingdom revealed similar rates of victimisation, with 19 per cent of the sample reporting that they were the victim of an assault in the last month (Edgar, O'Donnell, & Martin, 2004). Rates of sexual violence are also high in prisons (Wolff, Blitz, & Shi, 2007).

The harmful effects of prisons have been exacerbated in recent decades due to chronic overcrowding. This is largely a consequence of the rapid rise in rates of incarceration described earlier. In the United Kingdom, the problem of overcrowding has meant that in 2003/2004 around a fifth of prisoners were required to share a cell that had been originally designed for one inmate, and rates of occupancy were well over 100 per cent of maximum capacity (Coyle, 2005). Despite a massive programme of prison construction in the United States, overcrowding also still remains a problem: in 2006, 23 states operated at higher than 100 per cent of their highest capacity, and the Federal prison system was operating at 37 per cent above its rated capacity (Sabol, Couture, & Harrison, 2007). In the United States, an increasing number of prisoners – an estimated 25,000 or more – are also being held in supermax facilities that impose long periods of solitary confinement on prisoners and remove almost all opportunities for any meaningful social interaction. Prisoners in supermax prisons are typically confined in, often windowless, 7ft by 12ft (2.1m by 3.7m) cells for 22 to 23 hours a day and rarely engage in any social contact with other individuals; they are fed through a food port in the cell door, and visits and consultations with doctors and psychiatrists may be conducted via tele-conferencing (Haney, 2003; Pizarro & Narag, 2008).

Prisons are environments that, by their very nature, impose sometimes severe deprivations on inmates. Violence, overcrowding, and, in some cases, solitary confinement contribute significantly to the impact of prisons on physical, social, and psychological functioning. The effects of adverse environmental contexts have been well researched, and psychologists have an important role to play both in understanding the psychological impact of prisons and in attempting to ameliorate this impact through the provision of mental health services (Haney, 2005; Haney & Zimbardo, 1998).

One of the more visible impacts of prisons on inmates is reflected in the comparatively high rates of suicide in custody. Most studies find that suicide occurs comparatively more frequently in prison than in does in the community (Daniel, 2006; Liebling, 2007). For example, in England and Wales 78 individuals committed suicide in custody in 2005. This translates to a rate of 102.6 individuals per 100,000 compared to a rate of 10–12 per 100,000 in the community (Liebling, 2007). It should be noted, however, that young males – who have a higher rate of suicide in general – are over-represented in prisons, accounting for some of the differences in rates of suicide between prisons and the community. The majority of suicides occur during the earliest periods of custody. Prisoners on remand and those in their first month of imprisonment are at a particularly high risk of suicide. Individuals sentenced to life imprisonment are also at greater risk (Liebling, 2007). Individual risk factors for suicide in prisons largely mirror those found in the general community and include youth, social exclusion, substance abuse, and mental health problems (Daniel, 2006).

Mental health problems are particularly prevalent among prisoners, as a number of studies have illustrated (Brinded et al., 2001; Butler et al., 2005). For example, Butler et al. (2005) in a study of 953 reception and 579 sentenced prisoners in New South Wales, Australia found that 43 per cent of the sample were assessed as suffering from at least one mental illness within the last 12 months. The results from a large-scale international review of 62 studies from 12 countries confirmed these general findings as the authors concluded that 'typically about one in seven prisoners in Western countries have psychotic illnesses or major depression (disorders that might be risk factors for suicide), and about one in two male prisoners and about one in five female prisoners have antisocial personality disorders' (Fazel & Danesh, 2002, p. 548). These rates are significantly higher than those found in the general population with prisoners at a two- to four-fold risk of suffering from psychotic disorders and depression and a ten-fold risk of having antisocial personality disorder. To what extent these results reflect the *impact* of prisons on mental health rather than the pre-existing health problems of prisoners is clearly an important issue. As we have seen in Chapter 3, offenders are at a greater risk of suffering from mental health problems in general, accounting for some of the high rates of mental illness in prison. Most researchers, however, also argue that the prison environment has a negative effect on mental health (Birmingham, 2004).

The high rates of mental illness among prisoners and the negative psychological effects of prisons mean that prison mental health services have an important role to play in the assessment, management, and treatment of mental disorder. It is essential that prisoners are thoroughly assessed in order to establish their suicide risk and overall mental health needs. The provision of treatment and the implementation of risk management strategies should also feature in prison environments (Steel et al., 2007).

The collateral effects of imprisonment on family members

The individuals who most visibly experience the negative impacts of prison life are the prisoners themselves. It is also important to recognise the collateral impact of imprisonment: for families, children, and the community (Hagan & Dinovitzer, 1999). A large number of individuals have parents, partners, or other family members who are either currently in prison or have been imprisoned in the past. Exact figures are not available for all English-speaking Western countries, but in the United States over 1.5 million children under the age of 18 have a parent in prison (Mumola, 2000). In Australia it is estimated that around 38,000 children currently have an incarcerated parent each year, and some 145,000 children have ever had a parent in prison. This means that some 5 per cent of all children and 20 per cent of indigenous Australians have experienced parental incarceration (Quilty, 2005; Quilty et al., 2004).

Not all children or partners of prisoners will necessarily experience negative effects from their family member's incarceration. However, having a partner in prison can result in loss of income, relationship problems, and additional burdens relating to child care. For children, parental imprisonment can lead to an array of psychological problems including depression, aggressive behaviour, sleep problems, truancy, and delinquency (Murray, 2005). There are a number of reasons why having a parent in prison may result in these kinds of problems. First, the experience of parental separation and loss may have a direct effect on child adjustment, as attachment theory would suggest. This is likely to be compounded by fears about the parent's safety. Second, children may overtly model their incarcerated parent's criminal behaviour and become involved in antisocial acts. Third, children may experience stigma due their parent's incarceration. This can lead to bullying and teasing from other children or negative labelling from others. Fourth, having a parent in prison may result in a loss of income and reduced parental supervision, both of which can contribute to negative outcomes for children (Murray, 2005; Murray & Farrington, 2005).

Of course, children who have parents in prison are likely to also have a number of other risk factors for delinquency and antisocial behaviour that predate their parent's imprisonment. These might include genetic factors, poor parenting, the modelling of antisocial behaviour, and social factors such as employment and low socioeconomic status. Very few studies have attempted to tease out the direct effects of imprisonment from these pre-existing risk factors. One exception is provided in Murray and Farrington's (2005) research on the effects of parental imprisonment on boys' antisocial behaviour using longitudinal data from the Cambridge Study in Delinquent Development. The results of their study found that the boys who had experienced parental imprisonment were at an elevated risk on a range of antisocial and delinquent outcomes compared to boys who had not experienced parental incarceration or had experienced parental separation due to other reasons. Importantly, the association between parental imprisonment and antisocial outcomes remained after controlling for a range of other parenting and family risk factors, thus providing support for the direct negative impact of parental imprisonment on children.

In this section we have focused on the various harms that arise from punishment, particularly those that occur in the context of prison. Prison environments vary significantly from country to country and even within countries to a considerable degree. Different individuals also respond to the same environment in different ways – prison will not be experienced as an overwhelmingly negative experience for all inmates. However, a good deal of research has clearly documented that prison can have many detrimental physical, psychological, and social effects on prisoners.

REVIEW AND REFLECT

1 What are some of the features of prison life that are likely to contribute to the high rates of mental health problems in correctional facilities?
2 What are some of the 'collateral' impacts on family members?

RATIONALES FOR PUNISHMENT

A 23-year-old man breaks into a school room on the weekend and sexually assaults and murders a 60-year-old female school teacher who is catching up on grading students' assignments. The man is subsequently apprehended by police. Should he be punished by the criminal justice system for his crime? For most people (probably everyone) it doesn't take much reflection to answer this question in the affirmative: of course he should be punished. But why? Why do we accept that, by and large, individuals who break the law should be punished for their offending? Many different answers have been offered to this seemingly straightforward question. Before reading further you may want to consider in more detail the reasons that *you* believe are most important in justifying punishment (Activity 12.1). Given that, as we have seen, punishment involves the infliction of harms on others it is important to able to provide a sound rationale for punishing law breakers. In the following sections we first examine the main philosophical rationales for punishment. Then, we examine psychological research that has explored the reasons that people – either implicitly or explicitly – believe are the reasons behind the infliction of punishment on those individuals who break the law.

ACTIVITY 12.1 **RATIONALES FOR PUNISHMENT**

Read through the following two scenarios about people who have committed an offence. For each scenario indicate what sentence you think would be appropriate and the most important aim or purpose of that sentence.

Scenario 1

Walter, a 35-year-old father of three, was caught trying to smuggle heroin into the country for resale. The heroin has an estimated street value of $250,000. Walter has no previous convictions.

What sentence would you hand down to Walter? (You may choose more than one option.)

- Prison <5 years
- Prison >5 years
- Community service
- Fine
- Rehabilitation

What was the main reason or purpose for the sentencing option(s) that you chose above? (Select one only.)

- To discourage others from committing the crime.
- To discourage the offender from committing any further crimes.
- To prevent the offender from committing further crimes through imprisonment.
- To punish the offender in a way that reflects the seriousness of the offence.
- To show society's disapproval of the crime.
- To rehabilitate the offender.

Scenario 2

Simon, aged 22 and unemployed, broke into an elderly couple's house. When the elderly man got up to investigate the noise, Simon knocked him to the floor with a baseball bat and fled the premises. The victim required 16 stitches to his head and spent a week in hospital as a result of the attack.

What sentence would you hand down to Simon? (You may choose more than one option.)

- Prison <5 years
- Prison >5 years
- Community service

- Fine
- Rehabilitation

What was the main reason or purpose for the sentencing option(s) that you chose above? (Select one only.)

- To discourage others from committing the crime.
- To discourage the offender from committing any further crimes.
- To prevent the offender from committing further crimes through imprisonment.
- To punish the offender in a way that reflects the seriousness of the offence.
- To show society's disapproval of the crime.
- To rehabilitate the offender.

Source: This exercise was adapted from the research carried out by Paulin, Searle, and Knaggs (2003)

Philosophical perspectives

It is generally recognised that rationales for punishment fall under two main categories (Cavadino & Dignan, 2006; Hudson, 1996). The first category can be described as utilitarian or consequentialist in nature: individuals are punished in order to reduce the likelihood of future offending. This approach to punishment is thus forward looking: punishment serves to control or reduce crime in society. The second main category is generally known as retributivist. Crimes are punished primarily to extract retribution from offenders. This approach to punishment is backward looking in nature: punishment is inflicted because the offending warranted it, not in order to alter future behaviour (Marsh, 2004).

One of the most widely recognised utilitarian goals of punishment is **deterrence**. The core idea of deterrence is that the infliction of punishment serves to reduce the likelihood of offending because individuals will be motivated to avoid punishment and thus will be more likely to obey the law. For the punishment to act as a deterrent it has to be harsh enough in order to outweigh any benefits that might arise from committing the crime. Two forms of deterrence are generally recognised (Hudson, 1996). The first is **general deterrence**: punishment is believed to affect the community as a whole by signalling that certain behaviours result in certain consequences. People do not want to end up in prison or have other such punishments imposed on them, and thus they are deterred from committing crimes that might be punished in these ways. When an offender is punished for a crime by, say, being sent to prison, it sends a clear message to the rest of society that behaviour of this sort will result in an unpleasant response from the criminal justice system. To the extent that individuals are motivated to avoid having the same pain inflicted upon them, then they should avoid committing the same criminal act. **Individual** (or specific) **deterrence** refers to the effects of punishment on the individual who commits the crime. By imposing negative sanctions on an individual who commits an offence it is believed that the individual will be less likely to offend again. Offenders should recognise the harmful consequence of their actions to themselves and change their behaviour accordingly.

Another important utilitarian, or consequentialist, rationale for punishment is **incapacitation**. Some forms of punishment – especially imprisonment, but to a lesser extent probation, intense supervision, and electronic monitoring – serve to incapacitate an offender. By imposing restrictions on an offender's freedom to act we are thus reducing the possibility that they can commit crimes (in the community at least). Capital punishment, of course, might be viewed as the ultimate way in which an individual's ability to offend is curtailed. Contemporary penal policy has typically focused on the idea of *selective* incapacitation. Because research clearly demonstrates that a relatively small percentage of offenders commit a vastly disproportionate amount of crime, then selectively incapacitating these offenders should effectively reduce overall amounts of crime (Bartol & Bartol, 2008). Although the idea of selection incapacitation makes sense from a crime control perspective, identifying this sub-group of problem or persistent offenders is a more difficult task (Newburn, 2013).

Punishment may, in principle, be able to reduce crime by deterring or incapacitating offenders. The criminal justice system may also be able to prevent crime by intervening in offenders' lives in ways that make re-offending less likely. The idea that offenders should be reformed or rehabilitated played an important role in criminal justice responses to crime for much of the nineteenth and twentieth century, although it lost favour as a correctional philosophy in the 1970s and 1980s (Bartol & Bartol, 2008). The topic of rehabilitation is taken up in more detail in Chapter 13.

The core feature of retributivist rationales for punishment is the idea that certain acts, by their very nature, *deserve* to be punished. Individuals should be held accountable to their crimes and receive punishment that is commensurate with the seriousness or gravity of their offending. Retributivist accounts are, therefore, backward looking in nature: they focus on meting out appropriate responses for past wrongdoing. Punishment, from this perspective, can be viewed as an end in itself, rather than a means to some other end, like crime prevention. The idea of retribution has a rich historical pedigree, perhaps best represented in the biblical concept of *lex talionis*: an eye for an eye, a tooth for a tooth, a life for a life (Hudson, 1996).

Contemporary retributivist accounts highlight the importance of censure and **proportionality** (von Hirsch, 1998). Punishment communicates the idea that an individual has committed an act that deserves punishment: 'The criminal sanction censures: punishing consists of doing something unpleasant to someone, because he purportedly has committed a wrong, under circumstances and in a manner that conveys disapprobation of the person for his wrong' (von Hirsch, 1998, p. 169). Punishment, however, need not involve inflicting the same harm on the individual that they have inflicted on others, as the idea of lex talionis suggests. Rather, punishment should be *proportionate* to the seriousness of the offence – murderers, for instance, should be punished more harshly than shoplifters. Proportionality is central to the retributivist account offered by von Hirsch (1998) because more serious offences that involve greater harm deserve a commensurate level of censure (embodied in punishment) to convey to the individual the harm that they have caused.

A number of contemporary retributivist accounts admit some consequentialist goals or aims within their theoretical frameworks. Von Hirsch (1998), for instance, recognises that punishment, in addition to censuring an act, adds a 'prudential disincentive' that provides a further discouragement for offending. The idea that censure serves a critical consequentialist or crime prevention function is most fully developed in the work of Duff (1998, 2003). Duff argues that punishment not only condemns a given act as wrong, but also promotes change in an offender by focusing their attention on their wrongdoing in a way that might induce 'repentance, reform and reconciliation' (Duff, 1998, p. 165). Punishment, therefore, is viewed as a communicative act that portrays to individual offenders, and to others in society, that a wrong has been done and that this kind of behaviour should be avoided.

Psychological perspectives

Understanding the rationale for punishment has provided fertile ground for debate by philosophers, criminologists, and other legal scholars. But what do the public, in general, believe are, or should be, the main reasons why we punish criminal offenders? Finkel (1995; Finkel & Sales, 1997) has introduce the notion of **common-sense justice** – people's sense of what is fair and just – to capture the idea that individuals have, perhaps firmly entrenched, beliefs about what kinds of acts should be punished and for what reasons. Understanding people's common-sense ideas of justice is important, Darley (2001, 2009) argues, because the ideas that people hold might conflict with those that are formalised within the criminal justice system. When this is the case, compliance with legal codes might be diminished, and individuals will have a sense that the system is 'unfair'.

Survey research generally finds that the public endorse multiple sentencing goals, including deterrence, incapacitation, retribution, rehabilitation, and censure (Doble, 2002). When give the option to agree with a range of different rationales for punishment, respondents typically strongly endorse a number of different options. For instance, in a national sample of American households, researchers asked respondents to rate their agreement with a number of different statements about punishment (Cullen et al., 2002). Some 92 per cent of the sample agreed with the statement 'criminals deserve to be punished because they have harmed society', providing strong support for retributivist goals. However, 91 per cent of the sample also agreed that 'we should put criminals in jail so that innocent citizens will be protected from criminals who victimise them – rob them – if given the chance' suggesting that incapacitation is also a punishment goal held by the public. To complicate the picture, when asked which of three goals of prison they thought were important, respondents thought that the goals of rehabilitation (87 per cent), punishment (86 per cent), and deterrence (93 per cent) were all important.

It is clear from public opinion research that the full range of rationales for punishment identified by philosophers and legal scholars may play an important role in people's beliefs about the aims of punishment. Perhaps, however, the way individuals respond to explicit questions regarding the aims of punishment fails to accurately capture their actual reasons for why they think offenders should be punished (Carlsmith, Darley, & Robinson, 2002). In an experimental study designed to explore the competing rationales of deterrence and just deserts as motives for punishment, Carlsmith et al.

(2002) presented participants with vignettes of offences that varied in terms of variables that would tap into just deserts thinking (e.g., magnitude of harm associated with the crime – punishment severity should be in proportion to the seriousness of offences) and deterrence thinking (e.g., the detection rate of the crime – difficult crimes to catch should, from a deterrence perspective, be punished more harshly). The results of the study found that people's punitiveness was more strongly influenced by variables associated with a just deserts perspective than it was be deterrence-related variables, leading the researchers to conclude: 'When faced with a prototypical wrongdoing action, a harm intentionally inflicted on another by a perpetrator, people assign punishment to give the perpetrator his or her just deserts rather than to achieve any future utility' (Carlsmith et al., 2002, p. 295).

Other experimental research has provided additional support for the idea that the desire to punish is prominently driven by retributivist concerns (e.g., Gromet & Darley, 2006; Rucker et al., 2004; see also Hoffman, 2014). We should, though, be somewhat cautious in generalising too much from these studies on college students to the wider population. Certainly, however, deviant acts have the capacity to evoke strong emotional feelings that can promote the desire to punish offenders. Vidmar (2001), in an analysis of real-world cases, suggests that when criminal offences threaten, or are perceived to threaten, group norms and values then retributive emotions and impulses are likely to be evoked. The outrage that is often invoked among community members by particularly heinous crimes or crimes that go unpunished (or in the eyes of the public, *under*-punished – see Research in Focus 12.1) provide some support for the idea that retributive justice is deeply engrained and may serve the important function, as Durkheim (1893/1984) argued, of re-affirming group norms and values (Box 12.1).

RESEARCH IN FOCUS 12.1 PUBLIC ATTITUDES TOWARDS SENTENCING IN AUSTRALIA

Title: Sentencing and public confidence: Results from a national Australian survey on public opinions towards sentencing

Author: Mackenzie, G., et al.   **Year:** 2012

Source: *Australian and New Zealand Journal of Criminology,* 45, 45–65

Aims: To explore public attitudes towards sentencing in Australia

Method: Computer-assisted interviewing on a stratified random sample of 6,005 Australians on questions relating to confidence in sentencing, attitudes towards punishment, and alternatives to prison.

Key results:
- Confidence in sentencing practices and processes was fairly limited, e.g., over half the sample disagreed or strongly disagreed with the statement 'I am satisfied with decisions that the courts make'.

- The majority of participants believed that penalties for offenders should be more severe, e.g., 56 per cent of the sample agreed or strongly agreed with the statement 'People who break the law should receive stiffer sentences'.
- There was strong support for the use of alternatives to prison, particularly for certain groups of offenders, e.g., 82 per cent of the sample agreed or strongly agreed with the statement 'Instead of going to prison, mentally ill offenders should receive treatment in mental health facilities'.

Conclusion: 'The present findings confirm that the Australian public lacks confidence in sentencing, is dissatisfied with the quantum of penalties and believes that harsher sentencing is needed ... however ... there was widespread support for the use of alternatives to imprisonment for young, mentally ill and non-violent offender' (pp. 56–57).

Question for discussion

To what extent should sentencing practices reflect or take in to account public opinion on crime and punishment? (See Roberts & de Keijser, 2014.)

BOX 12.1 THE ORIGINS OF PUNISHMENT

Imagine that you are a participant in a behavioural experiment known as the ultimatum game. Another player is given $100 (in real money) and is told that they can split it with you anyway they like – they can give you the full $100, nothing, or anything in between. If you accept their offer then you both get to keep the money; if you reject it, you both get nothing. The other player offers your $20, what do you do? If you are being rational, then you should keep the money – after all $20 is better than nothing. If, however, you are like the vast majority of individuals who have participated in these games all across the world then you will probably reject their offer (Henrich et al., 2006). Why? One explanation for the apparently irrational response of most participants is that individuals perceive very uneven splits to violate norms of fairness (after all, the other player got *given* the money), and they are willing to pay a cost (in hard cash) to punish that individual. Similar types of economic games involving more participants produce similar responses: individuals are willing to pay a cost in order to punish those individuals who violate perceived social norms. Of course, in the real world, we go to a great deal of effort to ensure that individuals that offend against society are punished and feel a sense of injustice if they are not. Why are we so motivated to punish those individuals that violate important social norms?

From an evolutionary perspective, it has been argued that the motivation to punish (and the sense of moral outrage over violations of social norms) evolved because punishment promotes cooperation in social groups (Boyd et al., 2003; Henrich, 2006). In short, small groups – of the type that constituted most of our evolutionary history – in which there were individuals willing to incur costs to punish norm violators were more successful than groups in which such individuals were absent. By punishing norm violations, groups could be more cooperative because free riders – those individuals who took the benefits afforded by the group but contributed nothing – could be either brought into line or, in extreme cases, excluded from the group. In modern societies, the criminal justice system has taken over the role of punishing those individuals that violate a particular class of social norms (i.e., criminal offences), and the history of punishment tells us that the kind of offence punished and the mode of punishment reflect, to some extent, specific cultural and historical contexts. However, it is also reasonable to suggest that humans have shared 'intuitions of justice' (Decety & Yoder, 2016; Robinson, Kurzban, & Jones, 2007), which reflect our evolutionary history as hunter gatherers in small groups, and which motivate us to punish those individuals who engage in behaviours that violate social norms, particularly those that pose a perceived threat to the effective functioning of the social group.

REVIEW AND REFLECT

1   What are some of the main philosophical rationales for punishment?
2   Read through some newspaper reports of sentences handed down by judges. What rationale for punishment appears to feature most prominently in such reports?
3   Darley (2001) argues that it is important to understand people's common-sense beliefs about justice. Why is this important, and what happens when these beliefs conflict with the operation of the criminal justice system?

DOES PUNISHMENT WORK?

What would our world be like if the criminal justice system decided, overnight, to abolish all forms of punishment? Would mayhem necessarily ensue and previously law-abiding citizens become robbers, rapists, and murderers? Almost certainly not. Indeed, although most people would rather not live in such a world, and perhaps the overall amount of crime would increase, as Tyler (2006; see also Trinkner & Tyler, 2016) has argued most people don't obey the law primarily out of fear of punishment per se. Rather, respect for the law (and lawmakers and enforcers) as legitimate authorities and conformity to widely shared social norms predominantly guide law-abiding behaviour. That is not to say that a criminal justice system that metes out punishment for law breaking has no deterrent effect. Most scholars would agree that the threat of punishment in general makes some contribution to the prevention of offending (Apel & Nagin, 2011; Nagin, 1998, 2013). However, there is less certainty, and considerable disagreement, as to whether or to what extent specific sentences or changes to sentencing severity can meaningfully affect levels of crime. In other words, there is considerable doubt that the criminal law deters (Robinson & Darley, 2004). This is obviously an important issue because the primary rationale for the punitive turn in many Western countries over the last couple of decades is that harsher punishments should work to deter offending. In this section we first review the available evidence base for deterrent effects and then discuss some of the psychological and social factors that can explain why strong deterrent effects have proven so elusive to find.

The evidence base for deterrent effects

The logic of deterrence is deceptively straightforward: if the penalties for breaching the law are substantial enough then individuals will reason that the consequences of crime are simply not worth the risk and will therefore not offend. It should follow that increasing the severity of penalties for offending will result in a commensurate reduction in crime. However, most systematic reviews of the effects of sentencing severity on crime conclude, with a few exceptions, that there is little or no evidence that increasing the punitiveness of criminal sanctions exerts an effect on offending (Doob & Webster, 2003; MacKenzie, 2002; Tonry, 2008). For example, Doob and Webster (2003) in a comprehensive review of the general deterrent effects of sentence severity urge us to 'accept the null hypothesis: severity of sentences does not affect crime levels' (p. 191).

Reviews of the effects of specific deterrence (that is, the effects of actual punishment on offenders' rates of recidivism), largely reach the same conclusion. In a large-scale meta-analysis of the effects of prison sentences on recidivism, Gendreau et al. (2001) reviewed studies that compared the impact of (a) prison versus community sentences, and (b) longer versus shorter prison sentences on rates of recidivism among convicted offenders. The offenders in the different groups in all the studies were matched in terms of their general risk factors for offending (e.g., criminal history, severity of index offence), although only one study in the sample used random assignment. In sum, 57 studies were included involving more than 350,000 offenders. The results of the meta-analysis revealed no support for the deterrent effects of punishment. Imprisonment (compared to community sentences) was associated with a small *increase* in the risk of offending, and longer (compared to shorter sentences) had a negligible effect on rates of recidivism. It would appear, based on this study, that harsher and longer punishment does not impact on rates of offending as would be assumed if punishment had a deterrent effect. The results of this study are largely supported in other research on individual deterrent effects (Nagin, 2013). Reviews of 'enhanced punishment' such as boot camps, intensive supervision, scared straight programmes, and electronic monitoring are typically consistent with the thesis that increasing the severity of punishment does not act a significant deterrent to offenders (MacKenzie, 2006; Petrosino, Turpin-Petrosino, & Buehler, 2003).

It could be argued that the punitive 'bite' represented in many of the above studies is simply not sufficient to deter offenders and that deterrent effects should emerge with harsher punishments such as long mandatory minimum sentences (e.g., three strike laws in the United States) and the death penalty. One common justification for the retention of the death penalty in some countries and states (in America) is that it can serve as a potent deterrent for the most serious offences, such as murder. In an early and often-referred-to study, Ehrlich (1975) claimed that the death penalty acts as a significant deterrent, with each execution resulting in a reduction in 7 or 8 homicides. Other research has also supported the notion that capital punishment deters, with Dezhbakha, Rubin, and Shepherd (2003) suggesting that each execution results in an estimated 18 fewer murders. However, other researchers have failed to find significant deterrent effects of the death penalty (e.g., Hood, 2001), and estimates appear to be dependent on the specific model used by researchers suggesting that methodological issues play an important role in evaluations of the efficacy of capital punishment (Cohen-Cole et al., 2006; Fagan, 2006; Nagin, 2013). One significant problem in evaluating the effectiveness of the death penalty as a deterrent in the United States (where most research has been carried out) is that so few individuals are executed in the states where capital punishment has been retained. As Fagan (2006) points out, even if we assume that offenders are rational (and can, therefore, be amenable to deterrence), the rare and somewhat arbitrary use of execution in retentionist states means that it 'serves no deterrent function, because no would-be murderer can reasonably expect to be executed' (p. 290). Given the politically charged nature of the debate over the death penalty in the United States the safest conclusion based on the available evidence is that capital punishment probably does not deter potential offenders; however, we are lacking the kind of robust evidence that would allow a definitive conclusion either way.

The overall thrust of this section so far is that sentence severity and changes in the severity of punishments for offences have negligible impact on rates of crime. In short, firm evidence for robust deterrent effects is lacking. However, we shouldn't conclude that the criminal law has absolutely no deterrent effects. As mentioned previously, the mere presence of criminal justice sanctions for offences surely deters some individuals who might otherwise commit crimes, and it is likely that legal sanctions exert general deterrent effects (Apel & Nagin, 2011). Evidence for, often localised, deterrent effects have also been found in a number of studies. A good example is provided by Weisburd, Einat, and Kowalski (2008). In this study, a sample of New Jersey probationers that were seriously arrears in paying court-ordered fines were randomly assigned to either a regular probation group or one of two other groups in which there was a threat of incarceration for non-payment of fines. The results of the study indicated that individuals who were threatened with imprisonment for non-payment of fines were significantly more likely to have paid their fines than the control group. This study supports the idea that the threat of (a specific and well-advertised) punishment can deter a specific form of offending (the non-payment of fines). This study suggests that it is important to investigate under what conditions and for what groups of individuals criminal justice sanctions are most likely to work as a deterrent. This suggests that understanding whether and how punishment can deter offending requires an understanding of the psychological and social factors that underlie criminal decision making.

Understanding deterrence: A psychological perspective

Before reading further, consider the factors that might influence your decision to engage (or not to engage) in a criminal act like the illegal downloading of movies from the internet (Activity 12.2). One prominent tradition in criminological thought is the idea that criminal activities are determined by rational, cost–benefit analyses. Jeremy Bentham argued that offenders weigh up the costs and benefits of committing crimes, and if the benefits outweigh the costs then they will be more likely to offend. This idea has undergone a number of revisions and extensions (Becker, 1968; Matsueda, Kreager, & Huizinga, 2006), but we can capture the core elements in a fairly straightforward formula, in which offending will occur if the benefits of offending multiplied by the likelihood of receiving

---

ACTIVITY 12.2 **TO COPY OR NOT TO COPY?**

A person that you are extremely attracted to asks you to do them a favour. They want you to download pirated copies of recently released films using software on your computer. They tell you they are for their personal use and hints that you could 'get together' afterwards for a coffee. Would you copy the movies?

In making your decision on this venture rank order the following factors in terms of how important they are in influencing your decision (from most important to least important).

Factors influencing your behaviour	Order
The certainty of punishment (i.e., the chances of getting caught by the police).	
The severity of punishment (your likely sentence).	
Your personal beliefs about the morality of the suggestion (your sense of right and wrong).	
How important to you doing a favour for this person is.	

Which of the following would most likely to deter you if you were to copy the movies? (Circle one.)

1 If your chances of getting caught were only 1% but your punishment would be 1 year in prison; or
2 If your chances of getting caught were 50% but your punishment would be $500.

Think about your answers to this activity. What do they tell you about the factors that might influence offending and the factors that might work to deter criminal behaviour?

those benefits outweighs the sum of the costs multiplied by the probability of incurring those costs:

$$P * U_{\text{(rewards from offending)}} > P * U_{\text{(costs from offending)}}$$

Where U represents the amount of reward or cost experienced translated to a common unit of measurement, and P represents the probability of receiving the benefit or cost.

Consider a hypothetical example. Sam is trying to work out whether or not to burgle a residential property a few streets over from where he lives. According to this utility model, Sam will first consider the possible benefits that he might obtain from the crime (loot, thrills, status among his peers) and the likelihood that he will receive those benefits (maybe a burglar alarm or a guard dog will interrupt him, maybe the house doesn't have much in the way of portable goods to steal). Sam will also ponder the likely costs of the offence: criminal justice sanctions if caught, retaliation from the home owners, and other, non-legal sanctions such as shame, guilt, and stigmatisation (Nagin & Pogarsky, 2001). He will also consider the probability that these costs will be incurred (e.g., what are the chances that the police will catch him). Sam's thought processes might pan out as follows: 'the amount of reward that I will get from this burglary is about a "5£" and the chances of getting those rewards are around 75 per cent. I ranks the potential costs at "20" and the probability of those costs happening at about 10 per cent. So 0.75 multiplied by 5 equals 3.75, and 0.10 multiplied by 20 equals 2.0. Because 3.75 is greater than 2.0 I will dust off my balaclava and rob the house!' Now of course, proponents of rational choice theory do not believe that potential offenders like Sam actually go through these calculations in the manner illustrated above, crunching the numbers into their calculators prior to committing every criminal act. However, it is assumed that something like this mental cost–benefit calculus is undertaken.

The relevance of rational choice theory for deterrence should be clear: if the certainty and severity of punishment (many researchers also add the *celerity*, or swiftness of punishment into this equation) are appropriately calibrated, they should outweigh the benefits of offending, and deterrence will be achieved. In practice, there are several difficult hurdles to surmount before any likely deterrent effects can be expected to occur (McGuire, 2004; Robinson & Darley, 2004) (see Figure 12.3 for a schematic overview). The first hurdle, as Robinson & Darley (2004, p. 175) have pointed out, is *legal knowledge*:

Does the potential offender know, directly or indirectly, and understand the implications for him, of the law this is meant to influence him? That is, does the potential offender know which actions are criminalized by criminal codes, which actions are required, and which conditions will excuse actions which are otherwise criminal?

In short, individuals have to be *aware* of what the sanctions are for a given act before there can be any deterrent effects.

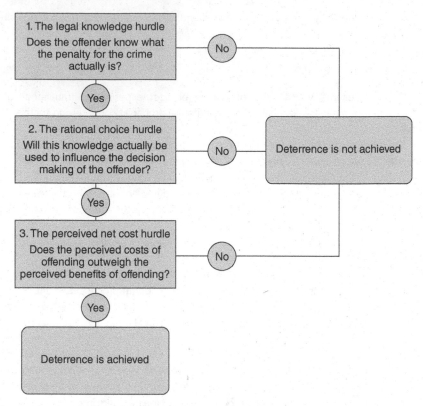

Figure 12.3 Hurdles to overcome before deterrence can be achieved.
Source: Based on the analysis by Robinson and Darley (2004).

The department in which I teach, for example, has some strict regulations regarding late assignments: any assignment without an extension handed in after the cut-off date receives a 5-mark deduction for each 24 hours that it is late. If this stipulation is tucked away in small print in a footnote on page 37 of a 42-page course outline then students are unlikely to aware of it, and therefore the regulation will be ineffective as a deterrence against late assignments (students who are penalised for late assignments are also likely to feel somewhat aggrieved as well!). Although many offenders will be aware that assault, heroin trafficking, robbery, rape, and murder are punishable offences, fine-grained knowledge of specific penalties is likely to be lacking. Do you, for instance, know the likely penalty for cultivating cannabis for supply where you live? Anderson (2002), in a study of 278 convicted offenders, found that only 22 per cent of their sample 'knew exactly what the penalties would be' when they committed their crime. This finding is important because many changes to the severity of penalties that are implemented are based on the assumption that tougher penalties will result in less offending. Clearly if offenders do not have any precise idea what the penalties are then they cannot be deterred (or, specifically, *more* deterred) from offending as a result of the policy change.

The second hurdle to be surmounted before deterrence can work is the assumption that offenders, even if they have accurate knowledge of the likely penalties, actually consider this information prior to offending (Robinson & Darley, 2004). Do burglars like Sam, in our hypothetical example above, actually consider the potential costs? Most research suggests that the answer to this question is no, or, at best, such considerations are rarely prominent in offenders' minds. In the research carried out by Anderson (2002), 35 per cent of the sample 'didn't think about' the likely punishment prior to the offence, and other studies confirm that thoughts about getting caught and being punished are not in the forefront of offenders' minds prior to committing crime (McGuire, 2004). Many offences are also, of course, to some degree impulsive in nature; they are carried out 'in the heat of the moment' with little forethought or planning (see the discussion on instrumental and expressive violence in Chapter 4). Offenders as a group are also, as we have discussed at various points in this book, more likely to be impulsive in nature and less likely to consider the future consequences of their actions (Nagin & Pogarsky, 2004). In combination, the impulsive nature of a good proportion of offending and the fact that offenders are less likely as a group to consider the potential costs of their actions suggest that the cost–benefit calculus that underpins deterrence theory is relatively unlikely to be implemented in a rigorous fashion.

If these two hurdles are surmounted – offenders have knowledge of the costs of crime and bring this knowledge to bear on their behaviour – then they, in principle, can be deterred from offending assuming that the perceived costs (certainty multiplied by severity) outweigh the perceived benefits of offending. Probably the most important component on the 'cost' side of the equation is the perceived probability of being punished for a given offence (Apel & Nagin, 2011). How likely is it that if you commit a crime you will be arrested and punished for that offence? If you are to believe the vision of crime portrayed on television shows where the police typically 'get their man' you would probably conclude that the risk of punishment is relatively high. Indeed, researchers have confirmed that naïve individuals inhabit a 'shell of illusion' (Tittle, 1980) in which they believe that there is a significant chance of getting caught if they commit an offence. Generally speaking, research supports the idea that the perceived *certainty* of punishment (or, rather, of apprehension) is a more important factor in influencing whether or not punishment deters than is the severity of punishment (Nagin, 2013).

This widespread belief in the risk of punishment is probably a good thing! However, in reality the vast majority of offences go undetected by law enforcement officials and therefore go unpunished. In the United Kingdom, figures suggest that only an estimated 2 per cent of offences result in conviction, and only 1 in 7 of those convictions result in a custodial sentence. The probability of being sent to prison for a crime, therefore, is about 1 in 300 (Home Office, 1993, cited in McGuire, 2004). Similar figures can be provided for the United States, where it has been calculated that only 10 in every 1,000 burglaries result in a custodial sentence (Felson, 1994, cited in McGuire, 2004). The chances of getting caught are even less for crimes like drug use: for every time an individual uses an illicit drug like cannabis or cocaine their chance of being punished (by the criminal justice system) is extremely remote – less than 1 in 3000 in the United States (MacCoun & Reuter, 2001). The cumulative risk of getting caught is obviously higher, but it is only calculated to be at 3 per cent per year for cannabis users. This means on average that you will need to smoke cannabis regularly for over 30 years before you are punished through the criminal justice system.

What is important for deterrence theory is not the risk of getting punished per se, but rather *perceptions* of risk. Given the figures cited above, it is not surprising that active offenders tend to rate their risk of being punished by the criminal justice system as quite low. In the study of offenders by Anderson (2002), 76 per cent of the sample either did not think about getting caught or thought that the chances of getting caught were not likely (see also Decker, Wright, & Logie, 1993; Piquero & Rengert, 1999). Offenders who are successful in evading detection and punishment are particularly likely to discount the probability of getting caught. Piquero and Paternoster (1998), for example, found that drink-drivers who had successfully avoided punishment were more likely to report intentions to drink-drive in the future, and Carmichael and Piquero (2006), in a study of 1,146 incarcerated offenders, reported that 'for all crimes except burglary, perceptions of sanction certainty for each crime type decreased as participation in that crime type increased during the 12 street months' (p. 79). In other words, individuals who are more likely to commit certain crimes perceived that they were less likely to get apprehended for those crimes. In this study it was also found that, for four out of the eight crimes studied, as arrest ratios (the number of arrests relative to the number of crimes committed) increased, so did the perceptions of punishment certainty. In sum, although research findings are somewhat inconsistent, it is clear that for any given offence the chances of actually getting punished by the criminal justice system are quite slim, and active criminals are well aware of these favourable odds, thus undermining the potential deterrent effects of punishment.

The other two key components in the cost–benefit analysis of offending described above are the perceived benefits and costs of offending. One seemingly straightforward assumption is that increasing the severity of punishment (all else being equal) should increase the costs of offending and therefore make offending less likely (deterrence will be achieved). In practice there are limits to the punitive severity that can be imposed by the criminal justice system because it is widely accepted that the gravity of offending should be at least roughly proportionate to the severity of punishment meted out. Most people will recognise that the death penalty for jay walking (whatever its deterrent effects) is not a reasonable response to this offence. Punishment severity for more serious offences is typically calibrated in terms of prison length. As discussed earlier, there is little support for the idea that ramping up the prison time that can be meted out for offences actually results in any deterrent effect. In part this is because, at an individual level, offenders adjust or adapt to prison life so that (within reason) longer sentences are not perceived as more severe than shorter sentences (see Robinson & Darley, 2004, for a review of the relevant research).

Finally, it needs to be recognised that the benefits of offending in terms of material gain, thrills, satisfaction, and peer status may simply prove too attractive for many offenders, especially for those with little to lose. Moreover, the benefits obtained from offending are typically immediate, whereas the costs not only are unknown but, given the slow speed with which the criminal justice system usually operates, are typically in the distant future (Robinson & Darley, 2004).

The decision-making processes that underpin offending are clearly influenced by a number of factors. These are likely to include the perceived severity and certainty of sanctions but are also shaped by the rewards of offending, the possibility of extra-legal sanctions, and individual differences in criminal propensity (in terms of both self-control and the presence of other inhibitions against offending).

There is every reason to believe that offenders can, in principle, be deterred. Increasing the certainty of punishment would appear to provide the best avenue to obtain deterrent effects, although increasing the severity of offending and reducing the benefits of offending (and the probability of obtaining those benefits) are both likely to exert some deterrent effects. The main problem is that, in practice, it can be very difficult to manage the criminal justice system in ways that can meaningfully promote deterrent effects in most cases. There are, for example, as noted above, clear limits to the capacity to increase either the certainty or severity of punishment, even if this information can be successfully conveyed to potential offenders. Situational crime prevention initiatives, such as increasing security measures or improving street lighting (see Chapter 11), may reduce the rewards of some kinds of offences by reducing the probability of successful offending. There is also scope for reducing offending through the promotion of *informal* social controls, although this avenue is largely neglected within the conventional criminal justice system.

REVIEW AND REFLECT

1   What is more important in deterring offenders – the severity or the certainty of punishment?
2   Do you think that the public would be less willing to endorse more punitive responses to crime if they were to review the evidence base for deterrent effects?
3   Given your understanding of the psychological factors underlying deterrent effects how would you go about reducing the incidence of drink-driving in your local community?

SUMMARY

There is a wide range of responses to crime employed by the criminal justice system. These responses include non-custodial sanctions, custodial sanctions, corporal punishment and the death penalty (in some countries), and restorative justice. The use of these different responses varies considerably among different countries with the United States having the highest rate of imprisonment in the world.

Over the last couple of decades in many Western countries an increasingly greater proportion of individuals have become incarcerated in correctional facilities. Although not all countries share this penal trend, many scholars recognise a move towards greater punitiveness, reflected not only in the number of individuals in prison, but also in the enactment of harsh penal policies, such as mandatory minimum sentences and 'three strike' laws.

Prisons are environments that impose a number of important deprivations on inmates, including the loss of liberty, autonomy, and security. These features of prison life are likely to contribute to the high rates of suicide and mental health problems that are found in correctional facilities. The negative impact of prison extends beyond the offender to their partners, family, and community. Having a parent or partner in prison is associated with a number of negative outcomes. Having a parent in prison is a risk factor for a number of psychological problems in children, including depression and antisocial behaviour.

A number of rationales for the punishment of offenders have been identified. These can be broadly categorised into two main types: consequentialist and retributivist. Consequentialist rationales (such as deterrence and incapacitation) justify punishment because of the role it can play in preventing or reducing crime. Retributivist rationales, in contrast, see punishment as an end in itself and an appropriate response to criminal offending. Public opinion research typically finds that people endorse a number of rationales for punishment although the type of rationale varies according to the type of offender and the type of crime. Experimental research carried out by psychologists tends to support the notion that people's motivations to punish are largely driven out of a desire for retribution.

Although some studies support the idea that criminal justice sanctions can act as a deterrent, most researchers conclude that increasing the severity of criminal justice sanctions exerts little or no deterrent effects either on the individuals who are punished or on the general population. There are three main hurdles that need to be surmounted before criminal justice sanctions can be said to exert deterrent effects on individuals: (a) individuals must be aware of the penalties for specific offences; (b) they must bring this knowledge to bear on their actions; and (c) the costs of offending must outweigh the benefits. In practice, it is difficult to manage the criminal justice system in a way that would overcome these three hurdles to achieving deterrent effects.

FURTHER READING

Roth, M. P. (2014). *An Eye for an Eye: A Global History of Punishment.* London: Reaktion Books.
A good, readable account of punishment in history.

Hoffman, M. B. (2014). *The Punisher's Brain: The Evolution of Judge and Jury.* New York, NY: Cambridge University Press.
An excellent exploration of some of the psychological and neurobiological underpinnings of punishment.

Nagin, D. S. (2013). Deterrence in the twenty-first century. *Crime and Justice,* 42, 199–263.
A comprehensive review of the research on deterrence.

Darley, J. M. (2009). Morality in the law: The psychological foundations of citizens' desires to punish transgressions. *Annual Review of Law and Science,* 5, 1–23.
A good review of the psychological foundations of punishment.

WEB RESOURCES

Two good sources for information about the death penalty are the death penalty information centre (www.deathpenaltyinfo.org) and Amnesty International (www.amnesty.org). The International Centre of Prison Studies provides a lot of useful information and contains updated information about prison numbers in different countries (www.prisonstudies.org). For an opportunity to sentence a case check out http://ybtj.justice.gov.uk.

KEY CONCEPTS

- common-sense justice
- death penalty
- deterrence
- general deterrence
- incapacitation
- individual deterrence
- proportionality
- punitiveness
- supermax prisons
- three strike laws

Rehabilitation and reintegration

LEARNING OBJECTIVES

On completion of this chapter you should:

➤ recognise the problem of offender recidivism and the major risk factors for re-offending;
➤ understand the various different approaches to rehabilitation and reintegration;
➤ be familiar with the risk-need-responsivity and good lives models of offender rehabilitation;
➤ be able address the question of whether offender rehabilitation is effective.

Unfortunately, a significant majority of offenders re-offend within a relatively short time of being released from prison or completing their non-custodial sentence. As we have discussed in Chapter 12, although punishment is an essential component of our efforts to manage crime, by itself it does little to change offending behaviour. Indeed, the experience of imprisonment may well, in itself, be criminogenic. What, then, can be done with offenders to make them less likely to re-offend? In this chapter we first consider the problem of offender recidivism and risk assessment. We then explore approaches to the rehabilitation of offenders focusing on the different types of programme that have been developed. We then examine the available literature on offender effectiveness, before exploring two prominent models or theories of offender rehabilitation – the risk-need-responsivity model and the good lives model. On completion of this chapter you should have a good understanding of what offender rehabilitation is and whether it is effective in reducing re-offending.

THE PROBLEM OF OFFENDER RECIDIVISM

Recidivism, or re-offending, remains a persistent problem: it is widely recognised that a significant proportion of offenders that are arrested and punished for a given offence re-offend within three to five years of serving their sentence. This is clearly illustrated in a comprehensive study of recidivism in the United States for two cohorts of offenders: one that was released from prison in 1999 and another that was released from prison in 2004 (Pew Centre on the States, 2011). The researchers found that of the cohort that was released in 1999, 45.4 per cent were re-imprisoned within the next three years, and for those released in 2004 the comparable figure was 43.4 per cent. In other words, close to half of all prisoners released in the United States during this period re-offended and were re-imprisoned within three years of their release.

Rates of re-offending do vary somewhat across countries and by offence type. Clearly rates of re-offending are also sensitive to the time frame of the follow-up period and the criteria involved for re-offending (some studies measure re-arrest or re-conviction rather than re-imprisonment). Figure 13.1, for instance, illustrates re-conviction and re-imprisonment rates for a sample of close to 5,000 offenders in New

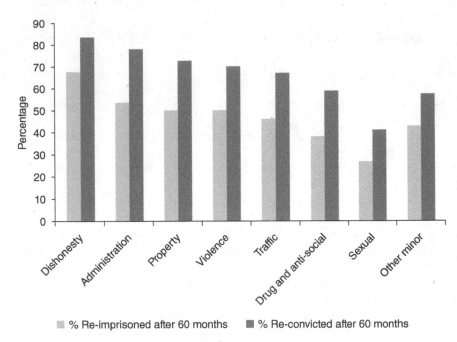

% Re-imprisoned after 60 months   ■ % Re-convicted after 60 months

Figure 13.1 The percentage of individuals who were re-imprisoned and re-convicted after five years based on the most serious offence that they were initially imprisoned for.
Source: Nadesu (2009).

Zealand who were released from prison in 2002/2003 and were followed up for a five-year period (Nadesu, 2009). As you can see, rates of re-conviction and re-imprisonment differ significantly by offence type with individuals imprisoned for dishonesty offences most likely to re-offend. This study also illustrated that rates of re-offending vary by gender and age. For instance, 71.4 per cent of men were re-convicted after five years compared to 62 per cent of women, and close to 88 per cent of those under 20 were re-convicted compared to only 41.7 per cent of those aged 40 and above. Of course, these various figures almost certainly underestimate the total amount of recidivism because they do not capture those individuals who offend but are not apprehended (or who are apprehended but not prosecuted) by the criminal justice system. These figures also reinforce the point made in Chapter 12: punishment in and of itself does very little to change the likelihood of future criminal behaviour.

Risk assessment and re-offending

Not everyone who is convicted, however, re-offends. This raises the possibility that we can employ various measures to predict which individuals are more likely to re-offend. Risk assessment plays a prominent role in criminal justice systems around the world and is used for a diverse range of purposes including decisions regarding bail, parole, rehabilitation, and civil commitment (Monahan & Skeem, 2014; Singh, Grann, & Fazel, 2011). Although there are multiple ways of assessing risk, increasingly criminal justice systems employ actuarial methods that calculate risk of re-offending based on what is empirically known about the relationship between specific risk factors and recidivism. A **risk factor** for re-offending is, pretty straightforwardly, any characteristic of an individual that is statistically correlated with recidivism (Kraemer et al., 1997). Two different types of risk factor dominate risk assessment measures: **static risk factors** are those characteristics of individuals that are not amenable to change (e.g., gender, number of prior convictions); **dynamic risk factors** are those characteristics that predict re-offending but are – in principle at least – amenable to change (e.g., substance abuse problems, antisocial cognitions). Table 13.1 outlines some of the main static and dynamic risk factors for offending that have been identified in the literature (Andrews & Bonta, 2010a).

Two questions immediately arise in connection with risk factors. First, do they actually do a good job at predicting re-offending? Second, how might we use this information to better design and implement rehabilitation programmes so as to reduce the likelihood of re-offending? The answer to the first question – do they predict re-offending – is a clear yes. There is good evidence to support the idea that the use of risk assessment tools can successfully predict whether or not individuals will re-offend in a given period (normally three to five years) with a good degree of accuracy (Yang, Wong, & Coid, 2010). Although some assessment tools incorporate dynamic risk factors, most use static factors such as age, gender, and criminal history variables. Indeed, the inclusion of dynamic risk factors does very little to improve the predictive accuracy of such tools (Caudy, Durso, & Taxman, 2013). Static risk factors are, however, of relatively little value in efforts to rehabilitate offenders – after all, it is not possible to change an offender's age, gender, ethnicity, or criminal history within a treatment context. If dynamic risk factors predict re-offending, and they are amenable to change, they can become targets for treatment, and many rehabilitation programmes do just that (see discussion below on the risk-need-responsivity model). Before we turn to a discussion of specific rehabilitation programmes it will be useful to briefly consider what we mean by the term 'rehabilitation' and how it is related to other overlapping concepts such as 'desistance', 'treatment', and 're-integration'.

Table 13.1 The main static and dynamic risk factors for offending

Static risk factors	Dynamic risk factors
Age (younger)	Antisocial personality (impulsivity, risk taking, antisocial personality disorder)
Gender (male)	Antisocial cognition (offence-supportive beliefs, values, and attitudes)
Ethnicity (ethnic minority)	Antisocial associates (association with criminals)
Criminal history (number, type, seriousness, frequency, and recency of prior convictions)	Substance use problems, family/marital problems, school/work problems

Source: Andrews and Bonta (2010a).

REVIEW AND REFLECT

1   What is recidivism, and why is it a 'problem'?
2   Outline the main differences between static and dynamic risk factors.
3   The use of dynamic risk factors in forensic practice has recently come under the critical spotlight in a special issue of the journal *Psychology, Crime, and Law* (2016, volume 22, numbers 1–2). Read one (or more!) of the articles in this special issue and summarise the main concerns of the author(s).

THE NATURE OF REHABILITATION

As Ward and Maruna (2006) note, there are a large number of different terms that have been employed to refer to the processes involved in reducing re-offending among groups of offenders. Criminal and forensic psychologists tend to use the terms **treatment** or **rehabilitation** to capture the idea that offenders are being changed or altered in ways that make them less likely to re-offend and more likely to be productive and responsible members of society. Many offenders, however, don't particularly like these terms because it implies that something is wrong with them and they need to be 'fixed'. Indeed, many criminologists prefer to talk in terms of 'integration' or **desistance** to capture the idea that the key task involves assisting offenders to 'go straight' and avoid a life of crime. In an influential paper, criminologist Fergus McNeill (2012, p. 31) suggests that we need to recognise that rehabilitation is 'a social project as well as a personal one' and that although it may entail addressing individual psychological factors it also needs to consider the wider social, cultural, and moral context of offenders' lives. Ultimately, individuals need to 'decide' to turn away from offending and lead prosocial lives, and this, in part, is due to the way that they view the overarching narratives of their lives (see Box 13.1). Given its widespread use in the literature we will stick with the term 'rehabilitation' in this chapter, which can be conceptualised quite inclusively as the 'broad array of psychosocial programs and services that are designed to assist offenders in addressing a range of needs related to their offending behaviour and in achieving a more productive and satisfying lifestyle' (Wormith et al., 2007, p. 880).

The idea that offenders should not only be punished, but also be assisted in ways that help them to avoid re-offending has a long history (Cullen & Smith, 2011; Smith & Schweitzer, 2012). Indeed, prisons have long been viewed as places of 'reform', as reflected in the widely used term 'correctional facility'. Rehabilitation programmes were widespread in prison in the 1960s and early 1970s, but this was to change in the mid-1970s due, in part, to a well-known and influential review of the effectiveness of rehabilitation by Robert Martinson (1974). Martinson reviewed relevant studies from the period 1945–1967 and concluded that 'with few and isolated exceptions, the rehabilitative efforts that have been reported so far have had no appreciable effect on recidivism' (p. 25). In many Western countries there was a subsequent shift away from the use of rehabilitation programmes, and a strong emphasis was placed on punitive criminal justice polices. This situation was to change slowly but surely in the

BOX 13.1 A NARRATIVE PERSPECTIVE ON OFFENDER CHANGE

Why do offenders made the decision to change their lifestyles and become crime-free? Many factors are important, but Maruna (2001) has argued that the way an offender views their life story (their 'narratives') may play an important role. As part of the Liverpool desistance study Maruna interviewed a large number of offenders to explore their qualitative experiences of offending and desistance. He found that persistent offenders – those that did not see themselves as giving up an offending lifestyle – lived their lives according to what he referred to as a *condemnation script*. They viewed themselves more as victims than as offenders and believed that the nature of their lives was set in concrete. In short, they felt powerless to change the fate that was set out for them, and their antisocial behaviour helped them to create a sense of control over the nature and pattern of their lives. Here is an example of a condemnation script (Maruna, 2001, p. 73) from one of the participants:

> The reality is I'll never be able to get a straight, decent job unless I was working for myself or something. So, it looks like I'm back to crime, doesn't it? I mean, I'd love to go to work for £200 a week plastering walls, but I just can't see it. I'm now a single man. I've met people from all over the world who have offered me illegal jobs ... So, it looks like that's what I'm going to do. Isn't it?
>
> (Male, age 28)

In contrast, offenders who managed to desist from offending and take up prosocial lives followed a different narrative, what Marina referred to as a *redemption script*. These offenders viewed themselves as essentially good people who had taken a wrong direction as a result of the experiences that they had been exposed to and thus had the capacity to turn away from offending. Here is an example of a redemption script (Maruna, 2001, p. 92) from one of the participants:

> It was just that, um, I realized that the entire thing had all been an act, my entire life, all me criminal offences, all me drug taking, it was all a sham ... It was just like what it was, was right at the core of me, I am how I am now, who I've always been inside. I've always been intelligent, honest, hard working, truthful, erm, nice, you know, loving. I've always like. But it was always wrapped up in so much shit it couldn't get out.

Questions for discussion

1   Are the narratives identified by Maruna in this research likely to reflect important instigators of change or post hoc reflections on what factors led to change?

2   How might an offenders' condemnation narrative be turned into a redemption narrative during rehabilitation?

1980s and 1990s as a number of systematic reviews and meta-analyses of treatment programmes – discussed below – suggested that rehabilitation *can* work (Cullen & Smith, 2011). Moreover, a consensus has emerged regarding the important factors that make offender rehabilitation effective and what kind of programmes are most likely to result in reductions in re-offending.

REVIEW AND REFLECT

1   Does is matter what label we employ to refer to the processes that lead offenders to lead crime-free lives? Why?

APPROACHES TO REHABILITATION

So what does rehabilitation actually involve in practice? There are a huge range of different types of programmes and initiatives that fall broadly under the scope of offender rehabilitation. As Wilson (2016, p. 194) notes in a systematic review of correctional programmes, these vary from the 'standard' to the 'just plain wacky'. We make no attempt here to review all of the different approaches that have been employed, instead focusing on the main types of programmes that have been offered. We begin by briefly discussing educational and works-based programmes, then turn to a more detailed discussion of cognitive behavioural programmes. Finally, we consider, again in brief, the range of other specific programmes that have been developed. There will be a focus on programmes developed within a New Zealand context for specific examples, so students from other countries are encouraged to find out more about the programmes available within their prison systems.

Educational and works-based programmes

Many prisoners have limited education, often poor numeracy and literacy skills, and a limited or patchy work history. There is general agreement that finding meaningful employment can be an important component of desisting from an offending lifestyle. If individuals have a reliable and liveable income and are involved in activities that promote a sense of self-worth and social bonding then, all other things being equal, they are less likely to re-offend. Perhaps unsurprisingly, then, many correctional facilities offer a range of educational, vocational, and work-based programmes designed to enhance literacy and numeracy skills, and to enable inmates to obtain relevant qualifications and skills. Often programmes will be implemented within a prison context, but will also include ongoing assistance in finding employment when prisoners are released.

Wilson (2016) provides a useful review of systematic reviews of educational, vocational, and work programmes. Although the methodological quality of evaluation studies in this area is not consistently high, meta-analyses of the effectiveness of educational, vocational, and work programmes suggest that all three types of approach can be effective in reducing offender recidivism. It is worth noting, however, that such programmes tend to more effective for adult offenders, and there remain substantial barriers to offenders obtaining work outside of the prison environment as a result of the offender's criminal convictions. Even given these limitations there is every reason to believe that such programmes should be part of the suite of programmes available to offenders in prison. Of course, such programmes do not necessarily address many of the underlying psychological causes of offending. As such, they will need to be supplemented with other types of programme that target changes in the psychological characteristics of offenders.

Cognitive behavioural treatment programmes

Approaches to changing human behaviour, including criminal behaviour, are largely dominated by **cognitive behavioural treatment programmes** (Hollin, 2006; McGuire, 2006; Wilson, 2016). Cognitive behavioural treatment programmes are predicated on the idea that criminal offending is importantly related to offender cognition. In other words, they are based on the idea that the beliefs, values, and norms that an offender has and the way that they think and reason play an important causal role in their offending. Moreover, it is assumed that, to a significant extent, criminal cognition is learned and therefore is amenable to change. Cognitive behavioural approaches to rehabilitation, therefore, focus on changing the way that offenders think and behave so as to make offending less likely. Typically speaking, cognitive-behavioural treatment programmes are 'manual-based' (i.e., follow clear guidelines) and are run in small groups by a facilitator who is often (but, now always) a clinical psychologist. The precise content of the programme will vary depending on the specific group of offenders (e.g., violent vs. child sex offenders), and programmes will incorporate a variety of different techniques and approaches.

There are a wide range of different cognitive behavioural treatment programmes that are employed internationally, including 'reasoning and rehabilitation', 'enhanced thinking skills', and 'think first' (McGuire, 2006). We will explore in more detail a specific programme for child sex offenders below, but most programmes include a common core of elements such as the developmental of cognitive skills, interpersonal problem-solving strategies, anger control, and **relapse prevention** (Wilson, 2016). The Department of Correction in New Zealand offers a range of different types of programme, but many are based on a cognitive behavioural approach. For example, a family violence programme targeted at male offenders 'adopts a strengths-based, cognitive-behavioural approach teaching men new skills to manage their emotions and change their beliefs and attitudes that underlie their abuse and violence. The Family Violence Programme also ensures men have strategies in place to maintain their positive changes' (Department of Corrections Website, 2017).

Let's explore in a bit more detail the concept of relapse prevention as it underpins many such programmes. Relapse prevention is an approach to behaviour change that was originally developed in the context of treating people with alcohol and drug problems (Marlatt & Gordon, 1985), but has since been extended to other contexts, most prominently in the treatment of sex offenders (Laws, Hudson, & Ward, 2000). One difficulty that many people have in changing problem behaviours − whether it is addiction to heroin, smoking, over-eating, or compulsive shopping − is that gains that are made during treatment are often hard to maintain. In short, individuals relapse to problem behaviours at a relatively high rate. Relapse prevention, therefore, involves the construction of detailed plans to prevent relapse. These include the development of specific skills and the identification of important support people. Plans will also involve strategies for negotiating high-risk situations and the 'seemingly irrelevant decisions' that individuals recovering from behavioural problems tend to take (e.g., an individual recovering from alcohol dependence just 'happens' to decide on a new route to work past the liquor store). Another important component of relapse prevention is managing the so-called **abstinence violation effect** (AVE) (Wheeler, George, & Marlatt, 2006). This effect refers to the fact that when a self-imposed rule (e.g., not drinking for someone recovering from alcohol dependence) is broken, then there is tendency for individuals to believe that they are unable to maintain abstinence, and a lapse (a single drink) rapidly and destructively can turn into a relapse (an all-night drinking session). A key task, therefore, is to facilitate a different way of thinking about the lapse ('OK, I have had a single drink, but that doesn't mean I have returned to my problem drinking') that doesn't result in a full-blown relapse. This task is especially important for violent and sex offenders as a 'relapse' can have negative consequences not only for the individual concerned but also for their potential victims.

Because cognitive behavioural programmes are probably the most widespread in correctional facilities internationally, we shall discuss the research that has explored their effectiveness in more detail below.

Other programmes

There are numerous other types of programmes that have been tried over the years in correctional facilities and in the community with varying degrees of success. These include motivational programmes, reintegration programmes, faith-based or religious programmes, biological treatments, 'alternative' programmes, and various offence (and offender) specific programmes (which often employ a cognitive behavioural approach). Here we will briefly consider this range of approaches and then focus in a bit more detail on a specific programme for child sex offenders.

It may seem obvious to us that offenders *want* to change their behaviour. However, this not always the case. Many offenders do not think that there is anything 'wrong' with them and have no desire to engage in a lengthy treatment programme that they might view as a complete waste of time – as evidenced by the often high drop-out rate that is found from such programmes (Olver, Stockdale, & Wormith, 2011) (see Research in Focus 13.1). The aim of motivational programmes is, therefore, to get individuals to a position where they are willing to accept change and thus might be more amenable to participation in a rehabilitation programme.

Faith-based or religious programmes have a long history in corrections and are reasonably widely employed, most notably in the United States (Johnson, 2013; Wilson, 2016). They may be delivered in prisons or in the community and variously target youth and adults. Such programmes aim to achieve personal transformations in offenders in ways that encourage them to embrace religion and turn away from their former offending lifestyles. For example, the InnerChange programme in Minnesota incorporates life skills development, educational attainment, and religious instruction based on the teachings of Jesus Christ (Duwe & King, 2012). The programme is run initially in prison but

RESEARCH IN FOCUS 13.1 HOW MANY OFFENDERS FAIL TO COMPLETE TREATMENT, AND HOW DOES THIS AFFECT THEIR CHANCES OF REOFFENDING?

Title: A meta-analysis of predictors of offender treatment attrition and its relationship to recidivism

Author: Olver, M. E., et al.   **Year**: 2011

Source: *Journal of Consulting and Clinical Psychology, 79, 6-21*

Aims: To review the literature on attrition from offender rehabilitation programmes and to investigate the relationship between attrition and recidivism

Method: Relevant databases were searched yielding 114 studies, involving 41,438 offenders

Key results:
- An overall attrition rate of 27% was found across programmes with the highest dropout rate found for domestic violence programmes (37.8%)
- Those individuals who fail to complete an offender rehabilitation programme are significantly more likely to reoffend

Conclusion: "The problem of offender treatment attrition remains an ongoing and serious concern" (p. 17). Those individuals who are in most in need of treatment are the ones that are most likely to fail to complete a rehabilitation programme.

continues on the participants' release to the community through one-on-one mentoring and support. The available literature base doesn't allow us to conclude with any degree of certainty that such programmes are effective in reducing re-offending, but most have positive outcomes that are 'encouraging' (Wilson, 2016, p. 204). As Wilson notes, most such programmes are firmly based on the Christian religion, and there remains scope for the development of such programmes based on other faiths and denominations such as Islam, Hinduism, and Buddhism.

Offender rehabilitation programmes generally focus on psychological and social factors. If offending also has, in part, a biological basis there is clearly scope for treatment programmes that aim to change biological processes and functions. Most of the focus in this area has been on the use of surgical or chemical castration for sex offenders. Surgical castration involves the removal of the man's testes in a procedure known as a bilateral orchiectomy. This substantially reduces the amount of circulating testosterone and thus significantly attenuates (but does not entirely remove) the recipient's sexual motivation. So-called chemical castration achieves the same effect, except via the use of anti-androgen drugs. The available evidence suggests that these interventions can be effective in reducing sexual recidivism, although the scope and quality of relevant evaluations remains somewhat limited (Maletzky, Tolan, & McFarland, 2006; Rice & Harris, 2011; Weinberger et al., 2005). Rapid advances in our understanding of the neurobiological underpinnings of offending may see a wider range of biological treatments proposed for different types of offence and offender in the future. Understandably, many have voiced concern over the ethical issues that such approaches raise, particularly when they result in permanent changes to an individual or are accompanied by the risk of negative side effects (McMillan, 2014; Shaw, 2015)

The all-embracing term 'alternative programmes' covers a lot of ground, but the pressing problem of offender recidivism has led many to explore a range of different approaches that fall outside of what is currently recognised as 'mainstream' practice. These include 'mindfulness-based stress reduction' and other types of meditation practices, capoeira (a type of African-Brazilian martial arts), yoga, 'equine-facilitated psychotherapy', various forms of art, theatre, and music programmes, and numerous programmes that focus on physical education and sporting activities (see Joseph & Crichlow, 2015). It may be easy to dismiss this potpourri of strategies as largely misguided, and the evidence base for the effectiveness of most of the approaches is limited. However, given the high rates of recidivism demonstrated by offenders it would be unwise to dismiss any 'alternative' approach out of hand, and there is an accumulating body of evidence that, at least, suggests that such approaches are promising (e.g., Muirhead & Fortune, 2016).

Finally, we need to recognise that there are a number of different programmes that directly target specific types of offender or specific types of problems that offenders have. Given the high prevalence of substance use problems among offenders (see Chapter 8), it is not surprising that substance abuse programmes for offenders are common both within and outside the prison context. There are also specific programmes for serious violent offenders, and for both adult and child sex offenders. In New Zealand, for example, there are a number of 'special treatment units' that provide focused cognitive behavioural based rehabilitation to high-risk violent and sexual offenders (Polaschek & Kilgour, 2013). One such dedicated treatment programme targets child sex offenders with currently two specific prison-based units – one in Auckland (Te Piriti) and one in Christchurch (Kia Marama)

Kia Marama – a programme for child sex offenders

A good example of a child sex offender treatment programmes is provided by Kia Marama, which is based in a dedicated prison unit in Rolleston prison, Christchurch, New Zealand (Hudson et al., 2002; Hudson, Wales, & Ward, 1998). An overview of the treatment programme is provided in Figure 13.2. Participation in the programme is voluntary, and the timing is typically organised towards the end of an offender's sentence. Referrals are made from psychological service staff from eligible volunteers in prisons. The programme begins with a two-week assessment period involving in-depth clinical interviews, phallometric testing (which is used to measure sexual arousal to deviant stimuli), and completion of self-report scales. The programme runs for eight months and involves the completion of seven treatment modules.

Module 1 involves a general orientation to the programme including a discussion of group norms and the sharing of personal details. In Module 2, the offender will come to

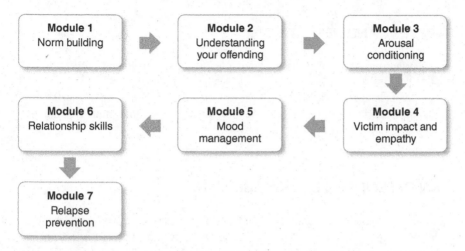

Figure 13.2 Key rehabilitation modules in the Kia Marama programme for child sex offenders.

understand his offence chain and the various distal and proximate factors that contributed to his offending. This module also provides opportunities to challenge offence-supportive thinking or implicit theories relating to offending (see Chapter 6). Module 3 targets deviant sexual interests, and entails two key approaches. *Covert sensitisation* involves the pairing of thoughts of offending right up to the point of offending with negative consequences of the offending (e.g., the humiliation of arrest) and thoughts of escaping the situation. *Directed masturbation* involves the offender becoming sexually aroused and then switching to a non-deviant sexual fantasy until orgasm in order to pair sexual pleasure with 'normal' sexual relations. Module 4 involves developing victim empathy. This can be obtaining by reading victim impact statements, brainstorming possible harms associated with offending, and watching videotapes of child sex abuse survivors. Module 5 targets problems in self-regulation and the management of negative mood states. Module 6 deals with issues relating to intimacy problems including effective strategies for communication in close relationships, resolving conflict, and so forth. The final module focus on relapse prevention strategies and plans including the development of skills to manage relapse and the identification of relevant support people in the community. Evaluations of this programme suggest that it can be effective in reducing re-offending (Hudson et al., 2002; Hudson et al., 1998).

Summary

There is no shortage of different programmes designed to reduce re-offending and help offenders live prosocial, crime-free lives. Of course, their availability to offenders varies enormously from location to location, and many individuals who go through the criminal justice system will receive little in the way of assistance from such programmes and initiatives. Inevitably, budgets for such efforts are limited, and thus it becomes crucial to establish with a relatively high degree of confidence that any particular type of programme can be effective in reducing re-offending. It is to this issue that we turn to next.

CAN OFFENDERS BE REHABILITATED?

Cognitive behavioural programmes, then, tend to dominate the correctional landscape in most Western countries, but what evidence is there that they are effective? Can offenders actually be rehabilitated? The answer to this question is, almost certainly, 'yes', but the task of successfully rehabilitating offenders is a challenging one. The challenges involved in successfully *evaluating* rehabilitation programmes are also formidable, and before we discuss research that has looked at the effectiveness of rehabilitation programmes it will be useful to briefly consider some important methodological issues (Hollin, 1999, 2006; McGuire, 2002).

Methodological issues

In the field of public health and medicine the gold standard for evaluating the outcome of intervention programmes is the randomised double-blind design (see Figure 13.3). This involves randomly allocating participants (drawn from the same pool) into either treatment or control groups. This ensures that individuals in both groups are likely to be similar on characteristics that might be relevant to the outcome of the study. Individuals in the treatment group receive the actual treatment while those in the control group receive a placebo. Neither the participants nor the people administering the experiment know which groups receives which, ensuring that the outcomes of the study are not influenced by 'experimenter bias' or how people expect they should respond. At the end of (and often during) the study the participants are measured on a variety of outcomes relevant to the intervention. If those in the treatment group do significantly better than those in the control or placebo group then we have some warrant to claim that the treatment was effective.

It shouldn't take more than a moment's reflection to recognise that the randomised double-blind treatment design is next to impossible to implement in the context of evaluating offender rehabilitation programmes. The requirement that both the participants and the administrators of the programme are blind as to whether individuals are in the treatment or control group is impossible to meet because anyone who is chosen to run a treatment programme will *know* whether it is a 'real' one or not. In principle it is possible to implement randomised controlled trials, and some evaluations of treatment programmes are based on this design. However, randomisation is hard to implement in practice for several important reasons. First, offenders who end up in treatment

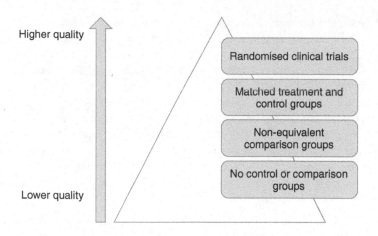

Higher quality

Randomised clinical trials

Matched treatment and control groups

Non-equivalent comparison groups

No control or comparison groups

Lower quality

Figure 13.3 Methods for evaluating rehabilitation programmes from lower quality to higher quality.

programmes are usually referred by the court, are volunteers, or are selected on the basis that they are likely to benefit from treatment. Each of these procedures inevitably introduces an element of bias as offenders are selected for treatment programmes (reasonably enough) on the basis of their perceived need and/or motivation. Second, if participants were chosen randomly this would inevitably mean that some individuals who might be in need to treatment are excluded, and this might have implications for their parole outcomes and the public (if they re-offend once released) (Hollin, 2006). Given these issues, most treatment programmes compare individuals who participate in the treatment programme with a group of **matched controls** – individuals who don't participate in the treatment programme but who possess similar characteristics in terms of their likelihood of re-offending to those that do.

A second crucial issue concerns the problem of non-completion. For a variety of reasons many offenders who participate in treatment programmes do not complete them (Hollin, 2006; McMurran & Ward, 2010). Indeed, rate of non-completion can be significant. For example, one review of cognitive behavioural programmes found that, on average, 15 per cent of individuals in institutional programmes and 46 per cent of individuals in community programmes failed to complete the programme (McMurran & Theodosi, 2007), while a meta-analysis of 114 studies revealed an overall attrition rate of 27.1 per cent, suggesting that close to one third of participants fail to complete (Olver et al., 2011). These high rates of non-completion raise some important questions about the ability of treatment programmes to engage clients, as we discuss below, but they also create problems for effective evaluation. Typically speaking, those individuals who drop out of treatment programmes are more likely to re-offend than those that complete them. This may be, of course, because the treatment programme actually works, but it could also be because non-completers are more likely to re-offend anyway. This means that if the effectiveness of treatment programmes is based only on a comparison between those that complete and a control group the success of the programme may be inflated because those who were more likely to re-offend actually dropped out (Parker, Bush, & Harris, 2014).

A final methodological issue concerns the appropriate use of outcome measures. In other words, how are we going to measure the effectiveness of our treatment programme? A standard approach is to measure rates of reconviction and/or re-imprisonment after a set time period – usually two or three years. Researchers are also typically interested in the offence that resulted in re-conviction as a successful rehabilitation programme may have both general effects on offending and/or specific effects on specific types of offence such as sexual offending. More fine-grained analyses may also involve time to first arrest or re-conviction and the seriousness of re-offending. Most researchers typically use criminal justice data as a basis for re-offending because it is relatively easy to obtain and provides 'objective' evidence for re-offending. Of course, not all individuals who re-offend are re-convicted, and so there is also scope to use self-report measures where relevant.

The effectiveness of offender rehabilitation

Now that we have considered some of the important methodological issues in evaluating offender treatment programmes we can turn to the question of whether such programmes do, in fact, reduce re-offending. The results of over 30 meta-analytic reviews of the effectiveness of offender rehabilitation published since 1985 indicate that treatment, in general, has a positive impact (McGuire, 2002). For example, Lipsey, Landenberger, and Wilson (2007) in a meta-analysis of 58 studies found a mean recidivism rate of .40 for controls compared to .30 for treatment groups. In other words, an average of only 30 per cent of the individuals who participated in treatment groups re-offended in the study period compared to 40 per cent in the control groups. A more recent review of 100 meta-analyses and systematic reviews by McGuire (2013) found that almost all treatment effects were positive, although small to moderate in size. A similar conclusion was drawn by Wilson (2016, p. 210) in another review of systematic reviews of cognitive behavioural programmes, concluding 'Overall, the empirical evidence for the effectiveness of CBT programs is relatively strong with numerous high-quality randomised trials demonstrating positive results across a diversity of approaches and therapeutic elements'.

Evaluation studies have also looked at particular types of treatment programmes and for specific types of offender. A number of reviews have found significantly positive effects for structured cognitive behavioural programmes on recidivism (Pearson et al., 2002; Tong & Farrington, 2006; Wilson, Bouffard, & Mackenzie, 2005). For example, Tong and Farrington (2006) conducted a meta-analysis of 16 evaluations of the 'reasoning and rehabilitation' cognitive behavioural programme for offenders and found that there was an average of a 14 per cent decrease in re-offending for participants in the treatment group compared to the control group. A number of studies have also focused on the effectiveness of treatment for specific types of offender. In a comprehensive review of meta-analyses of treatment outcomes for violent offender programmes, McGuire (2008, p. 2586) concluded that, despite a need 'for more, better controlled outcome studies' the results of 11 meta-analyses 'permit reasonable confidence in the broad conclusion that it is possible to reduce violent recidivism by systematic and carefully designed intervention'. As Polaschek (2011) notes, however, there are still some important challenges in effectively treating high-risk men with an extensive history of violent behaviour. Several meta-analyses also have supported the effectiveness of treatment programmes for sex offenders (Hanson et al., 2002; Kim, Benekos, & Merlo, 2016; Lösel & Schmucker, 2005; Schmucker & Lösel, 2015). Lösel and Schmucker (2005), for instance, drew on 69 studies involving a total of 9,512 treated and 12,669 untreated sex offenders and found an average of 6.4 per cent reduction in sexual recidivism in the treatment compared to the control group. However, many treatment programmes for sex offenders include individuals who sexually offend against adults as well as those that offend against children (see Chapter 6) in the same treatment groups. This may be problematic for a variety of reasons, especially as the available evidence seems to indicate that it is more difficult to reduce the re-offending of adult sex offenders, compared to child sex offenders (Gannon et al., 2008; Marques et al., 2005).

What then can we conclude about the effectiveness of offender rehabilitation programmes? The first important point to note is that the available evidence clearly supports the idea that offenders *can* be rehabilitated. However, the overall effect of treatment programmes on recidivism, although meaningful, is somewhat modest. It is also clear that some programmes work better than others with the strongest support for structured cognitive behavioural programmes. Finally, some offenders seem more amenable to treatment than others with currently limited available evidence in support of the efficacy of programmes for serious repeat violent offenders and adult sex offenders.

REVIEW AND REFLECT

1   What are some of the important methodological issues involved in evaluating the effectiveness of offender rehabilitation programmes?
2   What evidence is there that offender rehabilitation programmes are effective in reducing re-offending?

MODELS OF OFFENDER REHABILITATION

It is clear from the previous section that offenders can be rehabilitated, although there also appears to be some scope for improvement both in the overall effectiveness of treatment programmes and in their efficacy for certain types of offender. In order to develop the most effective treatment programmes for different types of offender it is important that we develop clear theories or models of offender rehabilitation. Ward, Rose, and Willis (2012, p. 408) argue that a good rehabilitation theory is a 'conceptual map' that 'will provide guidance on pressing matters such as the overall aims of intervention, what constitutes risk, what the general causes of crime are, how best to manage and work with individuals, and how best to balance offender needs with the interests of the community'. In this section we will consider two prominent models or theories of offender rehabilitation: the **risk-need-responsivity model** and the **good lives model**.

The risk-need-responsivity model

Rehabilitation programmes for offenders in many countries have been guided by the principles of risk, need, and responsivity that are the core elements of the – appropriately named – risk-need-responsivity model (Andrews & Bonta, 2010a; Andrews, Bonta, & Wormith, 2006, 2011) (see Figure 13.4). According to the **risk principle** it is important that the intensity of treatment should match an offender's risk of re-offending. Individuals who are at a low risk of re-offending are less likely to benefit from treatment than individuals who are at a high risk of re-offending. Although this may sound somewhat counter-intuitive it makes sense because low-risk offenders, by definition, are unlikely to re-offend so intensive treatment programmes are not going to make much of a difference compared to those for high-risk offenders. In practical terms, the risk principle means that intensive treatment services should be targeted at high-risk offenders whereas low-risk offenders should receive minimal or no treatment services.

Whereas the risk principle specifics *who* should be treated, the **need principle** speaks to the *targets* of treatment programmes. Specifically, Andrews and Bonta argue that treatment programmes must target **criminogenic needs**. As Andrews and Bonta (2010b, pp. 45–46) explain:

> Offenders have many needs. Some are functionally related to criminal behaviour (i.e., dynamic risk factors or criminogenic needs) and others have a very minor or no causal relationship to criminal behaviour (i.e., noncriminogenic needs) … Criminogenic needs are dynamic risk factors and, most importantly, serve as the intermediate targets of change in rehabilitation programing.

Examples of criminogenic needs include pro-criminal attitudes (e.g., attitudes, values and beliefs supportive of criminal behaviour), antisocial personality characteristics (e.g., low self-control, callousness), pro-criminal associates, and substance abuse problems (Andrews & Bonta, 2010b). Specific criminogenic needs will, however, vary depending on the type of offender. For instance, for child sex offenders, important criminogenic needs may include deviant sexual arousal (that is, sexual preference for

Risk	Need	Responsivity
• The intensity of treatment should be related to the risk of re-offending • Treatment should be preferentially directed at high-risk offenders	• Only those characteristics associated with reductions in recidivism should be targeted in treatment • Treatment should target 'criminogenic needs' (dynamic risk factors)	• Treatment should be tailored to the individual characteristics of offenders

Figure 13.4 The risk-need-responsivity model.

pre-pubescent children), distorted cognitions, and intimacy deficits (see Chapter 7). The logic of targeting criminogenic needs is fairly straightforward: because these needs are functionally related to and predictive of re-offending, if they can be changed during treatment then, in theory, individuals should be less likely to re-offend.

The final component of the RNR model is the **responsivity principle**, and it relates to the way that offender rehabilitation is implemented. There are two aspects to this principle (Andrews & Bonta, 2010b). The first relates to *general responsivity* and concerns the best overall practice for interacting with offenders. Thus it addresses issues to do with general rehabilitation approaches and the development of effective therapeutic relationships. The second aspect is *specific responsivity* and concerns the importance of tailoring interventions to offender's cognitive abilities and learning styles.

In sum, the RNR model provides an overarching framework for rehabilitation that specifies who should be rehabilitated (the risk principle), the nature of the intervention or treatment targets (the need principle), and how the rehabilitation programme should be implemented (the responsivity principle). Research on offender rehabilitation suggests that programmes that adhere to each of these three principles are more effective in reducing re-offending (Andrews & Bonta, 2010a).

The good lives model

Despite the relative success of the RNR model in rehabilitating offenders and its widespread implementation in correctional facilities the model has received criticism from some scholars. For example, Ward and colleagues (Ward & Gannon, 2006; Ward & Steward, 2003) have argued that although the targeting of risk factors is a necessary component of rehabilitation it is not a sufficient one. In other words, although offenders' criminogenic needs are a legitimate treatment target, effective intervention needs to focus not only on negative treatment goals (the elimination of risk factors) but also on positive goals. Moreover, it is suggested that the RNR model tends neglect the important role of personal agency and the wider social and cultural context in the rehabilitation of offenders.

An alternative rehabilitation framework developed by Ward and that attempts to address these issues is known as the good lives model (GLM) (Laws & Ward, 2011; Ward, 2002; Ward & Brown, 2004; Ward & Maruna, 2007). The GLM is a strength-based approach to treating offenders that focuses on the enhancement of positive factors that can help individuals desist from offending (alongside reducing their ability to harm others). A primary assumption of the GLM is that humans are goal-directed organisms that are motivated to seek a number of primary goods such as relatedness (intimate, family, and social relationships), knowledge, excellence in work and play, excellence in agency, and happiness. The realisation of these primary goods is a central component in leading a rich and meaningful life. Offenders, like everyone else, are motivated to seek these primary goods. However, for a variety of reasons they have a tendency to pursue primary goods in ways that are personally and socially destructive. For instance, a child sex offender may seek the primary good of relatedness (sexual intimacy with others) through the illegitimate means of offending against children.

Effective rehabilitation from a GLM perspective, therefore, involves the therapist providing opportunities for offenders to fashion a more adaptive sense of self that includes the pursuit of primary goods through means that do not involve harming others. Thus a treatment plan needs to incorporate various primary goods and aim to provide the internal (e.g., skills, competencies, beliefs) and external (e.g., relational, social, cultural, and ecological) conditions necessary to achieve these goods. In other words treatment needs to take into account an offender's strengths, primary goods, and relevant environments, and detail on an individual basis what competencies and resources are necessary in order to realise these goods (Ward & Brown, 2004). As Ward and Brown (2004, p. 244) clearly state:

> We argue that the management of risk is a necessary but not sufficient condition for the rehabilitation of offenders. We propose that the best way to lower offending recidivism rates is to equip individuals with the tools to live more fulfilling lives rather than to simply use increasingly sophisticated risk management measures and strategies. At the end of the day most offenders have more in common with us than not, and like the rest of humanity have needs to be loved, valued, to function competently, and to be part of a community.

The GLM framework for offender rehabilitation provides a theoretically well-grounded and promising approach to working with offenders in ways that can help them to desist from crime. Although the GLM has not been subject to as many evaluations as other programmes there is an accumulating body of research that indicates it is a promising new direction that might help to improve the success of rehabilitation programmes, and many of the core features of the GLM are becoming more widely included in such programmes (Netto, Carter, & Bonell, 2014; Willis & Ward, 2013).

REVIEW AND REFLECT

1   How do the principles of 'risk', 'need', and 'responsivity' guide rehabilitation in the RNR model?
2   How does the good lives model differ from the risk-need-responsivity model?

SUMMARY

Many individuals who are convicted for criminal offences re-offend within two to three years of serving their sentence. This suggests that programmes that attempt to treat or rehabilitate offenders have an important role to play in reducing crime. Most contemporary approaches to rehabilitation involve cognitive behavioural treatment programmes that target the way that offenders think. Although there are some important methodological issues to negotiate in evaluating the effectiveness of offender treatment programmes a good deal of research now indicates that such programmes can, indeed, work. Two important models or theories of offender rehabilitation have been considered in this chapter: the risk-need-responsivity model and the good lives model.

FURTHER READING

Casey, S., Day, A., Vess, J., & Ward, T. (2013). *Foundations of Offender Rehabilitation*. London: Routledge.
A good, readable introduction to the topic of offender rehabilitation.

Andrews, D. A., & Bonta, J. (2010a). *The Psychology of Criminal Conduct* (5th edition). Newark, NJ: Anderson Publishing.
A comprehensive overview of the RNR model.

McGuire, J. (2013). 'What works' to reduce re-offending: 18 years on. In L. A. Craig, L. Dixon, & T. A. Gannon (eds.), *What Works in Offender Rehabilitation: An Evidence-Based Approach to Assessment and Treatment* (pp. 20–49). Hoboken, NJ: Wiley.
A cutting-edge review of the research that has examined the effectiveness of offender rehabilitation programmes.

Joseph, J., & Crichlow, W. (eds.). (2015). *Alternative Offender Rehabilitation and Social Justice: Arts and Physical Engagement in Criminal Justice and Community Settings*. New York, NY: Springer.
A useful resource for those interested in 'alternative' approaches to offender rehabilitation.

WEB RESOURCES

Provides systematic reviews of crime prevention initiatives: www.campbellcollaboration.org/CCJG/index.asp.
 The home page for the good lives model provides a wealth of useful information on this approach to offender rehabilitation: www.goodlivesmodel.com/glm/Home.html.

 KEY CONCEPTS

- abstinence violation effect
- cognitive behavioural treatment programmes
- criminogenic needs
- desistance

- dynamic risk factors
- good lives model
- matched controls
- need principle
- recidivism
- rehabilitation
- relapse prevention

- responsivity principle
- risk factor
- risk-need-responsivity model
- risk principle
- static risk factors
- treatment

REFERENCES

Abadinsky, H. (2014). *Drug Use and Abuse: A Comprehensive Introduction* (8th edition). Belmont, CA: Wadsworth.

Abbey, A., Zawacki, T., Buck, P. O., Clinton, A. M., & McAuslan, P. (2001). Alcohol and sexual assault. *Alcohol Research and Health*, 24, 43–51.

Abbott, J. H. (1981). *In the Belly of the Beast: Letters from Prison*. New York, NY: Random House.

Adams, D. (1989). The Seville statement on violence: A progress report. *Journal of Peace Research*, 26, 113–121.

Adamson, S. J., Todd, F. C., Sellman, J. D., Huriwai, T., & Porter, J. (2006). Co-existing psychiatric disorders in a New Zealand outpatient alcohol and other drug clinical population. *Australian and New Zealand Journal of Psychiatry*, 40, 164–170.

Adler, R. N., Smith, J., Fishman, P., & Larson, E. B. (2004). To prevent, react, and rebuild: Health research and the prevention of genocide. *Health Services Research*, 39, 2027–2051.

Adler, F., Mueller, G. O. W., & Laufer, W. S. (2007). *Criminology* (6th edition). Boston, MA: McGraw Hill.

Agnew, R. (2003). An integrated theory of the adolescent peak in offending. *Youth and Society*, 34, 263–299.

Agnew, R. (2006). *Pressured into Crime: An Overview of General Strain Theory*. Los Angeles, CA: Roxbury Publishing.

Agnew, R. (2007). Strain theory and violent behaviour. In D. J. Flannery, A. T. Vazsonyi, & I. D. Waldman (eds.), *Cambridge Handbook of Violent Behaviour* (pp. 519–529). Leiden: Cambridge University Press.

Agnew, R. (2009). *Juvenile Delinquency: Causes and Control* (3rd edition). New York, NY: Oxford University Press.

Agnew, R. (2010). A general strain theory of terrorism. *Theoretical Criminology*, 14, 131–153.

Agnew, R. (2011). *Toward a Unified Criminology: Integrating Assumptions About Crime, People, and Society*. New York, NY: New York University Press.

Agnew, R. (2012a). Dire forecast: A theoretical model of the impact of climate change on crime. *Theoretical Criminology*, 16, 21–42.

Agnew, R. (2012b). It's the end of the world as we know it: The advance of climate change from a criminological perspective. In R. White (ed.), *Climate Change from a Criminological Perspective* (pp. 13–25). New York, NY: Springer.

Agnew, R., & Brezina, T. (2010). Strain theories. In E. McLaughlin & T. Newburn (eds.), *The Sage Handbook of Criminological Theory* (pp. 96–113). London: Sage Publications.

Aitchison, A. (2010). Genocide and 'ethnic cleansing'. In F. Brookman, M. Maguire, H. Pierpoint, & T. Bennett (eds.), *Handbook on Crime* (pp. 762–784). Cullompton: Willan Publishing.

Akers, R. L. (1977). *Deviant Behaviour: A Social Learning Approach* (2nd edition). Belmont, CA: Wadsworth Publishing.

Akers, R. L., & Jensen, G. F. (2010). Social learning theory: Process and structure in criminal and deviant behaviour. In E. McLaughlin & T. Newburn (eds.), *The Sage Handbook of Criminological Theory* (pp. 56–71). London: Sage Publications.

Albanese, J. S. (2014). The Italian-American mafia. In L. Paoli (ed.), *The Oxford Handbook of Organised Crime* (pp. 142–158). Oxford: Oxford University Press.

Alden, A., Brennan, P., Hodgins, S., & Mednick, S. (2007). Psychotic disorders and sex offending in a Danish birth cohort. *Archives of General Psychiatry*, 64, 1251–1258.

Ali, P. A., Dhingra, K., & McGarry, J. (2016). A literature review of intimate partner violence and its classifications. *Aggression and Violent Behavior*, 31, 16–25.

Allely, C. S., Minnis, H., Thompson, L., Wilson, P., & Gillberg, C. (2014). Neurodevelopmental and psychosocial risk factors in serial killers and mass murderers. *Aggression and Violent Behavior*, 19, 288–301.

Allen, M., Emmers, T., Gebhardt, L., & Giery, M. A. (1995). Exposure to pornography and acceptance of rape myth. *Journal of Communication*, 45, 5–25.

American Psychiatric Association. (2000). *Diagnostic and Statistical Manual of Mental Disorders* (4th ed., text rev.). Washington, DC: American Psychiatric Association.

American Psychiatric Association. (2013). *Diagnostic and Statistical Manual of Mental Disorders* (5th edition). Arlington, VA: American Psychiatric Association.

Amnesty International. (2016). Death sentences and executions in 2015. Retrieved from www.amnesty.org/en/latest/research/2016/04/death-sentences-executions-2015/ on January 19, 2017.

Anderson, C. A. (2001). Heat and violence. *Current Directions in Psychological Science*, 10, 33–38.

Anderson, C. A., & Anderson, K. B. (1998). Temperature and aggression: Paradox, controversy, and a (fairly) clear picture. In R. G. Green & E. Donnerstein (eds.), *Human Aggression: Theories, Research, and Implications for Social Policy*. San Diego, CA: Academic Press.

Anderson, C. A., Berkowitz, L., Donnerstein, E., Huesmann, L. R., Johnson, J. D., Linz, D., ... Wartella, E. (2003). The influence of media violence on youth. *Psychological Science in the Public Interest*, 4, 81–110.

Anderson, C. A., & Bushman, B. J. (2002). Human aggression. *Annual Review of Psychology*, 53, 27–51.

Anderson, C. A., Bushman, B. J., Donnerstein, E., Hummer, T. A., & Warburton, W. (2015). SPSSI research summary on media violence. *Analyses of Social Issues and Public Policy*, 15, 4–19.

Anderson, C. A., & Carnagey, N. L. (2007). Violent evil and the general aggression model. In A. G. Miller (ed.), *The Social Psychology of Good and Evil* (pp. 168–190). New York, NY: The Guilford Press.

Anderson, C. A., Shibuya, A., Ibori, N., Wing, E. L., Bushman, B. J., Sakamoto, A., ... Saleem, M. (2010). Violent video game effects on aggression, empathy, and prosocial behaviour in Eastern and Western countries: A meta-analytic review. *Psychological Bulletin*, 136, 151–173.

Anderson, D. A. (2002). The deterrence hypothesis and picking pockets at the pickpocket's hanging. *American Law and Economics Review*, 4, 295–313.

Anderson, E. (1994). The code of the streets. *Atlantic Monthly*, 273, 81–94.

Anderson, E. (1999). *Code of the Street: Decency, Violence, and the Moral Life of the Inner City*. New York, NY: Norton.

Anderson, J., & Linden, R. (2014). Why steal cars? A study of young offenders involved in auto theft. *Canadian Journal of Crime and Criminal Justice*, 56, 241–260.

Andersson, M. (1994). *Sexual Selection*. Princeton, NJ: Princeton University Press.

Andrews, D. A., & Bonta, J. (2010a). *The Psychology of Criminal Conduct* (5th edition). Newark, NJ: Anderson Publishing.

Andrews, D. A., & Bonta, J. (2010b). Rehabilitating criminal justice policy and practice. *Psychology, Public Policy, and Law*, 16, 39–55.

Andrews, D. A., Bonta, J., & Wormith, J. S. (2006). The recent past and near future of risk and/or need assessment. *Crime and Delinquency*, 52, 7–27.

Andrews, D. A., Bonta, J., & Wormith, J. S. (2011). The risk-need-responsivity (RNR) model: Does adding the good lives model contribute to effective crime prevention? *Criminal Justice and Behavior*, 38, 735–755.

Apel, R., & Nagin, D. S. (2011). General deterrence. In M. Tonry (ed.), *The Oxford Handbook of Crime and Criminal Justice* (pp. 179–206). Oxford: Oxford University Press.

Aquino, K., Reed, A., Thau, S., & Freeman, D. (2007). A grotesque and dark beauty: How moral identity and mechanisms of moral disengagement influence cognitive and emotional reactions to war. *Journal of Experimental Social Psychology*, 43, 385–392.

Archer, J. (2002). Sex differences in physically aggressive acts between heterosexual partners: A meta-analytic review. *Aggression and Violent Behaviour*, 7, 313–351.

Archer, J. (2004). Sex differences in aggression in real-world settings: A meta-analytic review. *Review of General Psychology*, 8, 291–322.

Archer, J. (2006a). Cross-cultural differences in physical aggression between partners: A social-role analysis. *Personality and Social Psychology Review*, 10, 133–153.

Archer, J. (2006b). Testosterone and human aggression: An evaluation of the challenge hypothesis. *Neuroscience and Biobehavioral Reviews*, 30, 319–345.

Archer, J. (2009a). Does sexual selection explain human sex differences in aggression? *Behavioral and Brain Sciences*, 32, 249–311.

Archer, J. (2009b). The nature of human aggression. *International Journal of Law and Psychiatry*, 32, 202–208.

Archer, J. (2013). Can evolutionary principles explain patterns of family violence? *Psychological Bulletin*, 139, 403–440.

Archer, J., Birring, S. S., & Wu, F. C. W. (1998). The association between testosterone and aggression among young men: Empirical findings and a meta-analysis. *Aggressive Behavior*, 24, 411–420.

Archer, J., & Coyne, S. M. (2005). An integrated review of indirect, relational, and social aggression. *Personality and Social Psychology Review*, 9, 212–230.

Arnett, J. J. (1999). Adolescent storm and stress, reconsidered. *American Psychologist*, 54, 317–326.

Arnett, J. J. (2000). Emerging adulthood: A theory of development from the late teens through the twenties. *American Psychologist*, 55, 469–480.

Arrigo, B. A., & Purcell, C. E. (2001). Explaining paraphilias and lust murder: Toward an integrated model. *International Journal of Offender Therapy and Comparative Criminology*, 45, 6–31.

Arseneault, L., Cannon, M., Witton, J., & Murray, R. M. (2004). Causal association between cannabis and psychosis: Examination of the evidence. *British Journal of Psychiatry*, 184, 110–117.

Arsenault, L., Moffitt, T. E., Caspi, A., & Taylor, P. J. (2000). Mental disorder and violence in a total birth cohort. *Archives of General Psychiatry*, 57, 979–986.

Ashton, M. C., Lee, K., & de Vries, R. E. (2014). The HEXACO honesty-humility, agreeableness, and emotionality factors: A review of research and theory. *Personality and Social Psychology Review*, 18, 139–152.

Atran, S. (2003, March 7). Genesis of suicide terrorism. *Science*, 299, 1534–1539.

Atran, S., & Ginges, J. (2012). Religious and sacred imperatives in human conflict. *Science*, 336(6083), 855–857.

Atran, S., Sheikh, H., & Gómez, A. (2014). For cause and comrade: Devoted actors and willingness to fight. *Cliodynamics: The Journal of Quantitative History and Cultural Evolution*, 5, 41–57.

Australian Institute of Criminology. (2016). *Australian Crime: Facts and Figures 2007.* Canberra: Australian Institute of Criminology. Retrieved from www.aic.gov.au/media_library/publications/facts/2014/facts_and_figures_2014.pdf on February 1, 2017.

Australian Institute of Health and Welfare. (2007). *Statistics on Drug Use in Australia, 2006.* Canberra: Australian Institute of Health and Welfare.

Australian Institute of Health and Welfare. (2014). *2013 National Drug Strategy Household Survey Report.* Canberra: Australian Institute of Health and Welfare. Retrieved from www.aihw.gov.au/alcohol-and-other-drugs/data-sources/ndshs-2013/ on February 1, 2017.

Babchishin, K. M., Hanson, R. K., & VanZuylen, H. (2015). Online child pornography offenders are different: A meta-analysis of the characteristics of online and offline sex offenders against children. *Archives of Sexual Behavior, 44,* 45–66.

Bachman, R., & Schutt, R. K. (2014). *The Practice of Research in Criminology and Criminal Justice* (5th edition). Thousand Oaks, CA: Sage Publications.

Badenes-Ribera, L., Bonilla-Campos, A., Frias-Navarro, D., Pons-Salvador, G., & Montervede-i-Bort, H. (2016). Intimate partner violence in self-identified lesbians: A systematic review of its prevalence and correlates. *Trauma, Violence, and Abuse, 17,* 284–297.

Bahr, S. J., & Hoffmann, J. P. (2015). Social scientific theories of drug use, abuse, and addiction. In H. H. Brownstein (ed.), *The Handbook of Drugs and Society.* Hoboken, NJ: Wiley.

Baker, L. A., Bezdjian, S., & Raine, A. (2006). Behavioral genetics: The science of antisocial behaviour. *Law and Contemporary Problems, 69,* 7–46.

Baker, L. A., Tuvblad, C., & Raine, A. (2010). Genetics and crime. In E. McLaughlin & T. Newburn (eds.), *The SAGE Handbook of Criminological Theory* (pp. 21–40). Los Angeles, CA: Sage Publications.

Ballard, E., & Teasdale, B. (2016). Reconsidering the criminalization debate: An examination of the predictors of arrest among people with major mental disorders. *Criminal Justice Policy Review, 27,* 22–45.

Baller, R. D., Zevenbergen, M. P., & Messner, S. F. (2009). The heritage of herding and southern homicide: Examining the ecological foundations of the code of honor thesis. *Journal of Research in Crime and Delinquency, 46,* 275–300.

Bandura, A. (1973). *Aggression: A Social Learning Analysis.* Englewood Cliffs, NJ: Prentice Hall.

Bandura, A. (1999). Moral disengagement in the perpetration of inhumanities. *Personality and Social Psychology Review, 3,* 193–209.

Bandura, A. (2002). Selective moral disengagement in the exercise of moral agency. *Journal of Moral Education, 31,* 101–118.

Bannon, S. M., Salis, K. L., & O'Leary, K. D. (2015). Structural brain abnormalities and violent behaviour. *Aggression and Violent Behavior, 25,* 323–331.

Barash, D. P., & Webel, C. P. (2009). *Peace and Conflict Studies* (2nd edition). Los Angeles, CA: Sage Publications.

Barker, V. (2013). Nordic exceptionalism revisited: Explaining the paradox of a Janus-faced penal regime. *Theoretical Criminology, 17,* 5–25.

Barkley, R. A. (2006). *Attention-Deficit Hyperactivity Disorder: A Handbook for Diagnosis and Treatment* (3rd edition). London: The Guilford Press.

Barkley, R. A. (2016). Recent longitudinal studies of childhood attention-deficit/hyperactivity disorder: Important themes and questions for further research. *Journal of Abnormal Psychology, 125,* 248–255.

Barlow, D. H., & Durand, V. M. (2005). *Abnormal Psychology: An Integrated Approach* (4th edition). Southbank: Thomson/Wadsworth.

Barnes, J. C., Boutwell, B. B., & Beaver, K. M. (2016). Contemporary biosocial criminology: A systematic review of the literature, 2000–2012. In A. R. Piquero (ed.), *The Handbook of Criminological Theory* (pp. 75–99). Chichester: Wiley-Blackwell.

Barnes, J. C., Wright, J. P., Boutwell, B. B., Schwartz, J. A., Connolly, E. J., Nedelec, J. L., & Beaver, K. M. (2014). Demonstrating the validity of twin research in criminology. *Criminology*, 52, 588–626.

Barnett, O. W., Miller-Perrin, C. L., & Perrin, R. D. (2004). *Family Violence Across the Lifespan: An Introduction* (2nd edition). Thousand Oaks, CA: Sage Publications.

Baron, R. A. (1977). *Human Aggression*. New York, NY: Plenum Press.

Barratt, M. J., Seear, K., & Lancaster, K. (2017). A critical examination of the definition of 'psychoactive effect' in Australian drug legislation. *International Journal of Drug Policy*, 40, 16–25.

Barrowcliff, A. L., & Haddock, G. (2006). The relationship between command hallucinations and factors of compliance: A critical review of the literature. *The Journal of Forensic Psychiatry and Psychology*, 17, 266–298.

Barrowcliffe, E. R., & Gannon, T. A. (2016). Comparing the psychological characteristic of un-apprehended firesetters and non-firesetters living in the UK. *Psychology, Crime and Law*, 22, 382–404.

Bartlett, C. P., & Anderson, C. A. (2012). Direct and indirect relations between Big 5 personality traits and aggressive and violent behaviour. *Personality and Individual Differences*, 52, 870–875.

Bartol, C. R., & Bartol, A. M. (2008). *Criminal Behaviour: A Psychosocial Approach* (8th edition). Upper Saddle River, NJ: Pearson Prentice Hall.

Bartol, C. R., & Bartol, A. M. (2012). *Introduction to Forensic Psychology: Research and Application* (3rd edition). Thousand Oaks, CA: Sage Publications.

Baskin-Sommers, A. R., & Hearon, B. A. (2015). The intersection between neurobiological and psychological theories of substance use disorders. In H. H. Brownstein (ed.), *The Handbook of Drugs and Society*. Hoboken, NJ: Wiley.

Baumeister, R. F. (1997). *Evil: Inside Human Violence and Cruelty*. New York, NY: Holt.

Baumeister, R. F., & Boden, J. M. (1998). Aggression and the self: High self-esteem, low self-control, and ego threat. In R. G. Green & E. Donnerstein (eds.), *Human Aggression: Theories, Research, and Implications for Social Policy* (pp. 111–137). San Diego, CA: Academic Press.

Baumeister, R. F., Bushman, B. J., & Campbell, W. K. (2000). Self-esteem, narcissism, and aggression: Does violence result from low self-esteem or from threatened egotism? *Current Directions in Psychological Science*, 9, 26–29.

Baumeister, R. F., & Leary, M. R. (1995). The need to belong: Desire for interpersonal attachments as a fundamental human motivation. *Psychological Bulletin*, 117, 497–529.

Baumeister, R. F., & Vohs, K. D. (2003). Four roots of evil. In A. G. Miller (ed.). *The Social Psychology of Good and Evil* (pp. 85–101). New York, NY: The Guilford Press.

Baumeister, R. F., & Vohs, K. D. (2016). Strength model of self-regulation as a limited resource: Assessment, controversies, update. *Advances in Experimental Social Psychology*, 54, 67–127.

Bean, P. (2008). *Madness and Crime*. Cullompton: Willan Publishing.

Bean, P. (2014). *Drugs and Crime* (4th edition). London: Routledge.

Beaver, K. M. (2009). Molecular genetics and crime. In A. Walsh & K. M. Beaver (eds.), *Biosocial Criminology: New Directions in Theory and Research* (pp. 50–73). New York, NY: Routledge.

Beaver, K. M. (2013). The familial concentration of crime. *Criminal Justice and Behavior*, 40, 139–155.

Beaver, K. M., & Connolly, E. J. (2013). Genetic and environmental influences on the development of childhood antisocial behavior: Current evidence and directions for future research. In M. DeLisi & K. M. Beaver (eds.), *Criminological Theory: A Life-Course Approach* (2nd edition), (pp. 43–55). Burlington, MA: Jones and Bartlett Learning.

Beaver, K. M., Nedelec, J. L., Schwartz, J. A., & Connolly, E. J. (2014). Evolutionary behavioral genetics of violent crime. In *The Evolution of Violence* (pp. 117–135). New York, NY: Springer.

Beaver, K. M., Wright, J. P., & DeLisi, M. (2007). Self-control as an executive function: Reformulating Gottfredson and Hirschi's parental socialization thesis. *Criminal Justice and Behavior*, 34, 1345–1361.

Becker, G. S. (1968). Crime and punishment: An economic approach. *Journal of Political Economy*, 76, 169–217.

Becker, J. B., McLellan, M., & Reed, B. G. (2016). Sociocultural context for sex differences in addiction. *Addiction Biology*, 21, 1052–1059.

Beech, A., Elliott, I. A., Birgden, A., & Findlater, D. (2008). The internet and child sexual offending: A criminological review. *Aggression and Violent Behaviour*, 13, 216–228.

Beech, A., Fisher, D., & Ward, T. (2005). Sexual murderers' implicit theories. *Journal of Interpersonal Violence*, 20, 1366–1389.

Beech, A. R., Miner, M. H., & Thornton, D. (2016). Paraphilias in the DSM–5. *Annual Review of Clinical Psychology*, 12, 383–406.

Beeson, J. G. (2014). Psychology of human trafficking. In M. J. Palmiotto (ed.), *Combating Human Trafficking: A Multidisciplinary Approach* (pp. 47–60). London: CRC Press.

Benjamin, A. J., & Bushman, B. J. (2016). The weapons priming effect. *Current Opinion in Psychology*, 12, 45–48.

Benjamin, L. T., & Simpson, J. A. (2009). The power of the situation: The impact of Milgram's obedience studies on personality and social psychology. *American Psychologist*, 64, 12–19.

Bennett, T., & Brookman, F. (2010). Street robbery. In F. Brookman, M. Maguire, H. Pierpoint, & T. Bennett (eds.), *Handbook on Crime* (pp. 270–289). Cullompton: Willan Publishing.

Bennett, T., & Edwards, J. (2015). What has been learned from research on the drugs-crime connection? In H. H. Brownstein (ed.), *The Handbook of Drugs and Society*. Hoboken, NJ: Wiley.

Bennett, T., & Holloway, K. (2005). *Understanding Drugs, Alcohol and Crime*. New York, NY: Open University Press.

Bennett, T., & Holloway, K. (2006). Variations in drug users' accounts of the connection between drug misuse and crime. *Journal of Psychoactive Drugs*, 38, 243–254.

Benson, M. L., & Simpson, S. S. (2014). *Understanding White-Collar Crime: An Opportunity Perspective* (2nd edition). London: Routledge.

Berkowitz, L. (1988). Frustrations, appraisals, and aversively stimulated aggression. *Aggressive Behavior*, 14, 3–11.

Berkowitz, L. (1990). On the formation and regulation of anger and aggression: A cognitive-neoassociationistic analysis. *American Psychologist*, 45, 494–503.

Berkowitz, L. (1993). *Aggression: Its Causes, Consequences, and Control*. New York, NY: McGraw-Hill.

Berkowitz, L. (1999). Evil is more than banal: Situationism and the concept of evil. *Personality and Social Psychology Review*, 3, 246–253.

Berkowitz, L., & LePage, A. (1967). Weapons as aggression-eliciting stimuli. *Journal of Personality and Social Psychology*, 7, 202–207.

Bernasco, W. (2010). A sentimental journey to crime: Effects of residential history on crime location choice. *Criminology*, 48, 389–416.

Bernasco, W., Johnson, S. D., & Ruiter, S. (2015). Learning where to offend: Effects of past on future burglary locations. *Applied Geography*, 60, 120–129.

Bernasco, W., & Nieuwbeerta, P. (2005). How do residential burglars select target areas? A new approach to the analysis of criminal location choice. *British Journal of Criminology*, 45, 296–315.

Bettencourt, B. A., Talley, A., Benjamin, A. J., & Valentine, J. (2006). Personality and aggressive behaviour under provoking and neutral conditions: A meta-analytic review. *Psychological Bulletin*, 132, 751–777.

Betzig, L. (2012). Means, variances, and ranges in reproductive success: Comparative evidence. *Evolution and Human Behavior*, 33, 309–317.

Beyers, J. M., Toumbourou, J. W., Catalano, R. F., Arthur, M. W., & Hawkins, D. (2004). A cross-national comparison of risk and protective factors for adolescent substance use: The United States and Australia. *Journal of Adolescent Health*, 35, 3–16.

Bickley, J., & Beech, A. R. (2001). Classifying child abusers: Its relevance to theory and clinical practice. *International Journal of Offender Therapy and Comparative Criminology*, 45, 51–69.

Birmingham, L. (2004). Mental disorder and prisons. *Psychiatric Bulletin*, 28, 393–397.

Bjorkly, S. (2002a). Psychotic symptoms and violence toward others – a literature review of some preliminary findings: Part 1. Delusions. *Aggression and Violent Behavior*, 7, 617–631.

Bjorkly, S. (2002b). Psychotic symptoms and violence toward others – a literature review of some preliminary findings: Part 2. Hallucinations. *Aggression and Violent Behavior*, 7, 605–615.

Blackburn, R. (1996). What is forensic psychology? *Legal and Criminological Psychology*, 1, 3–16.

Blair, J., Mitchell, D., & Blair, K. (2005). *The Psychopath: Emotion and the Brain*. Malden, MA: Blackwell Publishing.

Blair, R. J. R. (2013). The neurobiology of psychopathic traits. *Nature Reviews Neuroscience*, 14, 786–799.

Blair, R. J. R. (2015). Psychopathic traits from an RDoC perspective. *Current Opinion in Neurobiology*, 30, 79–84.

Blair, R. J. R., Peschardt, K. S., Budhani, S., Mitchell, D. G. V., & Pine, D. S. (2006). The development of psychopathy. *Journal of Child Psychology and Psychiatry*, 47, 262–275.

Blanchard, R., Kuban, M. E., Blak, T., Cantor, J. M., Klassen, P., & Dickey, R. (2006). Phallometric comparison of pedophilic interest in nonadmitting sexual offenders against stepdaughters, biological daughters, other biologically related girls, and unrelated girls. *Sexual Abuse: A Journal of Research and Treatment*, 18, 1–14.

Blass, T. (2004). *The Man Who Shocked the World: The Life and Legacy of Stanley Milgram*. New York, NY: Basic Books.

Bloxham, D., & Moses, A. D. (eds.). (2010). *The Oxford Handbook of Genocide Studies*. Oxford: Oxford University Press.

Boardman, J. D., Finch, B. K., Ellison, C. G., Williams, D. R., & Jackson, J. S. (2001). Neighborhood disadvantage, stress, and drug use among adults. *Journal of Health and Social Behavior*, 42, 151–165.

Boddy, C., Miles, D., Sanyal, C., & Hartog, M. (2015). Extreme managers, extreme workplaces: Capitalism, organizations and corporate psychopaths. *Organization*, 22, 530–551.

Boden, J. M., Fergusson, D. M., & Horwood, L. J. (2013). Alcohol misuse and criminal offending: Findings from a 30-year longitudinal study. *Drug and Alcohol Dependence*, 128, 30–36.

Boland, M. J. (2007, July 11). Child in time. *Sunday Star Times*, p. 9.

Boles, S. M., & Miotto, K. (2003). Substance abuse and violence: A review of the literature. *Aggression and Violent Behavior*, 8, 155–174.

Bondü, R., & Richter, P. (2016). Linking forms and functions of aggression in adults to justice and rejection sensitivity. *Psychology of Violence*, 6, 292–302.

Bor, W., McGee, T. R., & Fagan, A. A. (2004). Early risk factors for adolescent antisocial behaviour: An Australian longitudinal study. *Australian and New Zealand Journal of Psychiatry*, 38, 365–372.

Bourgois, P. (1995). *In Search of Respect: Selling Crack in El Barrio*. Cambridge: Cambridge University Press.

Bowers, K. J., & Johnson, S. D. (2016). Situational crime prevention. In D. Weisburd, D. P. Farrington, & C. Gill (eds.), *What Works in Crime Prevention and Rehabilitation* (pp. 111–135). New York, NY: Springer.

Bowie, N. G., & Schmid, A. P. (2011). Databases on terrorism. In A. P. Schmid (ed.), *The Routledge Handbook of Terrorism Research* (pp. 294–341). London: Routledge.

Boyd, R., Gintis, H., Bowles, S., & Richerson, P. J. (2003). The evolution of altruistic punishment. *Proceedings of the National Academy of Sciences*, 100(6), 3531–3535.

Boyd, S. (2002). Media constructions of illegal drugs, users, and sellers: A closer look at traffic. *International Journal of Drug Policy*, 13, 397–407.

Braams, B. R., van Duijvenvoorde, A. C. K., Peper, J. S., & Crone, E. A. (2015). Longitudinal changes in adolescent risk-taking: A comprehensive study of neural responses to rewards, pubertal development, and risk-taking behaviour. *The Journal of Neuroscience*, 35, 7226–7328.

Bradley, T., & Walters, R. (2011). *Introduction to Criminological Thought* (2nd edition). Auckland: Pearson Education.

Braga, A. A. (2006). Policing crime hot spots. In B. C. Welsh & D. P. Farrington (eds.), *Preventing Crime: What Works for Children, Offenders, Victims, and Places* (pp. 179–193). Dordrecht: Springer.

Braga, A. A. (2016). The continued importance of measuring potentially harmful impacts of crime prevention programs: The Academy of Experimental Criminology 2014 Joan McCord Lecture. *Journal of Experimental Criminology*, 12, 1–20.

Brantingham, P., & Brantingham, P. (2008). Crime pattern theory. In R. Wortley & L. Mazzerolle (eds.), *Environmental Criminology and Crime Analysis* (pp. 78–92). Cullompton: Willan Publishing.

Brantingham, P., & Faust, F. L. (1976). A conceptual model of crime prevention. *Crime and Delinquency*, 22, 284–296.

Brassett-Harknett, A., & Butler, N. (2007). Attention-deficit/hyperactivity disorder: An overview of the etiology and a review of the literature relating to the correlates and life course outcomes for men and women. *Clinical Psychology Review*, 27, 188–210.

Brinded, P. M. J., Simpson, I. F., Laidlaw, T. M., Fairley, N., & Malcolm, F. (2001). Prevalence of psychiatric disorders in New Zealand prisons: A national study. *Australian and New Zealand Journal of Psychiatry*, 35, 166–173.

Bronfenbrenner, U. (1977). Toward an experimental ecology of human development. *American Psychologist*, 32, 513–531.

Bronfenbrenner, U. (1986). Ecology of the family as a context for human development: Research perspectives. *Developmental Psychology*, 22, 723–742.

Brookman, F. (2010). Homicide. In F. Brookman, M. Maguire, H. Pierpoint, & T. Bennett (eds.), *Handbook on Crime* (pp. 217–245). Cullompton: Willan Publishing.

Brown, G. R., Dickens, T. E., Sear, R., & Laland, K. N. (2011). Evolutionary accounts of behavioural diversity. *Philosophical Transactions of the Royal Society of London B*, 366, 313–324.

Brown, J., Shell, Y., & Cole, T. (2015). *Forensic Psychology: Theory, Research and Practice*. Los Angeles, CA: Sage Publications.

Brown, J. M., & Walklate, S. L. (eds.). (2012). *Handbook on Sexual Violence*. London: Routledge.

Brown, R. (2010). Vehicle crime. In F. Brookman, M. Maguire, H. Pierpoint, & T. Bennett (eds.), *Handbook on Crime* (pp. 26–47). Cullompton: Willan Publishing.

Brown, R. (2015). Explaining the property crime drop: The offender perspective. *Trends and Issues in Criminal Justice* (495).

Brown, S. E., Esbensen, F., & Geis, G. (2015). *Criminology: Explaining Crime and Its Contexts* (9th edition). New York, NY: Routledge.

Browne, K. D., & Hamilton-Giachritsis, C. (2005, February). The influence of violent media on children and adolescents: A public-health approach. *The Lancet*, 365, 702–710.

Browning, C. R. (1992). *Ordinary Men: Reserve Battalion 101 and the Final Solution in Poland*. London: Penguin Books.

Brownmiller, S. (1975). *Against Our Will: Men, Women and Rape*. New York, NY: Simon & Schuster.

Brownstein, H. H. (2015). Drugs and violent crime. In H. H. Brownstein (ed.), *The Handbook of Drugs and Society*. Hoboken, NJ: Wiley.

Brownstein, H. H., Crimmins, S. M., & Spunt, B. J. (2000). A conceptual framework for operationalizing the relationship between violence and drug market stability. *Contemporary Drug Problems*, 27, 867–888.

Bruinsma, G. (2015). Criminology and transnational crime. In G. Bruinsma (ed.), *Histories of Transnational Crime* (pp. 1–8). New York, NY: Springer.

Bryant, P. (2009). Predicting internet pornography use and arousal: The role of individual difference variables. *Journal of Sex Research*, 46, 344–357.

Bufkin, J. L., & Luttrell, V. R. (2005). Neuroimaging studies of aggressive and violent behaviour: Current findings and implications for criminology and criminal justice. *Trauma, Violence, and Abuse*, 6, 176–191.

Bumby, K. M. (1996). Assessing the cognitive distortions of child molesters and rapists: Development and validation of the MOLEST and RAPE scales. *Sexual Abuse: A Journal of Research and Treatment*, 8, 37–54.

Bureau of Justice Statistics. (2007). Number of persons under correctional supervision, 1980–2006. Retrieved from www.ojp.gov/bjs/glance/tables/corr2tab.htm on June 1, 2008.

Burger, J. M. (2009). Replicating Milgram: Would people still obey today? *American Psychologist*, 64, 1–11.

Burke, M., Hsiang, S. M., & Miguel, E. (2015). Climate and conflict. *Annual Review of Economics*, 7, 577–617.

Burroughs, W. (1953). *Junky*. New York, NY: Penguin Books.

Burt, C. H., & Simons, R. L. (2014). Pulling back the curtain on heritability studies: Biosocial criminology in the postgenomic era. *Criminology*, 52, 223–262.

Burt, M. R. (1980). Cultural myths and supports for rape. *Journal of Personality and Social Psychology*, 38, 217–230.

Burton, P. R. S., McNiel, D. E., & Binder, R. L. (2012). Firesetting, arson, pyromania, and the forensic mental health expert. *Journal of American Academy of Psychiatry and Law*, 40, 355–365.

BushFIRE Arson Bulletin (No. 1). (2004). Canberra: Australian Institute of Criminology.

Bushman, B. J., & Anderson, C. A. (1998). Methodology in the study of aggression: Integrating experimental and nonexperimental findings. In R. G. Green & E. Donnerstein (eds.), *Human Aggression: Theories, Research, and Implications for Social Policy* (pp. 23–48). San Diego, CA: Academic Press.

Bushman, B. J., & Anderson, C. A. (2001). Is it time to pull the plug on the hostile versus instrumental dichotomy? *Psychological Review*, 108, 273–279.

Bushman, B. J., & Baumeister, R. F. (1998). Threatened egotism, narcissism, self-esteem and direct and displaced aggression: Does self-love or self-hate lead to violence? *Journal of Personality and Social Psychology*, 75, 219–229.

Bushman, B. J., & Huesmann, L. R. (2006). Short-term and long-term effects of violent media on aggression in children and adults. *Archives of Pediatric Adolescent Medicine*, 160, 348–352.

Buss, D. M. (1995). Evolutionary psychology: A new paradigm for psychological science. *Psychological Inquiry*, 6, 1–49.

Buss, D. M., & Duntley, J. D. (2011). The evolution of intimate partner violence. *Aggression and Violent Behavior*, 16, 411–419.

Buss, D. M., & Duntley, J. D. (2015). Intimate partner violence in evolutionary perspective. In T. K. Shackelford & R. D. Hansen (eds.), *The Evolution of Violence* (pp. 1–21). New York, NY: Springer.

Buss, D. M., Haselton, M. G., Shackelford, T. K., Bleske, A. L., & Wakefield, J. C. (1998). Adaptation, exaptations, and spandrels. *American Psychologist*, 53, 533–548.

Buss, D. M., & Shackelford, T. K. (1997). Human aggression in evolutionary psychological perspective. *Clinical Psychology Review*, 17, 605–619.

Butcher, J. N., Hooley, J. M., & Mineka, S. M. (2015). *Abnormal Psychology.* New York, NY: Pearson Higher Education.

Butler, H., & Gannon, T. A. (2015). The scripts and expertise of firesetters: A preliminary conceptualization. *Aggression and Violent Behavior,* 20, 72–81.

Butler, T., Allnutt, S., Cain, D., Owens, D., & Muller, C. (2005). Mental disorder in the New South Wales prisoner population. *Australian and New Zealand Journal of Psychiatry,* 39, 407–413.

Byrd, A. L., & Manuck, S. B. (2014). MAOA, childhood maltreatment, and antisocial behavior: Meta-analysis of a gene-environment interaction. *Biological Psychiatry,* 75, 9–17.

Byrnes, J. P., Miller, C. C., & Schafer, W. D. (1999). Gender differences in risk taking: A meta-analysis. *Psychological Bulletin,* 125, 367–383.

Cale, E. M. (2006). A quantitative review of the relations between the 'big 3' higher order personality dimensions and antisocial behaviour. *Journal of Research in Personality,* 40, 250–284.

Campbell, A. (2006). Sex differences in direct aggression: What are the psychological mediators? *Aggression and Violent Behavior,* 11, 237–264.

Campbell, A. (2007). Sex differences in aggression. In R. I. M. Dunbar & L. Barrett (eds.), *Oxford Handbook of Evolutionary Psychology* (pp. 366–380). Oxford: Oxford University Press.

Campbell, A. (2013a). *A Mind of Her Own: The Evolutionary Psychology of Women* (2nd edition). Oxford: Oxford University Press.

Campbell, A. (2013b). The evolutionary psychology of women's aggression. *Philosophical Transactions of the Royal Society of London B: Biological Sciences,* 368, 20130078.

Cann, J., Friendship, C., & Gozna, L. (2007). Assessing crossover in a sample of sexual offenders with multiple victims. *Legal and Criminological Psychology,* 12, 149–163.

Canter, D. V., & Youngs, D. (2009). *Investigative Psychology: Offender Profiling and the Analysis of Criminal Action.* Chichester: John Wiley & Sons.

Carlsmith, K. M., Darley, J. M., & Robinson, P. H. (2002). Why do we punish? Deterrence and just deserts as motives for punishment. *Journal of Personality and Social Psychology,* 83, 284–299.

Carlson, M., Marcus-Newhall, A., & Miller, N. (1990). Effects of situational aggression cues: A quantitative review. *Journal of Personality and Social Psychology,* 58, 622–633.

Carlsson, C., & Sarnecki, J. (2016). *An Introduction to Life-Course Criminology.* London: Sage Publications.

Carmichael, S. E., & Piquero, A. R. (2006). Deterrence and arrest ratios. *International Journal of Offender Therapy and Comparative Criminology,* 50, 71–87.

Carré, J. M., & Olmstead, N. A. (2015). Social neuroendocrinology of human aggression: Examining the role of competition-induced testosterone dynamics. *Neuroscience,* 286, 171–186.

Cartwright, J. (2000). *Evolution and Human Behaviour.* London: Macmillan Press.

Casey, B. J., & Caudle, K. (2013). The teenage brain: Self control. *Current Directions in Psychological Science,* 22, 82–87.

Casey, S., Day, A., Vess, J., & Ward, T. (2013). *Foundations of Offender Rehabilitation.* London: Routledge.

Caspi, A. (2000). The child is father of the man: Personality continuities from childhood to adulthood. *Journal of Personality and Social Psychology,* 78, 158–172.

Caspi, A., McClay, J., Moffitt, T. E., Mill, J., Martin, J., Craig, I. W., … Poulton, R. (2002). Role of genotype in the cycle of violence in maltreated children. *Science,* 297, 851–854.

Caudy, M. S., Durso, J. M., & Taxman, F. S. (2013). How well do dynamic needs predict recidivism? Implications for risk assessment and risk reduction. *Journal of Criminal Justice,* 41, 458–466.

Cauffman, E., Cavanagh, C., Donley, S., & Thomas, A. G. (2016). A developmental perspective on adolescent risk-taking and criminal behaviour. In A. R. Piquero (ed.), *The Handbook of Criminological Theory* (pp. 100–120). Chichester: Wiley-Blackwell.

Cavadino, M., & Dignan, J. (2006). *Penal Systems: A Comparative Approach.* Thousand Oaks, CA: Sage Publications.

Center for Behavioral Health Statistics and Quality. (2015). *Behavioral Health Trends in the United States: Results from the 2014 National Survey on Drug Use and Health* (HHS Publication No. SMA 15-4927, NSDUHSeries H-50). Retrieved from: www.samhsa.gov/data/sites/default/files/NSDUH-FRR1-2014/NSDUH-FRR1-2014.pdf.

Chagnon, N. A. (1988, February 26). Life histories, blood revenge, and warfare in a tribal population. *Science*, 239, 958–992.

Chan, H. C., & Heide, K. M. (2009). Sexual homicide: A synthesis of the literature. *Trauma, Violence, and Abuse*, 10, 31–54.

Chan, H. C., Heide, K. M., & Beauregard, E. (2011). What propels sexual murderers: A proposed integrated theory of social learning and routine activities theories. *International Journal of Offender Therapy and Comparative Criminology*, 55, 228–250.

Chang, L. W., Krosch, A. R., & Cikara, M. (2016). Effects of intergroup threat on mind, brain, and behaviour. *Current Opinion in Psychology*, 11, 69–73.

Chang, Z., Larsson, H., Lichtenstein, P., & Fazel, S. (2015). Psychiatric disorders and violent reoffending: A national cohort study of convicted prisoners in Sweden. *Lancet Psychiatry*, 2, 891–900.

Charlesworth, A., & Glantz, S. A. (2005). Smoking in the movies increases adolescent smoking: A review. *Pediatrics*, 116, 1516–1528.

Chen, F. R., Gao, Y., Glenn, A. L., Niv, S., Portnoy, J., Schug, R., … Raine, A. (2016). Biosocial bases of antisocial and criminal behaviour. In A. R. Piquero (ed.), *The Handbook of Criminological Theory* (pp. 355–379). Chichester: Wiley-Blackwell.

Cheng, J. T., & Tracy, J. L. (2014). Toward a unified science of hierarchy: Dominance and prestige are two fundamental pathways to human social rank. In J. T. Cheng, J. L. Tracy, & C. Anderson (eds.), *The Psychology of Social Status* (pp. 3–27). New York, NY: Springer.

Child Rights International Network. (2016). *Minimum Ages of Criminal Responsibility Around the World*. Retrieved from www.crin.org/en/home/ages on May 30, 2016.

Chin, K.-L. (2014). Chinese organized crime. In L. Paoli (ed.), *The Oxford Handbook of Organised Crime* (pp. 219–233). Oxford: Oxford University Press.

Choe, J. Y., Teplin, L. A., & Abram, K. M. (2008). Perpetrators of violence, violent victimization, and severe mental illness: Balancing public health concerns. *Psychiatric Services*, 59, 159–164.

Choi, J.-K., & Bowles, S. (2007, October). The coevolution of parochial altruism and war. *Science*, 318, 636–640.

Chon, D. S. (2017). Residential burglary victimization: Household and country level mixed modelling. *International Review of Victimology*, 23, 47–61.

Cikara, M. (2015). Intergroup schadenfreude: Motivating participation in collective violence. *Current Opinion in Behavioral Sciences*, 3, 12–17.

Cikara, M., Botvinick, M. M., & Fiske, S. T. (2011). Us versus them: Social identity shapes neural responses to intergroup competition and harm. *Psychological Science*, 22, 306–313.

Cikara, M., Bruneau, E., van Bavel, J. J., & Saxe, R. (2014). Their pain gives us pleasure: How intergroup dynamics shape empathic failures and counter-empathic responses. *Journal of Experimental Social Psychology*, 55, 110–125.

Cikara, M., & Van Bavel, J. J. (2014). The neuroscience of intergroup relations: An integrative review. *Perspectives on Psychological Science*, 9, 245–274.

Clarke, R. V. (1980). 'Situational' crime prevention: Theory and practice. *British Journal of Criminology*, 20, 136–146.

Clarke, R. V. (1999). *Hot Products: Understanding, Anticipating, and Reducing the Demand for Stolen Goods*. London: Home Office.

Clarke, R. V. (2008). Situational crime prevention. In R. Wortley & L. Mazerolle (eds.), *Environmental Criminology and Crime Analysis* (pp. 178–192). Cullompton: Willan Publishing.

Cleave, L. (2005, March 26). A powder keg ignited by P. *The New Zealand Herald.* Retrieved from www.nzherald.co.nz/nz/news/article.cfm?c_id=1&objectid=10117138.

Cleckley, H. M. (1964). *The Mask of Sanity: An Attempt to Clarify some Issues about the So-Called Psychopathic Personality* (4th edition). St Louis, MO: Mosby Co.

Cleveland, H. H., Scholmer, G. L., Vandenbergh, D. J., & Wieber, R. P. (2016). Gene x environment intervention designs: A promising step toward understanding etiology and building better preventive interventions. *Criminology and Public Policy*, 15, 711–720.

Coccaro, E. F. (2012). Intermittent explosive disorder as a disorder of impulsive aggression for the DSM–5. *American Journal of Psychiatry*, 169, 577–588.

Coghlan, S., Gannoni, A., Goldsmid, S., Patterson, E., & Willis, M. (2015). *Drug Use Monitoring in Australia: 2013–2014 Report on Drug Use Among Police Detainees.* Canberra: Australian Institute of Criminology.

Cohen, A. O., & Casey, B. J. (2014). Rewiring juvenile justice: The intersection of developmental neuroscience and legal policy. *Trends in Cognitive Sciences*, 18, 63–65.

Cohen, D., Nisbett, R. E., Bowdle, B. F., & Schwarz, N. (1996). Insult, aggression, and the southern culture of honor: An 'experimental ethnography'. *Journal of Personality and Social Psychology*, 70, 945–960.

Cohen, D., & Strayer, J. (1996). Empathy in conduct-disordered and comparison youth. *Developmental Psychology*, 32, 988–998.

Cohen, L. E., & Felson, M. (1979). Social change and crime rate trends: A routine activity approach. *American Sociological Review*, 44, 588–608.

Cohen-Cole, E., Durlauf, S., Fagan, J., & Nagin, D. (2006). *Re-Evaluating the Deterrent Effect of Capital Punishment: Model and Data Uncertainty* (Report submitted to the U.S. Department of Justice). Retrieved from https://pdfs.semanticscholar.org/daf3/73fd7cf48f9dc6a1bd7b72b3d9fe2f33c692.pdf.

Coid, J. W., Gonzalez, R., Igoumenou, A., Zhang, T., Yang, M., & Bebbington, P. (2016). Personality disorder and violence in the national household population of Britain. *The Journal of Forensic Psychiatry and Psychology*, 1–19.

Collins Atlas of Military History. (2006). London: Collins.

Colson, M. H., Boyer, L., Baumstarck, K., & Loundou, A. D. (2013). Female sex offenders: A challenge to certain paradigms. Meta analysis. *Sexologies*, 22, e109–e117.

Confer, J. C., Easton, J. A., Fleischman, D. S., Goetz, C. D., Lewis, D. M. G., Perilloux, C., & Buss, D. M. (2010). Evolutionary psychology: Controversies, questions, prospects, and limitations. *American Psychologist*, 65, 110–126.

Convention on the Prevention and Punishment of the Crime of Genocide (1948, December 9). Retrieved from www.icrc.org/ihl.nsf/full/357?OpenDocument on February 6, 2012.

Cooke, D. J. (2008). Psychopathy as an important forensic construct: Past, present, and future. In D. Canter & R. Žukasukiene (eds.), *Psychology and Law: Bridging the Gap* (pp. 167–191). Aldershot: Ashgate.

Cooke, D. J., & Michie, C. (1999). Psychopathy across cultures: North America and Scotland compared. *Journal of Abnormal Psychology*, 108, 55–68.

Cooke, D. J., Michie, C., Hart, S. D., & Clark, D. (2005). Searching for the pan-cultural core of psychopathic personality disorder: Continental Europe and North America compared. *Personality and Individual Differences*, 39, 283–295.

Copes, H., Vieraitis, L. M., Cardwell, S. M., & Vasquez, A. (2013). Accounting for identify theft: The roles of lifestyle and enactment. *Journal of Contemporary Criminal Justice*, 29, 351–368.

Cornish, D. B., & Clarke, R. V. (2008). The rational choice perspective. In R. Wortley & L. Mazzerolle (eds.), *Environmental Criminology and Crime Analysis* (pp. 21–46). Cullompton: Willan Publishing.

Cornish, D. B., & Clarke, R. V. (eds.). (2014). *The Reasoning Criminal: Rational Choice Perspectives on Offending*. Piscataway, NJ: Transaction.

Cortoni, F., & Gannon, T. A. (2016). Female sex offenders: An overview. In A. Phenix & H. M. Hoberman (eds.), *Sexual Offending* (pp. 213–224). New York, NY: Springer.

Cosmides, L., & Tooby, J. (2013). Evolutionary psychology: New perspectives on cognition and motivation. *Annual Review of Psychology*, 64, 201–229.

Cossins, A. (2000). *Masculinities, Sexualities and Child Sexual Abuse*. The Hague: Kluwer Law International.

Costa, P. T., & McCrae, R. R. (1994). Set like plaster? Evidence for the stability of adult personality. In T. F. Heatherton & J. L. Weinberger (eds.), *Can Personality Change?* (pp. 21–40). Washington, DC: APA Press.

Coyle, A. (2005). *Understanding Prisons: Key Issues in Policy and Practice*. New York, NY: Open University Press.

Coyne, J. A. (2009). *Why Evolution is True*. New York, NY: Viking.

Cozens, P., & Love, T. (2015). A review and current status of crime prevention through environmental design (CPTED). *Journal of Planning Literature*, 30, 393–412.

Crenshaw, M. (2011). *Explaining Terrorism: Causes, Processes, and Consequences*. London: Routledge.

Crick, N. R., & Dodge, K. A. (1994). A review and reformulation of social information-processing mechanisms in children's social adjustment. *Psychological Bulletin*, 115, 74–101.

Cromwell, P., & Thurman, Q. (2003). The devil made me do it: Use of neutralizations by shoplifters. *Deviant Behavior*, 24, 535–550.

Cross, C. P., & Campbell, A. (2011). Women's aggression. *Aggression and Violent Behavior*, 16, 390–398.

Cross, C. P., Copping, L. T., & Campbell, A. (2011). Sex differences in impulsivity: A meta-analysis. *Psychological Bulletin*, 137, 97–130.

Cuellar, A. E., Snowden, L. M., & Ewing, T. (2007). Criminal records of persons served in the public mental health system. *Psychiatric Services*, 58, 114–120.

Cullen, F. T., Pealer, J. A., Fisher, B. S., Applegate, B. K., & Santana, S. A. (2002). Public support for correctional rehabilitation in America: Change or consistency? In J. V. Roberts & M. Hough (eds.), *Changing Attitudes to Punishment: Public Opinion, Crime and Justice* (pp. 128–146). Cullompton: Willan Publishing.

Cullen, F. T., & Smith, P. (2011). Treatment and rehabilitation. In M. Tonry (ed.), *The Oxford Handbook of Crime and Criminal Justice* (pp. 156–178). Oxford: Oxford University Press.

Cullen, F. T., Unnever, J. D., Wright, J. P., & Beaver, K. M. (2008). Parenting and self-control. In E. Goode (ed.), *Out of Control: Assessing the General Theory of Crime* (pp. 61–74). Stanford, CA: Stanford University Press.

Cussen, T., & Bryant, W. (2015). *Domestic/family homicide in Australia* (Research in Practice No. 38). Canberra: Australian Institute of Criminology.

Dackis, C., & O'Brien, C. (2005). Neurobiology of addiction: Treatment and public policy ramifications. *Nature Neuroscience*, 8, 1431–1436.

Dahl, R. E. (2004). Adolescent brain development: A period of vulnerabilities and opportunities. *Annals of the New York Academy of Sciences*, 1021, 1–22.

Dalton, M. A., Sargent, J. D., Beach, M. L., Titus-Ernstoff, L., Gigson, J. J., Ahrens, M. B., ... Heatherton, T. F. (2003). Effect of viewing smoking in movies on adolescent smoking initiation: A cohort study. *The Lancet*, 362, 281–285.

Daly, M. (2016). *Killing the Competition: Economic Inequality and Homicide*. New Brunswick, NJ: Transaction Publishers.

Daly, M., Delaney, L., Egan, M., & Baumeister, R. F. (2015). Childhood self-control and unemployment throughout the life span: Evidence from two British cohort studies. *Psychological Science*, 26, 709–723.

Daly, M., & Wilson, M. (1988). *Homicide*. Hawthorne, NY: Aldine.

Daly, M., & Wilson, M. (1990). Killing the competition: Female/female and male/male homicide. *Human Nature*, 1, 81–107.

Daly, M., & Wilson, M. (1996). Violence against stepchildren. *Current Directions in Psychological Science*, 5, 77–80.

Daly, M., & Wilson, M. (1997). Crime and conflict: Homicide in evolutionary psychological perspective. *Crime and Justice*, 22, 51–100.

Daly, M., & Wilson, M. (2008). Is the 'Cinderella Effect' controversial? A case study of evolution-minded research and critiques thereof. In C. Crawford & D. Krebs (eds.), *Foundations of Evolutionary Psychology* (pp. 383–400). London: Lawrence Erlbaum Associates.

Daly, M., & Wilson, M. (2010). Cultural inertia, economic incentives, and the persistence of 'Southern violence'. In M. Schaller, A. Norenzayan, S. J. Heine, T. Yamagishi, & T. Kameda (eds.), *Evolution, Culture, and the Human Mind* (pp. 229–241). New York, NY: Psychology Press.

Daly, M., Wilson, M., & Vasdev, S. (2001). Income inequality and homicide rates in Canada and the United States. *Canadian Journal of Criminology*, 43, 210–236.

Dammer, H. R., & Fairchild, E. (2006). *Comparative Criminal Justice Systems* (3rd edition). Belmont, CA: Thomson Wadsworth.

Daniel, A. (2006). Preventing suicide in prison: A collaborative responsibility of administrative, custodial, and clinical staff. *Journal of American Academy of Psychiatry and Law*, 34, 165–175.

Darley, J. M. (2001). Citizens' sense of justice and the legal system. *Current Directions in Psychological Science*, 10, 10–13.

Darley, J. M. (2009). Morality in the law: The psychological foundations of citizens' desires to punish transgressions. *Annual Review of Law and Science*, 5, 1–23.

Darwin, C. (1859). *On the Origin of Species by Means of Natural Selection or the Preservation of Favoured Races in the Struggle for Life*. London: John Murray.

David, O., & Bar-Tal, D. (2009). A sociopsychological conception of collective identity: The case of national identity as an example. *Personality and Social Psychology Review*, 13, 354–379.

Davies, G., Hollin, C., & Bull, R. (2008). Introduction. In G. Davies, C. Hollin, & R. Bull (eds.), *Forensic Psychology* (pp. XIII–XXIII). Chichester: Wiley.

Davies, N. (2016). *Cuckoo: Cheating by Nature*. London: Bloomsbury.

Dawkins, R. (2009). *The Greatest Show on Earth: The Evidence for Evolution*. London: Bantam.

D'Cruze, S. (2012). Sexual violence in history: A contemporary heritage? In J. M. Brown & S. L. Wallklate (eds.), *Handbook on Sexual Violence* (pp. 23–51). New York, NY: Routledge.

de Almeida, R. M. M., Cabral, J. C. C., & Narvaes, R. (2015). Behavioural, hormonal and neurobiological mechanisms of aggressive behaviour in human and non-human primates. *Physiology and Behavior*, 143, 121–135.

De Castro, B. O., Veerman, J. W., Koops, W., Bosch, J. D., & Monshouwer, H. J. (2002). Hostile attribution of intent and aggressive behaviour: A meta-analysis. *Child Development*, 73, 916–934.

Decety, J., & Yoder, K. J. (2016). The emerging social neuroscience of justice motivation. *Trends in Cognitive Sciences*, 21, 6–14.

Decker, S., Wright, R., & Logie, R. (1993). Perceptual deterrence among active residential burglars: A research note. *Criminology*, 31, 135–147.

De Dreu, C. K. W., Greer, L. L., Handgraaf, M. J. J., Shalvi, S., Van Kleef, G. A., Baas, M., ... Feith, S. W. W. (2010, June 11). The neuropeptide oxytocin regulates parochial altruism in intergroup conflict among humans. *Science*, 328, 1408–1411.

De Dreu, C. K. W., Greer, L. L., Van Kleef, G. A., Shalvi, S., & Handgraaf, M. J. J. (2011, January 25). Oxytocin promotes human ethnocentrism. *Proceedings of the National Academy of Sciences*, 108, 1262–1266.

DeFronzo, J., Ditta, A., Hannon, L., & Prochnow, J. (2007). Male serial homicide: The influence of cultural and structural variables. *Homicide Studies*, 11, 3–14.

DeLisi, M. (2016). *Psychopathy as Unified Theory of Crime*. New York, NY: Palgrave Macmillan.

DeLisi, M., Nelson, E. J., Vaughn, M. G., Boutwell, B. B., & Salas-Wright, C. P. (2016). An epidemiological study of burglary offenders: Trends and predictors of self-reported arrests for burglary in the United States, 2002–2013. *International Journal of Offender Therapy and Comparative Criminology*. Advance online publication. DOI: 10.1177/0306624X16670178.

DeLisi, M., & Scherer, A. M. (2006). Multiple homicide offenders: Offense characteristics, social correlates, and criminal careers. *Criminal Justice and Behavior*, 33, 367–391.

Denson, T. F., de Wall, C. N., & Finkel, E. J. (2012). Self-control and aggression. *Current Directions in Psychological Science*, 21, 20–25.

Department of Corrections (2017). Retrieved from www.corrections.govt.nz/working_with_ offenders/community_sentences/employment_and_support_programmes/rehabilitation_and_ treatment_programmes.html.

Derefinko, K. J., & Widiger, T. A. (2008). Antisocial personality disorder. In S. H. Fatemi & P. J. Clayton (eds.), *The Medical Basis of Psychiatry* (pp. 213–225). Totowa, NJ: Humana Press.

De Ridder, D. T. D., Lensvelt-Mulders, G., Finkenauer, C., Stok, F. M., & Baumeister, R. F. (2012). Taking stock of self-control: A meta-analysis of how trait self-control relates to a wide range of behaviours. *Personality and Social Psychology Review*, 16, 76–99.

De Wall, C. N., Anderson, C. A., & Bushman, B. J. (2011). The General Aggression Model: Theoretical extension to violence. *Psychology of Violence*, 3, 245–258.

Diem, C., & Pizarro, J. M. (2010). Social structure and family homicides. *Journal of Family Violence*, 25, 521–532.

Dingwall, G. (2006). *Alcohol and Crime*. Cullompton: Willan Publishing.

Dobash, R. E., & Dobash, R. (1979). *Violence Against Wives: A Case Against Patriarchy*. New York, NY: Free Press.

Doble, J. (2002). Attitudes to punishment in the US – punitive and liberal opinions. In J. V. Roberts & M. Hough (eds.), *Changing Attitudes to Punishment: Public Opinion, Crime and Justice* (pp. 148–161). Cullompton: Willan Publishing.

Dodge, K. A. (2006). Translational science in action: Hostile attributional style and the development of aggressive behaviour problems. *Development and Psychopathology*, 18, 791–814.

Dodge, K. A., Malone, P. S., Lansford, J. E., Sorbring, E., Skinner, A. T., Tapanya, S., … Pastorelli, C. (2015). Hostile attributional bias and aggressive behavior in global context. *Proceedings of the National Academy of Sciences*, 112, 9310–9315.

Dollard, J., Doob, L., Miller, N. E., Mowrer, O. H., & Sears, R. R. (1939). *Frustration and Aggression*. New Haven, CT: Yale University Press.

Domínguez, P., & Raphael, S. (2015). The role of cost-of-crime literature in bridging the gap between social science research and policy making. *Criminology and Public Policy*, 14, 589–632.

Doob, A. N., & Webster, C. M. (2003). Sentence severity and crime: Accepting the null hypothesis. *Crime and Justice: A Review of Research*, 30, 143–195.

Doosje, B., Moghaddam, F. M., Kruglanski, A. W., de Wolf, A., Mann, L., & Feddes, A. R. (2016). Terrorism, radicalization and de-radicalization. *Current Opinion in Psychology*, 11, 79–84.

Dorfman, H. M., Meyer-Lindenberg, A., & Buckholtz, J. W. (2014). Neurobiological mechanisms for impulsive-aggression: The role of MAOA. *Current Topics in Behavioral Neuroscience*, 17, 297–313.

Drieschner, K., & Lange, A. (1999). A review of cognitive factors in the etiology of rape: Theories, empirical studies, and implications. *Clinical Psychology Review*, 19, 57–77.

Drug trafficking deserves death penalty. (2005). ABC news online. Retrieved from www.abc.net.au/news/newsitems/200511/s1519531.htm on June 1, 2008.

Ducat, L., & Ogloff, J. R. P. (2011). Understanding and preventing bushfire-setting: A psychological perspective. *Psychiatry, Psychology, and Law,* 18, 341–356.

Duckworth, A. L., & Kern, M. L. (2011). A meta-analysis of the convergent validity of self-control measures. *Journal of Research in Personality,* 45, 259–268.

Due, P., Holstein, B. E., Lynch, J., Diderichesen, F., Gabhain, N., Scheidt, P., & Currie, C. (2005). Bullying and symptoms among school-aged children: International comparative cross sectional study in 28 countries. *European Journal of Public Health,* 5, 128–132.

Due, P., Holstein, B. E., & Soc, M. S. (2008). Bullying victimization among 13–15-year-old school children: Results from two comparative studies in 66 countries and regions. *International Journal of Adolescent Mental Health,* 20, 209–221.

Duff, R. A. (1998). Desert and penance. In A. Von Hirsch & A. Ashworth (eds.), *Principled Sentencing: Readings on Theory and Policy* (2nd edition, pp. 161–168). Oxford: Hart Publishing.

Duff, R. A. (2003). *Punishment, Communication and Community.* Oxford: Oxford University Press.

Duke, A. A., Begue, L., Bell, R., & Eisenlohu-Moul, T. (2013). Revisiting the serotonin-aggression relation in humans: A meta-analysis. *Psychological Bulletin,* 139, 1148–1172.

Duntley, J. D., & Shackelford, T. K. (eds.). (2008). *Evolutionary Forensic Psychology: Darwinian Foundations of Crime and Law.* Oxford: Oxford University Press.

Durkheim, E. (1984). *The Division of Labour in Society.* Basingstoke: Macmillan. (Original work published 1893).

Durrant, R. (2011). Collective violence: An evolutionary perspective. *Aggression and Violent Behavior,* 16, 428–436.

Durrant, R. (2016). Putting risk factors in their place: An evolutionary-developmental approach to understanding risk. *Psychology, Crime and Law,* 22, 17–32.

Durrant, R., Adamson, S., Todd, F., & Sellman, D. (2009). Drug use and addiction: An evolutionary perspective. *Australian and New Zealand Journal of Psychiatry,* 43, 1049–1056.

Durrant, R., & Ellis, B. J. (2013). Evolutionary psychology. In R. J. Nelson & S. J. Y. Mizumori (eds.), *Handbook of Psychology: Vol. 3. Behavioural Neuroscience* (2nd edition), (pp. 26–51). Hoboken, NJ: John Wiley & Sons.

Durrant, R., & Thakker, J. (2003). *Substance Use and Abuse: Cultural and Historical Perspectives.* Thousand Oaks, CA: Sage Publications.

Durrant, R., & Ward, T. (2011). Evolutionary explanations in the social and behavioural sciences: Introduction and overview. *Aggression and Violent Behaviour,* 16, 361–370.

Durrant, R., & Ward, T. (2012). The role of evolutionary explanations in criminology. *Journal of Philosophical and Theoretical Criminology,* 4, 1–37.

Durrant, R., & Ward, T. (2015). *Evolutionary Criminology: Toward a Comprehensive Explanation for Crime.* London: Academic Press.

Dutton, D. G., Boyanowsky, E. O., & Bond, M. H. (2005). Extreme mass homicide: From military massacre to genocide. *Aggression and Violent Behavior,* 10, 437–473.

Duwe, G., & King, M. (2012). Can faith-based correctional programs work? An outcome evaluation of the InnerChange freedom initiative in Minnesota. *International Journal of Offender Therapy and Comparative Criminology,* 57, 813–841.

Easton, S., & Piper, C. (2005). *Sentencing and Punishment: The Quest for Justice.* Oxford: Oxford University Press.

Eck, J. E. (2002). Preventing crime at places. In L. W. Sherman, D. P. Farrington, B. C. Welsh, & D. L. MacKenzie (eds.), *Evidence-Based Crime Prevention* (revised edition), (pp. 241–295). New York, NY: Routledge.

Edgar, K., O'Donnell, I., & Martin, C. (2004). *Prison Violence: The Dynamics of Conflict, Fear, and Power.* Cullompton: Willan Publishing.

Egger, S. A. (2002). *The Killers Among Us: An Examination of Serial Murder and Its Investigation.* Upper Saddle River, NJ: Prentice Hall.

Ehrensaft, M. K., Cohen, P., Brown, J., Smailes, E., Chen, H., & Johnson, J. G. (2003). Intergenerational transmission of partner violence: A 20-year prospective study. *Journal of Consulting and Clinical Psychology*, 71, 741–753.

Ehrlich, I. (1975). The deterrent effect of capital punishment: A question of life and death. *American Economic Review*, 65, 397–417.

Ehrlich, P. R., & Ehrlich, A. H. (2013). Can a collapse of global civilization be avoided? *Proceedings of the Royal Society of London B*, 280, 20122845.

Eisner, M. (2003). Long-term historical trends in violent crime. *Crime and Justice*, 30, 83–142.

Eisner, M. (2013). What causes large-scale variation in homicide rates? In H. Juergen & K. Henning (eds.), *Aggression in Humans and Other Primates* (pp. 137–162). Berlin: de Gruyter.

Eisner, M. (2014). From swords to words: Does macro-level change in self-control predict long-term variation in levels of homicide? *Crime and Justice*, 43, 65–134.

Ekblom, P. (2008). Designing products against crime. In R. Wortley & L. Mazerolle (eds.), *Environmental criminology and crime analysis* (pp. 195–217). Cullompton: Willan.

Elbogen, E. B., Dennis, P. A., & Johnson, S. C. (2016). Beyond mental illness: Targeting stronger and more direct pathways to violence. *Clinical Psychological Science*, 4, 747–759.

Elliott, M. C., Dupéré, V., & Leventhal, T. (2015). Neighborhood context and the development of criminal and antisocial behaviour. In J. Morizot & L. Kazemian (eds.), *The Development of Criminal and Antisocial Behaviour* (pp. 253–265). New York, NY: Springer.

Ellis, B. J., Volk, A. A., Gonzalez, J.-M., & Embry, D. D. (2016). The meaningful roles intervention: An evolutionary approach to reducing bullying and increasing prosocial behaviour. *Journal of Research on Adolescence*, 26, 622–637.

Ellis, L. (2005). A theory explaining biological correlates of criminality. *European Journal of Criminology*, 2, 287–315.

Ember, C. R., & Ember, M. (1996). Violence in the ethnographic record: Results of cross-cultural research on war and aggression. In D. L. Martin & D. W. Frayer (eds.), *Troubled Times: Violence and Warfare in the Past* (pp. 1–20). Amsterdam: Gordan and Breach Publishers.

Ennett, S. T., Tobler, N. S., Ringwalt, C. L., & Flewelling, R. L. (1994). How effective is Drug Abuse Resistance Education? A meta-analysis of Project DARE outcome evaluations. *American Journal of Public Health*, 84, 1394–1401.

Eriksson, L., & Mazerolle, P. (2013). A general strain theory of intimate partner homicide. *Aggression and Violent Behavior*, 18, 462–470.

Exum, M. L. (2006). Alcohol and aggression: An integration of findings from experimental studies. *Journal of Criminal Justice*, 34, 131–145.

Fagan, J. (2006). Death and deterrence redux: Science, law and causal reasoning on capital punishment. *Ohio State Journal of Criminal Law*, 4, 255–319.

Fahey, S., & LaFree, G. (2015). Does country-level social disorganization increase terrorist attacks? *Terrorism and Political Violence*, 27, 81–111.

Farrell, A. L., Keppel, R. D., & Titterington, V. B. (2011). Lethal ladies: Revisiting what we know about female serial murderers. *Homicide Studies*, 15, 228–252.

Farrell, A. L., Keppel, R. D., & Titterington, V. B. (2013). Testing existing classifications of serial murder considering gender: An exploratory analysis of solo female serial murderers. *Journal of Investigative Psychology and Offender Profiling*, 10, 268–288.

Farrell, G. (2015). Crime concentration theory. *Crime Prevention and Community Safety*, 17, 233–248.

Farrell, G., Tilley, N., & Tseloni, A. (2014). Why the crime drop? *Crime and Justice*, 43, 421–490.

Farrell, G., Tilley, N., Tseloni, A., & Mailley, J. (2010). Explaining and sustaining the crime drop: Clarifying the role of opportunity related theories. *Crime Prevention and Community Safety*, 12, 24–41.

Farrington, D. P. (1991). Childhood aggression and adult violence: Early precursors and later life outcomes. In D. J. Pepler & K. H. Rubin (eds.), *The Development and Treatment of Childhood Aggression* (pp. 5–25). Hillsdale, NJ: Lawrence Erlbaum.

Farrington, D. P. (2003). Developmental and life course criminology: Key theoretical and empirical issues – the 2002 Sutherland Award Address. *Criminology*, 41, 221–255.

Farrington, D. P. (2005). Childhood origins of antisocial behaviour. *Clinical Psychology and Psychotherapy*, 12, 177–190.

Farrington, D. P. (2006). Key longitudinal-experimental studies in criminology. *Journal of Experimental Criminology*, 2, 121–141.

Farrington, D. P. (2007). Family background and psychopathy. In C. J. Patrick (ed.). *Handbook of Psychopathy* (pp. 229–250). New York, NY: The Guilford Press.

Farrington, D. P. (2010a). Life-course and developmental theories in criminology. In E. McLaughlin & T. Newburn (eds.), *The Sage Handbook of Criminological Theory* (pp. 249–270). London: Sage Publications.

Farrington, D. P. (2010b). The developmental evidence base: Psychosocial research. In G. J. Towl & D. A. Crighton (eds.), *Forensic Psychology* (pp. 95–112). Chichester: John Wiley & Sons.

Farrington, D. P. (2015). The developmental evidence base: Psychosocial research. In D. A. Crighton & G. J. Towl (eds.), *Forensic Psychology* (2nd edition), (pp. 162–181). Hoboken, NJ: John Wiley & Sons.

Farrington, D. P., Jolliffe, D., Loeber, R., Southamer-Loeber, M., & Kalb, L. M. (2001). The concentration of offenders in families, and family criminality in the prediction of boys' delinquency. *Journal of Adolescence*, 24, 579–596.

Farrington, D. P., Piquero, A. R., & Jennings, W. G. (2013). *Offending from Childhood to Late Middle Age: Recent Results from the Cambridge Study in Delinquent Development.* New York, NY: Springer.

Farrington, D. P., Ttofi, M. M., & Lösel, F. A. (2016). Developmental and social prevention. In D. Weisburd, D. P. Farrington, & C. Gill (eds.), *What Works in Crime Prevention and Rehabilitation* (pp. 15–75). New York, NY: Springer.

Farrington, D. P., & Welsh, B. C. (2003). Family-based prevention of offending: A meta-analysis. *Australian and New Zealand Journal of Criminology*, 36, 127–145.

Farrington, D. P., & Welsh, B. C. (2007). *Saving Children from a Life of Crime: Early Risk Factors and Effective Interventions.* Oxford: Oxford University Press.

Fattore, L., & Melis, M. (2016). Sex differences in impulsive and compulsive behaviors: A focus on drug addiction. *Addiction Biology*, 21, 1043–1051.

Faulkner, J., Schaller, M., Park, J. H., & Duncan, L. A. (2004). Evolved disease-avoidance mechanisms and contemporary xenophobic attitudes. *Group Processes and Intergroup Relations*, 7, 333–353.

Fazel, S., & Danesh, J. (2002). Serious mental disorder in 23000 prisoners: A systematic review of 62 surveys. *The Lancet*, 359, 545–550.

Fazel, S., & Grann, M. (2006). The population impact of severe mental illness on violent crime. *American Journal of Psychiatry*, 163, 1397–1403.

Fazel, S., Långström, N., Hjern, A., Grann, M., & Lichtenstein, P. (2009). Schizophrenia, substance abuse, and violent crime. *The Journal of the American Medical Association*, 301, 2016–2023.

Federal Bureau of Investigation. (2006). *Terrorism 2002–2005.* U. S. Department of Justice. Retrieved from www.fbi.gov/stats-services/publications/terrorism-2002-2005 on February 14, 2012.

Felson, M. (2008). Routine activity approach. In R. Wortley & L. Mazzerolle (eds.), *Environmental Criminology and Crime Analysis* (pp. 70–76). Cullompton: Willan Publishing.

Felson, R. B. (2002). *Violence and Gender Re-Examined*. Washington, DC: American Psychological Association.

Felson, R. B., & Feld, S. L. (2009). When a man hits a woman: Moral evaluations and reporting violence to the police. *Aggressive Behavior*, 35, 477–488.

Ferguson, C. J. (2015). Do angry birds make for angry children? A meta-analysis of video game influences on children's and adolescents' aggression, mental health, prosocial behavior, and academic performance. *Perspectives on Psychological Science*, 10, 646–666.

Ferguson, C. J., Farza, A., Jerabeck, J., Ramos, R., & Fgalindo, M. (2013). Not worth the fuss after all? Cross-sectional and prospective data on violent video game influences on aggression, visuospatial cognition and mathematics ability in a sample of youth. *Journal of Youth and Adolescence*, 42, 109–122.

Ferguson, C. J., & Hartley, R. D. (2009). The pleasure in momentary … the expense damnable? The influence of pornography on rape and sexual assault. *Aggression and Violent Behavior*, 14, 323–329.

Ferguson, C. J., & Rueda, S. M. (2009). Examining the validity of the modified Taylor competitive reaction time test of aggression. *Journal of Experimental Criminology*, 5, 121–137.

Ferguson, R. B. (1996). Violence and war in prehistory. In D. L. Martin & D. W. Frayer (eds.), *Troubled Times: Violence and Warfare in the Past* (pp. 321–355). Amsterdam: Gordan and Breach Publishers.

Fergusson, D. M., Boden, J. M., & Horwood, J. (2015). From evidence to policy: Findings from the Christchurch health and development study. *Australian and New Zealand Journal of Criminology*, 48, 386–408.

Fergusson, D. M., & Horwood, L. J. (2000). Alcohol abuse and crime: A fixed-regression analysis. *Addiction*, 95, 1525–1536.

Fergusson, D. M., Horwood, L. J., & Ridder, E. M. (2005). Show me the child at seven II: Childhood intelligence and later outcomes in adolescence and young adulthood. *Journal of Child Psychology and Psychiatry*, 46, 850–858.

Fergusson, D. M., Swain-Campbell, N., & Horwood, J. (2004). How does childhood economic disadvantage lead to crime? *Journal of Child Psychology and Psychiatry*, 45, 956–966.

Finkel, N. J. (1995). *Commonsense Justice: Jurors' Notions of the Law*. Cambridge, MA: Harvard University Press.

Finkel, N. J., & Sales, B. D. (1997). Commonsense justice: Old roots, germinant ground, and new shoots. *Psychology, Public Policy and Law*, 3, 227–241.

Finkelhor, D. (1984). *Child Sexual Abuse: New Theory and Research*. New York, NY: Free Press.

Finneran, C., & Stephenson, R. (2012). Intimate partner violence among men who have sex with men: A systematic review. *Trauma, Violence, and Abuse*, 14, 168–185.

Fisher, P. A., Beauchamp, K. G., Roos, L. E., Noll, L. K., Flannery, J., & Delker, B. C. (2016). The neurobiology of intervention and prevention in early diversity. *Annual Review of Clinical Psychology*, 12, 331–357.

Flatley, J. (2015). *Crime in England and Wales: Year Ending June 2015*. Retrieved from www.ons.gov.uk/peoplepopulationandcommunity/crimeandjustice/bulletins/crimeinengland andwales/2015-10-15#robbery.

Flatley, J. (2016a). *Crime in England and Wales: Year Ending June 2016*. Office for National Statistics. Retrieved from www.ons.gov.uk/peoplepopulationandcommunity/crimeandjustice/ bulletins/crimeinenglandandwales/yearendingjune2016.

Flatley, J. (2016b). *Experimental Statistics 1: New Data on Police Recorded Violent and Sexual Offences, Year Ending March 2015*. Office for National Statistics. Retrieved from www.ons.gov.uk/peoplepopulationandcommunity/crimeandjustice/compendium/focuson

violentcrimeandsexualoffences/yearendingmarch2016experimentalstatisticsvictimsofpolice recordedviolentandsexualoffences.

Flatley, J. (2016c). *Focus on Violent Crime and Sexual Offences: Year Ending 2015*. Office for National Statistics. Retrieved from www.ons.gov.uk/peoplepopulationandcommunity/crimeandjustice/compendium/focusonviolentcrimeandsexualoffences/yearendingmarch2015.

Flatley, J., Kershaw, C., Smith, K., Chaplin, R., & Moon, D. (2010). *Crime in England and Wales 2009–2010. Findings from the British Crime Survey and Police Recorded Crime*. London: Home Office.

Fletcher, G. J. O., Simpson, J. A., Campbell, L., & Overall, N. C. (2015). Pair-bonding, romantic love, and evolution: The curious case of Homo sapiens. *Perspectives on Psychological Science*, 10, 20–36.

Flood-Page, C., Campbell, S., Harrington, V., & Miller, J. (2000). *Youth Crime: Findings from the 1998/1999 Youth Lifestyles Survey*. London: Home Office.

Flynn, A., & Graham, K. (2010). 'Why did it happen?' A review and conceptual framework for research on perpetrators' and victims' explanations for intimate partner violence. *Aggression and Violent Behavior*, 15, 239–251.

Flynn, C., & Heitzmann, D. (2008). Tragedy at Virginia Tech: Trauma and its aftermath. *The Counselling Psychologist*, 36, 479–489.

Foster, H., & Brooks-Gunn, J. (2013). Neighborhood influences on antisocial behaviour during childhood and adolescence. In C. L. Gibson & M. D. Krohn (eds.), *Handbook of Life Course Criminology: Emerging Trends and Direction for Future Research* (pp. 69–90). New York, NY: Springer.

Fotaine, R. G., & Dodge, K. A. (2006). Real-time decision making and aggressive behaviour in youth: A heuristic model of response evaluation and decision (RED). *Aggressive Behavior*, 32, 604–624.

Fox, B. H., Farrington, D. P., & Ttofi, M. M. (2012). Successful bullying prevention programs: Influence of research design, implementation features, and program components. *International Journal of Conflict and Violence*, 6, 273–283.

Fox, J. A., & DeLateur, M. J. (2014). Mass shootings in America: Moving beyond Newtown. *Homicide Studies*, 18, 125–145.

Fox, J. A., & Levin, J. (2005). *Extreme Killing: Understanding Serial and Mass Murder*. Thousand Oaks, CA: Sage Publications.

Freilich, J. D., & LaFree, G. (2015). Criminological theory and terrorism: Introduction to the special issue. *Terrorism and Political Violence*, 27, 1–8.

Frick, P. J., & Nigg, J. T. (2012). Current issues in the diagnosis of attention deficit hyperactivity disorder, oppositional defiant disorder, and conduct disorder. *Annual Review of Clinical Psychology*, 8, 77–107.

Frick, P. J., Ray, J. V., Thornton, L. C., & Kahn, R. E. (2014a). Annual research review: A developmental psychopathology approach to understanding callous-unemotional traits in children and adolescents with serious conduct problems. *Journal of Child Psychology and Psychiatry*, 55, 532–548.

Frick, P. J., Ray, J. V., Thornton, L. C., & Kahn, R. E. (2014b). Can callous-unemotional traits enhance the understanding, diagnosis, and treatment of serious conduct problems in children and adolescents? A comprehensive review. *Psychological Bulletin*, 140, 1–57.

Fry, D. P. (2007). *Beyond War: The Human Potential for Peace*. Oxford: Oxford University Press.

Funder, D. C. (2001). Personality. *Annual Review of Psychology*, 52, 197–221.

Funder, D. C. (2004). *The Personality Puzzle* (3rd edition). New York, NY: W. W. Norton and Company.

Gable, R. S. (2004). Comparison of acute lethal toxicity of commonly abused psychoactive substances. *Addiction*, 99, 686–696.

Gailliot, M. T., & Baumeister, R. F. (2007). The physiology of willpower: Linking blood glucose to self-control. *Personality and Social Psychology Review*, 11, 303–327.

Gajos, J. M., Fagan, A. A., & Beaver, K. M. (2016). Use of genetically informed evidence-based prevention science to understand and prevent crime and related behavioral disorders. *Criminology and Public Policy*, 15, 683–701.

Galvan, A. (2013). The teenage brain: Sensitivity to rewards. *Current Directions in Psychological Science*, 22, 88–93.

Gangestad, S. W., & Simpson, J. A. (2007). Whither science of the evolution of mind? In S. W. Gangestad & J. A. Simpson (eds.), *The Evolution of Mind: Fundamental Questions and Controversies* (pp. 397–437). New York, NY: Guilford Press.

Gannon, T. A. (2009). Social cognition in violent and sexual offending: An overview. *Psychology, Crime and Law*, 15, 97–118.

Gannon, T. A. (2016). Explanations of firesetting: Typologies and theories. In T. Gannon, G. Dickens, & R. M. Doley (eds.), *The Psychology of Arson: A Practical Guide to Understanding and Managing Deliberate Firesetters* (pp. 23–34). London: Routledge.

Gannon, T. A., & Barrowcliffe, E. (2012). Firesetting in the general population: The development and validation of the fire setting and fire proclivity scales. *Legal and Criminological Psychology*, 17, 105–122.

Gannon, T. A., Collie, R. M., Ward, T., & Thakker, J. (2008). Rape: Psychopathology, theory and treatment. *Clinical Psychology Review*, 28, 982–1008.

Gannon, T. A., Ó Ciardha, C., Doley, R. M., & Alleyne, E. (2012). The multi-trajectory theory of adult firesetting (M-TTAF). *Aggression and Violent Behavior*, 17, 107–121.

Gannon, T. A., & Pina, A. (2010). Firesetting: Psychopathology, theory and treatment. *Aggression and Violent Behavior*, 15, 224–238.

Gannon, T. A., Ward, T., & Collie, R. (2007). Cognitive distortions in child molesters: Theoretical and research developments over the past two decades. *Aggression and Violent Behavior*, 12, 402–416.

Gardner, H. (1983). *Frames of Mind: The Theory of Multiple Intelligences*. London: Fontana Press.

Gardner, M., & Steinberg, L. (2005). Peer influence on risk taking, risk preference, and risky decision making in adolescence and adulthood: An experimental study. *Developmental Psychology*, 41, 625–635.

Gat, A. (1999). The pattern of fighting in simple, small-scale, prestate societies. *Journal of Anthropological Research*, 55, 563–583.

Gat, A. (2006). *War in Human Civilization*. Oxford: Oxford University Press.

Gat, A. (2009). So why do people fight? Evolutionary theory and the causes of war. *European Journal of International Relations*, 15, 571–599.

Gat, A. (2015). Proving communal warfare among hunter-gatherers: The quasi-Rousseauan error. *Evolutionary Anthropology*, 24, 111–126.

Geary, D. C. (2000). Evolution and proximate expression of human paternal investment. *Psychological Bulletin*, 126, 55–77.

Gelles, R. J. (2007). Family violence. In D. J. Flannery, A. T. Vazsonyi, & I. D. Walman (eds.), *Cambridge Handbook of Violent Behaviour* (pp. 403–417). Leiden: Cambridge University Press.

Gendreau, P., Goggin, C., Cullen, F. T., & Andrews, D. A. (2001). The effects of community sanctions and incarceration on recidivism. *Compendium 2000 on Effective Correctional Programming*. Ottawa: Correctional Services Canada.

Giancola, P. R. (2000). Executive functioning: A conceptual framework for alcohol-related aggression. *Experimental and Clinical Psychopharmacology*, 8, 576–597.

Giancola, P. R. (2002). Irritability, acute alcohol consumption and aggressive behaviour in men and women. *Drug and Alcohol Dependence*, 68, 263–274.

Giancola, P. R. (2013). Alcohol and aggression: Theories and mechanisms. In M. McMurran (ed.), *Alcohol-Related Violence: Prevention and Treatment* (pp. 19–34). Chichester: Wiley.

Giancola, P. R., Josephs, R. A., Parrott, D. J., & Duke, A. D. (2010). Alcohol myopia revisited: Clarifying aggression and other acts of disinhibition through a distorted lens. *Perspectives on Psychological Science*, 5, 265–278.

Gilbert, R., Widom, C. P., Browne, K., Fergusson, D., Webb, E., & Janson, S. (2009). Burden and consequences of child maltreatment in high-income countries. *Lancet*, 373, 68–81.

Gill, C. (2016). Community interventions. In D. Weisburd, D. P. Farrington, & C. Gill (eds.), *What Works in Crime Prevention and Rehabilitation* (pp. 77–109). New York, NY: Springer.

Gill, M., & Goldstraw-White, J. (2010). Theft and fraud by employees. In F. Brookman, M. Maguire, H. Pierpoint, & T. Bennett (eds.), *Handbook on Crime* (pp. 100–119). Cullompton: Willan Publishing.

Ginges, J., Hansen, I., & Norenzayan, A. (2009). Religion and support for suicide attacks. *Psychological Science*, 20, 224–230.

Glenn, A. L., Johnson, A. K., & Raine, A. (2013). Antisocial personality disorder: A current review. *Current Psychiatry Reports*, 15, 1–8.

Glenn, A. L., Kurzban, R., & Raine, A. (2011). Evolutionary theory and psychopathy. *Aggression and Violent Behavior*, 16, 371–380.

Glick, A. R. (2015). The role of serotonin in impulsive aggression, suicide, and homicide in adolescents and adults: A literature review. *International Journal of Adolescent Medical Health*, 27, 143–150.

Global Commission on Drug Policy. (2016). *Advancing Drug Policy Reform: A New Approach to Decriminalization*. Retrieved from www.globalcommissionondrugs.org/reports/advancing-drug-policy-reform on February 1, 2017.

Glowacki, L., & Wrangham, R. W. (2013). The role of rewards in motivating participation in simple warfare. *Human Nature*, 24, 444–460.

God ordered Dixon 'to chop off heads'. (2005, March 5). *The Christchurch Press*, p. 17.

Goetz, A. T., Shackelford, T. K., & Camilleri, J. A. (2008). Proximate and ultimate explanations are required for a comprehensive understanding of partner rape. *Aggression and Violent Behavior*, 13, 119–123.

Goldhagen, D. J. (1996). *Hitler's Willing Executioners: Ordinary Germans and the Holocaust*. London: Abacus.

Goldhagen, D. J. (2009). *Worse than War: Genocide, Eliminationism, and the Ongoing Assault on Humanity*. New York, NY: Public Affairs.

Goldstein, E. B. (2005). *Cognitive Psychology: Connecting Mind, Research, and Everyday Experience*. Belmont, CA: Thomson/Wadsworth.

Goldstein, P. J. (1985). The drugs/violence nexus: A tripartite conceptual framework. *Journal of Drug Issues*, 39, 143–174.

Goldstein, P. J., Brownstein, H. H., Ryan, P. J., & Bellucci, P. A. (1997). Crack and homicide in New York City: A case study in the epidemiology of violence. In C. Reinarman & H. G. Levine (eds.), *Crack in America: Demon Drugs and Social Justice* (pp. 113–130). Berkeley, CA: University of California Press.

Golub, A., & Johnson, B. D. (2004). How much do Manhattan-arrestees spend on drugs? *Drug and Alcohol Dependence*, 76, 235–246.

Gossop, M., Marsden, J., Stewart, D., & Kidd, T. (2003). The National Treatment Outcomes Research Study (NTORS): 4–5 year follow-up results. *Addiction*, 98, 291–303.

Gottfredson, G. D., & Gottfredson, D. C. (2007). School violence. In D. J. Flannery, A. T. Vazsonyi, & I. D. Walman (eds.), *Cambridge Handbook of Violent Behaviour* (pp. 344–358). Leiden: Cambridge University Press.

Gottfredson, M. R., & Hirschi, T. (1990). *A General Theory of Crime*. Palo Alto, CA: Stanford University Press.

Gottschall, J. A., & Gottschall, T. A. (2003). Are per-incident rape-pregnancy rates higher than per-incident consensual pregnancy rates? *Human Nature*, 14, 1–20.

Gotzsche-Astrup, O., & Moskowitz, A. (2016). Personality disorders in the DSM–5: Scientific and extra-scientific factors in the maintenance of the status quo. *Australian and New Zealand Journal of Psychiatry*, 50, 119–127.

Gowlett, J. A. J. (2016). The discovery of fire by humans: A long and convoluted process. *Philosophical Transactions of the Royal Society of London B*, 371, 20150164.

Green, A. E., Gesten, E. L., Greenwald, M. A., & Salcedo, O. (2008). Predicting delinquency in adolescence and young adulthood: A longitudinal analysis of early risk factors. *Youth Violence and Juvenile Justice*, 6, 323–342.

Green, A. I., Drake, R. E., Brunette, M. F., & Noordsy, D. L. (2007). Schizophrenia and co-occurring substance use disorder. *American Journal of Psychiatry*, 164, 402–408.

Green, D. A. (2007). Comparing penal cultures: Child-on-child homicide in England and Norway. *Crime and Justice: A Review of Research*, 36, 591–643.

Green, D. A. (2008). Suitable vehicles: Framing blame and justice when children kill a child. *Crime, Media and Culture*, 4, 197–220.

Griffin, T., & Stitt, B. G. (2010). Random activities theory: The case for 'black swan' criminology. *Critical Criminology*, 18, 57–72.

Griffiths, R. (2016). Criminalising bribery in a corporate world. *Current Issues in Criminal Justice*, 27, 251–268.

Gromet, D. M., & Darley, J. M. (2006). Restoration and retribution: How including retributive components affects the acceptability of restorative justice procedures. *Social Justice Research*, 19, 395–432.

Grossman, L. C. D. (1995). *On Killing: The Psychological Costs of Learning to Kill in War and Society*. New York, NY: Back Bay Books.

Guo, G. (2011). Gene-environment interactions for delinquency: Promises and pitfalls. In K. A. Dodge & M. Rutter (eds.), *Gene-Environment Interactions in Developmental Psychopathology* (pp. 121–139). New York, NY: Guilford Press.

Haapasalo, J., & Pokela, E. (1999). Child-rearing and child abuse antecedents of criminality. *Aggression and Violent Behavior*, 4, 107–127.

Haas, H., Farrington, D. P., Killias, M., & Sattar, G. (2004). The impact of different family configurations on delinquency. *British Journal of Criminology*, 44, 520–532.

Hagan, J., & Dinovitzer, R. (1999). Collateral consequences of imprisonment for children, communities, and prisoners. *Crime and Justice*, 26, 121–162.

Hagan, J., Rymond-Richmond, W., & Parker, P. (2005). The criminology of genocide: The death and rape of Darfur. *Criminology*, 43, 525–562.

Hair, E. C., Moore, K. A., Garrett, S. B., Ling, T., & Cleveland, K. (2008). The continued importance of quality parent–adolescent relationships during late adolescence. *Journal of Research on Adolescence*, 18, 187–200.

Hald, G. M., & Malamuth, N. N. (2015). Experimental effects of exposure to pornography: The moderating effect of personality and mediating effect of sexual arousal. *Archives of Sexual Behavior*, 44, 99–109.

Hald, G. M., Malamuth, N. M., & Yuen, C. (2010). Pornography and attitudes supporting violence against women: Revisiting the relationship in nonexperimental studies. *Aggressive Behavior*, 36, 14–20.

Hald, G. M., Seaman, C., & Linz, D. (2014). Sexuality and pornography. In D. L. Tolman & L. M. Diamond (eds.), *APA Handbook of Sexuality and Psychology* (Vol. 2, pp. 3–35). Washington, DC: American Psychological Association.

Hall, G. C. N., & Hirschman, R. (1991). Toward a theory of sexual aggression: A quadripartite model. *Journal of Consulting and Clinical Psychology*, 59, 662–669.

Hall, G. C. N., & Hirschman, R. (1992). Sexual aggression against children: A conceptual perspective of etiology. *Criminal Justice and Behaviour*, 19, 8–23.

Hall, W. (2016). Alcohol and cannabis: Comparing their adverse health effects and regulatory regimes. *International Journal of Drug Policy*. Advance online publication. DOI: 10.1016/j.drugpo.2016.10.021.

Hallsworth, S., & Young, T. (2010). Street collectives and group delinquency: Social disorganization, subcultures and beyond. In E. McLaughlin & T. Newburn (eds.), *The Sage Handbook of Criminological Theory* (pp. 72–95). London: Sage Publications.

Hammersley, R., Forsyth, A., Morrison, V., & Davies, J. B. (1989). The relationship between crime and opioid use. *Addiction*, 84, 1029–1043.

Haney, C. (2003). Mental health issues in long-term solitary and 'supermax' confinement. *Crime and Delinquency*, 49, 124–156.

Haney, C. (2005). The contextual revolution in psychology and the question of prison effects. In A. Liebling & S. Maruna (eds.), *The Effects of Imprisonment* (pp. 66–93). Cullompton: Willan Publishing.

Haney, C., & Zimbardo, P. (1998). The past and future of U.S. prison policy: Twenty-five years after the Stanford prison experiment. *American Psychologist*, 53, 709–724.

Hanson, R. K., Gordon, A., Harris, A. J. R., Marques, J. K., Murphy, W., Quinsey, V. L., & Seto, M. C. (2002). First report of the collaborative outcome data project on the effectiveness of psychological treatment for sex offenders. *Sexual Abuse: A Journal of Research and Treatment*, 14, 169–194.

Hare, R. D. (1996). Psychopathy: A clinical construct whose time has come. *Criminal Justice and Behavior*, 23, 25–54.

Hare, R. D. (1999). Psychopathy as a risk factor for violence. *Psychiatric Quarterly*, 7, 181–197.

Hare, R. D. (2001). Psychopaths and their nature: Some implications for understanding human predatory violence. In A. Raine & J. Sanmartin (eds.), *Violence and Psychopathy* (pp. 5–34). New York, NY: Kluwer Academic/Plenum Publishers.

Hare, R. D., Clark, D., Grann, M., & Thornton, D. (2000). Psychopathy and the predictive validity of the PCL-R: An international perspective. *Behavioral Sciences and the Law*, 18, 623–645.

Harris, G. T., Hilton, N. Z., Rice, M. E., & Eke, A. W. (2007). Children killed by genetic parents versus stepparents. *Evolution and Human Behavior*, 28, 85–95.

Harris, G. T., & Rice, M. E. (2007). Treatment of psychopathy: A review of empirical findings. In C. J. Patrick (ed.). *Handbook of Psychopathy* (pp. 555–572). New York, NY: The Guilford Press.

Harrison, M. A., & Bowers, T. G. (2010). Autogenic massacre as maladaptive response to status threat. *The Journal of Forensic Psychiatry and Psychology*, 21, 916–932.

Harrison, M. A., Murphy, E. A., Ho, L. Y., Bowers, T. G., & Flaherty, C. V. (2015). Female serial killers in the United States: Means, motives, and makings. *The Journal of Forensic Psychiatry and Psychology*, 26, 383–406.

Hart, C., de Vet, R., Moran, P., Hatch, S. L., & Dean, K. (2012). A UK population-based study of the relationship between mental disorder and victimisation. *Social Psychiatry and Psychiatric Epidemiology*, 47, 1581–1590.

Hart, S. D., & Hare, R. D. (1997). Psychopathy: Assessment and association with criminal conduct. In D. M. Stoff, J. Breiling, & J. D. Maser (eds.), *Handbook of Antisocial Behavior* (pp. 22–35). New York, NY: John Wiley & Sons.

Hasan, Y., Bégue, L., Scharkow, M., & Bushman, B. J. (2013). The more you play, the more aggressive you become: A long-term experimental study of cumulative violent video game effects on hostile expectations and aggressive behavior. *Journal of Experimental Social Psychology*, 49, 224–227.

Hasin, D., Hatzenbuehler, M., & Waxman, R. (2006). Genetics of substance use disorders. In R. Miller & K. M. Carroll (eds.), *Rethinking Substance Abuse: What the Science Shows, And What We Should Do About It* (pp. 61–81). New York, NY: The Guilford Press.

Haslam, N. (2006). Dehumanization: An integrative review. *Personality and Social Psychology Review*, 10, 252–264.

Haslam, N., & Stratemeyer, M. (2016). Recent research on dehumanization. *Current Opinion in Psychology*, 11, 25–29.

Hatzfeld, J. (2005). *A Time for Machetes: The Rwandan Genocide: The Killers Speak.* London: Serpent's Tail.

Heath, D. B. (2000). *Drinking Occasions: Comparative Perspectives on Alcohol and Culture.* Ann Arbor, MI: Brunner/Mazel, Taylor & Francis Group.

Helmus, L., Hanson, R. K., Babchishin, K. M., & Mann, R. E. (2013). Attitudes supportive of sexual offending predict recidivism: A meta-analysis. *Trauma, Violence & Abuse*, 14, 34–53.

Henrich, J. (2006, April 7). Cooperation, punishment, and the evolution of human institutions. *Science*, 312, 60–61.

Henrich, J. (2016). *The Secret of Our Success: How Culture is Driving Human Evolution, Domesticating Our Species, and Making Us Smarter.* Princeton, NJ: Princeton University Press.

Henrich, J., McElreath, R., Barr, A., Ensminger, J., Barrett, C., Bolyanatyz, A., … Ziker, J. (2006, June 23). Costly punishment across human societies. *Science*, 312, 1767–1770.

Hesselbrock, V. N., & Hesselbrock, M. N. (2006). Developmental perspectives on the risk for developing substance abuse problems. In W. R. Miller & K. M. Carroll (eds.), *Rethinking Substance Abuse: What the Science Shows, and What We Should Do About It* (pp. 97–114). New York, NY: The Guilford Press.

Hickey, E. W. (2002). *Serial Murderers and Their Victims.* Belmont, CA: Wadsworth.

Hiday, V. A. (1997). Understanding the connection between mental illness and violence. *International Journal of Law and Psychiatry*, 20, 399–417.

Hiday, V. A. (2006). Putting community risk in perspective: A look at correlations, causes and controls. *International Journal of Law and Psychiatry*, 29, 316–331.

Higgins, P., Short, D., & South, N. (2013). Protecting the planet: A proposal for a law of ecocide. *Crime, Law, and Social Change*, 59, 251–266.

Hilal, S. M., Densley, J. A., Li, S. D., & Ma, Y. (2014). The routine of mass murder in China. *Homicide Studies*, 18, 83–104.

Hill, P. (2014). The Japanese Yakuza. In L. Paoli (ed.), *The Oxford Handbook of Organised Crime* (pp. 234–253). Oxford: Oxford University Press.

Hirschi, T. (1969). *Causes of Delinquency.* Berkeley, CA: University of California Press.

Hirschi, T., & Gottfredson, M. (1983). Age and the explanation of crime. *American Journal of Sociology*, 89, 552–584.

Hirtenlehner, H., & Hardie, B. (2016). On the conditional relevance of controls: An application of situational action theory to shoplifting. *Deviant Behavior*, 37, 315–331.

Hitchcock, T., & Shoemaker, R. (2006). *Tales from the Hanging Court.* London: Hodder Arnold.

Hoaken, P. N. S., & Stewart, S. H. (2003). Drugs of abuse and the elicitation of human aggressive behaviour. *Addictive Behaviors*, 28, 1533–1554.

Hodgins, S. (2008). Criminality among persons with severe mental illness. In K. Soothill, P. Rogers, & M. Dolan (eds.), *Handbook of Forensic Mental Health* (pp. 400–422). Cullompton: Willan Publishing.

Hodgkinson, T., Andresen, M. A., & Farrell, G. (2016). The decline and locational shift of automotive theft: A local level analysis. *Journal of Criminal Justice*, 44, 49–57.

Hoffman, M. B. (2014). *The Punisher's Brain: The Evolution of Judge and Jury.* New York, NY: Cambridge University Press.

Hogg, M. A., & Abrams, D. (2003). Intergroup behavior and social identity. In M. A. Hogg & J. Cooper (eds.), *The Sage Handbook of Social Psychology* (pp. 407–431). London: Sage Publications.

Holligan, C. (2015). Breaking the code of the street: Extending Elijah Anderson's encryption of violent street governance to retaliation in Scotland. *Journal of Youth Studies,* 18, 634–648.

Hollin, C. R. (1999). Treatment programs for offenders: Meta-analysis, 'what works', and beyond. *International Journal of Law and Psychiatry,* 22, 361–372.

Hollin, C. R. (2006). Offending behaviour programmes and contention: Evidence-based practice, manuals, and programme evaluation. In C. R. Hollin & E. J. Palmer (eds.), *Offending Behaviour Programmes: Development, Application and Controversies.* New York, NY: John Wiley & Sons.

Hollin, C. R. (2013). *Psychology and Crime: An Introduction to Criminological Psychology.* New York, NY: Routledge.

Hollin, C. R., Hatcher, R. M., & Palmer, E. J. (2010). Sexual offences against adults. In F. Brookman, M. Maguire, H. Pierpoint, & T. Bennett (eds.), *Handbook on Crime* (pp. 505–524). Cullompton: Willan Publishing.

Holloway, K., & Bennett, T. (2004). *The Results of the First Two Years of the NEW-ADAM programme.* London: Home Office.

Holmes, R., & Holmes, S. T. (1992). Understanding mass murder: A starting point. *Federal Probation,* 56, 53–61.

Hood, R. (2001). Capital punishment: A global perspective. *Punishment and Society,* 3, 331–354.

Horgan, J. (2008). From profiles to pathways and roots to routes: Perspectives from psychology on radicalization into terrorism. *The Annals of the American Academy of Political and Social Science,* 618, 80–94.

Howard, A. (2010). A timeline of serial killers. In J. M. Doris (ed.). *Serial Killers: Being and Killing.* Chichester: Wiley-Blackwell.

Huang, Y., Kotov, R., de Girolamo, G., Preti, A., Angermeyer, M., Benjet, C., … Kessler, R. C. (2009). DSM-IV personality disorders in the WHO world mental health surveys. *British Journal of Psychiatry,* 195, 46–53.

Hudson, B. A. (1996). *Understanding Justice: An Introduction to Ideas, Perspectives and Controversies in Modern Penal Theory.* Buckingham: Open University Press.

Hudson, S. M., Wales, D. S., Bakker, L., & Ward, T. (2002). Dynamic risk factors: The Kia Marama evaluation. *Sexual Abuse: A Journal of Research and Treatment,* 14, 103–119.

Hudson, S. M., Wales, D. S., & Ward, T. (1998). Kia Marama: A treatment program for child molesters in New Zealand. In W. Marshall et al. (eds.), *Sourcebook of Treatment Programs for Sexual Offenders.* New York, NY: Plenum Press.

Huesmann, L. R. (1988). An information processing model for the development of aggression. *Aggressive Behavior,* 14, 13–24.

Huesmann, L. R. (1998). The role of social information processing and cognitive schema in the acquisition and maintenance of habitual aggressive behaviour. In R. G. Green & E. Donnerstein (eds.), *Human Aggression: Theories, Research, and Implications for Social Policy* (pp. 73–105). San Diego, CA: Academic Press.

Huesmann, L. R. (2007). The impact of electronic media violence: Scientific theory and research. *Journal of Adolescent Health,* 41, S6–S13.

Huesmann, L. R., Eron, L. D., Lefkowitz, M. M., & Walder, L. O. (1984). The stability of aggression over time and generations. *Developmental Psychology,* 20, 1120–1134.

Huff-Corzine, L., McCutcheon, J. C., Corzine, J., Jarvis, J. P., Tetzlaff-Bemiller, M. J., Weller, M., & Landon, M. (2014). Shooting for accuracy: Comparing data sources on mass murder. *Homicide Studies,* 18, 105–124.

Huss, M. T. (2009). *Forensic Psychology: Research, Clinical Practice, and Applications.* Chichester: Wiley-Blackwell.

Imogen, N. (2011, June 28). Kahui twins' brain injuries 'extensive'. *The Press,* p. 5.

Indermaur, D. (2006). Changing attitudes to the death penalty: An Australian perspective. *Current Issues in Criminal Justice*, 17, 444–450.

Indig, D., Gear, C., & Wilhelm, K. (2016). *Comorbid Substance Use Disorders and Mental Health Disorders Among New Zealand Prisoners.* Wellington: New Zealand Department of Corrections.

Inglehart, R. F., Puranen, B., & Welzel, C. (2015). Declining willingness to fight for one's country: The individual-level basis of the long peace. *Journal of Peace Research*, 52, 418–434.

Ingram, J. R., Patchin, J. W., Huebner, B. M. McCluskey, J. D., & Bynum, T. S. (2007). Parents, friends, and serious delinquency: An examination of direct and indirect effects among at-risk early adolescents. *Criminal Justice Review*, 32, 380–400.

Intergovernmental Panel on Climate Change. (2015). *Climate Change 2014: Synthesis Report.* Retrieved from www.ipcc.ch/report/ar5/syr.

International Humanitarian Law (2012). Retrieved from www.icrc.org/ihl.nsf/full/357?Open Document on February 6, 2012.

Irwin, J., & Owen, B. (2005). Harm and the contemporary prison. In A. Liebling & S. Maruna (eds.), *The Effects of Imprisonment* (pp. 94–117). Cullompton: Willan Publishing.

Ishikawa, S., & Raine, A. (2003). Prefrontal deficits and antisocial behaviour. In B. Lahey, T. Moffitt, & A. Caspi (eds.), *Causes of conduct disorder and juvenile delinquency* (pp. 277–304). New York, NY: Guilford Press.

Itzin, C. (2002). Pornography and the construction of misogyny. *The Journal of Sexual Aggression*, 8, 4–42.

Jackson, L. E., & Gaertner, L. (2010). Mechanisms of moral disengagement and their differential use by right-wing authoritarianism and social dominance orientation in support of war. *Aggressive Behaviour*, 36, 238–250.

Jacobs, B. A., & Wright, R. (1999). Stick-up, street culture, and offender motivation. *Criminology*, 37, 149–173.

Jacobs, B. A., & Wright, R. (2008). Moralistic street robbery. *Crime and Delinquency*, 54, 511–531.

Jacobs, D., & Richardson, A. M. (2008). Income inequality and homicide in the developed nations from 1975–1995. *Homicide Studies*, 12, 28–45.

Jefferson, T. (2010). Psychosocial criminology. In E. McLaughlin & T. Newburn (eds.), *The SAGE Handbook of Criminological Theory* (pp. 284–302). Los Angeles, CA: Sage Publications.

Jenkins, P. (1999). *Synthetic Panics.* New York, NY: New York University Press.

Jenkins, J. E., & Zunguze, S. T. (1998). The relationship of family structure to adolescent drug use, peer affiliation, and perception of peer acceptance of drug use. *Adolescence*, 33, 811–822.

Jespersen, A. F., Lalumière, M. L., & Seto, M. C. (2009). Sexual abuse history among adult sex offenders and non-sex offenders: A meta-analysis. *Child Abuse and Neglect*, 33, 179–192.

Johnson, B. R. (2013). Religious participation and criminal behaviour. In J. A. Humphrey & P. Cordella (eds.), *Effective Interventions in the Lives of Criminal Offenders* (pp. 3–18). New York, NY: Springer.

Johnson, H. (2006). Factors associated with drug and alcohol dependence among women in prison. *Trends and Issues in Crime and Criminal Justice* (318).

Johnson, H., & Hotton, T. (2003). Losing control: Homicide risk in estranged and intact intimate relationships. *Homicide Studies*, 7, 58–84.

Johnson, M. P. (2006). Conflict and control: Gender symmetry and asymmetry in domestic violence. *Violence Against Women*, 12, 1003–1018.

Johnson, M. P. (2008). *A Typology of Domestic Violence: Intimate Terrorism, Violent Resistance, and Situational Couple Violence.* Boston, MA: Northeastern University Press.

Johnson, M. P. (2011). Gender and types of intimate partner violence: A response to an anti-feminist literature review. *Aggression and Violent Behavior*, 16, 289–296.

Jolliffe, D., & Farrington, D. P. (2004). Empathy and offending: A systematic review and meta-analysis. *Aggression and Violent Behaviour*, 9, 441–476.

Jolliffe, D., & Farrington, D. P. (2007). Examining the relationship between low empathy and self-reported offending. *Legal and Criminological Psychology*, 12, 265–287.

Jones, A. (2011). *Genocide: A Comprehensive Introduction* (2nd edition). London: Routledge.

Jones, D. W. (2008). *Understanding Criminal Behaviour: Psychosocial Approaches to Criminality*. Cullompton: Willan Publishing.

Jordan, J. (2012). Silencing rape, silencing women. In M. Brown & S. L. Wallklate (eds.), *Handbook on Sexual Violence* (pp. 253–286). New York, NY: Routledge.

Jorm, A. F., Reavley, N. J., & Ross, A. M. (2012). Belief in the dangerousness of people with mental disorders: A review. *Australian and New Zealand Journal of Psychiatry*, 46, 1029–1045.

Joseph, J., & Crichlow, W. (eds.). (2015). *Alternative Offender Rehabilitation and Social Justice: Arts and Physical Engagement in Criminal Justice and Community Settings*. New York, NY: Springer.

Jost, J. T. (2006). The end of ideology. *American Psychologist*, 61, 651–670.

Juby, H., & Farrington, D. P. (2001). Disentangling the link between disrupted families and delinquency. *British Journal of Criminology*, 41, 22–40.

Julien, R. M. (1998). *A Primer of Drug Action* (8th edition). New York, NY: W. H. Freeman and Company.

Juvonen, J., & Graham, S. (2014). Bullying in schools: The power of bullies and the plight of victims. *Annual Review of Psychology*, 65, 159–185.

Kanazawa, S. (2008). Theft. In J. Duntley & T. K. Shackelford (eds.), *Evolutionary Forensic Psychology* (pp. 160–175). New York, NY: Oxford University Press.

Kay, M. (2002, September 10). Killer had daily welfare contact. *The Dominion Post*, p. 1.

Kazemian, L. (2015). Desistance from crime and antisocial behaviour. In J. Morizot & L. Kazemian (eds.), *The Development of Criminal and Antisocial Behaviour* (pp. 295–312). New York, NY: Springer.

Keeley, L. H. (1996). *War Before Civilization: The Myth of the Peaceful Savage*. New York, NY: Oxford University Press.

Keers, R., Ullrich, S., DeStavola, B. L., & Coid, J. W. (2014). Association of violence with emergence of persecutory delusions in untreated schizophrenia. *American Journal of Psychiatry*, 171, 332–339.

Kelling, G. (2015). An author's brief history of an idea. *Journal of Research in Crime and Delinquency*, 52, 626–629.

Kelly, L. (1988). *Surviving Sexual Violence*. Cambridge: Polity.

Kelly, R. C. (2000). *Warless Societies and the Origin of War*. Ann Arbor, MI: The University of Michigan Press.

Keown, K., Gannon, T. A., & Ward, T. (2008). What were they thinking? An exploration of child sex offenders' beliefs using a lexical decision task. *Psychology, Crime & Law*, 14, 317–337.

Keown, K., Gannon, T. A., & Ward, T. (2010). What's in a measure? A multi-method study of child sexual offenders' beliefs. *Psychology, Crime & Law*, 16, 125–143.

Kerig, P. K., & Becker, S. P. (2015). Early abuse and neglect as risk factors for the development of criminal and antisocial behaviour. In J. Morizot & L. Kazemian (eds.), *The Development of Criminal and Antisocial Behaviour* (pp. 181–197). New York, NY: Springer.

Ketelaar, T., & Ellis, B. J. (2000). Are evolutionary explanations unfalsifiable? Evolutionary psychology and the Lakatosian philosophy of science. *Psychological Inquiry*, 11, 1–22.

Khantzian, E. J. (1997). The self-medication hypothesis of substance use disorders: A reconsideration and recent applications. *Harvard Review of Psychiatry*, 4, 231–244.

Kim, B., Benekos, P. J., & Merlo, A. V. (2016). Sex offender recidivism revisited: Review of recent meta-analyses on the effects of sex offender treatment. *Trauma, Violence, and Abuse*, 17, 105–117.

Kim, B. K. E., Gilman, A. B., & Hawkins, J. D. (2015). School and community-based preventive interventions during adolescence: Preventing delinquency through science-guided collective action. In J. Morizot & L. Kazemian (eds.), *The Development of Criminal and Antisocial Behaviour* (pp. 447–460). Cham: Springer.

Kim-Cohen, J., Caspi, A., Taylor, A., Williams, B., Newcombe, R., Craig, I. W., & Moffitt, T. E. (2006). MAOA, maltreatment, and gene-environment interaction predicting children's mental health: New evidence and meta-analysis. *Molecular Psychiatry*, 11, 903–913.

King, C., & Murphy, G. H. (2014). A systematic review of people with autism spectrum disorder and the criminal justice system. *Journal of Autism and Developmental Disorders*, 44, 2717–2733.

Kingston, D. A., Malamuth, N. M., Fedoroff, P., & Marshall, W. L. (2009). The importance of individual differences in pornography use: Theoretical perspectives and implications for treating sex offenders. *Journal of Sex Research*, 46, 219–232.

Kirsch, L. G., & Becker, J. V. (2007). Emotional deficits in psychopathy and sexual sadism: Implications for violent and sadistic behaviour. *Clinical Psychology Review*, 27, 904–922.

Knoll, J. L. (2010). The 'pseudocommando' mass murderer: Part 1. The psychology revenge and obliteration. *Journal of the American Academy of Psychiatry and Law*, 38, 87–94.

Kokkevi, A., Richardson, C., Florescu, S., Kuzman, M., & Stergar, E. (2007). Psychosocial correlates of substance use in adolescence: A cross-national study in six European countries. *Drug and Alcohol Dependence*, 86, 67–74.

Kolb, B., & Whishaw, I. Q. (2011). *An Introduction to Brain and Behaviour.* New York, NY: Worth Publishers.

Komro, K. A., Flay, B. R., Biglan, A., & Promise Neighborhoods Research Consortium. (2011). Creating nurturing environments: A science-based framework for promoting child health and development within high-poverty neighborhoods. *Clinical Child and Family Psychology Review*, 14, 111–134.

Koob, G. F. (2006). The neurobiology of addiction: A hedonic Calvinist view. In W. R. Miller & K. M. Carroll (eds.), *Rethinking Substance Abuse: What the Science Shows, and What We Should Do About It* (pp. 25–45). New York, NY: The Guilford Press.

Koob, G. F., & Le Moal, M. (2006). *The Neurobiology of Addiction.* Amsterdam: Elsevier.

Kosslyn, S. M., & Rosenberg, R. S. (2004). *Psychology: The Brain, the Person, the World* (2nd edition). Boston, MA: Pearson.

Kraemer, H. C., Kazdin, A. E., Offord, D. R., Kessler, R. C., Jensen, P. S., & Kupfer, D. J. (1997). Coming to terms with the terms of risk. *Archives of General Psychiatry*, 54, 338–344.

Kramer, R. C., & Michalowski, R. J. (2007). War, aggression, and state crime: A criminological analysis of the invasion and occupation of Iraq. In N. Larsen & R. Smandych (eds.), *Global Criminology and Criminal Justice: Current Issues and Perspectives* (pp. 489–515). Peterborough: Broadview Press.

Krasnovsky, T., & Lane, R. C. (1998). Shoplifting: A review of the literature. *Aggression and Violent Behavior*, 3, 219–235.

Krueger, R. B., & Kaplan, M. S. (2016). Noncontact paraphilic sexual offences. In A. Phenix & H. M. Hoberman (eds.), *Sexual Offending* (pp. 79–102). New York, NY: Springer.

Kruger, D. J., Fisher, M. L., & Wright, P. (2014). Patriarchy, male competition, and excess male mortality. *Evolutionary Behavioral Sciences*, 8, 3–11.

Kruger, D. J., & Nesse, R. M. (2006). An evolutionary life-history framework for understanding sex differences in human mortality rates. *Human Nature*, 17, 74–97.

Kruglanski, A. W., Gelfand, M. J., Bélanger, J. J., Sheveland, A., Hetiarachchi, M., & Gunaratna, R. (2014). The psychology of radicalization and deradicalization: How significance quest impacts violent extremism. *Advances in Political Psychology*, 35, 69–93.

Kubrin, C. E. (2003). Structural covariates of homicide rates: Does type of homicide matter? *Journal of Research in Crime and Delinquency*, 40, 139–170.

Kulper, D. A., Kleiman, E. M., McCloskey, M. S., Berman, M. E., & Coccaro, E. F. (2015). The experience of aggressive outbursts in intermittent explosive disorder. *Psychiatry Research*, 225, 710–715.

Lab, S. P. (2016). *Crime Prevention: Approaches, Practices, and Evaluations* (9th edition). New York, NY: Routledge.

Lacina, B., Gleditsch, N. P., & Russett, B. (2006). The declining risk of death in battle. *International Studies Quarterly*, 50, 673–680.

Lader, D. (2015). *Drug Misuse: Findings from the 2014/15 Crime Survey for England and Wales.* Retrieved from www.gov.uk/government/statistics/drug-misuse-findings-from-the-2014-to-2015-csew.

LaFree, G., & Dugan, L. (2007). Introducing the Global Terrorism Database. *Terrorism and Political Violence*, 19, 181–204.

Lambe, S., Hamilton-Giachritsis, C., Garner, E., & Walker, J. (2016). The role of narcissism in aggression and violence: A systematic review. *Trauma, Violence, and Abuse*. Advance online publication. DOI: 10.1177/1524838016650190.

Lambie, I., Ioane, J., & Randell, I. (2016). Understanding child and adolescent firesetting. In R. M. Doley, G. L. Dickens, & T. A. Gannon (eds.), *The Psychology of Arson: A Practical Guide to Understanding and Managing Deliberate Firesetters* (pp. 35–44). Oxford: Routledge.

Lambie, I., Ioane, J., Randell, I., & Seymour, F. (2013). Offending behaviours of child and adolescent firesetters over a 10-year follow-up. *The Journal of Child Psychology and Psychiatry*, 54, 1295–1307.

Lamsma, J., & Harte, J. M. (2015). Violence in psychosis: Conceptualising its causal relationship with risk factors. *Aggression and Violent Behavior*, 24, 75–82.

Land, K. C., McCall, P. L., & Cohen, L. E. (1990). Structural covariates of homicide rates: Are there any invariances across time and social space? *American Journal of Sociology*, 95, 922–963.

Lantz, B., & Ruback, R. B. (2015). A networked boost: Burglary co-offending and repeat victimization using a network approach. *Crime and Delinquency*, 1–25. Advance online publication. DOI: 10.1177/1057567716666642.

Larson, M., Vaughn, M. G., Salas-Wright, C. P., & DeLisi, M. (2015). Narcissism, low self-control, and violence among a nationally representative sample. *Criminal Justice and Behavior*, 42, 644–661.

Lasky, N., Jacques, S., & Fisher, B. S. (2015). Glossing over shoplifting: How thieves act normal. *Deviant Behavior*, 36, 293–309.

Lassek, W. D., & Gaulin, S. J. C. (2009). Costs and benefits of fat-free muscle mass in men: Relationship to mating success, dietary requirements, and native immunity. *Evolution and Human Behavior*, 30, 322–328.

Lawrence, D., Hafekost, J., Johnson, S. E., Saw, S., Buckingham, W. J., Sawyer, M. G., ... Zubrick, S. R. (2015). Key findings from the second Australian Child and Adolescent Survey of Mental Health and Wellbeing. *Australian and New Zealand Journal of Psychiatry*, 50, 876–886.

Laws, D. R., Hudson, S. M., & Ward, T. (2000). *Remaking Relapse Prevention with Sex Offenders: A Sourcebook.* New York, NY: Guilford Press.

Laws, D. R., & Ward, T. (2011). *Desistance from Sex Offending: Alternatives to Throwing Away the Keys.* New York, NY: The Guilford Press.

Leary, M. R., Kowalski, R. M., Smith, L., & Phillips, S. (2003). Teasing, rejection, and violence: Case studies of the school shootings. *Aggressive Behavior*, 29, 202–214.

Leary, M. R., Twenge, J. M., & Quinlivan, E. (2006). Interpersonal rejection as a determinant of anger and aggression. *Personality and Social Psychology Review*, 10, 111–132.

Le Blanc, M. (2015). Developmental criminology: Thoughts on the past and insights for the future. In J. Morizot & L. Kazemian (eds.), *The Development of Criminal and Antisocial Behaviour* (pp. 507–537). Cham: Springer.

Le Blanc, S. A. (2003). *Constant Battles: The Myth of the Peaceful, Noble Savage.* New York, NY: St Martin's Press.

Lee, B. X. (2015). Causes and cures: 1. Toward a new definition. *Aggression and Violent Behaviour*, 25, 199–203.

Lee, M. R., Bankston, W. B., Hayes, T. C., & Thomas, S. A. (2007). Revisiting the Southern culture of violence. *Sociological Quarterly*, 48, 253–275.

Lee, M. R., & Shihadeh, E. (2009). The spatial concentration of Southern Whites and argument based lethal violence. *Social Forces*, 87, 1671–1694.

Lee, R. M., & Stanko, E. A. (eds.). (2003). *Researching Violence: Essays on Methodology and Measurement*. London: Routledge.

Lee, W. E. (2016). *Waging War: Conflict, Culture and Innovation in World History*. Oxford: Oxford University Press.

Leigh, V. (2007, August 5). New trial likely in samurai case. *Sunday Star Times*, p. 3.

Leonard, K. F., Quigley, B. M., & Collins, R. L. (2003). Drinking, personality, and bar environmental characteristics as predictors of involvement in barroom aggression. *Addictive Behaviors*, 28, 1681–1700.

Leshner, A. I. (1997, October 3). Addiction is a brain disease, and it matters. *Science*, 278, 45–47.

Levenson, J. S., & Socia, K. M. (2015). Adverse childhood experiences and arrest patterns in a sample of sexual offenders. *Journal of Interpersonal Violence*, 31, 1–39.

Levin, J., & Madfis, E. (2009). Mass murder at school and cumulative strain: A sequential model. *American Behavioral Scientist*, 52, 1227–1245.

Liddle, J. R., Shackelford, T. K., & Weekes-Shackelford, V. A. (2012). Why can't we all just get along? Evolutionary perspectives on violence, homicide, and war. *Review of General Psychology*, 16, 24–36.

Liebling, A. (2007). Prison suicide and its prevention. In Y. Jewkes (ed.). *Handbook of Prisons* (pp. 423–446). Cullompton: Willan Publishing.

Liebling, A., & Maruna, S. (eds.). (2005). *The Effects of Imprisonment*. Cullompton: Willan Publishing.

Liem, M., & Reichelmann, A. (2014). Patterns of multiple family homicide. *Homicide Studies*, 18, 44–58.

Lilienfeld, S. O., Watts, A. L., & Smith, S. F. (2015). Successful psychopathy: A scientific status report. *Current Directions in Psychological Science*, 24, 298–303.

Link, B. G., Monahan, J., Stueve, A., & Cullen, F. T. (1999). Real in their consequences: A sociological approach to understanding the association between psychotic symptoms and violence. *American Sociological Review*, 64, 316–332.

Link, B. G., Phelan, J. C., Bresnahan, M., Stueve, A., & Pescosolido, B. A. (1999). Public conceptions of mental illness: Labels, causes, dangerousness, and social distance. *American Journal of Public Health*, 89, 1328–1333.

Link, B. G., & Stueve, A. (1994). Psychotic symptoms and the violent/illegal behaviour of mental patients compared to community controls. In J. Monahan & H. J. Steadman (eds.), *Violence and Mental Disorder: Developments in Risk Assessment* (pp. 137–160). Chicago, IL: University of Chicago Press.

Link, N. W., Cullen, F. T., Agnew, R., & Link, B. G. (2016). Can general strain theory help us to understand violent behaviors among people with mental illnesses? *Justice Quarterly*, 33, 729–754.

Lipsey, M. W., Landenberger, N. A., & Wilson, S. J. (2007). Effects of cognitive-behavioral programs for criminal offenders. *Campbell Systematic Reviews*, 6, 27.

Listenbee, R. L. (2014). *Highlights of the 2012 National Youth Gang Survey*. U. S. Department of Justice. Retrieved from www.ojjdp.gov/pubs/248025.pdf on February 1, 2017.

Littman, R., & Paluck, E. L. (2015). The cycle of violence: Understanding individual participation in collective violence. *Advances in Political Psychology*, 36, 79–99.

Loeber, R. (2012). Does the study of the age-crime curve have a future? In R. Loeber & B.C. Welsh (eds.), *The Future of Criminology* (pp. 11–19). Oxford: Oxford University Press.

Loeber, R., Pardini, D., Homish, D. L., Wei, E. H., Crawford, A. M., Farrington, D. P., ... Rosenfeld, R. (2005). The prediction of violence and homicide in young men. *Journal of Consulting and Clinical Psychology*, 73, 1074–1088.

Lopez, A. C. (2016). The evolution of war: Theory and controversy. *International Theory*, 8, 97–139.

Lorber, M. F. (2004). Psychophysiology of aggression, psychopathy, and conduct problems: A meta-analysis. *Psychological Bulletin*, 130, 531–552.

Lorenz, K., & Ullman, S. E. (2016). Alcohol and sexual assault victimization: Research findings and future directions. *Aggression and Violent Behavior*, 31, 82–94.

Lösel, F., & Beelman, A. (2005). Social problem solving programs for preventing antisocial behaviour in children and youth. In M. McMurran & J. McGuire (eds.), *Social Problem Solving and Offending: Evidence, Evaluation and Evolution*. New York, NY: Wiley.

Lösel, F., & Schmucker, M. (2005). The effectiveness of treatment for sexual offenders: A comprehensive meta-analysis. *Journal of Experimental Criminology*, 1, 117–146.

Luckenbill, D. F. (1977). Criminal homicide as a situated transaction. *Social Problems*, 25, 176–186.

Lüscher, C. (2016). The emergence of a circuit model for addiction. *Annual Review of Neuroscience*, 39, 257–276.

Lussier, P., & Cale, J. (2016). Understanding the origins and development of rape and sexual aggression against women: Four generations of research and theorizing. *Aggression and Violent Behavior*, 21, 66–81.

Lykken, D. T. (1957). A study of anxiety in the sociopathic personality. *Journal of Abnormal Psychology*, 55, 6–10.

Maas, C., Herrenkohl, T. I., & Sousa, C. (2008). Review of research on child maltreatment and violence in youth. *Trauma, Violence and Abuse*, 9, 56–67.

MacCoun, R. J. (2013). The puzzling uniformity of DSM–5 substance use disorder diagnoses. *Frontiers in Psychiatry*, 4, 1–5.

MacCoun, R., Kilmer, B., & Reuter, P. (2003). *Research on Drugs–Crime Linkages: The Next Generation*. Washington, DC: National Institute of Justice.

MacCoun, R. J., & Reuter, P. (2001). *Drug War Heresies: Learning from Other Vices, Times, and Places*. Cambridge: Cambridge University Press.

MacKenzie, D. L. (2002). Reducing the criminal activities of known offenders and delinquents. In L. Sherman et al. (eds.), *Evidence-Based Crime Prevention* (pp. 331–404). New York, NY: Routledge.

MacKenzie, D. L. (2006). *What Works in Corrections: Reducing the Criminal Activities of Offenders and Delinquencies*. Cambridge: Cambridge University Press.

Mackenzie, G., Spiranovic, C., Warner, K., Stobbs, N., Gelb, K., Indermaur, D., ... Bouhours, T. (2012). Sentencing and public confidence: Results from a national Australian survey on public opinions towards sentencing. *Australian and New Zealand Journal of Criminology*, 45, 45–65.

Mackenzie, S. (2010a). Fakes. In F. Brookman, M. Maguire, H. Pierpoint, & T. Bennett (eds.), *Handbook on Crime* (pp. 120–136). Cullompton: Willan Publishing.

Mackenzie, S. (2010b). Scams. In F. Brookman, M. Maguire, H. Pierpoint, & T. Bennett (eds.), *Handbook on Crime* (pp. 137–152). Cullompton: Willan Publishing.

Macmillan, M. (2008). Phineas Gage – Unravelling the myth. *The Psychologist*, 21, 828–831.

Maguire, M., Wright, R., & Bennett, T. (2010). Domestic burglary. In F. Brookman, M. Maguire, H. Pierpoint, & T. Bennett (eds.), *Handbook on Crime* (pp. 3–25). Cullompton: Willan Publishing.

Maher, J. (2010). Youth gang violence. In F. Brookman, M. Maguire, H. Pierpoint, & T. Bennett (eds.), *Handbook on Crime* (pp. 308–330). Cullompton: Willan Publishing.

Maibom, H. L. (2014). Introduction: (Almost) everything you wanted to know about empathy. In H. L. Maibom (ed.), *Empathy and Morality* (pp. 1–40). Oxford: Oxford University Press.

Maisto, S. A., Galizio, M., & Connors, G. J. (2004). *Drug Use and Abuse* (4th edition). Belmont, CA: Wadsworth/Thomson Learning.

Malamuth, N. M. (1996). Sexually explicit media, gender differences, and evolutionary theory. *Journal of Communication*, 46, 8–31.

Malamuth, N. M. (2003). Criminal and non-criminal sexual aggressors: Integrating psychopathy in a hierarchical-mediational confluence model. *Annals of the New York Academy of Sciences*, 989, 33–58.

Malamuth, N. M., Linz, D., Heavey, C. L., et al. (1995). Using the confluence model of sexual aggression to predict men's conflict with women: A 10 year follow-up study. *Journal of Personality and Social Psychology*, 69, 353–369.

Malby, R. I. (2001). *Burglary.* Cullompton: Willan Publishing.

Maletzky, B. M., Tolan, A., & McFarland, B. (2006). The Oregon depo-Provera program: A five-year follow-up. *Sex Abuse*, 18, 303–316.

Marlatt, G. A., & Gordon, J. R. (1985). *Relapse Prevention: Maintenance Strategies in the Treatment of Addictive Behaviour.* New York, NY: Guilford Press.

Marques, J. K., Wiederanders, M., Day, D. M., Nelson, C., & Van Ommeren, A. (2005). Effects of a relapse prevention program on sexual recidivism: Final results from California's Sex Offender Treatment and Evaluation Project (SOTEP). *Sexual Abuse: A Journal of Research and Treatment*, 17, 79–107.

Marsden, S. V., & Schmid, A. P. (2011). Typologies of terrorism and political violence. In A. P. Schmid (ed.), *The Routledge Handbook of Terrorism Research* (pp. 158–200). London: Routledge.

Marsh, A. A., & Blair, R. J. R. (2008). Deficits in facial affect recognition among antisocial populations: A meta-analysis. *Neuroscience and Biobehavioral Reviews*, 32, 454–465.

Marsh, I. (2004). *Criminal Justice: An Introduction to Philosophies, Theories and Practice.* London: Routledge.

Marshall, W. L. (2006). Diagnostic problems with sexual offenders. In W. L. Marshall, Y. M. Fernandez, & L. E. Marshall (eds.), *Sexual Offender Treatment: Controversial Issues.* Hoboken, NJ: John Wiley & Sons.

Marshall, W. L., & Barbaree, H. E. (1990). An integrated theory of the etiology of sexual offending. In W. L. Marshall, D. R. Laws, & H. E. Barbaree (eds.), *Handbook of Sexual Assault: Issues, Theories, and Treatment of the Offender* (pp. 257–275). New York, NY: Plenum.

Marshall, W. L., & Fernandez, Y. M. (2000). Phallometric testing with sex offenders: Limits to its value. *Clinical Psychology Review*, 20, 807–820.

Marshall, W. L., & Marshall, L. E. (2000). The origins of sexual offending. *Trauma, Violence and Abuse*, 1, 250–263.

Martinson, R. (1974). What works? Questions and answers about prison reform. *The Public Interest*, 35, 22–54.

Maruna, S. (2001). *Making Good: How Ex-Convicts Reform and Build Their Lives.* Washington, DC: APA Press.

Marziano, V., Ward, T., Beech, A. R., & Pattison, P. (2006). Identification of five fundamental implicit theories underlying cognitive distortions in child abusers: A preliminary study. *Psychology, Crime & Law*, 12, 97–105.

Mason, T. B., Lewis, R. J., Milletich, R. J., et al. (2014). Psychological aggression in lesbian, gay, and bisexual individuals' intimate relationships: A review of prevalence, correlates, and measurement issues. *Aggression and Violent Behavior*, 19, 219–234.

Mata, R., Josef, A. K., & Hertwig, R. (2016). Propensity for risk taking across the life span and around the globe. *Psychological Science*, 27, 231–243.

Matsueda, R. L., Kreager, D. A., & Huizinga, D. (2006). Deterring delinquents: A rational choice model of theft and violence. *American Sociological Review*, 71, 95–122.

Mayhew, P. & Reilly, J. (2007). *The New Zealand Crime & Safety Survey 2006: Key Findings.* Wellington: Ministry of Justice.

Mays, G. L., & Winfree, L. T. (2006). *Juvenile Justice* (2nd edition). Long Grove, IL: Waveland Press Inc.

Mazerolle, L., Wickes, R., & McBroom, J. (2010). Community variations in violence: The role of social ties and collective efficacy in comparative context. *Journal of Research in Crime and Delinquency*, 47, 3–30.

Mazur, A. (2009). Testosterone and violence among young men. In A. Walsh & K. M. Beaver (eds.), *Biosocial Criminology: New Direction in Theory and Research* (pp. 191–204). New York, NY: Routledge.

McAdams, D. P. (2006). *THE person: A New Introduction to Personality Psychology*. Hoboken, NJ: John Wiley & Sons.

McAlister, A. L. (2006). Acceptance of killing and homicide rates in nineteen nations. *European Journal of Public Health*, 16, 259–265.

McCall, G. S., & Shields, N. (2008). Examining the evidence from small-scale societies and early prehistory and implications for modern theories of aggression and violence. *Aggression and Violent Behavior*, 13, 1–9.

McCall, P. L., Land, K. C., & Parker, K. F. (2010). An empirical assessment of what we know about structural covariates of homicide rates: A return to a classic 20 years later. *Homicide Studies*, 14, 219–243.

McCall, P. L., & Nieuwbeerta, P. (2007). Structural covariates of homicide rates: A European city cross-national comparative analysis. *Homicide Studies*, 11, 167–178.

McCord, J. (2003). Cures that harm: Unanticipated outcomes of crime prevention programs. *Annals of the American Academy of Political and Social Science*, 587, 16–30.

McCrae, R. R., & Costa, P. T. (1997). Personality trait structure as a human universal. *American Psychologist*, 52, 509–516.

McDonald, M. M., Navarrete, C. D., & van Vugt, M. (2012). Evolution and the psychology of intergroup conflict: The male warrior hypothesis. *Philosophical Transactions of the Royal Society B*, 367, 670–679.

McGee, T. R., & Farrington, D. P. (2016). Developmental and life-course theories of crime. In A. R. Piquero (ed.), *The Handbook of Criminological Theory* (pp. 336–354). Chichester: Wiley-Blackwell.

McGloin, J. M., Pratt, T. C., & Piquero, A. R. (2006). A life-course analysis of the criminogenic effects of maternal cigarette smoking during pregnancy: A research note on the mediating impact of neuropsychological deficit. *Journal of Research in Crime and Delinquency*, 43, 412–426.

McGloin, J. M., Sullivan, C. J., & Kennedy, L. W. (eds.). (2012). *When Crime Appears: The Role of Emergence*. New York, NY: Routledge.

McGregor, J. (2012). The legal heritage of the crime of rape. In J. M. Brown & S. L. Wallklate (eds.), *Handbook on Sexual Violence* (pp. 69–89). New York, NY: Routledge.

McGuire, J. (2002). Integrating findings from research reviews. In J. McGuire (ed.). *Offender Rehabilitation and Treatment: Effective Programmes and Policies to Reduce Re-Offending*. New York, NY: John Wiley & Sons.

McGuire, J. (2004). *Understanding Psychology and Crime: Perspectives on Theory and Action*. New York, NY: Open University Press.

McGuire, J. (2006). General offending behaviour programmes: Concept, theory, and practice. In C. R. Hollin & E. J. Palmer (eds.), *Offending Behaviour Programmes: Development, Application and Controversies*. New York, NY: John Wiley & Sons.

McGuire, J. (2008). A review of effective interventions for reducing aggression and violence. *Philosophical Transactions of the Royal Society of London B*, 363, 2577–2597.

McGuire, J. (2013). 'What works' to reduce re-offending: 18 years on. In L. A. Craig, L. Dixon, & T. A. Gannon (eds.), *What Works in Offender Rehabilitation: An Evidence-Based Approach to Assessment and Treatment* (pp. 20–49). Hoboken, NJ: Wiley.

McKetin, R., McLaren, J., Lubman, D. I., & Hides, L. (2006). The prevalence of psychotic symptoms among methamphetamine users. *Addiction*, 101, 1473–1478.

McKetin, R., McLaren, J., Riddell, S., & Robins, L. (2006). The relationship between methamphetamine use and violent behaviour. *Crime and Justice Bulletin*, 97, 1–15.

McKibbin, W. F., Shackelford, T. K., Goetz, A. T., & Starratt, V. G. (2008). Why do men rape? An evolutionary psychological perspective. *Review of General Psychology*, 12, 86–97.

McLean, S. J., Worden, R. E., & Kim, M. (2013). Here's looking at you: An evaluation of public CCTV cameras and their effects on crime and disorder. *Criminal Justice Review*, 38, 303–334.

McMillan, J. (2014). The kindest cut? Surgical castration, sex offenders and coercive offers. *Journal of Medical Ethics*, 40, 583–590.

McMurran, M. (ed.). (2013). *Alcohol-Related Violence: Prevention and Treatment.* Chichester: Wiley.

McMurran, M., & Theodosi, E. (2007). Is treatment non-completion associated with increased reconviction over no treatment? *Psychology, Crime and Law*, 13, 333–343.

McMurran, M., & Ward, T. (2010). Treatment readiness, treatment engagement and behaviour change. *Criminal Behaviour and Mental Health*, 20, 75–85.

McNeil, D. E. (1994). Hallucinations and violence. In J. Monahan & H. J. Steadman (eds.), *Violence and Mental Disorder: Developments in Risk Assessment* (pp. 183–203). Chicago, IL: University of Chicago Press.

McNeill, F. (2012). Four forms of 'offender' rehabilitation: Towards an interdisciplinary perspective. *Legal and Criminological Psychology*, 17, 18–36.

McSweeney, T., Hough, M., & Turnbull, P. J. (2007). Drugs and crime: Exploring the links. In M. Simpson, T. Shildrick, & R. MacDonald (eds.), *Drugs in Britain: Supply, Consumption and Control* (pp. 95–108). New York, NY: Palgrave Macmillan.

McWilliams, J., Brown, J., Sanders, M. R., & Jones, L. (2016). The Triple P implementation framework: The role of purveyors in the implementation and sustainability of evidence-based programs. *Prevention Science*, 17, 636–645.

Mead, M. (1940). Warfare is only an invention – not a biological necessity. *Asia XL*, 40, 402–405.

Mealey, L. (1995). The socio-biology of sociopathy: An integrated evolutionary model. *Behavioural and Brain Sciences*, 18, 523–599.

Meehan, J., Flynn, S., Hunt, I. M., Robinson, J., Bickley, H., Parsons, R., ... Shaw, J. (2006). Perpetrators of homicide with schizophrenia: A national clinical survey in England and Wales. *Psychiatric Services*, 57, 1648–1651.

Mehta, P. H., & Prasad, S. (2015). The dual-hormone hypothesis: A brief review and future research agenda. *Current Opinion in Behavioral Science*, 3, 163–168.

Melde, C. (2015). Gang membership in developmental perspective. In J. Morizot & L. Kazemian (eds.), *The Development of Criminal and Antisocial Behaviour* (pp. 349–363). Cham: Springer.

Meloy, J. R. (2006). Empirical basis and forensic application of affective and predatory violence. *Australian and New Zealand Journal of Psychiatry*, 40, 539–547.

Meloy, J. R., Hempel, A. G., Gray, B. T., Mohandie, K., Shiva, A., & Richards, T. C. (2004). A comparative analysis of North American adolescent and adult mass murderers. *Behavioural Sciences and the Law*, 22, 291–309.

Mesoudi, A. (2011). *Cultural Evolution: How Darwinian Theory Can Explain Human Culture and Synthesize the Social Sciences.* Chicago, IL: University of Chicago Press.

Messerschmidt, J. W. (1993). *Masculinities and Crime: Critique and Reconceptualization of Theory.* Lanham, MD: Rowman & Littlefield.

Messner, S. F., & Rosenfeld, R. (2013). *Crime and the American Dream* (5th edition). Belmont, CA: Wadsworth.

Metzl, J. M., & MacLeish, K. T. (2015). Mental illness, mass shootings, and the politics of American firearms. *American Journal of Public Health*, 105, 240–249.

Meyer, J., & O'Malley, P. (2005). Missing the punitive turn? Canadian criminal justice, 'balance', and penal modernism. In J. Pratt, D. Brown, M. Brown, S. Hallsworth, & W. Morrison (eds.), *The New Punitiveness: Trends, Theories, Perspectives* (pp. 201–218). Cullompton: Willan Publishing.

Meyer, J. S., & Quenzer, L. F. (2005). *Psychopharmacology: Drugs, the Brain, and Behaviour.* Sunderland, MA: Sinauer Associates.

Mildner, S., Lauster, G., & Wodni, W. (2011). Scarcity and abundance revisited: A literature review on natural resources and conflict. *International Journal of Conflict and Violence*, 5, 155–172.

Milgram, S. (1963). Behavioral study of obedience. *Journal of Abnormal and Social Psychology*, 67, 371–378.

Milgram, S. (1965). Some conditions of obedience and disobedience to authority. *Human Relations*, 18, 57–76.

Miller, A. G. (2004). What can the Milgram obedience experiments tell us about the holocaust? Generalising from the social psychology laboratory. In A. G. Miller (ed.), *The Social Psychology of Good and Evil* (pp. 193–239). New York, NY: The Guilford Press.

Miller, A. G. (2016). Why are the Milgram obedience experiments still so extraordinarily famous – and controversial. In A. G. Miller (ed.), *The Social Psychology of Good and Evil* (2nd edition), (pp. 185–222). New York, NY: Guilford Publications.

Miller, J. D., & Lynam, D. (2001). Structural models of personality and their relations to antisocial behaviour: A meta-analytic review. *Criminology*, 39, 765–798.

Miller, L. (2014a). Serial killers I: Subtypes, patterns, and motives. *Aggression and Violent Behavior*, 19, 1–11.

Miller, L. (2014b). Serial killers II: Development, dynamics, and forensics. *Aggression and Violent Behavior*, 19, 12–22.

Miller, S. L., Maner, J. K., & Becker, D. V. (2010). Self-protective biases in group categorization: Threat cues shape the psychological boundary between 'us' and 'them'. *Journal of Personality and Social Psychology*, 99, 62–77.

Ministry of Health (2007). *Alcohol Use in New Zealand. Analysis of the 2004 New Zealand Health Behaviours Survey – Alcohol Use.* Wellington: Ministry of Health.

Ministry of Health (2010). *Drug Use in New Zealand: Key Results of the 2007/2008 New Zealand Alcohol and Drug Use Survey.* Wellington: Ministry of Health.

Ministry of Justice. (2015). *2014 New Zealand Crime and Safety Survey: Main findings.* Retrieved from www.justice.govt.nz/assets/Documents/Publications/NZCASS-201602-Main-Findings-Report-Updated.pdf on February 1, 2017.

Ministry of Justice. (2016). *Trends in convictions and sentencing.* Retrieved from https://justice.govt.nz/assets/Documents/Publications/Adult-infographic-June-2016.pdf on January 19, 2017.

Minkes, J. (2010). Corporate financial crimes. In F. Brookman, M. Maguire, H. Pierpoint, & T. Bennett (eds.), *Handbook on Crime* (pp. 653–677). Cullompton: Willan Publishing.

Minkes, J., & Minkes, L. (2010). Income tax evasion and benefit fraud. In F. Brookman, M. Maguire, H. Pierpoint, & T. Bennett (eds.), *Handbook on Crime* (pp. 87–99). Cullompton: Willan Publishing.

Mitani, J. C. (2009). Cooperation and competition in chimpanzees: Current understanding and future challenges. *Evolutionary Anthropology*, 18, 215–227.

Moffitt, T. E. (1993). Adolescence-limited and life-course-persistent antisocial behaviour: A developmental taxonomy. *Psychological Review*, 100, 674–701.

Moffitt, T. E. (2005). The new look at behavioural genetics in developmental psychopathology: Gene-environment interplay in antisocial behaviors. *Psychological Bulletin*, 131, 533–554.

Moffitt, T. E. (2006). A review of research on the taxonomy of life-course persistent versus adolescence-limited antisocial behaviour. In F. T. Cullen, J. P. Wright, & K. R. Blevins (eds.), *Advances in Criminological Theory: Vol. 15. Taking Stock: The Status of Criminological Theory* (pp. 277–311). New Brunswick, NJ: Transaction Publishers.

Moffitt, T., & Caspi, A. (1998). Implications of violence between intimate partners for child psychologists and psychiatrists. *Journal of Child Psychology and Psychiatry,* 39, 137–144.

Moffitt, T. E., Caspi, A., Harrington, H., & Milne, B. J. (2002). Males on the life-course-persistent and adolescence-limited antisocial pathways: Follow-up at age 26 years. *Development and Psychopathology,* 14, 179–207.

Moghaddam, F. M. (2005). The staircase to terrorism: A psychological explanation. *American Psychologist,* 60, 161–169.

Moloney, C. J. (2014). Sociology of human trafficking. In M. J. Palmiotto (ed.), *Combating Human Trafficking: A Multidisciplinary Approach* (pp. 27–45). London: CRC Press.

Monahan, J. (1992). Mental disorder and violent behaviour: Perceptions and evidence. *American Psychologist,* 47, 511–521.

Monahan, J., & Skeem, J. L. (2014). Risk redux: The resurgence of risk assessment in criminal sanctioning. *Federal Sentencing Reporter,* 26, 158–166.

Montoya, E. R., Terburg, D., Bos, P. A., & van Honk, J. (2012). Testosterone, cortisol, and serotonin as key regulators of social aggression: A review and theoretical perspective. *Motivation and Emotion,* 36, 65–73.

Moore, D. S. (2015). *The Developing Genome: An Introduction to Behavioural Epigenetics.* Oxford: Oxford University Press.

Moore, T. M., Scarpa, A., & Raine, A. (2002). A meta-analysis of serotonin metabolite 5-HIAA and antisocial behaviour. *Aggressive Behavior,* 28, 299–316.

Morgan, A., & Louis, E. (2009). *Key issues in graffiti* (Research in Practice Summary Paper No. 6). Canberra: Australian Institute of Criminology.

Morris, I. (2014). *War! What Is It Good For? Conflict and the Progress of Civilization from Primates to Robots.* London: Macmillan.

Mosher, C. J., & Atkins, S. (2007). *Drugs and Drug Policy: The Control of Consciousness Alteration.* Thousand Oaks, CA: Sage Publications.

Mother only allowed to hold hands. (2005). *Sydney Morning Herald.* Retrieved from www.smh.com.au/news/national/barbaric-to-hang-him-ruddock/2005/12/01/1133311133346.html on June 1, 2008.

Mouzos, J., Hind, N., Smith, L., & Adams, K. (2007). *Drug Use Monitoring in Australia: 2006 Annual Report on Drug Use Among Police Detainees.* Canberra: Australian Institute of Criminology.

Mouzos, J., & West, D. (2007). An examination of serial murder in Australia. *Trends and Issues in Crime and Criminal Justice* (346). Retrieved from www.aic.gov.au/publications/current%20series/tandi/341-360/tandi346.html.

Mueser, K. T., & Drake, R. E. (2007). Comorbidity: What have we learned and where are we going? *Clinical Psychology: Science and Practice,* 14, 64–69.

Mueser, K. T., Drake, R. E., Turner, W., & McGovern, M. (2006). Comorbid substance use disorders and psychiatric disorders. In R. Miller & K. M. Carroll (eds.), *Rethinking Substance Abuse: What the Science Shows, and What We Should Do About It* (pp. 115–134). New York, NY: The Guilford Press.

Muftic, L. R. (2009). Macro-micro theoretical integration: An unexplored theoretical frontier. *Journal of Theoretical and Philosophical Criminology,* 1, 33–71.

Muirhead, J., & Fortune, C.-A. (2016). Yoga in prisons: A review of the literature. *Aggression and Violent Behavior,* 28, 57–63.

Mumola, C. J. (2000). *Incarcerated Parents and Their Children.* Washington, DC: U.S. Department of Justice.

Munice, J. (2010). Labelling, social reaction and social constructionism. In E. McLaughlin & T. Newburn (eds.), *The Sage Handbook of Criminological Theory* (pp. 139–152). London: Sage Publications.

Munice, J., & McLaughlin, E. (eds.). (2001). *The Problem of Crime* (2nd edition). London: Sage Publications.

Murray, J. (2005). The effects of imprisonment on families and children of prisoners. In A. Liebling & S. Maruna (eds.), *The Effects of Imprisonment* (pp. 442–462). Cullompton: Willan Publishing.

Murray, J., & Farrington, D. P. (2005). Parental imprisonment: Effects on boys' antisocial behaviour and delinquency through the life-course. *Journal of Child Psychology and Psychiatry*, 46, 1269–1278.

Nadesu, A. (2009). Reconviction patterns of released prisoners: A 60-months follow-up analysis. Retrieved from www.corrections.govt.nz/research/reconviction-patterns-of-released-prisoners-a-60-months-follow-up-analysis2.html on February 17, 2012.

Nagin, D. S. (1998). Criminal deterrence research at the outset of the twenty-first century. *Crime and Justice: A Review of Research*, 23, 51–91.

Nagin, D. S. (2013). Deterrence in the twenty-first century. *Crime and Justice*, 42, 199–263.

Nagin, D. S. (2016). The deterrent effect of stop, question, and frisk practices. *Criminology and Public Policy*, 15, 27–29.

Nagin, D. S., & Pogarsky, G. (2001). Integrating celerity, impulsivity, and extralegal sanction threats into a model of general deterrence: Theory and evidence. *Criminology*, 39, 865–892.

Nagin, D. S., & Pogarsky, G. (2004). Time and punishment: Delayed consequences and criminal behaviour. *Journal of Quantitative Criminology*, 20, 295–317.

Naterer, A. (2015). Violence and the code of the street: A study of social dynamics among street children in Makeevka, East Ukraine. *Journal of Interpersonal Violence*, 30, 1387–1402.

Neale, J., Bloor, M., & Weir, C. (2005). Problem drug users and assault. *International Journal of Drug Policy*, 16, 393–402.

Nelson, E. E., Jarcho, J. M., & Guyer, A. E. (2016). Social re-orientation and brain development: An expanded and updated view. *Developmental Cognitive Neuroscience*, 17, 118–127.

Nesse, R. M., & Berridge, K. C. (1997). Psychoactive drug use in evolutionary perspective. *Science*, 278, 63–66.

Netto, N. R., Carter, J. M., & Bonell, C. (2014). A systematic review of interventions that adopt the 'good lives' approach to offender rehabilitation. *Journal of Offender Rehabilitation*, 53, 403–422.

Neumann, C. S., & Hare, R. D. (2008). Psychopathic traits in a large community sample: Links to violence, alcohol use, and intelligence. *Journal of Consulting and Clinical Psychology*, 76, 893–899.

Neumann, C. S., & Hare, R. D., & Pardini, D. A. (2015). Antisociality and the construct of psychopathy: Data from around the globe. *Journal of Personality*, 83, 678–692.

Newbold, G. (2007). *The Problem of Prisons: Corrections Reform in New Zealand Since 1840*. Wellington: Dunmore Publishing.

Newbold, G. (2016). *Crime, Law and Justice in New Zealand*. New York, NY: Routledge.

Newburn, T. (2013). *Criminology* (2nd edition). London: Routledge.

Newcombe, R. (2007). Trends in the prevalence of illicit drug use in Britain. In M. Simpson, T. Shildrick, & R. MacDonald (eds.), *Drugs in Britain: Supply, Consumption and Control* (pp. 13–39). New York, NY: Palgrave.

New Zealand Crime and Safety Survey (NZCASS). (2015). *Main Findings*. Wellington: Ministry of Justice.

New Zealand Crime Statistics. (2015). *New Zealand Crime Statistics, 2014*. Retrieved from www.police.govt.nz/sites/default/files/publications/crime-stats-national-20141231.pdf on January 9, 2017.

New Zealand Police. (2016). *Recorded Offender Statistics, 2016*. Retrieved from www.police.govt.nz/about-us/publications-and-statistics/statistics/policedatanz on May 30, 2016.

New Zealand Statistics. (2017). *Criminal Convictions and Sentencing Tables.* Data retrieved from http://nzdotstat.stats.govt.nz/wbos/Index.aspx?DataSetCode=TABLECODE7373.

Nisbett, R. E. (1993). Violence and U.S. regional culture. *American Psychologist,* 48, 441–449.

Nivette, A. E. (2011a). Cross-national predictors of crime: A meta-analysis. *Homicide Studies,* 15, 103–131.

Nivette, A. E. (2011b). Violence in non-state societies: A review. *British Journal of Criminology,* 51, 578–598.

Nordmarker, A., Hjärthag, F., Perrin-Wallqvist, R., & Archer, T. (2016). The roles of gender and personality factors in vandalism and scrawl-graffiti among Swedish adolescents. *PsyCh Journal,* 5, 180–190.

Nowak, A., Gelfand, M. J., Borkowski, W., Cohen, D., & Hernandez, I. (2016). The evolutionary basis of honor cultures. *Psychological Science,* 27, 12–24.

Nutt, D., King, L. A., Saulsbury, W., & Blakemore, W. (2007). Development of a rational scale to assess the harm of drugs and of potential misuse. *The Lancet,* 369, 1047–1053.

Nutt, D. J., Lingford-Hughes, A., Erritzoe, D., & Stokes, P. R. A. (2015). The dopamine theory of addiction: 40 years of highs and lows. *Nature Reviews Neuroscience,* 16, 305–312.

Oakley, B. A. (2007). *Evil Genes: Why Rome Fell, Hitler Rose, Enron Failed, and My Sister Stole My Mother's Boyfriend.* New York, NY: Prometheus Books.

O'Brien, K., Daffern, M., Chu, C. M., & Thomas, S. D. M. (2013). Youth gang affiliation, violence, and criminal activities: A review of motivational, risk, and protective factors. *Aggression and Violent Behavior,* 18, 417–425.

Olds, D., Henderson, C. R., Jr., Cole, R., Eckenrode J., Kitzman, H., Luckey, D., … Powers, J. (1998). Long-term effects of nurse home visitation on children's criminal and antisocial behaviour: 15-year follow-up of a randomized controlled trial. *Journal of the American Medical Association,* 14, 1238–1244.

Olds, D. L., Sadler, L., & Kitzman, H. (2007). Programs for parents of infants and toddlers: Recent evidence from randomized trials. *Journal of Child Psychology and Psychiatry,* 35, 1171–1190.

Olivier, B., & van Oorschot, R. (2005). 5-HT$_{1B}$ receptors and aggression: A review. *European Journal of Pharmacology,* 526, 207–217.

Olver, M. E., Stockdale, K. C., & Wormith, S. J. (2011). A meta-analysis of predictors of offender treatment attrition and its relationship to recidivism. *Journal of Consulting and Clinical Psychology,* 79, 6–21.

Ostrowsky, M. K. (2010). Are violent people more likely to have low self-esteem or high self-esteem? *Aggression and Violent Behavior,* 15, 69–75.

Ousey, G. C., & Lee, M. R. (2010). The southern culture of violence and homicide-type differentiations: An analysis across cities and time points. *Homicide Studies,* 14, 268–295.

Owens, P. B., Su, Y., & Snow, D. A. (2013). Social scientific inquiry into genocide and mass killing: From unitary outcome to complex processes. *Annual Review of Sociology,* 39, 69–84.

Padilla, A., Hogan, R., & Kaiser, R. B. (2007). The toxic triangle: Destructive leaders, susceptible followers, and conducive environments. *The Leadership Quarterly,* 18, 176–194.

Palermo, G. B. (1997). The berserk syndrome: A review of mass murder. *Aggression and Violent Behavior,* 2, 1–8.

Pandit, S. A., Pradhan, G. R., Balashov, H., & van Schaik, C. P. (2016). The conditions favouring between-community raiding in chimpanzees, bonobos, and human foragers. *Human Nature,* 27, 141–159.

Paoli, L. (2014). The Italian mafia. In L. Paoli (ed.), *The Oxford Handbook of Organised Crime* (pp. 121–141). Oxford: Oxford University Press.

Paoli, L., & Vander Beken, T. V. (2014). Organized crime: A contested concept. In L. Paoli (ed.), *The Oxford Handbook of Organised Crime* (pp. 13–31). Oxford: Oxford University Press.

Pardini, D. A., Waller, R., & Hawes, S. W. (2015). Familial influences on the development of serious conduct problems and delinquency. In J. Morizot & L. Kazemian (eds.), *The Development of Criminal and Antisocial Behaviour* (pp. 201–220). Cham: Springer.

Paris, J. (2013). *The Intelligent Clinician's Guide to the DSM–5.* Oxford: Oxford University Press.

Parker, R., Bush, J., & Harris, D. (2014). Important methodological issues in evaluating community-based interventions. *Evaluation Review,* 38, 295–308.

Paternoster, R., & Bachman, R. (2010). Control theories. In E. McLaughlin & T. Newburn (eds.), *The Sage Handbook of Criminological Theory* (pp. 114–138). London: Sage Publications.

Paton-Simpson, G. (2001). Socially obligatory drinking: A sociological analysis of norms governing minimum drinking levels. *Contemporary Drug Problems,* 28, 133–177.

Patrick, C. J. & Drislane, L. E. (2014). Triarchic model of psychopathy: Origins, operationalizations, and observed linkages with personality and general psychopathology. *Journal of Personality,* 83, 627–643.

Paulin, J., Searle, W., & Knags, T. (2003). *Attitudes Towards Crime and Punishment: A New Zealand Study.* Wellington: Ministry of Justice.

Paunonen, S. V. (2003). Big five factors of personality and replicated predictions of behaviour. *Journal of Personality and Social Psychology,* 84, 411–424.

Pearson, F. S., Lipton, D. S., Cleland, C. M., & Yee, D. S. (2002). The effects of behavioral/cognitive-behavioral programs on recidivism. *Crime & Delinquency,* 48, 476–496.

Pennington, B. F. (2002). *The Development of Psychopathology: Nature and Nurture.* New York, NY: Guilford Press.

Peper, J. S., & Dahl, R. E. (2013). The teenage brain: Surging hormones – Brain-behavior interactions during puberty. *Current Directions in Psychological Science,* 22, 134–139.

Perri, F. S. (2013). Visionaries or false prophets. *Journal of Contemporary Criminal Justice,* 29, 331–350.

Pervin, L. A., Cervone, D., & John, O. P. (2005). *Personality: Theory and Research.* Hoboken, NJ: John Wiley & Sons.

Petrosino, A., Turpin-Petrosino, C., & Buehler, J. (2003). Scared straight and other juvenile awareness programs for preventing juvenile delinquency: A systematic review of the randomized experimental evidence. *Annals of the American Academy of Political and Social Science,* 589, 41–62.

Pettersson, T., & Wallensteen, P. (2015). Armed conflict, 1946–2014. *Journal of Peace Research,* 52, 536–550.

Pew Centre on the States. (2011). *State of recidivism: The revolving door of American prisons.* Washington, DC: The Pew Charitable Trusts. Retrieved from www.pewcenteronthestates.org/uploadedFiles/Pew_State_of_Recidivism.pdf on February 17, 2012.

Picciotto, M. R. (1998). Common aspects of the action of nicotine and other drugs of abuse. *Drug and Alcohol Dependence,* 51, 165–172.

Pinker, S. (2002). *The Blank Slate: The Modern Denial of Human Nature.* London: Penguin.

Pinker, S. (2011). *The Better Angels of Our Nature: Why Violence Has Declined.* London: Penguin.

Piquero, A. R., Hawkins, J. D., & Kazemian, L. (2012). Criminal Career Patterns. In R. Loeber & D. Farrington (eds.), *From Juvenile Delinquency to Adult Crime: Criminal Careers, Justice Policy, and Prevention* (pp. 14–46). Oxford: Oxford University Press.

Piquero, A. R., Jennings, W. G., Diamond, B., Farrington, D. P., Tremblay, R. E., Welsh, B. C., & Gonzalez, J. M. R. (2016). A meta-analysis update on the effects of early family/parent training programs on antisocial behavior and delinquency. *Journal of Experimental Criminology,* 12, 229–248.

Piquero, A., & Paternoster, R. (1998). An application of Stafford and Warr's re-conceptualization of deterrence to drinking and driving. *Journal of Research in Crime and Delinquency,* 35, 3–39.

Piquero, A., & Rengert, G. F. (1999). Studying deterrence with active residential burglars. *Justice Quarterly,* 16, 451–471.

Pizarro, J. M., & Narag, R. E. (2008). Supermax prisons: What we know, what we do not know, and where we are going. *The Prison Journal*, 88, 23–42.

Plenty, S., & Sundell, K. (2015). Graffiti: A precursor to future deviant behaviour during adolescence? *Deviant Behavior*, 36, 565–580.

Plomin, R., De Fries, J. C., McClearn, G. E., & McGuffin, P. (2008). *Behavioral Genetics* (5th edition). New York, NY: Worth Publishers.

Plotkin, H. (2004). *Evolutionary Thought in Psychology: A Brief History.* Oxford: Blackwell Publishing.

Polaschek, D. L. L. (2011). High intensity rehabilitation for violent offenders in New Zealand: Reconviction outcomes for high and medium risk prisoners. *Journal of Interpersonal Violence*, 26, 664–682.

Polaschek, D. L. L. (2014). Adult criminals with psychopathy: Common beliefs about treatability and change have little empirical support. *Current Directions in Psychological Science*, 23, 296–301.

Polaschek, D. L. L. (2015). (Mis)understanding psychopathy: Consequences for policy and practice with offenders. *Psychiatry, Psychology and Law*, 22, 500–519.

Polaschek, D. L., & Gannon, T. A. (2004). The implicit theories of rapists: What convicted offenders tell us. *Sexual Abuse: A Journal of Research and Treatment*, 16, 299–314.

Polaschek, D. L. L., & Kilgour, T. G. (2013). New Zealand's special treatment units: The development and implementation of intensive treatment for high-risk male prisoners. *Psychology, Crime and Law*, 19, 511–526.

Polaschek, D. L. L., & Ward, T. (2002). The implicit theories of potential rapists: What our questionnaires tell us. *Aggression and Violent Behavior*, 7, 385–406.

Polk, K. (1995). Lethal violence as a form of masculine conflict resolution. *Australian and New Zealand Journal of Criminology*, 28, 93–115.

Polk, K. (1999). Males and honor contest violence. *Homicide Studies*, 3, 6–29.

Porter, T., & Gavin, H. (2010). Infanticide and neonaticide: A review of 40 years of research literature on incidence and causes. *Trauma, Violence and Abuse*, 11, 99–112.

Post, J. M., Sprinzak, E., & Denny, L. M. (2003). The terrorists in their own words: Interviews with 35 incarcerated Middle Eastern terrorists. *Terrorism and Political Violence*, 15, 171–184.

Pratt, J. (2000). Emotive and ostentatious punishment: Its decline and resurgence in modern society. *Punishment and Society*, 2, 417–439.

Pratt, J. (2006). *Penal Populism.* New York, NY: Routledge.

Pratt, J., Brown, D., Brown, M., Hallsworth, S., & Morrison, W. (2005). *The New Punitiveness: Trends, Theories, Perspectives.* Cullompton: Willan Publishing.

Pratt, J., & Eriksson, A. (2014). *Contrasts in Punishment: An Explanation of Anglophone Excess and Nordic Exceptionalism.* New York, NY: Routledge.

Pratt, T. C., & Cullen, F. T. (2000). The empirical status of Gottfredson and Hirschi's general theory of crime: A meta-analysis. *Criminology*, 38, 931–964.

Pridemore, W. A., & Trent, C. L. S. (2010). Do the invariant findings of Land, McCall and Cohen generalize to cross-national studies of social structure and homicide? *Homicide Studies*, 14, 296–335.

Prot, S., Anderson, C. A., Saleem, M., Groves, C. L., & Allen, J. J. (2016). Understanding media violence effects. In A. G. Miller (ed.), *The Social Psychology of Good and Evil* (2nd edition), (pp. 119–139). New York, NY: The Guilford Press.

Pudney, S. (2002). *The Road to Ruin? Sequences of Initiation to Drug Use and Offending by Young People in Britain.* London: Home Office.

Puts, D. A. (2010). Beauty and the beast: Mechanisms of sexual selection in humans. *Evolution and Human Behavior*, 31, 157–175.

Puts, D. (2016). Human sexual selection. *Current Opinion in Psychology*, 7, 28–32.

Quilty, S. (2005). The magnitude of experience of parental incarceration in Australia. *Psychiatry, Psychology and Law*, 12, 256–257.

Quilty, S., Levy, M., Howard, K., Barratt, A., & Butler, T. (2004). Children of prisoners: A growing public health problem. *Australian National Journal of Public Health*, 28, 339–343.

Rafter, P., Posick, C., & Rocque, M. (2016). *The Criminal Brain: Understanding Biological Theories of Crime* (2nd edition). New York, NY: New York University Press.

Ragatz, L., & Fremouw, W. (2010). A critical examination of research on the psychological profiles of white-collar criminals. *Journal of Forensic Psychology Practice*, 10, 373–402.

Ragatz, L. L., Fremouw, W., & Baker, E. (2012). The psychological profile of white-collar offenders: Demographics, criminal thinking, psychopathic traits, and psychopathology. *Criminal Justice and Behavior*, 39, 978–997.

Raine, A. (2008). From genes to brain to antisocial behaviour. *Current Directions in Psychological Science*, 17, 323–328.

Raine, A. (2013). *The Anatomy of Violence: The Biological Roots of Crime*. New York, NY: Pantheon Books.

Raine, A., Buchsbaum, M., & LaCasse, L. (1997). Brain abnormalities in murderers indicated by positron emission tomography. *Biological Psychiatry*, 42, 495–508.

Raine, A., Laufer, W. S., Yang, Y., Narr, K. L., Thompson, P., & Toga, A. W. (2012). Increased executive functioning, attention, and cortical thickness in white-collar criminals. *Human Brain Mapping*, 33, 2932–2940.

Ramsey, M. (2003). *Prisoners' Drug Use and Treatment: Seven Research Studies*. London: Home Office.

Randall, M., Sciberras, E., Brignell, A., Ihsen, E., Lfron, D., Dissanayake, C., & Williams, K. (2016). Autism spectrum disorder: Presentation and prevalence in a nationally representative Australian sample. *Australian and New Zealand Journal of Psychiatry*, 50, 243–253.

Ranson, M. (2014). Crime, weather, and climate change. *Journal of Environmental Economics and Management*, 67, 274–302.

Reuter, P. (2016). On the multiple sources of violence in drug markets. *Criminology and Public Policy*, 15, 1–7.

Reuter, P., & Pardo, B. (2016a). Can new psychoactive substances be regulated effectively? An assessment of the British Psychoactive Substances Bill. *Addiction*, 112, 25–31.

Reuter, P., & Pardo, B. (2016b). New psychoactive substances: Are there any good options for regulating new psychoactive substances? *International Journal of Drug Policy*, 40, 117–122.

Reyna, V. F., & Farley, F. (2006). Risk and rationality in adolescent decision making. *Psychological Science in the Public Interest*, 7, 1–44.

Reyna, V. F., & Farley, F. (2007). Is the teen brain too rational? *Scientific American Mind*, January, 58–65.

Rhee, S. H., & Waldman, I. D. (2002). Genetic and environmental influences on antisocial behaviour: A meta-analysis of twin and adoption studies. *Psychological Bulletin*, 128, 490–529.

Rhee, S. H., & Waldman, I. D. (2007). Behavior-genetics of criminality and aggression. In D. J. Flannery, A. T. Vazsonyi, & I. D. Waldman (eds.), *Cambridge Handbook of Violent Behaviour* (pp. 77–90). Leiden: Cambridge University Press.

Rice, M. E., & Harris, G. T. (2011). Is androgen deprivation therapy effective in the treatment of sex offenders? *Psychology, Public Policy, and Law*, 17, 315–332.

Richerson, P. J., & Boyd, R. (2005). *Not by Genes Alone: How Culture Transformed Human Evolution*. Chicago, IL: Chicago University Press.

Riek, B. M., Mania, E. W., & Gaertner, S. L. (2006). Intergroup threat and outgroup attitudes: A meta-analytic review. *Personality and Social Psychology Review*, 10, 336–353.

Ritter, D., & Eslea, M. (2005). Hot sauce, toy guns, and graffiti: A critical account of current laboratory aggression paradigms. *Aggressive Behavior*, 31, 407–419.

Roberts, J. V., & de Keijser, J. W. (2014). Democratising punishment: Sentencing, community views and values. *Punishment and Society*, 16, 474–498.

Roberts, J. V., & Hough, M. (2005). The state of the prisons: Exploring public knowledge and opinion. *The Howard Journal*, 44, 286–306.

Roberts, L. D., & Indermaur, D. (2007). Predicting punitive attitudes in Australia. *Psychiatry, Psychology and Law*, 14, 56–65.

Robins, L. N., Helzer, J. E., & Davis, D. H. (1975). Narcotic use in southeast Asia and afterward: An interview study of 898 Vietnam returnees. *Archives of General Psychiatry*, 32, 955–961.

Robins, L. N., & Slobodyan, S. (2003). Post-Vietnam heroin use and injection by returning US veterans: Clues to preventing injection today. *Addiction*, 98, 1053–1060.

Robinson, A. (2010). Domestic violence. In F. Brookman, M. Maguire, H. Pierpoint, & T. Bennett (eds.), *Handbook on Crime* (pp. 245–270). Cullompton: Willan Publishing.

Robinson, P. H., & Darley, J. M. (2004). Does criminal law deter? A behavioural science investigation. *Oxford Journal of Legal Studies*, 24, 173–205.

Robinson, P. H., Kurzban, R., & Jones, O. D. (2007). The origins of shared intuitions of justice. *Vanderbilt Law Review*, 60, 1633–1688.

Robinson, T. E., & Berridge, K. C. (2001). Incentive-sensitization and addiction. *Addiction*, 96, 103–114.

Robinson, T. E., & Berridge, K. C. (2003). Addiction. *Annual Review of Psychology*, 54, 25–53.

Room, R. (2006). The dangerousness of drugs. *Addiction*, 101, 166–168.

Room, R. (2013). Legalizing a market for cannabis for pleasure: Colorado, Washington, Uruguay and beyond. *Addiction*, 109, 345–351.

Rosenfeld, R. (2011). The big picture: 2010 presidential address to the American Society of Criminology. *Criminology*, 49, 1–26.

Rossow, I., & Bye, E. K. (2013). The problem of alcohol-related violence: An epidemiological and public health perspective. In M. McMurran (ed.), *Alcohol-Related Violence: Prevention and Treatment* (pp. 3–18). Chichester: Wiley.

Roth, M. P. (2014). *An Eye for An Eye: A Global History of Punishment*. London: Reaktion Books.

Roth, P. A. (2011). Social psychology and genocide. In D. Bloxham & A. D. Moses (eds.), *The Oxford Handbook of Genocide Studies* (pp. 198–216). Oxford: Oxford University Press.

Rowe, M., & Hutton, F. (2012). 'Is your city pretty anyway?' Perspectives on graffiti and the urban landscape. *Australian and New Zealand Journal of Criminology*, 45, 66–86.

Rucker, D. D., Polifroni, M., Tetlock, P. E., & Scott, A. L. (2004). On the assignment of punishment: The impact of general-societal threat and the moderating role of severity. *Personality and Social Psychological Bulletin*, 30, 673–684.

Ruddiman, W. F. (2013). The Anthropocene. *Annual Review of Earth and Planetary Science*, 41, 45–68.

Russett, B., & Oneal, J. (2001). *Triangulating Peace: Democracy, Interdependence and International Organizations*. New York, NY: Norton.

Rutter, M. (2003a). Commentary: Causal processes leading to antisocial behaviour. *Developmental Psychology*, 39, 372–378.

Rutter, M. (2003b). Crucial paths from risk indicator to causal mechanism. In B. B. Lahey, T. E. Moffitt, & A. Caspi (eds.), *Causes of Conduct Disorder and Juvenile Delinquency* (pp. 5–24). New York, NY: The Guilford Press.

Rutter, M. (2007). Gene-environment interdependence. *Developmental Science*, 10, 12–18.

Sabol, W. J., Couture, H., & Harrison, P. M. (2007). *Prisoners in 2006* (Bureau of Justice Statistics Bulletin). Washington, DC: U.S. Department of Justice.

Sachs, J. D. (2015). *The Age of Sustainable Development*. New York, NY: Columbia University Press.

Salekin, R. T. (2002). Psychopathy and therapeutic pessimism: Clinical lore or clinical reality? *Clinical Psychology Review*, 22, 79–112.

Salekin, R. T. (2008). Psychopathy and recidivism from mid-adolescence to young adulthood: Cumulating legal problems and limiting life opportunities. *Journal of Abnormal Psychology*, 117, 386–395.

Salekin, R. T., & Frick, P. J. (2005). Psychopathy in children and adolescents: The need for a developmental perspective. *Journal of Abnormal Child Psychology*, 33, 403–409.

Sampson, R. J. (2012). *Great American City: Chicago and the Enduring Neighborhood Effect.* Chicago, IL: University of Chicago Press.

Sampson, R. J., & Laub, J. H. (2005). A life-course view of the development of crime. *Annals of the American Academy of Political and Social Sciences*, 602, 12–45.

Sampson, R. J., & Laub, J. H. (2016). Turning points and the future of life-course criminology: reflections on the 1986 Criminal Careers Report. *Journal of Research in Crime and Delinquency*, 53, 321–335.

Sampson, R. J., Raudenbush, S. W., & Earls, F. (1997). Neighborhoods and violent crime: A multilevel study of collective efficacy. *Science*, 277, 918–924.

Samuel, D. B., & Widiger, T. A. (2008). A meta-analytic review of the relationships between the five-factor model and DSM-IV-TR personality disorders: A facet level analysis. *Clinical Psychology Review*, 28, 1326–1342.

Samúni, L., Preis, A., Mundry, R., Deschner, T., Crockford, C., & Wittig, R. M. (2017). Oxytocin reactivity during intergroup conflict in wild chimpanzees. *Proceedings of the National Academy of Sciences*, 114, 268–273.

Sanders, M. R., Kirby, J. N., Tellegen, C. L., & Day, J. J. (2014). The Triple P-positive parenting program: A systematic review and meta-analysis of a multi-level system of parenting support. *Clinical Psychology Review*, 34, 337–357.

Saradjian, A., & Nobus, D. (2003). Cognitive distortions of religious professionals who sexually abuse children. *Journal of Interpersonal Violence*, 18, 905–923.

Sargent, J. D., Wills, T. A., Stoolmiller, M., Gibson, J., & Gibbons, F. X. (2006). Alcohol use in motion pictures and its relation with early-onset teen drinking. *Journal of Studies on Alcohol*, 67, 54–65.

Savage, J. (2004). Does viewing violent media really cause criminal violence? A methodological review. *Aggression and Violent Behavior*, 10, 99–128.

Savage, J., & Yancey, C. (2008). The effects of media violence exposure on criminal aggression: A meta-analysis. *Criminal Justice and Behavior*, 35, 772–791.

Schanda, H., Knecht, G., Schreinzer, D., Stompe, T., Ortwwin-Swoboda, G., & Waldhoer, T. (2004). Homicide and major mental disorders: A 25-year study. *Acta Psychiatrica Scandinavica*, 110, 98–107.

Schindler, H. S., & Black, C. F. D. (2015). Early prevention of criminal and antisocial behaviour: A review of interventions in infancy and childhood. In J. Morizot & L. Kazemian (eds.), *The Development of Criminal and Antisocial Behaviour* (pp. 433–446). New York, NY: Springer.

Schlesinger, L. B., Kassen, M., Mesa, B., & Pinizzotto, A. J. (2010). Ritual and signature in serial sexual homicide. *Journal of American Academy of Psychiatry and Law*, 38, 239–246.

Schloenhardt, A., & Laura-Rose, L. (2013). McIvor and Tanuchit: A truly 'heinous' case of sexual slavery. *The University of Queensland, TC Beirne School of Legal Studies Research Paper Series*, 13–15.

Schlomer, G. L., Del Giudice, M., & Ellis, B. J. (2011). Parent-offspring conflict theory: An evolutionary framework for understanding conflict within human families. *Psychological Review*, 118, 496–521.

Schmid, A. P. (2011). The definition of terrorism. In A. P. Schmid (ed.), *The Routledge Handbook of Terrorism Research* (pp. 39–157). London: Routledge.

Schmucker, M., & Lösel, F. (2015). The effects of sexual offender treatment on recidivism: An international meta-analysis of sound quality evaluations. *Journal of Experimental Criminology*, 11, 597–630.

Schrock, D., & Schwalbe, M. (2009). Men, masculinity, and manhood acts. *Annual Review of Sociology*, 35, 277–295.

Schug, R. A., & Fradella, H. F. (2015). *Mental Illness and Crime*. Thousand Oaks, CA: Sage Publications.

Schultes, R. E. (1990). An overview of hallucinogens in the Western hemisphere. In P. T. Furst (ed.), *Flesh of the Gods: The Ritual Use of Hallucinogens* (2nd edition). Prospect Heights, IL: Waveland Press Inc.

Schwartz, S. J., Dunkel, C. S., & Waterman, A. A. (2009). Terrorism: An identity theory perspective. *Studies in Conflict and Terrorism*, 32, 537–559.

Seddon, N., Mace, G. M., Naeem, S., Tobias, J. A., Pigot, A. L., Cavanagh, R., ... Walpole, M. (2016). Biodiversity in the Anthropocene: Prospects and policy. *Proceedings of the Royal Society B*, 283, 20162094.

Séguin, J. R., Sylvers, P., & Lilienfeld, S. O. (2007). The neuropsychology of violence. In D. J. Flannery, A. T. Vazsonyi, & I. D. Waldman (eds.), *Cambridge Handbook of Violent Behaviour* (pp. 187–214). Leiden: Cambridge University Press.

Sellers, C. S., Cochran, J. K., & Branch, K. A. (2005). Social learning theory and partner violence: A research note. *Deviant Behavior*, 26, 379–395.

Semmens, N. (2010). Identity theft and fraud. In F. Brookman, M. Maguire, H. Pierpoint, & T. Bennett (eds.), *Handbook on Crime* (pp. 172–190). Cullompton: Willan Publishing.

Seo, D., Patrick, C. J., & Kennealy, P. J. (2008). Role of serotonin and dopamine system interactions in the neurobiology of impulsive aggression and its comorbidity with other clinical disorders. *Aggression and Violent Behavior*, 13, 383–395.

Seto, M. C., Maric, A., & Barbaree, H. E. (2001). The role of pornography in the etiology of sexual aggression. *Aggression and Violent Behavior*, 6, 35–53.

Sexual Offences Act. (2003). Retrieved from www.legislation.gov.uk/ukpga/2003/42/contents on April 8, 2017.

Shackelford, T. K., Buss, D. M., & Peters, J. (2000). Wife killing: Risk to women as a function of age. *Violence and Victims*, 15, 273–281.

Shackelford, T. K., & Mouzos, J. (2005). Partner killing by men in cohabiting and marital relationships: A comparative, cross-national analysis of data from Australia and the United States. *Journal of Interpersonal Violence*, 20, 1310–1324.

Shapiro, H. (2005). *Shooting Stars: Drugs, Hollywood and the Movies*. New York, NY: Serpent's Tail.

Shaw, E. (2015). The use of brain interventions in offender rehabilitation programmes: Should it be mandatory, voluntary, or prohibited? In J. Clausen & N. Levy (eds.), *Handbook of Neuroethics* (pp. 1381–1398). Dordrecht: Springer.

Shaw, J., Hunt, I. M., Flynn, S., Amos, T., Meehan, J., Robinson, J., ... Appleby, L. (2006). The role of alcohol and drugs in homicides in England and Wales. *Addiction*, 101, 1117–1124.

Shaw, V. N. (2002). *Substance Use and Abuse: Sociological Perspectives*. Westport, CT: Praegar.

Shepherd, S. M., Campbell, R. E., & Ogloff, J. R. P. (2016). Psychopathy, antisocial personality disorder, and reconviction in an Australian sample of forensic patients. *International Journal of Offender Therapy and Comparative Criminology*. Advance online publication. DOI: 10.1177/0306624X16653193.

Sherif, M., Harvey, O. J., White, B. J., Hood, W. R., & Sherif, C. W. (1961). *Intergroup Conflict and Cooperation: The Robber's Cave Experiment*. Norman, OK: The University Book Exchange.

Shulman, E. P., Harden, K. P., Chein, J. M., & Steinberg, L. (2014). Sex differences in the developmental trajectories of impulse control and sensation-seeking from early adolescence to early adulthood. *Journal of Youth and Adolescence*, 44, 1–17.

Shulman, E. P., Smith, A. R., Silva, K., Icenogle, G., Duell, N., Chein, J., & Steinberg, L. (2016). The dual systems model: Review, reappraisal, and reaffirmation. *Developmental Cognitive Neuroscience*, 17, 103–117.

Silke, A. (2008). Holy warriors: Exploring the psychological processes of Jihadi radicalization. *European Journal of Criminology*, 5, 99–123.

Silver, E., Felson, R. B., & Vaneseltine, M. (2008). The relationship between mental health problems and violence among criminal offenders. *Criminal Justice and Behavior*, 35, 405–426.

Silver, E., Mulvey, E. P., & Monahan, J. (1999). Assessing violence risk among discharged psychiatric patients: Toward an ecological approach. *Law and Human Behavior*, 23, 237–255.

Silver, E., & Teasdale, B. (2005). Mental disorder and violence: An examination of stressful life events and impaired social support. *Social Problems*, 52, 62–78.

Silverstein, S. M., Del Pozzo, J., Roché, M., Boyle, D., & Miskimen, T. (2015). Schizophrenia and violence: Realities and recommendations. *Crime Psychology Review*, 1, 21–42.

Simmons, F., O'Brien, B., David, F., & Beacroft, L. (2013). Human trafficking and slavery offenders in Australia. *Trends and Issues in Crime and Criminal Justice* (464), 1–13.

Simons, D. A., Wurtele, S. K., & Durham, R. L. (2008). Developmental experiences of child sexual abusers and rapists. *Child Abuse and Neglect*, 32, 549–560.

Simons, R. L., Simons, L. G., Chen, Y-F., Brody, G. H., & Lin, K.-H. (2007). Identifying the psychological factors that mediate the association between parenting practices and delinquency. *Criminology*, 45, 481–517.

Simpson, S. S. (2013). White-collar crime: A review of recent developments and promising directions for future research. *Annual Review of Sociology*, 39, 309–331.

Singh, J. P., Grann, M., & Fazel, S. (2011). A comparative study of violence risk assessment tools: A systematic review and metaregression analysis of 68 studies involving 25,980 participants. *Clinical Psychology Review*, 31, 499–513.

Sirdifield, C., Gojkovic, D., Brooker, C., & Ferriter, M. (2009). A systematic review of research on the epidemiology of mental health disorders in prison populations: A summary of findings. *The Journal of Forensic Psychiatry and Psychology*, 20, S1, S78–S101.

Skardhamar, T., Savolainen, J., Aase, K. N., & Lyngstad, T. H. (2015). Does marriage reduce crime? *Crime and Justice*, 44, 385–557.

Skeem, J. L., & Cooke, D. J. (2010). Is criminal behaviour a central component of psychopathy? Conceptual directions for resolving the debate. *Psychological Assessment*, 22, 433–445.

Skeem, J. L., Kennealy, P., Monahan, J., Peterson, J., & Appelbaum, P. (2016). Psychosis uncommonly and inconsistently precedes violence among high risk individuals. *Clinical Psychological Science*, 4, 40–49.

Skeem, J. L., Polaschek, D. L. L., Patrick, C. J., & Lilienfeld, S. O. (2011). Psychopathic personality: Bridging the gap between scientific evidence and public policy. *Psychological Science in the Public Interest*, 12, 95–162.

Smith, D. L. (2011). *Less than human: Why we demean, enslave, and exterminate others*. New York, NY: St Martin's Press.

Smith, E. A., Borgerhoff Mulder, M., & Hill, K. (2001). Controversies in the evolutionary social sciences: A guide for the perplexed. *Trends in Ecology and Evolution*, 16, 128–135.

Smith, P., & Schweitzer, M. (2012). The therapeutic prison. *Journal of Contemporary Criminal Justice*, 28, 7–22.

Smith, S. F., & Lilienfeld, S. O. (2013). Psychopathy in the workplace: The known and the unknowns. *Aggression and Violent Behavior*, 18, 204–218.

Somerville, L. H. (2013). The teenage brain: Sensitivity to social evaluation. *Current Directions in Psychological Science*, 22, 121–127.

Sommers, I., & Baskin, D. (2006). Methamphetamine use and violence. *Journal of Drug Issues*, 36, 77–96.

Soussan, C., & Kjellgren, A. (2016). The users of novel psychoactive substances: Online survey about their characteristics, attitudes and motivations. *International Journal of Drug Policy*, 32, 77–84.

Spear, L. P. (2013). Adolescent neurodevelopment. *Journal of Adolescent Health*, 52, S7–S13.

Stadler, W. A., & Benson, M. L. (2012). Revisiting the guilty mind: The neutralization of white-collar crime. *Criminal Justice Review*, 37, 494–511.

Stake, J. E. (2004). The property 'instinct'. *Philosophical Transactions of the Royal Society of London B*, 359, 1763–1774.

Stanton, J., & Simpson, A. (2002). Filicide: A review. *International Journal of Law and Psychiatry*, 25, 1–14.

Steadman, H. J., Mulvey, E. P., Monahan, J., Robbins, P. C., Appelbaum, P. A., Grisso, T., ... Silver, E. (1998). Violence by people discharged from acute psychiatric inpatient facilities and by others in the same neighborhoods. *Archives of General Psychiatry*, 55, 393–401.

Steel, J., Thornicroft, G., Birmingham, L., Brooker, C., Mills, A., Harty, M., & Shaw, J. (2007). Prison mental health inreach services. *British Journal of Psychiatry*, 190, 373–374.

Stein, M. L., Schlesinger, L. B., & Pinizzotto, A. J. (2010). Necrophilia and sexual homicide. *Journal of Forensic Sciences*, 55, 443–446.

Steinberg, L. (2007). Risk taking in adolescence: New perspectives from brain and behavioural science. *Current Directions in Psychological Science*, 16, 55–59.

Steinberg, L. (2009). Adolescent development and juvenile justice. *Annual Review of Clinical Psychology*, 5, 47–73.

Steinberg, L. (2013). The influence of neuroscience on US Supreme Court decisions about adolescents' criminal culpability. *Nature Reviews Neuroscience*, 14, 513–518.

Steinberg, L. (2014). *Age of Opportunity: Lessons from the New Science of Adolescence*. Boston, MA: Houghton Mifflin Harcourt.

Stephens, S., Seto, M. C., Goodwill, A. M., & Cantor, J. M. (2016). Age diversity among victims of hebephilic sexual offenders. *Sexual Abuse: A Journal of Research and Treatment*. Advance online publication. DOI: 10.1177/1079063216665837.

Stevens, M. (2016). *Cheats and Deceits: How Animals and Plants Exploit and Mislead*. Oxford: Oxford University Press.

Stewart, E. A., & Simons, R. L. (2010). Race, code of the street, and violent delinquency: A multilevel investigation of neighbourhood street culture and individuals' norms of violence. *Criminology*, 48, 569–605.

Stewart-Williams, S., & Thomas, A. G. (2013). The ape that thought it was a peacock: does evolutionary psychology exaggerate human sex differences? *Psychological Inquiry*, 24, 137–168.

Stiles-Shields, C., & Carroll, R. A. (2015). Same-sex domestic violence: Prevalence, unique aspects, and clinical implications. *Journal of Sex and Marital Therapy*, 41, 636–648.

Stinson, J. D., & Becker, J. V. (2016). Pedophilic disorder. In A. Phenix & H. M. Hoberman (eds.), *Sexual Offending* (pp. 15–27). New York, NY: Springer.

Stith, S. M., Liu, T., Davies, C., Boykin, E. L., Alder, M. C., Harris, J. M., ... Dees, J.E.M.E.G. (2009). Risk factors in child maltreatment: A meta-analytic review of the literature. *Aggression and Violent Behavior*, 14, 13–29.

Stith, S. M., Rosen, K. H., Middleton, K. A., Busch, A. L., Lundeberg, K., & Carlton, R. P. (2000). The intergenerational transmission of spouse abuse: A meta-analysis. *Journal of Marriage and the Family*, 62, 640–654.

Stith, S. M., Smith, D. B., Penn, C. E., Ward, D. B., & Tritt, D. (2004). Intimate partner physical abuse perpetration and victimization risk factors: A meta-analytic review. *Aggression and Violent Behaviour*, 10, 65–98.

Stöckl, H., Devries, K., Rotstein, A., Abrahams, N., Campbell, J., Watts, C., & Moreno, C. G. (2013). The global prevalence of intimate partner homicide: A systematic review. *The Lancet*, 382, 859–865.

Stöckl, H., March, L., Pallitto, C., & Garcia-Moreno, C. (2014). Intimate partner violence among adolescents and young women: Prevalence and associated factors in nine countries: A cross-sectional study. *BMC Public Health*, 14, 751.

Stoltenborgh, M., Bakermans-Kranenburg, M. J., Lenneke, R. A. A., & van Ijzendoorn, M. H. (2015). The prevalence of child maltreatment across the globe: Review of a series of meta-analyses. *Child Abuse Review*, 24, 37–50.

Stone, M. H. (2007). Violent crimes and their relationship to personality disorders. *Personality and Mental Health*, 1, 138–153.

Straus, M. A. (2008). Bucking the tide in family violence research. *Trauma Violence Abuse*, 9, 191–213.

Straus, M. A. (2011). Gender symmetry and mutuality in perpetration of clinical-level partner violence: Empirical evidence and implications for prevention and treatment. *Aggression and Violent Behavior*, 16, 279–288.

Straus, M. A., & Gozjolko, K. L. (2016). Concordance between partners in 'intimate terrorism': A comparison of two typologies. *Aggression and Violent Behavior*, 29, 55–60.

Sugarman, D. P., & Frankel, S. L. (1996). Patriarchal ideology and wife-assault: A meta-analytic review. *Journal of Family Violence*, 11, 13–40.

Sullivan, D. H., & Mullen, P. E. (2006). Forensic mental health. *Australian and New Zealand Journal of Psychiatry*, 40, 505–507.

Sutton, A., Cherney, A., & White, R. (2008). *Crime Prevention: Principles, Perspectives, and Practices*. Cambridge: Cambridge University Press.

Sutton, A., Cherney, A., & White, R. (2014). *Crime Prevention: Principles, Perspectives, and Practices* (2nd edition). New York, NY: Cambridge University Press.

Swann, W. B., & Buhrmester, M. D. (2015). Identity fusion. *Current Directions in Psychological Science*, 24, 52–57.

Swann, W. B., Buhrmester, M. D., Gómez, A., Jetten, J., Bastian, B., Vázquez, A., ... Zhang, A. (2014). What makes a group worth dying for? Identity fusion fosters perception of familial ties, promoting self-sacrifice. *Journal of Personality and Social Psychology*, 106, 912–926.

Swann, W. B., Gómez, Á., Dovidio, J. F., Hart, S., & Jetten, J. (2010). Dying and killing for one's group: Identity fusion moderates responses to intergroup versions of the trolley problem. *Psychological Science*, 21, 1176–1183.

Swann, W. B., Gómez, Á., Huici, C., Morales, J. F., & Hixon, J. G. (2010). Identity fusion and self-sacrifice: Arousal as a catalyst of pro-group fighting, dying, and helping behavior. *Journal of Personality and Social Psychology*, 5, 824–841.

Swanson, J. W. (1994). Mental disorder, substance abuse, and community violence: An epidemiological approach. In J. Monahan & H. J. Steadman (eds.), *Violence and Mental Disorder: Developments in Risk Assessment* (pp. 101–136). Chicago, IL: University of Chicago Press.

Swanson, J. W., Holzer, C. E., Ganju, V. K., & Jono, R. T. (1990). Violence and psychiatric disorder in the community: Evidence from the Epidemiologic Catchment Area surveys. *Hospital and Community Psychiatry*, 41, 761–770.

Swanson, J. W., Swartz, M. S., Van Dorn, R. A., Elbogen, E. B., Wagner, H. R., Rosenheck, R. A., ... Lieberman, J. A. (2006). A national study of violent behavior in persons with schizophrenia. *Archives of General Psychiatry*, 63, 490–499.

Sweeten, G., Piquero, A. R., & Steinberg, L. (2013). Age and the explanation of crime, revisited. *Journal of Youth and Adolescence*, 42, 921–938.

Sykes, G. M., & Matza, D. (1957). Techniques of neutralization: A theory of delinquency. *American Sociological Review*, 22, 664–670.

Taleb, N. N. (2007). *The Black Swan: The Impact of the Highly Improbable*. New York, NY: Random House.

Tangney, J. P., Baumeister, R. F., & Boone, A. L. (2004). High self-control predicts good adjustment, less pathology, better grades, and interpersonal success. *Journal of Personality*, 72, 271–323.

Tanner, E. E., Wilson, S. J., & Lipsey, M. W. (2013). Risk factors and crime. In F. T. Cullen & P. Wilcox (eds.), *Criminological Theory* (pp. 89–111). Oxford: Oxford University Press.

Taylor, E. (2014). Honour among thieves? How morality and rationality influence the decision-making processes of convicted burglars. *Criminology and Criminal Justice*, 14, 487–502.

Taylor, E. (2016a). On the edge of reason? Armed robbery affective transgression, and bounded rationality. *Deviant Behavior.* Advance online publication. DOI: 10.1080/01639625.2016.1229929.

Taylor, E. (2016b). Supermarket self-checkouts and retail theft: The curious case of SWIPERS. *Criminology and Criminal Justice*, 16, 552–567.

Taylor, N., Prichard, J., & Charlton, K. (2004). *National Project on Drink Spiking: Investigating the Nature and Extent of Drink Spiking in Australia.* Canberra: Australian Institute of Criminology.

Teasdale, B. (2009). Mental disorder and violent victimization. *Criminal Justice and Behavior*, 36, 513–535.

Tedeschi, J., & Quigley, B. (1996). Limitations of laboratory paradigms for studying aggression. *Aggression and Violent Behavior*, 1, 163–177.

Temrin, H., Nordlund, J., Rying, M., & Tullberg, B. S. (2011). Is the higher rate of parental child homicide in stepfamilies an effect of non-genetic relatedness? *Current Zoology*, 57, 253–259.

Theisen, O. M. (2008). Blood and soil? Resources scarcity and internal armed conflict revisited. *Journal of Peace Research*, 45, 801–818.

Themnér, L., & Wallensteen, P. (2011). Armed conflict, 1946–2010. *Journal of Peace Research*, 48, 525–536.

Theobald, D., & Farrington, D. P. (2009). Effects of getting married on offending: Results from a prospective longitudinal study of males. *European Journal of Criminology*, 6, 496–516.

Theobald, D., & Farrington, D. P. (2011). Why do the crime-reducing effects of marriage on offending vary with age? *British Journal of Criminology*, 51, 136–158.

Theobald, D., Farrington, D. P., & Piquero, A. R. (2014). Does the birth of a first child reduce the father's offending? *Australian and New Zealand Journal of Criminology*, 48, 3–23.

Thompson, M. E. (2009). Human rape: Revisiting evolutionary perspectives. In M. M. Muller & R. W. Wrangham (eds.), *Sexual Coercion in Primates and Humans: An Evolutionary Perspective on Male Aggression Against Females* (pp. 346–374). Cambridge, MA: Harvard University Press.

Thompson, S., & Kyle, K. (2005). Understanding mass school shootings: Links between personhood and power in the competitive school environment. *The Journal of Primary Prevention*, 26, 419–438.

Thornberry, T., Lizotte, A., Krohn, M., Farnworth, M., & Jang, S. (1994). Delinquent peers, beliefs, and delinquent behaviour: A longitudinal test of interactional theory. *Criminology*, 32, 47–83.

Thornhill, R., & Palmer, C. T. (2000). *A Natural History of Rape: Biological Bases of Sexual Coercion.* Cambridge: MIT Press.

Thoumi, F. E. (2014). Organized crime in Colombia: The actors running the illegal drug industry. In L. Paoli (ed.), *The Oxford Handbook of Organised Crime* (pp. 177–195). Oxford: Oxford University Press.

Tilley, N. (2009). *Crime Prevention.* Cullompton: Willan Publishing.

Tilley, N. (2010). Shoplifting. In F. Brookman, M. Maguire, H. Pierpoint, & T. Bennett (eds.), *Handbook on Crime* (pp. 48–67). Cullompton: Willan Publishing.

Timeline: The life of Van Nguyen. (2005). *ABC news online.* Retrieved from www.abc.net.au/news/indepth/featureitems/s1520853.htm on June 1, 2008.

Tinbergen, N. (1963). On the aims and methods of ethology. *Zeitschrift Fur Tierpsychologie*, 20, 410–433.

Tittle, C. R. (1980). *Sanctions and Social Deviance: The Question of Deterrence.* New York, NY: Praegar.

Tolan, P., Gorman-Smith, D., & Henry, D. (2006). Family violence. *Annual Review of Psychology,* 57, 557–583.

Tomlinson, M. F., Brown, M., & Hoaken, P. N. S. (2016). Recreational drug use and aggressive behaviour: A comprehensive review since 2003. *Aggression and Violent Behaviour,* 27, 9–29.

Tong, L. S., & Farrington, D. P. (2006). How effective is the 'reasoning and rehabilitation' programme in reducing reoffending? A meta-analysis of evaluations in four countries. *Psychology, Crime and Law,* 12, 3–24.

Tonry, M. (2008). Learning from the limitations of deterrence research. *Crime and Justice,* 37, 279–311.

Townsley, M., Birks, D., Bernasco, W., Ruiter, S., Johhnson, S. D., White, G., & Baum, S. (2015). Burglar target selection: A cross-national comparison. *Journal of Research in Crime and Delinquency,* 52, 3–31.

Trinkner, R., & Tyler, T. R. (2016). Legal socialization: Coercion versus consent in an era of mistrust. *Annual Review of Law and Social Science,* 12, 417–429.

Trivers, R. L. (1972). Parental investment and sexual selection. In B. Campbell (ed.), *Sexual Selection and the Descent of Man, 1871–1971* (pp. 136–179). Chicago, IL: Aldine.

Truman, J. L., & Rand, M. R. (2010). *Criminal Victimization, 2009.* Washington, DC: U.S. Department of Justice.

Ttofi, M. M., & Farrington, D. P. (2010). School bullying: risk factors, theories and interventions. In F. Brookman, M. Maguire, H. Pierpoint, & T. Bennett (eds.), *Handbook on Crime* (pp. 427–457). Cullompton: Willan Publishing.

Ttofi, M. M., Farrington, D. P., Piquero, A. R., Losel, F., DeLisi, M., & Murray, J. (2016). Intelligence as a protective factor against offending: A meta-analytic review of prospective longitudinal studies. *Journal of Criminal Justice,* 45, 4–18.

Turchin, P. (2016). *Ultrasociety: How 10,000 Years of War Made Humans the Greatest Cooperators on Earth.* Chaplin, CT: Beresta Books.

Twain, M. (1966). *Letters From the Earth.* New York, NY: Fawcett Cress Publishing.

Tyler, T. R. (2006). *Why People Obey the Law.* Princeton: Princeton University Press.

United Nations Office on Drugs and Crime. (2013). *Global Study on Homicide 2013.* Retrieved from www.unodc.org/gsh/ on February 1, 2017.

United Nations Office on Drugs and Crime. (2016a). *Global Report on Trafficking in Persons 2016.* New York, NY: United Nations.

United Nations Office on Drugs and Crime. (2016b). *World Drug Report, 2016.* Retrieved from www.unodc.org/wdr2016/ on February 1, 2017.

Urbas, B. (2000). The age of criminal responsibility. *Australian Institute of Criminology Trends and Issues in Crime and Criminal Justice* (181).

U.S. Department of Justice. (2016). *Crime in the United States, 2015* (Uniform Crime Reports 2015). Retrieved from https://ucr.fbi.gov/crime-in-the-u.s/2015/crime-in-the-u.s.-2015 on February 1, 2017.

Vachon, D. D., Lynam, D. R., & Johnson, J. A. (2014). The (non)relation between empathy and aggression: Surprising results from a meta-analysis. *Psychological Bulletin,* 140, 751–773.

Vance, A. (2011, March 19). Children's story has no happy ending. *Dominion Post,* p. 8.

Van de Weijer, S. G. A., Bijleveld, C. C. J. H., & Blokland, A. A. J. (2014). The intergeneration transmission of violent offending. *Journal of Family Violence,* 29, 109–118.

Van der Dennen, J. M. G. (1995). *The Origin of War: Evolution of a Male-Coalitional Reproductive Strategy.* Groningen: Origin Press.

Van der Linden, S. (2015). The social-psychological determinants of climate changes risk perceptions: Towards a comprehensive model. *Journal of Environmental Psychology*, 41, 112–124.

Van Dijk, J. (2008). *The World of Crime: Breaking the Silence on Problems of Security, Justice, and Development Across the World*. Los Angeles, CA: Sage Publications.

Van Dorn, R., Volavka, J., & Johnson, N. (2012). Mental disorder and violence: Is there a relationship beyond substance use? *Social Psychiatry and Psychiatric Epidemiology*, 47, 487–503.

Van Lange, P. A. M., Rinderu, M. I., & Bushman, B. J. (2016). Aggression and violence around the world: A model of Climate, Aggression, and Self-control in Humans (CLASH). *Behavioral and Brain Sciences*. Advance online publication. DOI: 10.1017/S0140525X16000406.

Van Langen, M. A. M., Wissink, I. B., van Vugt, E. S., van der Stouwe, T., & Stams, G. J. J. M. (2014). The relation between empathy and offending: A meta-analysis. *Aggression and Violent Behavior*, 19, 179–189.

Van Mastrigt, S. B., & Farrington, D. P. (2009). Co-offending, age, gender and crime type: Implications for criminal justice policy. *British Journal of Criminology*, 49, 552–573.

Van Vugt, M., Griskevicius, V., & Schultz, P. W. (2014). Naturally green: Harnessing stone age psychological biases to foster environmental behaviour. *Social Issues and Policy Review*, 8, 1–32.

Van Wees, H. (2010). Genocide in the ancient world. In D. Bloxham & A. D. Moses (eds.), *The Oxford Handbook of Genocide Studies* (pp. 240–258). Oxford: Oxford University Press.

Vassos, E., Collier, D. A., & Fazel, S. (2014). Systematic meta-analyses and field synopsis of genetic association studies of violence and aggression. *Molecular Psychiatry*, 19, 471–477.

Vaughn, M. G. (2016). Policy implications of biosocial criminology: Toward a renewed commitment to prevention science. *Criminology and Public Policy*, 15.

Vega, V., & Malamuth, N. M. (2007). Predicting sexual aggression: The role of pornography in the context of general and specific risk factors. *Aggressive Behavior*, 33, 104–117.

Viding, E., Blair, R. J. R., Moffitt, T. E., & Plomin, R. (2005). Evidence for substantial genetic risk for psychopathy in 7-year-olds. *Journal of Child Psychology and Psychiatry*, 46, 592–597.

Vidmar, N. (2001). Retributive justice: Its social context. In M. Ross & D. T. Miller (eds.), *The Justice Motive in Everyday Life*. Cambridge: Cambridge University Press.

Von Hirsch, A. (1998). Proportionate sentences: A desert perspective. In A. Von Hirsch & A. Ashworth (eds.), *Principled Sentencing: Readings on Theory and Policy* (2nd edition, pp. 168–180). Oxford: Hart Publishing.

Wacquant, L. (2005). The great penal leap backward: Incarceration in America from Nixon to Clinton. In J. Pratt, D. Brown, M. Brown, S. Hallsworth, & W. Morrison (eds.), *The New Punitiveness: Trends, Theories, Perspectives* (pp. 3–27). Cullompton: Willan Publishing.

Wagers, M., Sousa, W., & Kelling, G. (2008). Broken windows. In R. Wortley & L. Mazerolle (eds.), *Environmental Criminology and Crime Analysis* (pp. 247–262). Cullompton: Willan Publishing.

Wakefield, J. C. (1992). The concept of mental disorder: On the boundary between biological facts and social values. *American Psychologist*, 47, 373–388.

Wakefield, J. C. (2016). Diagnostic issues and controversies in DSM–5: Return of the false positives problem. *Annual Review of Clinical Psychology*, 12, 105–132.

Walker, J. S., & Bright, J. A. (2009). False inflated self-esteem and violence: A systematic review and cognitive model. *The Journal of Forensic Psychiatry and Psychology*, 20, 1–32.

Wall, T., & Horwood, A. (2003, January 23). Drug 'pure' linked to sword attacks and gunshot death. *The New Zealand Herald*. Retrieved from www.nzherald.co.nz/nz/news/article.cfm?c_id=1&objectid=3097885.

Wallace, C., Mullen, P. E., & Burgess, P. (2004). Criminal offending in schizophrenia over a 25-year period marked by deinstitutionalization and increasing prevalence of comorbid substance use disorders. *American Journal of Psychiatry*, 161, 716–727.

Walmsley, R. (2016). *World Prison Population List* (11th edition). Institute of Criminal Policy Research. Retrieved from www.icpr.org.uk/media/41356/world_prison_population_list_11th_edition.pdf.

Walsh, A. (2009a). Crazy by design: A biosocial approach to the age-crime curve. In A. Walsh & K. M. Beaver (eds.), *Biosocial Criminology: New Directions in Theory and Research* (pp. 154–175). New York, NY: Routledge.

Walsh, A. (2009b). Criminal behaviour from heritability to epigenetics: How genetics clarifies the role of the environment. In A. Walsh & K. M. Beaver (eds.), *Biosocial Criminology: New Directions in Theory and Research* (pp. 28–48). New York, NY: Routledge.

Walsh, A., & Bolen, D. (2012). *The Neurobiology of Criminal Behaviour: Gene-Brain-Culture Interaction.* Burlington, VT: Ashgate.

Walsh, A., & Ellis, L. (2007). *Criminology: An Interdisciplinary Approach.* Thousand Oaks, CA: Sage Publications.

Walsh, A., & Wu, H.-H. (2008). Differentiating antisocial personality disorder, psychopathy, and sociopathy: Evolutionary, genetic, neurological, and sociological considerations. *Criminal Justice Studies*, 21, 135–152.

Warburton, W. A., & Anderson, C. A. (2015). Aggression, social psychology of. In *International Encyclopaedia of the Social and Behavioural Sciences* (2nd edition, Vol. 1), (pp. 373–380). Amsterdam: Elsevier.

Ward, T. (2002). Good lives and the rehabilitation of offenders: Promises and problems. *Aggression and Violent Behavior*, 7, 513–528.

Ward, T., & Beech, A. (2006). An integrated theory of sexual offending. *Aggression and Violent Behavior*, 11, 44–63.

Ward, T., & Brown, M. R. (2004). The Good Lives Model and conceptual issues in offender rehabilitation. *Psychology, Crime & Law*, 10, 243–257.

Ward, T., & Durrant, R. (2014). Psychological altruism, empathy, and offender rehabilitation. In H. L. Maibom (ed.), *Empathy and Morality* (pp. 210–229). Oxford: Oxford University Press.

Ward, T., Fisher, S., & Beech, A. (2016). An integrated theory of sexual offending. In A. Phenix & H. M. Hoberman (eds.), *Sexual Offending* (pp. 1–11). New York, NY: Springer.

Ward, T., & Gannon, T. A. (2006). Rehabilitation, etiology, and self-regulation: The comprehensive good lives model of treatment for sexual offenders. *Aggression and Violent Behavior*, 11, 77–94.

Ward, T., & Keenan, T. (1999). Child molesters' implicit theories. *Journal of Interpersonal Violence*, 14, 821–838.

Ward, T., Mann, R. E., & Gannon, T. A. (2007). The good lives model of offender rehabilitation: Clinical implications. *Aggression and Violent Behavior*, 12, 87–107.

Ward, T., & Maruna, S. (2007). *Rehabilitation: Beyond the Risk Paradigm.* London: Routledge.

Ward, T., Polaschek, D. L. L. & Beech, A. R. (2006). *Theories of Sexual Offending.* Hoboken, NJ: John Wiley & Sons.

Ward, T., Rose, C., & Willis, G. M. (2012). Offender rehabilitation: Good lives, desistance and risk reduction. In G. Davies & A. Beech (eds.), *Forensic Psychology: Crime, Justice, Law, and Interventions* (2nd edition), (pp. 407–424). Chichester: John Wiley & Sons.

Ward, T., & Siegert, R. J. (2002a). Rape and evolutionary psychology: A critique of Thornhill and Palmer's theory. *Aggression and Violent Behavior*, 7, 145–168.

Ward, T., & Siegert, R. J. (2002b). Toward a comprehensive theory of child sexual abuse: A theory knitting perspective. *Psychology, Crime, and Law*, 8, 319–351.

Ward, T., & Stewart, C. (2003). Criminogenic needs and human needs: A theoretical model. *Psychology, Crime and Law*, 9, 125–143.

Waring, T. M. (2016). An evolutionary approach to sustainability science. *Cliodynamics*, 7, 119–167.

Warr, M. (2002). *Companions in Crime: The Social Aspects of Criminal Conduct.* Cambridge: Cambridge University Press.

Warr, M. (2005). Making delinquent friends: Adult supervision and children's affiliations. *Criminology,* 43, 77–106.

Weatherburn, D. (2016). 'Rack 'em, pack 'em and stack 'em': Decarceration in an age of zero tolerance. *Current Issues in Criminal Justice,* 28, 137–156.

Weber, S., Hable, U., Amunts, K., & Schneider, F. (2008). Structural brain abnormalities in psychopaths – A review. *Behavioral Sciences and the Law,* 26, 7–28.

Weigard, A., Chein, J., Albert, D., Smith, A., & Steinberg, L. (2014). Effects of anonymous peer observation on adolescents' preferences for immediate rewards. *Developmental Science,* 17, 71–78.

Weinberger, L. E., Sreenivasan, S., Garrick, T., & Osran, H. (2005). The impact of surgical castration on sexual recidivism risk among sexually violent predatory offenders. *Journal of American Academy of Psychiatry and the Law,* 33, 16–36.

Weisburd, D., & Eck, J. E. (2004). What can police do to reduce crime, disorder, and fear? *Annals of the American Academy of Political and Social Sciences,* 593, 42–65.

Weisburd, D., Einat, T., & Kowalski, M. (2008). The miracle of the cells: An experimental study of interventions to increase payment of court-ordered financial obligations. *Criminology & Public Policy,* 7, 9–36.

Weisburd, D., Wooditch, A., Weisburd, S., & Yang, S.-M. (2016). Do stop, question, and frisk practices deter crime? *Criminology and Public Policy,* 15, 31–55.

Welch, M. (2004). *Corrections: A Critical Approach.* Boston, MA: McGraw-Hill.

Wells, S., Graham, K., & West, P. (2000). Alcohol-related aggression in the general population. *Journal of Studies on Alcohol,* 61, 626–632.

Welsh, B. C., Braga, A. A., & Bruinsma, G. J. N. (2015). Reimaging broken windows: From theory to policy. *Journal of Research in Crime and Delinquency,* 52, 447–463.

Welsh, B. C., & Farrington, D. P. (2007). Scientific support for early prevention of delinquency and later offending. *Victims and Offenders,* 2, 125–140.

Welsh, B. C., & Farrington, D. P. (2012). Crime prevention and public policy. In B. C. Welsh. & D. P. Farrington (eds.), *The Oxford Handbook of Crime Prevention* (pp. 3–19). Oxford: Oxford University Press.

Welsh, B. C., & Farrington, D. P. (2015). Monetary value of early developmental crime prevention and its policy significance. *Criminology and Public Policy,* 14, 673–680.

Welsh, B. C., Farrington, D. P., & Taheri, S. A. (2015). Effectiveness and social costs of public area surveillance for crime prevention. *Annual Review of Law and Social Science,* 11, 111–130.

Welsh, B. C., & Rocque, M. (2014). When crime prevention harms: A review of systematic reviews. *Journal of Experimental Criminology,* 10, 245–266.

West, R. (2001). Theories of addiction. *Addiction,* 96, 3–13.

Wheeler, J. G., George, W. H., & Marlatt, G. A. (2006). Relapse prevention for sexual offenders: Considerations for the 'abstinence violation effect'. *Sex Abuse,* 18, 233–248.

Whitaker, D. J., Le, B., Hanson, R. K., Baker, C. K., McMahon, P. M., Ryan, G., ... Rice, D. D. (2008). Risk factors for the perpetration of child sexual abuse: A review and meta-analysis. *Child Abuse and Neglect,* 32, 529–548.

White, H. R. (2015). A developmental approach to understanding the substance use-crime connection. In J. Morizot & L. Kazemian (eds.), *The Development of Criminal and Antisocial Behaviour* (pp. 379–397). Cham: Springer.

White, J. L., Moffitt, T. E., Caspi, A., Bartusch, D. J., Needles, D. J., & Stouthamer-Loeber, M. (1994). Measuring impulsivity and examining its relationship to delinquency. *Journal of Abnormal Psychology,* 103, 192–205.

White, M. (2012). *Atrocities: The 100 Deadliest Episodes in Human History.* New York, NY: W. W. Norton.

White, R., & Heckenberg, D. (2014). *Green Criminology: An Introduction to the Study of Environmental Harm.* London: Routledge.

Whitehead, A. (2005). Man to man violence: How masculinity may work as a dynamic risk factor. *The Howard Journal,* 44, 411–422.

Widiger, T. A., & Trull, T. J. (2007). Plate tectonics in the classification of personality disorder: Shifting to a dimensional model. *American Psychologist,* 62, 71–83.

Widom, C. S. (1989). The cycle of violence. *Science,* 244, 160–166.

Wike, T. L., & Fraser, M. W. (2009). School shootings: Making sense of the senseless. *Aggression and Violent Behavior,* 14, 162–169.

Wikström, P. H. (2006). Individuals, settings, and acts of crime: Situational mechanisms and the explanation of crime. In P. H. Wikström & R. J. Sampson (eds.), *The Explanation for Crime: Context, Mechanisms and Development* (pp. 61–107). Cambridge: Cambridge University Press.

Wikström, P. H., & Treiber, K. (2016). Situational theory: The importance of interactions and action mechanisms in the explanation of crime. In A. R. Piquero (ed.), *The Handbook of Criminological Theory* (pp. 415–444). Chichester: John Wiley & Sons.

Wilcox, A. J., Dunson, D. B., Weinberg, C. R., Trussell, J., & Baird, D. D. (2001). Likelihood of conception with a single act of intercourse: Providing benchmark rates for assessment of post-coital contraceptives. *Contraception,* 63, 211–215.

Wilkins, C., & Casswell, S. (2003). Cannabis cultivation and organised crime in New Zealand. *Contemporary Drug Problems,* 30, 757–777.

Wilkins, C., Jawalker, P., Barnes, H. M., Parker, K., Asiasiga, L. (2013). *New Zealand Arrestee Drug Use Monitoring Report (NZ-ADUM).* Retrieved from www.police.govt.nz/sites/default/files/publications/2013-nz-adum-report.pdf on February 1, 2017.

Wilkins, C., Pledger, M., Lee, A., Adams, R., & Rose, E. (2004). *A Local Pilot of the New Zealand Arrestee Drug Abuse Monitoring (NZ-ADAM) System.* Auckland: Centre for Social Health Outcomes Research and Evaluation.

Williams, J. (2010). Elder abuse. In F. Brookman, M. Maguire, H. Pierpoint, & T. Bennett (eds.), *Handbook on Crime* (pp. 415–426). Cullompton: Willan Publishing.

Williams, M., Zalasiewicz, J., Haff, P. K., Schwägerl, C., Barnosky, A. D., & Ellis, E. C. (2015). The Anthropocene biosphere. *The Anthropocene Review,* 2, 196–219.

Williams, P. (2014). Nigerian criminal organizations. In L. Paoli (ed.), *The Oxford Handbook of Organised Crime* (pp. 254–269). Oxford: Oxford University Press.

Willis, G. M., & Ward, T. (2013). The good lives model: Does it work? Preliminary evidence. In L. A. Craig, L. Dixon, & T. A. Gannon (eds.), *What Works in Offender Rehabilitation: An Evidence-Based Approach to Assessment and Treatment* (pp. 305–317). Hoboken, NJ: Wiley.

Wilson, D. B. (2016). Correctional programs. In D. Weisburd et al. (eds.), *What Works in Crime Prevention and Rehabilitation* (pp. 193–217). New York, NY: Springer.

Wilson, D. B., Bouffard, L., & Mackenzie, D. L. (2005). A quantitative review of structured, group-oriented, cognitive-behavioral programs for offenders. *Criminal Justice and Behavior,* 32, 172–203.

Wilson, J. Q., & Kelling, G. L. (1982, March). Broken windows. *The Atlantic Monthly,* 29–38.

Wilson, M. I., & Daly, M. (1996). Male sexual proprietariness and violence against wives. *Current Directions in Psychological Science,* 5, 2–7.

Wilson, M., Daly, M., & Daniele, A. (1995). Familicide: The killing of spouse and children. *Aggressive Behavior,* 21, 275–291.

Wilson, M., Johnson, H., & Daly, M. (1995). Lethal and nonlethal violence against wives. *Canadian Journal of Criminology,* 331–361.

Winterdyk, J. (2009). Genocide: International issues and perspectives worthy of criminal justice attention. *International Criminal Justice Review*, 19, 101–114.

Witt, K., van Dorn, R., & Fazel, S. (2013). Risk factors for violence in psychosis: Systematic review and meta-regression analysis of 110 studies. *PLoS ONE*, 8(2), e55942.

Wohl, M. J. A., & Branscombe, N. R. (2008). Remembering historical victimization: Collective guilt for current ingroup transgressions. *Journal of Personality and Social Psychology*, 94, 988–1006.

Wolff, N., Blitz, C. L., & Shi, J. (2007). Rates of sexual victimization in prison inmates with and without mental disorders. *Psychiatric Services*, 58, 1087–1094.

Wolff, N., Blitz, C. L., Shi, J., Siegel, J., & Bachman, R. (2007). Physical violence inside prisons: Rates of victimization. *Criminal Justice and Behavior*, 34, 588–599.

World Health Organization. (2002a). *The ICD-10 Classification of Mental and Behavioural Disorders*. Geneva: World Health Organization.

World Health Organization. (2002b). *World Report on Violence and Health*. Geneva: World Health Organization.

World Health Organization. (2005). *WHO Multi-Country Study on Women's Health and Domestic Violence Against Women*. Geneva: World Health Organization.

Wormith, J. S., Althouse, R., Simpson, M., Reitzel, L. R., Fagan, T. J., & Morgan, R. D. (2007). The rehabilitation and reintegration of offenders: The current landscape and some future directions for correctional psychology. *Criminal Justice and Behavior*, 34, 879–892.

Worrall, A., & Hoy, C. (2005). *Punishment in the Community: Managing Offenders, Making Choices* (2nd edition). Cullompton: Willan Publishing.

Wortley, R. (2011). *Psychological Criminology: An Integrative Approach*. London: Routledge.

Wrangham, R. (1999). Evolution of coalitionary killing. *Yearbook of Physical Anthropology*, 42, 1–30.

Wrangham, R., & Carmody, R. (2010). Human adaptation to the control of fire. *Evolutionary Anthropology*, 19, 187–199.

Wrangham, R., & Peterson, D. (1996). *Demonic Males: Apes and the Origin of Human Violence*. London: Bloomsbury.

Wright, J. P., & Beaver, K. M. (2005). Do parents matter in creating self-control in their children? A genetically informed test of Gottfredson and Hirschi's theory of low self-control. *Criminology*, 43, 1169–1202.

Wright, R., Brookman, F., & Bennett, T. (2006). The foreground dynamics of street robbery in Britain. *British Journal of Criminology*, 46, 1–15.

Wright, S., & Klee, H. (2001). Violent crime, aggression and amphetamine: What are the implications for drug treatment services? *Drugs: Education, Prevention and Policy*, 8, 73–90.

Yang, M., Wong, S. C. P., & Coid, J. (2010). The efficacy of violence prediction: A meta-analytic comparison of nine risk assessment tools. *Psychological Bulletin*, 136, 740–767.

Yang, S. (2014). 5 Years ago Bernie Madoff was sentenced to 150 years in prison – here's how his scheme worked. *Business Insider Australia*. Retrieved from www.businessinsider.com.au/how-bernie-madoffs-ponzi-scheme-worked-2014-7?r=US&IR=T on January 18, 2017.

Yang, Y., & Raine, A. (2009). Prefrontal structural and functional brain imaging findings in antisocial, violent, and psychopathic individuals: A meta-analysis. *Psychiatry Research: Neuroimaging*, 174, 81–88.

Young, S., Moss, D., Sedgwick, O., Fridman, M., & Hodgkins, P. (2015). A meta-analysis of the prevalence of attention deficit hyperactivity disorder in incarcerated populations. *Psychological Medicine*, 45, 247–258.

Yu, R., Geddes, J. R., & Fazel, S. (2012). Personality disorder, violence and antisocial behaviour: A systematic review and meta-regression analysis. *Journal of Personality Disorders*, 26, 775–792.

Zefferman, M. R., & Mathew, S. (2015). An evolutionary theory of large-scale human warfare: Group-structured cultural selection. *Evolutionary Anthropology*, 24, 50–61.

Zhang, Z. (2003). *Drug and Alcohol Use and Related Matters Among Arrestees*. Washington, DC: National Institute of Justice.

Zimbardo, P. G. (2003). A situationist perspective on the psychology of evil: Understanding how good people are transformed into perpetrators. In A. G. Miller (ed.), *The Social Psychology of Good and Evil* (pp. 21–50). New York, NY: The Guilford Press.

Zimbardo, P. G. (2007). *The Lucifer Effect*. New York, NY: Random House.

Zimring, F. E. (2012). *The City That Became Safe: New York's Lessons for Urban Crime and Its Control*. Oxford: Oxford University Press.

Zuckerman, M. (1979). *Sensation Seeking: Beyond the Optimal Level of Arousal*. Hillsdale, NJ: Erlbaum.

Zuravin, S. J. (1989). The ecology of child abuse and neglect: Review of the literature and presentation of data. *Violence and Victims*, 4, 101–120.

Zych, I., Ortega-Ruiz, R., & Del Ray, R. (2015). Systematic review of theoretical studies on bullying and cyberbullying: Facts, knowledge, prevention, and intervention. *Aggression and Violent Behavior*, 23, 1–21.

INDEX